T0214339

Lecture Notes in Computer Science　　8938

Commenced Publication in 1973
Founding and Former Series Editors:
Gerhard Goos, Juris Hartmanis, and Jan van Leeuwen

More information about this series at http://www.springer.com/series/7408

Carlos Canal · Akram Idani (Eds.)

Software Engineering and Formal Methods

SEFM 2014 Collocated Workshops: HOFM,
SAFOME, OpenCert, MoKMaSD, WS-FMDS
Grenoble, France, September 1–2, 2014
Revised Selected Papers

 Springer

Editors
Carlos Canal
University of Malaga
Malaga
Spain

Akram Idani
LIG Lab
Saint Martin d'Hères Cedex
France

ISSN 0302-9743   ISSN 1611-3349 (electronic)
Lecture Notes in Computer Science
ISBN 978-3-319-15200-4 ISBN 978-3-319-15201-1 (eBook)
DOI 10.1007/978-3-319-15201-1

Library of Congress Control Number: 2014960220

LNCS Sublibrary: SL2 – Programming and Software Engineering

Springer Cham Heidelberg New York Dordrecht London

Printed on acid-free paper

Springer International Publishing AG Switzerland is part of Springer Science+Business Media
(www.springer.com)

Preface

This volume contains the technical papers presented in the five high-quality workshops associated to SEFM 2014 (12th International Conference on Software Engineering and Formal Methods, held in Grenoble, September 1–5, 2014). SEFM 2014 was organized by Inria and supported by Grenoble INP, Joseph Fourier University, LIG, and CNRS.

SEFM 2014 brought together practitioners and researchers from academia, industry, and government to advance the state of the art in formal methods, to facilitate their uptake in the software industry, and to encourage their integration with practical engineering methods. Satellite workshops provided further opportunities for collaborating and exchanging ideas about specific topics of Formal Methods and Software Engineering, from conceptual to practical aspects.

The workshops focused on specific topics in the Software Engineering and Formal Methods related domains: the First Workshop on Human-Oriented Formal Methods – From Readability to Automation (HOFM 2014), the Third International Symposium on Modeling and Knowledge Management Applications – Systems and Domains (MoKMaSD 2014), the Eighth International Workshop on Foundations and Techniques for Open Source Software Certification (OpenCert 2014), the First Workshop on Safety and Formal Methods (SaFoMe 2014), and the Fourth Workshop on Formal Methods in the Development of Software (WS-FMDS 2014). The review and the selection process was performed rigorously, with each paper being reviewed by at least three Program Committee (PC) members. A brief description of each workshop follows, written by their organizers.

For each of the workshops at SEFM 2014, we thank the organizers for these interesting topics and resulting talks. We also thank the paper contributors to these workshops and those who attended them. We would like to extend our thanks to all keynote speakers for their support and excellent presentations, and also, members of each workshop's Program Committee.

September 2014   Carlos Canal
                                                                                  Akram Idani

HOFM Organizers' Message

While designing and applying formal methods, computer scientists have dominantly focused on two factors only: first, a method must be precise and sound, and secondly, it must be mathematically concise and aesthetic. Other important characteristics such as simplicity, learnability, readability, memorability, ease of use and communication or, even support for integrating tools into larger development tool chains are ignored too often. These nonfunctional properties, however, are key attributes of usability and user satisfaction. If usability is compromised, methods are not fit for the purpose of documenting, reproducing, and communicating key design and realization decisions, or analysis results, especially when these need to communicate or mediate between expertise in different disciplines, different tool chains, or across technological or organizational boundaries. For these reasons, many engineers and practitioners largely reject formal methods and formal specification languages as "too hard to understand and use in practice" while admitting that they are powerful and precise.

With increasing computing power and its consequent automation capabilities, the research and development community, however, is slowly but definitely focusing on usability in combination with automation. Moreover, practitioners across numerous domains are increasingly interested in formal domain-specific modeling, simulation, and validation, whether in application areas of energy, robotics, health, biology, climate, and sustainable development, or, for specific technologies of importance such as data analytics and user interface specification for an exponentially growing number of handheld or wearable devices. While there are many applications of formal methods to analyze human-machine interaction and to construct user interfaces, the field of application of human factors to the analysis and to the optimization of formal methods area is almost unexplored.

The HOFM workshop was held on September 1, 2014 in Grenoble, France. This international workshop was affiliated to the 12th International Conference on Software Engineering and Formal Methods (SEFM). The goal of the HOFM (Human-Oriented Formal Methods) workshop was to bring together researchers, engineers, and practitioners from academia and industry to baseline the state of the art in this increasingly important domain. Every submitted paper was reviewed by at least three Program Committee members, four regular papers were accepted for presentation at HOFM 2014. An introduction to the first HOFM workshop was given by Maria Spichkova on "Human-Oriented Formal Methods: Human Factors + Formal Methods." The program of the workshop was enriched by two keynote talks:

- Arkady Zaslavsky, CSIRO, Australia, "Internet of Things: New Dimensions of Modelling, Usability and Human-Computer Interaction"
- Martin Glinz, University of Zurich, Switzerland, "Advantages and Pitfalls of Formal or Formalizable Graphic Requirements Models"

The HOFM 2014 pre-proceedings, which include all papers presented at the workshop, are available online at the workshop site http://hofm2014.wordpress.com.

All authors of the HOFM workshop were invited to submit extended versions of their papers, taking into account discussions made during the workshop.

We would like to thank all authors who contributed to HOFM 2014 as well as all attendees to the workshop. We hope that the attendees found the program relevant to their interests and inspiring. We also thank the Program Committee members for their support and considered reviews, and the SEFM workshop chairs and local organizers for their help.

Maria Spichkova
Heinz W. Schmidt

Program Committee

Katherine Blashki	Noroff University College, Norway
Manfred Broy	Technical University of Munich, Germany
Jan Carlson	Mälardalen University, Sweden
Pedro Isaas	Universidade Aberta, Portugal
Lalchandani Jayprakash	IIIT Bangalore, India
Margaret Hamilton	RMIT University, Australia
Peter Herrmann	NTNU Trondheim, Norway
Tim Miller	The University of Melbourne, Australia
Srini Ramaswamy	ABB Bangalore, India
Daniel Ratiu	Siemens AG, Germany
Bernhard Schätz	fortiss GmbH, Germany
Heinz W. Schmidt (Chair)	RMIT University, Australia
Carol Smidts	Ohio State University, USA
Maria Spichkova (Chair)	RMIT University, Australia
Judith Stafford	University of Colorado, USA

SaFoMe Organizers' Message

The enhancement of quality of service (QoS) and the reduction of the risk of fatalities and injuries of strategic industrial products is a real need in many domains, including for instance automotive, avionics, and rail. To achieve this, there is a need for cost-efficient processes and methods supporting the development and operation of safety enabling embedded systems.

Among several approaches, Component-Based Development (CBD) has emerged as suitable to improve both the reuse and maintainability of systems. Many CBD techniques use the concept of a contract, which describes what a component interface provides and what it expects from other components. During system composition contracts are compared to determine system compatibility. The majority of these works has concentrated on the functional properties of systems. Much less work has been devoted to apply CBD while dealing with nonfunctional properties, including dependability properties such as safety, reliability, performance, and availability.

Formal methods have traditionally been advocated for improving the reliability of safety-relevant systems. The First International Workshop on Safety and Formal Methods, SaFoMe 2014, which was held in Grenoble, France, on September 1, 2014, aimed at providing a forum for people from academia and industry to communicate their latest results on theoretical advances, industrial case studies, and lessons learned in the application of formal methods to safety certification, verification, and/or validation in (but not limited to) component-based systems.

Papers submitted to SaFoMe 2014 were carefully reviewed by at least three members of the Program Committee. From nine submissions, five papers were finally selected to discuss the following topics: survivability, diagnosis, verification of safety contracts, and formalization of behavioral patterns and shared resources. Prof. Dr. Jan Jürgens from TU Dortmund and Fraunhofer ISST gave an invited talk on Security Certification in the Presence of Evolution: Models vs. Code. A Round Table was held at the end of the workshop where current challenges in industrial application of Formal Methods in the safety context were actively discussed by the attendees, which consisted of people both from academia and industry. The conclusion was that we are still far from applying formal methods to deal with safety concerns in industrial contexts, since there are too many modeling languages and tools that partially analyze safety concerns while considering the evolving requirements.

Several people contributed to the success of SaFoMe 2014. We would like to express our gratitude to all members of the Program Committee for their efforts and commitment. The SEFM workshop's organizers deserve special thanks for their dedication and good work, which clearly made our organization tasks easier. We also thank the nSafeCer project (EU ARTEMIS Joint Undertaking under grant agreement no. 295373) for their support. Finally, thanks to the authors and attendees for their passion and interest.

Program Co-chairs

Hans Hansson
Clara Benac Earle

Organization Committee

Elena Gómez-Martínez
Ricardo J. Rodríguez
Catia Trubiani

Program Committee

Clara Benac Earle	Universidad Politécnica de Madrid, Spain
Simona Bernardi	Centro Universitario de la Defensa, Universidad de Zaragoza, Spain
Jan Carlson	Mälardalen University, Sweden
David Garcia-Rosado	Universidad de Castilla-La Mancha, Spain
Christophe Gaston	Institut CARNOT CEA LIST, France
Elena Gómez-Martínez	Universidad Politécnica de Madrid, Spain
Hans Hansson	Mälardalen University, Sweden
José Merseguer	Universidad de Zaragoza, Spain
Sasikumar Punnekkat	Mälardalen University, Sweden
Nicolas Rapin	Institut CARNOT CEA LIST, France
Ricardo J. Rodríguez	Universidad de León, Spain
Fernando Rosa-Velardo	Universidad Complutense de Madrid, Spain
Stefano Tonetta	Fondazione Bruno Kessler, Italy
Catia Trubiani	Gran Sasso Science Institute, Italy
Xavier Zeitoun	Institut CARNOT CEA LIST, France

OpenCert Organizers' Message

OpenCert provides for a unique venue advancing the state of the art in the analysis and assurance of open-source software with an ultimate aim of achieving certification and standards. The dramatic growth in open-source software over recent years has provided for a fertile ground for fundamental research and demonstrative case studies. Over the years, OpenCert has enabled a thriving community, small but focused, examining issues ranging from certification to security and safety analysis for applications areas as diverse as railways, aviation, knowledge management, sustainable development, and the open-source developers community.

The OpenCert workshop has successfully been held for seven consecutive editions. The 8th year's edition was colocated with SEFM 2014, being held in Grenoble, France. The workshop attracted a total of six papers, out of which three were accepted (an acceptance rate of 50 %). Each paper was reviewed by two to three reviewers. The accepted papers offer a diverse range of topics from modeling approaches to learning processes to state-of-the-art reviews on open-source software development processes.

The organizers are grateful to the Program Committee for their contribution in terms of reviews and discussions.

Victor Fonte
Siraj Ahmed Shaikh

Program Committee

Bernhard Aichernig	Technical University of Graz, Austria
Luis Barbosa	University of Minho, Portugal
Alessandro Bessani	Lisbon, Portugal
Peter Breuer	Birmingham City University, UK
Antonio Cerone	University of Pisa, Italy
Yannis Dimitriadis	University of Valladolid, Spain
Fabrizio Fabbrini	ISTI-CNR, Italy
Jesus Arias Fisteus	Carlos III University of Madrid, Spain
Victor Fonte (Co-chair)	University of Minho, Portugal
Maria João Frade	University of Minho, Portugal
Paddy Krishnan	Oracle Labs, Australia
Imed Hammouda	Tampere University of Technology, Finland
Alexandre Madeira	HASLab INESC TEC, Portugal
Paolo Milazzo	University of Pisa, Italy
John Noll	Lero – The Irish Software Engineering Research Centre, Ireland
Alexander K. Petrenko	ISP RAS, Russia
Simon Pickin	Universidad Complutense de Madrid, Spain
Miguel Rio	University College London, UK

WS-FMDS Organizers' Message

The Fourth International Workshop on Formal Methods in the Development of Software, WS-FMDS 2014, was held in Grenoble, France, on September 2, 2014. The purpose of WS-FMDS is to bring together scientists and practitioners who are active in the area of formal methods and interested in exchanging their experiences in the industrial usage of these methods. This workshop also strives to promote research and development for the improvement of theoretical aspects of formal methods and tools focused on practical usability for industrial applications.

After a careful reviewing process in which every paper was reviewed by at least three WS-FMDS PC members and additional reviewers, the Program Committee accepted seven regular papers, which is around half of the submitted papers. The program of WS-FMDS 2014 was enriched by the keynote speech of Radu Mateescu, on "Mu-Calculus Property-Dependant Reductions for Divergence-Sensitive Branching Bisimilarity."

Several people contributed to the success of WS-FMDS 2014. We are grateful to the general chair of the 12th International Conference on Software Engineering and Formal Methods SEFM 2013, Prof. Radu Mateescu, for his support and help. We also would like to thank the Program Committee members as well as the additional reviewers for their work on selecting the papers. The process of reviewing and selecting papers was significantly simplified using Easy-Chair. We would like to thank the attendees of the workshop and hope that they found the program useful, interesting, and challenging.

Carlos Gregorio-Rodríguez
Fernando L. Pelayo

Program Committee

Mario Bravetti	University of Bologna, Italy
Carlos Gregorio-Rodríguez	Universidad Complutense de Madrid, Spain
Raluca Lefticaru	University of Bucharest, Romania
Luis LLana	University Complutense de Madrid, Spain
Jasen Markovski	Eindhoven University of Technology, The Netherlands
Fernando L. Pelayo	Universidad de Castilla-La Mancha, Spain
Pascal Poizat	Université Paris Ouest Nanterre La Défense and LIP6, France
Fernando Rosa-Velardo	Universidad Complutense de Madrid, Spain
Franz Wotawa	Graz University of Technology, Austria
Fatiha Zadi	University of Paris-Sud, France

Additional Reviewers

Souheib Baarir	Paris-Sorbonne University and LIP6, France
M. Emilia Cambronero	Universidad de Castilla-La Mancha, Spain
Fernando Cuartero	Universidad de Castilla-La Mancha, Spain
Miguel Palomino	Universidad Complutense de Madrid, Spain
Ismael Rodriguez	Universidad Complutense de Madrid, Spain

MoKMaSD Organizers' Message

The Third International Symposium on Modelling and Knowledge Management applications: Systems and Domains (MoKMaSD 2014) was held in Grenoble, France, on September 2, 2014. The aim of the Symposium is to bring together practitioners and researchers from academia, industry, government, and non-government organizations to present research results and exchange experiences, ideas, and solutions for modeling and analyzing complex systems and using knowledge management strategies, technology, and systems in various domain areas such as ecology, biology, medicine, climate, governance, education, and social software engineering. In particular, the focus is on synergistic approaches that integrate modeling and knowledge management/discovery or exploit knowledge management/discovery to develop/synthesise system models.

After a careful review process, the Program Committee accepted seven papers. The program of MoKMaSD 2014 was enriched by keynote speeches by Alberto d'Onofrio entitled "Human Behavior and the Spread of Infectious Diseases: A Challenge for Modeling" and by Elisa Fromont entitled "Mine First to See Better."

Several people contributed to the success of MoKMaSD 2014. We are grateful to Antonio Cerone, who invited us to chair this edition of the Symposium and assisted us in some organization aspects of the event. We would like to thank the organizers of SEFM 2014, and in particular the General Chair Radu Mateescu, the Workshop Chairs Carlos Canal and Akram Idani, and the Program Chair Gwen Salaun. We would also like to thank the Program Committee and the additional reviewers for their work on reviewing the papers. The process of reviewing and selecting papers was significantly simplified using EasyChair.

We welcome all attendees to the symposium and hope that this event will enable good exchange of ideas and generate new collaborations among attendees.

Paolo Milazzo
Anna Monreale

Program Committee

Orlando Belo	University of Minho, Portugal
Paloma Cáceres	Rey Juan Carlos University, Spain
Giulio Caravagna	University of Milano-Bicocca, Italy
Antonio Cerone	University of Pisa, Italy
Michele Coscia	Harvard Kennedy School, USA
Andrea Esuli	ISTI-CNR, Pisa, Italy
Alexeis Garcia-Perez	Coventry University, UK
Jane Hillston	University of Edinburgh, UK
Joris Hulstijn	Delft University of Technology, The Netherlands
Marijn Janssen	Delft University of Technology, The Netherlands
Ferenc Jordan	COSBI, Italy

Wei-chung Liu	Academia Sinica, Taiwan, R.O.C
Donato Malerba	University of Bari, Italy
Stan Matwin	University of Ottawa, Canada
Paolo Milazzo (Co-chair)	University of Pisa, Italy
Anna Monreale (Co-chair)	University of Pisa, Italy
Siegfried Nijssen	KU Leuven, Belgium and Leiden University, The Netherlands
Adegboyega Ojo	DERI, National University of Ireland, Ireland
Giovanni Pardini	University of Pisa, Italy
Matteo Pedercini	Millennium Institute, USA
Nikos Pelekis	University of Piraeus, Greece
Anna Philippou	University of Cyprus, Cyprus
Marco Scotti	GEOMAR Centre, Germany
Luca Tesei	University of Camerino, Italy
Daniel Villatoro	IIIA-CSIC and Universitat Autònoma de Barcelona, Spain
Hui Xiong	Rutgers, The State University of New Jersey, USA

Additional Reviewer

Pasquale Bove

Internet of Things: New Dimensions of Modelling, Usability and Human-Computer Interaction

Arkady Zaslavsky

CSIRO, Australia

Keynote Speaker of HOFM 2014

The Internet of Things (IoT) is one of the pillars of Future Internet and will connect billions of "things", where things include computers, smartphones, sensors, objects from everyday life with embedded computational and communication capabilities and the list goes on and on. Each of those things will have their physical and/or virtual identity, attributes, intelligent and human-oriented interfaces, componentised functionality and standardised communication protocols.

The Internet of Things will be generating massive amounts of data that will have to be stored, validated, processed and communicated to relevant services, applications and systems. This means also new dimensions of modelling, usability, and human-computer interaction.

This talk focuses on the challenges of developing tools, middleware and software platforms for the IoT, disruptively big data it generates, discovery of things for various services and applications, representing semantics and enriching IoT data with semantics, transforming IoT data into context and integrating these into knowledge. The talk will also present various CSIRO projects in IoT, including EU FP7 OpenIoT which developed open source flexible sensor-based system middleware platform. OpenIoT brings together sensing and cloud computing and is an efficient platform for handling big IoT data. Another advantage of the platform is human-orientation and usability – OpenIoT offers users zero-programming integrated development environment.

Advantages and Pitfalls of Formal or Formalizable Graphic Requirements Models

Martin Glinz

University of Zurich, Switzerland

Keynote Speaker of HOFM 2014

Every formal requirements specification needs to be validated by the stakeholders of the system to be built. This is a major challenge as stakeholders typically have no training in formal methods, thus making validation of formal requirements specifications a difficult or even impossible task. Formal or formalizable graphic models of requirements have the potential of providing a solution to this problem as they are demonstrative and can be simulated or executed. However, graphic formal models also have pitfalls and limitations.

In my talk I will first introduce and situate the problem. Then I will take the audience on a guided tour through some typical formal or formalizable graphic requirements modeling languages such as statecharts, labeled transition systems, Petri nets, and UML activity diagrams, highlighting advantages, pitfalls and limitations.

Security Certification in the Presence of Evolution: Models vs. Code

Jan Jürjens

Technical University of Dortmund and Fraunhofer Institute for Software
and Systems Technology ISST, Dortmund (Germany)
http://jan.jurjens.de

Keynote Speaker of SaFoMe 2014

Security certification of complex systems requires a high amount of effort. As a particular challenge, today's systems are increasingly long-living and subject to continuous change. After each change of some part of the system, the whole system needs to be re-certified from scratch (since security properties are not in general modular), which is usually far too much effort.

We present a tool-supported approach for security certification that minimizes the amount of effort necessary in the case of re-certification after change. It is based on an approach for model-based development of secure software which makes use of the security extension UMLsec of the Unified Modeling Language (UML) [Jur05]. It allows the user to integrate security requirements such as secure information flow [Jur00] and audit security [Jur01] into a system design model and has been applied to a number of industrial applications such as an electronic purse system [JW01].

The approach presented is based on results that determine under which conditions change preserves security properties (for example in the context of structuring techniques such as refinement or architectural principles such as modularization). The approach supports an automated difference-based security analysis, at the level of design models as well as the implementation code (using static security analysis [AGJ11] or run-time verification). It has been applied e.g. to cryptographic protocols, distributed security infrastructures, and identity management systems, and there are empirical results comparing it to classical techniques for security certification. In the outlook, we briefly present current research directions, such as applying the approach to the security certification of cloud-based systems.

References

[Jur00] Jürjens, J.: Secure information flow for concurrent processes. In: Palamidessi, C. (ed.) CONCUR 2000. LNCS, vol. 1877, pp. 395–409. Springer, Heidelberg (2000)

[Jur01] Jürjens, J.: Modelling audit security for smart-cart payment schemes with UML-SEC. In: IFIP TC11 Sixteenth Annual Working Conference on Information Security (IFIP/Sec'01), pp. 93–108. Kluwer, Norwell (2001)

[Jur05] Jürjens, J.: Secure systems development with UML. Springer, Heidelberg (2005)

[JW01]   Jürjens, J., Wimmel, G.: Security modelling for electronic commerce: the common electronic purse specifications. In: Schmid, B., Stanoevska-Slabeva, K., Tschammer, V. (eds.) Towards the E-Society. IFIP, vol. 74, pp. 489–506. Springer, Heidelberg (2001)

[AGJ11] Aizatulin, M., Gordon, A.D., Jürjens, J.: Extracting and verifying cryptographic models from C protocol code by symbolic execution. In: 18th ACM Conference on Computer and Communications Security (CCS 2011), pp. 331–340 (2011)

Static Analysis by Abstract Interpretation and Decision Procedures

Matthieu Moy

Verimag, France
Joint work with Julien Henry and David Monniaux

Keynote Speaker of OpenCert 2014

Abstract interpretation techniques can be made more precise by distinguishing paths inside loops, at the expense of possibly exponential complexity. SMT-solving techniques and sparse representations of paths and sets of paths avoid this pitfall.

We improve previously proposed techniques for guided static analysis and the generation of disjunctive invariants by combining them with techniques for succinct representations of paths and symbolic representations for transitions based on static single assignment.

Because of the non-monotonicity of the results of abstract interpretation with widening operators, it is difficult to conclude that some abstraction is more precise than another based on theoretical local precision results. We thus conducted extensive comparisons between our new techniques and previous ones, on a variety of open-source packages.

Human Behavior and the Spread of Infectious Diseases: A Challenge for Modeling

Alberto d'Onofrio

International Prevention Research Institute (iPRI), France

Keynote Speaker of MoKMaSD 2014

This talk concerns a fast growing research area: modeling the influence of information-driven human behavior on the spread and control of infectious diseases. In particular, we shall focus on two main and inter-related "core" topics: behavioral changes in response to global (or "perceived global"...) threats, and the pseudo-rational opposition to vaccines. Indeed, people are likely to change their behavior and their propensity to vaccinate themselves and their children based on information and, even more often, rumors about the spread of a disease. This, implicitly, induces a feedback that can deeply affect the dynamics of epidemics and endemics. In order to make realistic predictions, modelers must go beyond classical mathematical epidemiology, where, in anology with systems biology, the individuals are abstracted as particles in brownian motion.

Mine First to See Better

Elisa Fromont

Université de Lyon, Université de St-Etienne, France

Keynote Speaker of MoKMaSD 2014

I will explain how data mining techniques such as pattern mining or (semi-supervised) clustering can and should be used to improve fundamental computer vision tasks such as image classification, image or video retrieval or object tracking in videos. The main idea is to build on low level vision features such as segmentations or SIFT bag-of-visual-words to construct more discriminant and invariant "mid-level" descriptors. I will show examples of success stories that have used this pattern mining phase in the last years. On the algorithmic point of view, I will focus on a dynamic plane graph mining algorithm that integrates spatio-temporal constraints and can be used to help tracking objects in videos in an unsupervised way.

Mu-Calculus Property-Dependent Reductions for Divergence-Sensitive Branching Bisimilarity

Radu Mateescu

Head of the CONVECS Research Team, INRIA Grenoble, France
Chair of the FMICS working group of ERCIM

Keynote Speaker of WS-FMDS 2014

When analyzing the behavior of finite-state concurrent systems by model checking, one way of fighting state space explosion is to reduce the model as much as possible whilst preserving the properties under verification. We consider the framework of action-based systems, whose behaviors can be represented by labeled transition systems (LTSs), and whose temporal properties of interest can be formulated in modal mu-calculus (Lmu). First, we determine, for any Lmu formula, the maximal set of actions that can be hidden in the LTS without changing the interpretation of the formula. Then, we define Lmu-dsbr, a fragment of Lmu adequate w.r.t. divergence-sensitive branching bisimilarity. This enables one to apply the maximal hiding and to reduce the LTS modulo this relation when verifying any formula of Lmu-dsbr. We show that this fragment is equally expressive to mu-ACTL, the action-based counterpart of CTL extended with fixed point operators. The experiments that we performed on various examples of communication protocols and distributed systems show that this reduction approach can significantly improve the performance of verification.

Contents

MoKMaSD 2014

WS-FMDS 2014

HOFM 2014

A Usability Evaluation of Interactive Theorem Provers Using Focus Groups

Bernhard Beckert, Sarah Grebing$^{(\boxtimes)}$, and Florian Böhl

Karlsruhe Institute of Technology (KIT), Karlsruhe, Germany
{beckert,sarah.grebing,boehl}@kit.edu

Abstract. The effectiveness of interactive theorem provers (ITPs) increased such that the bottleneck in the proof process shifted from effectiveness to efficiency. While in principle large theorems are provable, it takes much effort for the user to interact with the system. A major obstacle for the user is to understand the proof state in order to guide the prover in successfully finding a proof. We conducted two focus groups to evaluate the usability of ITPs. We wanted to evaluate the impact of the gap between the user's model of the proof and the actual proof performed by the provers' strategies. In addition, our goals are to explore which mechanisms already exist and to develop, based on the existing mechanisms, new mechanisms that help the user in bridging this gap.

1 Introduction

Motivation. The degree of automation of interactive theorem provers (ITPs) has increased to a point where complex theorems over large formalisations for real-world problems can be proven effectively. But even with a high degree of automation, user interaction is still required on different levels. On a global level, users have to find the right formalisation and have to decompose the proof task by finding useful lemmas. On a local level, when automatic proof search for a lemma fails, they have to either direct the proof search or understand why no proof can be constructed and fix the lemma or the underlying formalisation. As the degree of automation increases, the number of interactions decreases. But the remaining interactions get more and more complex as ITPs are applied to more and more complex problems.

When proving theorems, the automated proof search often leads the proof into a direction that differs from the way a human would conduct the proof. To interact with the theorem prover in a meaningful way during the proof process, users have to understand the prover's strategy and the state of proof construction and, thus, have to bridge the gap between their own model of the proof search and the current proof state of the tool. Open goals in partial proofs are the result of syntactic transformations that may not be intended to make it easy for humans to understand them. The intention of the transformations is rather

---

This work is part of the project Usability of Software Verification Systems within the BMBF-funded Software Campus. Florian Böhl was funded by MWK grant "MoSeS".

C. Canal and A. Idani (Eds.): SEFM 2014 Workshops, LNCS 8938, pp. 3–19, 2015.
DOI: 10.1007/978-3-319-15201-1_1

to get the automated proof search closer to a complete proof. Therefore, users need to understand the prover's strategy and often have to look at *intermediate proof states*, resulting from rule applications onto the original proof obligation, to comprehend the current state.

Although it is easy to accept that there is a gap between a human user's model of the proof resp. proof search and the actual automated proof search, it is rather unclear how large its impact on interactive theorem proving is for typical proof obligations. Nevertheless, the following is a central hypothesis for our work, which we wanted to test during the usability evaluation:

> Bridging the gap between the user's model of the proof state and the state of the theorem prover at interaction points is *the* paramount and prominent challenge for efficient and effectively usable general theorem provers.

In addition, we are interested in evaluating which tools or mechanisms are already present in today's provers that help to bridge the gap and how to extend existing mechanisms to help the user in understanding the proof states.

Our contribution in this work is that we conducted an experiment using the survey method focus groups to get a first evaluation of whether our hypothesis is true and to gain answers to our two questions: (a) Which mechanisms of this kind are already used in theorem provers? (b) What mechanisms are missing?

Survey method. We have carried out two experiments, where we applied the focus group method [10,16] to two different ITPs: the tactical theorem prover Isabelle/HOL [18] and the interactive program verification system KeY [7].

Focus groups are a qualitative survey method typically used in an early stage of the usability engineering process [12,17]. Based on their results, (prototypical) mechanisms for improving usability can be developed, which can then be evaluated with methods such as usability testing and user questionnaires to quantitatively measure increases in usability. While focus groups explore the subjective experience of users, they are designed to eliminate experimenter-bias and to provide more objective results. The number of participants required to get significant results is much smaller than for quantitative evaluations, which makes focus groups well-suited for the relatively small user base of ITPs.

Background. Our work is part of the BMBF-funded Software Campus programme. We apply various methods known from the field of human-computer-interaction (HCI) to ITPs, including focus group discussions, usability testing, and user experience questionnaires. Since expertise from both fields (ITP and HCI) is required, we cooperate with user experience experts from DATEV eG who are well-versed in the ergonomic evaluation of standard software.

Structure of this paper. Section 2 briefly reviews related work on usability evaluations of ITPs. The focus group method is introduced in Sect. 3. In Sect. 4 we present the results of the experiments and relate them to our hypothesis. Section 4.5 presents our results regarding mechanisms and tools for understanding the proof state. We conclude and discuss future work in Sect. 5.

2   Related Work

The ITP community has noticed the need to evaluate and improve usability, but so far structured usability evaluation methods have rarely been applied to ITPs.

In previous work [5], we have performed a questionnaire-based evaluation of the KeY system based on Green and Petre's Cognitive Dimensions questionnaire [9] to get a first impression of the user's perception and to develop first hypotheses about the usability of the KeY system. Beyond that Kadoda et al. [14] evaluated proof systems using Green and Petre's Cognitive Dimensions questionnaire to develop a list of desirable features for educational theorem provers.

Aitken and Melham [1–3] evaluated the interactive proof systems Isabelle and HOL using recordings of user interactions with the systems in collaboration with HCI experts. During the proof process the users were asked to think aloud and after the recordings the users were interviewed. The goal of this work was to study the activities performed by users of interactive provers during the proof process to obtain an interaction model of the users. They propose to use typical user errors as usability metric and they compared provers w.r.t. these errors. Also, suggestions for improvements of the systems have been proposed by the authors based on the evaluation results, including, besides others, improved search mechanisms and improved access to certain proof-relevant components.

Jackson et al. used co-operative evaluation methods on the CLAM Proof Planner [13]. Users were asked to perform predefined tasks while using the "think-aloud technique" to comment on what they were doing.

Vujosevic and Eleftherakis used questionnaires and interviews to explore why Formal Methods Tools are not used in industry [20]. Their work includes evaluations of usability aspects of several formal methods tools, such as the Alloy Analyzer. For improving the interface of the prover NuPRL, a self-designed questionnaire was used to evaluate the users' perceptions of the interface [11].

Similar to our findings, Archer and Heitmeyer [4] also realized the gap between the prover's and the user's model of the proof. They have developed the TAME interface on top of the prover PVS to reduce the distance between manual proofs and proofs by automation. TAME is able to prove properties of timed automata using so called *human-style reasoning*. Proof steps in TAME are intended to be close to the large proof steps performed in manual proofs. The authors have developed strategies on top of the PVS strategies that match more closely the steps performed by humans. The goal is to provide evidence and comprehension of proofs for domain but not proof experts.

Lowe et al. describe in their work [15] their approach to building a co-operative theorem prover and describe some undesirable features of ITPs focussing on feedback of the system. They have implemented the BARNACLE interface for the CLAM prover which allows explanations for failing preconditions, which should make proofs more comprehensible for the users.

Ouimet identified different issues, e.g., large proof size and number of proof steps, that have to be addressed in order to have a widespread use of theorem provers in [19] and evaluated the system ESC/Java against these issues. The issues were identified by examining a large case study conducted at Motorola.

3   Survey Method: Focus Groups

Focus group discussions are a qualitative method to explore opinions of users about specific topics or products, e.g., in market research. In the field of human-computer interaction (HCI) they are used to explore user perspectives on software systems and their usability in an early stage of the usability engineering process [12,17]. As already mentioned in the introduction, they provide the subjective experience of the users and require only a small number of participants (five to ten). The duration of the discussion groups is around one to two hours and it is guided by a moderator who uses a script to structure the discussion. Focus groups have three phases: Recruiting participants, performing the discussion and post-processing. In the following we will briefly give an insight into the script which was used to guide the discussion. The full description of the setup and script can be found in [6].

Script for the discussions. The main questions and tasks in the script were the same for both conducted focus groups as we wanted to compare the results. Adaptations of the questions and presented mock-ups to the specifics of the two systems were the main differences. As a warm-up task, we asked about typical application areas of the systems and about their strengths and weaknesses related to the proof process. In the main part of the discussion, we had two topics: (1) Support during the proof process and (2) Mechanisms for understanding proof states. As a cool-down task, we asked the participants to be creative and imagine their ideal interactive proof system. The full scripts with all questions for our experiments are available at http://formal.iti.kit.edu/~grebing/SWC.

4   Evaluation of the Focus Groups and Analysis Results

4.1   The User's and the Tool's Model of the Proof Process

ITPs are used to aid users in proving complex theorems in many areas of computer science and mathematics. For using such systems, the user needs to have a certain level of experience in proving theorems. In general, the user has a concept or plan of how to prove the desired theorem. We call this concept *user's model of the proof.* This can either be already a whole proof plan or just first ideas on the proof process. This model also includes an assumption about the theorem prover's strategies as we do not consider the proof plan for a pen and paper proof as being the user's model, but the proof plan for how the user would prove the problem using a theorem prover.

One big difference between the user's model of the proof and the current partial proof is that the proof steps in the model are coarser and have an intuitive (summing up) semantic for the user (such as "simplification of the proof obligation"), whereas the prover's steps are more fine-grained and are a syntactic manipulation of the proof state. While an intuitive semantic for each rule application exists (as given by the rule's author), a sequence of consecutive rule applications in the system may not have a clear intuitive semantic for the user.

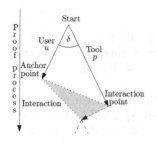

Fig. 1. Model of the proof process

In Fig. 1 we have sketched our idea of the relation between the actual proof performed by the prover's search strategy (p) and the user's proof model (u). At the beginning of the proof process the user's model is identical with or close to the proof obligation in the proof system. However, the more the automatic strategies of the prover try to prove the proof obligation (arrow p), the more the actual proof state in the system differs from the user's model (arrow u). As the user has to guide the prover by interacting with it, the user has to understand the process of the prover and relate the actual proof state to the user's model. For this relation the user has to inspect the current proof state (*interaction point*) and find a corresponding state in the own model (*anchor point*). After the user interacts with the prover, the proof of the system below the interaction point is proceeding to some extent into the direction of the user's model, reducing the gap.

In some cases, no useful anchor point may exist. Then the user has to follow and understand the automatic proof construction and, in doing so, construct a new model u that is identical with or an abstraction of p. In contrast, if the user only applies rules manually and there is no automatic proof search, then p is identical to u (in case the user fully understands the effect of the applied rules).

In the standard case, however, where there is a gap between u and p, there should be mechanisms in the systems that help the user in relating the anchor point with the interaction point (dotted line). In general, we can identify two parameters which can differ from system to system: the size of the gap between the actual proof and the user's model (δ), and the mechanisms that help to relate the user's model and the current proof state to aid the user in comprehending the proof state (dotted line between anchor and interaction point).

Apart from the gap it could be that the user does not have a clear model of the proof or even none at all. Here the gap, as described is not applicable. In this case the user uses the automation of the prover without any model in mind in order to use the resulting proof state to concretize the own fuzzy model and therefore the user has to comprehend the resulting proof state.

4.2   The Participants of Our Focus Group Discussions

We conducted two focus groups, one for the Isabelle system and one for the KeY system. To categorize the participants, we draw a distinction between tool knowledge and domain knowledge. Most of them were at expert or intermediate level w.r.t. domain knowledge. With respect to tool expertise, the Isabelle group consisted of five participants: one less experienced, two intermediate, and two expert users. The KeY group consisted of seven participants: one less experienced, two intermediate, and four expert users.

4.3   Targets of Evaluation

In the following we will briefly introduce the two systems under evaluation with the focus on those parts that were mentioned by the participants. Here, we start with the application areas of the systems as given by the participants.

KeY system. The KeY system is an interactive verification system for programs written in Java annotated with the Java Modelling Language (JML). As such it is mostly used for the verification of Java programs w.r.t. a formal specification (usually a functional specification but also, for example, information-flow properties). KeY is also used for teaching and demonstrating formal methods, and as verification condition generator for other systems. KeY has an explicit proof object, i.e., all intermediate proof states can be inspected by the user. KeY uses a sequent calculus for Java Dynamic Logic [8]. Its user interface shows proofs as a tree, the nodes of the tree contain intermediate proof goals (i.e., sequents). Each node N is annotated with the rule that was applied to some formula in N's parent node to construct N.

Isabelle. Isabelle is a theorem prover for higher-order logic. As mentioned by the participants, it is especially used for the formalization, verification and execution of algorithms, for proving in general and for the development of formal models. It has an implicit proof object, i.e., not all intermediate proof states are shown to the user, only goal-states where the system stops its automatic strategies. These automatic strategies are called *methods*, however the participants used the term *tactics*, therefore we use this term throughout the paper. Isabelle' proof tactics are basically sets of rules or lemmas that can be applied to the goal state. In this paper, the *auto* tactic will often be mentioned, which applies a large number of rule sets automatically, and the *simp* tactic, which applies rules that simplify the goal-state. Within Isabelle also different tools can be invoked that generate counterexamples (e.g., *nitpick*, *quickcheck*) or that invoke SMT solvers to find a (sub-)proof (e.g., *sledgehammer*).

4.4   Strengths and Weaknesses of the Targets of Evaluation

Here, we discuss the strengths and weaknesses of the systems with respect to the proof process as mentioned by the participants. Interestingly, some characteristics of the systems that were first named as a strength lead to lively discussions in later phases, which often brought up negative aspects of the same characteristics.

Strengths. First, we discuss results of the focus groups w.r.t. the strengths of the systems, which are summarized in Table 1.

KeY System. The group on KeY agreed that the expressiveness of the system is an important strength. The participants like how the Java Modeling Language can be used to annotate Java code. They appreciated that a proof with the KeY system always follows a certain structure, that this structure is visualized

Table 1. Strengths of the two systems according to the participants. The labels indicate whether a characteristic is linked to our (M)odel of the proof process (see Sect. 4.1) or rather to (O)ther aspects of interactive theorem proving (the classification is our own and not the focus group's).

KeY	Isabelle
· Expressive specification language (O)	· Underlying language very intuitive (M)
· Proof can be inspected in detail (M)	· Helpful community (O)
· KeY tries to simplify open goals (M)	· Large public library of theorems (O)
· High degree of automation for simple problems (O)	· Automatic tactics and tools ease proof process (M)
· All proofs follow a similar structure (M)	· Proofs can be modularized (M)
· Intuitive presentation of proof by using macros and proof tree (M)	· Flexible w.r.t. use of top down or bottom up approach (O)
· Allows user-defined rules (M)	· Code export for testing the model (M)
· Support of JML (O)	· User-adjustable syntax (M)

in form of the proof tree, and that this tree can be inspected at an arbitrary level of detail. Macros, which group rules similar to tactics in Isabelle, ease the interaction process and help to give the proof the direction intended by the user. According to the participants, the KeY system can solve easy problems without any or with only very little interaction. Furthermore, KeY supports user-defined rules. These rules can be of help during the proof process.

Isabelle. The group on Isabelle considers the underlying proof input language Isar to be one of the system's main advantages. It allows for proofs to be structured and presented in a standard textbook style that is very intuitive for humans. The large user community of Isabelle is considered to be an important strength. It provides a growing (and already quite extensive) library of theorems available to everyone. Furthermore, the community is a good resource of knowledge and friendly towards beginners. Isabelle provides a variety of tools that help during the proof process, e.g., *sledgehammer* and *nitpick*. The system can be used for a top-down as well as for a bottom-up proof approach.

Weaknesses. The results of the focus groups w.r.t. weaknesses of the systems, i.e., room for improvements are shown in Table 2. For this brief overview, we omit some of the more technical remarks by participants that are not related to the general proof process in our opinion. For example, regarding KeY there were complaints about an unstable proof loading mechanism and memory leaks. Some Isabelle users complained about specific features of jEdit – a widespread editor for Isabelle proofs.

KeY System. Interestingly, several characteristics of KeY that were named as strengths by the focus group were also identified as areas with potential for

Table 2. Weaknesses of the two systems according to the participants. The labels indicate whether a characteristic is linked to our (M)odel of the proof process (see Sect. 4.1) or rather to (O)ther aspects of interactive theorem proving (the classification is our own and not the focus group's).

KeY	Isabelle
· Necessity of repeated trivial manual interactions (M)	· Finding the right tactic for a proof state is a non-trivial explorative task (M)
· Not possible to get practically usable counterexamples (M)	· Unexpected inference of types leads to unintuitive errors (M)
· Proof tree too detailed (M)	· Bloated formulas (M)
· Interaction on low-level logic formulas required (M)	· No insight into automatic tactics; unintuitive (M)
· Unintuitive mapping between formula and program (M)	· Messy downward compatibility for older proofs in newer system versions (O)
· Performance of automatic strategy (O)	· No support for proof refactoring (O)
· Practical scalability (O)	· Library: important mathematical foundations are missing (O)

improvement. The proof tree – whose existence was perceived as a strength of KeY – was considered to be too detailed. Some stated that linking proof states to Java code would be helpful. Interaction on the low-level logic formulas is necessary, sometimes trivial and tedious. Manual interaction often has to be repeated in similar situations. There are no useful tools to generate counterexamples.

Isabelle. According to the participants, an important downside of Isabelle is that the process of choosing the right tactics and tactic parameters to conduct a proof is not always intuitive. If a tactic cannot be applied successfully in a situation it is hard to find the reason. A technical problem is that type inference sometimes leads to very unintuitive errors. Additionally, formulas belonging to different properties that could be checked (and thus presented) independently are all combined in a single goal state which increases the size of the formula (e.g., invariants encoding type information for functions).

An often recurring task when working with Isabelle is to refactor proofs towards better understandability, however, tools for refactoring are missing. While the public library of theorems was also mentioned as a strength, a weakness is that some important mathematical foundations are still missing, i.e., in some theories lemmas are still missing.

Observations and Relation of Results to Our Model. Here, we relate results of the focus groups to our model of the proof process (Sect. 4.1) and to our hypothesis. We evaluate the characteristics (Tables 1 and 2) w.r.t. to three challenges an ITP has to solve:

(A) Keeping the gap small. In general, mechanisms that help to keep the gap between the tool's proof state and the user's mental model small are seen as strengths of the systems – unintuitive behavior of the tools in the proof process is often mentioned as a problem. Several strengths of KeY help to keep the gap small: Proofs follow the same structure, macros help to guide the proof into the expected direction (similar to tactics which were mentioned as a strength of Isabelle), and users can introduce new rules that match their intuition (these rules have to be proven correct). Both tools allow the proof to be modularized (in Isabelle it can be split up into lemmas, in KeY into contracts) – this allows structuring the proof as a sequence of statements intuitive for humans. Some KeY users stated that they use the automatic proof search only if it closes a branch as otherwise the resulting state is too unintuitive to continue interactively.

(B) Bridging the gap. Understanding a given proof state is an important challenge for users of both systems during the proof process. Consequently, mechanisms and characteristics of the systems that help the user's understanding are considered to be important strengths. Here, Isabelle provides a couple of useful tools (quickcheck and nitpick to name two). Furthermore, the intuitive structure of the underlying language Isar is named as an important strength. Correspondingly, the absence of suitable mechanisms for certain situations is an important weakness. For example, our participants criticized that KeY does not provide a useful tool to generate counterexamples. Such a tool is necessary to detect whether the prover is stuck because further user input is needed or the property does not hold and no proof exists. While there are tools to generate counterexamples for Isabelle, the counterexample representation could be improved in the eyes of some participants in case proof obligations contain functions. Currently it is difficult to find the part of a proposition that is not provable.

(C) Supporting Interaction. Finally, as soon as users have a sufficient understanding of the proof state, they need to interact with the tool in an effective way. In this area there still seems to be a lot of room for improvement for both tools. The participants of the KeY focus group criticized that the interaction often has to be performed not on the annotation level but on low-level logic formulas. Furthermore, low-level steps have to be repeated by hand in similar situations. The Isabelle users were unhappy about the tedious task of finding the correct tactic to continue.

Conclusion. We observe a strong connection between the named strengths and weaknesses and our model of the proof process from Sect. 4.1. More than half of the mentioned characteristics can be associated with concepts introduced by the model. Furthermore, the results support our hypothesis that bridging the gap between the user's model of the proof and the ITP's proof state is very important during the proof process.

4.5   User Support During the Proof Process

We divided the part of the discussion about the proof processes into two parts, namely the *global* proof process (finding the right formalization and decomposing the proof task) and the *local* proof process (proving a single lemma or theorem). The participants were asked to describe their typical proof process respectively, and to name feedback mechanisms that the systems provide. Our expectations were that existing prover support and mechanisms to aid the user are adapted to the respective abstraction levels of the two processes.

4.6   State-of-the-Art in User Support

Global proof process. For both, KeY and Isabelle, the participants described a similar proof process: it starts with the formalization of the system/problem and its main properties. Users considered the modeling task to be among the most time-consuming ones. However, system feedback in this phase is restricted to syntactical and simple consistency tests. Instead, feedback causing the user to revise the model on the global level results from the *local* proof process. It is not surprising that there is only little user support for the global process, as the tasks often require creativity and depend on the particular problem.

Local proof process. In the local proof process, the users are guided by their individual impression of the complexity of open goals/proof obligations. If the user considers the obligation to be "easy enough", he or she tries a fully automatic strategy. Otherwise, or if the automation fails, the user tries to prove the obligation interactively. In this case there are two options: structured proofs (Isar/macros) or proof exploration (manual application of rules resp. tactics).

The case where the problem is considered to be easy and is tried to be proven automatically fits our model: It is the case where the user's proof plan has only one step leading to the proof state "proof complete". In the other case, proof exploration corresponds to the user having only a partial proof model, or a set of different models from which the appropriate one has to be determined. In terms of Fig. 1, we observe multiple arrows originating from the proof obligation.

Both KeY and Isabelle aid the user by providing search mechanisms or suggestion mechanisms for proof rules resp. lemmas: As stated by the participants, Isabelle supports the user in finding the right proof technique with a search mechanism for theorems in the library. KeY offers different search mechanisms and suggests applicable rules for a user-selected formula.

System feedback for the local process. In the local processes the systems give different kinds of feedback, e.g., counterexamples, open or closed goals, and (partial) proofs. Some of these are explicit (e.g., message boxes), others are implicit in a changed proof state.

The main difference between both tools is that KeY provides the full path to the open goals as proof tree, while no explicit tree is available in Isabelle.

Which part of the system (e.g., sequent, proof tree, formalization) is inspected by the user to decide on how to continue the proof depends on the problem, but we also learned that different users use different information.

From an abstract perspective the approach of inspecting the proof state, especially in KeY, corresponds to top-down analysis of the proof: the focus moves from the specification to single goals/sequents. At the beginning of the proof process, the specification is inspected more often and the shape of the proof tree plays an important role. Later in the process, the branches in the proof tree and the sequents in the open goals become more important. Also, problem complexity influences whether the sequents of the open goals are helpful or not.

In Isabelle, the strategy *try* (that carries out the complexity estimation in a simple form) and other tools and tactics (e.g., *sledgehammer*, *quickcheck*, *nitpick*, *auto*) give feedback about the goal-state. If the tactics cannot find a proof, the resulting goal-states have to be inspected by the user. However, Isabelle does not provide information about the used rules or lemmas leading to an open goal. As stated especially in the Isabelle group, it is a matter of experience to decide how proof search should proceed.

The comments on the feedback mechanisms of the proof systems support our hypothesis: the user has to understand the system's proof. The different proof artifacts are inspected and the user tries to recognize certain familiar shapes, for which he or she knows from experience how to continue in the proof process.

Proof granularity in the local process. One part of our hypothesis is that the granularity of the automatic strategies as presented to the user does not match the granularity in the user's proof model.

When the application of automatic strategies and tools does lead to open goals instead of a closed proof, information about used lemmas or rules is often missing. An example is the *auto* tactic: if it finds a proof, showing only a single proof step is appropriate. If it does not find a proof, it does not provide information about the concrete proof rules it applied and the resulting intermediate states (although this information is available internally). Only the remaining goal-states are presented to the user. Better feedback is provided by sledgehammer, as it displays the lemmas used in the underlying SMT proof.

Granularity of the proof and feedback of single steps also plays a role when publishing or refactoring a proof depending on the intended audience. In user-constructed proofs Isabelle allows different levels of granularity. Often proofs in Isabelle are more fine grained than proofs on paper.

In KeY, there are three different granularity levels (in this case for proof construction): (a) each rule application individually, (b) using the full automatic strategy, and (c) proof macros together with one step-simplification as middle-course. Proof macros are a preferred way of proving. However, they are not applicable in every proof situation.

In both systems, the granularity of the proof steps can be too fine-grained or too coarse, depending on the proof situation (e.g., failed proof attempts) and the purpose of the proof (e.g., publishing a proof). We conclude that there should be a compromise between the two extremes, e.g., a mechanism that allows to get insight into the Isabelle tactics if required. For the KeY system, a mechanism would be useful that summarizes steps in the proof tree and only unfolds them on user inspection – extending existing mechanisms that collapse/unfold certain kind of proof nodes like intermediate steps or closed proof branches.

Time-consuming tasks during the proof process. We suspected that inspecting open goals resp. finding relations between different proof artifacts would be time-consuming tasks. To test this, we asked for time-consuming actions in the proof processes. As mentioned above, in the global process the modelling and specification task is time-consuming as well as the proof attempts in the local process. Additionally, when the user wants to minimize the proof attempts in the local process, the setup for the automatic strategies is time-consuming in both systems. Other time-consuming tasks that were mentioned, are the decision when to reconsider the whole model, proof refactoring (in Isabelle), and model refactoring (in KeY).

In the local process, the following time-consuming actions are related to *understanding the proof state*: analyzing open goals, finding counterexamples, identifying the cause of a failed proof, as well as systematic proof exploration (in KeY), and *find_theorems* and proof exploration by using apply scripts (in Isabelle). These answers support our hypothesis, as they provide evidence that understanding the proof state is a laborious task. Also, other costly tasks were mentioned: automatic proofs (as the user has to wait for the prover) and trivial repetitive instantiations on different branches (in KeY), as well as redoing a proof and especially finding the correct point to which to backtrack before correcting the model or specification. In Isabelle, cleaning up proofs takes time as well.

Conclusion. Our observation is that a lot of answers focused on understanding the proof state. For example, Isabelle users spend a lot of time cleaning up their proofs to make them accessible and understandable for other users. The answers related to the topic "understanding the proof state" in the part about time-consuming actions also support this observation. To conclude, the answers support our hypothesis that understanding a proof is a central and important task in theorem proving. The participants spend time on understanding the proof state in order to be able to proceed with the proof or find the cause for a failed proof attempt. Comprehending the proof state is also necessary for proof exploration, e.g., when the user only has parts of the proof process in mind or when the user does not know how to start or proceed.

4.7 Mechanisms Supporting the Comprehension of the Proof State

Prior to the discussion, we developed paper mock-ups of mechanisms for both verification tools which we believe aid the user in understanding the proof (state) and therefore help to overcome the discrepancy between the proof model of the user and the actual proof of the system. Implementing these remains for future work. These mock-ups were presented to the focus groups as a sequence of screenshots that show how to invoke the mechanism and the effect of the mechanism in a particular proof situation.[1] Our intention was to gain feedback whether our developed mechanisms are comprehensible, serve our intended purpose (bridge or reduce the gap) and are of interest for the participants. The task for the participants was to describe the purpose and effect of the mechanism (as they saw it) and share their opinion about it.

Tracing Terms/formulas/variables. We showed two mock-ups (designs) for each system for the mechanism of tracing the origin of formulas respectively variables in an open goal: In Isabelle we showed the parent formula of an open goal with renamed variables. Additionally, the relation between the original and the renamed variables was depicted. As a second mock-up we showed a state with a number of open goals. By clicking on one of the goals, some of the used lemmas and definitions leading to that goal were shown.

For the KeY system, the starting point for both designs was the same: we selected one (sub-)formula of the sequent in the open goal. Then, for the first design, we depicted a new window showing the selected formula and its ancestors up to the original proof obligation (we summarized some of the intermediate parent formulas to not clutter up the screen). In addition, the names of the rules producing the formulas were given. The top-most parent shown was that part of the specification where the formula had its origin. In the second design we did not use a new window, instead we highlighted the parents in each inner node of the proof tree up to the root, which contains the original proof obligation.

When the groups where shown the mock-up of the mechanism for tracing formulas, the first reaction was clearly positive, particularly in the Isabelle group for the first mock-up. Almost all participants intuitively understood the mechanism. One participant reported that he simulates this mechanism by manual "reverse-renaming" in an external text editor. However, the question came up whether the additional information may be confusing or clutter the screen. It was suggested to implement the mechanism carefully, possibly using mouse-over tags and – in particular for KeY – include it into the existing GUI concept.

Inspired by the second mechanism for Isabelle (showing the used lemmas) some participants stated that it would be useful to have a mechanism showing the path or case distinctions leading to selected open goals on demand.

The second design in the KeY group triggered a new idea: some participants suspected a filtering mechanism and discussed about filtering the sequent and the proof tree.

What Needs to Be Proven? For the Isabelle system, a mock-up was given, showing which lemmas and theorems contribute to a proof (depicted as a simple coloured graph). Unproven lemmas were coloured red, lemmas whose proofs used unproven lemmas were coloured orange, and fully proven lemmas were coloured green. The lemmas already proven were depicted with a box with an ellipsis as description. The red and orange boxes were labelled with the name of the

---

[1] The screenshots may be found at http://formal.iti.kit.edu/~grebing/SWC/.

lemma that still needs to be proven resp. uses unproven lemmas. The participants described the mechanism as separating the used from the unused lemmas and that it would be useful in combination with, e.g., the automatic strategy *simp*.

Most of the participants showed a positive reaction to this mechanism. Some participants would prefer a textual representation of the used and unused lemmas. The design of our mock-up can be improved in general. The level of detail should be chosen carefully in order not to clutter up the screen (e.g., fold proven lemmas with the option to unfold) and the view should be hierarchic.

What Happened During the Proof Process? For the KeY system, the mock-up showed a diff mechanism relating two nodes in the proof tree (not necessarily adjacent nodes). We designed the mock-up such that all unchanged parts of the sequent were blurred out and the relevant changes were shown directly above each other. The participants needed some time to understand the idea and the blurring was found to be confusing, as the presentation of two different sequent parts can be mistaken as belonging to the same single sequent.

One participant noticed that something similar is implemented in the KeY system already as string diff mechanism, where the diff between two sequents is shown in one new window. However, this participant also claimed that the mechanism needs improvement, which supports our idea that such a functionality should be implemented in the KeY system.

Already during the discussion, ideas for improvement came up, e.g., that the diff between two sequents should be shown in two windows adjacent to each other or above each other. Also, like in a text-diff viewer, the changes should be marked using colours or typographical presentations. And in the proof tree, the two nodes which are being compared should be marked.

In conclusion, we suggest to develop a user-configurable diff mechanism which shows the two sequents being compared in two windows. One window depicts the old sequent and one depicts the new sequent. In addition, the algorithm for comparing two sequents has to be chosen carefully and consider the tree-structure of the sequent. A string diff algorithm is not sufficient for comparing tree-shaped sequents, as certain differences are recognized in the wrong way. For example, it is wrong to assume that replacing n by `null` results from appending `ull` to n.

4.8   The Ideal Interactive Proof System

As a cool-down task, we asked the participants to name properties that an ideal interactive verification system should or should not have. Our goal here was twofold – we wanted to collect more ideas about desirable features of ITPs and evaluate our hypothesis at the same time. For the sake of brevity, we can only present some of the mentioned features here. We decided to omit comments that were of technical nature (e.g., "It should not have memory leaks.") as well as points that have already been mentioned in previous phases.

Intuitive proof process. Both groups wished that an ideal interactive proof system would produce proofs "close to what an experienced user would expect."

This perfectly supports our paradigm of reducing the gap resp. keeping the gap small between the user's model of the proof and the ITP's current proof state.

Understandable proof states. The focus group on KeY prefers more interaction in terms of the original proof obligation (e.g., specification and program) while the Isabelle group wishes for semi-automatic proof steps (instead of the fully automatic tactics). In our opinion this illustrates that too many as well as too few details have a negative effect on understandability of the ITP.

Convenient interaction. One important feature that was wished for by both groups is a good performance of the ITP. The performance can impede usability if the user has to wait too long between interaction steps.

Conclusion. In summary, participants of our focus groups asked for an ITP that (i) produces intuitive proofs, (ii) can present proof steps in an understandable way (and give counterexamples if the proof can not be closed), and (iii) provides a convenient interface for interaction.

5   Conclusion and Future Work

We conducted two focus group discussions to evaluate the usability of ITPs. Our goal was to find evidence that a gap between the user's model of the proof and the system's current proof state exists and that this gap is a central problem for the usability of ITPs. In addition, we have developed mock-ups for mechanisms that help to bridge this gap or keep it small. We have developed a first model of the proof process with the focus on the relation between the user's (partial) model of the proof process and the current proof state.

In this evaluation we have found evidence that our model of the proof process is reasonable: the model does not fully represent the complexity of interactive proof search but captures already a lot of peculiarities. Our findings also indicate that the gap between the user's model of the proof and the system's current proof state is a central problem in interactive theorem proving.

We have also encountered related topics, such as counterexample generators and finding the correspondence between the current proof state and the program (in the KeY system) that clearly show that our model does not capture all the details of proving yet and therefore for future work this model will be extended. We have also discovered other usability issues in the systems not related to our hypothesis. These are often either technical or relate to other topics, e.g., performance of the automatic strategies. We believe that attention has to be drawn to these as well to enhance the user experience for ITPs.

We have presented functionalities that should help to bridge the gap or reduce the gap concentrated on providing the user insights into what happened during the automatic proof search. The participants reacted positively towards the mechanisms and provided feedback for improvements or new ideas, such as user defined filter mechanisms for the proof tree in KeY.

For future work we will extend the proposed mechanisms and prototypically implement them in the KeY system and perform usability tests to evaluate our solutions. Additionally, we plan to extend the model to take into account that there are also different proof strategies for one proof and it is often user-dependent which proof style is used for a proof.

Acknowledgements. We thank the participants of our focus group discussions on the usability of KeY and of Isabelle and, in particular, the two moderators for their great work. In addition, we thank our project partners from DATEV eG for sharing their expertise in how to prepare and analyse focus group discussions.

References

1. Aitken, J.S., Gray, P., Melham, T., Thomas, M.: Interactive theorem proving: an empirical study of user activity. J. Symb. Comp. **25**(2), 263–284 (1998)
2. Aitken, J.S., Melham, T.F.: An analysis of errors in interactive proof attempts. Interact. Comput. **12**(6), 565–586 (2000)
3. Aitken, S., Gray, P., Melham, T., Thomas, M.: A study of user activity in interactive theorem proving. In: Task Centred Approaches To Interface Design, pp. 195–218. GIST Technical. Report G95.2, Department of Computing Science (1995)
4. Archer, M., Heitmeyer, C.: Human-style theorem proving using PVS. In: Ait Mohamed, O., Muoz, C., Tahar, S. (eds.) LNCS. Springer, Heidelberg (1997)
5. Beckert, B., Grebing, S.: Evaluating the usability of interactive verification systems. In: Proceedings, 1st International Workshop on Comparative Empirical Evaluation of Reasoning Systems (COMPARE), Manchester, UK, June 30, 2012, CEUR Workshop Proceedings, vol. 873, pp. 3–17. CEUR-WS.org (2012)
6. Beckert, B., Grebing, S., Böhl, F.: How to put usability into focus: using focus groups to evaluate the usability of interactive theorem provers. In: Benzmüller, C., Woltzenlogel Paleo, B. (eds.) Proceedings, Workshop on User Interfaces for Theorem Provers (UITP), Vienna. EPTCS, July 2014 (to appear)
7. Beckert, B., Hähnle, R., Schmitt, P.H. (eds.): Verification of Object-Oriented Software: The KeY Approach. LNCS, vol. 4337. Springer, Heidelberg (2007)
8. Beckert, B., Klebanov, V., Schlager, S.: Dynamic logic. In: Beckert et al. [7], chapter 3, pp 69–175
9. Blackwell, A., Green, T.R.: A cognitive dimensions questionnaire (v. 5.1.1) Feb 2007. www.cl.cam.ac.uk/~afb21/CognitiveDimensions/CDquestionnaire.pdf
10. Caplan, S.: Using focus group methodology for ergonomic design. Ergonomics **33**(5), 527–533 (1990)
11. Cheney, J.: Project report - theorem prover usability. Technical report, 2001. Report of project COMM 641. http://homepages.inf.ed.ac.uk/jcheney/projects/tpusability.ps
12. Ferré, X., Juzgado, N.J., Windl, H., Constantine, L.L.: Usability basics for software developers. IEEE Softw. **18**(1), 22–29 (2001)
13. Jackson, M., Ireland, A., Reid, G.: Interactive proof critics. Formal Aspects Comput. **11**(3), 302–325 (1999)

14. Kadoda, G., Stone, R., Diaper, D.: Desirable features of educational theorem provers: a cognitive dimensions viewpoint. In: Proceedings of the 11th Annual Workshop of the Psychology of Programming Interest Group (1996)
15. Lowe, H., Cumming, A., Smyth, M., Varey, A.: Lessons from experience: making theorem provers more co-operative. In: Proceedings 2nd Workshop User Interfaces for Theorem Provers (1996)
16. Morgan, D.L.: Focus groups. Annu. Rev. Sociol. **22**(1), 129–152 (1996)
17. Nielsen, J.: Usability Engineering. Morgan Kaufmann Publishers Inc., San Francisco (1993)
18. Nipkow, T., Paulson, L.C., Wenzel, M.: Isabelle/HOL: A Proof Assistant for Higher-Order Logic. LNCS, vol. 2283. Springer, Heidelberg (2002)
19. Ouimet, M., Lundqvist, K.: Formal software verification: model checking and theorem proving. Technical report, March 2007
20. Vujosevic, V., Eleftherakis, G.: Improving formal methods' tools usability. In: Eleftherakis, G. (ed.) 2nd South-East European Workshop on Formal Methods (SEEFM 05), Formal Methods: Challenges in the Business World, Ohrid, 18–19 Nov 2005. South-East European Research Centre (SEERC) (2006)

An Approach for Creating Domain Specific Visualisations of CSP Models

Lukas Ladenberger[✉], Ivaylo Dobrikov, and Michael Leuschel

Institut für Informatik, Universität Düsseldorf, Düsseldorf, Germany
{ladenberger,dobrikov,leuschel}@cs.uni-duesseldorf.de

Abstract. A domain specific visualisation can greatly contribute to better understanding of formal models. In this work we propose an approach that supports the user in creating domain specific visualisations of CSP models. CSP (Communicating Sequential Processes) is a formal language that is mainly used for specifying concurrent and distributed systems. We have successfully created various visualisations of CSP models in order to demonstrate our approach. The visualisations of two case studies are presented in this paper: the bully algorithm and a level crossing gate. In addition, we discuss possible applications of our approach.

Keywords: Formal methods · CSP · Domain specific visualisation · Validation · Method · Tool support · Graphical editor

1 Introduction and Motivation

The feedback from a domain expert is crucial in the process of creating a formal model since certain types of errors can only be detected by a domain expert. Moreover, it is very important for the domain expert to make sure that his expectations are met in the formal model. However, the communication between the developer of a formal model and the domain expert can be challenging. One reason for this is the fact that discussing a formal model requires knowledge about the mathematical background of the respective formalism that the domain expert might not have. To overcome this challenge, it may be useful to create domain specific visualisations of formal models.

Inspired by the successful application of domain specific visualisations [1,6] of Event-B models [3], we have started an attempt to develop an approach for creating domain specific visualisations for CSP (Communicating Sequential Processes). CSP is a notation used mainly for describing concurrent and distributed systems. There are two major CSP dialects: CSP-M [15] and CSP# [17]. The most popular tools that support model checking of CSP-M specifications are FDR [19] and PROB [10]. Support for animating processes of CSP-M specifications is provided by ProB and ProBE [5]. The more recent CSP# [17] is

---

The work in this paper is partly funded by ADVANCE, an European Commission Information and Communication Technologies FP7 project.

C. Canal and A. Idani (Eds.): SEFM 2014 Workshops, LNCS 8938, pp. 20–35, 2015.
DOI: 10.1007/978-3-319-15201-1_2

supported by the PAT system [18]. In this work, we concentrate on the creation of domain specific visualisations for CSP-M models.

Some of the tools provide features for visualising some aspects of the formal CSP model. For instance, ProB, PAT, and FDR can provide visualisations of counter examples that come in form of graphs. On the other hand, this work is concerned with creating domain specific visualisations. This means that if we were modelling, an interlocking system we could create a domain specific visualisation that shows a track layout with blocks and points as well as signals and trains. From now on, when we speak about a visualisation we mean a domain specific visualisation.

In this work we present an approach (method and tool) for visualising CSP-M models. We describe the method and present an implementation that comes as an extension for BMotion Studio [8]. BMotion Studio is a visual editor that supports the user in creating domain specific visualisations for Event-B, a formal language for state-based modelling and verification of systems.

The difference between our contribution and the original visualisation approach of BMotion Studio is imposed by the specifics of the CSP formal language. The basic idea of BMotion Studio is to visualise the information that is encoded in the states of an Event-B model (e.g. the values of variables), where each state of the model is mapped to a particular visualisation. In contrast to Event-B, in CSP the states of the modelled system are left uninterpreted and the behaviour is defined in terms of sequences of events (*traces*). Thus, the concepts of BMotion Studio are not longer applicable on event-based formalisms as CSP. The intention of our approach is to visualise the traces of the underlying CSP model.

In order to demonstrate our approach, we have created visualisations for various CSP-M models that we have found in the literature. In this paper, we focus on the presentation of the visualisations of the bully algorithm [13] and of a level crossing gate [14]. We also discuss how our approach can be of use in the process of analysing and validating CSP specifications.

The paper is organised as follows: Sects. 2 and 3 describe the method and tool support, respectively. The presentation of the visualisation of both case studies is given in Sect. 4. The discussion of possible applications of our approach is outlined in Sect. 5. Finally, we present our conclusions and compare our work with related work.

Tool Website. The tool, various case studies, and a tutorial can be found at http://www.stups.hhu.de/bmotionstudio/index.php/CSP.

2   The Method

The mathematical semantics of CSP are mainly based on *traces*. A trace is a sequence of events performed by a process that can communicate and interact with other processes within the CSP model. The basic idea of our approach is to visualise the information encoded in the given sequence of events (*trace*). However, a process may perform many different traces and thus creating a visualisation manually for each possible trace is an almost impossible task.

Our method requires the user to set up only one visualisation that may be capable of representing any possible trace of a CSP process of a particular model. This is achieved by means of *observers* that are used to link the visualisation with the model. Formally, one can describe the method by means of Algorithm 1.

Algorithm 1. Visualising a CSP trace

---

1 **procedure** visualiseTrace(trace $\langle e_1, e_2, \ldots, e_n \rangle$, observers *obs*)
2   **for** *i=1* **to** n **do**
3   **foreach** $o \in obs$ **do**
4   **if** $member(e_i, o.exp)$ **then**
5                  $trigger(o.acts)$
6   **end if**
7   **end foreach**
8   **end for**
9 **end proc**

For visualising a particular trace $tr = \langle e_1, e_2, \ldots, e_n \rangle$, we sequentially go through each event e_i of tr with $i \in \{1..n\}$ and execute all established observers *obs* for e_i. Note that by "visualisation of a trace" we mean the visualisation of the state reached after the sequential execution of the events of a trace.

Each observer o has a user-defined CSP expression $o.exp$ that constitutes a set of observed events. For instance, the CSP expression $\{e.x \mid x \leftarrow \{0..3\}\}$ will constitute the set of observed events $\{e.1, e.2, e.3\}$. In addition, an observer defines a list of actions $o.acts$ that determine the appearance and the behaviour of the visualisation. The actions are only triggered when the currently processed event e_i of the given trace is a member of the respective set of observed events defined by $o.exp$. More precisely, the actions are triggered (line 5) whenever the expression $member(e_i, o.exp)$ evaluates to *true* (line 4).

3 Tool Support

Figure 1 shows an overview of the tools and components that are used in this work, as well as how our contribution fits into this overview (marked with dotted border).

We implemented the method presented in Sect. 2 as an extension for the new version[1] of BMotion Studio [8]. BMotion Studio is a visual editor for creating domain specific visualisations of formal models. It uses PROB [9] to interact with the model, to obtain trace information and to evaluate expressions. PROB is a validation tool for model checking and animating Event-B, Classical-B and CSP-M models [10], as well as other formalisms (e.g. [7,12]). The current version of BMotion Studio supports the user in creating visualisations for Event-B models [8]. This work extends BMotion Studio to support the creation of visualisations for CSP-M models.

---

[1] The new version of BMotion Studio is not officially released yet, but the source code is available from http://www.stups.hhu.de/bmotionstudio/index.php/Source.

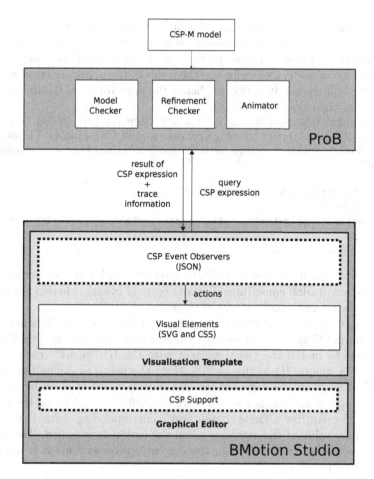

Fig. 1. Overview of the components that are used in this work

In BMotion Studio, a visualisation is described by a *visualisation template* that contains *visual elements* and *observers*. Visual elements may be, for instance, shapes or images that represent some aspects of the model. For example, in case of modelling a communication protocol, we can use circles for representing the communicating entities of the protocol and arrows for the message exchanges between the entities. The new version of BMotion Studio uses web technologies like Scalable Vector Graphics (SVG) [21] and Cascading Style Sheets (CSS) [20] for this purpose. SVG is an XML-based markup language for describing two-dimensional vector graphics. It comes with a number of visual elements like shapes, images and paths. On the other hand, CSS is a language that can be used to describe the style of SVG visual elements (e.g. the colour or the dimension).

Observers are used to link visual elements with the model. An observer is notified whenever a model change its state, e.g. an event was executed. In response, the observer will query the model's state and triggers actions on the linked visual elements in respect to the new state. BMotion Studio comes with a number of default observers for creating visualisations for Event-B. For instance, BMotion Studio provides an observer that takes a user-defined predicate that is to be evaluated in every state. Depending on the result of the predicate (true or false), the observer will trigger an action to change the appearance of the linked visual elements (e.g. the colour of a shape).

We extended BMotion Studio with a new observer type called *CSP event observer* in order to support creating visualisations of CSP models. The observer has the following JSON structure (in BMotion Studio an observer is represented in JSON [2]):

```
{ "exp": "<user-defined CSP expression>",
  "actions": [
    {"selector":"<selector>", "attr":"<attribute>", "value":"<value>" },
    { ... }
  ] }
```

Each observer has a *user-defined CSP expression* and a list of *actions*. The user-defined expression constitutes a set of observed events, whereas the actions determine the changes made on visual elements.

An action defines a *selector* that matches a set of visual elements in the visualisation (SVG graphic). A selector follows the syntax provided by jQuery[2]. For instance, to match the visual element with the ID "elem1" (each element should have a unique ID in the visualisation) the user can define the selector "#elem1". The prefix "#" is used for matching a visual element by its ID in jQuery. An action also defines an *attribute* (e.g. "fill" for colouring the interior of a visual element like a circle shape) and a corresponding *value* that will be set as the new value of the attribute when the action is triggered. The actions of an observer o are triggered when the currently processed event is in the set of observed events of o.

The user can refer to the information given by the arguments of the currently processed event within the action fields (selector, attribute and value). This is achieved by means of the construct "{{aN}}" where aN refers to the N-th argument of the event. For instance, if the event has two arguments, then the first and the second one can be obtained with "{{a1}}" and "{{a2}}", respectively. To illustrate this, consider an event $evt.x$ with $x \leftarrow 0..4$. One may want to use the information given by the first argument x of evt within a selector in order to match visual elements that have an ID of the form "elem$x$". This can be done by defining the selector "#elem{{a1}}". The construct "{{a1}}" will be replaced by the value of the first argument of the currently processed event in the observer. For instance, if the currently processed event is $evt.2$, the selector "#elem{{a1}}" will become "#elem2".

Figure 2 illustrates the function of the CSP event observer on a simple example. The visualisation consists of an SVG graphic with a text field element with the ID "txt" and one CSP event observer. The CSP event observer defines an

---

[2] For more information about jQuery and selectors we refer the reader to the jQuery API documentation http://api.jquery.com/category/selectors/.

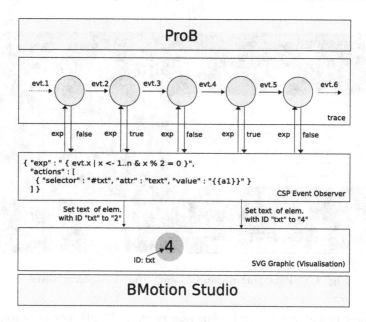

Fig. 2. The function of the CSP event observer

expression that constitutes the set of observed events $evt = \{evt.2, evt.4, evt.6, ..\}$ and one action $act1$ that changes the value of the attribute "text" to "{{a1}}" of the visual element with the ID "txt" (the text field). According to our method (see Sect. 2), the observer is executed for each event of a given trace. This means that, whenever the currently processed event is in the set of observed events evt, the observer will trigger the defined action $act1$. For instance, the execution of the event $evt.4$ causes the observer to set the value of the text field element to "4" as demonstrated in Fig. 2.

Creating a Visualisation. BMotion Studio provides a graphical editor with different views and wizards that supports users in creating visualisations for formal models. Figure 3 shows the bully algorithm visualisation template opened in the graphical editor (the bully algorithm visualisation will be introduced in Sect. 4). The editor consists of a set of tools (1) for creating SVG widgets (e.g. visual elements as shapes and images), a canvas (2) holding the actual visual elements, a view (3) for editing observers, and another view (4) for manipulating the attributes of the currently selected visual element in the canvas. The corresponding JSON file which contains the observers is created by the editor automatically. We extended the graphical editor of BMotion Studio in order to support the editing of CSP event observers.

Running a Visualisation. Once a visualisation template is created, it can be started with BMotion Studio as shown in Fig. 4. BMotion Studio uses the default web browser of the user's operating system to view the visualisation and the PROB tool to animate the corresponding CSP-M model.

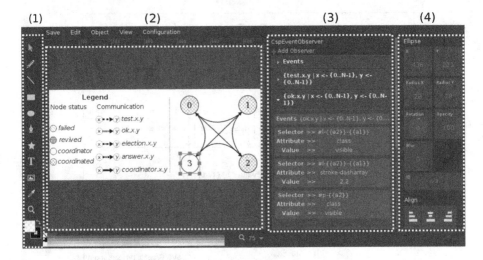

Fig. 3. CSP support within BMotion Studio graphical editor

The user can access the entire function range of PROB. For instance, Fig. 4 shows two views (Events and History) that come from PROB. The first one (Events) lists all possible events that are available in the current state of the animation. The second one (History) shows the executed events so far. The left side of Fig. 4 shows the visualisation of the trace that is displayed in the History view. If the user executes an event in the Events view, a new trace (the trace generated so far plus the recently executed event) is provided which is visualised according to our approach.

4 Case Studies

In order to test our approach, we successfully created various visualisations for CSP specifications that we have found in the literature. In this work we present the visualisation of the bully algorithm specification from [13] and of the level crossing gate specification from [14]. The specifications are written in the machine readable dialect CSP-M and have not been modified for the visualisation we have created. Both visualisations were created by means of the built-in graphical editor of BMotion Studio. However, for presentation purposes the observers of the visualisations are described in the JSON notation in this section.

4.1 The Bully Algorithm

The algorithm represents a method of distributed computing for electing a node to be the coordinator amongst a group of nodes. Each node has a unique ID and the algorithm intends to select the node with the highest ID to be the coordinator. It is assumed that the nodes may fail and revive from time to time and the communication between the nodes is reliable. Three types of messages

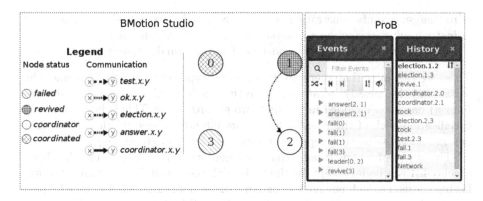

Fig. 4. The bully algorithm visualisation

are defined within the design of the algorithm: *election* (announcing an election), *answer* (responding to an election message), and *coordinator* (announcing the identity of the coordinator).

The specification from [13] defines six additional types of events needed for the formalisation of the algorithm in CSP: the *fail* and *revive* events (for modelling failing and reviving of a node), the *test* and *ok* events (for simulating a test-response communication), the *leader* events (for indicating the coordinator of a living node), and the *tock* event (for modelling timeouts and time).

Visualising the Bully Algorithm. In general, we want to visualise the process of electing a leader in the network. More precisely, we aim to visualise the *Network* process of the CSP specification. As the bully algorithm specification in [13] is presented for a network with four nodes, we also intend to create a visualisation for four nodes (the nodes are enumerated from 0 to 3). Figure 4 demonstrates the visualisation of a particular trace.

There are two major aspects of the specification that we want to visualise: the nodes and the communication between the nodes. Each node is visualised by means of a circle in which the respective ID is positioned, whereas the communication between the nodes is illustrated by directed arrows. Each directed arrow is made up of a line and a corresponding arrowhead.

To each visual element in the visualisation we assign a unique ID referring to the elements in the CSP specification. Thus, the node with ID x in the CSP specification is presented by the circle with ID "n-x" in the visualisation. Additionally, a message transfer from the node with ID x to the node with ID y is represented by the line with ID "l-x-y" and the arrowhead with ID "p-y" (i.e. the arrow connecting "n-x" and "n-y"). In this section, both symbols x and y stand for an integer ranging from 0 to 3.

We can classify all types of events in the specification into the following groups:

– **status:** Events that can change the status of a particular node x: $fail.x$, $revive.x$, $coordinator.x.y$, and $leader.x.y$.

- **message:** Events illustrating a message transfer from node x to node y: *test.x.y, ok.x.y, election.x.y, answer.x.y,* and *coordinator.x.y.*
- **hidden:** Events that are not considered in the visualisation: *tock.*

Thus, we can infer that there are two general types of observers to define: the *status* and the *message* observers. Note that each *coordinator* event (*coordinator.x.y*) has been included in the first two groups above. This is because in the specification each of the *coordinator* events intends to identify the coordinator (x) and at the same time represents a message transfer (to node y).

The status of a node usually changes when one of the *status* events has been executed. Each node, except for the node with the lowest ID[3], can have the following status: `failed`, `revived`, `coordinator`, or `coordinated`. A unique fill pattern has been selected for distinguishing each possible status of a node (see legend in Fig. 4).

In order to associate a *status* event from the CSP specification with a node in the visualisation, we use the selector "#n-{{a1}}" in the definition of the respective observer. The construct "{{a1}}" is used in the selector for obtaining the value of the first argument of the respective *status* event. For example, the observer for changing a status of a node to `failed` can be defined as follows:

```
{ "exp": "{fail.x | x <- {0..N-1}}",
  "actions": [ {"selector":"#n-{{a1}}",
                "attr":"fill", "value":"url(#diagonalHatch) "} ] }
```

The observer will fill the respective node with a diagonal hatch pattern whenever a *fail* event has been processed. For instance, the node with ID "n-3" will be filled with a diagonal hatch pattern when the event *fail.3* has been processed. In a similar fashion we have defined the observers for the other node status changes.

For creating the *message* observers we need to consider both arguments of the *message* events. The types of the messages are distinguished by different stroke patterns (see Fig. 4). Thus, each *message* observer, except for the *coordinator* observer (this observer has three actions), has two actions: one action for appearing the arrow (the line and arrowhead constituting the respective arrow in the visualisation) and one action for changing the stroke pattern of the arrow. For instance, the observer for visualising the election message can be defined as follows:

```
{ "exp": "{election.x.y | x <- {0..N-1}, y <- {0..N-1}}",
  "actions": [ { "selector": "#l-{{a1}}-{{a2}}, #p-{{a2}}",
                 "attr": "class", "value": "visible" },
               { "selector": "#l-{{a1}}-{{a2}}",
                 "attr": "stroke-dasharray", "value": "5,2,2,2" } ] }
```

To provide a clear visualisation an additional observer has been added to hide all arrows after performing an arbitrary event. This observer is applied on the currently processed event before all other defined observers.

---

[3] The node with ID 0 can never be a coordinator as there is no node with a lower ID.

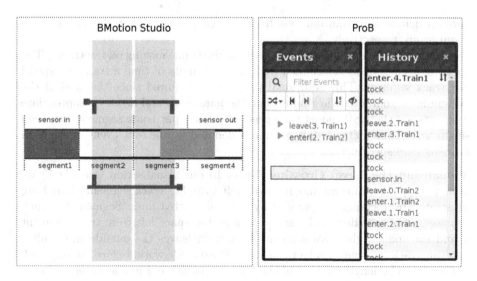

Fig. 5. The level crossing gate visualisation

The initial state of the specification and the visualisation is the state in the network where all nodes are alive and the coordinator is the node with the ID 3 (the node with the greatest ID). Additionally, no message exchanges are performed.

4.2   Level Crossing Gate

The model of the first case study introduced in [14] specifies a level crossing gate of a single railway track along which trains move only in one direction. The track is divided into segments such that each of the segments is at least as long as any train. There are five track segments considered for the level crossing gate where one of the track segments represents the outside world.

The track segments are numbered. The input sensor is placed in segment 1 and the crossing and output sensors in segment 4. The outside world segment is identified by 0. A train enters segment $(i+1)$ before it leaves segment i. Entering and leaving of a segment are specified by the events *enter* and *leave*, respectively. The entering of train t into segment j is described by *enter.j.t*. Accordingly, the leaving of train t from segment j is designed by means of the event *leave.j.t*.

The sensors send control signals to the gate. The gate goes down after a train enters segment 1 and accordingly the gate goes up after the train leaves segment 3 and no train is moving along the segments 1 to 2. The control signals sent by the input and output sensors are specified by the events *sensor.in* and *sensor.out*, respectively. The communication between the controller and the gate processes is specified by the channel *gate* which defines four different events. The events *gate.go_down* and *gate.go_up* represent the commands from the controller to the gate for moving the barriers down or up. And the events *gate.down* and *gate.up* denote the confirmations from the gate sensors that the barriers are down or up, respectively.

In addition, timing constraint are set for the trains moving on the tracks. The speed of each train is determined by how many units of time a train can spend per track segment. This additional property is required since the goal of the system is to guarantee via timing that the gate is up and down at appropriate moments. In the CSP model the speed of a train per track segment has been set to three time units. A unit of time is denoted by the *tock* event in the level crossing gate specification.

Visualising the Level Crossing Gate. In our visualisation (see Fig. 5) we assume that the trains are moving from left to right. Track segments 1 to 4 are illustrated by rectangles separated by vertical, dotted lines. Segment 0, which represents the outside world, can be seen as the space left from track segment 1 and the space right from segment 4. A train leaves the outside world after entering track segment 1 and a train enters the outside world before leaving track segment 4. The length of each of the track segments 1–4 in the visualisation is considered to be 100 pixels.

Since the model from [14] handles two trains, we also intend to visualise only two trains (these are indicated as *Train1* and *Train2*). Both trains are represented by two boxes coloured in grey and slate grey, respectively. Moving of a train along the track is simulated by shifting the respective box from left to right. In order to simulate a movement along the track segments, we shift the respective box 50 pixels from left to right. In doing so, entering of a new segment is represented such that the box is laid half on the new segment and half on the previous. On the other hand, when the train leaves a track segment, the box is moved fully on the recently entered segment. Referring to Fig. 5, the grey box representing *Train1* is laid half on segment 4 and half on segment 3 after executing the event *enter.4.Train1*, whereas *Train2* (the slate grey box) is moved fully on segment 1 after performing consecutively the events *enter.1.Train2* and *leave.0.Train2*. We have set each box representing a train to the length of 100 pixels.

For visualising the movement of the trains, we defined two observers that listen respectively to the events *enter.j.t* and *leave.j.t*. Both observers contain an action that changes the *transform* attribute [21] of the matched visual element. For instance, the *leave* observer is defined such that by executing an event *leave.j.t* the visual element with the ID "train-*t*" (*t* refers to the second argument of the *leave* events) will be moved 50 pixels to right by setting the *transform* attribute to the value *translate*(50, 0). Thus, the observer for leaving a track is defined as follows:

```
{ "exp": "{leave.j.t | j <- {0..3}, t <- {Train1,Train2}}",
  "actions": [ { "selector":"#train-{{a2}}",
                 "attr":"transform", "value":"translate(50,0)" } ] }
```

Note that the *leave* observer does not fire its actions when an event *leave.4.t* is executed since in our visualisation the respective box "train-t" is intended to be moved on the left site of track segment 1 when the event *enter.0.t* is executed.

We decided to define the observers in this way because after entering the outside world (track segment 0) and leaving at last track segment 4, the same train can enter the crossing gate segments once again.

For the overall visualisation we defined four different observers. The other two observers are responsible for simulating the up and down movement of the barriers in the visualisation after proceeding of the events *gate.up* and *gate.down*, respectively. For this, we created for each of the barriers two visual elements that illustrate accordingly the two possible states of the appropriate barrier: barrier is up and barrier is down. This means that we have four visual elements illustrating the different positions of the barriers. When, for example, the event *gate.down* is processed, then the *go-down* observer executes two actions. The first is to hide all barrier elements and the second action is to display the visual elements representing that the barriers are down. The hiding and displaying of the barriers are realised by setting the "opacity" attribute of the visual elements to 0 and 100, respectively. The *go-down* observer is given as follows:

```
{ "exp":"{gate.down}",
  "actions": [
    { "selector":"g[id^=gate]", "attr":"opacity", "value":"0" }
    { "selector":"g[id^=gate-go_down]", "attr":"opacity", "value":"100" }]}
```

Analogously, we defined the *go-up* observer. The initial state of the specification and its visualisation is the state in which both trains are in the "outside world" track segment and both barriers are up.

5 Application of the Approach

Using validation tools for performing various consistency checks automatically is a powerful technique for verifying the correctness of the analysed specification. A failure of a consistency check is mostly reported by producing of a counterexample (very often presented as a trace leading to an error state). However, trying to understand the failure behaviour of the model by simply examining the trace can sometimes be difficult as the error trace may, for example, be the result of the interaction of various components in the specified system. Thus, using a visualisation in order to facilitate the effort of understanding the error trace can be very useful.

In this Section we show how the bully algorithm visualisation introduced in Sect. 4 may, for example, contribute to the better understanding of an erroneous behaviour in the models.

For example, the trace of the *Network* process of the bully algorithm model

$$\langle fail.2, fail.3, test.1.3, tock, election.1.3, election.1.2, revive.2, revive.3,$$
$$coordinator.3.2, fail.3, test.0.3, tock, coordinator.1.0, leader.2.3 \rangle$$

represents a sequence of events leading to a state in the network in which the elected leader is not the living node with the greatest ID. In general, the false

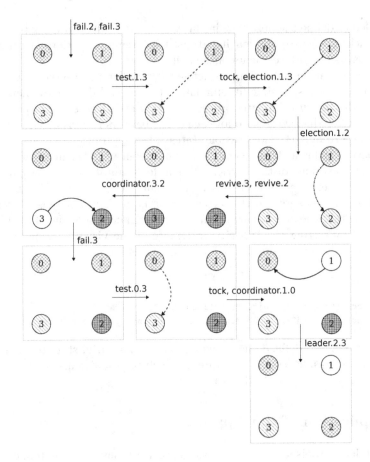

Fig. 6. A stepwise visualisation of a trace of the bully algorithm model

behaviour that is explicitly discussed in [13] illustrates a problem occurring by a certain combination of node failures and mixing up various elections.

While examining the given error trace, it is hard for the user to reproduce and to see the actual problem. In contrast, Fig. 6 shows a stepwise graphical representation of the error trace. The user can see at a glance the erroneous behaviour that is shown in the last step of the trace (after performing leader.2.3) in the graphical representation.

6   Conclusion

In this paper, we presented an approach for creating domain specific visualisations of CSP-M models and an implementation based on BMotion Studio. In particular, we extended BMotion Studio and the built-in graphical editor with a new observer type (CSP event observer) that implements the algorithm presented in Sect. 2.

The difference between our contribution and the primary approach of BMotion Studio (the domain specific visualisation of Event-B models) is imposed by the question of what is to be visualised of a model. On the one hand, in CSP each trace is mapped to a particular visualisation. On the other hand, in Event-B the information to be visualised is given by the states (e.g. the values of variables) of an Event-B model, where each state is mapped to an individual visualisation.

We tested our approach by creating visualisations of various CSP-M models. A demonstration of our approach is given by visualising the bully algorithm specification from [13] and the level crossing gate specification from [14]. We also have shown how our approach could be of use in the process of analysing and validating CSP specifications.

Our tool comes with a graphical editor that can be used to create easily visualisations. The developer of a visualisation remains in the CSP domain. This means that only CSP expressions and jQuery selectors (see Sect. 3) are required for establishing the link between a visualisation and the CSP model. Moreover, a modification of the CSP model is not necessary to create a visualisation for it.

A domain specific visualisation of a CSP model can be useful in various ways. For example, the graphical representation of the behaviour of the CSP processes can be helpful for discussing the specification with non-formal method experts and for the further development of the specification.

We also believe that our approach may be of use to identify inconsistencies or unexpected behaviours within the specification. Indeed, in the process of examining the various case studies, the visualisation helped us to better understand some of the unexpected behaviours (error traces) discovered by validating the corresponding specification (see Sect. 5).

Finally, we believe that our approach may be useful for teaching formal methods, as the execution of a specification with a graphical representation may give a better idea and overview of the system being modelled. For instance, we used our approach successfully in our lectures as a way to present formal models to students and to motivate them to write their own formal models.

Related Work. BMotion Studio was initially developed for creating domain specific visualisations of Event-B models [8]. Our approach extends BMotion Studio to permit users to also create visualisations for CSP-M.

The tools presented in [4,16] support the creation of domain specific visualisations for Classical-B. In contrast to our approach, both tools require the user to set up scripts in order to link the visualisation to the model.

Our approach uses ProB [10] to execute a CSP-M specification. ProB and other CSP tools [18,19] are capable of displaying graphs of processes and counterexamples. Whereas, the purpose of our work is to provide a tool that allows the user to create custom visualisations that are specific to a domain.

A central goal of our work is to gain a better understanding of CSP models by creating domain specific visualisations. A different approach has been taken by [11], which presents a tool for visualising CSP in UML.

References

1. ADVANCE Deliverable D4.2 (Issue 2). Methods and tools for simulation and testing I, March 2013
2. ECMA-404 The JSON Data Interchange Standard. Ecma International, October 2013
3. Abrial, J.: Modeling in Event-B: System and Software Engineering. Cambridge University Press, New York (2010)
4. Bendisposto, J., Leuschel, M.: A generic flash-based animation engine for ProB. In: Julliand, J., Kouchnarenko, O. (eds.) B 2007. LNCS, vol. 4355, pp. 266–269. Springer, Heidelberg (2006)
5. Formal Systems (Europe) Ltd., Process Behaviour Explorer (ProBE User Manual, version 1.30). http://www.fsel.com/probe_manual.html
6. Hansen, D., Ladenberger, L., Wiegard, H., Bendisposto, J., Leuschel, M.: Validation of the ABZ landing gear system using ProB. In: Boniol, F., Wiels, V., Ait Ameur, Y., Schewe, K.-D. (eds.) ABZ 2014. CCIS, vol. 433, pp. 66–79. Springer, Heidelberg (2014)
7. Hansen, D., Leuschel, M.: Translating TLA$^+$ to B for validation with ProB. In: Derrick, J., Gnesi, S., Latella, D., Treharne, H. (eds.) IFM 2012. LNCS, vol. 7321, pp. 24–38. Springer, Heidelberg (2012)
8. Ladenberger, L., Bendisposto, J., Leuschel, M.: Visualising event-B models with B-motion studio. In: Alpuente, M., Cook, B., Joubert, C. (eds.) FMICS 2009. LNCS, vol. 5825, pp. 202–204. Springer, Heidelberg (2009)
9. Leuschel, M., Butler, M.: ProB: an automated analysis toolset for the B method. STTT 10(2), 185–203 (2008)
10. Leuschel, M., Fontaine, M.: Probing the depths of CSP-M: a new FDR-compliant validation tool. In: Liu, S., Araki, K. (eds.) ICFEM 2008. LNCS, vol. 5256, pp. 278–297. Springer, Heidelberg (2008)
11. Ng, M.Y., Butler, M.: Tool support for visualizing CSP in UML. In: George, C.W., Miao, H. (eds.) ICFEM 2002. LNCS, vol. 2495, pp. 287–298. Springer, Heidelberg (2002)
12. Plagge, D., Leuschel, M.: Validating Z specifications using the ProB animator and model checker. In: Davies, J., Gibbons, J. (eds.) IFM 2007. LNCS, vol. 4591, pp. 480–500. Springer, Heidelberg (2007)
13. Roscoe, A.: Understanding Concurrent Systems, 1st edn. Springer-Verlag New York Inc., New York (2010)
14. Roscoe, A.W., Hoare, C.A.R., Bird, R.: The Theory and Practice of Concurrency. Prentice Hall PTR, Upper Saddle River (1997)
15. Scattergood, B., Armstrong, P.: CSP-M: A Reference Manual (2011)
16. Servat, T.: BRAMA: a new graphic animation tool for B models. In: Julliand, J., Kouchnarenko, O. (eds.) B 2007. LNCS, vol. 4355, pp. 274–276. Springer, Heidelberg (2006)
17. Sun, J., Liu, Y., Dong, J.S., Chen, C.: Integrating specification and programs for system modeling and verification. In: Chin, W.-N., Qin, S. (eds.) Proceedings TASE 2009, pp. 127–135. IEEE Computer Society (2009)
18. Sun, J., Liu, Y., Dong, J.S., Pang, J.: PAT: towards flexible verification under fairness. In: Bouajjani, A., Maler, O. (eds.) CAV 2009. LNCS, vol. 5643, pp. 709–714. Springer, Heidelberg (2009)

19. Gibson-Robinson, T., Armstrong, P., Boulgakov, A., Roscoe, A.W.: FDR3 — a modern refinement checker for CSP. In: Ábrahám, E., Havelund, K. (eds.) TACAS 2014 (ETAPS). LNCS, vol. 8413, pp. 187–201. Springer, Heidelberg (2014)
20. W3C CSS Working Group. Cascading Style Sheets (CSS) Snapshot 2010. http://www.w3.org/TR/css-2010/, May 2011
21. W3C SVG Working Group. Scalable Vector Graphics (SVG) 1.1 (Second Edition), August 2011. http://www.w3.org/TR/SVG11/

Using Z in the Development and Maintenance of Computational Models of Real-World Systems

Shahrzad Moeiniyan Bagheri[1,2]([✉]), Graeme Smith[1], and Jim Hanan[2]

[1] School of Information Technology and Electrical Engineering,
The University of Queensland, Brisbane, Australia
[2] Queensland Alliance for Agriculture and Food Innovation,
The University of Queensland, Brisbane, Australia
shahrzad.moeiniyanbagheri@uqconnect.edu.au

Abstract. There are two main challenges in developing computational models of a real-world phenomena. One is the difficulty in ensuring clear communication between the scientists, who are the end-users of the model, and the model developers. This results from the difference in their backgrounds and terminologies. Another challenge for the developers is to ensure that the resultant software satisfies all the requirements accurately. Utilising a formal notation such as Z which is easy to learn, read, understand and remember can address these issues by (a) acting as a means to unambiguously communicate between scientists and simulation developers, and (b) providing a basis for systematically producing and maintaining simulation code that meets the specification. In this paper, we describe a translation scheme for producing code for the widely used agent-based simulation environment NetLogo from Z specifications. Additionally, we report on the use of the approach on a real project studying the movement of *chyme*, i.e. food undergoing digestion, through a pig's intestine as a means of understanding the effect of dietary fibre on human health.

1 Introduction

Studying real-world processes through experimental observation can be technically difficult. It can also be costly both in time and resources, and in certain areas ethical issues can arise. A more convenient approach is to develop a computational model of the system. Such a model allows scientists to uncover patterns in the studied system and to determine the system parameters and factors that are the most influential. While the visualisations provided by a computational model allows scientists to observe macro-level behaviour, this behaviour is only representative of their understanding of how the system works when that understanding has been accurately encoded. Furthermore, such visualisations represent specific system behaviours, not the general system behaviour. Ensuring an accurate encoding of the general behaviour can be difficult to achieve, particularly when the developers of the model are not part of the scientific team and are from different backgrounds. The situation can become even worse if developers

© Springer International Publishing Switzerland 2015
C. Canal and A. Idani (Eds.): SEFM 2014 Workshops, LNCS 8938, pp. 36–53, 2015.
DOI: 10.1007/978-3-319-15201-1_3

and scientists have different and even sometimes conflicting terminologies. For example, they may use different terms for the same concepts, or a single term for different concepts.

An additional problem is that the scientists' understanding of the system may evolve over time and the model needs to be modified to reflect this. Again it is important that the modifications are an accurate reflection of the required change. This is facilitated if the model is expressed in terms of constructs that are easy to learn and remember. The constructs of the implementation language of a typical simulation environment are too low-level (i.e., too close to programming constructs) to satisfy this criteria for scientists who are not familiar with programming.

To overcome these issues, two considerations are essential. Firstly, the system needs to be specified and the design ideas and decisions documented using a method that is easy to learn, read, understand and remember by all the people involved, both during the development and for future purposes like testing and maintenance. Such a method should make the communication between the scientists and developers, and also between the development team members, more convenient, efficient and well-documented. Secondly, the applied method for specifying the system should provide a basis for ensuring efficient and accurate implementation of the specified requirements. Not only should this facilitate the production of the code, but also its maintenance. The changes in the scientists' understanding of the system, and as a result in the specification, should be readily incorporated into the code. This reduces the burden of the resultant model's integrity assurance and its maintenance on the developers' shoulders.

To achieve these two goals, formal methods can be utilised. Formal specifications provide a communication method that does not include the ambiguities that are found in informal (e.g., natural language) specifications [3]. These methods also allow the developers to gain a clear understanding of the system, before starting the implementation process. Moreover, such specifications can form the basis of a systematic approach for deriving simulation code. This is in contrast to semi-formal specifications (e.g., UML [2]) that only achieve the first goal.

Recently, we developed simulation software for biologists at the Centre for Nutrition and Food Sciences (CNAFS), The University of Queensland, who are examining the effect of dietary fibre on human health. To facilitate the communication in the development process and future maintenance of the software, we utilised the formal notation Z [10,13]. Z was chosen due to it being a simple extension of set theory and first-order predicate logic which is relatively easy to learn. Since the biologists are not necessarily familiar with programming, notations supporting program-like constructs (such as B [1]) or program-like structuring (such as Object-Z [9]) were seen as having more concepts to learn, and hence being less suitable. It should be noted that in order to achieve the goal of having a fairly simple and easy to learn notation, the use of Z in this research was restricted to avoid more complex notations and certain modelling techniques, such as promotion [13], which are regarded as difficult to understand for non-computer scientists.

For the purpose of implementing this simulator, the NetLogo [11] simulation environment was chosen. NetLogo is a modelling language and environment that is widely used for developing agent-based simulation software. The agent-based approach considers smaller components of the system as autonomous entities (agents) that can form more complex system-level behaviours while performing relatively simple interactions with each other and with their environment [8]. Additionally, a systematic translation scheme from Z to NetLogo code was defined. This made the implementation much easier and enabled us to ensure that the simulation software behaved as required and specified.

Mens and Van Gorp [6] argue that even source code can act as the specification of a system being studied. As a result, the need for utilising Z for specifying the system requirements might be questioned in this research, especially when a Z specification block and its equivalent NetLogo code are almost of similar length. However, what makes a Z specification a more appropriate means of communication than NetLogo code is that it is based on first-order predicate logic. This makes the Z notation easy to learn, read, understand and remember. On the other hand, in order to understand the logic behind NetLogo source code, the reader is required to learn quite a large amount of syntax as well. Consequently, like with many other programming languages, it is not easy and straightforward to learn NetLogo and more importantly memorise its syntax for future references, modifications and maintenance.

In this paper, we present an approach for systematically translating Z specifications to NetLogo code that was developed while working on the CNAFS case study. We begin in Sect. 2 with an overview of NetLogo syntax. In Sect. 3 we provide the translation scheme and illustrate its application on part of the CNAFS case study in Sect. 4. We then conclude with a discussion of lessons learnt and future directions in Sect. 5.

2   Overview of NetLogo

In this section we describe the syntax of NetLogo [11] relevant to the case study described in Sect. 4. A comprehensive documentation of NetLogo can be found in the NetLogo User Manual [12].

2.1   Agents

NetLogo allows developers to define specific *breeds* of agents using the syntax

    breed[*MyBreeds mybreed*]

where *MyBreeds* is the plural, or *agentset*, form of the breed name and *mybreed* is the singular form.

Each type of breed can have its own *properties*. These are a set of attributes that are specific to agents of the breed and, for a given agent, can only be accessed and modified by the agent itself. For example, the following defines agents of type *MyBreeds* as having properties x, y and z.

MyBreeds-own$[x\ y\ z]$

A number of commands exist for creating and accessing agents. For example,

create-*MyBreeds* 2 [set x 0
        set y 100]

creates two agents of type *MyBreeds* where the brackets enclose a sequence of tasks which are applied to the agents upon creation. In this case NetLogo's set keyword is used to set the agents' property x to 0 and property y to 100. Note that when agents are created, a unique non-negative integer is automatically assigned to them, no matter which agentset they are from. This unique number is called who number.

In NetLogo, in order to update the property values of an agent, the ask command, which takes an agent or agentset as its input, is used. Thus, the value of z can be set to 10 for all existing agents of type *MyBreeds* as follows.

ask *MyBreeds* [set z 10]

2.2 Procedures

Procedures in NetLogo enable developers to modularise their code. A procedure includes a group of statements that aims to perform a particular task on agents, their environment, interface controls, inputs or outputs to the system. NetLogo procedures can be defined either as a *reporter* or as a *command* procedure. A reporter procedure is one that reports a value when it is called somewhere in the code, whereas a command procedure only performs some tasks. Additionally, both reporter and command procedures can take input variables. When a procedure, which takes n inputs, is called elsewhere in the code, the first n words after the procedure name are considered as its inputs.

Procedures of each type can be defined using the syntax

```
to mycommand [myinput]          to-report myreporter
    print myinput                   report myval
end                             end
```

where *mycommand* is a command procedure that takes *myinput* as its input and, using the print command, prints its value in the NetLogo Command Center which is part of NetLogo's interface. Also, *myreporter* is a reporter procedure that uses the report keyword to report the value of the *myval* variable. Having defined these two procedures, the following code prints the value of the *myval* variable to the Command Centre

mycommand myreporter

where the value reported by *myreporter* is passed to *mycommand* as an input.

2.3   Data Structures

NetLogo is an untyped programming language, which allows a variable to take different types of values whenever required. In order to define a variable, therefore, it is not required to identify its data type. This section describes the main types of data structures that have been used in the case study.

Globals are those types of variables in the system that can be accessed by all procedures. Such variables can be defined either by using the `globals` keyword as follows

> `globals`[*myglobal1 myglobal2*]

or by assigning a name to an interface control such as a slider or switch, which can then be treated as a global variable throughout the code. It should be noted that the defined breeds are also accessible globally.

Locals, on the other hand, are the variables that can only be accessed within the scope of the procedure in which they have been defined. A local can be defined using the `let` keyword and is accessible to following statements within the procedure.

```
to myprocedure
   let mylocal myvalue
      ...       ; other statements
end
```

Strings, numbers, booleans and lists are the main data types that exist in NetLogo. For instance, a string, number and boolean can be defined as follows.

```
let mystring "my string value"
let mynumber 1000
let myboolean? false
```

It is common in the NetLogo user community to add a '?' to the end of a boolean variable name, however it is not compulsory.

Lists allow developers to define more complex data structures. Each element of a list can be a number, string, agent, agentset or a list. A list can be defined as follows.

```
let mylist list 1 2       ; a list with the two elements 1 and 2
```

2.4   Operators and Reporters

NetLogo supports the usual range of arithmetic (e.g., $+, -, *, /$), comparison (e.g., $<=, >=, =$ and $! =$) and logical operators (e.g., **and**, **or** and **not**). NetLogo also has a range of built-in reporters that are explained in the rest of this section.

The **with** reporter can be used to report only those agents from an agentset that satisfy the given conditions as follows

ask *MyBreeds* **with** $[x = 10]$ [**set** z 10]

where z will be set to 10 only for those agents with $x = 10$. The **with** reporter can be used together with all of the following reporters when required.

The **one-of** reporter can be used to randomly choose a single agent from an agentset. For example, the following equates to an agent with $x = 10$.

one-of *MyBreeds* **with** $[x = 10]$

The **min-one-of** reporter can be used to randomly choose an agent with the minimum value for a given property. For example, the following equates to an agent with the minimum value of z out of all those agents with $x = 10$.

min-one-of *MyBreeds* **with** $[x = 10]$ $[z]$

Note that in both the **one-of** and **min-one-of** examples, a reserved value in NetLogo, **nobody** (representing no agent), is reported in the case where no *mybreed* with $x = 10$ is found.

Additionally, whenever it is required to get the value of any agent's properties, the **of** reporter can be used. For example, the x property of an agent can be accessed as follows

$[x]$ **of** *mybreed* 0

where *mybreed* 0 refers to the agent of type *MyBreeds* with **who** number equal to 0.

The **member?** reporter can be used to check that an agent *mb* (defined, for example, as a local variable) is a member of the agentset *MyBreeds* as follows.

member? *mb MyBreeds*

The **all?** or **any?** reporters, which report **true** or **false**, can be used to check conditions on all or any agents in an agentset. For example,

set *myboolean?* (**all?** *MyBreeds* **with** [color = **green**] $[x = 0]$)

sets *myboolean?* to **true** when all agents of type *MyBreeds* with **color green** have their x property equal to 0, or when there is no **green** *mybreed*[1]. Otherwise, *myboolean?* will be set to **false**. Also,

set *myboolean?* (**any?** *MyBreeds* **with** [color = **green** and $x = 0$])

sets *myboolean?* to **true** when at least one agent of type *MyBreeds* with **color green** and $x = 0$ exists. Otherwise, *myboolean?* will be set to **false**.

---

[1] **color** is a property of all agents, and **green** is a constant that may be assigned to **color**.

2.5 Branching

The main branching structures in NetLogo, as in most programming languages, are the `if` and `ifelse` commands. The latter can be used to control the flow of the program under two opposite conditions as follows.

> `ifelse` *mytotal* < 1000
> [create-*MyBreeds* 1 [set color green]]
> [ask *MyBreeds* with [color = green] [die]]

In this example, if *mytotal* is less than 1000, the commands within the first brackets will be executed and as a result, one agent of type *MyBreeds* will be created and its initial `color` will be set to `green`. However, if *mytotal* is greater than or equal to 1000, then the commands inside the second brackets will be executed and consequently, all the green *MyBreeds* will `die`. The `die` command can be applied on all agents of the system and removes the specified agent from its agentset.

3 Translating Z to NetLogo

The goal of this section is to describe how a Z specification can be systematically translated into NetLogo code. We adopt the guarded (or blocking) interpretation of Z [4] in which operations can only occur when their pre-state predicates, i.e., their predicates describing the state before the operation, hold. In the traditional (or non-blocking) interpretation of Z, operations can always occur but have an undefined effect when their pre-state predicates do not hold.

It should be noted that not all of the Z notation has been investigated in this work. Rather we have considered a subset of Z that we believe satisfies our requirements of being easy to learn, read, understand and remember while also being adequate for modelling the kinds of systems we are targeting. In particular, all updates of variables are written in the form $x' = e$, where e is an expression, facilitating translation to NetLogo `set` commands. Similarly, all initialisations of variables are written $x = e$. Also, some constructs which are not readily translated are avoided. For example, nested quantifiers are avoided in operation guards. Also, use of *promotion* schemas (used in Z to promote operations on local state spaces to the global system state) is avoided by specifying all operations directly on the global system state.

Additionally, as in other programming languages, there are alternative ways to implement a single task in NetLogo, each of which differs in terms of performance, efficiency, readability and other characteristics. Consequently, the translation examples in this section are not necessarily the best or the most efficient way to implement a Z specification. Instead, they represent how a Z specification could be translated into NetLogo code effortlessly. In this section, we use a car racing game as an example.

3.1   Type Definitions

In addition to the predefined types such as $\mathbb{N}$ (natural numbers) and $\mathbb{Z}$ (integers), Z also supports definition of other types [10,13], such as *free types*. Free types represent the fact that a variable of this type can take a value from the set of distinct specified constants. For instance,

$$LicenceClass ::= Car \mid Lightrigid \mid Mediumrigid \mid Heavyrigid$$

represents a type for specifying different kinds of a driver's licence.

Schemas in Z can also be used as (record) types. This is useful for expressing more details regarding the format of a defined type. For instance, the following schema defines a *Driver* type

```
┌─ Driver ──────────────────────────────────────────
│ licence : LicenceClass
│ age : ℕ
└──────────────────────────────────────────────────
```

where *licence* and *age* represent the driver's licence type and age respectively.

Since NetLogo does not support type definition, it is the implementer's responsibility to ensure that the values of variables of such types satisfy the specified constraints throughout the program.

3.2   Global Constants

Z supports the definition of global constants which are accessible throughout a specification. They are defined using an axiomatic definition as follows

```
┌──────────────────────────────
│ SPEED_LIMIT : ℕ
├──────────────────────────────
│ SPEED_LIMIT = 200
```

where $SPEED\_LIMIT$ represents the highest speed allowed for cars on a road.

In NetLogo, global constants can be defined like global variables using the following syntax.

```
globals[SPEED_LIMIT]
```

The value of $SPEED\_LIMIT$ should then be set in the first procedure that will be run in the NetLogo code (usually called *setup*), so that its value can be used throughout the program. This value should not be changed anywhere else in the code as it is a constant.

```
to setup
    set SPEED_LIMIT 200
    ...      ; other tasks, which should be performed in the setup procedure
end
```

3.3   State and Initial State Schemas

As mentioned in Sect. 3.1, schemas can be used as types in Z. State schemas are also used for specifying the main entities of a system. In our car racing game, cars are the main entities (agents) of the system and are specified with the following state schema

```
┌─ Car ─────────────────────────────────────────
│ ID : ℕ
│ fuelAmount : ℕ
│ speed : ℕ
├───────────────────────────────────────────────
│ speed ≤ SPEED_LIMIT
└───────────────────────────────────────────────
```

where ID, $fuelAmount$ and $speed$ (in the declaration part of the schema) represent the car's unique ID in the race, amount of fuel and speed respectively. In NetLogo, the main system's entities can be implemented as *breeds* of agents using the following syntax.

breed $[Cars\ Car]$
$Cars$-**own** $[ID\ fuelAmount\ speed]$

In Z, the invariant part of the Car state schema ($speed \leq SPEED\_LIMIT$) is implicitly included in all other schemas in which Car is included. However, in NetLogo, such invariants need to be implemented explicitly. For example, whenever the $speed$ variable changes, the programmer needs to check its new value to ensure that it satisfies the specified constraint.

State schemas are also used to model the entire system of agents. For example, given the type definition

$GameStatus ::= Normal \mid Dangerous$

$CarRacingGame$ is a multi-agent system with a set of *cars* as the agents of the system and *status* as the game status.

```
┌─ CarRacingGame ──────────┐   ┌─ InitCarRacingGame ──────────┐
│ cars : ℙ Car             │   │ CarRacingGame                │
│ status : GameStatus      │   ├──────────────────────────────┤
│                          │   │ status = Normal              │
└──────────────────────────┘   │ ∀ c : cars •                 │
                                │    c.fuelAmount = 100 ∧ c.speed = 0 │
                                └──────────────────────────────┘
```

In NetLogo, the variables of the multi-agent system schema can be defined as globals (as described in Sect. 2.3).

The $InitCarRacingGame$ specifies that the game *status* is *Normal* in the initial state of the system. This can be implemented by setting the value of the global variable *status* to *Normal* at the beginning of the program (usually in the *setup* procedure). The next predicate starts with a universal quantifier ($\forall$), where the • symbol reads *such that* and states that there are some constraints on the quantified variable c. The constraint part of the predicate then specifies that, in the initial state of the system, each member (c) of the *cars* set has a fuel amount of 100 ($c.fuelAmount = 100$) and a speed of 0 ($c.speed = 0$). These values can be set when the agents are created as described in Sect. 2.1.

3.4 Operation Schemas

In NetLogo, operation schemas of Z can be implemented using procedures. As an example, consider the following operation schemas on the state space of *CarRacingGame*.

Assume that for safety reasons, all moving cars should have a fuel amount higher than 10. If this is the case, the game status would be *Normal*; otherwise, the game status would be *Dangerous* and one of the unsafe cars is reported. In Z, a variable followed by ! specifies an output of the operation. Also, the Δ symbol represents that one or more variables of the following state schema will be changed as a result of the operation being performed. Note that the post-state variables in Z are displayed using the prime symbol ($'$).

GameStatusNormal	*GameStatusDangerous*
$\Delta CarRacingGame$	$\Delta CarRacingGame$
	unsafe! : *Car*
$\forall c : cars \bullet c.speed > 0 \Rightarrow$ $c.fuelAmount > 10$ $status' = Normal \wedge cars' = cars$	$\exists c : cars \bullet c.speed > 0 \wedge$ $c.fuelAmount \leq 10 \wedge unsafe! = c$ $status' = Dangerous$

The *GameStatusNormal* and *GameStatusDangerous* operation schemas can be implemented in NetLogo as follows. Note that in translating an operation no action is required if a variable remains unchanged (e.g., as in the predicate $cars' = cars$).

```
to game-status-normal
     if all? Cars with [speed > 0][fuelAmount > 10]
     [set status "Normal"]
end
to-report game-status-dangerous
     ifelse any? Cars with [speed > 0 and fuelAmount <= 10]
     [report one-of Cars with [speed > 0 and fuelAmount <= 10]
     set status "Dangerous"]
     [report nobody]
end
```

As can be seen, we use nearly direct translation from the quantified expressions of the operation schemas in Z to the NetLogo statements inside the procedures. These expressions are guards of the operations and hence checked using an `if` or `ifelse` statement. The `with` reporter can be used in the `all?` statement to introduce constraints on the quantified variable. Such constraints would appear in Z as proposition $P(x)$ in predicates of the form $\forall x : X \mid P(x) \bullet Q(x)$ or $\forall x : X \bullet P(x) \Rightarrow Q(x)$. The translation of $Q(x)$ comes within the last brackets in the `all?` statement. Similar constraints $P(x)$ in Z predicates of the form $\exists x : X \mid P(x) \bullet Q(x)$ appear in the single set of brackets after the `with`, combined with the translation of $Q(x)$ using `and`. To access an existentially quantified variable, such as c in *GameStatusDangerous*, we utilise the `one-of` reporter. Note that if the existentially quantified variable is required to have the minimum value for a given property (as in the case study of Sect. 4) we use the `min-one-of` reporter instead.

Whenever a Z operation has an output, it needs to be translated as a reporter procedure in NetLogo. Hence, the *game-status-dangerous* procedure is defined as a reporter. The output is `nobody` in the case where the Z operation's guard is false.

In Z such outputs can be used as inputs to other schemas using the piping operator ($\gg$) [10]. For example, *RefuelUnsafe* specifies an operation in which an unsafe car is refuelled. In this operation the output *unsafe!* of *GameStatus Dangerous* is equated with the input *unsafe?* of *Refuel*. In Z, a variable followed by ? denotes an input to the operation.

Refuel
$\Delta CarRacingGame$
$unsafe? : Car$

$unsafe? \in cars$
$\exists uc : Car \bullet uc.ID = unsafe?.ID \wedge uc.fuelAmount = 100 \wedge uc.speed = 0$
     $\wedge \ cars' = cars \setminus \{unsafe?\} \cup \{uc\}$

$$RefuelUnsafe \mathrel{\hat{=}} GameStatusDangerous \gg Refuel$$

The $\exists$ quantifier in *Refuel* is used to define a new car uc, which has the same ID as the *unsafe?*, fuel amount of 100 and speed of 0. The last part of the predicate specifies that the new car uc is replaced with the unsafe car *unsafe?* in the *cars* set. The union symbol ($\cup$) can be translated into NetLogo code by creating a new agent. This agent will automatically be added to the agentset. Also, the set difference symbol ($\setminus$) is translated by using the `die` command which removes the old agent from the agentset. Hence, the above operations can be translated as

```
to refuel [unsafe]
    if (member? unsafe Cars)
    [create-Cars 1 [set ID ([ID] of unsafe)
                    set fuelAmount 100
                    set speed 0]
        ask Cars with [self = unsafe][die]]
end
to refuel-unsafe
    if game-status-dangerous != nobody
    [refuel game-status-dangerous]
end
```

where **self** is a reporter used to refer to the current agent at each iteration of the *ask* command. Note that equality between two agents (= operator) is checked according to their **who** numbers. Additionally, in order to access the state variables of a variable that is of type schema in Z a dot (.) is used. This dot can be translated using the **of** reporter in NetLogo, e.g., *unsafe?.ID* in Z is translated into [*ID*] *of unsafe*.

4 Case Study

In this section, we illustrate the translation scheme on a small part of the CNAFS case study: a model of movement of *chyme*, i.e., food undergoing digestion, through the small intestine of a pig. In their experiments, the researchers consider the small intestine as comprising 6 different intestine segments (SI1–SI6). One of the main reasons for this segmentation is that the movement rate of chyme varies in each of these segments. To allow results of the simulation to be verified against experimental data, most parts of the specification are based on CNAFS researchers' hypotheses and their methods of running their experiments. Additional biological details of small intestine functionality are derived from Guyton and Hall [5]. Using the built-in NetLogo visualisation facilities, the outcome of this simulation provides the biologists with a visualisation of the system at each time step and some statistical results, such as total amount of chyme content and marker content in each intestine segment at each time step.

4.1 State Definitions

All non-schema types used in this section are defined as appropriate global types in Z. The agents of the system are intestine segments and packets of chyme. The idea of considering chyme as a collection of discrete packets is derived from the functionality of the *pyloric valve* which controls chyme entry to the small intestine [5].

   An intestine segment is specified in terms of its length, the total amount of chyme content that exists in the segment, and the movement rate of chyme packets in the segment. Also, each segment can only take up to a certain amount of chyme because of physical limits on its expansion. This value is represented by *contentThreshold*. When the total amount of chyme content in a segment reaches this threshold, the variable *entryBlocked* of the segment will be set to *Yes* to specify that the segment cannot take any more packets. The value of *entryBlocked* will be changed back to *No* whenever the total amount of chyme content is decreased to a value less than *contentThreshold*.

IntestineSegment

length : *NonNegativeReal*
totalExistingChymeContent : *NonNegativeReal*
chymePassageRate : *NonNegativeReal*
contentThreshold : *NonNegativeReal*
entryBlocked : *YesOrNo*

$totalExistingChymeContent \geq contentThreshold \Leftrightarrow entryBlocked = Yes$

A schema *Position* represents a chyme packet's current position in the small intestine. In the *Position* schema, *segNum* represents the ID of the segment that the packet is currently in and *posInSeg* specifies the packet's distance from the beginning of the segment. Each chyme packet contains specific amounts of nutrients, markers and water. Markers are consumable, but non-absorbable materials used in experiments for different purposes such as calculation of passage rate in the gastrointestinal tract [7]. All these contents together have a total mass that is represented by the variable *totalContent*.

Position

segNum : *SegmentID*
posInSeg : *NonNegativeReal*

ChymePacket

Position
nutrients : $\mathbb{P}$ *Nutrient*
markers : $\mathbb{P}$ *Marker*
waterAmount : *NonNegativeReal*
totalContent : *NonNegativeReal*

The (multi-agent) system is a small intestine comprising a sequence of intestine segments and set of chyme packets that have entered, but not left the small intestine. The variables *totalLength*, *chymeEntryRate* and *emptyingBlocked* represent the small intestine length, the rate at which the chyme packets enter the small intestine and whether the packets can leave the small intestine or not, respectively.

─── *SmallIntestine* ──────────────────────────────────
$segments : SegmentID \rightarrow IntestineSegment$
$chymePackets : \mathbb{F}\ ChymePacket$
$totalLength : NonNegativeReal$
$chymeEntryRate : NonNegativeReal$
$emptyingBlocked : YesOrNo$
─────────────────────────────────────
$\forall c1, c2 : chymePackets \bullet$
    $c1.segNum = c2.segNum \wedge c1.posInSeg = c2.posInSeg \Leftrightarrow c1 = c2$
$(segments\ 1).length = (segments\ 6).length = 1$
$\forall segID : SegmentID \bullet segID \neq 1 \wedge segID \neq 6 \Rightarrow$
    $(segments\ segID).length = (totalLength - 2)\ \mathrm{div}\ 4$
$\forall c : chymePackets;\ segID : SegmentID \bullet$
    $c.segNum = segID \Rightarrow c.posInSeg \leq (segments\ segID).length$
──

The predicate of *SmallIntestine* states that no chyme packets have the same position. Additionally, according to the experiments at CNAFS, both the first and the last segments (SI1 and SI6) of the small intestine are considered to be 1 metre long and the other four segments are each one quarter of the remaining length of the small intestine. Finally, the position of each chyme packet in each segment must be less than or equal to the segment length.

When translating a schema such as *ChymePacket* that includes another schema, we include the variables of the included schema as properties of the NetLogo breed. When translating collections of agents such as *segments* which are specified in terms of a function, we include the domain value associated with an agent, as a property of the NetLogo breed. Effectively, we are using the Z interpretation of the function as a set of ordered pairs of domain and range values [10]. Hence, the NetLogo translation of the above is as follows. As mentioned in Sect. 3.3, state invariants need to be implemented explicitly in operations.

    breed [IntestineSegments IntestineSegment]
    breed [ChymePackets ChymePacket]
    IntestineSegments-own [segmentID length chymePassageRate ...]
    ChymePackets-own [segNum posInSeg nutrients markers ...]
    globals [totalLength chymeEntryRate emptyingBlocked ...]

4.2 Operations

This section describes the case in which a chyme packet wants to move through one intestine segment, but will be blocked by another packet. One of the assumptions made in the specification is that chyme packets move through and leave the small intestine in the same order as they arrive. Therefore, packets cannot pass each other and sometimes packets may be blocked.

An operation *MovingBlocked* in the Z specification specifies the movement of a packet *pkt?* being blocked by another packet *blocking!* in the same segment. The function *Min* is a predefined global constant in the specification which returns the minimum of a set of real numbers (defined similarly to Z's *min* function for integers [10]).

$\rule[0.5ex]{0.15em}{0pt}$ *MovingBlocked* $\rule{8cm}{0.4pt}$

Ξ *SmallIntestine*

$pkt? : ChymePacket$

$blocking! : ChymePacket$

$pkt? \in chymePackets$

$pkt?.posInSeg +$
    $(segments\ pkt?.segNum).chymePassageRate * TIMESTEP \le$
        $(segments\ pkt?.segNum).length$

$\exists\, c : chymePackets \bullet$
    $c.segNum = pkt?.segNum \wedge c.posInSeg > pkt?.posInSeg \wedge$
    $c.posInSeg \le pkt?.posInSeg +$
        $(segments\ pkt?.segNum).chymePassageRate * TIMESTEP \wedge$
    $c.posInSeg = Min(\{ch : chymePackets \mid ch.segNum = pkt?.segNum \wedge$
                $ch.posInSeg > pkt?.posInSeg \bullet ch.posInSeg\}) \wedge$
    $blocking! = c$

The first two predicates state that *pkt?* is a chyme packet in a segment of the small intestines which, if unblocked, would not leave that segment in the next time step (*TIMESTEP* is a global constant representing the time step in our NetLogo simulation). The final predicate states there exists another packet *c* which will block *pkt?*'s movement and assigns that packet to the output variable *blocking!*. Following the translation scheme in Sect. 3, the operation is translated as follows. Note that in order to access agents which are specified in the range of a function, such as *segments*, the **one-of** and **with** reporters are used, where the desired domain value comes inside the brackets after **with**.

```
to-report MovingBlocked [pkt]
    ifelse (member? pkt ChymePackets) and
        ([posInSeg] of pkt +
            ([chymePassageRate] of one-of IntestineSegments with
                [segmentID = [segNum] of pkt] * TIMESTEP) <=
                [length] of one-of IntestineSegments with
                    [segmentID = [segNum] of pkt]) and
        (any? ChymePackets with [(segNum = [segNum] of pkt) and
            (posInSeg > [posInSeg] of pkt) and
            (posInSeg <= [posInSeg] of pkt +
                ([chymePassageRate] of one-of IntestineSegments with
                    [segmentID = [segNum] of pkt] * TIMESTEP))])
        [report min-one-of ChymePackets with
            [segNum = [segNum] of pkt and
            posInSeg > [posInSeg] of pkt] [posInSeg]]
        [report nobody]
end
```

The operation *MoveUntilBlocked* specifies that a chyme packet *pkt?* moves to right behind another packet *blocking?* which is blocking it.

```
┌─ MoveUntilBlocked ─────────────────────────────────────────────
│ ΔSmallIntestine
│ pkt? : ChymePacket
│ blocking? : ChymePacket
├────────────────────────────────────────────────────────────────
│ pkt? ∈ chymePackets ∧ blocking? ∈ chymePackets
│ ∃ updPkt : ChymePacket • updPkt.segNum = pkt?.segNum ∧
│    ((blocking?.posInSeg − PKTSIZE > pkt?.posInSeg ⇒
│        updPkt.posInSeg = blocking?.posInSeg − PKTSIZE)
│    ∨ (blocking?.posInSeg − PKTSIZE ≤ pkt?.posInSeg ⇒
│        updPkt.posInSeg = pkt?.posInSeg))
│    updPkt.nutrients = pkt?.nutrients ∧ updPkt.markers = pkt?.markers ∧
│    updPkt.waterAmount = pkt?.waterAmount ∧
│    updPkt.totalContent = pkt?.totalContent ∧
│    chymePackets' = chymePackets \ {pkt?} ∪ {updPkt}
│    totalLength' = totalLength ∧ emptyingBlocked' = emptyingBlocked
│    segments' = segments ∧ chymeEntryRate' = chymeEntryRate
└────────────────────────────────────────────────────────────────
```

The first predicate of this schema states that *pkt?* and *blocking?* are chyme packets within the small intestine. The second predicate replaces *pkt?* with a new chyme packet *updPkt* which is in the position the blocked packet would move to, and is otherwise identical to *pkt?* (*PKTSIZE* is a global constant representing the size of chyme packets in our NetLogo simulation). The remaining predicates indicate that the small intestine is otherwise unchanged.

MoveUntilBlocked is combined with the operation schema *MovingBlocked*, which provides the input *blocking?*, as follows.

$$PacketMoveInSegmentBlocked \,\hat{=}\, MovingBlocked \gg MoveUntilBlocked$$

This part of the specification is translated into the following NetLogo code.

```
to MoveUntilBlocked [pkt blocking]
    if(member? pkt ChymePackets) and (member? blocking ChymePackets)
    [create-ChymePackets 1 [
        set segNum ([segNum] of pkt)
        ifelse ([posInSeg] of blocking − PKTSIZE) > ([posInSeg] of pkt)
            [set posInSeg ([posInSeg] of blocking − PKTSIZE)]
            [set posInSeg ([posInSeg] of pkt)]
        set nutrients ([nutrients] of pkt)
        set markers ([markers] of pkt)
        set waterAmount ([waterAmount] of pkt)
        set totalContent ([totalContent] of pkt)]
    ask ChymePackets with [self = pkt] [die]]
end
to PacketMoveInSegmentBlocked [pkt]
    if MovingBlocked pkt != nobody
    [MoveUntilBlocked pkt (MovingBlocked pkt)]
end
```

5   Conclusion

This research combined the use of the Z formal notation with computational modelling in the NetLogo simulation language. This reduced a large amount of effort required for the developer of the simulation to firstly understand the system requirements and functionality clearly, and to secondly efficiently derive code directly from the specification of these requirements. The approach was trialled on a real project studying digestion in pigs' intestines. During simulations, the emergent property of total contents in different segments increased along the intestine in a manner qualitatively in agreement with the patterns seen in experimental data. Additionally, modifications to the model were readily integrated into the Z specification and, via translation, into the NetLogo simulation. Overall, the application of the approach was successful in the sense that it made the development process more convenient for all the people involved. This warrants its ongoing use as well as use in similar projects in the future.

A major lesson learnt is that the usability and effectiveness of formal methods is influenced by human-factors such as the background of the people involved in the development process. Consequently, one important step before applying formal methods is to choose a suitable formal modelling language that makes the software development process more efficient and convenient for all the people involved.

Acknowledgements. This project was jointly supported by the Queensland Alliance for Agriculture and Food Innovation (QAAFI) and Australian Research Council (ARC) Discovery Grant DP110101211.

References

1. Abrial, J.-R.: The B-Book: Assigning Programs to Meanings. Cambridge University Press, Cambridge (1996)
2. Booch, G., Rumbaugh, J., Jacobson, I.: The Unified Modeling Language User Guide. Addison-Wesley, Reading (1999)
3. Bowen, J.P.: Formal Specification and Documentation Using Z: A Case Study Approach. International Thomson Computer Press, London (1996)
4. Derrick, J., Boiten, E.: Refinement in Z and Object-Z, Foundations and Advanced Applications, 2nd edn. Springer, London (2014)
5. Guyton, A.C., Hall, J.E.: Guyton and Hall Textbook of Medical Physiology, 12th edn. Saunders/Elsevier, Philadelphia (2011)
6. Mens, T., Van Gorp, P.: A taxonomy of model transformation. Electron. Notes Theor. Comput. Sci. **152**, 125–142 (2006)
7. Owens, F.N., Hanson, C.F.: External and internal markers for appraising site and extent of digestion in ruminants. J. Dairy Sci. **75**(9), 2605–2617 (1992)
8. Singh, V.K., Gautam, D., Singh, R.R., Gupta, A.K.: Agent-based computational modeling of emergent collective intelligence. In: Nguyen, N.T., Kowalczyk, R., Chen, S.-M. (eds.) ICCCI 2009. LNCS, vol. 5796, pp. 240–251. Springer, Heidelberg (2009)

9. Smith, G.: The Object-Z Specification Language. Kluwer Academic Publishers, Dordrecht (2000)
10. Spivey, J.M.: The Z Notation: A Reference Manual. Prentice Hall, 2nd edition, (1992)
11. Tisue, S., Wilensky, U.: Netlogo: a simple environment for modeling complexity. In: International Conference on Complex Systems, pp. 16–21 (2004)
12. Wilensky, U.: NetLogo User Manual. Center for Connected Learning and Computer-Based Modeling, Northwestern University, Evanston, IL, 5.0.5 edition (2013)
13. Woodcock, J.C.P., Davies, J.: Using Z: Specification, Refinement, and Proof. Prentice Hall, New York (1994)

When a Formal Model Rhymes
with a Graphical Notation

Akram Idani[1,2]([⊠]) and Nicolas Stouls[3]

[1] LIG, University of Grenoble Alpes, 38000 Grenoble, France
[2] LIG, CNRS, 38000 Grenoble, France
Akram.Idani@imag.fr
[3] CITI-INRIA, Université de Lyon, INSA-Lyon, 69621 Lyon, Villeurbanne, France
Nicolas.Stouls@insa-lyon.fr

Abstract. Formal methods are based on mathematical notations which allow to rigorously reason about a model and ensure its correctness by proofs and/or model-checking. Unfortunately, these notations are complex and often difficult to understand from a human point of view especially for engineers who are not familiar with formal methods. Several research works have proposed tools to support formal models using graphical views. On the one hand, such views are useful to make formal documents accessible to humans, and on the other hand they ease the verification of some behavioral properties. However, links between graphical and formal models proposed by these approaches are often difficult to put into practice and depend on the targeted formal language. In this paper, we discuss these links from a practical approach and show how a behavioral description can be computed from a formal model based on two complementary paradigms: under-approximation (or animation-based) and over-approximation (or proof-based). We applied these paradigms in order to produce behavioural state/chart views from B models and we carried out an empirical study to assess the quality and relevance of these graphical representations for humans.

Keywords: B method · Symbolic LTS · Animation · Abstraction

1 Introduction

Several research works are devoted to bridge the gap between formal and semi-formal methods considering their complementary aspects and cross contributions. Indeed, on the one hand, semi-formal methods (thanks to their support for graphical notations such as UML) are synthetic, structuring and more intuitive for humans, and on the other hand, formal methods (thanks to their mathematical notations) are precise and support automated reasonings. These works were widely interested by translations from a semi-formal UML model to a formal specification: from UML to B [15], from UML to Z [10], from UML to Alloy [3], etc. Their main motivations are to provide precise semantics to UML notations in order to remedy the lack of tools for formally analyzing UML models.

© Springer International Publishing Switzerland 2015
C. Canal and A. Idani (Eds.): SEFM 2014 Workshops, LNCS 8938, pp. 54–68, 2015.
DOI: 10.1007/978-3-319-15201-1_4

Despite of these numerous tools dedicated to such translation, several companies have an established software development process entirely based on a formal method. For example, Siemens Transport [7], Clearsy [13], Gemplus [5] have used the B method as its core development method without any accompanying UML model. Indeed, since the targeted formal language is not object oriented, translations from UML often lead to a complex specification which is, on the one hand, far from what a developer could write directly, and on the other hand incomplete for a safety critical system. This motivates other kind of works to define a formal link between a formal model and its behavioral representation. For example, works of C. Snook and M. Butler [15] ant its support tool iUML-B [14], provide a graphical front end, used conjointly with a formal B specification in order to keep the distance between both formal and graphical models as thin as possible. We can also cite the ProB tool [11] which is an animator and a model-checker able to draw an accessibility graph after an exhaustive exploration of the specification state space. However, it considers concrete states rather than symbolic ones and the resulting graphical representation is complex because of the combinatorial explosion problem. In order to remedy this shortcoming, [12] provides some heuristics to reduce the accessibility graph size by using a symmetry analysis technique. Furthermore, it was not dedicated to make the focus on the understanding of some particular properties, since the abstract state space could not be provided by an expert user.

In this paper, the starting point is a B or Event-B formal model [1,2]. Our aim is to provide tools able to extract graphical views representing some properties of the formal model and hence increase its understanding by humans who are not trained with such a formal notation. We discuss and compare two paradigms: **under-approximation** (or animation-based) and **over-approximation** (or proof-based). We applied these paradigms in order to produce behavioural views from B models and then we carried out an empirical study to assess the quality and relevance of these graphical representations for humans.

In Sect. 2 we give a simple example in order to illustrate contributions of this paper. Section 3 discusses the under-approximation approach and presents an algorithm which improves automation of this technique. Section 4 describes the over approximation technique and presents the *GénéSyst*-tool. Results of our empirical study are discussed in Sect. 5. Finally, Sect. 6 summarizes our comparative study of both techniques and draws the conclusions and perspectives of this work.

2   Case-Study

Figure 1 gives a simple scheduler specification taken from [6] and written in B. It models exclusive access of processes to a unique resource. Variables *waiting*, *ready* and *active* model states of processes managed by the system. The set of all processes is an abstract set (set *PID*). An idle process which doesn't request access to the unique resource is introduced by the system using the *waiting* variable. Variable *ready* is the set of processes that have requested access to the resource. Finally, variable *active* contains the active process to which the resource is assigned. Evolutions of these variables are performed by three events. Event NEW(pp) creates a new waiting process. Event READY(pp) changes process pp from the waiting state to the ready state. If there is no active process it directly activates process pp. Finally, event SWAP puts the active process in the waiting state and activates non-deterministically some ready process.

SYSTEM SCHEDULER
SETS
　PID
VARIABLES
　active, ready, waiting
INVARIANT
　active $\subseteq$ PID $\wedge$ ready $\subseteq$ PID $\wedge$ waiting $\subseteq$ PID $\wedge$
　ready $\cap$ waiting $= \emptyset \wedge$ active $\cap$ waiting $= \emptyset \wedge$ active $\cap$ ready $= \emptyset \wedge$
　card(active) $\leq 1 \wedge$ (active $= \emptyset \Rightarrow$ ready $= \emptyset$)
INITIALISATION
　active, ready, waiting $:= \emptyset, \emptyset, \emptyset$
EVENTS
　NEW(pp) $\hat{=}$　**SELECT** (pp $\in$ PID) $\wedge$ (pp $\notin$ (ready $\cup$ waiting $\cup$ active))
　　　　　　　THEN　waiting := waiting $\cup$ {pp}
　　　　　　　END;
　READY(pp) $\hat{=}$ **SELECT** pp $\in$ waiting
　　　　　　　THEN　waiting := (waiting - {pp})||
　　　　　　　IF (active $= \emptyset$) **THEN** active := {pp}
　　　　　　　ELSE　ready := ready $\cup$ {pp}
　　　　　　　END

　　　　　　　END;
　SWAP $\hat{=}$　　**SELECT** active $\neq \emptyset$
　　　　　　　THEN　waiting := waiting $\cup$ active ||
　　　　　　　IF (ready $= \emptyset$) **THEN** active := $\emptyset$
　　　　　　　ELSE
　　　　　　　　　ANY pp **WHERE** pp $\in$ ready **THEN**
　　　　　　　　　　active := {pp} || ready := ready - {pp}
　　　　　　　　　END
　　　　　　　END
　　　　　　　END
END

Fig. 1. Scheduler Specification from [6]

A palette of graphical representations that can be issued from the scheduler example can be found in [8]. These representations provide a graphical documentation of the behaviour of B specifications and allow to identify different viewpoints potentially useful for humans. IFor example, a B analyst may be interested by a graphical representation of the SCHEDULER that intuitively show a process life cycle. Hence, the abstract graphical view may deal with three states corresponding to the fact that a process p_i (such that $p_i \in PID$) is in state *waiting*, *ready* or *active*. In other words, states of the abstract view are: (1) $p_i \in waiting$, (2) $p_i \in ready$, and (3) $p_i \in active$. Figure 2, built manually, gives an abstract view of the SCHEDULER system based on these three states.

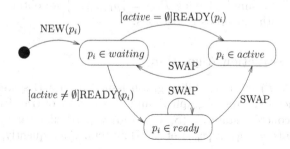

Fig. 2. Example of an intuitive abstract view of the SCHEDULER system

From a documentation point of view the interest of this representation is to emphasize graphically some intrinsic properties of the SCHEDULER system, for example:

- The process equity property, indicating that every process may be activated, is not verified by the specification. Indeed, Fig. 2 shows that in state $p_i \in ready$, SWAP has a non-deterministic behaviour justified by the existence of two transitions with the same label. This means that event *SWAP* can block a process p_i indefinitely in state $p_i \in ready$.
- The non-blocking property, indicating that after being active a process does not stop the system is verified by the specification. Indeed, in Fig. 2 the transition *SWAP* is triggered on from the state ($p_i \in active$) and always leads to state ($p_i \in waiting$).

This paper shows how these graphical representations can be extracted automatically using two kinds of techniques: **under-approximation** (or animation-based) and **over-approximation** (or proof-based).

3   Under-Approximation Approach

Under-approximation is based on exploration of a useful subset of the state space. We apply this technique in order to draw a graphical representation which is useful from a documentation point of view but which may miss some behaviours.

3.1   Construction Method and Usability Constraints

One way to build an under-approximating graphical abstraction is to exhaustively explore the concrete state space of the B specification and then to apply an abstraction algorithm to group concrete states. For a bounded state space, animators such as ProB [11] can help to explore all states. In other cases, such as for the SCHEDULER example, we must start by bounding unbounded elements (i.e. specifying *PID* with a bounded set). If we introduce only two processes p_1 and p_2 in the system, we obtain ten accessible states (Fig. 3). If the number of processes increases, the accessibility graph becomes too large and difficult to understand. For example, having *PID* = $\{p_1, p_2, p_3\}$ we obtained thirty five accessible states with numerous transitions.

3.2 Graph Abstraction Algorithm

We note $\mathcal{G} = (N, T)$ an accessibility graph issued from a B system, where N is the set of concrete states of graph $\mathcal{G}$, and T is the set of transitions between states of N. A concrete state S_v ($S_v \in N$) gives particular values assigned to state variables v ($v = \{v_1, \ldots, v_n\}$) of the B system. Consequently, each state s

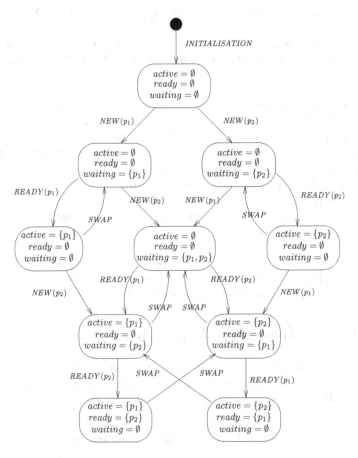

Fig. 3. Accessibility Graph of the SCHEDULER for *PID* = $\{p_1, p_2\}$

can be formally expressed by a predicate $P(S_v)$ as the conjunction of equality predicates that associate to each state variable v_i its value in S_v:

$$P(S_v) \triangleq \bigwedge_{i=1}^{n} (v_i = val_j)$$

Where val_j is a value of v_i allowed by the invariant. A concrete state S_v satisfies an abstract state $S_{abstract}$ (noticed $S_v \vdash S_{abstract}$), defined by a predicate R (e.g. $p_1 \in ready$), if and only if we can prove that $P(S_v) \Rightarrow R$.

Hence, according to an accessibility graph and a set of abstract states, the following algorithm can produce a symbolic representation by grouping concrete states satisfying a same abstract state predicate. The inputs are: (i) an accessibility graph $\mathcal{G} = (N, T)$ and (ii) a set of abstract state predicates $N_{abstract}$ (Fig. 4).

```
For  each  abstract state S_abstract from N_abstract do
 |     N := N ∪ {S_abstract}
 |     For each concrete state S_v such that
 |     |      S_v ∈ N − N_abstract  ∧  S_v ⊢ S_abstract
 |     do
 |     |     For each state S and transition t such that
 |     |     |      S ∈ N ∧ t ∈ T ∧ t = S ⟶ S_v
 |     |     do
 |     |     |    t := (S ⟶ᵒ S_abstract)
 |     |     End do
 |     |     For each state S and transition t such that
 |     |     |      S ∈ N ∧ t ∈ T ∧ t = S_v ⟶ᵒ S
 |     |     do
 |     |     |    t := (S_abstract ⟶ᵒ S)
 |     |     End do
 |     |     N := N − {S_v}
 |     End do
 |     Delete redundant transitions
End do
```

Fig. 4. Under approximation algorithm.

The algorithm checks each concrete state against each abstract state predicate, using the *AtelierB* prover. If the proof succeeds, then an abstract state has been found for the concrete state. The next step in the construction of the abstract state-transition diagram is to identify the transitions. Since each node of the concrete graph corresponds to a node of the abstract diagram, each transition of the concrete graph can be translated into a transition in the abstract diagram. In order to decrease the number of transitions, the tool groups all transitions which correspond to the same pair of nodes, and to the same B event.

Our algorithm links concrete states to abstract ones, and hence the nodes of the abstract state-transition diagram are: (a) the abstract state predicates given by the user, and (b) the concrete nodes which don't appear in the domain of the abstraction function. This guarantees that each concrete node will correspond to a node of the abstract diagram. Furthermore, in order to obtain a relevent abstract view, two conditions should be verified:

1. abstract state predicates are disjoint, *i.e.* each concrete state corresponds to at most one abstract state.
2. abstract state predicates cover all the state space allowed by the invariant, *i.e.* the nodes of the abstract diagram only correspond to the abstract predicates.

The abstract view of Fig. 2 respects only the first condition because it misses all concrete states reached from the initialization. These states can be grouped in an abstract state $p_i \notin (waiting \cup active \cup ready)$ which is reached when the system is initialized. The left hand side of Fig. 6 shows the result of this technique when applied to accessibility graph of Fig. 3 in which set PID contains two processes p_1 and p_2.

4   Over-Approximation Approach

The under-approximation technique is useful when the accessibility graph explores a relevant finite subset of state space from which we can exhibit a useful abstract view for a documentation purpose. If some interesting behaviours are not included in the concrete graph, they will not appear in the abstract diagram. An over-approximation technique is then more interesting because it allows to produce a symbolic transition system that represent a potentially infinite set of values. Such tools reason on event *enabledness* and state *reachability* properties.

4.1   Construction Method and Usability Constraints

Our objective is to directly compute an abstract view from the B model properties, rather than to reason on a concrete graph. For instance, if an over-approximation view shows that a state is not reached by any transition, then one can conclude that associated concrete valuations could not be reachable by any execution of the B model.

Our approach tries first to prove, for each event e and each couple of abstract states S_1 and S_2, that no execution of event e from state S_1 can reach state S_2. This goal is a proof obligation (PO) assuming that if state predicate $P(S_1)$ is true then event e establishes the negation of state predicate $P(S_2)$:

$$P(S_1) \Rightarrow [e]\neg P(S_2)$$

This first step allows to identify by proofs, all uncrossable transitions between states S_1 and S_2. In fact, if the above PO is solved, then we assert that event e never reaches S_2 from S_1. Variations of this PO allow to compute whether S_2 is always or possibly reached by e from S_1:

- S_2 always reached from S_1: $P(S_1) \Rightarrow [e]P(S_2)$
- S_2 possibly reached from S_1: $P(S_1) \Rightarrow \neg[e]\neg P(S_2)$.

For example, the following proofs (but not only) should succeed for event SWAP[1]:

- it always deactivate an active process: $(p_i \in active) \Rightarrow [\text{SWAP}](p_i \in waiting)$
- it never activate a waiting process: $(p_i \in waiting) \Rightarrow [\text{SWAP}](p_i \notin active)$
- it may activate a ready process: $(p_i \in ready) \Rightarrow \neg[\text{SWAP}](p_i \notin active)$

As for the under-approximation approach, two conditions must be verified: abstract state predicates are disjoint and cover all the state space allowed by the invariant. The first condition avoids states overlapping and the second one allows to have a global view on the complete system. An important proof obligation is then to establish the completeness of the state predicates according to the invariant:

$$I \implies \bigvee_{i=1}^{n} P(S - v)$$

4.2   The *GénéSyst* Tool

The *GénéSyst* tool[2] [4] implements the ideas of this approach. It computes a Symbolic Labelled Transition System (SLTS) describing all possible behaviours of a given event-B model, according to a given set of disjoint state predicates. Generated proof obligations are discharged by means of the *AtelierB* automatic prover.

The overall *GénéSyst* algorithm is presented in Fig. 5, where we distinguish transitions from the initialization, and transitions associated to other events. In this algorithm, conditions are written under a negative form (*i.e.* if $\neg A$ can not be established), since a formula that has not been proved is not necessarily true. In this algorithm, no any information is presented to consider simplification of the conditions. The reader can refer to [4] for further semantical details.

In order to restrict the undecidability problem of proofs, heuristics are used to compute the over-approximation graph (the SLTS). One of them is to split proofs into two parts: **enabledness** and **reachability**. In this approach, for each pair of abstract states S_1 and S_2, and each event e, a transition t of the SLTS is defined by $(S_1 \xrightarrow{(D,A,e)} S_2)$, where D is the *enabledness* condition (condition under which the event e can be triggered from S_1) and A is the *reachability* condition (condition under which the event e can reach the state S_2). We define *enabledness* and *reachability* as follows:

- *Enabledness* condition D : $P(S_1) \Rightarrow (D \Leftrightarrow guard(e))$
- *Reachability* condition A : $P(S_1) \wedge D \Rightarrow (A \Leftrightarrow \neg[action(e)]\neg P(S_2))$.

---

[1] These properties are not all properties of event SWAP.

[2] *GénéSyst*: http://perso.citi.insa-lyon.fr/nstouls/?ZoomSur=Logiciels.

```
// Initialization of the result: set of transitions is empty
T := ∅

// Defining states reachable by the initialization
For   each state S, except S_init do
|       // Define the condition A under which the initialization reaches S
|       A := ¬[init]¬P(S)
|       If ¬A can not be established then
|       |       T := T ∪ {(S_init ⟶^(true,A,init) S)}
|       End if
End do

// Defining existing transitions
For   each state S₁, except S_init, and each event e do
|       //Define the condition D under which e can be trigger from S₁
|       D := guard(e)
|       If (P(S₁) ⇒ ¬D) can not be established then
|       |       For   each state S₂, except S_init, do
|       |       |       // Define the condition A under which event e reaches S₂
|       |       |       A := ¬[action(e)]¬P(S₂)
|       |       |       If (P(S₁) ∧ D ⇒ ¬A) can not be established then
|       |       |       |       T := T ∪ {(S₁ ⟶^(D,A,e) S₂)}
|       |       |       End if
|       |       End do
|       End if
End do
```

Fig. 5. *GénéSyst* main algorithm

In the context of the starting state, the *enabledness* condition D is equivalent to the B event guard (denoted $guard(e)$). Technically, the tool asks *AtelierB* to prove if D can be reduced to *true*, by trying to proof the assertion $I \wedge P(S_1) \Rightarrow guard(e)$, where I is the invariant. If this proof succeeds, it concludes that e can always be enabled from S_1; otherwise it asks *AtelierB* to prove if D can be reduced to *false*, by trying to proof $I \wedge P(S_1) \Rightarrow \neg guard(e)$. If this second proof succeeds then the tool concludes that e can't be enabled from S_1. The same principle is applied for the *reachability* property. Condition A is equivalent to $\neg[action(e)]\neg P(S_2)$ which means that if A is reduced to true, then e may reach S_2. But if it is reduced to *false* then e cannot reach S_2. By the way, a transition $(S_1 \xrightarrow{(D,A,e)} S_2)$ is said valid if and only if $\exists x \cdot (P(S_1) \wedge D \wedge A)$.

Right hand side of Fig. 6 is produced by this technique without any bounding of set PID. It describes all possible behaviours around states focused on a process life-cycle. The two crossing conditions between brackets represent respectively conditions D and A, for *enabledness* and *reachability*. Empty brackets mean that the condition is proved true. A cross X on a condition means that this condition has not been proved neither true, nor false.

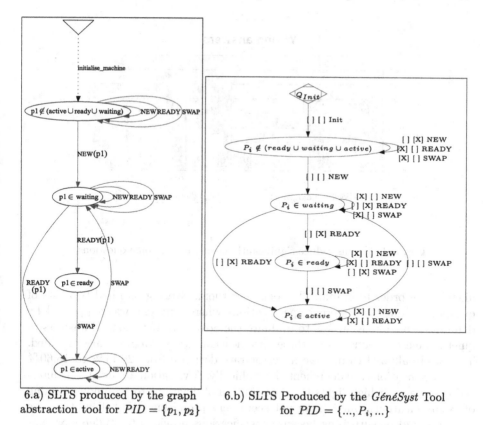

6.a) SLTS produced by the graph abstraction tool for $PID = \{p_1, p_2\}$

6.b) SLTS Produced by the *GénéSyst* Tool for $PID = \{..., P_i, ...\}$

Fig. 6. Results of Under and Over-Approximation Techniques

Compared to the under-approximation diagram produced for two processes, some transitions exhibited by *GénéSyst* don't correspond to any transition of the concrete representation (*New*, *ready* and *swap* transitions, reflexive on state $P_i \in Ready$). Indeed, limited to two processes for this example the under-approximation technique didn't explore a sufficient number of states.

5 Human Oriented Empirical Study

Techniques discussed in the previous sections allow to produce behavioural views from a formal B specification depending on the abstraction chosen by the analyst. We have conducted experimentally a qualitative study with students from a master's degree specialized on software engineering, and who have finished a detailed course about the B method. We formed two groups of 17 students to which we provided two different specifications: the scheduler example discussed in this paper, and a B specification modelling access control mechanisms to buildings. We applied our tools to these specifications and produced various

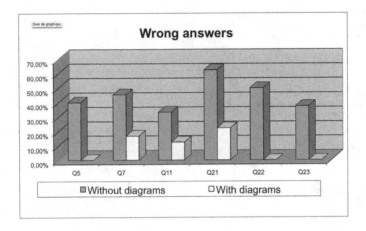

Fig. 7. Diagrams reduce significantly error rate for some questions

diagrams in order to graphically document them. Every group had two lists of questions about two different specifications where only one was supported by diagrams. Our intension was to evaluate the error rate variations of answers to quiet simple questions about these specifications when diagrams are provided. This study allowed to observe an error rate decrease from 26.14 % to 15.60 % when specifications are documented graphically. A variation about 11 % is interesting, because it hightlights the contribution of diagrams to the understanding of B specifications, but it may not seem very promising. We believe that the inverse would be surprising because specifications provided to students are not complex and should be accessible for them. Indeed, a global error rate near 26 % may be acceptable for persons who are not skilled with formal techniques, but 15 % is better. More specifically, we observed that diagrams reduce significantly the number of wrong answers for several questions. Figure 7 gives wrong answers proportions with and without diagrams and shows that the error rate can be divided by three and sometimes it is reduced from around 50 % to zero.

Questions G5-Q23 will be detailed further. 30 % of students to whom we didn't provide diagrams, misunderstood the equity property and considered that a process can't be bloqued indefinitely in the ready state (question Q11

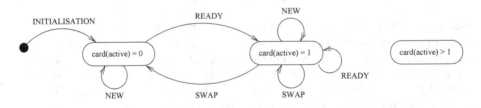

Fig. 8. State/Transition diagram focused on active processes

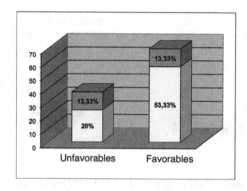

Fig. 9. Did the diagrams help you to understand specifications?

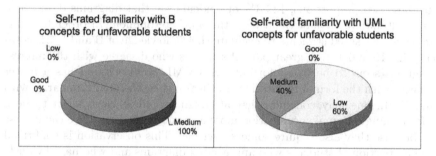

Fig. 10. Self-rated familiarity with B and UML for unfavourable students

in Fig. 7). However, when the diagram of Fig. 2 is provided, only 10 % gave the wrong answer. We believe that such a property is somehow difficult to perceive from a human point of view. Indeed, in order to be verifyied, the equity property needs more automated tool analysis or other formal languages, such as LTL, because it is a kind of behavioural properties not explicit in the B model. Nevertheless, invariant properties can be illustrated graphically using state transition diagrams. For example, Fig. 8, produced by our tools, shows that state $card(active) > 1$ is not reached by any transition and hence it is conformant to invariant $card(active) \leq 1$.

Without this diagram, about 40 % of students said that there may be several active processes at the same time (question Q5 in Fig. 7). Although invariant $card(active) \leq 1$ is clearly mentioned in the scheduler specification, students were not able to attest that the scheduler operations preserve such a trivial property. This result emphasizes the interest to document graphically an invariant property for a better human understanding. Indeed, we obtained 100 % of good answers when Fig. 8 is provided.

An overall appreciation of the graphical views is given in Fig. 9 and shows that two out of three students think that diagrams helped them to understand specifications and the remaining one third expresses an unfavourable opinion.

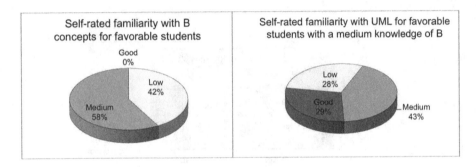

Fig. 11. Self-rated familiarity with B and UML for favourable students

In these two proportions, 13.33 % of students say that diagrams didn't help them at all and 13.33 % of them have the opposite opinion. In order to refine these results we asked students to evaluate their knowledge of B and UML notations (Figs. 10 and 11). A great part of students who disagree with the interest of diagrams seem to be uncomfortable with UML notations and has a better familiarity with the formal B notation. Basing on this self-rated familiarity with B and UML, one may conclude that although graphical views seem to be a way for making a formal specification more accessible, they can have the inverse effect because they also require some knowledge. This observation is confirmed by the proportion of students who appreciated diagrams and who has obviously a better mastering of graphical UML notations.

6   Conclusion

It is commonly known that formal specifications are complex because of notations that need a great mathematical background. In this paper, we focused our interest on a B specification which is based on a verbose notation, close to a programming language, and which should be more affordable than other formal notations. Our empirical study showed that the language itself is not the main reason to be less at ease with a formal method. Obviously, the difficulty for humans is to have an overall view on the formal model.

This paper has presented two complementary approaches providing a behavioural abstract view from a formal specification, in order to ease its understanding. Figure 6 shows an example of results issued from under and over-approximation techniques. We can observe from these diagrams that the *GénéSyst* tool associates guards to events in order to describe their *enabledness* and *reachability* properties. However, reflexive transitions SWAP, READY and NEW in state $p_i \in ready$ are not possible when the scheduler system deals with only two processes. For this particular set of processes the graph abstraction tool produced a more precise diagram. *GénéSyst* being based on proof techniques, it suffers the usual limitations of automatic provers: some theorems cannot be proved automatically and require user interaction. Furthermore, if the under-approximation approach can be used to verify reachability properties, then the over-approximation approach is mainly interesting in case of safety properties. Both techniques have some restrictions such as a limited state space for the first one and a too large abstraction in case of leak of proof for the second one.

We also measured the computational time of each approach and we noticed that the graph abstraction tool produced the state/transition diagram of a process life cycle in 7 s for $PID = \{p_1, p_2\}$ and 13 s for $PID = \{p_1, p_2, p_3\}$; while the *GénéSyst* tool produced this diagram in 80 s for an unbounded state space. This confirms that under-approximation tools are interesting when the state space can be reduced to a small finite space. Furthermore, if some interesting behaviours are not included in the concrete graph, they will not appear in the abstract diagram. Given sets, such as *PID*, can be turned into enumerated sets but numerical data structures such as *NAT* are less easy to address. Over-approximation tools are much more interesting for such complex data structures because they may be used to provide more formal evidence on the diagram transitions.

Over-approximation, can be dedicated to verify safety properties as proposed in [4] and [16]. It has the advantage to preserve infinite concrete state space without any constraint, and hence safety properties could be established on the symbolic transition system. The resulting LTS could also be used like a test oracle which brings some interesting perspectives [9].

References

1. Abrial, J.-R.: Extending B without changing it (for developing distributed systems). In: Habrias, H. (ed.) First Conference on the B method, France, pp. 169–190 (1996)
2. Abrial, J.-R.: The B-Book. Cambridge University Press, Cambridge (1996)
3. Anastasakis, K., Bordbar, B., Georg, G., Ray, I.: UML2Alloy: a challenging model transformation. In: Engels, G., Opdyke, B., Schmidt, D.C., Weil, F. (eds.) MODELS 2007. LNCS, vol. 4735, pp. 436–450. Springer, Heidelberg (2007)
4. Bert, D., Potet, M.-L., Stouls, N.: GeneSyst: a tool to reason about behavioral aspects of B event specifications. Application to security properties. In: Treharne, H., King, S., C. Henson, M., Schneider, S. (eds.) ZB 2005. LNCS, vol. 3455, pp. 299–318. Springer, Heidelberg (2005)
5. Casset, L.: Development of an embedded verifier for java card byte code using formal methods. In: Eriksson, L.-H., Lindsay, P.A. (eds.) FME 2002. LNCS, vol. 2391, pp. 290–309. Springer, Heidelberg (2002)
6. Dick, J., Faivre, A.: Automating the generation and sequencing of test cases from model-based specifications. In: Woodcock, J.C.P., Larsen, P.G. (eds.) FME '93: Industrial Strength, Formal Methods. LNCS, vol. 670, pp. 268–284. Springer, London (1993)
7. Essamé, D., Dollé, D.: B in large-scale projects: the Canarsie line CBTC experience. In: Julliand, J., Kouchnarenko, O. (eds.) B 2007. LNCS, vol. 4355, pp. 252–254. Springer, Heidelberg (2006)
8. Idani, A., Ledru, Y.: Dynamic graphical UML views from formal B specifications. Int. J. Inf. Softw.Technol. **48**(3), 154–169 (2006). Elsevier
9. Julliand, J., Stouls, N., Bué, P.-C., Masson, P.-A.: B model slicing and predicate abstraction to generate tests. Softw. Qual. J. **21**(1), 127–158 (2013)

10. Ledru, Y.: Using Jaza to animate RoZ specifications of UML class diagrams. In: SEW, pp. 253–262. IEEE Computer Society (2006)
11. Leuschel, M., Butler, M.: ProB: a model checker for B. In: Araki, K., Gnesi, S., Mandrioli, D. (eds.) FME 2003. LNCS, vol. 2805, pp. 855–874. Springer, Heidelberg (2003)
12. Leuschel, M., Butler, M., Spermann, C., Turner, E.: Symmetry reduction for B by permutation flooding. In: Julliand, J., Kouchnarenko, O. (eds.) B 2007. LNCS, vol. 4355, pp. 79–93. Springer, Heidelberg (2007)
13. Pouzancre, G.: How to diagnose a modern car with a formal B model? In: Bert, D., Bowen, J.P., King, S., Waldén, M. (eds.) ZB 2003. LNCS, vol. 2651, pp. 98–100. Springer, Heidelberg (2003)
14. Savicks, V., Snook, C.: A framework for diagrammatic modelling extensions in Rodin. In: Rodin Workshop (2012)
15. Snook, C., Butler, M.: UML-B: formal modeling and design aided by UML. ACM Trans. Softw. Eng. Method. (TOSEM) **15**(1), 92–122 (2006)
16. Vu, D-H., Chiba, Y., Yatake, K., Aoki, T.: Model checking conformance of design model to its formal specification, Research report (2014)

SaFoMe 2014

On a Process Algebraic Representation
of Sequence Diagrams

Jaco Jacobs$^{(\boxtimes)}$ and Andrew Simpson

Department of Computer Science, University of Oxford, Oxford, UK
{jaco.jacobs,andrew.simpson}@cs.ox.ac.uk

Abstract. Sequence diagrams depict the interaction between entities as a sequence of messages arranged in a temporal order. However, they lack a formal execution semantics: the *Unified Modeling Language* (UML) specification opts to use natural language to describe fundamental concepts such as interaction operators that alter the behaviour of a fragment. *Communicating Sequential Processes* (CSP) is a process-algebraic formalism that is suited to modelling patterns of behavioural interaction. Moreover, the associated refinement checker, *Failures-Divergence Refinement* (FDR), gives rise to a practical approach that enables us to reason about these interactions in a formal setting. In this paper, we show how CSP and FDR have been used to provide a process-algebraic representation of sequence diagrams that is amenable to refinement-checking.

1 Introduction

Sequence diagrams are used to depict the interactions between entities in a sequential, temporal order and have been applied in a wide range of contexts, including: the automatic generation of test cases [1]; the specification of interaction protocols in multi-agent systems [2]; and in technical documentation outlining the specification and design of a product [3]. In this paper, we give consideration to sequence diagrams within the context of the *Systems Modeling Language* (SysML),[1] an extension of a subset of the *Unified Modeling Language*.[2]

The UML specification makes use of meta-models in order to capture the abstract syntax of a diagram. While the benefits of this approach are significant, a drawback is that the execution semantics are expressed using natural language [4,5]. The lack of sufficient formalism in the specification makes it problematic to interpret the precise meaning of a complex diagram [5]. In addition, the use of natural language may lead to ill-defined semantics, or induce further confusion with regards to how a diagram ought to be interpreted. Thus, approaches that translate UML diagrams into formal representations are advantageous. Our focus is the process algebra *Communicating Sequential Processes* (CSP) [6], with a view to establishing a formal framework that supports the automated reasoning about patterns of behaviour exhibited by sequence diagrams.

---

[1] www.sysml.org.
[2] www.uml.org.

© Springer International Publishing Switzerland 2015
C. Canal and A. Idani (Eds.): SEFM 2014 Workshops, LNCS 8938, pp. 71–85, 2015.
DOI: 10.1007/978-3-319-15201-1_5

One notable reference where sequence diagrams are translated into CSP (via a model-driven engineering approach) is that of Li and Li [7], where the emphasis is placed on the translation process, which is insightful in terms of a mechanised implementation approach. In contrast, we direct our efforts towards the definition of adequate and succinct CSP processes in an implementation-independent manner. Our objective therefore is to provide concise definitions — using the process algebra CSP — of the patterns of behaviour represented by the different interaction operators. This is done in the spirit of work undertaken by Ng and Butler for state machines [8], and Dong *et al.* for activity diagrams [9]. We view the mechanised translation, using, for example, model-driven techniques, as an implementation of our approach; as such, will address this separately. While these contributions have their benefits, none of them provide a satisfactory (for our purposes) behavioural semantics for sequence diagrams in terms of CSP.

2 Background

2.1 Communicating Sequential Processes

Events are at the heart of CSP, with an event being an indivisible communication or interaction. We denote by Σ the set of all possible events for a particular specification. We can also give consideration to the *alphabet* of a process — the events that it can perform. We write αP to denote the alphabet of a process P.

A communication takes place when two or more processes agree on an event. The communication can either be a primitive event, or can take a more structured, message-passing form, utilising channels. The message-passing mechanism is based on the principle of a rendezvous between a sending and a receiving process: if the communication takes place on channel c, and a sending process wants to output a value e, the receiving process has to allow for this (by inputting on c). Once this has happened, the event is abstracted as $c.e$.

CSP is compositional in that it provides operators that allow us to define a process in terms of other, constituent processes. The CSP syntax utilised in this paper can be defined thus (where P, P_1 and P_n denote processes, e denotes an event, X and Y denotes sets of events, and b denotes a Boolean condition):

$$P \mathrel{\widehat{=}} P \mid Stop \mid Skip \mid e \to P \mid$$
$$P \mathbin{\square} P \mid \square\, e : X \bullet e \to P \mid P \sqcap P \mid \sqcap\, e : X \bullet e \to P \mid$$
$$P \setminus X \mid P \mathbin{\fatsemi} P \mid \text{if } b \text{ then } P \text{ else } P \mid$$
$$P\,[\,X \parallel Y\,]\,P \mid P\,[\!|\,X\,|\!]\,P \mid \big\Vert\, i \bullet [X_i] P_i \mid P \,\vert\!\vert\!\vert\, P \mid \big\vert\!\big\vert\!\big\vert\, i \bullet P_i \mid$$

Stop is the deadlocked CSP process: it will refuse to participate in all events. *Skip* models successful termination: it performs the special internal event $\checkmark$, before behaving like *Stop*. The process $e \to P$, modelled using the *prefixing* operator, performs the event e and subsequently behaves as P.

CSP provides two choice operators: the *external* or *deterministic choice* operator, $\square$, offers the environment the choice between the initial events of its argument processes; conversely, the *internal* or *nondeterministic choice* operator, $\sqcap$,

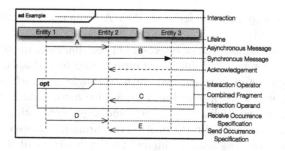

Fig. 1. Relevant constructs of the sequence diagram.

offers no such choice and the observed behaviour may be that of either process. Indexed versions exist for both operators.

The *hiding* operator, $\backslash$, conceals the events of X from the view of the external environment of P. The process $P_1 \, \S \, P_2$ represents the *sequential composition* of P_1 and P_2. This process behaves as P_1 until it terminates successfully, after which it behaves as P_2. A conditional choice construct is available in the form *if b then P_1 else P_2*, where a process behaves as P_1 if b is true and P_2 otherwise.

The process $P_1 \, [\![\, X \,]\!] \, P_2$ uses the *generalised parallel* operator to define an interface on which P_1 and P_2 must synchronise. Events outside X may occur independently in either process. The process $P_1 \, [\, X \, \| \, Y \,] \, P_2$ denotes *alphabetised parallel*, where synchronisation takes place on events in the set $X \cap Y$. The *interleaving* operator, $\| \! \|$, expresses the unsynchronised concurrent interleaving of the events of its constituent processes. Indexed forms exist for each.

The refinement checker Failures-Divergence Refinement (FDR) — which uses the machine-readable dialect of CSP, CSP_M [10] — employs CSP's theory of refinement to investigate whether a potential design meets its specification. If such a test fails, a counter-example is returned to indicate why this is so. We write $P \sqsubseteq_T Q$ when the process Q is a traces-refinement of the process P. While other forms of refinement exist, traces-refinement is sufficient for our purposes.

2.2   Sequence Diagrams

Sequence diagrams facilitate the modelling of interactions between structural constructs as sequences of temporal occurrences. These *interaction occurrences*, or *occurrence observations*, can be broadly categorised into three classes: the sending or receiving of a message; the creation or destruction of an instance; and the start or end of another behaviour. In the interests of brevity, we restrict our treatment to the first class of occurrence observations.

Messages can be exchanged either *synchronously* or *asynchronously*. If the communication is synchronous, the sender blocks until the arrival of a response. Conversely, during an asynchronous exchange, the sender does not block; rather, it continues execution after sending the message. In SysML, for example, an interaction executes within the context of its owning block, and specifies the interaction between parts or references [11]. A sequence diagram depicts this interaction graphically.

Figure 1 shows the notation of interest. On the diagram, lifelines correspond to the parts (or references). A lifeline is represented as a dashed line with the name of the reference or part enclosed in a rectangle. A synchronous message exchange is indicated using a solid line with a filled arrowhead from the sending lifeline to the receiving lifeline; the return message, unblocking the sender, is a dashed line with opposite direction. An asynchronous message is represented using a solid line from the sending lifeline to the receiving lifeline; there is no associated return message as the interaction does not block. When an interaction executes, it produces a sequence of interaction occurrences, termed a *trace*.

Several interaction operators exist. An operator either alters the behaviour of the prescribed sequence, or alters our interpretation of the trace. Examples include the optional interaction operator, *opt*, and the assertion operator, *assert*.

3 Formalisation Using CSP

An interaction, I, is a quintuple of the form $I \cong (L_I, E_I, M_I^S, M_I^O, O_I)$, where:

- L_I denotes the set of lifelines of the sequence diagram, I;
- E_I denotes the set of event types (partitioned by disjoint sets for the signals, E_I^S, or operations, E_I^O, that type messages);
- $M_I^S : ID \rightarrowtail E_I^S$ uniquely identifies the asynchronous messages of an interaction and associates a message with the signal that typed it;
- $M_I^O : ID \rightarrowtail E_I^O$ uniquely identifies the synchronous messages of an interaction and associates a message with the operation that typed it; and
- $O_I \subseteq L_I \times seq\,(ID \times \{snd, rcv, ack\})$ describes all interaction occurrences as a set of pairs, with the first element being the lifeline and the second being a sequence of occurrence observations.

We partition E_I into two disjoint sets, E_I^S and E_I^O, representing *signal events* and *operation events*, respectively. An instance of a signal event corresponds to the sending and receiving of an asynchronous message in the interaction; similarly, an *operation event* types an operation call and can be either synchronous or asynchronous. For the purposes of this paper, we will treat all call operations as synchronous (asynchronous call operations are similar to signals).

To provide each message (we view the acknowledgement message as part of the synchronous message) with a unique identifier, we require that the domains of the functions M_I^S and M_I^O be pairwise disjoint: $\mathrm{dom}\,(M_I^S) \cap \mathrm{dom}\,(M_I^O) = \emptyset$.

As an additional constraint, we assume that each synchronous message has an associated acknowledgement (with opposite direction). This acknowledgement is not a message in the conventional sense — it merely exists in order to unblock the sender. We can think of the acknowledgement as a rendezvous between the communicating lifelines in order to unblock the sender. As such, we do not associate it with its own identifier (it uses that of the corresponding synchronous message); nor do we associate with it *snd* or *rcv* occurrence observations. In order for the communicating lifelines to synchronise on this event, both observe it as an *ack*.

In addition, we define the following auxiliary functions:

- $sd : ID \nrightarrow L_I$ returns, for a message identifier, the sending lifeline;
- $rv : ID \nrightarrow L_I$ returns, for a message identifier, the receiving lifeline; and
- *occurrences* $: L_I \nrightarrow seq(ID \times \{snd, rcv, ack\})$ denotes the sequence of event occurrences on the argument lifeline in temporal order.

Interaction occurrences appear in temporal order on a lifeline, with time progressing downwards. An interaction implicitly imposes an order on the messages sent between lifelines. This *weak sequencing* implies that the order of interaction occurrences on a particular lifeline is significant, but that ordering between occurrences on different lifelines can be interleaved. An additional (and seemingly obvious) constraint is that, for a particular message, the send occurrence must happen before the receive occurrence. For example, consider again Fig. 1. Message A (and all other messages) must be sent before it can be received. Additionally, for entity 2, A must be received before B can be sent. However, there are no direct constraints between the send occurrences of messages D and E.

Our approach for translating sequence diagrams to CSP is based on mirroring the structure of the corresponding diagram. Broadly, each lifeline is mapped to a process and each occurrence observation is mapped to a CSP event. The process then enforces weak sequencing by insisting that the occurrence observations appear in the temporal order specified on the corresponding lifeline. The acts of sending and receiving a message are completely detached; as such, we require an additional constraint process to enforce the fact that a message cannot be received before it was sent.

We treat the various interaction operators of sequence diagrams using template processes that describe their respective patterns of behaviour. These are defined formally in Sect. 4.

Consider an interaction, I, with a corresponding sequence diagram. Our approach can be outlined as follows.

- With each lifeline, $l \in L_I$, we associate a sequence of events of the same temporal order. The sequence of events is given by *occurrences* (l). An element of this sequence is a pair of the form (id, obs), where $id \in ID$ and $obs \in \{snd, rcv, ack\}$.
- We model each occurrence observation with a corresponding CSP event. The unique identifier is communicated as part of the event due to the finer nuances of weak sequencing semantics. Let $obs' \in \{snd, rcv\}$. Recall that for acknowledgements we use the same id as that of the associated synchronous message. Depending on the observation and the nature of the message, the event takes the following form:
  - for asynchronous messages, $msg.asynch.id.obs'.sd(id).rv(id).M_I^S(id)$
  - for synchronous messages, $msg.synch.id.obs'.sd(id).rv(id).M_I^O(id)$
  - for acknowledgements, $msg.synch.id.ack.rv(id).sd(id).M_I^O(id)$

- Each lifeline has a corresponding CSP process that communicates the events in the required order (defined in the template process).
- For each message in an interaction, we associate a triple, (*from, to, name*), where {*from, to*} $\subseteq L_I$ and *name* $\in E_I$.
- Each message has an associated process with send and receive occurrence events that synchronise with the appropriate sending and receiving lifelines (defined in the template process).
- Depending on the interaction, we instantiate the correct template process (as defined in the next section) to describe the behaviour.
- A sequence diagram that consists of more than one interaction operator is subsequently defined as the sequential composition of the CSP template processes that describe the respective interaction operators.

The approach does not require fixed sized buffers to model asynchrony, as the sending and receiving lifelines do not synchronise on a message. This allows for a uniform treatment of synchronous and asynchronous messages: in an asynchronous exchange neither the sending nor the receiving lifelines are blocked; conversely, for a synchronous exchange, the sending lifeline blocks until the receiving lifeline communicates the acknowledgement.

In order to simplify the CSP presented here, we do not model passing arguments for call operations or signals; however, these can be readily incorporated via the use of CSP channels.

4   Complex Interactions

Combined fragments allow for the description of complex patterns of interaction in a concise and compact manner. UML (and, therefore, SysML) defines different *interaction operators*, each enabling the specification of different rules with regards to the ordering of messages (and their associated occurrence observations). A combined fragment is an *interaction* operator with associated *operands*. Figure 1 gives an example of the use of the *opt* interaction operator.

The operands of an interaction operator is dependant upon the type of the operator: the alternative and parallel operator each "have multiple horizontal partitions, separated by dashed lines that correspond to their operands. Others have just a single partition" [11]. For single partition operators, their operands correspond to the messages enclosed in the combined fragment. In addition, the operands of the interaction operators follow weak sequencing semantics (unless it is the strict operator): "During execution of an interaction, all operands use weak sequencing semantics on their contents" [11].

The weak sequencing interaction operator, *seq*, is the default. The operator imposes a weak sequencing semantics on its operands, with the operands of the weak sequencing operator being the messages contained within the combined fragment. The UML specification [4] defines weak sequencing as follows.

1. "The ordering of occurrence specifications within each of the operands [messages] are maintained in the result."

2. "Occurrence specifications on different lifelines from different operands [messages] may come in any order."
3. "Occurrence specifications on the same lifeline from different operands [messages] are ordered such that an occurrence specifications of the first operand [message] comes before that of the second operand [message]."

Thus: a message needs to be sent before it can be received; occurrence specifications between different lifelines (also between different messages) impose no additional ordering constraints upon each other; and the temporal order of the occurrence specifications on each lifeline must be honoured.

The process *Message* asserts that the sending of a message necessarily occurs before its reception, as per condition 1. The parameters *type* and *id* correspond to the type (synchronous or asynchronous) and unique identifier, respectively; *from* and *to* model the sending and receiving lifelines; and *name* corresponds to the signal or operation (an instance of an event type).

$$Message\,(type, id, from, to, name) =$$
$$msg.type.id.snd.from.to.name \rightarrow msg.type.id.rcv.from.to.name \rightarrow Skip$$
$$\alpha\,Message\,(type, id, from, to, name) =$$
$$\{|\ msg.type.id.snd.from.to.name, msg.type.id.rcv.from.to.name\ |\}$$

PrefixComposition, if supplied a sequence as input, is the process that communicates the events in order and then behaves as *Skip*. Given a temporal sequence of interaction occurrences for a lifeline, we use *PrefixComposition* to enforce condition 3:

$$PrefixComposition\,(s) =$$
$$\text{if } null\,(s) \text{ then } Skip \text{ else } head\,(s) \rightarrow PrefixComposition\,(tail\,(s))$$

The process *Lifelines* models the parallel composition of a set of lifelines. The process takes as input a set of sequences, where each sequence describes occurrence specifications for a lifeline in temporal order. Each lifeline in the composition synchronises on its entire alphabet. (In the following, the function *set* converts a sequence to a set.)

$$Lifelines\,(l) = \|\ line : l \bullet [set\,(line)]\,PrefixComposition\,(line)$$
$$\alpha\,Lifelines\,(l) = \bigcup\{line : l \bullet set\,(line)\}$$

The process *Messages* is the parallel composition of the *Message* processes, with each taking a quintuple of the form $(type, id, from, to, name)$ as input.

$$Messages\,(m) =$$
$$\|(t, id, from, to, n) : m \bullet$$
$$[\alpha\,Message\,(t, id, from, to, n)]\,Message\,(t, id, from, to, n)$$
$$\alpha\,Messages\,(m) =$$
$$\bigcup\{(t, id, from, to, n) : m \bullet \alpha\,Message\,(t, id, from, to, n)\}$$

We can now model weak sequencing behaviour. By placing *Messages* and *PrefixComposition* in parallel, we restrict the traces to adhere to the behaviours

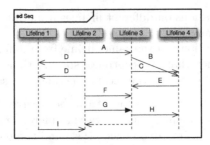

Fig. 2. The default seq operator (adapted from [11]).

imposed by the first and last condition. Condition 2 places no further restrictions on the behaviour, and, as the interaction occurrences between different lifelines do not have any shared events in common, we require no process to model this behaviour. *Seq*, which models weak sequencing, is defined thus (for brevity, we write α *Lifelines* (l) and α *Messages* (m) as L_α and M_α, respectively):

$$Seq\,(l, m) = Lifelines\,(l)\,[\,L_\alpha \parallel M_\alpha\,]\,Messages\,(m)$$

The operands of the strict sequencing operator, *strict*, are the messages contained within the combined fragment: "the semantics of strict sequencing defines a strict ordering of the operands [messages]" [4].

Strict sequencing semantics therefore impose an additional constraint upon weak sequencing, in that the operands (messages) must be sequenced across all participating lifelines [11]. This implies that, for a particular message, the send and receive occurrences must occur in strict succession.

We can subsequently define strict sequencing by placing another process (*Enforce*) in parallel to constrain the behaviour of weak sequencing.

The process *Strict* is defined as follows:

$$Strict\,(l, m) = (Lifelines\,(l)\,[\,L_\alpha \parallel M_\alpha\,]\,Messages\,(m))\,[\!|\,M_\alpha\,|\!]\,Enforce\,(m)$$
$$Enforce\,(m) = \Box\,(msg.m.i.snd.f.t.n) : M_\alpha \bullet$$
$$msg.m.i.snd.f.t.n \rightarrow msg.m.i.rcv.f.t.n \rightarrow Enforce\,(m)$$
$$\Box\,Skip$$

Our approach allows for detecting when the operands of an interaction operator are not well-defined. For example, when we try and enforce strict semantics on the sequence of Fig. 2, FDR detects a *deadlock* and returns a counter-example — message overtaking is not possible using strict semantics.

The parallel operator, *par*, designates an interleaving between its operands. The horizontal partitions (within the combined fragment) correspond to the operands. The *interleaving* operator of CSP models this pattern of behaviour perfectly. We therefore define the *par* interaction operator as the interleaved behaviour of sequentially interleaved processes. For readability, the definition below assumes that there are only two partitions within the combined fragment;

we can, however, easily extend this to cover more partitions, or even generalise the definition to cover an arbitrary number of horizontal partitions.

$$Par\,(l_1, m_1, l_2, m_2) = Seq\,(l_1, m_1) \; ||| \; Seq\,(l_2, m_2)$$

The alternative operator, *alt*, offers the choice between the behaviours of its operands, based on the guard associated with each partition. Recall that the horizontal partitions (within the combined fragment) correspond to the operands. In a scenario in which more than one guard evaluates to true, the choice is nondeterministic; if none evaluate to true, an optional else partition is selected [11]. We can use the *nondeterministic* and *conditional choice* constructs to model this behaviour. Below we provide a definition for a combined fragment consisting of two conditionally guarded partitions and one else clause. This definition can be generalised to handle an arbitrary number of conditional clauses, but a simplified version is presented here to illustrate the concepts.

$$\begin{aligned} Alt\,(l_1, m_1, g_1, l_2, m_2, g_2, l_3, m_3) = \\ \text{if } (g_1 \wedge g_2) \text{ then } Seq\,(l_1, m_1) \sqcap Seq\,(l_2, m_2) \\ \text{else if } g_1 \text{ then } Seq\,(l_1, m_1) \\ \text{else if } g_2 \text{ then } Seq\,(l_2, m_2) \text{ else } Seq\,(l_3, m_3) \end{aligned}$$

The operator *opt* models optional behaviour. The operand (messages contained within the combined fragment) is only executed if the guard condition is true. This behaviour is precisely that of an *alt* operator with a single operand.

$$Opt\,(l, m, g) = \text{if } (g) \text{ then } Seq\,(l, m) \text{ else } Skip$$

The *break* interaction operator is used to model a breaking scenario from another enclosing fragment. The behavioural semantics is such that if the guard associated with the break evaluates to true, then its operand is executed (rather than the remainder of the enclosing fragment). For example, consider a break nested within an enclosing *seq* fragment, which we model in terms of the process *Break*. The first two parameters (l_{pre} and m_{pre}) describe the lifelines and messages of the enclosing fragment preceding the break; the final two parameters (l_{post} and m_{post}) model the remainder of the enclosing behaviour. The l, m and g parameters correspond to the operands of the break fragment.

$$\begin{aligned} Break\,(l_{pre}, m_{pre}, l, m, g, l_{post}, m_{post}) = \\ Seq\,(l_{pre}, m_{pre}) \,\mathring{\,}\, (\text{if } g \text{ then } Seq\,(l, m) \text{ else } Seq\,(l_{post}, m_{post})) \end{aligned}$$

The *loop* operator repeats its operand (the messages contained within the combined fragment) until the termination condition imposed upon it is satisfied. The semantics of the loop operator allows for the termination condition to be expressed as either: an iteration bound (of the form (*lower*, *upper*) or (*exact*)); a Boolean condition; or a combination of both. (In practice, however, one would use one or the other, rather than a combination.)

The UML specification is ambiguous with regards to the semantics when the termination condition is expressed as a combination of an iteration bound and Boolean guard: it is unclear what happens if the Boolean condition evaluates to false before the minimum number of iterations have executed. This ambiguity arises as a result the following two quotes from the UML specification: "after the minimum number of iterations have executed and the Boolean expression is false the loop will terminate" [4], and "the loop will only continue if that specification evaluates to true during execution regardless of the minimum number of iterations specified in the loop" [4]. As such, we consider in our treatment only the cases where either an iteration bound or Boolean guard is specified.

The *sequencing* operator of CSP is used to express behaviour as a sequence of process executions. We can convey the desired behaviour of the loop operator through successive application of the sequencing operator (to the CSP process modelling the behaviour of the operand) in accordance with the stated termination condition. Consider the case where there is a single integer iteration bound is specified as the termination condition. The process *Loop* models this:

$$Loop\,(l, m, e) = \text{if } (e \geq 1) \text{ then } (Seq\,(l, m) \,\mathring{,}\, Loop\,(l, m, e - 1)) \text{ else } Skip$$

5   Interaction Interpretation

The interaction operators described in the previous section allowed us to model different forms of control flow — alternative or parallel behaviour, for example. In this section, we introduce the three operators that change our interpretation of a particular interaction sequence. We discuss these in the context of how they might possibly be used in a refinement check. In addition, we motivate why it is inappropriate to define process definitions in the spirit of the preceding section.

The *ignore* interaction operator provides, as part of the combined fragment, a set of messages that are to be ignored. Consequently, the messages are not allowed within the interaction fragment. The interpretation is that the messages are insignificant and irrelevant and are to be ignored if they appear in the interaction. An alternative interpretation is that the ignored messages can appear anywhere in a trace and still be considered valid.

It is possible to model this as a template process, where the ignored traces are interleaved with those of the interaction (assuming we followed the second interpretation, and *ignore* contained all the valid observations of the ignored events between participating lifelines):[3]

$$Ignore\,(l, m, ignore) = Seq\,(l, m) \,\|\|\, Run\,(ignore)$$

A more elegant solution can be achieved via the hiding operator and the first interpretation: in a refinement, we simply hide the ignored events from any behaviour we are comparing against. For example, $StateMachines \setminus ignore \sqsubseteq_T$

---

[3] Here, $Run\,(E) = \Box\, e : E \bullet e \to Run\,(E)$.

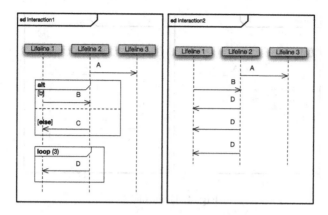

Fig. 3. Example 1

$Seq\,(lifelines, messages)$ would test if an interaction is valid for a pair of communicating state machines, $StateMachines$.

The *consider* interaction operator specifies a set of messages that are to be considered as part of this combined fragment; all other messages are ignored. Consequently, the combined fragment can only contain the considered messages. The semantics is interpreted to mean that other messages might occur as part of the interaction, but that these are irrelevant and ought to be ignored. The *consider* operator can be defined in terms of *ignore*: ignore all other messages not considered. As was the case for *ignore*, there exists an alternative interpretation, where all messages that are not considered may appear anywhere in the traces. (In the interests of brevity, we do not expand further on the *consider* operator.)

The assertion operator, *assert*, declares that the interaction fragment models the only valid continuations; any other eventuality is considered invalid. In this case, we need the refinement relation to hold in both directions.

6   Examples

Having defined a process-algebraic formal semantics for sequence diagrams, we can test whether the behaviour of one interaction sequence is contained within another by considering trace semantics. Consider Fig. 3. If we regard the behaviour (in terms of traces) of $I_2 = Seq\,(L_2, M_2)$ as the valid behaviours (a *safety specification*), and we want to test whether another interaction sequence, $I_1 = Seq\,(L_{11}, M_{11})\ \r{\circ}\ Alt\,(L_{12}, M_{12}, b, L_{13}, M_{13})\ \r{\circ}\ Loop\,(L_{14}, M_{14}, 3)$, does not deviate from this, we can use a traces-refinement ($I_2 \sqsubseteq_T I_1$) to confirm this.

As another example, we might want to be sure that interaction diagrams at different levels of the specification are consistent (see Fig. 4). Such *vertical consistency* problems are induced by a development process where models are iteratively refined: we start with an interaction sequence at a higher level and add more detail as we move closer to the implementation level specification. Assuming $Higher = Seq\,(L_h, M_h)$ and $Lower = Seq\,(L_l, M_l)$, we can check whether

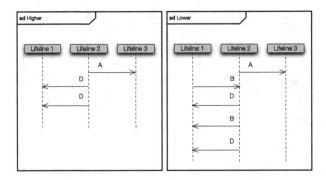

Fig. 4. Example 2

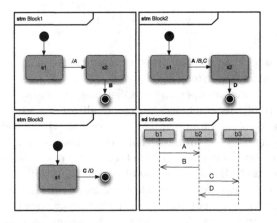

Fig. 5. Example 3

Higher $\sqsubseteq_T$ *Lower* \ *hidden* (where *hidden* denotes those occurrence observations present at the lower level, but not at the higher level).

Finally, we might make use of sequence diagrams to check the validity of communicating state machines, as described in [12,13]. We can, for example, test whether a particular sequence of events is possible when we consider the combined behaviour of a set of communicating state machines. We can check *Blocks* $\sqsubseteq_T$ *SEQ*, where *SEQ* = *Seq* (*L*, *M*). Here, *Blocks* denotes the compositional process describing the combined behaviour of the communicating state machines. We would also expect to make use of the CSP renaming operator in order to consolidate the events of our interaction semantics with the events of the state machine semantics, as proposed in [13] (Fig. 5).

7   Related Work

State machine diagrams were given a CSP semantics by Ng and Butler in [8]; activity diagrams were formalised by Dong *et al.* [9]. To the best of our knowledge, there has been no such mapping done in the spirit of the aforementioned

papers for sequence diagrams. Both [8,9] focus on the provision of a CSP semantics in an implementation-independent fashion; this was our goal for sequence
diagrams. Other examples where state-based graphical models have been given
a formal CSP semantics include [14,15].

Li and Li [7] considered the automatic translation of sequence diagrams to
CSP using a model-driven approach. Sibertin-Blanc *et al.* [16] showed four possible semantic interpretations of sequence diagrams, partly due to the semi-formal
nature of the UML specification. Rasch and Wehrheim [17] used sequence diagrams to check the validity of scenarios in a UML model. Our work differs, in
that they define a semantics for sequence diagrams in terms of the messages
communicated; in addition, they exclude the interaction operators from their
analysis. Our work considers sequence diagrams in terms of occurrence observations, rather than messages, and extends to all operators. The checking of the
validity of scenarios, using our semantics as a model of interaction, will be a focus
of future research. Other notable works of reference can be found in [18,19].

8   Discussion

We have introduced patterns of behaviour to model the interaction operators as
per the UML standard. In addition, we have provided a uniform treatment of
synchronous and asynchronous messages. Furthermore, our approach does not
rely on fixed size buffers in order to model asynchronous exchanges. Finally, we
are able to deal with lost and found messages, as well as message overtaking.

The process-algebraic approach suggested enables us to compare the behaviour of a sequence of interactions against another interaction in a natural fashion.
This is in contrast to approaches that rely on traditional model checking, such
as the work of Lima *et al.* [20] — where such comparisons are not possible. Furthermore, the only other formalisation of the semantics of sequence diagrams
that makes use of CSP that we are aware of is that of Li and Li [7]. Our approach differs in that we define our semantics for sequence diagrams in terms of
templates that describe the patterns of behaviour for the various interaction
operators. Additionally, we consider the *seq, strict, ignore, consider*, and *assert*
operators. The advantage of our approach is that any implementation of an automated translation mechanism would only have to instantiate the proposed CSP
processes in order to describe the behaviour of the desired interaction operator.

The work of Li and Li [7] models the sending of a message between lifelines
L_1 and L_2 using the channel construct, with the lifelines synchronising on the
message being exchanged. The problem here, from our perspective, is that we
require the sending and receiving of a message to be modelled as two, separate,
detached events (the sending and receiving occurrence specifications related to
the message exchange). However, the suggested approach abstracts them into
a single event. This might have been appropriate, for example, if we were only
concerned with the act of exchanging a message. However, this is not our desire
here. Instead, we wish to decompose the exchange into two separate events. In
doing so, we will be able to operate our CSP models at a finer granularity.

Consider making use of sequence diagrams to check the validity of communicating state machines, as described by the present authors in [12,13]. Activities are used to augment the behaviour of state machines in [21]. Using our model for sequence diagrams, we would be able to make use of events (like a state machine sending an asynchronous message) that correspond to interaction occurrences on the sequence diagram. Of course, the sending of an asynchronous message by one state machine does not guarantee that the message is received by another. Even if it is received immediately, it might still be placed in an event queue, so the receiving state machine might only process it later. If we operated at a coarser granularity, we would have to be content with only modelling the exchange of the message, making it impossible to distinguish between when it was sent and when it was received.

The approach presented here is novel as we give a detailed account of interaction operators. Moreover, due to the nature of a process-algebraic formalism like CSP, where the focus is on describing intricate patterns of behaviour, we are able to deal with interaction operators that alter our interpretation of an interaction sequence more naturally that in approaches that rely on traditional model checking using temporal logics [20]. In addition, the refinement checker, FDR, which allows the behaviour of one process to be compared against that of another in terms of a refinement hierarchy, provides a practical means of comparing behaviour of one sequence diagram against that of another (incorporating the operators that alter interaction interpretation, for example).

Possible areas of future work include checking the validity of scenarios.

References

1. Swain, S.K., Mohapatra, D.P., Mall, R.: Test case generation based on use case and sequence diagram. Int. J. Softw. Eng. **3**(2), 21–52 (2010)
2. Odell, J.J., Van Dyke Parunak, H., Bauer, B.: Representing agent interaction protocols in UML. In: Ciancarini, P., Wooldridge, M.J. (eds.) AOSE 2000. LNCS, vol. 1957, pp. 121–140. Springer, Heidelberg (2001)
3. Bist, G., MacKinnon, N., Murphy, S.: Sequence diagram presentation in technical documentation. In: Proceedings of the 22nd International Conference on Design of Communication: The Engineering of Quality Documentation, SIGDOC 2004, pp. 128–133. ACM (2004)
4. Object Management Group: Unified Modeling Language Specification, version 2.4.1 (2011)
5. Kim, S.-K., Carrington, D.: A formal model of the UML metamodel: the UML state machine and its integrity constraints. In: Bert, D., Bowen, J.P., C. Henson, M., Robinson, K. (eds.) ZB 2002. LNCS, vol. 2272, pp. 497–516. Springer, Heidelberg (2002)
6. Hoare, C.A.R.: Communicating Sequential Processes. Prentice Hall, Upper Saddle River (1985)
7. Li, D., Li, D.: An approach to formalize UML sequence diagrams in CSP. Int. Proc. Comput. Sci. Inf. Technol. **53**(2), 109–115 (2010)
8. Ng, M.Y., Butler, M.: Towards formalizing UML state diagrams in CSP. In: Proceedings of the 1st International Conference on Software Engineering and Formal Methods, SEFM 2003, pp. 138–147. IEEE (2003)

9. Dong, X., Philbert, N., Zongtian, L., Wei, L.: Towards formalizing UML activity diagrams in CSP. In: Proceedings of the International Symposium on Computer Science and Computational Technology, ISCSCT 2008, pp. 450–453. IEEE (2008)
10. Roscoe, A.W.: The Theory and Practice of Concurrency. Prentice Hall, Upper Saddle River (1997)
11. Friedenthal, S., Moore, A., Steiner, R.: A Practical Guide to SysML: The Systems Modeling Language. Morgan Kaufmann Publishers, San Francisco (2008)
12. Jacobs, J., Simpson, A.C.: A process algebraic approach to decomposition of communicating SysML blocks. Int. J. Model. Opt. **3**(2), 153–157 (2013)
13. Jacobs, J.: A Formal Refinement Framework for the Systems Modeling Language. Department of Computer Science, University of Oxford, Doctor of Philosophy thesis (2015)
14. Yeung, W.L., Leung, K.R.P.H., Dong, W., Wang, J.: Improvements towards formalising UML state diagrams in CSP. In: Proceedings of the 12th Asia-Pacific Software Engineering Conference, APSEC 2005, pp. 176–182. IEEE (2005)
15. Roscoe, A.W., Chakraborty, S.: Verifying statemate statecharts using CSP and FDR. In: Liu, Z., Kleinberg, R.D. (eds.) ICFEM 2006. LNCS, vol. 4260, pp. 324–341. Springer, Heidelberg (2006)
16. Sibertin-Blanc, C., Hameurlain, N., Tahir, O.: Ambiguity and structural properties of basic sequence diagrams. Innov. Syst. Softw. Eng. **4**(3), 275–284 (2008)
17. Rasch, H., Wehrheim, H.: Checking the validity of scenarios in UML models. In: Steffen, M., Zavattaro, G. (eds.) FMOODS 2005. LNCS, vol. 3535, pp. 67–82. Springer, Heidelberg (2005)
18. Sibertin-Blanc, C., Tahir, O., Cardoso, J.: Interpretation of UML sequence diagrams as causality flows. In: Ramos, F.F., Larios Rosillo, V., Unger, H. (eds.) ISSADS 2005. LNCS, vol. 3563, pp. 126–140. Springer, Heidelberg (2005)
19. Bernardi, S., Merseguer, J.: Performance evaluation of UML design with stochastic well-formed nets. J. Syst. Softw. **80**(11), 1843–1865 (2007)
20. Lima, V., Talhi, C., Mouheb, D., Debbabi, M., Wang, L., Pourzandi, M.: Formal verification and validation of UML 2.0 sequence diagrams using source and destination of messages. Electron. Notes Theor. Comput. Sci. **254**, 143–160 (2009)
21. Jacobs, J., Simpson, A.C.: On the formal interpretation of SysML blocks using a safety critical case study. In: Proceedings of the 8th Brazilian Symposium on Software Components, Architectures, and Reuse, SBCARS 2014. IEEE (2014)

Modelling and Verification of Survivability Requirements for Critical Systems

Simona Bernardi[1]([✉]), Lacramioara Dranca[1], and José Merseguer[2]

[1] Centro Universitario de la Defensa, Academia General Militar,
Zaragoza, Spain
{simonab,licri}@unizar.es
[2] Dpto. Informática e Ing. de Sistemas, Universidad de Zaragoza,
Zaragoza, Spain
jmerse@unizar.es

Abstract. Survivability is a property of systems that guarantees services which operate safe and timely. Safety-critical services must survive despite the presence of faults or attacks. The contribution of the paper is twofold: construction of a survivability assessment model (SAM) and its transformation to a model checking problem. Our SAM is automatically obtained from an improved specification of misuse cases, which encompasses essential services, threats and survivability strategies. The SAM is automatically converted, using model-driven techniques, into a Petri Net model for verifying survivability properties through model checking. The method has been applied to a military command-and-control information system.

Keywords: Safety assessment · Survivable services · Petri Nets

1 Introduction

Critical systems offer services that must operate safe and timely, despite the presence of faults or attacks. This is the case, for example, of military Command and Control Information Systems (C2IS). For these systems, "essential services" must survive even when the system is infiltrated, compromised or crashed. Survivability strategies, *resistance, recognition* and *recovery*, are in this case cornerstone system capabilities. In particular, resistance is the capability to repeal attacks and to mask faults, recognition is the capability to detect attacks and faults and to evaluate damage and, recovery is the capability to restore services after intrusions or failures.

We propose a method to obtain a system survivability assessment model (SAM), which can be formally verified. The method is based on misuse cases [1], which we enhance with a QoS definition for the essential services and with a survivability specification. The latter consists of a specification of faults and attacks, threatening essential services, and of survivable strategies for threats mitigation. The language used for specification is UML [16] and its extension

C. Canal and A. Idani (Eds.): SEFM 2014 Workshops, LNCS 8938, pp. 86–100, 2015.
DOI: 10.1007/978-3-319-15201-1_6

mechanisms. As a byproduct of the improved misuse cases, our method automatically yields a *service modes specification*, which we call SAM. It comprises full service and degraded modes and paths that account for threats and survivable strategies. Special feature of the method is its ability to verify whether fundamental properties for survivable systems are considered in the requirements specification, such as the capability of the system to recover the full service mode. The method then provides a support for the engineer to identify lacks or errors in the SAM.

The method primarily focuses on how to represent system requirements for getting an appropriate SAM, rather than addressing the issues of eliciting and gathering the requirements, which definitely are in the use case technique [10]. Model-driven techniques are used to derive from the SAM a Petri net model [15], where model-checking is applied for a system survivable verification.

The paper is organized as follows. Section 2 describes our method. Section 3 illustrates the method using a military C2IS case study. Section 4 reviews the literature. Conclusions are drawn in Sect. 5.

2   Survivability Assessment Method

We propose a method, as a four steps process, for creating a survivability assessment model (SAM) and for verifying survivability properties on this SAM. Figure 1 outlines the method, the first two steps comply with the SNA method [7]. Our method is primarily proposed to be used within iterative and incremental processes, such as the Rational unified process [12], in the requirements stage. It is also worth noting that the method resorts to the *(mis)use cases* technique [1]. Today, most development processes include use cases, being then the method also practicable in prototype-based or agile processes.

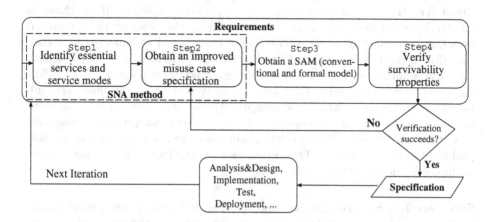

Fig. 1. Method overview

2.1   Identify Essential Services and Service Modes

From a use case list the engineer selects those that must not collapse, even when operating in adverse conditions of fault or attack. Our process supplements a use case specification as follows:

- Each selected use case is an essential service stereotyped as `service`.
- The engineer develops a QoS specification for essential services, see Table 2 for an example. She identifies the system service modes, the metrics (e.g., availability, response time) and indicators (e.g., confidence level) of interest and she decides the acceptable metric's (indicator's) thresholds.

Regarding service modes, it is expected to have a low number; three or four different services modes can be reasonable even for large systems. Service modes in Table 2 describe a paradigmatic case.

2.2   Obtain an Improved Misuse Case Specification

The objective is to develop an improved misuse case specification, which consists of both a specification of the threats to the system and a set of survivable strategies - resistance, recognition and recovery -. The former is a faults and attacks specification. Our method supplements the well-known misuse case technique as follows to get an improved specification.

Sub-step 2.1. Threats Specification. Fault and attack scenarios *threatening* each essential service are discovered and represented by misuse cases stereotyped as `misuse`. Similarly to use cases, also misuse cases are detailed with informal descriptions; Table 3 shows an example. Each misuse case is annotated with tagged-values that describe the characteristics of the threat, according to the classification in [3]. The engineer should specify at least the *persistency* of the threat (i.e., transient or permanent), the *origin* (i.e., malicious, if the threat is an attack, or not malicious if the threat is a fault), the *effect* on the threatened essential services, that is the service failure modes, and the affected QoS (i.e., the affected metrics/indicators defined in the QoS specification). In particular, the service failure modes characterize the incorrect service according to different viewpoints: the *domain* (i.e., content, early or late timing, halt, erratic), the *detectability* (i.e., signaled or unsignaled), the *consistency* (i.e., consistent or inconsistent) and the *consequence* on the environment (application-specific severity levels are normally used which are associated to maximum acceptable probabilities of occurrence). The misuse case annotations in Figs. 4 and 7 show examples of the threats characterization.

Sub-step 2.2. Survivable Strategies. For each misuse case, survivability strategies need to be specified to *mitigate* its effects on the essential services. A strategy is stereotyped either `resistance`, `recognition` or `recovery` according to the classification in [7]. The survivability strategies mitigating a given misuse case are identified as follows:

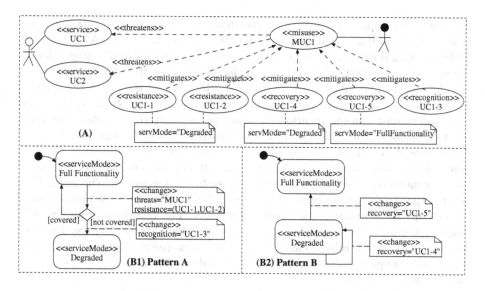

Fig. 2. Service modes specification patterns.

1. The engineer studies if one or more *resistance* strategies can be devised, and creates one use case per strategy. The interpretation is that the resistance introduced by *UC1-1* AND *UC1-2*, see Fig. 2, when applied to *MUC1* would leave the system in full functionality. But it is also possible that the resistance does not succeed, then the system reaches a degraded service mode. The reached service mode is specified as a tagged-value associated to the UCs (*servMode* in Fig. 2(A)).

2. The engineer studies a strategy for the system to *recognize* the degraded service mode induced by the success of the misuse case. If she identifies such strategy, she creates the corresponding use case (*UC1-3* in Fig. 2(A)).

3. The engineer identifies one or more strategies to *recover* the system, and creates one use case for each strategy. Each use case is annotated with a tagged value indicating the impact of the strategy. For example, one strategy could recover the system to full functionality, but other can get less impact (see Fig. 2(A), *UC1-5* and *UC1-4* respectively).

Sub-step 2.3. Review the QoS Specification. The improved misuse case specification -created by Steps 2.1 and 2.2- will help the engineer to review the QoS specification initially proposed in the first step of the method. So, new service modes can be added, new metrics can be devised, and modifications in the thresholds introduced. Again a few experience in QoS is required.

2.3 Obtain a Survivability Assessment Model

Two equivalent survivability assessment models (SAM) are obtained through two sequential steps. First, a semi-formal SAM is automatically obtained by leveraging the improved misuse case specification and QoS specification. Then, a new SAM is also automatically obtained from the semi-formal SAM. The last SAM is a formal model, in terms of Petri Nets, where survivability properties of the system can be verified. Let us detail the obtention of the semi-formal SAM.

The semi-formal SAM is a UML state-machine whose states are the system service modes in the QoS specification. The transitions are obtained from the improved misuse case specification. We consider two patterns to obtain the transitions. For each misuse case we first apply pattern A and then pattern B.

Pattern A (in Fig. 2-B1). We create a choice node[1] whose input is the full functionality state. The choice has two output transitions. One to full functionality mode to represent that the resistance to the misuse case succeeds. The other output leads to the degraded mode specified by the *servMode* tagged-value associated to the resistance strategies (Fig. 2-A). The transition from the full functionality state to the choice node is labelled **change** and the tagged-values specify the mitigated misuse case (*threats*) as well as the resistance strategy use cases. The **change** transition from the choice node to the degraded state specifies the recognition use case.

Pattern B (in Fig. 2-B2). We review the recovery strategies for the misuse case. For each one we create a transition whose input is the degraded mode induced by the misuse case and its output the target mode indicated by the strategy (*servMode* tagged-value). The transition is labelled **change** to indicate the recovery use case.

The SAM Petri Net model is derived by applying a model-to-model transformation to the semi-formal SAM.

Figure 3 sketches the mapping: the SAM on the left is actually the one produced in next section, C2IS case study, for the first iteration (cf. Fig. 5, white part). The translation approach is quite intuitive: SAM states are mapped to single PN places, while SAM transitions correspond to sequences of causally connected PN transitions where the number of the latter depends on the annotations associated to the former. In particular, a change of service mode can be characterized by a threat causing it (*threats* tagged-value) and/or by a survivability strategy aimed at mitigating it (*resistance, recognition, recovery*). So each tagged-value, annotated to a **change** SAM transition, is mapped to a PN transition with the same name. The causality of the threat occurrence and the consequent resistance and/or recognition and/or recovery is captured by the causal connection of the corresponding PN transitions. The choice in the SAM is translated to a free-choice conflict between two PN transitions: one representing the successful coverage of the resistance strategy (e.g., *coveredUC4*) and the other the unsuccessful case (e.g., *notcoveredUC4*). Finally there is a unique marked place (initial marking), which is the one corresponding to the initial state of the SAM.

---

[1] The choice node is graphically represented by the diamond shape.

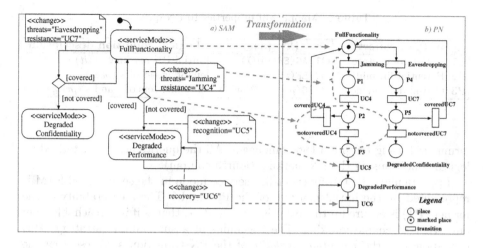

Fig. 3. Model transformation.

2.4 Verify Survivability Properties

In the last step, the formal SAM, Petri Net model, is used for verifying survivability properties through model-checking techniques. The step aims at providing a feedback to the engineer about the completeness and correctness of the service modes specification. In particular, considering that the SAM represents the acceptable service modes of the essential services and the change of service modes due to adverse conditions (attacks or faults), it may be interesting to check, at least, the following properties of survivability:

P1. The system should always be able to recover to full functionality.
P2. The survivability strategy S is feasible.
P3. As a response to the occurrence of an adverse condition C, the system should be able to carry out the survivability strategy S.

Model checking techniques [8] are state space based techniques that consist in verifying logical properties on the reachability graph of the PN model. Logical properties need to be formally specified as queries in order to be processed by a model checker: there exist different temporal logic languages that can be applied (e.g., CTL [4], LTL [14]), depending on the type of property to be checked and on the type of model checking technique. On the other hand, we need to interpret the survivability properties in terms of logical properties of the PN model, which will be then expressed as queries on the PN reachability graph using a formal language.

Table 1 shows the PN properties[2] (second column) that ensure the satisfiability of the properties **P1–P3** and the PN queries (third column) that can be

---

[2] Petri Nets have well-established properties, such as home state, which are usually defined in terms of place markings and transition firings [15].

Table 1. Mapping of properties to PN queries.

	PN property	PN query	Logical condition description
P1	Initial home state	Q1: AG(EF($init$))	initial PN marking ($init$)
P2	Potential firability	Q2: EF(pre_s)	enabling set of s (pre_s)
P3	Causal dependence	Q3: G($pre_c \Rightarrow$F pre_s)	enabling sets of c and s (pre_c, pre_s)

formulated using temporal logic languages. All the queries are characterized by logical conditions on the PN marking (fourth column).

In particular, the full functionality service mode in the semi-formal SAM is represented by the initial marking of the PN model. The recoverability of the former (**P1**) is ensured if the latter is a *home state*, that is if it is reachable from any other reachable marking. The feasibility of a survivability strategy (**P2**) corresponds to the *potential fireability* of the PN transition s representing the strategy, that is the latter belongs at least to a firing sequence. Finally, the cause-effect relationship between the occurrence of an adverse condition C and the execution of a survivability strategy S (**P3**) corresponds to the *causal dependence* between the PN transitions c and s modeling C and S, respectively. Observe that, for a given PN property, different possible queries can be formulated; in Table 1, Q1 and Q2 are CTL formulas and Q3 is an LTL formula.

Once the PN queries have been defined, they can be executed using a PN model checker: besides the true/false answer, usually the model checker produces a counter-example path for queries of universal type (e.g., Q1 and Q3) and a witness path for queries of existential type (e.g., Q2). For example, using PROD [17], the query Q1 on the PN model of Fig. 3(b) returns a false value. A counter-example path is also produced that indicates a path, on the reachability graph of the PN model, leading to a deadlock marking (i.e., *DegradedConfidentiality* place marked).

3   The C2IS Case Study

We consider a military Command and Control Information System (C2IS) [6]. Regardless the levels of command at which military C2IS systems are used, they generally share information to synchronize the *Situational Awareness* and the *Purpose of the Chief* in order to (1) provide timely an accurate view of what is happening in the theater of operations to the officers in charge and (2) send timely their orders to subordinates. In particular, they incorporate messaging capabilities and a map situation.

We exemplify the method application considering two consecutive iterations within the development process.

3.1   First Iteration

In the first step, three essential services related to information exchange are identified: send reports, transmit orders and request supplies. Figure 4 (left part) shows use cases (UCs) stereotyped **service**[3]. The exchange information functionalities are all characterized by QoS requirements, that are considered in the definition of the system service modes (see Table 2): *full functionality* defines the required QoS under normal condition, i.e., assuming no threats affecting the essential services. The other two modes define the required QoS under degraded conditions, either considering *degraded performance* or *degraded confidentiality*. The QoS metrics of interest are the steady state availability (*ssAvail*) and response time (*respTime*), while confidentiality is a qualitative indicator (*confLevel*) that enables to restrict the information exchange depending on the NATO clearance levels (i.e., top secret, secret, confidential, restricted). For example, a *high* confidence level indicates that the information can be exchanged at all clearance levels, while a *medium* one limits the exchange of confidential and restricted information. Finally, metric (indicator) threshold values are assigned to the essential services: an exemplification is provided in Table 2.

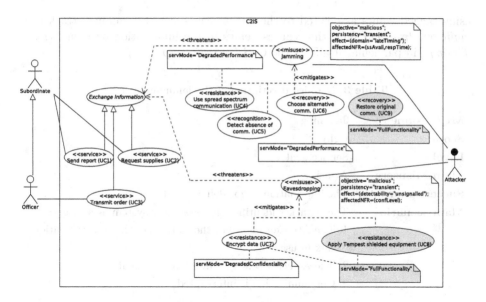

Fig. 4. Misuse case diagram (Iteration 1)

In the second step a vulnerability analysis is carried out first, to identify potential threats affecting essential services. Two types of attacks are considered specifically: sending radio signals to disrupt communication (*jamming*) and accessing to the information exchanged between officers and subordinates (*eavesdropping*). The attacks are represented by **misuse** cases (see Fig. 4), they are described in natural language using templates (see Table 3) and classified using the taxonomy in [3]. The result of such classification is specified in the diagram

---

[3] To avoid cluttering, the figure shows only the essential services considered in this iteration.

Table 2. Specification of QoS for each service mode

Full Functionality	UC1	UC2	UC3
ssAvail	99%	99%	99%
respTime	(10,sec,max)	(10,sec,max)	(100,sec,max)
confLevel	high	high	high
Degraded Performance	UC1	UC2	UC3
ssAvail	95%	95%	95%
respTime	(100,sec,max)	(100,sec,max)	(1000,sec,max)
confLevel	high	high	high
Degraded Confidentiality	UC1	UC2	UC3
ssAvail	99%	99%	99%
respTime	(10,sec,max)	(10,sec,max)	(100,sec,max)
confLevel	medium	medium	medium

using tagged-values associated to the misuse cases: e.g., a jamming attack is a *malicious transient* fault that causes delays in the information exchange (*lateTiming*), in particular it affects the QoS (*ssAvail, respTime*).

Table 3. Detailed description of the jamming attack.

MUC Name	Jamming
Scope	C2IS
Level	Service goal
Main Misusers	Attacker
Success guarantee	The information is not delivered timely
Main scenario	The Attacker identifies the messaging system as a target:
	1. The Attacker identifies the features of the communication link in use
	2. The Attacker sends an interference signal
	3. Communication is interrupted

Once threats affecting essential services have been identified, survival strategies to mitigate them are devised. Several strategies are required to mitigate a jamming attack (Fig. 4, white UCs): use of spread spectrum communication (**resistance** strategy that may not provide a 100 % threat coverability), detection of absence of communication in case the resistance does not succeed (**recognition**) and consequent reconfiguration with an alternative communication mean (**recovery**). Both the above resistance and the recovery strategies should guarantee an acceptable degraded performance service mode (*servMode* tagged value). On the other hand, to mitigate an eavesdropping attack only data encryption is required (**resistance**) that may lead to a degraded confidentiality service mode in case of successful intrusion.

In the third step, the SAM shown in Fig. 5 (white portion) is automatically obtained from Fig. 4, by applying the patterns described in the previous section. In particular, the states (`serviceMode`) represent the system service modes of Table 2, the transitions (`change`) model changes of service mode due to threat occurrence and consequent survivability strategies execution. Observe that the tagged values associated to `change` transitions refer to (mis)use cases of Fig. 4.

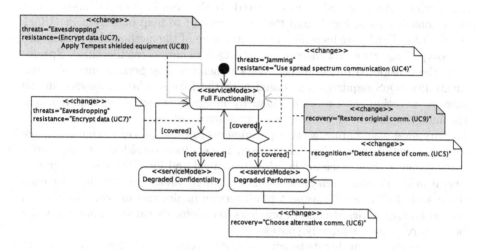

Fig. 5. SAM state-machine (Iteration 1)

In the fourth step, the Petri Net of Fig. 3(b) is used as a SAM formal model to verify properties as described in Sect. 2.4. The formal SAM was derived from the semi-formal SAM in Fig. 3(a), the same as in Fig. 5 (white portion). It is used to verify, through model-checking techniques, whether the system requirements specification satisfies the survivability properties described in Sect. 2.4. In particular, the recoverability property **P1** is not satisfied. As counterexample the model checker found that, once reached the *Degraded Confidentiality* mode is not still possible to recover to the *Full Functionality*. This result suggests to require a stronger resistance strategy to eavesdropping attacks, and the engineer decides to apply Tempest shielded equipment that together with data encryption should guarantee a 100 % of coverage. The misuse case diagram is updated accordingly by adding a new use case (*UC8* in Fig. 4) and new SAMs -semi-formal and formal- are generated. Property **P1** is newly checked and, again, a new counterexample is found since it is not possible to leave from a *Degraded Performance* mode. Then, the engineer needs to introduce a new recovery strategy to restore the original communication once a jamming attack disappears[4] (*UC9* in Fig. 4). The resulting semi-formal SAM is the one in Fig. 5 with the grey transitions and where the transition path from *Full Functionality* to *Degraded*

---

[4] Observe that attack is a transient fault.

Confidentiality is removed. All the survivability properties are satisfied in this SAM version, so the final misuse case specification can be used as input artifact for the design phase in this iteration.

3.2   Second Iteration

The application of the method in a next iteration restarts identifying new essential services. An essential service related to the coordination of land/sea/air operations (UC10 in Fig. 7) and two other related to map management (UC11 and UC12 in Fig. 7) are identified in the first step of the method. All of them are stereotyped **service** and their associated QoS requirements identified. Specifically, the considered functionalities are characterized by performance and confidentiality (QoS requirements shared with the functionalities analyzed in the previous iteration) and some of them by integrity (a new QoS requirement). The integrity metric of interest is a qualitative indicator (*integLevel*). A *high* integrity level would grant writing permissions to those processes that exchange critical, essential and routine information. The engineer considers the new metric in the scope of the service modes already defined and identifies a new degraded service mode *degraded integrity*. Initial threshold values are specified for each new essential service with respect to all service modes and metrics (see Fig. 6). Obviously, for metrics studied in previous iterations, its values remain the same for the service modes already considered.

In the second step threats to new essential services are identified. The threats analyzed in the previous iteration (*jamming* and *eavesdropping*) affect also some of the essential services considered in the running iteration and the relationship is reflected in the diagram in Fig. 7. Two new types of threats are considered: destroying a communication node (*destroy node*) and manipulation of the data sent by sensors or officers when updating the common situation map (*manipulate information*). Each of them is specified in the diagram with the QoS metrics affected, e.g., the latter attack is a *malicious transient* fault that affects the content of the information exchanged (*content*), and consequently the QoS of the confidence and integrity metrics (*confLevel, integLevel*).

Also in the second step survivable strategies are devised for the new threats in this iteration. First, the engineer specifies a **resistance** strategy (*Apply redundancy* - UC13 in Fig. 7) and a **recognition** strategy (*Monitor node status* - UC14 in Fig. 7) to mitigate the destruction of a communication node, these strategies should guarantee a 100 % of coverage. Next, a control access is required as **resistance** strategy to a manipulate information attack that may lead to a degraded integrity service mode in case the resistance fails. A **recognition** strategy (monitoring data quality) and **recovery** strategy (restore original mode) should eventually bring the system back to full functionality mode.

In the third step, a new semi-formal SAM is obtained considering the new essential services only. It is used further to automatically build a formal SAM - Petri Net-. In the fourth step, the verification of survivability properties on this model gives useful feedback to the engineer. Specifically, the recognition strategy *UC*14 does not satisfy the feasibility property **P2** (see Sub-sect. 2.4).

The engineer corrects the specification (Fig. 7, grey part), so that the `resistance` strategy *Apply redundancy* may lead to a degraded performance service mode and she adds a new `recovery` strategy (*Reconfigure* - UC18) that should eventually bring the system back to full functionality mode.

Full Functionality	UC1	UC2	UC3	UC10	UC11	UC12
ssAvail				99%	99%	99%
respTime				(10,sec,max)	(10,sec,max)	(20,sec,max)
confLevel				high	high	high
integLevel				high	——	high
Degraded Performance						
ssAvail				95%	95%	95%
respTime				(100,sec,max)	(100,sec,max)	(100,sec,max)
confLevel				high	high	high
integLevel				high	——	high
Degraded Confidentiality						
ssAvail				99%	99%	99%
respTime				(10,sec,max)	(10,sec,max)	(20,sec,max)
confLevel				medium	medium	medium
integLevel				high	——	high
Degraded Integrity						
ssAvail				99%	99%	99%
respTime				(10,sec,max)	(10,sec,max)	(20,sec,max)
confLevel				low	low	low
integLevel				medium	——	medium

First Iteration   *Second Iteration*

Fig. 6. Specification of QoS for each service mode (Iteration 2).

4 Related Work

Survivability has always been an important requirement in the military context for platforms, communication systems, and nowadays more generally to missions. It has also been a concern of those civil system domains (e.g., information systems and critical infrastructures) where it is crucial to guarantee certain QoS levels despite a set of pre-specified threats.

Ellison et al. [7] proposed a method (SNA) for survivability assessment of distributed software systems at architectural level, however we place our method in the requirements stage. The first two steps of our method comply with SNA and we have introduced a new survivability assessment model, based on (mis)use cases and QoS specifications, that is leveraged through model-checking for verification.

Knight and Strunk [11] proposed a formal definition for acceptable levels of service offered by a survivable system under different environment conditions.

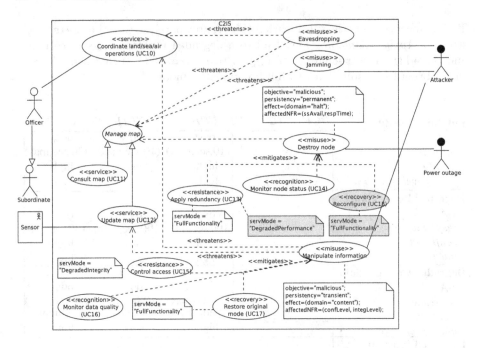

Fig. 7. Misuse case diagram (Iteration 2)

Each level is quantified by relative values (as perceived by the users) and can be expressed in terms of QoS requirements. The survivability specification is a graph, where the nodes represent the acceptable levels of service offered by the system and the edges model the change of levels when certain environment conditions are met. We have also used a graph representation for the different system service modes. Our work goes one step further by supporting the formal verification of the survivability properties.

Several approaches have been proposed in the literature to collect QoS requirements related to survivability. Mustafiz et al. [13] define a requirement engineering process to elicit reliability/safety requirements and degraded services. Similar to our proposal, use cases are profiled to model undesired situations that can interrupt the normal behavior of the system and handlers to guarantee reliable and safe services. In [5], a framework (UMD) has been proposed for eliciting and modeling dependability requirements that is designed around a basic modeling language defined by the authors. As in our proposal, UMD can be used to identify and define measurable dependability requirements and properties of the system. Allenby and Kelly [2] integrate use case and hazard identification techniques for safety requirements elicitation in aerospace application domain. The work in [9] inherits from [2] the use case specification and applies Practical Formal Specification to specify safety requirements and to verify them for completeness and consistency.

5   Conclusion

To the best of our knowledge, the task of verifying survivability requirements is an important issue not yet addressed in the literature. In particular, the derivation of service modes specification from the requirements and its formal verification are novel contributions of this work.

Reproducibility. Our method has been conceived to be easily reproduced in different software development processes (iterative and incremental, agile or prototype-based) through the use of the (mis)use case technique. In particular, Step1 and Step2 clearly identify how to supplement (mis)use cases, while Step3 and Step4 should be accomplished automatically. We are currently developing a framework based on the Eclipse platform as a support of the method.

Scalability. This is a strong point for the method. At this regard the main issue should be the model checking analysis of the SAM due to state space explosion. However, the number of states always remain low since they just indicate service modes, as previously discussed. Moreover, each new iteration gets a new SAM automatically, where only new essential services and new misuse cases are considered and consequently analyzed. For large systems the number of misuse cases could be large, however they only impact in the number of transitions, which is not a problem for the analysis. A large number of use cases does not hamper the method since they are not represented in the SAM for analysis. In our case study, the analyses carried out by PROD lasted for a few minutes.

Acknowledgements. Special thanks to the Lieutenant Colonel Félix Borque Pérez of the CASIOPEA centre at CENAD "San Gregorio'" (Zaragoza, Spain) for his help in gathering the C2IS requirements. This work has been supported by the Spanish projects TIN2011-24932 and TIN2013-46238-C4-1-R of the Ministerio de Economía y Competitividad, and by the Distributed Computation (DisCo) research group of the Aragonese Government (Ref. T94).

References

1. Alexander, I.: Misuse cases: use cases with hostile intent. IEEE Softw. **20**(1), 58–66 (2003)
2. Allenby, K., Kelly, K.: Deriving safety requirements using scenarios. In: International Conference on Requirements Engineering, pp. 228–235. IEEE Computer Society (2001)
3. Avizienis, A., Laprie, J.C., Randell, B., Landwehr, C.: Basic concepts and taxonomy of dependable and secure computing. IEEE Trans. Dependable Secure Comput. **01**(1), 11–33 (2004)
4. Clarke, E.M., Emerson, E.A., Sistla, A.P.: Automatic verification of finite-state concurrent systems using temporal logic specifications. ACM Trans. Program. Lang. Syst. **8**(2), 244–263 (1986)
5. Donzelli, P., Basili, V.: A practical framework for eliciting and modeling system dependability requirements: experience from the NASA high dependability computing project. J. Syst. Softw. **79**, 107–119 (2006)

6. Diedrichsen, L.D.: Command & Control operational requirements and system implementation. Inf. Secur. Int. J. **5**, 23–40 (2000)
7. Ellison, R.J., Linger, R.C., Longstaff, T., Mead, N.R.: Survivable network system analysis: a case study. IEEE Softw. **16**(4), 70–77 (1999)
8. Girault, C., Valle, R. (eds.): System Engineering: A Petri Net Based Approach to Modelling, Verification and Implementation, Chapter: State Space Based Methods and Model Checking, pp. 171–190. KRONOS (1998)
9. Iwu, F., Galloway, A., McDermid, J., Toyn, J.: Integrating safety and formal analyses using UML and PFS. Reliab. Eng. Syst. Saf. **92**(2), 156–170 (2007)
10. Jacobson, I., Booch, G., Rumbaugh, J.: The Unified Software Development Process. Addison Wesley, Reading (1999)
11. Knight, J.C., Strunk, E.A.: Achieving critical system survivability through software architectures. In: de Lemos, R., Gacek, C., Romanovsky, A. (eds.) Architecting Dependable Systems II. LNCS, vol. 3069, pp. 51–78. Springer, Heidelberg (2004)
12. Kruchten, P.: The Rational Unified Process: An Introduction. Addison-Wesley Longman Publishing, Boston (2003)
13. Mustafiz, S., Kienzle, J., Berlizev, A.: Addressing degraded service outcomes and exceptional modes of operation in behavioural models. In: Proceedings of the RISE/EFTS Joint International Workshop on Software Engineering for Resilient Systems, SERENE 2008, pp. 19–28. ACM, New York (2008)
14. Pnueli, A.: The temporal semantics of concurrent programs. Theor. Comput. Sci. **13**(1), 45–60 (1981)
15. Reisig, W.: Petri Nets. An Introduction. EATCS Monographs on Theoretical Computer Science. Springer, Heidelberg (1985)
16. Rumbaugh, J., Jacobson, I., Booch, G.: The Unified Modeling Language Reference Manual, 2nd edn. Addison Wesley, Reading (2004)
17. Varpaaniemi, K., Heljanko, K., Lilius, J.: PROD 3.2 — an advanced tool for efficient reachability analysis. In: Grumberg, O. (ed.) CAV 1997. LNCS, vol. 1254, pp. 472–475. Springer, Heidelberg (1997)

Model-Based Verification of Safety Contracts

Elena Gómez-Martínez[1], Ricardo J. Rodríguez[1([⊠])], Leire Etxeberria Elorza[2],
Miren Illarramendi Rezabal[2], and Clara Benac Earle[1]

[1] Babel Group, Universidad Politécnica de Madrid, Madrid, Spain
{egomez,rjrodriguez,cbenac}@babel.ls.fi.upm.es
[2] Embedded Systems Research Group, Mondragon Goi Eskola Politeknikoa (MGEP),
Arrasate-Mondragón, Spain
{letxeberria,millarramendi}@mondragon.edu

Abstract. The verification of safety becomes crucial in critical systems where human lives depend on the correct functioning of such systems. Formal methods have often been advocated as necessary to ensure the reliability of software systems, albeit with a considerable effort. In any case, such an effort is cost-effective when verifying safety-critical systems. Safety requirements are usually expressed using safety contracts, in terms of assumptions and guarantees. To facilitate the adoption of formal methods in the safety-critical software industry, we propose the use of well-known modelling languages, such as UML, to model a software system, and the use of OCL to express the system safety contracts within UML. A UML model enriched with OCL constraints is then transformed to a Petri net model that enables to formally verify such safety contracts. We apply our approach to an industrial case study that models a train doors controller in charge of the opening and closing of train doors. Our approach allows to perform an early safety verification, which increases the confidence of software engineers while designing the system.

Keywords: Safety contracts · Model-based · Verification · Petri nets

1 Introduction

With the growing adoption of software in safety-critical systems, safety assessment has become a crucial software engineering task as it has been recognised by several initiatives, for instance, the ARTEMIS JU nSafeCer project [1]. Moreover, software system safety engineering must be incorporated early in the software design process and be part of the development and operational lifecycle of the system.

Contract-based design is a popular approach for the design of complex component-based systems where safety properties are difficult to guarantee [2,3]. A key benefit of using contracts is that they follow the principle of separation

The research leading to these results has received funding from the ARTEMIS Joint Undertaking under grant agreement n° 295373 (project nSafeCer) and from National funding.

C. Canal and A. Idani (Eds.): SEFM 2014 Workshops, LNCS 8938, pp. 101–115, 2015.
DOI: 10.1007/978-3-319-15201-1_7

of concerns [4], separating assumptions that the environment of a component obeys from what a component guarantees under such an environment.

The Unified Modelling Language (UML) [5] is widely adopted to model the design of a system. By providing the means to include safety requirements in UML, the integration of safety activities in the normal software lifecycle is facilitated. For safety specification, two approaches have been proposed: (i) to use the Object Constraint Language (OCL) [6] which is a well-known language among modelisation engineering community, or (ii) to use specific UML profiles [7]. In previous work [8], we have proposed a technique that combines both approaches. In this paper, in contrast, we focus on the representation of safety contracts as OCL constraints.

For the verification of safety contracts, several formal verification techniques have been proposed, for instance [3], which uses model checking. Our proposal is to translate UML to Petri Nets and perform the analysis by computing probabilities using the GreatSPN tool [9]. By combining standard engineering practice, i.e., UML, with formal verification techniques, i.e. Petri nets, we provide a rigorous safety analysis available for software engineers.

Our approach has been used to verify a set of safety contracts on an industrial case study where the UML model of a train doors controller has been analysed. The train doors controller is the component in charge of opening and closing train doors. The CAF Power & Automation company[1] develops these train components. Thus, components like the train doors controller are modelled in UML previous to their implementation.

In summary, the contributions of the work presented in this paper are the following:

- a formal definition of the proposed transformation of a safety contract into an OCL constraint.
- an (informal) transformation of OCL constraints into Petri nets by means of the case-study.
- a (partly automatic/partly manual) translation of the case-study UML diagrams annotated with OCL to Petri Nets.
- the safety analysis of the case-sudy.

The rest of the paper contains the following sections. Firstly, Sect. 2 outlines the basic concepts. Section 3 details the train doors controller. Then, Sect. 4 describes a proposal of safety contract specification in OCL, and its transformation to Petri nets. It also introduces the safety contracts of the case study, which are analysed in Sect. 5. Finally, Sect. 6 covers related work and Sect. 7 states some conclusions.

2   Previous Concepts

UML [5,10] is a semi formal general-purpose visual modelling language used for specifying software systems. UML can be tailored for specific purposes by

---

[1] http://www.cafpower.com/es/.

profiling. A UML profile is a UML extension to enrich UML model semantics defined in terms of: *stereotypes* (concepts in the target domain), *tagged values* (attributes of the stereotypes) and *constraints* (formulae that apply to stereotypes and UML elements to extend their semantics). Numerous UML profiles can be found in the literature targeting different specific domains and non-functional properties system analysis (e.g., performance, dependability, security, etc.). For instance, MARTE (Modeling and Analysis of Real-Time and Embedded systems) profile [11] provides support for schedulability and performance analysis in real-time and embedded systems, while DAM (Dependability Analysis and Modelling) profile [12] supports dependability analysis and SecAM (Security Analysis and Modelling) profile [13] focuses on security aspects. In this paper, we use the MARTE profile to indicate the duration of activities in a UML model. The stereotype provided by MARTE to this goal is `gaStep` (`hostDemand` tagged value), within the MARTE analysis framework called Generic Quantitative Analysis Model (GQAM).

Another extension to enrich UML semantics is the Object Constraint Language (OCL) [6]. OCL is a pure expression language for describing constraints that apply to UML models. When an OCL expression is evaluated, it simply returns a value without further effects in the model. OCL allows to specify invariants (on classes and types), to describe pre- and post-conditions (on operations and methods), guards or either constraints (on operations). Note that although an OCL expression can be used to specify a state change (e.g., by means of a post-condition), the state of the system will never effectively change because of the evaluation of an OCL expression (that is, OCL only provides textual description).

Unfortunately, a UML model annotated with OCL and a profile that provides support for non-functional properties specification is not a suitable model to quantitatively or qualitatively evaluate such properties. For this aim, formal methods may help. In this paper, we consider Petri nets [14] as the formal modelling language. More precisely, we translate the annotated UML diagrams into Generalized Stochastic Petri Nets (GSPNs [15]), following the guidelines proposed in [16].

A GSPN is a graphical and mathematical formalism used for the modelling of concurrent and distributed systems. A gentle introduction to GSPN can be found in [15]. Informally, a GSPN is a bipartite graph of places and transitions joined by arcs (graphically represented by circles, bars and arrows respectively). They describe the flow of the system with concurrency and synchronous capabilities. Places can hold tokens, which represent system resources or system workload, while transitions represent system activities. The firing of transitions represents a change in the system state. When a transition fires, tokens from input places are placed in output places. A GSPN distinguishes two kind of transitions: immediate transitions, which fire at zero time (i.e. its firing does not consume any time); and timed transitions, which may follow different firing distributions such as uniform, deterministic or exponential distributions. In this paper, we consider timed transitions with exponentially distributed random firings. Immediate transitions, depicted as thin black bars, can have also associated probabilities to represent the system routing alternatives. Exponential transitions, drawn as white boxes, account for the time that takes an activity to complete.

3   Case Study: Train Doors Controller

As a case study in this paper, we consider the door control management performed by a Train Control and Monitoring System (TCMS). The TCMS is a complex distributed (along the train) system that controls many subsystems. It contains several Input/Output (IO) modules that gather data and send it to a PLC (Programmable Logic Controller) via a communication bus. Each of the IO modules has a CPU, digital/analogical inputs and outputs and is connected to the communication bus. The logic of the TCMS is performed in the PLC.

The system level requirements concerning the operation of opening and closing of doors are satisfied by the following components:

- the TCMS component that decides whether to enable or disable the doors. Doors must be enabled before they can be opened and disabled before closing;
- the Door component that effectively controls the opening or closing of a door;
- the Traction component that controls the train movement; and
- the MVB (Multifunction Vehicle Bus) component that communicates the components among them.

Figure 1 shows the composite diagram of the system. The subcomponents of the Door component, i.e., the controller (in the following we will refer to this component as the Door Controller), the limit sensors, the obstacle sensor, and a button for opening doors, are also depicted in the diagram.

In this paper, we focus on the control of doors. The case study presented here concerns a real system where some simplifications have been made. Namely, the interaction with other components of the TCMS and the dependencies with other subcomponents, and their communication has been omitted. Besides, concerning the closing of doors, in the original design there were different versions of the existence of obstacles, while here we have chosen only one of them.

In the following, we present the UML Sequence Diagrams (UML-SD) for the opening and closing of doors. Figure 2(a) depicts the UML-SD for opening the door. When a train driver requests the opening of doors, first the TCMS checks whether the train status is suitable for opening the doors without risk, checking that the train is really stopped before sending the "enable door" order to the Door Controller component. Thus, the TCMS system sends the "enable door" command request to the Door Controller component only when the train is in a safe condition (e.g. speed is zero) to perform the request properly and without risk for passengers. The Door Controller component opens the door only if it is enabled, i.e., it has received the "enable door" order from the TCMS and if some passenger has request the opening of a door ("open request") using any of the buttons (interior or exterior) of the door.

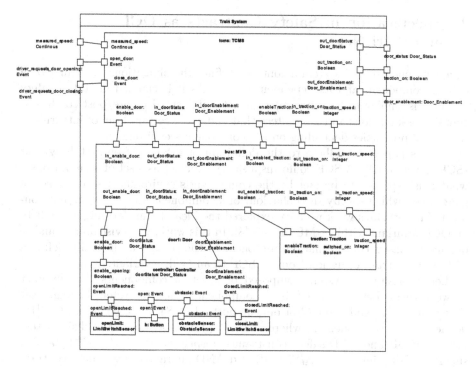

Fig. 1. The Composite diagram of the system.

The door closing operation is depicted in Fig. 2(b). When the driver commands doors closing, the TCMS system sends the "not enable door" command to the Door component. The Door component disables the door and closes the door if it is safe, i.e. there is no detected obstacle. When there is an obstacle, the door is opened and closed once such an obstacle has disappeared.

In order to enable an incremental certification process and to demonstrate the benefits of reusability, this case study adopts the methodology of contract-based design. In contract-based design each safety critical component of the system and non-critical components are seen as separate components [17] which interact with their environment. As we formally explain in the next section, we associate to each safety critical component C a safety contract, i.e. an abstract specification in the form of a tuple $S_C = \langle A, G \rangle$, where A represents the assumptions on the environment of the component, and G represents what the component guarantees under these assumptions. A contract is intended to expose enough information about the component, but not more than necessary. We say that a component *implements* its contract if it satisfies the guarantees when the environment meets the assumptions.

In the following section we introduce a framework for safety contract specification and the transformation to OCL constraints, which will be later used for formal safety assessment using Petri nets.

4 Specification of Safety Contracts as OCL and Petri Nets

In a component-based system a contract defines the obligations to be met by a certain component and its dependencies [18]. As it is claimed in [19], a safety contract is similar to a (software) contract but instead of pre/post-conditions contains assumptions and guarantees that endorse a certain level of integrity of functional properties depending on the component's environment.

In this paper, we adhere to the definition of a Safety Contract Fragment (SCF) given in [19]. A SCF conforms a safety contract as a set of assumptions – what it is expected to be met by the component's environment – and a set of guarantees, which specify the behaviour of a component under such an environment. In a previous work we have explored the idea of transforming an SCF to an OCL invariant within UML models [8]. In this work, we revise and formalise our model-based transformation approach. In the sequel, we formally define a SCF and the transformation from an SCF to an OCL invariant.

Let us assume a system composed of a set of components that interact between them. Let $\mathcal{C} = \langle \mathcal{I}, \mathcal{O} \rangle$ be a component of such a system having a set $\mathcal{I}$ of input ports and a set $\mathcal{O}$ of output ports. Let $\mathcal{S}_{\mathcal{C}} = \langle \mathcal{A}, \mathcal{G} \rangle$ be a SCF [19] defined over a component $\mathcal{C}$, where $\mathcal{A} = \mathcal{A}^+ \bigcup \mathcal{A}^*$ is a superset of disjoint sets $\mathcal{A}^+, \mathcal{A}^*$ of OR and AND safety constraints, respectively, and $\mathcal{G} = \mathcal{G}^+ \bigcup \mathcal{G}^*$ is a superset of disjoint sets $\mathcal{G}^+, \mathcal{G}^*$ of OR and AND guarantees[2]. A safety contract assumption $\mathcal{A}$ is a proposition that relates one or more of the input ports of a component. Similarly, a safety contract guarantee $\mathcal{G}$ is a proposition that relates one or more of the output ports of a component.

Recall that OCL is a UML extension to express constraints into UML models. An OCL constraint is defined over a context that describes where such a constraint is acting. As it is introduced in Sect. 2, OCL defines different constructs, such as **inv** to define invariants, which state conditions that must always be met by all instances of a context type, **pre** to state a condition that must be true when an operation starts its execution, or **post** to state a condition that must be true when an operation ends its execution. In this paper, we consider only OCL invariants. An OCL constraint can be formally defined as follows. Let $\mathcal{R} = \langle \mathcal{X}, \mathcal{V} \rangle$ be an OCL constraint defined over a context $\mathcal{X}$ and having an invariant formula $\mathcal{V} = \langle ls, rs \rangle$. An invariant formula is conformed by two propositions ls, rs joined by a boolean or **implies** operator. Note that the right-hand side of an invariant formula can be empty.

As it has been previously mentioned, an OCL constraint is defined over a context that describes where such a constraint is acting. In the proposed translation, a SCF corresponds to an OCL constraint. Since a SCF is specified over a component, it is reasonable to match the context of the corresponding OCL constraint to such a component as well. Thus, a transformation from SCF to OCL invariant can be straightforwardly defined as follows:

---

[2] As in [8], we restrict the logic of SCF assumptions and guarantees to AND and OR logic operators.

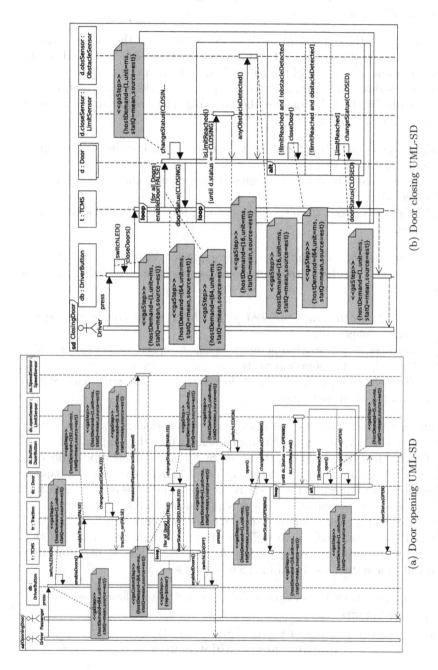

Fig. 2. (a) Door opening and (b) door closing UML sequence diagrams.

(a) Door opening UML-SD

(b) Door closing UML-SD

Proposition 1. *Let $\mathcal{C}$ be a component of a system on which a Safety Contract Fragment $\mathcal{S} = \langle \mathcal{A}, \mathcal{G} \rangle$ has been defined. Thus, an OCL $\mathcal{R} = \langle \mathcal{X}, \mathcal{V} \rangle$ can be built considering $\mathcal{X} = \mathcal{C}$ and $\mathcal{V} = \langle \mathcal{A}, \mathcal{G} \rangle$.*

As it can be seen, the component $\mathcal{C}$ defines the context $\mathcal{X}$ of the OCL constraint, while the content of such an OCL constraint (the invariant) is defined by the assumptions and guarantees of the Safety Contract Fragment $\mathcal{S}$ defined on $\mathcal{C}$.

Let us describe how our transformation approach works by means of the case study described in Sect. 3. Consider the following safety requirements given by the engineers designing the system:

SR1. The door opening is not enabled when the traction is on or the train speed is distinct than zero.

SR2. The door must be closed but remains open when some obstacle has been detected.

SR3. The door is closed when the door opening is enabled and the close event is received.

The above safety requirements can be expressed in terms of Safety Contract Fragments, considering the component-based system depicted in Fig. 1, as follows:

- $\mathcal{S}_1 = \langle (traction\ OR\ (tractionSpeed \neq 0)), (NOT\ enableOpening) \rangle$, defined on the TCMS component.
- $\mathcal{S}_2 = \langle obstacle, doorStatus = opening \rangle$. In this case, the component on which this SCF is defined is DoorController.
- $\mathcal{S}_3 = \langle (enableOpening\ AND\ close), doorStatus = isClosed \rangle$. This SCF is defined on the component Door.

Note that the assumptions and guarantees of the former SCFs relate, respectively, input and output ports of the components where they are defined.

Following the Proposition (1), the above SCFs can be straightforwardly converted to OCL invariants as it is listed in Code 1.1. Here, the task of a requirement engineer is to interpret the safety requirements in terms of SFC. This task is accomplished by matching the safety requirements to the UML component-based design. This task is surely a difficult one but once this task has been performed the transformation to OCL invariants becomes trivial. Recall that these OCL invariants that express safety requirements allow to perform safety assessment in a system, as shown in the following section.

Code 1.1. OCL constraints obtained from SCF transformation.

```
context  TCMS_SR1
    inv: (traction  or  tractionSpeed  <> 0)
                implies  not  enableOpening


context  DoorController_SR2
    inv:  obstacle
```

implies (doorStatus = opening)

context Door_SR3
    inv: (enableOpening and close)
        implies doorStatus = isClosed

Let us show how this OCL invariants can be transformed to Petri nets. Note that we use only the **implies** binary operator ($\rightarrow$) within the OCL invariant. Recall that in classical logic the **implies** binary operator can be transformed to an equivalent form using **or** and **not** operators, i.e., $p \rightarrow q$ is logically equivalent to $\neg p \lor q$. If we consider each proposition of OCL invariant as Petri net places, and transform the invariant to its logically equivalent, we obtain the Petri net models depicted in Fig. 3 for each safety contracts considered for the case under study[3].

The sink places (without output transitions) of each Petri net representation depicted in Fig. 3(a), (b) and (c) allow us to compute the probability of having a marking in such a place (post-condition) greater than zero, indicating that preconditions are fulfilled. Note that this solution does not provide us with information regarding the event order or any other kind of temporal information. This is an interesting issue that deserves further study, as discussed in the following section.

5   Safety Analysis

We describe the safety analysis we propose by means of the case study. In order to analyse the safety scenarios, i.e. the opening and closing of doors, the corresponding UML-SD diagrams annotated with OCL, respectively depicted in Fig. 2(a) and (b), are translated into GSPNs using the ArgoSPE tool [20] according to the algorithms proposed in [16]. The resulting GSPN is shown in Fig. 4. The left-hand side of the figure represents the door opening and the left-hand side, the door closing. Even though part of the translation is done automatically using the ArgoSPE tool some simple manual modifications to the GSPN are needed to represent OCL constraints. In particular, modifying this GSPN with the Great-SPN [9] tool, we have manually modelled the obstacle detection event as a place, named *p_Obstacle*, since it has associated an OCL constraint, as we explain in the following paragraph. Moreover, we have modelled the Traction operation without considering human interaction, thus, our system automatically speeds up after closing the door and it brakes when the traction receives a traction stop signal.

Since the OCL constraints are interpreted in a GSPN, they are equivalent to compute the probability of a condition. Each condition is represented by a place of the GSPN. For instance, the place *p_door_OPEN* represents the status in which a door is open and the place *p_switch_ON* represents when the door button is switched on. The probability of (eventually) reaching a condition is

---

[3] I. Sljivo, personal communication, April 1, 2014.

110   E. Gómez-Martínez et al.

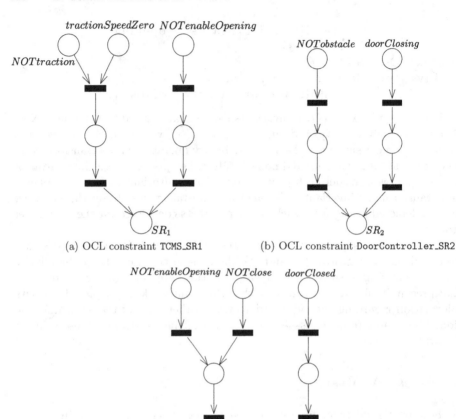

(a) OCL constraint TCMS_SR1   (b) OCL constraint DoorController_SR2

(c) OCL constraint Door_SR3

Fig. 3. Petri net representation of OCL constraints of the case study.

represented as a place being (eventually) marked. Note that a place eventually marked does not necessary mean a place eventually always marked.

The Petri nets representing the safety contracts, depicted in Fig. 3 can now be composed with the Petri net of the system depicted in Fig. 4. Both nets are merged using the transitions that create tokens in places representing the same issue, i.e., places *NOTtraction* and *tractionSpeedZero* in Fig. 3 represent the same state than $p\_traction\_on\_FALSE$ and $p\_traction\_STOP$, respectively, in Fig. 4. The connection to places representing safety contracts have been highlighted (grey colour) in Fig. 4.

Finally, we use the GreatSPN tool [9] to compute the steady-state probability of places SR_1, SR_2, SR_3 having a marking greater than zero (i.e. the place is eventually marked), which will indicate that the OCL constraints TCMS_SR1,

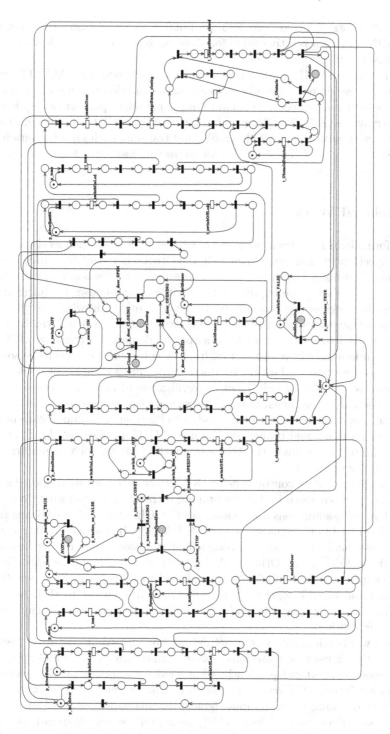

Fig. 4. Petri net corresponding to the opening and closing of a door.

`DoorController_SR2` and `Door_SR3` are fulfilled. A simulation of the net with GreatSPN returns a positive value for these probabilities, thus safety contracts are fulfilled in the system model.

Although the UML models that we use are enriched with MARTE profile annotations, we do not currently use such an information for the safety analysis even though it can be necessary for verifying some safety properties [18]. For this aim, we may use OCL/RT [21], an extension of native OCL to specify time issues, in conjunction with the MARTE profile, and translate such an information into the GSPN models. We consider this an interesting issue which deserves further study.

6   Related Work

Many formalisms have been proposed to express contracts, such as the Requirements Specification Language (RSL) [2], the Othello language [3], which is based on Linear Temporal Logic, or Modal Transmission Systems [22]. Unlike OCL, these languages are more expressive but OCL is a well-known language among modelisation engineering community. However, a major drawback of these formalisms is that the requirement engineers need to learn a new formalism each time they need to write contracts in a specific domain. In contrast, OCL is a well-known language in industry. Besides, to the best of our knowledge some of the proposed formalisms lack the means to verify that a component model fulfils their contracts [2,22], or only focus on verification of functional properties [3]. In this work, we have shown that OCL contracts can be used to perform safety assessment by translating the UML models to Petri nets. Although currently we also focus on functional properties, the use of UML profiles enables to analyse other non-functional properties that can affect to safety, such as performance, dependability or security.

Representing safety contracts using OCL has been previously proposed in [18]. The novelty of our work is that we propose a translation from safety contracts in the form of assumptions and guarantees to OCL. Our work complements the work of OTHELLO language [3] and OCRA [23]. In particular, the analysis of non-functional properties can complement the work on verifying functional properties in OCRA [23]. Other work similar to ours is [24], where UML/OCL is used to express system invariants, transformed to Place/Transition nets (without time) and to LTL logic for the verification. In contrast to their work, we formalise the safety contracts, and, moreover, our Petri net models capture the timing information.

Some works refine safety contract assumptions in strong and weak assumptions [2,25]. Strong assumptions specify what always is fulfilled by the environment, context-independently, while weak assumptions provide additional information about the context where a component could operate (e.g., the expected timing between input signals). In this paper, we consider the definition of safety contract as given in [19], having only strong assumptions. In our case, the weak assumptions can be implicitly described by UML annotations.

As future work, we aim at extending our safety contract specification to explicitly express timing issues.

7 Conclusions and Future Work

Safety assessment is a crucial software engineering activity in critical systems, since people integrity, and even their lives may depend on it. In the last years, contract-based design has emerged as a promising approach for designing safe systems, where contracts describe the expected behaviour of a component.

In this paper, we propose a specification of safety contracts as assumptions and guarantees based on the input and output ports of a component, and then translate these contracts to OCL in the UML context. Finally, these UML models are transformed into a formal model, in terms of Generalized Stochastic Petri nets (GSPN), to verify that safety contracts are fulfilled. As a case study, we have analysed three safety contracts on a train door controller designed by CAF Power & Automation. The most challenging tasks regarding the case study were the formalisation of safety contracts and the translation of UML models to GSPN. In the latter, although some automation exists, the complexity of some aspects of the case study (for instance, the existence of obstacles) required a manual translation to GSPN.

The specification of safety contracts in terms of OCL within UML models allows to recap safety requirements and system description in a single picture. Besides, the adoption of formal models, obtained after the transformation of UML/OCL models to Petri nets, are facilitated as UML/OCL are languages familiar to the industry engineers. The result is that we have sacrificed expression power to keep safety contracts expressed with OCL easier to understand than contracts written in more expressive languages like, for instance, Linear Temporal Logic (LTL). This issue can be overcome in the future by extending the native OCL with more operators.

As for further work, our aim is to keep on formalising more complex contracts expressed in OCL, as well as exploring how to provide the event order or any other kind of temporal information (or other non-functional property). Improving the automatic translation from the UML models to GSPN deserves also further study. In addition, we also plan to propose a well-established methodology to assess safety and to develop a tool that implements this methodology.

References

1. nSafeCer project: Safety Certification of Software-Intensive Systems with Reusable Components. Project Grant Agreement n° 295373. More information at: http://safecer.eu/
2. Damm, W., Hungar, H., Josko, B., Peikenkamp, T., Stierand, I.: Using contract-based component specifications for virtual integration testing and architecture design. In: Proceedings of the Design, Automation Test in Europe Conference Exhibition (DATE), pp. 1–6, March 2011

3. Cimatti, A., Tonetta, S.: A property-based proof system for contract-based design. In: Proceedings of the 38th EUROMICRO Conference on Software Engineering and Advanced Applications (SEAA), pp. 21–28, September 2012
4. Kath, O., Schreiner, R., Favaro, J.: Safety, security, and software reuse: a model-based approach. In: Proceedings of the Fourth International Workshop in Software Reuse and Safety (2009)
5. OMG: Unified Modeling Language (UML). Version 2.4.1, August 2011. Specification available at: http://www.omg.org/spec/UML/2.4.1/
6. OMG: Object Constraint Language (OCL). Object Management Group, v2.2, formal/2010-02-01, February 2010
7. OMG: UML Profile for Modeling Quality of Service and Fault Tolerance Characteristics and Mechanisms (QoS & FT). Version 1.1 (2008). Specification available at: http://www.omg.org/spec/QFTP/
8. Rodríguez, R.J., Gómez-Martínez, E.: Model-based safety assessment using OCL and Petri Nets. In: Proceedings of the 40th Euromicro Conference on Software Engineering and Advanced Applications (SEAA), pp. 56–59 (2014)
9. Baarir, S., Beccuti, M., Cerotti, D., De Pierro, M., Donatelli, S., Franceschinis, G.: The GreatSPN tool: recent enhancements. SIGMETRICS Perform. Eval. Rev. **36**(4), 4–9 (2009)
10. ISO/IEC: 19505-1:2012-Information technology-Object Management Group Unified Modeling Language (OMG UML)-Part 1: Infrastructure (2012)
11. OMG: A UML profile for Modeling and Analysis of Real Time Embedded Systems (MARTE). Version 1.1 (2011). Specification available at: http://www.omgmarte.org/
12. Bernardi, S., Merseguer, J., Petriu, D.C.: Dependability modeling and analysis of software systems specified with UML. ACM Comput. Surv. **45**(1), 2 (2012)
13. Rodríguez, R.J., Merseguer, J., Bernardi, S.: Modelling and analysing resilience as a security issue within UML. In: Proceedings of the 2nd International Workshop on Software Engineering for Resilient Systems, SERENE 2010, pp. 42–51. ACM, New York (2010)
14. Murata, T.: Petri Nets: properties, analysis and applications. Proc. IEEE **77**(4), 541–580 (1989)
15. Ajmone Marsan, M., Balbo, G., Conte, G., Donatelli, S., Franceschinis, G.: Modelling with Generalized Stochastic Petri Nets. John Wiley Series in Parallel Computing, Chichester (1995)
16. Bernardi, S., Merseguer, J.: Performance evaluation of UML design with Stochastic Well-formed Nets. J. Syst. Softw. **80**(11), 1843–1865 (2007)
17. Sangiovanni-Vincentelli, A., Damm, W., Passerone, R.: Taming Dr. Frankenstein: contract-based design for cyber-physical systems. Eur. J. Control **18**(3), 217–238 (2012)
18. Bate, I., Hawkins, R., McDermid, J.: A contract-based approach to designing safe systems. In: Proceedings of the 8th Australian Workshop on Safety Critical Systems and Software, SCS 2003, vol. 33, pp. 25–36. Australian Computer Society, Inc. (2003)
19. Söderberg, A., Johansson, R.: Safety contract based design of software components. In: IEEE International Symposium on Software Reliability Engineering Workshops (ISSREW), pp. 365–370 (2013)
20. Gómez-Martínez, E., Merseguer, J.: ArgoSPE: model-based software performance engineering. In: Donatelli, S., Thiagarajan, P.S. (eds.) ICATPN 2006. LNCS, vol. 4024, pp. 401–410. Springer, Heidelberg (2006)

21. Cengarle, M.V., Knapp, A.: Towards OCL/RT. In: Eriksson, L.-H., Lindsay, P.A. (eds.) FME 2002. LNCS, vol. 2391, pp. 390–409. Springer, Heidelberg (2002)
22. Bauer, S.S., David, A., Hennicker, R., Guldstrand Larsen, K., Legay, A., Nyman, U., Wąsowski, A.: Moving from specifications to contracts in component-based design. In: de Lara, J., Zisman, A. (eds.) FASE 2012. LNCS, vol. 7212, pp. 43–58. Springer, Heidelberg (2012)
23. Cimatti, A., Dorigatti, M., Tonetta, S.: OCRA: a tool for checking the refinement of temporal contracts. In: 28th IEEE/ACM International Conference on Automated Software Engineering (ASE), pp. 702–705. IEEE (2013)
24. Bouabana-Tebibel, T., Belmesk, M.: Integration of the association ends within UML state diagrams. Int. Arab. J. Inf. Technol. 5(1), 7–15 (2008)
25. Sljivo, I., Gallina, B., Carlson, J., Hansson, H.: Strong and weak contract formalism for third-party component reuse. In: IEEE International Symposium on Software Reliability Engineering Workshops (ISSREW), pp. 359–364, November 2013

A Testing-Based Approach to Ensure the Safety of Shared Resource Concurrent Systems

Lars-Åke Fredlund, Ángel Herranz, and Julio Mariño[✉]

Babel Group, Universidad Politécnica de Madrid, Madrid, Spain
{lfredlund,aherranz,jmarino}@fi.upm.es

Abstract. The paper describes an approach to testing a class of safety-critical concurrent systems implemented using shared resources.

Shared resources are characterized using a declarative specification, from which both an efficient implementation can be derived, and which serves as the first approximation of the state-based test model used for testing an implementation of the resource.

In this article the methodology is illustrated by applying it to the task of testing the safety-critical software that controls an automated shipping plant, specified as a shared resource, which serves shipping orders using a set of autonomous robots. The operations of the robots are governed by a set of rules limiting the weight of robots, and their cargo, to ensure safe operations.

1 Introduction

Developing reliable safety-critical software for concurrent systems is notoriously difficult, with subtle race conditions often going unnoticed by programmers and test personnel until disaster strikes.

Apart from the inherent complexity of the task, the situation can be made worse by the choice of an unsuitable programming language (or library). A case in point is Java. Programming safety-critical applications in Java is tempting (except if the targeted system has hard real-time constraints due to the e.g. presence of automatic garbage collection) since there is a large body of Java programmers available. However, the language and its libraries provide a large number of different concurrency primitives, and their limitations are often not well understood. Moreover, the Java concurrency primitives are generally low-level constructs, primarily targeting *efficient* execution rather than *safe* execution, thus constituting poor choices for implementing safety-critical systems.

In this work we attempt to improve the situation in two ways. First, we introduce a higher-level concurrency construct called *shared resources* [6]. Essentially a shared resource is a process (or thread) protecting some shared resource, and providing controlled methods for accessing the shared resource. The behaviour of a shared resource is specified declaratively, defining a set of operations whose behaviour is characterised using post/pre-conditions. To handle concurrency a new type of precondition is added: the *concurrency precondition*. These are preconditions expressing restrictions not only on the arguments of an operation,

C. Canal and A. Idani (Eds.): SEFM 2014 Workshops, LNCS 8938, pp. 116–130, 2015.
DOI: 10.1007/978-3-319-15201-1_8

but on the combination of the arguments of an operation and the resource state. Failing to satisfy a concurrency precondition does not imply that the operation fails (as is the case for normal preconditions), rather its execution is *postponed* until a time when the resource state changes leading the concurrency precondition to become true.

Still, even if the safety-critical problem has been structured well using a shared resource, if we wish to use Java to implement the resource we still have to use the somewhat inadequate language primitives and libraries in its implementation, and typical programmers commit many errors using such concurrency primitives, as we shall see in Sect. 6. Clearly we must at least test, systematically, the resulting implementation.

The second component of the methodology is thus the extensive use of property-based testing to automatically generate test cases (using the declarative specification as a base), and to automatically decide whether test execution is successful (again using the declarative specification as a base). The testing tool we use, Quviq QuickCheck [2], a variant of the well-known QuickCheck tool [4], has excellent support for testing stateful code. Essentially we build a model of the system under test (the shared resource), and use the model both to derive tests, and to judge the correctness of the execution of the system under test by comparing it with the execution of the system model.

To evaluate the efficacy of the approach, we apply it to the task of specifying and verifying a prototypical concurrent safety-critical system, a warehouse complex where autonomous robots move around fulfilling shipping orders. The safety-critical aspect we consider here is that the weight of the robots, in any given warehouse, should never exceed a certain maximum weight. To evaluate the usefulness of automatic testing, we proceed to test a large number of implementations of the warehouse control system by undergraduate students at the Polytechnic University of Madrid.

In Sect. 2 we introduce the QuickCheck property-based testing tool. Next the warehouse case study is described in Sect. 3. The shared resource formalism is introduced in Sect. 4, and Sect. 5 describes how shared resources based safety-critical systems are tested using our approach. The testing methodology is evaluated by applying to a number of implementations of the warehouse control system in Sect. 6. Finally, Sect. 7 draws conclusions from the work realised so far, and details issues for future work.

2   QuickCheck

The basic functionality of QuickCheck is simple: when supplied with a data term that encodes a boolean property, which may contain universally quantified variables, QuickCheck generates a random instantiation of the variables, and checks that the resulting boolean property is true. This procedure is by default repeated at most 100 times. If for some instantiation the property returns false, or a runtime exception occurs, an error has been found and testing terminates.

2.1 Erlang

Quviq QuickCheck uses the Erlang functional programming language [1,3] to express correctness properties and test models. This does not mean that the tested software must be written in Erlang; a good interface library for C code has e.g. permitted the testing of AUTOSAR components and infrastructure on a commercial basis [7]. In this article we focus on testing control systems written in Java using the JavaErlang interface library[1].

2.2 QuickCheck State Machines

For checking "stateful" code, QuickCheck provides a state machine library. Here the tested "object" is not a simple boolean property, but rather a sequence of function calls each with an associated post condition that determines whether the execution of a call was successful or not. A QuickCheck state machine has a state, obviously, which can be understood as the model state of the system under test. Given a model state, the library *generates* a suitable next API command, and proceeds to execute the call, checking after the call has completed whether the result was the expected one given the model state of the state machine. Next, a new model state is computed, and the generation of commands and their execution is repeated, until a test sequence of sufficient length has been generated and tested. In other words, the QuickCheck state machine acts as a *model* for the program under test.

To use the state machine library a user has to supply a "callback" Erlang module providing a set of functions with predefined names. The functions defined in the callback module are called by QuickCheck during test generation and test execution. The functions that should be implemented by a tester are enumerated below.

```
initial_state()
command(State)
precondition(State,Call)
next_state(State,Result,Call)
postcondition(State,Call,Result)
```

The model state is initialized by the initial_state function, and is updated by next_state. API calls are generated by the function command, which returns symbolic calls of the form {call,ModuleName,Function,Args}, which are then executed. The postcondition function checks that the return value of a call is correct, considering the current model test state.

3   Case Study

The case study used in the paper is the control system for a warehouse complex serviced by a set of autonomous robots. An example warehouse complex, with robots, is depicted in Fig. 1.

---
[1] https://github.com/fredlund/JavaErlang.git.

A robot must first enter warehouse 0, then it may load an item, and next it exits warehouse 0 and enters the corridor between warehouse 0 and warehouse 1. Then, it enters warehouse 1, etc., until it finally exits the warehouse complex by exiting the last warehouse (warehouse 2 in the figure).

Each robot has a weight, and the total weight of a robot and its cargo increases monotonically as it moves around in the warehouse complex.

A warehouse can admit any number of robots, but to ensure safe operations the total weight of robots and their cargo cannot exceed the constant MAX_WEIGHT_IN_WAREHOUSE when a new robot enters the warehouse. It is permitted that the total weight in a warehouse is temporarily above the limit, due to loading operations, but then no more robots can be admitted to the warehouse (until a robot leaves). A corridor has place for a single robot.

In Fig. 1, the constant MAX_WEIGHT_IN_WAREHOUSE is set to 1000 kg, and thus, for example, we can see that since the total weight in warehouse 0 is $500 + 200 + 200 = 900$ the robots with weights 200 and 300 that want to enter should be blocked, while the robot with weight 100 can be permitted to enter. Moreover, as the corridor between warehouse 1 and 2 is occupied, the robots inside warehouse 1 should be blocked from exiting it, until the robot occupying the corridor enters warehouse 2.

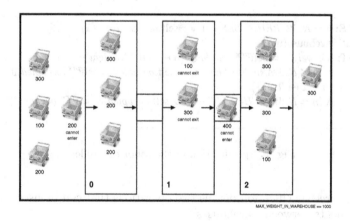

Fig. 1. Warehouses and robot movements

4 Resources

One commonly used mechanism for controlling interactions between concurrent processes is to impose some form of central control, to serialize potentially conflicting requests.

The *shared resources* introduced in [6] is one such centralized mechanism, and we will explain its syntax and semantics using the robot warehouse example. Figure 2 contains the specification of the control part of the robot warehouse example.

C-DAT WarehouseAccessControl
  OPERATIONS
    ACTION enterWarehouse: *Warehouse[i]* × *Weight*
    ACTION exitWarehouse: *Warehouse[i]* × *Weight*

BEHAVIOUR
  DOMAIN:
    TYPE: *WarehouseAccessControl = (weight: Warehouse → Weight × occupied:*
      Warehouse → $\mathbb{B}$)
      Warehouse = 0 .. N_WAREHOUSES - 1
      Weight = 0 .. MAX_WEIGHT_WAREHOUSE

  INITIAL: $\forall n \in$ *Warehouse* • self.*weight*$(n) = 0 \wedge \neg$self.*occupied*(n)
  INVARIANT: $\forall n \in$ *Warehouse* • self.*weight*$(n) \leq MAX\_WEIGHT\_WAREHOUSE$

  CPRE: $p +$ self.*weight*$(n) \leq MAX\_WEIGHT\_WAREHOUSE$
    enterWarehouse(n,p)
  POST: self.*weight* = self^{pre}.*weight* $\oplus \{n \mapsto$ self^{pre}.*weight*$(n) + p\}$
    $\wedge\ (n > 0 \Rightarrow$ self.*occupied* = self^{pre}.*occupied* $\oplus \{n \mapsto$ False$\})$
    $\wedge\ (n = 0 \Rightarrow$ self.*occupied* = self^{pre}.*occupied*$\})$

  CPRE: $n = N\_WAREHOUSES - 1 \vee \neg$self.*occupied*$(n + 1)$
    exitWarehouse(n,p)
  POST: self.*weight* = self^{pre}.*weight* $\oplus \{n \mapsto$ self^{pre}.*weight*$(n) - p\}$
    $\wedge\ (n < N\_WAREHOUSES - 1 \Rightarrow$ self.*occupied* = self^{pre}.*occupied*$\oplus$
    $\{n + 1 \mapsto$ True$\})$
    $\wedge\ (n = N\_WAREHOUSES - 1 \Rightarrow$ self.*occupied* = self^{pre}.*occupied*$)$

Fig. 2. Specification of the robot controller.

The resource specification details two operations that can be used to coordinate movements between warehouses:

enterWarehouse(n,w) – A request for permission for a robot to enter warehouse **n** carrying weight **w**.
exitWarehouse(n,w)] – A request for permission for a robot to exit a warehouse **n** towards a corridor carrying weight **w**.

The state of the resource has two fields: *weight*, a map from a warehouse to weight (a natural number), and *occupied*, a map from a warehouse to a boolean. Intuitively, *weight* should correspond to the accumulated weight in the warehouse, and *occupied[n]* is true if there is a robot present in the *corridor n* leading from the warehouse.

Initially, as specified in the **INITIAL** clause, the weight in all warehouses is zero, and no robot is present in any corridor. The resource has an invariant over the state, as specified by the **INVARIANT** clause, i.e., that the weight in a warehouse should always be less than or equal to the maximum weight *MAX_WEIGHT_WAREHOUSE*.

A robot that wants to enter warehouse n with weight w should first call **enterWarehouse(n,w)** to ask the resource (controller) for permission to do so. It is the task of the (implemented) resource to ensure that the call does not return (i.e., that it *blocks*) until it is safe for the robot to enter the warehouse. The *concurrency precondition* **CPRE** specifies when access is safe, i.e., when the accumulated weight of the robots already in the warehouse plus the weight of the new robot is less than or equal to the allowed maximum weight. The **POST** condition specifies the change on the resource state provoked by the completion of a call. It is possible to provide preconditions (**PRE**) for operations too, which specify requirements on the arguments to an operation that every call must satisfy.

Similarly, a robot should always call the operation **exitWarehouse(n,p)** to ask for permission to leave a warehouse. The **CPRE** condition of the resource specification ensures that the call does not return until the corridor leading away from the warehouse is free from robots. A restriction on the caller to these operations is that the weight w provided as argument to the operation **exitWarehouse(n,w)** when asking for permission for leaving a warehouse, must be identical to the weight provided when asking for permission to enter the warehouse, i.e., **enterWarehouse(n,w)**. That is, the exit weight should not reflect any cargo loaded in the warehouse, instead, the weight increase should be factored into the next call to **enterWarehouse**, e.g., **enterWarehouse(n+1,w+cargoWeight)**.

4.1   Resource Semantics

Conceptually a resource implements a recursive behaviour, serializing state updates. Below we depict the symbolic behaviour of a generic resource, as a recursive function *RESOURCE(state, Calls)*. We let *Calls* be the set of calls made to the resource, initially the empty set, and *state* is the state of the resource, its initial value provided by the **INITIAL** clause. The notation **CPRE**(*call, state*) is used to denote the calculation of the concurrency precondition of a call, given the current state of the resource, and **POST**(*pcall,state*) is the post condition function that given a call and the current state returns a new state.

RESOURCE(state, Calls) ≡

1. If a new *call* is pending add it to *Calls*

$$Calls' = Calls \cup \{call\}$$

2. Pick a *call* ∈ *Calls'* such that its concurrency precondition **CPRE**(*call, state*) is true, and remove it from *Calls'*, i.e.,

$$Calls'' = Calls' - \{call\}$$

3. If there is no such call, call $RESOURCE(state, Calls')$ recursively.
4. Otherwise modify the resource state according to the postcondition (**POST**) of the selected operation (and call parameters):

$$state' = \mathbf{POST}(call, state)$$

5. Signal to the caller that *call* has terminated.
6. Call $RESOURCE(state', Calls'')$ recursively.

4.2 Implementing a Resource

A correct implementation of a shared resource ensures that its operations are executed only when the concurrency precondition (**CPRE**) so permits, and in isolation. However, there may also be additional requirements on the order in which different calls are served which are not expressed by the resource specification. For instance, we may stipulate that calls (that meet the **CPRE**) should be served in a strictly first-come-first-served order (thus refining step 2 above).

A resource specification can be implemented in different languages, using different concurrency language primitives. We can implement a resource in Java, for instance, using e.g. the `Locks` and `Condition` classes provided by the `java.util.concurrent` package. As an example, Fig. 3 provides a (sketched) Java class that can serve as a starting point for a complete implementation. Note that the class is rather incomplete. It does for instance not address the special role of the last and first warehouses, i.e., that there is no corridor before the first warehouse, and the absence of a corridor after the last warehouse.

The `exitWarehouse(n,w)` method begins by acquiring a lock, ensuring that no other call executes simultaneously. Then, the concurrency precondition (CPRE) is continuously evaluated. If CPRE does not hold, because the corridor is not empty, the thread executing the method will wait on the condition `freedCorridor[n+1]` until another thread signals it (in `enterWarehouse(n,w)`).

Once the CPRE is established, the POST condition is established by modifying the state of the resource (not shown in the code excerpt). Then, finally, the method signals any other thread, corresponding to a robot waiting to enter warehouse n which the robot executing `exitWarehouse(n,w)` just left.

5   Testing Resources

There are different aspects of a system implemented using shared resources that we can test. We can for instance focus on testing the specification itself, to *validate* that the specification is internally consistent, and that it faithfully expresses the informal requirements an implemented system should satisfy. An example of a consistency property is that all post conditions should preserve the resource invariant.

Here, instead, we mainly focus on the task of *verifying* that an implemented system faithfully conforms to the resource specification on which it is based.

```java
public class WarehouseResource {
    // Resource state
    private int weight[];
    private boolean occupied[];

    // Handling concurrency
    private Lock lock;
    private Condition freedWarehouse[];
    private Condition freedCorridor[];

    public WarehouseResource() {
        // initialize state and create monitors and conditions
    }

    public void enterWarehouse(int n, int w) {
        lock.lock();

        // Check CPR -- coded in Java -- until it becomes true
        while (!CPRE(...)) freedWarehouse[n].await();

        // CPRE holds here, update resource state (POST)
        // ...

        // Signal waiters that the robot has left the corridor
        freedCorridor[n].signal();

        lock.unlock();
    }

    public void exitWarehouse(int n, int w) {
        lock.lock();

        // Check CPR -- coded in Java -- until it becomes true
        while (!CPRE(...)) freedCorridor[n+1].await();

        // CPRE holds here, update resource state (POST)
        // ...

        // Signal waiters that the robot has left the warehouse
        freedWarehouse[n].signal();

        lock.unlock();
    }
}
```

Fig. 3. An implementation sketch of the warehouse resource

However, we also test other aspects of the system which are not expressible in the resource specification, i.e., that the order in which the implemented system services the calls whose concurrency preconditions (**CPRE**s) hold, conforms to stated requirements.

For the warehouse example, there is just a single requirement on servicing calls, to enforce progress:

if the set of calls with true concurrency preconditions is non-empty, the system must eventually select a call to execute.

We can illustrate the semantics of this requirement by an example, assuming that the maximum weight permitted in warehouse 0 is 1000 kg:

```
enterWarehouse(0,900)    -- does not block
enterWarehouse(0,200)    -- blocks
enterWarehouse(0,100)    -- must not block
```

We assume that calls are made sequentially. The first call does not block, as $900 \leq 1000$. The second call blocks, as $900 + 200 > 1000$. The third call is permitted by the concurrency precondition as $900 + 100 \leq 1000$, and can thus not be blocked for infinitely long.

We will test a shared resource by developing a model for the behaviour of the resource as a Quviq QuickCheck [2] state machine. In the following we assume that the system is implemented using Java, although this is not crucial to the approach.

A first question to ask is what errors can we expect programmers to commit. We can separate the errors into three classes:

e_1: the evaluation of the concurrency precondition and postcondition, of different calls, are interleaved, although the precondition and postcondition of a given call should be evaluated in sequence. These errors are likely due to basic misunderstandings with regards to using Java concurrency primitives. To find such errors we must issue simultaneous calls to the controller.

e_2: either the **CPRE** or **POST** function is incorrectly implemented. To catch such errors issuing a sequence of sequential calls is sufficient.

e_3: the programmer may have made mistakes in the selection of a call candidate eligible to enter the resource; this can be a difficult task due to ordering constraints and the manner in which blocked tasks must be woken up. Correctly programming this functionality in Java is not an easy task, and we can expect to see many errors committed here. To detect such errors we must be able to observe which pending calls were unblocked by the execution of a non-blocking call. That is, if the concurrency preconditions for all pending calls in a shared resource are false, and a new call c_1 arrives whose precondition is true, we should observe which pending calls $c_2, \ldots, c_n$ are unblocked due to the execution of c_1.

Unfortunately we can in general not observe the exact order in which the calls $c_2, \ldots, c_n$ in errors of class e_3 are unblocked (we consider black-box testing only, i.e., we do not have access to the source code of the implementation of the resource).

In the following we consider the specific problem of testing the warehouse resource, but take care in pointing out what parts of the test model are generic, and what parts are specific to the task of testing the warehouse resource.

To develop a QuickCheck state machine for testing the system we have to decide on a model state, to decide which command to generate in a particular model state (i.e., implement the `command` function). Moreover we have to be able to decide whether the execution of a command was successful or not (i.e., implement the `postcondition` function), and to compute a next model state after a command has finished executing (i.e., implement the `next_state` function),

Using these functions, the QuickCheck state machine library repeatedly generates a test sequence of modest length composed of commands, where each individual command is generated by one call to the `command` function, executes the command sequence, and determines whether the execution revealed an error or not.

5.1   The State of a Resource

To produce more comprehensible tests we introduce the notion of a robot identifier, which is simply a natural number. In the model we extend the warehouse operations with a robot identifier as a first argument, i.e., a call is now `enterWarehouse(r,n,w)` where r is the robot identifier, n is the warehouse identifier, and w is the weight. However, before actually issuing the call to the implemented resource, the robot identifier is stripped. Thus robot identifiers are used only internally in the QuickCheck state model, and the resource specification need not change.

The state of a resource is represented as a record with fields `warehouses` and `corridor` which corresponds to the resource state; `num_enters` counts the number of robots that have entered warehouse 0, and `blocked_jobs` is a list with information about the currently blocked jobs (i.e., calls to the resource which have not completed yet).

The `blocked_jobs` field will be a component of any shared resource test model, whereas the other fields are specific to the warehouse example.

5.2   Generation of Commands

Clearly not all commands can be invoked in all situations, and thus test sequences must be generated that respect such restrictions. In the following we abbreviate `enterWarehouse` as `enter` and `exitWarehouse` as `exit`.

For instance, a test sequence containing only the test `exit(0,0,350)` is not very sensible, as there is no prior call in which robot 0 actually entered warehouse 0. Since robots are expected to move sequentially through the warehouse complex, entering warehouse 0, exiting warehouse 0, entering warehouse 1, etc., the test command sequences we generate should respect such sequential behaviour.

Similarly, if a call enter(0,0,350) blocks, it does not make sense to issue a call to exit(1,0,350) until the prior call is unblocked. Moreover, as commented earlier, it is expected that a call to exit(n,w) has the same weight parameter as the earlier call to enter the warehouse. Finally, the weight parameter w2 in a call to enter(r,n+1,w2) should be greater than or equal to the weight parameter w1 in a prior call exit(r,n,w1) (if any). Note that such restrictions are not inferrible from the warehouse resource specification in Fig. 2.

The actual command to generate in a model state is chosen randomly between all possible commands. As an example, we show below a QuickCheck generator that is capable of generating exit commands exit(r,n,w), using the current model state:

```
1  eqc_gen:oneof
2  ([{call,warehouse,exit,[R,N,W]} ||
3      N <- warehouses(),
4      {R,W} <- warehouse(N,State),
5      not(lists:member(R,blocked(State)))
6  ]).
```

A symbolic command calling the exit function (in the software module warehouse) is represented as {call,warehouse,exit,[R,N,P]} where [R,N,W] are the function arguments (robot identifier, warehouse identifier, and weight).

Such a command can be generated if N is a warehouse identifier (line 3), and R,W and the robot with identifier R and weight W is in warehouse N in the model state (line 4), and no call concerning robot R is currently blocked (line 5, also checked using the model state).

There may be several robots that are able to exit a warehouse at any given time, and the above generator chooses randomly between all such possible commands (line 1).

The full command generator also generates enter commands; we cut down on the number of possible commands by enforcing that robots enter warehouse 0 with sequentially increasing robot identifiers, starting with 0, and up to some small maximum (10). To increase the possibility that the sum of weights in a warehouse sum exactly to the maximum weight in a warehouse (normally 1000), starting weights for robots are chosen randomly using the QuickCheck generator[2] ?LET(X,eqc_gen:choose(1,11),X*100), i.e., the generator first chooses a random integer between 1 and 11, and multiplies it with 100. Thus possible weights are $100, 200, \ldots, 1100$.

A call to the command function to generate a command actually does not return a single command, but rather a small number of commands that should be invoked concurrently (to be able to detect errors of type e_1 above). The exact number of concurrent commands is chosen randomly. However, care must be taken that such concurrent calls are non-interfering, in the sense that the

---

[2] A QuickCheck generator is a function that is capable of, according to some probability distribution, generating an infinite number of elements for some type. The generator int(), for example, can generate random integers, and list(int()) generates lists of random length, containing random integers.

execution of one command cannot render another command non-executable (due to the restrictions above). In the case of the warehouse this corresponds to ensuring that concurrent calls concern distinct robots.

As an example, the following set of (concurrent) calls could be generated from the initial model state: $\{$enter$(0,0,300)$, enter$(1,0,700)$, enter$(2,0,300)\}$. Note that the concurrent calls concern different robots to prevent interference.

5.3   Execution of Commands

Commands are executed simply by invoking, in parallel, the Java methods corresponding to the resource operations, taking care to first strip the robot identifier. Next, the test code waits for a small interval of time, and checks which calls have completed. The result of executing the set of concurrent calls is a set of tuples ⟨*call, result*⟩ denoting a call *call* that has finished with some *result* (a normal return value, or a Java exception). The concurrent calls that have not yet completed are considered *blocked*.

Note that there may be more completed calls than the number of concurrent calls invoked, as a call may unblock calls blocked earlier in the execution of the test sequence.

Moreover, note also that there is no way to detect in which order the calls completed.

5.4   Computing the Next Model State

To compute the next model state, given the result of the execution of a set of concurrent calls, we must calculate a "feasible" ordering of the finished calls that permits all calls to execute, considering the restrictions enforced by the concurrency precondition **CPRE**.

Given the current model state s, and a set of finished calls $c_1, \ldots, c_n$, we explore all possible interleavings of these calls. That is, beginning with c_1, if c_1 should still block in the model state (according to the **CPRE**) it cannot have been the first call to terminate, and thus no interleavings beginning with c_1 needs to be considered further. If on the other hand c_1 should not block, we compute a new model state $s_2 = \mathbf{POST}(c_1, s)$, and explore all interleavings of the remaining commands $c_2, \ldots, c_n$. Similarly, we explore all interleavings beginning with c_2, etc. The successful interleavings are those which succeeded in executing (without blocking) all completed calls $c_1, \ldots, c_n$, and the successful new model states are the final new model states.

In general there may be more than one successful interleaving, e.g., consider the example with generated commands above. A potential execution result is that the two calls enter$(0,0,300)$ and enter$(0,0,700)$ finished (all three calls cannot finish). Clearly both possible interleavings of these calls are successful. However, the final model states are identical.

In fact, in this article we focus on a subclass of shared resource specifications, to permit "deterministic testing", where the following property holds:

given an execution $s_0, \ldots, s$ from the initial model state s_0 and ending in model state s, and a set of concurrent calls *Calls* generated from model state s, suppose that the concurrent execution of *Calls* causes the set of calls $Calls_1$ to finish, then the final model states computed from s and $Calls_1$ must all be identical.

This property holds of the warehouse example, but it is easy to construct a resource specification where the property does not hold. For instance, we can stipulate two operations a and b, where if a executes first the final model state is a (the execution of b has no effect, but does not block), and vice versa if b executes first the final model state is b.

This restriction can be lifted by generalizing a model state as a set of possible "simple" model states, corresponding to all possible final model states. However, we are then faced with the problem of generating commands that are permitted in all simple model states.

Note that if there exists no interleaving of the completed calls that is permitted according to the concurrency precondition, we have found a bug in the implementation of the shared resource.

The computation of all possible interleavings is done in a lazy manner, taking care not to generate all interleavings at once, but rather in a stepwise manner, discarding failed interleavings at once, and merging identical interleavings (i.e., whose model states are the same, and with the same remaining calls to consider) as soon as possible, to improve analysis efficiency. Nevertheless, in the worst case there may be an exponential number of interleavings to explore, although potential slow-downs caused by this are mitigated by the fact that we explore only tests of a limited size, and where the number of concurrent calls are severely limited by design. In practice we have so far not experienced any problems due to this potential inefficiency.

5.5   Checking if the Execution of a Command Was Correct

To check that the execution of a command was as predicted by the current model state, we compute the next model state s_{new} given the current one and the completed calls (as explained in the previous section).

Again, if there is no possible interleaving of the calls such that the concurrency precondition holds for all calls, we have found a bug in the implementation and testing can finish. Moreover, we examine the return values for all completed calls; if any call raised an exception we have found a bug in the implementation.

Finally, we consider all calls that have not completed but remain blocked. If, in the new model state, any of these calls can be completed, i.e., there exists a call $c_n \in blocked(s_{new}).\mathbf{CPRE}(c_n, s_{new})$, they should have already finished (due to the requirement on progress), and thus we have found a bug in the implementation.

6   Testing the Warehouse Resource

To validate the approach we developed a QuickCheck state machine according to the principles explained in the previous section, and used it to test 98 Java-based implementations of the Warehouse shared resource.

These implementations were written by undergraduate students attending a course on concurrency at the Polytechnic University of Madrid. The students were required to use a particular concurrency construct [5], which is an improvement on the lock and condition solution seen in Fig. 3, in that it is not needed to test the concurrency precondition using a while loop.

Before we ran the QuickCheck based test on the student programs, the students had already successfully tested their solutions on a small set of manually developed jUNIT test cases. Moreover, the students had a strong incentive in handing in good solutions, as the warehouse implementations were graded, and these grades were factored into the final course grade.

Although the task may not appear overly difficult, the results of our testing using QuickCheck are somewhat discouraging. Of the 98 solutions tested, we found errors in 33 of them, i.e., 34 % of the solutions handed contained at least one error. The following is a typical error report produced:

```
Test failed with reason {postcondition,false}

Generated test sequence:
----------------------------

  << enter(0,0,1000) >>   -- unblocks 0
  << enter(1,0,600) >>
  << exit(0,0,1000),
     enter(2,0,500) >>    -- unblocks 0,unblocks 1
  << enter(0,1,1000),
     enter(3,0,600),
     exit(1,0,600) >>     -- unblocks 0,unblocks 1,
                             unblocks 3,unblocks 2
```

In the error report we can see that robot tries to enter warehouse 0, carrying weight 1000 (the maximum allowed), and succeeds. Next, robot 1 tries to enter with weight 600, and blocks (correctly). Next two commands are executed concurrently, robot 0 exiting warehouse 0 to the following corridor, and robot 2 entering warehouse 0 with weight 500. The result is that the exiting operation succeed, and the previous request from robot 1 to enter warehouse 0 also succeeded. Finally, three commands are run in parallel, a request from robot 0 to enter warehouse 1, a request from robot 1 to exit warehouse 0, and a request from 3 to enter warehouse 0 with weight 600. All requests are successful, as well as the previous request of robot 2 to enter warehouse 0. Thus, both robot 2 and 3 have received permission to enter the warehouse, but the total weight of robots in the warehouse would then be $600 + 500$ which exceeds the permitted maximum of 1000; a safety critical bug!

7   Conclusions and Future Work

We have provided a methodology for developing and testing concurrent safety-critical systems, based on the use of a high-level concurrency mechanism: *shared resources*. The methodology was tested in a case study, and was found to be able to detect a large number of concurrency errors in a prototypical safety-critical system.

Items for future work includes providing the functionality of deriving individual test cases (and indeed entire test suites). This can be already achieved using the approach explained here, except the execution of a generated test case need not be deterministic, but instead depend on the particular implementation. Thus such a "pre-generated" test case may have to be aborted in mid-run because an invoked operation may be nonsensical (e.g., if a robot desires to exit a warehouse before it has been given permission to do so). In contrast, using the approach adopted in this article we do not have to abort test cases in mid-run, as the test case generation is *steered* by the actual implementation being tested.

References

1. Armstrong, J., Virding, R., Wikström, C., Williams, M.: Concurrent Programming in Erlang. Prentice-Hall, Englewood Cliffs (1996)
2. Arts, T., Hughes, J., Johansson, J., Wiger, U.T.: Testing telecoms software with quviq QuickCheck. In: Proceedings of the 2006 ACM SIGPLAN Workshop on Erlang, Portland, Oregon, USA, pp. 2–10 (2006)
3. Cesarini, F., Thompson, S.: Erlang Programming - A Concurrent Approach to Software Development. O'Reilly Media, Sebastopol (2009)
4. Claessen, K., Hughes, J.: Quickcheck: a lightweight tool for random testing of haskell programs. In: Proceedings of the Fifth ACM SIGPLAN International Conference on Functional Programming, ICFP 2000, pp. 268–279. ACM, New York (2000)
5. Herranz, Á., Mariño, J.: A verified implementation of priority monitors in Java. In: Beckert, B., Damiani, F., Gurov, D. (eds.) FoVeOOS 2011. LNCS, vol. 7421, pp. 160–177. Springer, Heidelberg (2012)
6. Herranz, A., Mariño, J., Carro, M., Moreno Navarro, J.J.: Modeling concurrent systems with shared resources. In: Alpuente, M., Cook, B., Joubert, C. (eds.) FMICS 2009. LNCS, vol. 5825, pp. 102–116. Springer, Heidelberg (2009)
7. Svenningsson, R., Johansson, R., Arts, T., Norell, U.: Testing AUTOSAR basic software models with quickcheck. In: Pavese, F., Bár, M., Filtz, J.-R., Forbes, A.B., Pendrill, L., Shirono, K. (eds.) Advanced Mathematical And Computational Tools In Metrology And Testing IX, pp. 391–395. World Scientific, Singapore (2012)

A Contracts-Based Framework for Systems Modeling and Embedded Diagnostics

Gregory Provan[✉]

Department of Computer Science, University College Cork, Cork, Ireland
g.provan@cs.ucc.ie

Abstract. Two key impediments for the commercial success of model-based diagnosis (MBD) include (a) a failure to integrate diagnostics modeling within the requirements and design phase, and (b) a high degree of diagnostic ambiguity during run-time. This article addresses both of these impediments by providing a formal framework that integrates requirements-based design with MBD modeling. The proposed framework extends the consistency-based theory of MBD with a requirements-based design theory based on contracts.

Keywords: Contracts · Model-based diagnostics · Systems modeling

1 Introduction

Model-based design has proven to be very effective for a range of systems. However, most companies still generate diagnostics models and simulation/control models independently, even though these models have significant overlap. For example, design models of autopilot systems incorporate many safety requirements, yet embedded autopilot diagnostics systems typically are designed and implemented independent of the simulation models. This approach creates multiple problems, such as conflicts between embedded diagnostics and control, and wasted resources during the design/implementation phases.

In this article, we address certain problems arising in on-board model-based diagnosis (MBD) software, which aims to isolate the components that are faulty during run-time. This differs from safety analysis, e.g., [13], which typically aims to identify, *a priori*, if unsafe states can be entered.

A problem with model-based diagnosis (MBD) is that there is no notion of "acceptable" inputs to a system/component. Hence the problem of *cascaded faults* occurs when an upstream fault in component C causes inconsistent data to be transmitted to components downstream of the original fault, which results in downstream components all signalling faults, when in fact only C is faulty. To circumvent such problems, we extend an MBD model with an A/G model, which explicitly rules out inconsistent input data as failing to fulfil the component/system model.

This article presents a formal framework that extends the consistency-based theory of MBD [17] with a component-based requirements/design theory based

Gregory Provan—Supported by SFI grant 12/RC/1189.

C. Canal and A. Idani (Eds.): SEFM 2014 Workshops, LNCS 8938, pp. 131–143, 2015.
DOI: 10.1007/978-3-319-15201-1_9

on contracts [9]. This assume/guarantee theory defines a system Φ in terms of an inter-connected collection of "rich" components [1], each of which must fulfil a contract (e.g., based on design requirements) given assumptions in which the component operates. Given a contract-based specification for Φ, one can prove properties about fulfilment of the design requirements. Contracts have been used for hardware design optimization [20], and also for software analysis during run-time [10]. Moreover, based on observations and the possibility of stochastic (or non-deterministic faults), one can then diagnose the reasons for the contracts violated during operation of Φ [18,21].

This approach offers a formal methodology not only to integrate requirements specification within diagnostics models, but also to significantly reduce the incidence of two challenging classes of ambiguous or "spurious" fault, commonly known as No-Fault-Found (NFF) and cascaded fault-reports. During run-time, many ambiguous diagnoses can arise due to inability to define models that adequately distinguish "local" faults from exogenous influences. For example, the No-Fault-Found is a common diagnosis that causes problems in many domains, particularly avionics: it is a fault that is isolated during device operation, but when the "faulty" component is replaced, the fault cannot be duplicated during testing of the component. In many cases, this fault occurs when the component is operated outside of its design intent. For example, fighter jets have many actuator faults that occur when the jets are operated outside of design specifications.

Cascaded faults are another difficult situation that arise in typical FDD situations: in avionics, for example, an upstream module will compute some faulty data, and then all downstream modules that process this faulty data will issue (erroneous) fault reports, when in fact downstream modules do not have hardware faults, but issue fault reports due to the incoming corrupted data. In this case, the failure to identify exogenous anomalies properly leads to many erroneous diagnoses.

Assume-guarantee reasoning considers components not in isolation, but in conjunction with assumptions about their context. Hence, the assume/guarantee (A/G) approach focuses on reasoning about a component in terms of the assumptions about its environment, and by proving that these assumptions are satisfied by the environment, establishing a set of *system obligations*, the contract. This approach has been use for (a) validating the requirements of a design (and thereby reducing the design-space that must be searched during design optimization [20]), and (b) during run-time for system-level verification [4].

The contributions of the article are as follows:

- We generalize the consistency-based theory of MBD to a contract-based theory that enables design models, with their environment-based requirements, to be integrated with an MBD model.
- We show how we can use the existing MBD inference to compute not only faults, but also operating-condition violations, and thereby rule out faults based on incorrect component inputs.
- We illustrate how our new approach can distinguish faults and assumption violations with a running example.

2 Related Work

This article synthesizes the notion of contracts with that of fault diagnosis of DESs, thereby extending both.

Previous work has been done on using LTL for model-based diagnostics [11,12]. This research has focused on mapping LTL specifications into propositional clauses that are amenable to MBD inference directly. In particular, [12] creates a structure-preserving SAT encoding for an LTL specification, such that inference based on Reiter's diagnosis theory [16] can be efficiently applied. In contrast, we do not focus on computationally efficient solutions, but rather aim towards *extending* Reiter's diagnosis theory with contracts. In future work we hope to explore the computational speedups possible within this MBD framework, using a tool-kit described in [14].

Sampath et al. [17] first proposed the framework for failure diagnosis of qualitative behaviors of discrete-event systems (DESs). They defined a DES executing a faulty event as *diagnosable* if it must be eventually diagnosed within a bounded number of state-transitions/events. To compute a diagnosis they define an automaton for that purpose, called a diagnoser, and showed necessary and sufficient conditions for diagnosability in terms of certain properties of the diagnoser. Subsequently, several researchers extended this work, e.g.,

In this paper, we adopt the failure diagnosis specification using linear-time temporal logic (LTL) [7]. Given a DES to be diagnosed, we use an LTL formula Φ for specifying a fault as follows: an infinite state-trace of the system is said to be faulty if it violates Φ. Thus for example, we can declare an infinite state-trace to be faulty if it visits a faulty state, which may be faulty by itself (as in [2] [24, 25, 45]), or may be a state introduced for representing a transition labeled by a faulty event (as in [4–6,11] [32, 35–37]). We can also have more general specifications for non-faulty state-traces in our setting such as a certain set of states should be visited infinitely often, or a certain set of states should be eventually invariant. Thus properties such as "invariance", "recurrence", "stability", etc. can be used to specify (non)-faulty behavior in our setting.

3 Running Example: TO/GA System

3.1 Example

This section introduces a simple example that we use throughout the article. The Take-off/Go Around (TO/GA) system is an autopilot sub-system that activates take-off or go-around thrust. During take-off, pressing the TO/GA switch causes the engines to increase their RPM to their computed take off power, as computed from parameters such as runway length, wind speed, temperature, and the weight of the aircraft. The go-around mode is engaged on approach to land, and switches the plane from autopilot approach mode by engaging the thrust levers until they reach the position go-around thrust.

Most commercial aircraft use some form of hardware/software redundancy to ensure high reliability of autopilot systems. For example, this may be a

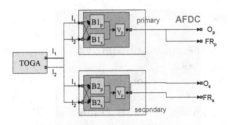

Fig. 1. Dual-dual autopilot TOGA sub-system, with TO/GA signals I_1, I_2 sent to primary and secondary AFDC computers.

dual-redundant or a triply-redundant approach, as in the Boeing 777 aircraft's TO/GA architecture. In this article we study a TO/GA System with a dual-dual redundant approach, as shown in Fig. 1. In such systems, the TO/GA commands are replicated and sent to two autopilot flight director control (AFDC) computers, which compute thrust levels in each of the AFDC computers. The AFDC outputs are sent to the engines, and any anomalies are sent to fault-report monitors. Each TO/GA signal is tagged with a time stamp, to ensure that the signals being compared are closely-spaced temporally and thus represent the same computation done in different downstream components.

We represent a state at time τ using the tuple $(I_1, I_2, \mu, O_P, O_S)$, where I_1 and I_2 are the two TO/GA inputs, $\mu = |\tau_{I_1} - \tau_{I_2}|$ is the input time difference, and O_P and O_S are the primary and secondary outputs, respectively.[1]

The aim of embedded diagnostics is to compute the primary and secondary fault reports, denoted FR_P and FR_S, respectively. The AFDC has primary and secondary computers; the primary AFDC is engaged as long as no possible data corruption is detected. If a signal mis-compare occurs, the primary AFDC issues a fault report and the secondary AFDC is also engaged. If the secondary AFDC does not detect a mis-compare, it is now used as the primary unit. If the secondary AFDC also detects a mis-compare, it also issues a fault report and a pilot-warning, which notifies the cockpit of TO/GA problems, with a recommendation to switch to manual TO/GA procedures.

Environment-Based Requirements Specification. This section defines two TOGA system signal requirements as propositions (R_1, R_2), in order to fit in with the MBD language. The requirements for the AFDC are that it must test signal equality for two asynchronous signals (R_1), which must be generated within a time difference μ no greater than a fixed constant δ (R_2). We formalise the two requirements as follows:

R_1 the time-difference between the AFDC input signals I_1 and I_2 must be such that $|\tau_{I_1} - \tau_{I_2}| < \delta$, when $\mu = t$; else $\mu = f$;

---

[1] Note that we suppress temporal indexing to simplify the notation.

Table 1. Set of states for dual-dual comparator, with state name x_i, inputs (I_1, I_2), time-difference μ for inputs, and outputs O_p and O_s

state	(I_1, I_2)	μ	O_p	O_s
x_1	(t,t)	t	t	t
x_2	(t,t)	t	f	t
x_3	(t,t)	t	f	f
x_4	(f,f)	t	t	t
x_5	(t,f)	f	f	f
x_6	(f,t)	f	f	f
x_7	(t,t)	f	f	f

R_2 if the TOGA outputs are both t, set the input flag $I = t$; else $I = f$. This is given by $(I_1 \cap I_2) \Leftrightarrow I$.

Hence, for this sub-system, we can define the requirements specification as $\mathcal{R} = \mu \wedge I$. We assume that the requirements are consistent.

A typical "run" of this system will consist of a sequence of states. For example, consider a state sequence $S = \{x_1, x_2, x_3, x_3, x_3, x_4\}$, as shown in Table 1. We can classify states as satisfying the requirements or not. For example, if we examine the input-equality and timing requirements for S, we see that x_4 through x_7 satisfy these requirements, and the other states do not.

4   Notation and Model

4.1   Components and System Composition

We adopt a component-based framework for systems. A component is an entity that represents a base-level unit of design. We create systems (hierarchically) by connecting components together such that connected components share and agree on the values of the connected ports and variables.

The environment of a component consists of a set of states over time (a trace or behaviour) external to the component. A system (or component) accepts as input a subset of exogenous traces (from its environment) and modifies these to produce an output trace.

We formalise a component using the notion of an interface and a set of behaviours over the interface. The interface is represented by a set P of input and output ports, which specify allowable values for the ports. The behaviour is characterised by sets of traces.

Definition 1 (Component). *A component C is a tuple $\langle P, \mathcal{T}_I, \mathcal{T}_O, \mathcal{T}_{obs} \rangle$ in which: P is the set of ports; $\mathcal{T}_I$ and $\mathcal{T}_O$ are disjoint sets referred to as inputs and outputs, respectively, (the union of which is denoted by $\mathcal{T}$); $\mathcal{T}_{obs} \subseteq \mathcal{T}$ is the subset of observable traces.*

A component modifies the input T_I to create the output T_O, and we use a model Φ to characterise this process. In the following we will specify models for diagnosis and for contracts.

In this article we focus on integrating a diagnosis and A/G model. We assume the well-known concepts of component composition to create a system model, and refer to articles such as [2,15,20] for details of model composition.

4.2 Model-Based Diagnosis Representation

This section described our fault model for discrete-event systems (DESs). Our work extends DES diagnosis by adding in the concept of contracts to rule out anomalous inputs that violate a contract. The research on DES diagnosis has a long history. Sampath et al. [17] first proposed a framework for failure diagnosis of qualitative behaviours of DESs. They defined a DES executing a faulty event as *diagnosable* if it can be diagnosed within a bounded number of state-transitions/events. They define an automaton, called a diagnoser, to compute a diagnosis, and show necessary and sufficient conditions for diagnosability in terms of properties of the diagnoser. Subsequently, several researchers extended this work, e.g., more general frameworks, as in timed systems in [5] and decentralized diagnosis [3], and improvements in efficiency from exponential-complexity diagnosability inference [17] to poly-time [6].

In this paper, we adopt the linear-time temporal logic (LTL) [19] failure diagnosis specification of [7]. In brief, LTL is built up from a finite set of propositional variables AP, the logical operators $\wedge$, $\vee$, $\neg$ and $\Rightarrow$, and the temporal modal operators $\bigcirc$ (next), $\square$ (always), $\diamond$ (eventually), U (until) and R (release). Formally, the set of LTL formulas over AP is inductively defined as follows:

- if $p \in AP$ then p is a LTL formula;
- if ψ and ξ are LTL formulas then $\neg\psi$, $\psi \vee \xi$, $\square\psi$, and $\psi \diamond \xi$ are LTL formulas.

Given a DES to be diagnosed, we use an LTL formula Φ for specifying a fault as follows: an infinite state-trace of the system is *faulty* if it violates Φ. In other words, a fault is *inconsistent* with the model Φ.

We represent a system as accepting as input a trace T_I and creates as output a trace T_O; our specification (model) of the system by Φ_Δ, an LTL formula that specifies the nominal (non-faulty) behavior of the system.

We formalise the model as follows:

Definition 2 (Model Φ). *A model Φ is defined by the tuple* $(X, \Sigma, R, X_0, \xi, \lambda)$, *where*

- X *is the set of states;*
- Σ *is a finite set of event labels;*
- $R : X \times (\Sigma \cup \epsilon) \times X$ *is a transition relation;*
- $X_0 \subseteq X$ *is the initial set of states;*
- ξ *is a finite set of proposition symbols;*
- $\lambda : X \to 2^\xi$ *is a labelling function.*

This model is capable of generating a trace as follows:

Definition 3 (Trace T). *A system S generates a finite or infinite state-trace $T = (x_1, ..., x_m)$ given as input $x_0 \in X_0$, such that $\forall i > 0$ there exists a $\sigma_i \in \Sigma \cup \{\epsilon\}$ such that $(x_{i-1}, \sigma_i, x_i) \in R$.*

A finite or infinite state-trace $T = (x_0, x_1, ...0)$ over $\Sigma \cup \{\epsilon\}$ is associated with a event-trace $\sigma = (e_0, e_1, ...)$ if $\forall i > 0$, $(x_{i-1}, e_i, x_i) \in R$.

If we represent a behaviour as $T = T_I \cup T_O$, a fault occurs if the behaviour is inconsistent with the diagnosis model Φ_Δ:

Definition 4. *Let S be a system, Φ_Δ be a LTL specification for S, and T be an infinite observed state-trace generated by S, then T is called a faulty state-trace if $T \nvDash \Phi_\Delta$.*

Given an anomalous observation T_Δ, we aim to compute the failure state of the system that is the "cause" of T_Δ. A key aspect for MBD is to take an observed event sequence (called an *observation*) and identify the fault status of the system based on the observation. Observations of events executed by system S are filtered through an observation mask $m : \Sigma \cup \{\epsilon\} \to \Gamma \cup \{\epsilon\}$ with $m(\epsilon) = \epsilon$, where Γ is the set of observed symbols.

Assume that system S has a set $\mathcal{F} = \{F_1, ..., F_n\}$ failures that can occur. We assume, using [17], that a failure event Σ_{F_i} precedes failure F_i. Hence, our task thus consists of isolating the failure events when an anomalous observation occurs. An anomalous observation is a faulty state-trace which is observable.

We can classify the states as being either faulty X_F or nominal (not faulty) X_N. Using the mapping from state-trace to event-trace, each faulty state-trace must be associated with one or more failure events. Further, based on [17], we associate to every failure event Σ_f one or more observable indicator events.

Definition 5. *Let S be a system and T be a finite state-trace generated by S, T is called an indicator if all its infinite extensions in S are faulty. We use Ind_S to denote the set of all indicators in S.*

Example: In our TO/GA example, we use the FR (fault-report) variable as our observable variable, i.e., we emit an observable signal to indicate the detection of a fault.

We can model each AFDC in our TO/GA example using the following:

$$(FR = OK) \Rightarrow \Box[(I_1 \land I_2) \Rightarrow O_i] \tag{1}$$

$$(FR = fault) \Rightarrow \Diamond[\neg O_i] \tag{2}$$

Equation 1 states that FR indicating it is OK means that the inputs should agree with output i, i.e., O_P and O_S. Equation 2 states that FR indicating it is *faulty* means that eventually we should obtain a *false* output.

The diagnosis model automaton shown in Fig. 2(a) depicts a transition relation that, starting from the *nominal* state (where $FR = OK$), constrains the system to continue in the *nominal* state or to move to a *fault* state (where $FR = fault$).

The two main inference techniques used for diagnostic state estimation are a diagnoser [6,17] or a diagnostics search engine built on top of a theorem prover (e.g., [8]).

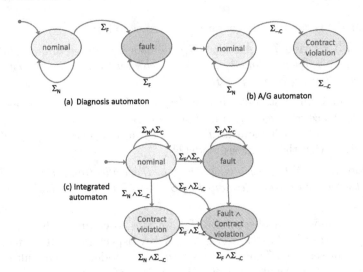

Fig. 2. Automata for diagnosis (a), and integrated (b), models

4.3 Assume/Guarantee Representation

This section describes a model Φ_{AG} that specifies the notion of a contract for a component. This can be extended to a system contract, as described in [2].

An AG specification consists of two (prefix-closed) sets of traces referred to as the assumption A and guarantee G. The assumption specifies the environment's allowable interaction sequences, while the guarantee is a constraint on the component's behaviour.

A component may include both implementations and contracts. An implementation M is an instantiation of a component and consists of a set P of ports and of a set of behaviours, or runs, also denoted by M, which assign a history of "values" to ports. Given an A/G specification Φ_{AG} for S, with assumption A and guarantee G, we informally characterize how a component S satisfies a contract as follows [2]. S satisfies Φ_{AG} if for any interaction between S and the environment characterised by a trace $\mathcal{T}$, if $\mathcal{T} \in A$, then $\mathcal{T} \in A$, and $\mathcal{T}$ cannot become inconsistent in S without further inputs from the environment. Components can thus be thought of as implementations of /AG specifications.

Given an MBD model Φ_Δ, an A/G model Φ_{AG} is defined over the same observable state-space, i.e., observations for the system and its sensors are the same. The A/G model is different in that it uses a model that constrains the transition relation to identify certain transitions as not fulfilling the contract. Hence, we must identify two classes of event label: events that satisfy the contract Σ_C and events that violate the contract $\Sigma_{\bar{C}}$, where these two classes form a partition of Σ. There is a corresponding partition of the complete state-space: $X = X_C \cup X_{\bar{C}}$. Figure 2(b) shows the automaton for this extended model.

In this new framework, an assumption that violates the contract is defined as follows:

Definition 6. *Given a system S, an A/G LTL specification Φ_{AG} for S, and an assumption A, i.e., an infinite state-trace, we say that A violates the contract for guarantee G if $A \not\models \Phi_{AG}$.*

Example: In our TO/GA example, we can model each AFDC using

$$(FR = OK) \Rightarrow \Box[A \Rightarrow O_i] \tag{3}$$
$$(FR = \bar{C}) \Rightarrow \Diamond[\neg O_i] \tag{4}$$

Equation 3 means that when the contract is satisfied the output O_i is assigned t. Equation 4 means that failure to satisfy the contract entails the output O_i eventually being assigned f.

The A/G model automaton shown in Fig. 2(b) depicts a transition relation that, starting from the *nominal* state (where $FR = OK$), constrains the system to continue in the *nominal* state or to move to a *Contract Violation* state (where $FR = \neg C$).

5 Assume/Guarantee and MBD Extended Model

This section describes how we extend our MBD model to incorporate A/G models.

5.1 Formal Model

In our framework, we assume a model Φ that accepts as input a trace $\mathcal{T}_I$ and creates as output a trace $\mathcal{T}_O$. If we represent a behaviour as $\mathcal{T} = \mathcal{T}_I \cup \mathcal{T}_O$, a fault occurs if the behaviour is inconsistent with the model Φ, i.e., $\mathcal{T} \not\models \Phi$.

Within the MBD framework, we model a system/component using an LTL model Φ_Δ (see Definition 2). Given an anomalous observation π_Δ, we aim to compute the failure state of the system that is the "cause" of π_Δ.

To extend Φ_Δ, we must define an A/G model Φ_{AG}, and then specify the extended model as $\Phi = \Phi_\Delta \cup \Phi_{AG}$.

The extended model thus has the following partition of the state set: $X = X_\Delta \times X_{AG} = (X_N \cup X_G) \times (X_C \cup X_{\bar{C}})$, which gives $X = X_N X_C \cup X_N X_{\bar{C}} \cup X_F X_C \cup X_F X_{\bar{C}}$. The extended model has the following analogous partition of the event label set: $\Sigma = \Sigma_\Delta \times \Sigma_{AG}$.

5.2 Example

We now describe how our running example covers this extended model.

The integrated diagnosis and A/G model automaton shown in Fig. 2(c) depicts a transition relation that, starting from the *nominal* state (where $FR = OK$), constrains the system to continue in the *nominal* state or to move to a *fault* state (where $FR = fault$), a *Contract Violation* state (where $FR = \neg C$), or a state where a fault exists and the contract is violated.

Table 2. Diagnostics and contract status for dual-dual comparator, with state name x_i, $i = 1, ..., 7$, inputs (I_1, I_2), time-difference μ for inputs, and outputs O_p and O_s

state	(I_1, I_2)	μ	O_p	O_s	Φ_Δ	Φ_{AG}	Φ_{Int}
x_1	(t,t)	t	t	t	-	-	-
x_2	(t,t)	t	f	t	✓	-	fault
x_3	(t,t)	t	f	f	-	✓	fault
x_4	(f,f)	t	t	t	-	-	-
x_5	(t,f)	f	f	f	✓	✓	$\neg C$
x_6	(f,t)	f	f	f	✓	✓	$\neg C$
x_7	(t,t)	f	f	f	✓	✓	fault $\wedge \neg C$

We can model each AFDC using

$$(FR = OK) \Rightarrow \Box[A \Rightarrow O_i] \tag{5}$$
$$(FR = fault) \Rightarrow \diamond[\neg O_i] \tag{6}$$
$$(FR = \bar{C}) \Rightarrow \diamond[\neg O_i] \tag{7}$$
$$(FR = fault \wedge \bar{C}) \Rightarrow \diamond[\neg O_i] \tag{8}$$

Table 2 depicts what can be computed from a given state x_i (assuming x_i is preceded by a nominal state sequence) by the different models: Φ_Δ, Φ_{AG}, and Φ_{Int}. Note that ✓ denotes that the particular model identifies either a fault or a contract violation. As examples of the computed results:

- State x_2 presents a fault in output O_P, and that is properly identified by Φ_Δ.
- State x_3 presents a fault in outputs O_P and O_S, and that is properly identified by Φ_Δ.
- State x_5 presents a contract violation in the inputs (which are t and f rather than t, t) which (correctly) produces a f output in O_P and O_S. However, that output is incorrectly identified as a fault by Φ_Δ. The combined model can rule out this as a fault, identifying this as a contract violation.
- State x_6 presents another example of a contract violation in the inputs (which are f and t rather than t, t); this (correctly) produces a f output in O_P and O_S. However, that output is incorrectly identified as a fault by Φ_Δ. The combined model can rule out this as a fault, but identifies it as a contract violation.

6   Properties of Extended Model

6.1   Diagnostic Soundness/Completeness

We can show that an A/G model Φ_{AG} can preserve all local component faults while excluding faults that the diagnosis model Φ_M incorrectly identifies based on contract violations.[2]

---

[2] The proof is provided in the supplementary material.

Theorem 1. *Given a diagnosis model Φ_Δ, a corresponding integrated model Φ_{Int}, and an observation α, Φ_{Int} is sound and complete with respect to the local component faults of Φ_Δ.*

Proof:

Sound: Since we are using a monotonic logic, adding extra clauses to any formula F will reduce the number of logical models (diagnoses) of F. If $\Omega(\Phi_\Delta, \alpha)$ and $\Omega(\Phi_{Int}, \alpha)$ denote the set of diagnoses given the diagnosis and integrated models, respectively, then $\Omega(\Phi_\Delta, \alpha) \supseteq \Omega(\Phi_{Int}, \alpha)$. Hence for a local component diagnosis ω, there is no $\omega \in \Omega(\Phi_{Int}, \alpha)$ such that $\omega \notin \Omega(\Phi_\Delta, \alpha)$.

Complete: Let $\tilde{\Omega}(\Phi_{Int}, \alpha)$ as the local component diagnoses, i.e., diagnoses with value *bad*. If $\exists \omega \in \tilde{\Omega}(\Phi_{Int}, \alpha)$ such that $\omega \notin \tilde{\Omega}(\Phi_M, \alpha)$, then we must have $\Omega(\Phi_\Delta, \alpha) \not\supseteq \Omega(\Phi_{Int}, \alpha)$, which is a contradiction. Hence we must have completeness of the local component faults of Φ_{Int} with respect to Φ_M. □

6.2 Ambiguity Reduction

We now show that, by using Φ_{AG}, we can reduce the number of ambiguous faults that arise during the fault isolation process without losing any true faults.

A complete test vector $\alpha = \{\alpha_1, \cdots \alpha_m\}$ for a fault ω and model Φ_Δ is a sequence of observations such that $\Phi_\Delta \cup \alpha \cup \omega \not\models \perp$ and there is no other fault $\omega' \neq \omega$ such that $\Phi_\Delta \cup \alpha \cup \omega' \not\models \perp$.

We now define the notion of fault ambiguity. Given a complete test $\alpha = \{\alpha_1, \cdots \alpha_m\}$, a "true" fault ω^* is such that $\Phi_\Delta \cup \alpha \cup \omega^* \not\models \perp$. An ambiguous fault is some $\omega \neq \omega^*$ such that ω is entailed by some observation $\alpha \in \alpha$, i.e., $\Phi_\Delta \cup \alpha \cup \omega \not\models \perp$, but not for a superset test of α, i.e., $\exists \alpha' \supset \alpha$ such that $\Phi_\Delta \cup \alpha' \cup \omega \models \perp$.

Given these definitions, we now prove that the strengthened model does not exclude any true faults.

Lemma 1. *Given an MBD model Φ_Δ and any observation vector α, $\not\exists \omega_R$ such that $(\Phi_{AG} \cup \Phi_\Delta) \cup \alpha \cup \omega_R \not\models \perp$ unless $\Phi_\Delta \cup \alpha \cup \omega_R \not\models \perp$.*

Proof: We perform a proof by contradiction. Assume that there exists some ω_R such that $(\Phi_{AG} \cup \Phi_\Delta) \cup \alpha \cup \omega_R \models \perp$ and $\Phi_\Delta \cup \alpha \cup \omega_R \not\models \perp$. In this case it must be that $\Phi_{AG} \models \perp$, i.e., the A/G model is inconsistent, which is a contradiction. □

7 Conclusions

This article has extended MBD to include contracts. This enables a diagnostic system to avoid false-positive faults to be signalled when contracts for components are being violated. It also indicates when poor requirements lead to excessive fault reporting even though contracts are not violated.

In future work we plan to examine more efficient LTL encoding, e.g., using [11], and to examine the impact of contract-based diagnostics on larger systems.

References

1. Benveniste, A., Caillaud, B., Ferrari, A., Mangeruca, L., Passerone, R., Sofronis, C.: Multiple viewpoint contract-based specification and design. In: de Boer, F.S., Bonsangue, M.M., Graf, S., de Roever, W.-P. (eds.) FMCO 2007. LNCS, vol. 5382, pp. 200–225. Springer, Heidelberg (2008)
2. Chilton, C., Jonsson, B., Kwiatkowska, M.: Compositional assume-guarantee reasoning for input/output component theories. Sci. Comput. Program. **91**, 115–137 (2014)
3. Debouk, R., Lafortune, S., Teneketzis, D.: Coordinated decentralized protocols for failure diagnosis of discrete event systems. Discrete Event Dyn. Syst. **10**(1–2), 33–86 (2000)
4. Giese, H., Henkler, S., Hirsch, M.: A multi-paradigm approach supporting the modular execution of reconfigurable hybrid systems. In: Transactions of the Society for Modeling and Simulation International (2010)
5. Hashtrudi Zad, S., Kwong, R., Wonham, W.: Fault diagnosis in timed discrete-event systems. In: Proceedings of the 38th IEEE Conference on Decision and Control, vol. 2, pp. 1756–1761. IEEE (1999)
6. Jiang, S., Huang, Z., Chandra, V., Kumar, R.: A polynomial algorithm for testing diagnosability of discrete-event systems. IEEE Trans. Autom. Control **46**(8), 1318–1321 (2001)
7. Jiang, S., Kumar, R.: Failure diagnosis of discrete-event systems with linear-time temporal logic specifications. IEEE Trans. Autom. Control **49**(6), 934–945 (2004)
8. Jobstmann, B., Staber, S., Griesmayer, A., Bloem, R.: Finding and fixing faults. J. Comput. Syst. Sci. **78**(2), 441–460 (2012)
9. Martin, A., Lamport, L.: Composing specifications. ACM Trans. Program. Lang. Syst. **15**, 73–132 (1993)
10. Meyer, B., Fiva, A., Ciupa, I., Leitner, A., Wei, Y., Stapf, E.: Programs that test themselves. Computer **42**(9), 46–55 (2009)
11. Pill, I., Quaritsch, T.: An ltl sat encoding for behavioral diagnosis. In: International Workshop on the Principles of Diagnosis, pp. 67–74 (2012)
12. Pill, I., Quaritsch, T.: Behavioral diagnosis of ltl specifications at operator level. In: Proceedings of the Twenty-Third International Joint Conference on Artificial Intelligence, pp. 1053–1059. AAAI Press (2013)
13. Prokhorova, Y., Troubitsyna, E.: A survey of safety-oriented model-driven and formal development approaches. Int. J. Crit. Comput.-Based Syst. **4**(2), 93–118 (2013)
14. Quaritsch, T., Pill, I.: Pymbd: A library of mbd algorithms and a light-weight evaluation platform. In: Proceedings of Dx-2014 (2014)
15. Raclet, J.B., Badouel, E., Benveniste, A., Caillaud, B., Legay, A., Passerone, R.: A modal interface theory for component-based design. Fundamenta Informaticae **108**(1), 119–149 (2011)
16. Reiter, R.: A theory of diagnosis from first principles. Artif. Intell. **32**(1), 57–95 (1987)
17. Sampath, M., Sengupta, R., Lafortune, S., Sinnamohideen, K., Teneketzis, D.C.: Failure diagnosis using discrete-event models. IEEE Trans. Control Syst. Technol. **4**(2), 105–124 (1996)
18. Slätten, V.: Model-Driven Engineering of Dependable Systems. In: 2010 Third International Conference on Software Testing, Verification and Validation, pp. 359–362. IEEE (2010)

19. Stirling, C.: Modal and temporal logics (1991)
20. Sun, X., Nuzzo, P., Wu, C., Sangiovanni-Vincentelli, A.: Contract-based system-level composition of analog circuits. In: Proceedings of the 46th Annual Design Automation Conference, pp. 605–610. ACM (2009)
21. Zulkernine, M., Seviora, R.: Towards automatic monitoring of component-based software systems. J. Syst. Softw. **74**(1), 15–24 (2005)

OpenCert 2014

Modelling and Verifying Smell-Free Architectures with the ARCHERY Language

Alejandro Sanchez[1,2], Luis S. Barbosa[2], and Alexandre Madeira[2](✉)

[1] Departamento de Informática, Universidad Nacional de San Luis,
Ejército de los Andes 950, D5700HHW San Luis, Argentina
asanchez@unsl.edu.ar
[2] HASLab INESC TEC and Universidade Do Minho,
Campus de Gualtar, 4710-057 Braga, Portugal
{asanchez,lsb,madeira}@di.uminho.pt

Abstract. Architectural (bad) smells are design decisions found in software architectures that degrade the ability of systems to evolve. This paper presents an approach to verify that a software architecture is smell-free using the ARCHERY architectural description language. The language provides a core for modelling software architectures and an extension for specifying constraints. The approach consists in precisely specifying architectural smells as constraints, and then verifying that software architectures do not satisfy any of them. The constraint language is based on a propositional modal logic with recursion that includes: a converse operator for relations among architectural concepts, graded modalities for describing the cardinality in such relations, and nominals referencing architectural elements. Four architectural smells illustrate the approach.

1 Introduction

Software systems evolve to cope with contextual change. This change compromises the value a system delivers as it might come, for instance, from the market or legislation in which the system is embedded. The principal design decisions governing a system, *i.e.*, the *software architecture* [14], play a fundamental role in its ability to evolve and address change.

Architectural (bad) smells are recurrent architectural decisions that have a negative impact on the ability of a system to evolve [5]. A catalogue is presented in [6], where they are characterized in terms of the basic building blocks that *architectural description languages* (ADL) offer, *i.e.*, components, connectors, interfaces, and configurations. These design decisions may not constitute an error or fault, but violate engineering principles such as isolation of change and separation of concerns. They affect the ability to evolve since they difficult understanding, testing, maintaining, extending and reusing parts of a system.

In the context of *open source software* (OSS), architectural smells acquire further relevance. This is because one of the most important success factors is the voluntary contribution of OSS community members [1]. Thus, the easier the system is to understand, test, maintain, extend and reuse, the greater the chances

C. Canal and A. Idani (Eds.): SEFM 2014 Workshops, LNCS 8938, pp. 147–163, 2015.
DOI: 10.1007/978-3-319-15201-1_10

of involving volunteers. Formal approaches enabling the automatic verification of smell-freeness of architectures will have a positive impact in both the quality of OSS projects and in the health of the involved community [2].

The work reported in this paper aims toward such end. The approach consists in using the ARCHERY language [8,9], an ADL with formal semantics, to verify constraints specifying the absence of architectural smells in software architectures. It does not aim at replacing existing practices in OSS communities, but to complement them, as suggested by the proposal discussed in [2]. ARCHERY is organized as a basic language, named ARCHERY-CORE, and extensions built on top of it. ARCHERY-CORE allows modelling the structure and behaviour of software architectures in terms of architectural patterns, and the extensions are for specifying reconfiguration scripts and constraints.

ARCHERY-CONSTRAINT is the extension for specifying constraints upon either structure, behaviour or reconfiguration processes of architectures. The specification language is based on a propositional modal logic. As a consequence, constraints become formulæ of a modal logic, interpreted over Kripke structures obtained from ARCHERY's specifications (see [10] for reconfiguration and [11] for structure). Since the proposed approach focuses on structural constraints, modalities allow inspecting the Kripke structure obtained from an architecture, by regarding the configuration constituents and their relationships as the Kripke structure's worlds and relationships, respectively.

The underlying logic is a fully enriched μ-calculus [3]. It includes fixed points, a converse operator, two graded modalities and hybrid features. Fixed points are for specifying recursive formulæ, and thus liveness and safety conditions. The converse operator allows exploring the converse of relations, and graded modalities allow describing their cardinalities. Hybrid features consist of a mechanism to explicitly refer to specific worlds through nominals, elementary propositions, each of which is only true at the world it identifies, and a reference operator which asserts that a formula is satisfied at the world named by a specific nominal. These features make possible, for instance, to express the equality between two worlds, to denote that a world is accessible through a relation from another world, or to assert the irreflexivity of a relation. Moreover, they make possible to describe acyclic structures when included in recursive constraints [11].

The approach can be used upon recovery techniques are applied to obtain an ARCHERY model. In fact, techniques were applied in [12] to recover an ARCHERY model for an existing software system, and subsequent model-based analysis and modifications were carried out. It is worth noting that the unrestricted access to source code renders OSS systems a natural target for the presented approach.

Architectural smells described in [6], and architectures of actual software systems illustrate the approach. The architectures were either documented during development, or recovered from source code, and are described in references also available in [6]. Observe that one of the example architectures was recovered from Linux [4], an open source operating systems widely adopted.

The obtained constraints correspond to decidable fragments of the underlying logic. The fully enriched μ-calculus is known to be not decidable, however, the fragments obtained by omitting one of either the converse operator, the graded modality operators, or the hybrid features, is [3]. None of the constraints that characterize the smells requires recursion, and three of them exclude either the converse operator, the graded modality operators, or the hybrid features.

The contribution of the paper is two fold. First, the constraint language presented in [11] is extended by including graded modalities. Second, the extended language is applied to precisely model architectural bad smells, which enables formally verifying the absence of these violations to design principles.

The rest of the paper is structured as follows: Sect. 2 briefly describes the ARCHERY language; Sect. 3 characterizes the smells as structural constraints; Sect. 4 describes the fully enriched μ-calculus, the translation of structural constraints to it, and illustrates how a constraint is verified; Sect. 5 summarizes results and describes future work.

2   The ARCHERY Language

This section describes ARCHERY-CORE in a brief and partial way (detailed descriptions can be found in [8,9]), and extends the structural part of ARCHERY-CONSTRAINT presented in [11]. The language is illustrated with an architectural pattern inspired in the Java Messaging Service (JMS). It prescribes three architectural elements: *queues*, where messages are kept in a specific order; *producers*, that send messages to the queue; and *consumers*, that receive messages from the queue. In the example pattern, a consumer provides one of three possible services, depending on the received message.

2.1   ARCHERY-CORE: Modelling Structure

An ARCHERY-CORE specification comprises one or more (architectural) patterns, a variable that references the main architecture, and global data specifications (not part of the examples in this paper). A *pattern* defines one or more (architectural) elements (connectors and components), such as the JMS pattern and the Queue, Producer and Consumer elements shown in Listing 1.

```
1   pattern JMS()
2   element Queue()   interface in rcvMsg; out dlvr;
3   element Producer()   interface in start; out sndMsg;
4   element Consumer()   interface in onMsg; out func;
5     act funcA, funcB, funcC;
6   end
7   jms:JMS = architecture JMS()
8     instances
9     q:Queue();
10    p:Producer=Producer();  c:Consumer=Consumer();
11    attachments
12    from p.sndMsg to q.rcvMsg;
13    from q.dlvr to c.onMsg;
```

```
14    interface p.start as produce;   c.func as consume;
15    end
```

Listing 1. JMS Pattern and architecture

Each *element* includes an *interface* that contains one or more ports. A *port* is defined by a polarity, either in or out and a name. For instance, the interface of Queue defines two ports in line 2. An element can optionally include a set of actions, and a set of process descriptions expressed in a subset of the mCRL2 process algebra. An *action* represents an event that is not a port activation, *e.g.*, see line 5. Process descriptions are not considered in the sequel.

A variable (see line 7) has an identifier and a type that must match an element or pattern name. Allowed values are instances of a type (element or pattern), that do not necessarily need to match the variable's own type.

An architecture describes the configuration a set of instances adopt. It contains a token that must match a pattern name, a set of variables, an optional set of attachments, and an optional interface. The type of each variable in the set is limited to an element in the pattern the architecture is instance of, such as in line 10. Each attachment includes port references to an output and an input port. A port reference is an ordered pair of identifiers: the first one matching a variable identifier, and the second matching a port of the variable's instance. Then, an attachment indicates which output port communicates with which input port – see e.g. p.sndMsg with q.rcvMsg in line 13. The architecture interface is a set of one or more port renamings. Each port renaming contains a port reference and a token with the external name of the port. An example interface is shown in line 14. Ports not included in this set are not visible from the outside.

2.2   ARCHERY-CONSTRAINT: Describing Structure

Structural constraints are verified over Kripke models obtained from ARCHERY-CORE specifications. Each model includes a set W of worlds and a family R of binary relations among them, with Mod a set of relation labels. The meta-model of ARCHERY's architectures is shown in Fig. 1. The worlds are the constituents: instances, ports, actions, variables, port references, attachments, names, and renamings. The relationships among constituents conform the family R of relations. The labels of relationships in Fig. 1 become the modality symbols $m \in Mod$. For convenience, modality symbols attd and evt are included. The former names the relationship that relates two worlds representing variables connected through an attachment. It is obtained as $\mathcal{R}[vref]^\circ \circ \mathcal{R}[strt]^\circ \circ \mathcal{R}[end] \circ \mathcal{R}[vref]$, where $\mathcal{R}^\circ$ denotes the converse of a relation. The latter is obtained as $\mathcal{R}[prt] \cup \mathcal{R}[act]$.

Propositions test if a specific condition is present at a (world) w. They are classified in: (*a*) *Naming* propositions exist for each action and port name, and hold when evaluated at a world representing the corresponding action or port. (*b*) *Meta-type* propositions hold when w belongs to a specific participant set, *e.g.*, PatternInstance. (*c*) *Emptiness* is checked by a single proposition, namely Empty, which holds when w is a variable with no associated instance. (*d*) *Type*

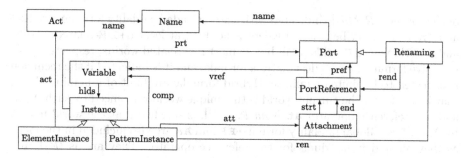

Fig. 1. Relations and roles in spatial specifications

propositions depend on the pattern definition. They test if w is an instance or a variable of a type. For example, the JMS pattern generates four proposition symbols: JMS, Queue, Producer and Consumer.

Each variable in a specification defines a nominal in the set Nom_{var}. In addition, depending on the variable's type, they are also included in a subset $Nom_{var:TYPEID}$. Then, each nominal holds exactly at the world that represents the corresponding variable.

Structural constraints are associated to a pattern or to a pattern instance. They allow precisely describing design decisions that characterize architectural patterns [11], and the absence of smells, as it is shown in this paper.

Pat	::=	**pattern** *THeader* Elem+ *SConsts*? **end**
PatInst	::=	**architecture** *IHeader* *ABody* *SConsts*? **end**
SConsts	::=	**structural constraints** *SConst*+
SConst	::=	**const** ID *Q*? *F*; *Rec** **end**
Q	::=	(**all** | **exists**) ID (: TYPEID)? .
Rec	::=	(**finite** | **infinite**) ID = *F*;
F	::=	**True** | **False** | PROP | **not** *F* | *F* **or** *F* | *F* **and** *F*
		| *F* **implies** *F* | *F* **iff** *F*
		| [*M*]*F* | <*M*>*F* | [(**Nat**,)?*M*]*F* | <(**Nat**,)?*M*>*F*
		| **A** *F* | **E** *F* | ID | NOM | **at** NOM *F*
M	::=	MOD | MOD-

Fig. 2. Grammar of structural constraints

A well-formed constraint is either a propositional formula, a modal formula, a converse formula, a graded modality formula, a recursive formula, or a hybrid formula (see grammar in Fig. 2). In a modal formula, a $\langle M \rangle F$ indicates that there exists a relationship M (named by expression M) between the present world and another world satisfying (formula) F, whereas a $[M]F$ indicates that any relationship M leads to a world satisfying F. An M non-terminal describes either a modal symbol Mod, that names a relation $\mathcal{R}[Mod]$ in the Kripke model, or the converse $\mathcal{R}[Mod]°$ indicated with Mod-. Graded modality formuæ, <n,M>F and [n,M]F, describe a world where F holds in at least n+1 M-related worlds, and a world where F holds in all but at most n M-related worlds, respectively. In recursive formulæ, an ID designates a formula, and it is indicated if the recursion is expected to be finite or infinite. Hybrid formulæ are built of a nominal *Nom*, that is satisfied if the current world is the unique world referenced by such *Nom*, and of a reference operator **at** *Nom F*, which is satisfied if at the world named by *Nom*, F is. Global modality formulæ **E**F and **A**F are also included in the logic, as they allow defining duals for the reference operator. They are as $\langle M \rangle F$ and $[M]F$ but with $W \times W$ as the underlying relation.

The quantifiers **all** and **exists** can only occur in the beginning of a constraint and have as domain the variables of the configuration. The meaning of an **all** x:TYPEID F is the conjunction of formulæ **at** i F, for each $i \in Nom_{var:TYPEID}$. The meaning of an **exists** x:TYPEID F, is a disjunction of formulæ **at** i F, for each $i \in Nom_{var:TYPEID}$.

3   Architectural Smells

In this section, the ARCHERY language is used to characterize the architectural smells in [6]: *connector envy, scattered parasitic functionality, ambiguous interfaces*, and *extraneous adjacent connector*. The smells are illustrated using the same examples used in [6], which are specified and then verified using ARCHERY. The examples do not aim at including an exact model of the software architecture, but to cover the fragment which is relevant to the smell.

3.1   Connector Envy

Components with connector envy assume responsibilities that a connector typically assumes. These responsibilities supporting interaction are classified as either concerning *communication, coordination, conversion*, or *facilitation* [7]. Communication and coordination services carry out the transfer of data and control, respectively. Conversion services address mismatches between required and provided interactions. Facilitation services cover streamlining and optimization needs in interactions.

The filesystem daemon of the Grid Datafarm [13] is an instance of connector envy [6]. The Grid Datafarm is a framework for petabyte scale data-intensive computing. It offers a filesystem distributed over the nodes of a PC cluster, where the operations in each node are facilitated by a daemon. The smell emerges as each daemon incorporates, besides its domain specific functionality, coordination behaviour that relies in a private remote procedure call (RPC) mechanism to interact with other daemons.

Listing 2 shows the specification of the pattern fragment and an instance. It only includes the daemon element GFSD, which has ports to coordinate work with peers through RPC (sndRpcCoord and rcvRpcCoord), and to allow accessing its functionality (sndResFun and rcvReqFun). The architecture consists of two instances of the daemon connected through the ports for RPC coordination.

```
1  pattern GDatafarm()
2  element GFSD()
3   interface
4     in rcvReqFun, rcvRpcCoord; out sndResFun, sndRpcCoord;
5  end
6  df:GDatafarm = architecture GDatafarm()
7   instances d1:GFSD=GFSD(); d2:GFSD=GFSD();
8   attachments
9     from d1.sndRpcCoord to d2.rcvRpcCoord;
10    from d2.sndRpcCoord to d1.rcvRpcCoord;
11 end
```

Listing 2. Fragment of Grid Datafarm pattern and example architecture

The constraint that verifies that an architecture does not suffer of connector envy is shown in Listing 3. It is divided in two parts, one that is generic and another that is specific to the pattern. The generic part comprises lines 1 to 4. It states that if a world represents an element instance, then it is not possible to access to a world that represent domain functionality and to a world that represent interaction (communication, coordination, conversion, or facilitation) from it. The specific part, line 4–8, establishes the worlds that represent functionality and interaction by indicating the propositions that hold in such worlds.

```
1  const ConnEnvy
2  A (ElementInstance implies
3     not (<evt> Function and <evt> Interaction));
4  finite Interaction = Comm or Coord or Conv or Fac;
5  finite Function = rcvReqFun or sndResFun;
6  finite Comm = False;
7  finite Coord = rcvRpcCoord or sndRpcCoord
8  finite Conv = False;  finite Fac = False;
9  end
```

Listing 3. Specification of connector envy for Grid Datafarm

3.2 Scattered Parasitic Functionality

The scattered parasitic functionality is found when a set of architectural elements share a concern while at the same time, some of them individually address an additional unrelated concern. Thus, the principle of separation of concerns is violated in two different ways: by scattering a concern among a set of elements, and by making a single element responsible of two concerns.

This smell is found in the Linux kernel architecture [6] as recovered in [4]. The PROC file system contains status information about the kernel, including its executing processes. However, it relies on other kernel subsystems to report their own status. As a result, the Process Scheduler and the Network Interface subsystems depend on the PROC file system.

Listing 4 shows an ARCHERY's specification for a fragment of the recovered architecture of the Linux kernel. The pattern includes a `ProcFS` element that receives status reports in port `rcvStatus`. It also includes the elements `NetInterface` and `ProcScheduler` that share a port `sndStatus` and an action `statusChk`, as their instances send a status report to an instance of `ProfFS`. These two elements also have unshared functionality, modelled by other actions. The architecture contains an instance of each element, and connects the other two with the `ProcFS` instance.

```
1   pattern Kernel()
2   element ProcFS()        interface in rcvStatus;
3   element NetInterface()  interface out sndStatus;
4    act connect, access, statusChk;
5   element ProcScheduler() interface out sndStatus;
6    act schedule, statusChk;
7   end
8   k:Kernel = architecture Kernel()
9    instances
10    prc:ProcFS=ProcFS(); sch:ProcScheduler=ProcScheduler();
11    net:NetInterface=NetInterface();
12    attachments
13     from sch.sndStatus to prc.rcvStatus;
14     from net.sndStatus to prc.rcvStatus;
15   end
```

Listing 4. Fragment of Linux kernel architecture

The constraint specifying the absence of the scattered parasitic functionality is shown in Listing 5. It requires that for each instance in an architecture, referenced by a nominal x, if there is a name that corresponds to an action of (the instance referenced by) x, then, it is not possible to find two actions with that name that belong to instances in the same architecture as x, which also have at least another action. The meaning of some of the expressions is as follows: <name-><act->x describes a name that corresponds to an action of x; <name-><2,act-> holds in a name shared by at least two actions; <comp-><comp>x holds in an instance placed in the same architecture as x; and <2,act>True holds in an instance with at least two actions.

```
1   const ScatteredParasiticFunc
2   all x. A ((Name and <name-><act->x) implies not
3    (<name-><2,act->(<comp-><comp>x and <2,act>True));
4   end
```

Listing 5. Specification of scattered parasitic functionality

3.3 Ambiguous Interfaces

An ambiguous interface offers a single entry point into an architectural element that offers multiple services. Instance of this smell are found in the JMS pattern, as reported in [6]. The example pattern is described in Sect. 2.

Listing 1 shows the specification that corresponds to a fragment of the JMS pattern and a software architecture. The smell is present in consumer instances that receive messages in port onMsg, but can perform any of three functionalities represented by actions FuncA, FuncB and FuncC.

The absence of cases of this smell is specified for the JMS example in Listing 6. The constraint detects the cases in which there is a single entry point, but multiple services are offered. The constraint holds if whenever there is an element instance, it is not the case that it has a number of ports less or equal to two, with one having inward direction, and it also has at least two actions that correspond to specific functionality. Note that the expressions [2,prt]False holds at worlds that represent instances that have at most two ports.

```
1  const AmbInt
2    A (ElementInstance implies not
3      ([2,prt]False and <prt>In and <2,act>Function);
4    finite Function = FuncA or FuncB or FuncC
5  end
```

Listing 6. Specification of ambiguous interfaces for JMS architectures

3.4 Extraneous Adjacent Connector

This smell occurs when two architectural elements interact through two different connector types. The presence of an extra connector type may cause a cancellation of the benefits that each of them offers individually.

The MIDAS System shows an instance of extraneous adjacent connector as reported in [6]. Communication in the system is mainly supported by event-based connectors, which are used by all high-level services. An exception is the *service discovery engine* that accesses the *service registry* using procedure calls. Then, the two components interact through two different connector types, which constitutes an instance of the extraneous adjacent connector.

The specification in Listing 7 characterizes a fragment of the pattern of the MIDAS system, and an architecture where the smell is found. It includes four elements: two connector types, and two component types. The former represent the event-based connector type Channel and the procedure call connector type PC. The component types are ServiceDiscovery and ServiceRegistry. The architecture includes an instance of each of the elements, and connects the two components using two connectors of different types. This configuration constitutes an instance of the extraneous adjacent connector.

```
1  pattern MIDAS()
2  element Channel()  interface in rcvEvnt; out sndNtf;
3  element PC()  interface in rcvPcComm; out sndPcComm;
4  element ServiceDiscovery()
5   interface in rcvNtf; out sndEvnt, sndPc;
6  element ServiceRegistry()
7   interface in rcvNtf, rcvPc; out sndEvnt;
8  end
9  m:MIDAS = architecture MIDAS()
10   instances c:Channel=Channel(); pc:PC=PC()
11   sd:ServiceDiscovery = ServiceDiscovery();
12   sr:ServiceRegistry = ServiceRegistry();
13   attachments
14     from sd.sndEvnt to c.rcvEvnt;
15     from sr.sndEvnt to c.rcvEvnt;
16     from c.sndNtf to sd.rcvNtf;  from c.sndNtf to c.rcvNtf;
17     from sd.sndPc to pc.rcvPcComm;
18     from pc.sndPcComm to sr.rcvPc;
19   end
```

Listing 7. Fragment of MIDAS Pattern and architecture

The constraint in Listing 8 specifies the absence of a case of extraneous adjacent connector. The constraint holds if whenever there is an element instance, it is not attached to connectors of different type. It is formulated in a very specific way, as it only considers the connector types of the pattern. If the pattern includes different connector types, the conjunction of the constraint needs to be reformulated, to consider all different pairs.

```
1  const ExtAdjConn
2  A (ElementInstance implies not
3   (<attd>PC and <attd>Channel));
4  end
```

Listing 8. Specification of extraneous adjacent connector for MIDAS

4   Verifying Architectural Constraints

This section describes the syntax and semantics of the fully enriched μ-calculus [3], provides a translation that takes a constraint and yields a formula in such logic, establishes the fragment of the logic used to characterize each architectural smell, and illustrates the logic with a manual verification of the formula that corresponds to the absence of the ambiguous interface smell on the model for the JMS example architecture.

The syntax of the fully enriched μ-calculus is shown in Definition 1.

Definition 1. Let *Prop* be a set of *propositional symbols*, *Mod* a set of *atomic modal symbols*, *XVar* a set of *states variables*, and *Nom* a set of *nominals*. A modal symbol β is either

(a) an atomic modal symbol α, or
(b) the converse of an atomic modal symbol (denoted as) α°.

Then, the set *SForm* of well-formed *state formulæ* of the *fully enriched μ-calculus* is the smallest set such that a state formula is either

(c) the top constant $\top$,
(d) a proposition p,
(e) a negation $\neg\varphi$,
(f) a conjunction $\varphi \wedge \psi$,
(g) a possibly operator $\langle\beta\rangle\varphi$,
(h) a state variable X,
(i) a maximal fixed point formula $\nu X.\varphi$, with every free X in φ occurring positively, *i.e.*, within the scope of an even number of negations,
(j) an at least graded modality $\langle n, \beta\rangle\varphi$ with $n \in \mathbb{N}$,
(k) a global possibly operator $\mathbf{E}\varphi$,
(l) a nominal i,
(m) a formula satisfaction operator $@_i\varphi$

where $p \in Prop$, $\{\varphi, \psi\} \subseteq SForm$, $X \in XVar$, and $i \in Nom$.   □

Derived constants and operators are obtained as follows:

$$\bot = \neg\top \qquad\qquad \varphi \vee \psi = \neg(\neg\varphi \wedge \neg\psi)$$
$$\varphi \rightarrow \psi = \neg\varphi \vee \psi \qquad\qquad \varphi \leftrightarrow \psi = \varphi \rightarrow \psi \wedge \psi \rightarrow \varphi$$
$$[\beta]\varphi = \neg\langle\beta\rangle\neg\varphi \qquad\qquad \neg\langle n, \beta\rangle\varphi = [n, \beta]\neg\varphi$$
$$\mathbf{A}\varphi = \neg\mathbf{E}\neg\varphi \qquad\qquad \mu X.\varphi = \neg\nu X.\neg\varphi[X/\neg X],$$

where $\varphi[X/\neg X]$ denotes a formula φ with all occurrences of X replaced with occurrences of $\neg X$.

Table 1. Fragments of the fully enriched μ-calculus

Logic	Clauses	Constraint (listing)
Fully enriched μ-calculus	(a)–(m)	Scattered parasitic func. (5)
Full graded μ-calculus	(a)–(j)	–
Full hybrid μ-calculus	(a)–(i), (k)–(m)	–
Hybrid graded μ-calculus	(a), (c)–(m)	Ambiguous interfaces (6)
Graded μ-calculus	(a), (c)–(j)	–
Hybrid μ-calculus	(a), (c)–(i), (k)–(m)	Extraneous adjacent conn. (8), Connector envy (3)

Restricted groups of clauses define less expressive, but useful logics. Five of these logics and the specific clauses that define them are shown in Table 1. The third column indicates which logic is required to specify each of the four architectural smells. Note that an actual recursion is not required by any of the four constraints, which may allow defining them in a less expressive logic. The translation in Definition 4 provides the correspondence between the structural constraint extension and the logic, which is used to classify the smells.

Fully enriched μ-calculus formulæ are interpreted over Kripke models.

Definition 2. A *Kripke model* for the fully enriched μ-calculus is a triple $\mathfrak{M} = (W, R, V)$ where

- W is a non-empty set of *worlds*, also called *states* or *points*;
- $R : Mod \to W \times W$ is a *relation function* that yields, for a given atomic modal symbol α, a binary relation on W; and
- $V = V : Prop \uplus Nom \to \mathcal{P}(W)$ is a *valuation function* that returns the set of worlds where a given propositional symbol or nominal holds. □

The interpretation of formulæ is described relying on the notation as follows: the expression $\mathfrak{m}[d \mapsto r]$ denotes a map $\mathfrak{m}'$ in which $\mathfrak{m}'(d') = \mathfrak{m}(d')$ for all $d' \neq d$ and $\mathfrak{m}'(d) = r$ otherwise; the set of values in the domain mapped by $\mathfrak{m}$ is called its *support*, and is denoted as $supp(\mathfrak{m})$.

The meaning of a state formula is defined in terms of sets of W, as it is described in Definition 3.

Definition 3. Let $\mathfrak{M}$ be a Kripke structure for the fully enriched μ-calculus, and $\mathfrak{s} : XVar \to \mathcal{P}(W)$ be a *state environment* that yields a set of worlds for a given state variable. The set of worlds that satisfy a state formula $\varphi \in SForm$ (Definition 1) is given by the interpretation function $[\![\cdot]\!]_\mathfrak{s} : SForm \to \mathcal{P}(W)$ inductively defined as

$$[\![\top]\!]_\mathfrak{s} \triangleq W \tag{1}$$

$$[\![p]\!]_\mathfrak{s} \triangleq \{w \in W : w \in V(p)\} \tag{2}$$

$$[\![\neg\varphi]\!]_\mathfrak{s} \triangleq W \setminus [\![\varphi]\!]_\mathfrak{s} \tag{3}$$

$$[\![\varphi \wedge \psi]\!]_\mathfrak{s} \triangleq [\![\varphi]\!]_\mathfrak{s} \cap [\![\psi]\!]_\mathfrak{s} \tag{4}$$

$$[\![\langle\beta\rangle\varphi]\!]_\mathfrak{s} \triangleq \{w \in W : \exists w' \in W.(w,w') \in \mathcal{S}[\beta] \wedge w' \in [\![\varphi]\!]_\mathfrak{s}\} \tag{5}$$

$$[\![X]\!]_\mathfrak{s} \triangleq \mathfrak{s}(X) \tag{6}$$

$$[\![\nu X.\varphi]\!]_\mathfrak{s} \triangleq \bigcup \{W' \subseteq W : W' \subseteq [\![\varphi]\!]_{\mathfrak{s}'}\} \text{ with } \mathfrak{s}' = \mathfrak{s}[X \mapsto W'] \tag{7}$$

$$[\![\langle n,\beta\rangle\varphi]\!]_\mathfrak{s} \triangleq \{w \in W : n <| \{w' \in W : (w,w') \in \mathcal{S}[\beta] \wedge w' \in [\![\varphi]\!]_\mathfrak{s}\} |\} \tag{8}$$

$$[\![\mathbf{E}\varphi]\!]_\mathfrak{s} \triangleq \begin{cases} W & \text{if } \exists w \in W.w \in [\![\varphi]\!]_\mathfrak{s} \\ \emptyset & otherwise \end{cases} \tag{9}$$

$$[\![i]\!]_{\mathfrak{s}} \triangleq \{V(i)\} \tag{10}$$

$$[\![@_i\varphi]\!]_{\mathfrak{s}} \triangleq \begin{cases} W & \text{if } V(i) \in [\![\varphi]\!]_{\mathfrak{s}} \\ \emptyset & \text{otherwise} \end{cases}, \tag{11}$$

provided that

$$\mathcal{S}[\beta] = \begin{cases} \mathcal{R}[\alpha] & \text{if } \beta = \alpha \\ \mathcal{R}[\alpha]^{\circ} & \text{if } \beta = \alpha^{\circ}, \end{cases}$$

$fsv(\varphi) \subseteq supp(\mathfrak{s})$, and $fsv(\varphi)$ denotes the free state variables of φ.   □

Definition 4 presents the translation that takes structural constraints, built as described in Fig. 2, and yields a fully enriched μ-calculus formula. A notational convention adopted to present the translation is to consider non-terminals of the grammar as sets. For instance, $f \in F$ is used to indicate that expression f is built according non-terminal F. In addition, the substitution of x by i in a constraint is denoted as $[x/i]$.

Definition 4. Given a constraint $c \in SConst$, consisting of an optional quantifier $q \in Q$, an expression $f \in F$ and optional recursion definitions $rs \in Rec*$, the translation $\mathcal{T} : SConst \to SForm$ is defined as follows:

$$\mathcal{T}(q, f, rs) = \begin{cases} \bigwedge_{i \in Nom_{var:type}} @_i \, \mathcal{T}(f, \mathcal{R}(rs))[x/i] & \text{for } q = \text{all x:type} \\ \bigvee_{i \in Nom_{var:type}} @_i \, \mathcal{T}(f, \mathcal{R}(rs))[x/i] & \text{for } q = \text{exists x:type} \\ \bigwedge_{i \in Nom_{var}} @_i \, \mathcal{T}(f, \mathcal{R}(rs))[x/i] & \text{for } q = \text{all x} \\ \bigvee_{i \in Nom_{var}} @_i \, \mathcal{T}(f, \mathcal{R}(rs))[x/i] & \text{for } q = \text{exists x} \end{cases}$$

$$\mathcal{T}(f, rs) = \mathcal{T}(f, \mathcal{R}(rs))$$

where the translation of the recursion definitions is carried out by function $\mathcal{R} : Rec* \to (ID \to SForm)$ defined as

$$\mathcal{R}(r \, rs, V) = \begin{cases} \mathcal{R}(rs, V[ID \to \mu \, ID.\mathcal{T}(f, rs)]) & \text{for } r = \text{finite ID f} \\ \mathcal{R}(rs, V[ID \to \nu \, ID.\mathcal{T}(f, rs)]) & \text{for } r = \text{infinite ID f} \end{cases}$$

$$\mathcal{R}([\,], V) = V$$

with $t \in (\texttt{finite}|\texttt{infinite})$, $f \in F$, $rs \in Rec*$, and $V \in ID \to SForm$, and the translation of $f \in F$ defined as

$$\mathcal{T}(\text{True}, V) = \top \qquad\qquad \mathcal{T}(\text{False}, V) = \bot$$
$$\mathcal{T}(\text{p}, V) = p \qquad\qquad \mathcal{T}(\text{not f}, V) = \neg \mathcal{T}(f, V)$$
$$\mathcal{T}(\text{f or g}, V) = \mathcal{T}(f, V) \vee \mathcal{T}(g, V) \qquad \mathcal{T}(\text{f and g}, V) = \mathcal{T}(f, V) \wedge \mathcal{T}(g, V)$$
$$\mathcal{T}(\text{f implies g}, V) = \mathcal{T}(f, V) \to \mathcal{T}(g, V) \qquad \mathcal{T}(\text{f iff g}, V) = \mathcal{T}(f, V) \leftrightarrow \mathcal{T}(g, V)$$
$$\mathcal{T}([\text{m}] \, \text{f}, V) = [\mathcal{M}(m)] \, \mathcal{T}(f, V) \qquad \mathcal{T}([\text{n,m}] \, \text{f}, V) = [n, \mathcal{M}(m)] \, \mathcal{T}(f, V)$$

$$T(\langle m\rangle f, V) = \langle \mathcal{M}(m)\rangle \, T(f, V) \qquad T(\langle n,m\rangle f, V) = \langle n, \mathcal{M}(m)\rangle \, T(f, V)$$
$$T(A \, f, V) = \mathbf{A} \, T(f, V) \qquad\qquad T(E \, f, V) = \mathbf{E} \, T(f, V)$$
$$T(\mathrm{id}, V) = V(\mathrm{id}) \qquad\qquad\qquad T(i, V) = i$$
$$T(\mathrm{at} \, i, V) = @_i$$
$$\mathcal{M}(m) = m \qquad\qquad\qquad\qquad \mathcal{M}(m\text{-}) = m^\circ$$

where $m \in Mod$. $\qquad\qquad\qquad\qquad\qquad\qquad\qquad\qquad\qquad$ □

Then, the translation of the constraint in Listing 6 yields formula

$$\mathbf{A} \, (ElementInstance \rightarrow \neg([2, prt]\bot \wedge \langle prt\rangle In$$
$$\wedge \, \langle 2, act\rangle \, \mu Function.(FuncA \vee FuncB \vee FuncC))).$$

A partial Kripke model for the architecture in Listing 1 is shown in Fig. 3. The model is partial since worlds representing names and their relationships are omitted. Each node in the graphic represents a world and includes: an identifier in the first line; the satisfied propositions in the second line; and the satisfied nominals

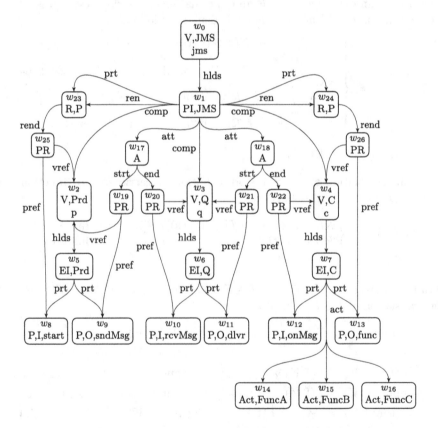

Fig. 3. Partial Kripke model for the JMS example configuration

in the third line. A short code is used instead of the actual name of propositions. The codes are: V (Variable), PI (PatternInstance), EI (ElementInstance), P (Port), I (In), O (Out), A (Attachment), R (Renaming), PR (PortReference), Act (Action), Q (Queue), Prd (Producer), and C (Consumer).

The verification of the formula is as follows:

$$\mathbf{A}\ (ElementInstance \rightarrow \neg([2, prt]\bot \land \langle prt \rangle In$$
$$\land\ \langle 2, act \rangle\ \mu Function.(FuncA \lor FuncB \lor FuncC)))$$
$$=\quad \{\ \text{duality and definition of implication}\ \}$$
$$\mathbf{A}\ (\neg ElementInstance \lor \neg(\neg \langle 2, prt \rangle \neg \bot \land \langle prt \rangle In$$
$$\land\ \langle 2, act \rangle\ \neg \nu Function.(\neg(FuncA \lor FuncB \lor FuncC))))$$
$$=\quad \{\ (2)\ \text{and duality}\ \}$$
$$\mathbf{A}\ (\neg\{w_5, w_6, w_7\} \lor \neg(\neg \langle 2, prt \rangle \top \land \langle prt \rangle \{w_8, w_{10}, w_{12}\}$$
$$\land\ \langle 2, act \rangle\ \neg \nu Function.(\neg FuncA \land \neg FuncB \land \neg FuncC)))$$
$$=\quad \{\ (1),\ \text{duality, and}\ (2)\ \}$$
$$\mathbf{A}\ \neg(\{w_5, w_6, w_7\} \land (\neg \langle 2, prt \rangle W \land \langle prt \rangle \{w_8, w_{10}, w_{12}\}$$
$$\land\ \langle 2, act \rangle\ \neg \nu Function.(\neg\{w_{14}\} \land \neg\{w_{15}\} \land \neg\{w_{16}\})))$$
$$=\quad \{\ (3), (4), (7),\ \text{and}\ (3)\ \text{again}\ \}$$
$$\mathbf{A}\ \neg(\{w_5, w_6, w_7\} \land (\neg \langle 2, prt \rangle W \land \langle prt \rangle \{w_8, w_{10}, w_{12}\}$$
$$\land\ \langle 2, act \rangle\ \{w_{14}, w_{15}, w_{16}\}))$$
$$=\quad \{\ \text{duality},\ (8),\ (5)\ \text{and}\ (8)\ \text{again}\ \}$$
$$\neg \mathbf{E}\ (\{w_5, w_6, w_7\} \land (\neg\emptyset \land \{w_5, w_6, w_7\} \land \{w_7\}))$$
$$=\quad \{\ (3)\ \text{and}\ (4)\ \}$$
$$\neg \mathbf{E}\ (\{w_7\})$$
$$=\quad \{\ (9)\ \text{and}\ (3)\ \}$$
$$\emptyset.$$

Then, the constraint is not satisfied by the architecture in Listing 1, *i.e.*, the architecture contains an instance of the ambiguous interface smell.

5   Conclusion and Future Work

This paper proposes the usage of the ARCHERY ADL to verify that software architectures are free of architectural smells found in catalogue [6]. The approach consists in specifying the absence of smells as constraints, and then verifying that architectures satisfy them. The constraint language is translated to a fully enriched μ-calculus, whose syntax and semantics are described. An architectural smell is detected in an example architecture, by showing that it fails to verify the corresponding constraint.

Future work includes the extension of the constraint language to cover the behaviour of instances and of reconfiguration scripts, and the development of a verification tool. The application of the language to case studies in Healthcare and e-Gov is also part of future developments.

Acknowledgment. This work was funded by ERDF - European Regional Development Fund, through the COMPETE Programme, and by National Funds through FCT within project FCOMP-01-0124-FEDER-028923.

References

1. Aberdour, M.: Achieving quality in open-source software. Softw. IEEE **24**(1), 58–64 (2007)
2. Barbosa, L.S., Henriquez, P.R., Sanchez, A.: Towards rigorous analysis of open source software. In: Proceedings of the 5th International Workshop on Harnessing Theories for Tool Support in Software, TTSS 2011, University of Oslo (2011)
3. Bonatti, P.A., Lutz, C., Murano, A., Vardi, M.Y.: The complexity of enriched μ-calculi. In: Bugliesi, M., Preneel, B., Sassone, V., Wegener, I. (eds.) ICALP 2006. LNCS, vol. 4052, pp. 540–551. Springer, Heidelberg (2006)
4. Bowman, I.T., Holt, R.C., Brewster, N.V.: Linux as a case study: its extracted software architecture. In: Proceedings of the 21st International Conference on Software Engineering, ICSE 1999, pp. 555–563. ACM, New York (1999)
5. Garcia, J., Popescu, D., Edwards, G., Medvidovic, N.: Identifying architectural bad smells. In: Proceedings of the 2009 European Conference on Software Maintenance and Reengineering, CSMR 2009, pp. 255–258. IEEE Computer Society, Washington, DC (2009)
6. Garcia, J., Popescu, D., Edwards, G., Medvidovic, N.: Toward a catalogue of architectural bad smells. In: Mirandola, R., Gorton, I., Hofmeister, C. (eds.) QoSA 2009. LNCS, vol. 5581, pp. 146–162. Springer, Heidelberg (2009)
7. Mehta, N.R., Medvidovic, N., Phadke, S.: Towards a taxonomy of software connectors. In: Proceedings of the 22Nd International Conference on Software Engineering, ICSE 2000, pp. 178–187. ACM, New York (2000)
8. Sanchez, A., Barbosa, L.S., Riesco, D.: A language for behavioural modelling of architectural patterns. In: Proceedings of the Third Workshop on Behavioural Modelling, BM-FA 2011, pp. 17–24. ACM, New York (2011)
9. Sanchez, A., Barbosa, L.S., Riesco, D.: Bigraphical modelling of architectural patterns. In: Arbab, F., Ölveczky, P.C. (eds.) FACS 2011. LNCS, vol. 7253, pp. 313–330. Springer, Heidelberg (2012)
10. Sanchez, A., Barbosa, L.S., Riesco, D.: Verifying bigraphical models of architectural reconfigurations (short paper). In: Proceedings of the 7th International Symposium on Theoretical Aspects of Software Engineering, TASE 2013, Birmingham, UK. IEEE (2013)
11. Sanchez, A., Barbosa, L.S., Riesco, D.: Specifying structural constraints of architectural patterns in the ARCHERY language. In: Proceedings of the International Conference of Numerical Analysis and Applied Mathematics 2014 (ICNAAM 2014): Symposium on Computer Languages, Implementations and Tools (SCLIT). AIP Proceedings (2014, to appear)
12. Sanchez, A., Oliveira, N., Barbosa, L.S., Henriques, P.: A perspective on architectural re-engineering. Sci. Comput. Program. **98**, 764–784 (2014)

13. Tatebe, O., Morita, Y., Matsuoka, S., Soda, N., Sekiguchi, S.: Grid datafarm architecture for petascale data intensive computing. In: 2nd IEEE/ACM International Symposium on Cluster Computing and the Grid, May 2002, pp. 102–102 (2002)
14. Taylor, R.N., Medvidovic, N., Dashofy, E.M.: Software Architecture: Foundations, Theory, and Practice. Wiley, Chichester (2009)

OntoLiFLOSS: Ontology for Learning Processes in FLOSS Communities

Patrick Mukala[✉], Antonio Cerone, and Franco Turini

Dipartimento di Informatica, University of Pisa, Pisa, Italy
{mukala,cerone,turini}@di.unipi.it

Abstract. Free/Libre Open Source Software (FLOSS) communities are considered an example of commons-based peer-production models where groups of participants work together to achieve projects of common purpose. In these settings, many occurring activities can be documented and have established them as learning environments. As knowledge exchange is proved to occur in FLOSS, the dynamic and free nature of participation poses a great challenge in understanding activities pertaining to Learning Processes.

In this paper we raise this question and propose an ontology (called OntoLiFLOSS) in order to define terms and concepts that can explain learning activities taking place in these communities. The objective of this endeavor is to define in the simplest possible way a common definition of concepts and activities that can guide the identification of learning processes taking place among FLOSS members in any of the standard repositories such as mailing list, SVN, bug trackers and even discussion forums.

1 Introduction

There is an increasing awareness for FLOSS environments as open participatory learning ecosystems [1,12,14] Given the structure and the volatile nature of these settings where people join and leave at any time and the lack of universal definition of concepts, understanding learning activities faces a big challenge. Moreover, empirically tracing and even studying these activities would be almost impossible without a clear understanding of key concepts.

In order to understand and document evidence of learning traces among participants in FLOSS repositories, we need a sort of guideline indication that provides a "generic" representation of the structure of information and conceptualization of knowledge pertaining to learning processes in these repositories. This can be achieved by means of ontologies, given their preponderant role in knowledge representation.

In describing the role of ontologies in computer science, Fonseca [6] supports that ontology is an engineering artifact that is constituted by a specific vocabulary used for the purpose of describing a specific reality or domain. Ontologies can also be useful for the validation of conceptual models and conceptual schemas [6]. Wilson [17] adds to this role by suggesting that ontologies "attempt to formulate

© Springer International Publishing Switzerland 2015
C. Canal and A. Idani (Eds.): SEFM 2014 Workshops, LNCS 8938, pp. 164–181, 2015.
DOI: 10.1007/978-3-319-15201-1_11

a thorough and rigorous representation of a domain by specifying all of its concepts, the relationships between them and the conditions and regulations of the domain". Furthermore, ontologies play a significant role in software engineering. Happel and Seedorf [8] advocate the adoption of ontologies to help the communities of Software Engineering and Knowledge Engineering make use of common topics and concepts. They claim that during the phase of requirements engineering, software engineers are seldom domain experts and must, therefore, learn about the problem domain from the customers. A different understanding of the concepts involved may lead to an ambiguous, incomplete specification and major rework after system implementation. Hence, it is important to ensure that all participants in this process share the same understanding of the requirements. Furthermore, Happel and Seedorf suggest that the use of a knowledge representation format would enable developers to discover sharable domain models and knowledge bases from internal and external repositories. In addition, the use of ontologies in various stages of the development lifecycle provides common grounds and vocabularies given their potential for knowledge representation and process support [8,9].

In Open Source, the adoption of ontologies is paramount. With millions of users converging on the same concepts and topics, a lack of common knowledge representation would be chaotic. Few attempts can be observed [10,13,15]. Mirbel [10] introduces and describes OFLOSSC (An Ontology for Supporting Open Source Development Communities) as an extension to the previous OSDO (Ontology for Open Source Software Development) [13]. Tifous *et al.* [15] introduce an ontology that specifies open source software environments as communities of practice from which Mirbel [10] borrows a few guidelines as well. While these ontologies describe classes and properties for participants as well as roles of individuals in Open Source environments, their scope of knowledge representation describes common concepts that need to be understood from a global perspective.

In our work instead, the focus is on learning processes in these communities. Hence, the premise of our task is predicated on the established assumption that in FLOSS communities, members engage in processes of knowledge exchange that can be regarded as learning processes. In order to explain how this takes place, we identify all relevant activities FLOSS members engage in and, on this basis, develop the ontology.

A number of studies have been critical in this instance [1–3,5,7,12]. Specifically the works conducted by Cerone [1] as well as Cerone and Sowe [2] provide ground for the identification of terms and concepts that can be used to explain learning activities, participants and related classes in FLOSS. Through an iterative process of ontologies design, the objective is to formalise and represent knowledge structures for the purpose of using them as a roadmap to understanding crucial learning resources and concepts that can be found in FLOSS repositories.

The rest of this paper is structured as follows. In Sect. 2 we discuss the adopted methodology and tools for the design of our ontology. In Sect. 3 we detail the elements of the ontology: classes and objects (Sect. 3.1) as well as properties and instances (Sect. 3.2). Section 4 concludes our paper.

2 Methodology

A wide range of methodologies exist as guidelines for the conceptualization and design of ontologies [4,11,16] For simplicity and user-friendliness, we have adopted a short methodology for designing our ontology. Based on the immense information and resources pertaining to FLOSS environments available in the literature that we have explored, we have design the ontology following a top-down approach comprising the following five steps:

1. *Information Collection*
   Our sources of information for the building of the ontologies are mainly studies on FLOSS environments in the literature [1–3,5,7,12,14] as well as generic assumptions about learning.
2. *Concepts Identification and classes? definition*
   Based on the availability of a plethora of materials on activities in FLOSS, we have defined some concepts and relations for the ontology to represent entities, resources and constraints of learning in FLOSS environments.
3. *Definition of Class Taxonomy*
   This helps in specifying and defining classes with their subclasses.
4. *Properties and Labels Definition*
   Properties give an indication of classes attributes as well as their connectivity.
5. *Ontology Formalisation*
   The language we chose for our ontology formalisation is OWL-DL given its large-scale semantic web support and the implementation is facilitated by the use of Protégé and OntVis.

Our ontology is called "OntoLiFLOSS". This is an acronym for "Ontology of Learning in FLOSS". Although we are not able to fully assert that there are empirical traces of all processes in CVS, mailing archives and bug reports, we think that the knowledge structural representation in the form of ontology may trigger further investigations and even additional research directions in FLOSS. Furthermore, we have chosen two main tools for the implementation and visualization of the ontology: Protégé 4.3 and Knoodl-OntVis. The former previews main classes as well as their subsequent subclasses while the latter helps in building graphs with relevant connecting properties between the classes.

   The previous studies on FLOSS environments [1–3,5,7,12,14] provide us with a lot of grounds for the identification of terms and concepts that can be used to identify learning activities, participants and related classes in FLOSS communities. Hence, we identified two main learning processes in FLOSS communities, Undirected Learning and Directed Learning. with Directed Learning unfolding from 2 perspectives in 4 different formats, thus totaling the number of processes to 9 (that constitute our instances in the ontology). These processes are:

Undirected Learning. This process can also be referred to as Peer-2-Peer or Reflective Learning. This kind of learning is assumed to take place between any numbers of participants. In this process, any participant can be both a receiver (Novice) and a sender (Expert). At this level, the assumption is that learning occurs between mates with a diversified expertise background who learn from each other.

Directed Learning. This process refers to involvement of more knowledgeable participants or expert members in helping less expert members to develop their skills with some level of guidance or supervision. The occurrence of the process is twofold:

Pulling. This is the process where a participant who is less expert on any topic would initiate a need to learn by reaching out to the more advanced participants that can culminate in a supervised or guided learning process. This can in turn occur according to the four formats as follow:

Modeling. In this process, the Expert's activities and actions are systematically monitored and observed by the Novice. This can happen as the receiver aims to emulate the sender given the latters reputation in their FLOSS contribution. An example could be tracking the senders commits in SVN, comments on mailing lists etc.;

Coaching. As the term explains, this involves giving direct monitoring and guidance to the requesters and then observing the requester's performance;

Scaffolding. In this process, the sender analyses and determines the receivers level of capacity and allows the receiver's opportunities to acquire knowledge accordingly. For example, supplying materials (tutorials etc.) on specific problems and a solution approach etc. based on the requesters background.

Fading. This process depicts involving a requester in practical execution of tasks for skills acquisition. However, as the requesters performance matures, the sender gradually gives the requester autonomy to apply skills.

Pushing. This is the type of directed learning that occurs when the sender takes the initiative to make available opportunities of knowledge acquisition for requesters. Just like the pulling, this process can also be understood in 4 formats: Modeling, Coaching, Scaffolding and Fading.

3 OntoLiFLOSS: Main Concepts

Based on the FLOSS information as obtained from the literature and given the purpose of our study, we have assumed that the ontology for learning processes in FLOSS called "OntoLiFLOSS" is made up of 138 entities (expandable as required) and detailed with the following main building blocks:

Classes (80). These classes are representation and classification of information on learning processes that are supported by a particular FLOSS project

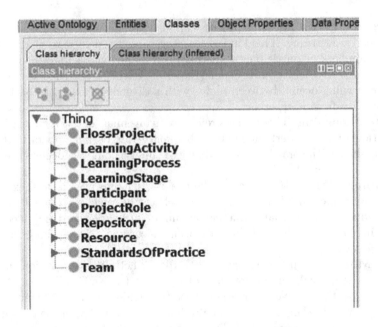

Fig. 1. Protégé snapshot of OntoliFLOSS super classes

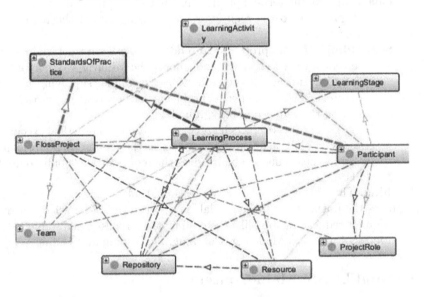

Fig. 2. Network graph of OntoliFLOSS super classes as they relate

through performing a certain number of activities referred to as "learning activities". Such activities are carried out by participants that can be either Experts or Novices with regards to their involvement in the learning process and can be organized into Teams. A number of resources are used to support

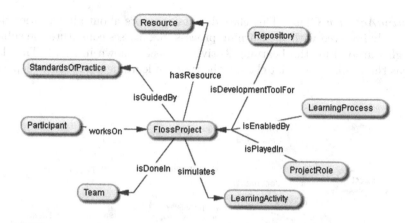

Fig. 3. Network graph of the *FLOSSProject* Class and related classes

the process that can be tracked through FLOSS repositories, to which inputs and learning outputs are committed.

Object Properties (38). These are associations or relationships that explain the link between the different classes/concepts as described above.

Data Properties (5). The data properties are attributes mainly for participants, whether they are Novices or Experts, that document their competency level, their experience, level of contributions as well as their skillset.

Annotation Properties (1). This is just a an explanatory comment on the ontology.

Individuals (9). These are the 9 identified learning processes that are represented in the Ontology as instances of the Concept/Object learning process.

Datatypes (3). These describe the data type for the 5 data properties.

3.1 Classes

Of the total of 80 classes in OntoLiFLOSS, 10 classes are super classes that can be expanded to identify subclasses at the appropriate granularity as needed. We give an abstract representation of these classes as well as their connecting associations in Figs. 1 and 2. We now give a detailed description of these 10 super classes as well as their subclasses with regard to the direct links they create with other classes.

***FLOSSProject* Class.** This class depicts any given project used in the investigation or evaluation of FLOSS environments. The instances of the class can be typical projects from Sourceforge.net or GitHub or any other FLOSS community platforms such as KDE, NetBeans or any other project of convenience.

Figure 3 reflects the direct neighbourhood for the *FLOSSProject* Class, which comprises 8 other super classes. Figure 3 gives a full visualisation graph of the neighbourhood for concepts and their related associations (through object properties).

LearningActivity **Class.** This class depicts concepts about all activities that are directly involved with the learning process. Six classes constitute the subnet or neighbourhood for the Learning Activity class as shown in Fig. 4. The class also has three subclasses that classify the types of learning activities as depicted in Fig. 4.

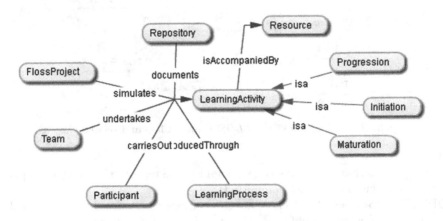

Fig. 4. Network graph of the *LearningActivity* Class, immediate subclasses and related classes

The three subclasses represent the following three stages of learning.

Initiation. Two main subclasses characterise and are part of this stage: *Observation* and *ContactEstablishement* as shown in in Fig. 5.

In *Observation*, it is implied that the learning activity or learning process spans as a result of some period of observation from either the Novice or Expert. This class also includes a number of self-explanatory subclasses such as *IdentifyExpert, FormulateQuestion, PostQuestions, ReadMessages, ReadPost, ReadSourceCode*, and *CommentPost*.

In *ContactEstablishment*, the focus of the representation is on the steps that any learning participant (Novice or Expert) undertakes to establish a contact between the actors and initiate the actual learning partnership. This happens through three activities: *ContactExpert, ContactNovice* and *SendDetailedRequest*.

Progression. In this stage, the ontology defines three subclasses: *Revert, Post* and *Apply*. Each of them further branches out with several subclasses as depicted in Fig. 6:

   Revert. This activity (class) encompasses all the steps Novice and Expert go through to provide the required information. Three basic classes or sub-activities occur here: *SendReply*, where there is a reaction to any attempt

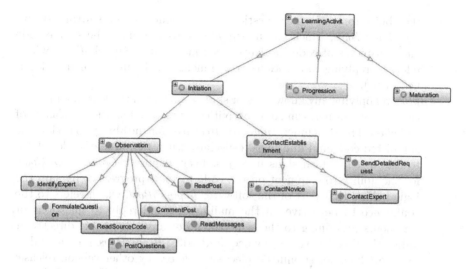

Fig. 5. Network graph representation of the *Initiation* Phase and related concepts

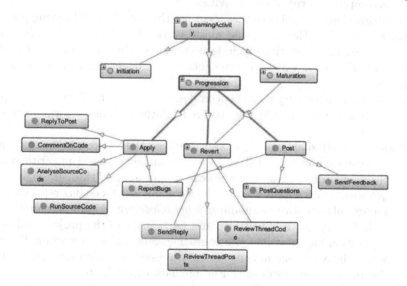

Fig. 6. Network graph representation of the *Progression* Phase and related concepts

of contact established from either the Novice or Expert; *ReviewThread-Posts* refers to the ability to analyse and react as needed to comments and posts related to a particular content that is the subject of learning; *ReviewThreadCode* concerns analysing the code (when applied) and engaging accordingly for a particular topic of interest.

Post. This is one of the basic activities that express the contributions of the Novice. It involves three activities: *PostQuestions*, which refers to the ability to ask further questions or comments on more advanced topics; *ReportBugs*, which entails the ability to scrutinize the source code and run pieces of code to identify potential flaws; *SendFeedback*, which refers to replying to questions or comments (including reporting identified flaws).

Apply. In applying any knowledge or skill as a result of the learning process, the Novice can perform some activities represented as the subclasses of this class. These include: *AnalyzeSourceCode*, for the ability to review the submitted code and find bugs, especially when the piece of code relates to the area in which skills have just been acquired; *CommentOnCode*, for the ability to comment on the code to show progress or explain the logic behind that part of the software; *ReplyToPost*, which refers to the confidence to be active on the mailing list and reply to questions or comments pertaining to the same thread or any other topic directly or indirectly linked to the newly acquired skills; *ReportBugs*, for the ability to report bugs for submitted piece of code or any other version release; *RunSourceCode*, where, in running a piece of code, the Novice is able to accomplish all the above activities.

Maturation. This class of activities identifies the last phase of learning process, which asserts how the Novice has mastered the skills learnt during the learning process. These activities include as subclasses *Analyze*, *Commit*, *Develop*, *Revert* and *Review*, which in turn contain subsequent child classes as shown in Fig. 7

Analyze. This activity (class) encompasses all the steps Novice and Expert go through to provide the required information or perform requested tasks.

Commit. With skills growing in a specific area, the Novice becomes confident and can commit some deliverables that can be evaluated and criticised by the community. These activities can be summarised through: *SubmitBugReport*, which entails the ability to commit any fix or bug report for the interest of the entire community; *SubmitCode*, which implies commit some code for any piece of software and participate to the project and build reputation for a possible role transition; *SubmitDocumentation*, through which the Novice submits documentation such as requirements elicitation documents, help document, user manuals, tutorials etc.

Develop. This basic activity summarised a set of tasks that the Novice carries out as a result of the skills learnt with regard to software development in FLOSS. These include: *FixBugs*, though which the Novice can identify possible bugs and fix them; *GiveSuggestion*, where The Novice can review peers? works and provide alternatives when needed, for example what the appropriate function might be to perform a particular task etc.; *PostCommentOnCode* refers to the ability to submit comments on the source code for enlightenment; *ReplyToSuggestion*, which entails reply and critique suggestions from other Experts or Novices in an active fashion; *WriteSourceCode*, through which the Novice can write and submit

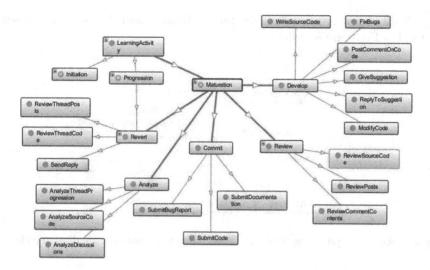

Fig. 7. Network graph representation of the *Maturation* Phase and related concepts

source code; *ModifySourceCode*, when the Novice can modify any code and implement suggestion as requested.

Revert. This is in essence the same activity as in the progress stage. In this class all activities through which the Novice and Expert exchange feedback are represented: *SendReply*, which entails react to any attempt of contact established from either the Novice or Expert; *ReviewThread-Posts*, which implies the ability to analyse and react as needed to comments and posts related to a particular content that is the subject of learning; *ReviewThreadCode*, which signifies analysing the code (when applied) and provide necessary suggestion if required.

Review. The Novice and Expert engage in a set of activities to examine the maturity of the learning process. These activities include: *ReviewCommentContents*, in which they actively engage and contribute to comments and posts in the team, about topics in the sphere of the skills acquired and possibly becoming an Expert to a new Novice; *Review-Posts*, which entails actively engaging and reacting as needed to comments and posts related to a particular content that is the subject of learning; *ReviewSourceCode*, in which they (Novice/Expert) analyse the code (when applied) and engage accordingly for a particular topic of interest.

Resource Class. This class refers to the resources used as part of learning during development in FLOSS. Such resources include the requirements description documents as well as any documentation needed for the project. Figure 8 depicts the class Resource with its direct neighbours as well as the categories of three subclasses which are part of the main resources used in FLOSS that can help identify learning processes. The three subclasses and their child subclasses, depicted in Fig. 9 are as follows:

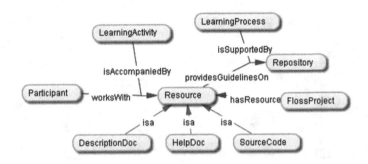

Fig. 8. Network graph of the *Resource* Class, immediate subclasses and related classes

DescriptionDoc. This class contains all the documents that provide the description for any activity or stage of the project in the team. The subclasses representing these documents include *BugReport*, which is a report outlining the description of a found reported bug in a code or piece of software at run time; *ProjectRequirementsDesc*, which encompasses the documents pertaining to the description of the project, including requirements and all related information regarding the project?s operations; *UserManuals*, which contains the guidelines for the users of the software.

HelpDoc. This class contains all the documents that provide information for any required help regarding the functionalities of the repositories and projects. These are: *FAQ*, *How-To*, and *Tutorial*.

SourceCode. This is the content of the Version Control System that contains all the coding done behind any application in FLOSS. It is a major resource of learning as it guides most the basic activities considered above.

Repository **Class.** This is the main class that represents a particular FLOSS repository where learning activities can be observed. Figure 10 depicts the class Repository as well as its neighbours and subclasses. The three subclasses are: *VersionControl*, where the source code is housed; *BugTracker*, which contains information about bugs, date of release, and description; *MailingList*, which represents the contents of interactions and discussions among participants online in FLOSS.

Team **Class.** This is the team of participants, the FLOSS community or forums where participants engage in knowledge exchange. Figure 11 depicts the properties and direct neighbours.

StandardOfPractice **Class.** These are rules of engagement that guide the interaction among participants, the usage and licensing of the deliverables in the FLOSS communities. Figure 12 shows the direct neighbourhood of classes

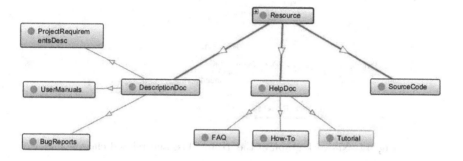

Fig. 9. Network graph of the *Resource* Class and subclasses

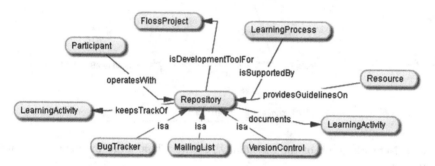

Fig. 10. Network graph of the *Repository* Class, immediate subclasses and related classes

as well as the different types of practices that can be subcategorised as follows: *GNULicense*, which represents a fundamental licensing guide for Open Source Software, and *PersonalGroundRules*, which are rules established and belonging to a given FLOSS Community.

***Participant* Class.** This class represents the participant of the learning process. The neighbouring classes are connected through associations as depicted in Fig. 13. The class has two important subclasses identified as *Novice* and *Expert*. These two concepts are critical in understanding and identifying role playing during knowledge exchange activities between FLOSS members. Subclass *Novice* represents a knowledge requester. This subclass is represented with its neighbours in Fig. 14.

With the *Expert* subclass, depicted in Fig. 15, the representation refers to the relative knowledge provider at any given point in time during interactions in FLOSS environments.

***LearningProcess* Class.** This class is the main focus and the reason of OntoLiFLOSS. To explain the existence of such a process in FLOSS, the rest of the classes in the ontology complete the need to define its semantic conceptualisation. Through a set of activities, by means of some resources, the ontology can

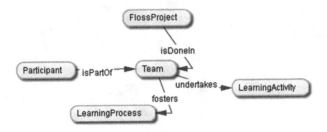

Fig. 11. Network graph of the *Team* Class and related classes

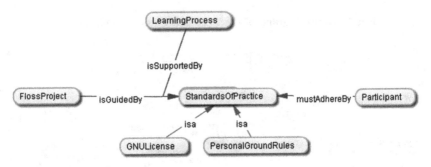

Fig. 12. Network graph of the *StandardOfPractice* Class, immediate subclasses and related classes

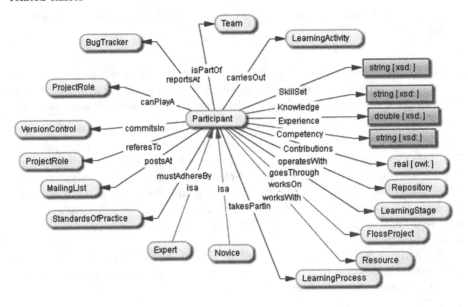

Fig. 13. Network graph of the *Participant* Class, immediate subclasses and related classes

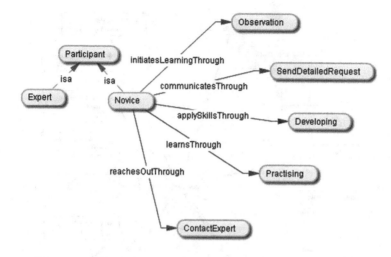

Fig. 14. Network graph of the *Novice* Class and related classes

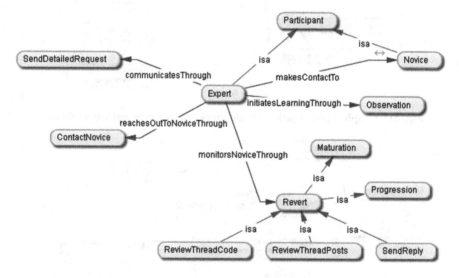

Fig. 15. Network graph of the *Expert* Class and related classes

express at some extent learning processes taking place between participants. In our context, we have identified based on some indications of studies in the literature as reported previously, nine learning processes which are shown as instances of the main *LearningProcess* class in Fig. 16. We give a more or less complete representation graph of the class and its neighbours in Fig. 17. The relationships between the connecting neighbours are given accordingly.

***ProjectRole* Class.** This subclass represents the basic roles any participants can be fulfilling in the FLOSS community. We consider the roles identified by

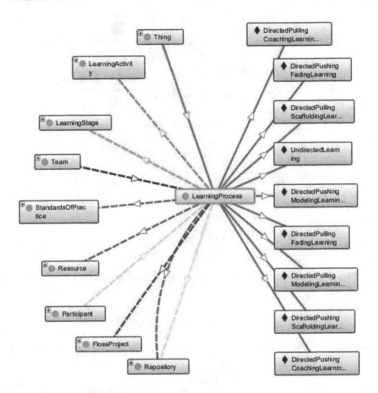

Fig. 16. Graph representation of instances of the *LearningProcess* Class

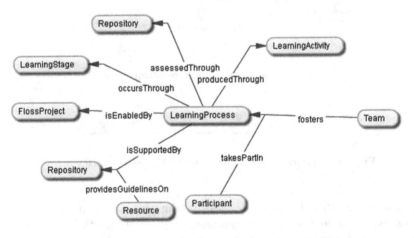

Fig. 17. Network graph of the *LearningProcess* Class and related classes

Cerone [1]: *Observer, PassiveUser, ActiveUSer, Developer,* and *CoreDeveloper.* The relationships between the connecting neighbours forming the network are given in Fig. 18.

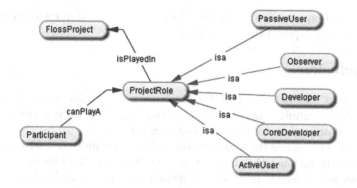

Fig. 18. Network graph of the *ProjectRole* Class, subclasses and related classes

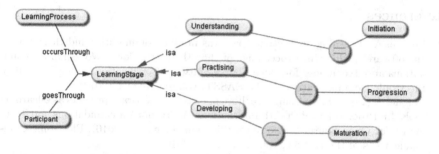

Fig. 19. Network graph of the *LearningStage* Class, subclasses and related classes

LearningStage **Class.** The objective of this class is to represent the different stages of learning that participants go through during a learning process. Hence, the *LearningStage* class clearly relates the performed activities to the different stages of learning.. Three stages can be identified relating to three layers of activities as in the *LearningActivity* class: *Understanding*, *Practicing* and *Developing*. Figure 19 depicts a different version of the representation with the subclasses *Understanding*, *Practicing* and *Developing* being depicted as equivalent classes of the *LearningActivity* class subclasses: *Initiation*, *Progression* and *Maturation*, respectively, with appropriate relationships.

3.2   Properties

Properties are ontology representations of concepts that establish links (relationship) between classes and form networks. Two main types of properties included in OntoLiFLOSS include Object and Data Properties.

About 38 Object Properties summarise the relationships and links between the different classes. Five data properties are representative of the main attributes of *Participant* (either Novice or Expert) relevant with learning. OntoLiFLOSS represents concepts for *Experience, Skill Set* (acquired through contribution),

Contributions (expressed through activities), *Competency* (built with experience) and *Knowledge* (acquired through learning).

4 Conclusion

We introduced and detailed OntoLiFLOSS as a knowledge representation for understanding learning concepts and activities in FLOSS environments. Details of classes and properties are provided and, given that the OntoLiFLOSS is specifically developed to guide the understanding of learning process in FLOSS repositories, it is fit to say that the choice of making these learning processes instances rather than subclasses is justifiable. Future work on this artifact would be to refine the ontology while we explore some empirical data in these environments.

References

1. Cerone, A.: Learning and activity patterns in OSS communities and their impact on software quality. In: Proceedings of the 5th International Workshop on Foundations and Techniques for Open Source Software Certification (OpenCert 2011). Electronic Communications of the EASST, vol. 48. EASST (2012)
2. Cerone, A., Sowe, S.K.: Using free/libre open source software projects as e-learning tools. In: Proceedings of the 4th International Workshop on Foundations and Techniques for Open Source Software Certification (OpenCert 2010). Electronic Communications of the EASST, vol. 33. EASST (2010)
3. Fernandes, S., Cerone, A., Barbosa, L.S.: Analysis of FLOSS communities as learning contexts. In: Counsell, S., Núñez, M. (eds.) SEFM 2013 Collocated Workshops. LNCS, vol. 8368, pp. 405–416. Springer, Heidelberg (2014)
4. Fernández-López, M.: Overview of methodologies for building ontologies (1999)
5. FLOSSCom Project. Using the principles of informal learning environments of FLOSScommunities to improve ICT supported formal education. http://openedworld.flossproject.org/index.php/flosscom-project-2006-to-2008
6. Fonseca, F.: The double role of ontologies in information science research. J. Am. Soc. Inf. Sci. Technol. **58**(6), 786–793 (2007)
7. Glott, R., Meiszner, A., Sowe, S.K.: FLOSSCom Phase 1 Report: Analysis of the informal learning environment of FLOSS communities. Technical report, FLOSSCom Project (2007)
8. Happel, H.J., Seedorf, S.: Applications of ontologies in software engineering. In: Proceedings of the Workshop on Sematic Web Enabled Software Engineering (SWESE) on the ISWC, pp. 5–9, November 2006
9. Hesse, W.: Ontologies in the software engineering process. In: Proceedings of the 2nd GI-Workshop on Enterprise Application Integration (EAI 2005) (2005)
10. Mirbel, I.: OFLOSSC, an ontology for supporting open source development communities. In: Proceedings of the 11th International Conference on Enterprise Information Systems (ICEIS 2009) (2009)
11. Noy, N.F., McGuinness, D.L.: Ontology development 101: A guide to creating your first ontology. Technical report, Stanford University (2001)
12. Rubin, V., Günther, C.W., van der Aalst, W.M.P., Kindler, E., van Dongen, B.F., Schäfer, W.: Process mining framework for software processes. In: Wang, Q., Pfahl, D., Raffo, D.M. (eds.) ICSP 2007. LNCS, vol. 4470, pp. 169–181. Springer, Heidelberg (2007)

13. Simmons, G.L., Dillon, T.S.: Towards an ontology for open source software development. In: Damiani, E., Fitzgerald, B., Scacchi, W., Scotto, M., Succi, G. (eds.) Open Source Systems. IFIP AICT, vol. 203, pp. 65–75. Springer, Boston (2006)
14. Sowe, S.K., Stamelos, I.: Reflection on knowledge sharing in F/OSS projects. In: Russo, B., Damiani, E., Hissam, S., Lundell, B., Succi, G. (eds.) Open Source Development, Communities and Quality. IFIP AICT, vol. 275, pp. 351–358. Springer, Boston (2008)
15. Tifous, A., Ghali, A.E., Dieng-Kuntz, A.E., Christina, A.G.C., Vidou, G.: An ontology for supporting communities of practice. In: Proceedings of the 4th International Conference on Knowledge Capture, pp. 39–46. ACM, October 2007
16. Uschold, M., Gruninger, M.: Ontologies: principles, methods and applications. Knowl. Eng. Rev. 11(02), 93–136 (1996)
17. Wilson, R.: The role of ontologies in teaching and learning. Technical report, TechWatch (2004)

Process Mining Event Logs from FLOSS Data: State of the Art and Perspectives

Patrick Mukala[✉], Antonio Cerone, and Franco Turini

Dipartimento di Informatica, University of Pisa, Pisa, Italy
{mukala,cerone,turini}@di.unipi.it

Abstract. Free/Libre Open Source Software (FLOSS) is a phenomenon that has undoubtedly triggered extensive research endeavors. At the heart of these initiatives is the ability to mine data from FLOSS repositories with the hope of revealing empirical evidence to answer existing questions on the FLOSS development process. In spite of the success produced with existing mining techniques, emerging questions about FLOSS data require alternative and more appropriate ways to explore and analyse such data.

In this paper, we explore a different perspective called *process mining*. Process mining has been proved to be successful in terms of tracing and reconstructing process models from data logs (event logs). The chief objective of our analysis is threefold. We aim to achieve: (1) conformance to predefined models; (2) discovery of new model patterns; and, finally, (3) extension to predefined models.

1 Introduction

Since the mid nineties, there has been considerable work in the field of process mining. A number of techniques and algorithms enable the reenactment and discovery of process models from event logs (data) [21]. As the field matures and achieves critical success in process modelling, we suggest applying such techniques and algorithms to software process modelling in order to document and explain activities involved in the software development process. Hence, a practical example would be process mining Software Configuration Management (SCM) systems, such as CVS or subversion systems, for the purpose of modelling software development processes. These systems are popular in the world of Free/Libre OpenSource Software (FLOSS). FLOSS repositories store massive volumes of data about the software development activities. Applying process mining carries a non-negligible potential for understanding patterns in these data.

However, there have been limited efforts in applying process mining to the analysis of data in FLOSS environments. The only attempt in our knowledge consists in combining a number of software repositories in order to generate a log for process mining and analysis [12]. Such work exemplifies how process mining can be applied to understand software development processes based on audit trail documents recorded by the SCM during the development cycle.

© Springer International Publishing Switzerland 2015
C. Canal and A. Idani (Eds.): SEFM 2014 Workshops, LNCS 8938, pp. 182–198, 2015.
DOI: 10.1007/978-3-319-15201-1_12

The objective of our work is to open the discussion and possibly pave a way in introducing and adopting process mining as a viable alternative in analysing and discovering workflow models from email discussions, code comments, bug reviews and reports that are widely found in FLOSS environments. Our discussion can be predicated on the assumption that by looking at some of the existing techniques in mining software repositories, some benchmarks and guidelines can be defined to explore similar questions via the use of process mining and possibly assess its potential in so doing.

In this paper we investigate some of the state of the art techniques and activities for mining software repositories. We refer the reader to a similar endeavor by Kagdi, Collard and Maletic [10] for a detailed report in this regard. Their survey is quite expressive of critical milestones reached as part of mining software repositories. Instead, we succinctly select and present some of these mining perspectives in convergence with the objectives of our endeavor. We consider these approaches in terms of the type of software repositories to be mined, the expected results guiding the process of mining as well as the methodology and techniques used herein.

The reminder of the paper is structured as follows. In Sect. 2 we discuss some leading factors taken into account while mining repositories. In Sect. 3 selected mining techniques are described. Section 4 gives a condensed overview of some tools developed over the years to mine software repositories. In Sect. 5 we describe process mining as related to the previous sections. Finally, Sect. 6 concludes our work with the prospects of process mining FLOSS repositories as well as directions for future related work.

2   Mining Software Repositories: Leading Factors

The analysis of software repositories is driven by a large variety of factors. We consider four factors outlined by Kagdi, Collard and Maletic [10]: information sources, the purpose of investigation, the methodology and the quality of the output.

The first factor, information resources, depicts the repositories storing the data to be mined. There is a wide literature on mining software repositories [7,8,13]. Some notable sources include source-control systems, defect-racking systems and archived communications as the main sources of data utilised while conducting investigations in FLOSS [7,10]. Source-control systems are repositories for storing and managing source code files in FLOSS. Defect-tracking systems, as the name suggests, manage bug and changes reporting. Archived communications encompass message exchanges via email in discussion groups and forums between FLOSS participants.

The next critical element at the heart of mining software repositories is the purpose. This is at the start of any research endeavor. It defines the objectives and produces questions whose answers are sought afterwards, during the investigation. This aims to determine what the output of process mining should be. After identifying the sources, determining the purpose, there is still room for deciding on the methodology for mining data and answering the questions. Due to the investigative nature of questions, available approaches present in the literature revolve around setting some metrics that need to be verified against the extracted data. For example, some metrics for assessing software complexity such as extensibility and defect density, can be verified on different versions of submitted software in SVN over a period of time and deduce properties that explain some form of software evolution.

The last factor paramount to the investigation of FLOSS repositories is evaluation. This is the evaluation of hypotheses that have been formulated according to the objectives of the investigation. In the context of software evolution, two assessment metrics for evaluation are borrowed from the area of information retrieval. These include precision and recall on the amount of information used as well as its relevance. In our case, the plan is to produce some models, process models primarily, and these models are to be evaluated and validated through a number of ways we deem appropriate.

3   Mining Techniques: Selected, Relevant Approaches

3.1   Bug Fixing Analysis

The first relevant attempt in mining software repositories pertains to analysing bug fixing in FLOSS. Śliwerski, Zimmermann and Zeller [18] present some results on their investigation on how bugs are fixed through introduced changes in FLOSS. The main repositories they used are CVS and Bugzilla along with the relevant metadata. While the purpose of their work was to locate changes that induce bug fixing by coupling a CVS to a BUGZILLA, our interest is to describe the methodology they used to investigate these repositories. Their methodology can be summarized in these three steps:

1. Starting with a bug report in the bug database, indicating a fixed problem.
2. Extracting the associated change from the version archive, this indicates the location of the fix.
3. Determining the earlier change at this location that was applied before the bug was reported.

Step 1 is to identify fixes. This is done on two levels: *syntactic* and *semantic* levels. At the syntactic level, the objective is to infer links from a CVS log to a bug report while at the semantic level the goal is to validate a link using the data from the bug report [18]. In practice, this is carried out as follows.

Syntactically, log messages are split into a stream of tokens in order to identify the link to Bugzilla. The split generates one of the following items as a token:

– a *bug number*, if it matches one of the following regular expressions (given in FLEX syntax[1]):

---

[1] FLEX syntax is used by Adobe Flex, a tool that generates programs for pattern matching in text. It receives user-specified input and produces a C source file.

- bug[# \t]*[0-9]+,
- pr[# \t]*[0-9]+,
- show_bug\.cgi\?id=[0-9]+,
- \[[0-9]+\];
- a *plain number*, if it is a string of digits [0-9]+;
- a *keyword*, if it matches the following regular expression:
  - fix(e[ds])?|bugs?|defects?|patch;
- a *word*, if it is a string of alphanumeric characters.

A syntactic confidence *syn* of zero is assigned to a link and its confidence raised by one if the number is a *bug number* and the log message contains a *keyword*, or if the log message contains only *plain numbers* or *bug numbers*. For example, the following log messages are considered:

- Fixed bug 53784: .class file missing from jar file export
  The link to the bug number 53784 gets a syntactic confidence of 2 because it matches the regular expression for bug and contains the keyword fixed.
- 52264,51529
  The links to bugs 52264 and 51529 have syntactic confidence 1 because the log message contains only numbers.

Furthermore, the role of the semantic level in Step 1 of the methodology is to validate a link (t, b) by taking information about its transaction t and check it against information about its bug report b. A semantic level of confidence is thus assigned to the link based on the outcome. This is raised accordingly and incremented by 1 following a number of conditions such as "the bug b has been resolved as FIXED at least once" or " the short description of the bug report b is contained in the log message of the transaction t". Two examples in ECLIPSE are as follows:

- Updated copyrights to 2004
  The potential bug report number "200" is marked as invalid and thus the semantic confidence of the link is zero.
- Support expression like (i)+= 3; and new int[] 1[0] + syntax error improvement
  1 and 3 are (mistakenly) interpreted as bug report numbers here. Since the bug reports 1 and 3 have been fixed, these links both get a semantic confidence of 1.

The rest of the process (Step 2 and 3) is performed manually. Returned links are inspected manually in order to eliminate those that do not satisfy the following condition

$$sem > 1 \vee (sem = 1 \wedge syn > 0)$$

As shown in Fig. 1, the process involves rigorous manual inspection of randomly selected links that are to be verified based on the above condition.

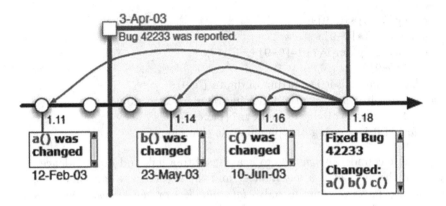

Fig. 1. Manual inspection of selected links

After applying this concept in ECLIPSE and MOZILLA with respectively 78,954 and 109,658 transactions for changes made until January 20, 2005, the authors presented their results based on their objectives for 278,010 and 392,972 individual revisions on these projects respectively. Some of these results concern the average size of transactions for fixes in both projects and the different days of the week during which most changes are projected to occur, etc.

3.2 Software Evolution Analysis

The second approach was conducted by German [5] to present the characteristics of different types of changes that occur in FLOSS. German used CVS and its related metadata as information sources. The collective nature of software development in FLOSS environments allows for incremental changes and modifications to software projects. These progressive changes can be retrieved from version control systems such as CVS or SVN and parsed for analysis. In his approach, German investigated changes made to files as well as the developers that mostly commit these changes over a period of time. His argument also suggests that analysing the changes would provide clarifications on the development stages of a project in light with addition and update of features [5].

A number of projects considered for this purpose include PostgreSQL, Apache, Mozilla, GNU gcc, and Evolution. Using a CVS analysis tool called softChange, CVS logs and metadata were retrieved from these projects for investigation. A new algorithm called *Modification Records (MRs)* is proposed by German, who also claims that the algorithm provides a fine-grained view of the evolution of a software product. Noticeable from the work is the methodology used for mining the chosen repositories. The first step was to retrieve the historical files from CVS and rebuild the Modification Records from this info as they do not appear automatically in CVS. SoftChange, through its component file revision makes use of sliding window algorithm heuristic (shown in Fig. 2) to help organize this information.

```
// front(List) removes the front of the list
// top(List) and last(List)
//    query the corresponding elements of the list
// Initialize set of all MRs to empty
MRS = ∅
for each A in Authors do
    List = Revisions by A ordered by date
    do
        MR.list = {front(List)}
        MR.sTime = time(MR.list₁)
        while first(List).time − MR.sTime ≤ δₘₐₓ∧
            first(List).time−
                last(MR.list).time ≤ τₘₐₓ∧
            first(List).log = last(MR.list).log∧
            first(List).file ∉ MR.list do
            queue(MR.list, front(List))
        od
        MRS = MRS∪ {MR}
    until List ≠ ∅
od
```

Fig. 2. Pseudocode for the *Modification Records (MRs)* algorithm

Briefly explained, the algorithm takes two parameters (δ_{max} and T_{max}) as inputs. Parameter δ_{max} depicts the maximum length of time that an MR can last while T_{max} is the maximum distance in time between two file revisions. The idea is that a file revision is included in a given MR on the basis of the following conditions:

- all file revisions in the MR and the candidate file revision were created by the same author and have the same log (a comment added by the developer when the file revisions are committed);
- the candidate file revision is at most T_{max} seconds apart from at least one file revision in the MR;
- the addition of the candidate file revision to the MR keeps the MR at most δ_{max} seconds long.

In order to conduct the analysis, knowledge of the nature and structure of codeMRs is required. Hence, the investigation is premised on an assumption that there exist six types of codeMRs reflecting different activities as undertaken by FLOSS developers. These include modifying code for Functionality improvement (addition of new features), Defect-fixing, Architectural Evolution and Refactoring (a major change in APIs or the reorganisation of the code base),

Relocating code, Documentation (reference to changes to the comments within files) and Branch-merging, e.g. code is merged from a branch or into a branch.

Rysselberghe and Demeyer [17] investigate FLOSS repositories using clone detection methods In their approach the source code in CVS as well as its meta-data are investigated in order to analyse frequently occurring changes (FACs) in source files. The idea is to document changes occurring in FLOSS using a technique tailored in the similar manner as the standard concept of frequently asked questions or FAQs. The rationale of FAQs is to gather some basic questions and answers that are representative of frequent questions and corresponding answers so as to reduce the continual posting of the same basic questions. Similarly, Rysselberghe and Demeyer consider this concept and apply it to frequent changes occurring in FLOSS. The objective is to identify frequently applied changes (FACs) since these changes record general solutions to frequent and recurring problems. Using proper CVS commands, such as some cvs log and cvs diff commands, change data can be extracted from CVS. These data include the difference in code before and after the change, the date and time of the change, the file involved. Once such information is obtained, the next step is to parse it and identify FACs. Locating FACs implies locating similar code fragments and this can be done by applying clone detection techniques.

Clone detection methods are developed to help identify duplicated or cloned code fragments in a program source code. During this process, a tool called CCFinder was used to analyze text files containing codes with FACs as retrieved using clone detection techniques. Based on some threshold values, the study asserts that high threshold values allow the identification of recurring and product-specific changes while low threshold values lead to the identification of frequently applied generic changes. Using Tomcat as a case study, observations drawn from the initial experiment include for instance that FACs identified with a high threshold and specific to one product and can be used to study and understand the motivation and success behind an applied change. Moreover, the removal of a recently added code fragment may give an indication for the reasons behind success or failure of changes in general. On the other hand, FACs with a low threshold can help in deriving low maintenance strategies automatically.

3.3   Identification of Developers Identities

The next case of FLOSS investigations is about the identification of developers identities in FLOSS repositories. Given the dynamic nature of developers behaviors in adopting different identities in distinct FLOSS projects, the task of identification becomes cumbersome. Nevertheless, one solution in this regards has been to integrate data from multiple repositories where developers contribute. Sowe and Cerone [19], using repositories from the FLOSSMetrics project, proposed a methodology to identify developers who make contributions both by committing code to SVN and posting messages to mailing lists.

Robles and Gonzalez-Barahona [14] conducted a similar study, based on the application of heuristics, to identify the many identities used by developers.

Their methodology was applied on the GNOME project where 464,953 messages from 36,399 distinct e-mail addresses were fetched and analysed, 123,739 bug reports from 41,835 reporters, and 382,271 comments from 10,257 posters were retrieved from the bug tracking system. Around 2,000,000 commits, made by 1,067 different committers, were found in the CVS repository. The results showed that 108,170 distinct identities could be extracted and for those identities, 47,262 matches were found, of which 40,003 were distinct (with the Matches table containing that number of entries). Using the information in the Matches table, 34,648 unique persons were identified.

3.4 Source Code Investigation

In his work Yao [25] has the objective to search through source code in CVS and related metadata to find lines of code in specific files etc. This is done through a tool called CVSSearch (see Sect. 4). The technique used here to analyse CVS comments allows to automatically find an explicit mapping of the commit comment and the lines of code that it refers to. This is useful as CVS comments provide additional information that one cannot find in code comments. For instance, when a bug is fixed, relevant information is not typically extracted from code comment but can be found in CVS. Moreover, as part of FLOSS investigation, one can search for code that is bug-prone or bug-free based on CVS comments where these lines of code can be referenced.

Hence, Yao's technique entails searching for lines of code by their CVS comments in producing a mapping between the comments and the lines of code to which they refer [25]. Unlike the CVS annotate command, which shows only the last revision of modification for each line, the algorithm used here records all revisions of modification for each line. The algorithm is highlighted as follows [25]:

- Consider a file f at version i which is then modified and committed into the CVS repository yielding version $i + 1$.
- Also, suppose the user entered a comment C which is associated with the triple $(f, i, i + 1)$.
- By performing a diff between versions i and $i+1$ of f, it is possible to determine lines that have been modified or inserted in version $i + 1$, the comment C is thus associated with such lines.
- Additionally, in order to search for the most recent version of each file, a propagation phase during which the comments associated with version $i + 1$ of f are "propagated" to the corresponding lines in the most recent version of f, say $j \geq i + 1$. This is done by performing diff on successive versions of f to track the movement of these lines across versions until version j is reached.

Ying, Wright and Abrams [26] use a different perspective to investigate source code. Using the source code in CVS, the authors propose an approach to study communication through source code comments using Eclipse as a case study. This is premised on a principle of good programming that asserts that comments should "aid the understanding of a program by briefly pointing out salient details or by providing a larger-scale view of the proceedings" [26]. As part of understanding FLOSS activities, it has been found that comments in these environments are sometimes used for communication purposes. An example of a comment such as "Joan, please fix this method" addresses a direct message to other programmers about a piece of code but it is usually located in a separate archive (e.g. CVS).

3.5   Supporting Developers and Analysing Their Contributions

Another approach to mining FLOSS repositories is about providing adequate information for new developers in FLOSS. Given the dynamic mode of operations in FLOSS, it is quite difficult for newcomers who join a project to come up-to-speed with a large volume of data concerning that project Hence, a new tool called Hipikat is introduced [2,3] to this end. The idea is that Hipikat can recommend to newcomers key artifacts from the project archives. Basically, this tool is assumed to form an implicit group memory from the information stored in a projects archives and, based on this information, gives a new developer information that may be related to a task that the newcomer is trying to perform [3]. The Eclipse open-source project is used as a case study in applying this approach.

The building blocks of this approach are twofold. Firstly, an implicit group memory is formed from the artifacts and communications stored in a projects history. Secondly, the tool presents to the new developer artifacts as selected from this memory in relevance to the task being performed. A group memory can be understood as a repository used in a FLOSS work group to solve present needs based on historical experience. In essence, the purpose of Hipikat is to allow newcomers to learn from the past by recommending items from the project memory made of source code, problem reports, newsgroup articles, relevant to their tasks [2].

This model depicts four types of artifacts that represent four main objects that can be found in FLOSS projects as shown in Fig. 3: change tasks (tracking and reporting bugs like in Bugzilla), source file versions (as recorded in CVS), mailing lists (messages posted on developer forums) and other project documents like requirements specification and design documents. An additional entity called Person is included to represent the authors of the artifacts.

Finally, Huang and Liu [9] analyse developer roles and contributions. Similar to numerous other studies available in the literature, this is based on a quantitative approach to analyse data in FLOSS. Using the CVS as the experimental repository, a network analysis is performed in order to construct social network graphs representing links between developers and different parts of a project. Standard graph properties are computed on the constructed networks and thus an overview in terms of developers activities is given to explain the fluctuations between developers with lower and higher degree.

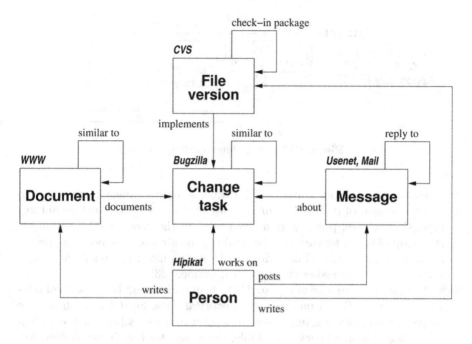

Fig. 3. Hipikat architectural model

4 Tools

Central to the sheer of work done with the purpose of mining software repositories are tools. A number of tools have been developed throughout this process,
and we look at a few to express what aspects of software repositories can be
mined using such tools.

CVSSearch. Used for mining CVS comments, the tool takes advantages of
two characteristics of CVS comments [25]. Firstly, a CVS comment more
likely describes the lines of code as involved in the commit; and secondly,
the description given in the comment can be used for many more versions
in the future. In other words, CVSSearch allows one to better search the
most recent version of the code by looking at previous versions to better
understand the current version. The tool is actually the implementation of
Yao's algorithm highlighted in Sect. 3.

CVSgrab. The objective of the tool is to visualise large software projects during their evolution. CV query mechanisms are embedded in the tool to access
CVS repositories both locally and over the internet. Using a number a metrics, CVSgrab is able to detect and cluster files with similar evolution patterns [23]. One of the key features is its particularity to interactively show
evolutions of huge projects on a single screen, with minimal browsing. The
tools architectural pipeline is given in the Fig. 4. As output, CVSgrab uses
a simple 2D layout where each file is drawn as a horizontal strip, made of

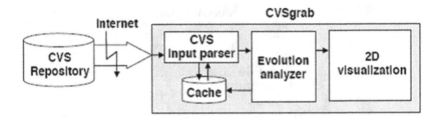

Fig. 4. CVSgrab architectural pipeline

several segments. The x-axis encodes time, so each segment corresponds to a given version of its file. Colour encodes version attributes such as author, type, size, release, presence of a given word in the versions CVS comment, etc. Atop of color, texture may be used to indicate the presence of a specific attribute for a version. File strips can be sorted along the y-axis in several ways, thereby addressing various user questions [23].

SoftChange. The purpose of this tool is to help understand the process of software evolution. Based on analysing historical data, SoftChange allows one to query who made a given change to a software project (authorship), when (chronology) and, whenever available, the reason for the change (rationale). Three basic repositories are used with SoftChange for analysis: CVS, bug tracking system (Bugzilla) and the software releases [6].

MLStats. This is a tool used for mailing lists analysis. The purpose of the tool is to extract details of emails from the repository. Data extracted from messages vary from senders and receivers to topics of message and time stamps as associated with the exchanged emails [1,15]. The tool makes use of the email headers to derive the analysis.

CVSAnalY. This is a CVS and Subversion repository analyser that extracts information from a repository. Embedded with a web interface, it outputs the analysis results and figures that can be browsed through the interface [16]. Specifically, CVSAnalY analyses CVS log entries that represent committers names, date of commit, the committed file, revision number, lines added, lines removed and an explanatory comment introduced by the committer. The tool provides statistical information about the database, compute several inequality and concentration indices and generate graphs for the evolution in time for parameters such as number of commits, number of committers etc. as needed.

5   Process Mining for Knowledge Discovery in Event Logs

Process mining is used as a method for reconstructing processes as executed from event logs [24]. Such logs are generated from process-aware information systems such as Enterprise Resource Planning (ERP), Workflow Management (WFM), Customer Relationship Management (CRM), Supply Chain Management (SCM) and Product Data Management (PDM) [20]. The logs contain records of events such as activities being executed or messages being exchanged on which process mining techniques can be applied in order to discover, analyse, diagnose and improve processes, organisational, social and data structures [4].

Van der Aalst *et al.* [20] describe the goal of process mining to be the extraction of information on the process from event logs using a family of *a posteriori* analysis techniques. Such techniques enable the identification of sequentially recorded events where each event refers to an activity and is related to a particular case (i.e. a process instance). They also can help identify the performer or originator of the event (i.e. the person/resource executing or initiating the activity), the timestamp of the event, or data elements recorded with the event.

Current process mining techniques evolved from Weijters and Van der Aalst's work [24] where the purpose was to generate a workflow design from recorded information on workflow processes as they take place. Assuming that from event logs, each event refers to a task (a well-defined step in the workflow), each task refers to a case (a workflow instance), and these events are recorded in a certain order. Weijters and Van der Aalst [24] combine techniques from machine learning and Workflow nets in order to construct Petri nets that provide a graphical but formal language for modeling concurrency as seen in Fig. 5.

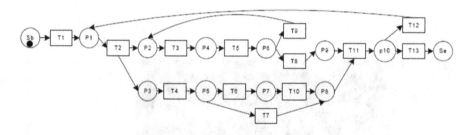

Fig. 5. Example of a workflow process modeled as a Petri net

The preliminaries of process mining can be explained starting with the following α-algorithm. Let W be a workflow log over T and $\alpha(W)$ be defined as follows.

1. $T_W = \{t \in T \mid \exists \sigma \in W.\ t \in \sigma\}$
2. $T_I = \{t \in T \mid \exists \sigma \in W.\ t = first(\sigma)\}$
3. $T_O = \{t \in T\mid \exists \sigma \in W.\ t = last(\sigma)\}$
4. $X_W = \{(A, B) \mid A \subseteq T_W \ \wedge \ B \subseteq T_W \wedge \forall a \in A \ \forall b \in B.\ a \to_W b \ \wedge$
   $\forall a_1, a_2 \in A.\ a_1 \#_W a_2 \ \wedge \ \forall b_1, b_2 \in B.\ b_1 \#_W b_2\}$
5. $Y_W = \{(A, B) \in X \mid \forall (A', B') \in X_A \subseteq A' \ \wedge \ B \subseteq B' \Longrightarrow (A, B) = (A', B')\}$
6. $P_W = \{p_{(A,B)} \mid (A, B) \in Y_W\} \ \cup \ \{i_W, o_W\}$
7. $F_W = \{(a, p_{(A,B)}) \mid (A, B) \in Y_W \ \wedge \ a \in A\} \cup$
   $\{(p_{(A,B)}, b) \mid (A, B) \in Y_W \ \wedge \ b \in B\} \cup$
   $\{(i_W, t) \mid t \in T_I\} \ \cup \ \{(t, o_W) \mid t \in T_O\}$
8. $\alpha(W) = (P_W, T_W, F_W)$.

The sequence of execution of the α-algorithm goes as follows [4]: the log traces are examined and the algorithm creates the set of transitions (T_W) in the workflow (Step 1) the set of output transitions (T_I) of the source place (Step 2) and the set of the input transitions (T_O) of the sink place (Step 3). Then the algorithm creates X_W (Step 4) and Y_W (Step 5) used to define the places of the mined workflow net. In Step 4, it discovers which transitions are causally related. Thus, for each tuple $(A, B) \in X_W$, each transition in set A causally relates to all transitions in set B, and no transitions in A and in B follow each other in some ring sequence. Note that the OR-split/join requires the fusion of places. In Step 5, the algorithm refines set X_W by taking only the largest elements with respect to set inclusion. In fact, Step 5 establishes the exact amount of places the mined net has (excluding the source place i_W and the sink place o_W). The places are created in Step 6 and connected to their respective input/output transitions in Step 7. The mined workflow net is returned in Step 8 [4].

From a workflow log, four important relations are derived upon which the algorithm is based. These are $>_W$, $\rightarrow_W$, $\#_W$ and $\|_W$ [4].

In order to construct a model such as the one in Fig. 5 on the basis of a workflow log, the workflow log has to be analysed for causal dependencies [22]. For this purpose, the log-based ordering relation notation is introduced: Let W be a workflow log over T, i.e. $W \in P(T*)$. Let $a, b \in T$. Then

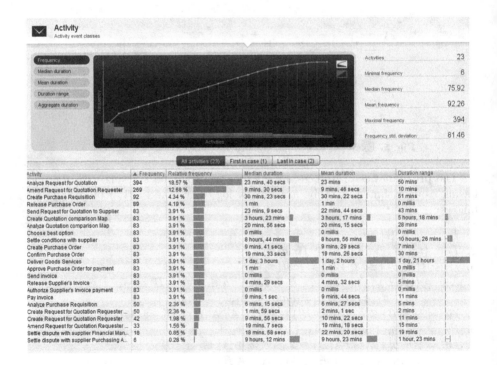

Fig. 6. A view of modeled activities in order and purchasing processes

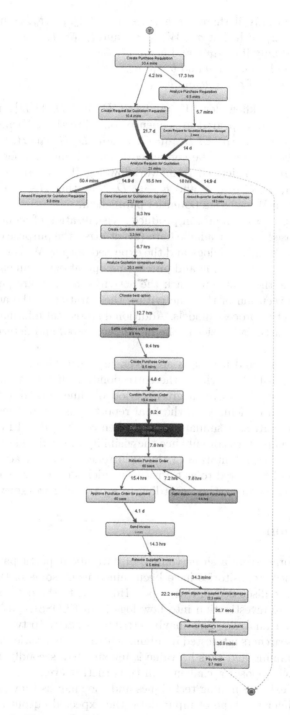

Fig. 7. Process model produced as a result of process mining

- $a >_W b$ if and only if there are a trace $\sigma = t_1 t_2 t_3 \ldots t_{n-1}$ and an integer $i \in \{1, \ldots, n-2\}$ such that $\sigma \in W$, $t_i = a$ and $t_{i+1} = b$;
- $a \rightarrow_W b$ if and only if $a >_W b$ and $b >_W a$;
- $a \#_W b$ if and only if $a >_W b$ and $b >_W a$;
- $a \parallel_W b$ if and only if $a >_W b$ and $b >_W a$.

Considering the workflow log $W = \{ABCD, ACBD, AED\}$, relation $>_W$ describes which tasks appeared in sequence (one directly following the other): $A >_W B$, $A >_W C$, $A >_W E$, $B >_W C$, $B >_W D$, $C >_W B$, $C >_W D$ and $E > WD$. Relation $\rightarrow_W$ can be computed from $>_W$ and is referred to as the (direct) causal relation derived from workflow log W: $A \rightarrow_W B$, $A \rightarrow_W C$, $A \rightarrow_W E$, $B \rightarrow_W D$, $C \rightarrow_W D$ and $E \rightarrow_W D$. Note that $B \rightarrow_W C$ follow from $C >_W B$. Relation W suggests potential parallelism.

In practice, process mining can produce a visualisation of models, as seen in Figs. 6 and 7, based on the available data (event logs), the purpose of the investigation as well as the methodology and the expected output. We consider a simple example of a log about ordering and purchasing operations in an enterprise. The core advantage is the ability to track the activities as they are performed, the authors in the execution of these activities, the duration of the activities with regards to the entire process models. Additional statistical information can also be provided about the activities in the model as rewired and determined by the goals of the analysis.

Details of events and activities are given in Fig. 6. Specifically, the user is presented with a list of activities, the corresponding timestamp as well as the authors of such activities over a given period of time. The duration of every single activity is also included in the final report as is the frequency of occurrence of these activities. A similar analysis when conducted in FLOSS promises to uncover hidden patterns or enhance the visibility of predicted occurrences. In Fig. 7, a graphical representation of the occurrence of flow of activities is constructed and can be referred to as a Process Model. This is a reenactment of all selected activities as they occur according to a particular workflow.

6   Conclusion

FLOSS repositories store a sheer volume of data about participants activities. A number of these repositories have been mined using some of the techniques and tools we have discussed in this paper. However, to the date, there has not been any concrete investigation into how logs from FLOSS repositories can be process mined for analysis. This maybe attributed partly to two apparent factors. Firstly, researchers interested in mining software repositories have not come across process mining and thus its value is unexploited; secondly, the format of recorded in FLOSS poses a challenge in constructing event logs. Nevertheless, after reviewing existing mining techniques and the analysis they provide on the data, one can infer the type of input data, the expected output and thus construct logs that can be used for analysis through any of process mining recognised tools such as the ProM framework or Disco. The example presented previously has been carried out using Disco as tool of visualisation. This approach can bring an additional flair and extensively enrich data analysis and visualisation in the realm of FLOSS data. In our future work, we plan to produce tangible examples of process models reconstructed with logs from data representing FLOSS members daily activities. These logs can be built from Mailing archives, CVS data as well as Bug reports. Our data source is OpenStack [11]. This is an environment that reunites thousands of developers and users as well as more than 180 participating organizations that work together on a number of projects and components for open source cloud operating systems. We make use of the dumps of data from this platform to produce empirical evidence of learning processes using Process Mining techniques. With a clearly defined objective and the type of data needed, process mining promises to be a powerful technique for empirical evidence provision in software repositories.

References

1. Bettenburg, N., Shihab, E., Hassan, A.E.: An empirical study on the risks of using off-the-shelf techniques for processing mailing list data. In: Proceedings of the IEEE International Conference on Software Maintenance, pp. 539–542. IEEE Computer Society (September 2009)
2. Cubranic, D., Murphy, G.C.: Hipikat: recommending pertinent software development artifacts. In: Proceedings of the 25th International Conference on Software Engineering, pp. 408–418. IEEE Computer Society (May 2003)
3. Cubranic, D., Murphy, G.C., Singer, J., Booth, K.S.: Hipikat: a project memory for software development. IEEE Trans. Softw. Eng. **31**(6), 446–465 (2005)
4. de Medeiros, A.K.A., van der Aalst, W.M.P., Weijters, A.J.M.M.T.: Workflow mining: current status and future directions. In: Meersman, R., Schmidt, D.C. (eds.) CoopIS 2003, DOA 2003, and ODBASE 2003. LNCS, vol. 2888, pp. 389–406. Springer, Heidelberg (2003)
5. German, D.M.: An empirical study of fine-grained software modifications. Empirical Softw. Eng. **11**(3), 369–393 (2006)
6. German, D.M., Hindle, A.: Visualizing the evolution of software using softchange. Int. J. Softw. Eng. Knowl. Eng. **16**(01), 5–21 (2006)
7. Hassan, A.E.: Mining software repositories to assist developers and support managers. In: Proceedings of the 22nd IEEE International Conference on Software Maintenance (ICSM'06), pp. 339–342. IEEE Computer Society (September 2006)
8. Hassan, A.E.: The road ahead for mining software repositories. In: Frontiers of Software Maintenance (FoSM 2008), pp. 48–57. IEEE Computer Society (September 2008)
9. Huang, S.K., Liu, K.M.: Mining version histories to verify the learning process of legitimate peripheral participants. ACM SIGSOFT Softw. Eng. Notes **38**(4), 1–5 (2005)
10. Kagdi, H., Collard, M.L., Maletic, J.I.: A survey and taxonomy of approaches for mining software repositories in the context of software evolution. J. Softw. Maint. Evol. Res. Pract. **19**(2), 77–131 (2007)
11. OpenStack. Openstack system usage data. http://www.openstack.org
12. Poncin, W., Serebrenik, A., van den Brand, M.: Process mining software repositories. In: Proceedings of the 15th European Conference on Software Maintenance and Reengineering (CSMR 2011), pp. 5–14. IEEE Computer Society (2011)

13. Robbes, R.: Mining a change-based software repository. In: Proceedings of the Fourth International Workshop on Mining Software Repositories, p. 15. IEEE Computer Society (2007)
14. Robles, C., Gonzalez-Barahona, J.M.: Developer identification methods for integrated data from various sources. ACM SIGSOFT Softw. Eng. Notes 38(4), 1–5 (2005)
15. Robles, G., Gonzalez-Barahona, J.M., Izquierdo-Cortazar, D., Herraiz, I.: Tools for the study of the usual data sources found in libre software projects. Int. J. Open Source Softw. Process. (IJOSSP) 1(1), 24–45 (2009)
16. Robles, G., Koch, S., Gonzalez-Barahona, J.M.: Remote analysis and measurement of libre software systems by means of the cvsanaly tool. In: Proceedings of the 2nd Workshop on Remote Analysis and Measurement of Software Systems (2004)
17. Rysselberghe, F.V., Demeyer, S.: Mining version control systems for facs (frequently applied changes). In: Proceedings of the International Workshop on Mining Software Repositories (MSR'04), pp. 48–52 (May 2004)
18. Śliwerski, J., Zimmermann, T., Zeller, A.: When do changes induce fixes? ACM SIGSOFT Softw. Eng. Notes 38(4), 1–5 (2005)
19. Sowe, S.K., Cerone, A.: Integrating data from multiple repositories to analyze patterns of contribution in foss projects. In: Proceedings of the 4th International Workshop on Foundations and Techniques for Open Source Software Certification (OpenCert 2010), Electronic Communications of the EASST, vol. 33. EASST (2010)
20. van der Aalst, W.M., Rubin, V., Verbeek, H.M.W., van Dongen, B.F., Kindler, E., Günther, C.W.: Process mining: a two-step approach to balance between underfitting and overfitting. Softw. Syst. Model. 9(1), 87–111 (2010)
21. van der Aalst, W.M., van Dongen, B.F., Herbst, J., Maruster, L., Schimm, G., Weijters, A.J.M.M.: Workflow mining: a survey of issues and approaches. Data Knowl. Eng. 47(2), 237–267 (2003)
22. van der Aalst, W.M., Weijters, T., Maruster, L.: Workflow mining: discovering process models from event logs. IEEE Trans. Knowl. Data Eng. 16(9), 1128–1142 (2004)
23. Voinea, L., Telea, A.: Mining software repositories with CVSgrab. In: Proceedings of the 2006 International Workshop on Mining Software Repositories, pp. 167–168. ACM (May 2006)
24. Weijters, A.J.M.M., der Aalst, W.M.P.V.: Process mining: discovering workflow models from event-based data. In: Proceedings of the 13th Belgium-Netherlands Conference on Artificial Intelligence (BNAIC 2001), pp. 283–290 (October 2001)
25. Yao, A.: Cvssearch: searching through source code using cvs comments. In: Proceedings of the IEEE International Conference on Software Maintenance (ICSM'01), p. 364. IEEE Computer Society (November 2001)
26. Ying, A.T., Wright, J.L., Abrams, S.: Source code that talks: an exploration of eclipse task comments and their implication to repository mining. ACM SIGSOFT Softw. Eng. Notes 30(4), 1–5 (2005)

MoKMaSD 2014

A Latent Representation Model for Sentiment Analysis in Heterogeneous Social Networks

Debora Nozza[1], Daniele Maccagnola[1]($\boxtimes$), Vincent Guigue[2], Enza Messina[1], and Patrick Gallinari[2]

[1] DISCo, University of Milano-Bicocca, Milano, Italy
Daniele.Maccagnola@disco.unimib.it
[2] LIP6, Université Pierre et Marie Curie - UPMC, Paris, France

Abstract. The growing availability of social media platforms, in particular microblogs such as Twitter, opened new way to people for expressing their opinions. Sentiment Analysis aims at inferring the polarity of these opinions, but most of the existing approaches are based only on text, disregarding information that comes from the relationships among users and posts. In this paper we consider microblogs as heterogeneous networks and we use an approach based on latent representation of nodes to infer, given a specific topic, the sentiment polarity of posts and users at the same time. The experimental investigation show that our approach, by taking into account both content and relationship information, outperforms supervised classifiers based only on textual content.

1 Introduction

"What other people think" has always been an important piece of information during the decision-making process [1], and this lead to a growing need of methods that could infer the opinion of people. The field of Sentiment Analysis (SA) aims to define automatic tools able to extract opinions and sentiments from texts written in natural language. The growing availability and popularity of social media platforms, such as online review sites, personal blogs and microblogs, opened the way to new opportunities for understanding the opinion of people. Companies, advertisers and political campaigners are seeking ways to analyze the sentiments of users through social media platform on their products, services and policies.

Several works in Sentiment Analysis, however, suffer of important limitations. Most prior work on SA applied to social network data has focused on understanding the sentiments of individual documents (posts) [2–6].

The problem of inferring the sentiment of the users has been only recently addressed by some authors [7,8]. Smith et al. [9] and Deng et al. [10] study both post-level and user-level sentiments, assuming that a users sentiment can be estimated by aggregating the sentiments of all his/her posts. Although the sentiment of users is correlated with the sentiment expressed in their posts, such simple aggregation can often produce incorrect results, because sentiment

C. Canal and A. Idani (Eds.): SEFM 2014 Workshops, LNCS 8938, pp. 201–213, 2015.
DOI: 10.1007/978-3-319-15201-1_13

extracted from short texts such as tweets (which in Twitter are limited to 140 characters) will generally be very noisy and error prone.

All of these approaches do not consider that microblogs are actually networked environments. Early studies for overcoming this limitation exploit the principle of homophily [11] for dealing with user connections. This principle could suggest that users connected by a personal relationship may tend to hold similar opinions. According to this social principle, friendship relations have been considered in few recent studies.

In [12], the authors showed that considering friendship connections is a weak assumption for modelling homophily, as two friends might not share the same opinion about a given topic. Instead, they proposed to use approval relationships (e.g. in Twitter represented by "retweets" and in Facebook represented by "like") which better represent the sharing of ideas between two users. However, in [12], the sentiment of the posts is used to infer the sentiment of the users, but not vice versa.

In order to overcome this limitation, in our approach we consider social network data as a heterogeneous network, whose nodes and edges can be of different types. Inspired by the work of Jacob et al. [13], who introduced an innovative method for classifying nodes in heterogeneous networks, we propose an approach that can infer at the same time the sentiment relative to each post and the sentiment relative to each user about a specific topic. This algorithm learns a latent representation of the network nodes so that all the nodes will share a common latent space, whatever their type is. This ensures that the sentiment of the posts can influence the sentiment of the users, and in the same way the sentiment of the posts is influenced by that of the users.

For each node type, a classification function will be learned together with the latent representation, which takes as input a latent node representation and computes the sentiment polarity (positive or negative) for the corresponding node.

The paper is structured as follows. In Sect. 2 we introduce the basic concepts that are used in our model, while in Sect. 3 we describe the model and the learning algorithm. In Sect. 4 we test our approach on a case study, a Twitter network about the topic 'Obama', and finally in Sect. 5 conclusions are drawn.

2   Preliminaries

In this section we introduce some preliminary concepts that will be used in our model. First, we give a definition of Heterogeneous Approval Network, which summarizes the structure of a social network and the information we require to determine the users' and posts' sentiment polarity. Then, we give a brief description of the techniques we use to represent and treat the textual data available in the posts.

2.1 Heterogeneous Approval Network

Following the work in [12], we assume that a user who approves a given message will share the same opinion with higher probability. Pozzi et al. defined as "approval network" a network where the nodes represent users of a social network, and a directed arc connects a user who has approved a post to the original author of that post. The most known example of approval relationship is the "retweet" feature in Twitter, which allows a user to share another user's post.

We start from the definition of "approval graph" in order to give a formal structure to our data.

Definition 1. *Given a topic of interest q, a **Directed Approval Graph** is a quadruple $DAG_q = \{V_q, E_q^{VV}, \mathbf{X}_q^V, \mathbf{X}_q^E\}$, where $V_q = \{v_1, \ldots, v_n\}$ represents the set of active users; $E_q^{VV} = \{(v_i, v_j) | v_i, v_j \in V_q\}$ is the set of approval edges, meaning that v_i approved v_j's posts; $\mathbf{X}_q^E = \{k_{i,j} | (v_i, v_j) \in E_q\}$ is the set of weights assigned to approval edges, where $k_{i,j}$ indicates the number of posts of v_j approved by v_i; $\mathbf{X}_q^V = \{c_i | v_i \in V_q\}$ is the set of coefficients related to nodes, where c_i represents the total number of posts of v_i.*

Starting from a DAG_q, the weight on the arc can be normalized to better reflect the importance of an approval.

Definition 2. *Given an Approval Graph $DAG_q = \{V_q, E_q^{VV}, \mathbf{X}_q^V, \mathbf{X}_q^E\}$, a **Normalised Directed Approval Graph** is derived as a triple $N\text{-}DAG_q = \{V_q, E_q^{VV}, \mathbf{W}_q^{VV}\}$, where $\mathbf{W}_q^{VV} = \{w_{i,j} = \frac{k_{i,j}}{c_j} | k_{i,j} \in \mathbf{X}_q^E, c_j \in \mathbf{X}_q^V\}$ is the set of normalised weights of approval edges.*

The $N\text{-}DAG_q$ represents a network with a single type of node, the users. In [12], Pozzi et al. defined a heterogeneous graph which could represent both the user-user and user-post relationships. However, the network they defined does not consider relationships among posts. In this paper, we extend their Heterogeneous Normalized Directed Approval Graph (HN-DAG_q) so that post-post relationships can be taken in account as well (Fig. 1):

Definition 3. *Given a $N\text{-}DAG_q = \{V_q, E_q^{VV}, \mathbf{W}_q^{VV}\}$, let $P_q = \{p_1, \cdots, p_m\}$ be the set of nodes representing posts about q and $E_q^{VP} = \{(v_i, p_t) | v_i \in V_q, p_t \in P_q\}$ be the set of arcs that connect the user v_i and the post p_t. Then, let $E_q^{PP} = \{(p_{t_1}, p_{t_2}) | p_{t_1}, p_{t_2} \in P_q\}$ be the set of arcs that connect a post p_{t_1} to another post p_{t_2}, and $\mathbf{W}_q^{PP} = \{w_{t_1, t_2} | (p_{t_1}, p_{t_2}) \in E_q^{PP}\}$ is the set of weights of the post-post edges. An **Heterogeneous Normalised Directed Approval Graph** is a septuple $HN\text{-}DAG_q = \{V_q, P_q, E_q^{VV}, E_q^{VP}, E_q^{PP}, W_q^{VV}, W_q^{PP}\}$.*

2.2 Vector Space Document Representation

The field of Sentiment Analysis requires the analysis of text documents, where the words occurring in a document are used to determine the opinion expressed in it. As described in the previous section, our heterogeneous network is composed

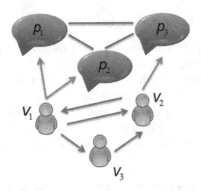

Fig. 1. Example of HN-DAG representing users and posts of a social network, connected by user-user (blue), post-post (red) and user-post (green) relationships (Color figure online).

not only by the users of a social network, but also by the textual posts every user has emitted.

For this reason, we require a way to model such text documents. The most common method applied in literature (in particular in the fields of information retrieval and text mining [14]) is the *bag of words* representation, where the words are assumed to appear independently and their order is not considered.

Given the set of posts P that are represented in our heterogeneous network, let $U = \{u_1, u_2, \ldots, u_m\}$ be the set of all the unique words occurring in P. Then, a post p_i can be represented by an m-dimensional vector $\vec{p_i}$. A usual document encoding for sentiment classification is $\mathrm{tf}(i, u)$, which is the frequency of a word $u \in U$ in post p_i. Then, the vector representation of the post is:

$$\vec{p_i} = (\mathrm{tf}(i, u_1), \mathrm{tf}(i, u_2), \ldots, \mathrm{tf}(i, u_m)) \tag{1}$$

In this work, we define the weights of the post-post edges as the value of similarity between each couple of posts. With document represented by vectors, we can measure the degree of similarity of two posts as the correlation between their corresponding vectors, which can be further quantified as the cosine of the angle between the two vectors (*Cosine Similarity*). Let $\vec{p_a}$ and $\vec{p_b}$ be the vector representation respectively of posts p_a and p_b. Their cosine similarity is computed as follows:

$$\text{similarity} = \frac{\vec{p_a} \cdot \vec{p_b}}{\|\vec{p_a}\|\|\vec{p_b}\|} = \frac{\sum_{j=1}^{l} p_{aj} \times p_{bj}}{\sqrt{\sum_{j=1}^{l} (p_{aj})^2} \sqrt{\sum_{j=1}^{l} (p_{bj})^2}} \tag{2}$$

3   Latent Space Heterogeneous Approval Model

Following the work of Jacob et al. [13], in this paper we propose a model that can, at the same time, learn the latent representation of the nodes and infer their sentiment polarity. Differently from previous works, this model performs sentiment polarity classification on all the nodes of the network HN-DAG shown in Sect. 2.1, that means we can infer the polarity for both users and posts simultaneously.

Each of the nodes, whatever their type is, is represented by a vector space model so that all of them will share the same common latent space.

The model we propose will therefore learn the proper representation of each node, and at the same time it will learn a classification function on the latent space. This ensures that the sentiment of the posts can influence the sentiment of the users, and vice versa.

The classification function will take as input a latent node representation in order to compute the polarity (positive or negative) for the corresponding node.

The proposed approach can be summarized with the following steps:

- Each node is mapped onto a latent representation in a vector space $\mathbb{R}^Z$ where Z is the dimension of this space. This latent representation will define a metric in the $\mathbb{R}^Z$ space such that two connected nodes will tend to have a close representation, depending on the weight of the connection (*smoothness assumption*).
  The latent representation for the nodes is initialized randomly.
- A classification function for inferring the polarity of the nodes is learned on the network starting from the latent representations. Nodes with similar representations will tend to have the same sentiment polarity.

In other words, both graph and label dependencies between the different types of nodes will be captured through this learned mapping onto the latent space.

In the following we describe in details the components of the proposed approach.

Given the latent representation $z_i \in \mathbb{R}^Z$ of the node x_i, we want to predict the related sentiment y_i. We are therefore searching for a linear classification function f_θ, where θ are the parameters of the linear regression. This function is learned by minimizing the classification loss on the training data:

$$\sum_{i \in \mathcal{T}} \Delta(f_\theta(z_i), y_i) \tag{3}$$

where $\Delta(f_\theta(z_i), y_i)$ is the loss to predict $f_\theta(z_i)$ instead of the real label y_i, and $\mathcal{T}$ is the training set.

In order to make sure that connected nodes have similar representations, we introduce the other following loss:

$$\sum_{i,j:w_{i,j}\neq 0} w_{i,j}\|z_i - z_j\|^2 \tag{4}$$

which forces the approach of the latent representation of connected nodes. The complete loss function is the aggregation of the classification and similarity loss:

$$L(z,\theta) = \sum_{i \in \mathcal{T}} \Delta(f_\theta(z_i), y_i) + \lambda \sum_{i,j:w_{i,j}\neq 0} w_{i,j}\|z_i - z_j\|^2 \tag{5}$$

This loss will allow us to find the best classification function and, at the same time, improve the meanings of the latent space.

In the original work of [13], the authors fixed a value of λ for all the possible edges. In our work, we decided to model the problem with three different parameters to give different weights to different types of edge, instead of a single parameter λ. Three new parameters are introduced: λ_{pp} refers to the edges connecting two posts, λ_{pv} refers to the edges connecting a post to a user and λ_{vv} refers to the edges connecting two users.

Following this idea, the loss function in Eq. 5 can be rewritten as follows:

$$L(z, \theta) = \sum_{i \in \mathcal{T}} \Delta(f_\theta(z_i), y_i) + \lambda_{vv} \sum_{\substack{i,j: w_{i,j} \neq 0 \\ i \in V \wedge j \in V}} w_{i,j} \| z_i - z_j \|^2 \tag{6}$$

$$+ \lambda_{pv} \sum_{\substack{i,j: w_{i,j} \neq 0 \\ i \in V \wedge j \in P}} w_{i,j} \| z_i - z_j \|^2$$

$$+ \lambda_{pp} \sum_{\substack{i,j: w_{i,j} \neq 0 \\ i \in P \wedge j \in P}} w_{i,j} \| z_i - z_j \|^2$$

The minimization of the loss function (Eq. 6) is performed by exploiting a Stochastic Gradient Descent Algorithm (see Algorithm 1). The algorithm first chooses a pair of connected nodes randomly. After that, if the node is in the training set $\mathcal{T}$ it modifies the parameters of the classification function and the latent representation according to the classification loss following Eq. 3. Successively, it updates the latent representation of both the nodes depending on the difference between the two representation presented in Eq. 4.

Algorithm 1. Learning$(x, w, \varepsilon, \lambda)$

1: **for** A fixed number of iterations **do**
2:    Choose (x_i, x_j) randomly with $w_{i,j} > 0$
3:    **if** $x_i \in \mathcal{T}$ **then**
4:       $\theta \longleftarrow \theta + \varepsilon \nabla_\theta \Delta(f_\theta(z_i), y_i)$
5:       $z_i \longleftarrow z_i + \varepsilon \nabla_{z_i} \Delta(f_\theta(z_i), y_i)$
6:    **end if**
7:    **if** $x_j \in \mathcal{T}$ **then**
8:       $\theta \longleftarrow \theta + \varepsilon \nabla_\theta \Delta(f_\theta(z_j), y_j)$
9:       $z_j \longleftarrow z_j + \varepsilon \nabla_{z_j} \Delta(f_\theta(z_j), y_j)$
10:   **end if**
11:   $z_i \longleftarrow z_i + \varepsilon \lambda \nabla_{z_i} w_{i,j} \| z_i - z_j \|^2$
12:   $z_j \longleftarrow z_j + \varepsilon \lambda \nabla_{z_j} w_{i,j} \| z_i - z_j \|^2$
13: **end for**

---

4 Experiments

4.1 Dataset

In order to evaluate the proposed approach, we used a dataset that contains enough information about users and posts to build a heterogeneous network as described in Sect. 2.1. Every user and post in the network has been labelled with its polarity (positive or negative).

We used the 'Obama' dataset available in [12], which has been collected from Twitter and contains the following data:

1. A set of users and their sentiment labels about the topic 'Obama' (obtained by manual tagging);
2. Tweets (posts) written by users about the topic 'Obama' with their sentiment labels (obtained by manual tagging);
3. The users' retweet network, which represent the approval connections between users.

This dataset contains 61 nodes and 187 tweets, and a total of 252 arcs representing retweet connections.

Starting from this dataset, we built a HN-DAG, where the set of nodes V_q represent the set of users who posted something about the topic 'Obama', and the set P_q represent the tweets that those users posted about 'Obama'.

We have three types of arcs connecting the nodes:

- the arcs connecting a user to another user, which weight is determined by the normalized number of retweets;
- the arcs connecting a user to a post, which in our case have 0/1 weights;
- the arcs connecting a post to another post, whose weight is determined by the cosine similarity between the two posts, as explained in Sect. 2.2.

4.2 Performance Evaluation and Settings

In order to assess the importance of relationships for determining the sentiment polarity of users and posts, we compare our method with two well-known approaches based only on the analysis of the textual data: a Support Vector Machine (SVM) and a L2-regularized logistic regression (LR). When only content is used, the posts are classified as positive or negative based on their content, while the users are classified based on the total polarity of their posts (the posts of a single user are merged and considered as a single document for determining the user's polarity).

We used the Support Vector Machine package available in LibSVM [15], using a linear kernel and default settings. The linear regression model was based on the library for large linear classification LibLinear [16].

We have considered as evaluation measures the well-known Precision(P), Recall(R) and F_1-measure:

$$P^+ = \frac{\text{\# of instances successfully predicted as positive}}{\text{\# of instances predicted as positive}} \tag{7}$$

$$R^+ = \frac{\text{\# of instances successfully predicted as positive}}{\text{\# of instances effectively labelled as positive}} \tag{8}$$

$$F_1^+ = \frac{2 \cdot P^+ \cdot R^+}{P^+ + R^+} \tag{9}$$

In the same way it is possible to compute the Precision, Recall and F-Measure for the negative class (P^-, R^-, F_1^-).

We also measured Accuracy as:

$$Acc = \frac{\text{\# of instances successfully predicted}}{\text{\# of instances}} \tag{10}$$

The performance of the proposed model can be affected by the randomness of the learning algorithm, leading to less-than-optimum results. In order to reduce this effect and improve the robustness of the classification, we used a majority voting mechanism to label the instances. In particular we performed k = 1, 5, 11, 15, 21 and 101 runs to get k predictions (votes) and we took a majority vote among the k possible labels for each node. For each k, we performed 100 experiments and considered their average performance. In the following, we report the results for $k = 21$, which show a good trade-off between the performance variability and the computational complexity.

The total number of iterations of the learning algorithm has been set to 4000000, while the gradient step ε have been set to 0.1. The size of the latent representation has been set to 40.

4.3   Results

Initially, we tested the performance of our approach by considering a case where 66 % of the nodes (randomly chosen) are considered as known. The proposed model is strongly influenced by the parameters λ_{pp}, λ_{pv} and λ_{vv} assigned to the different types of edges. Therefore, for each λ_i, where $i \in \{vv, pp, pv\}$, we investigated different values varying in the range $\{0.01, 0.05, 0.1\}$.

In Tables 1 and 2 we reported the best combinations of λ_i for classifying posts and users. The choice of the configuration is, at the current time, an empirical estimate. For the following experiments, we considered a trade-off between predicting the users and posts polarity, and therefore we chose as best configuration $\lambda_{pp} = 0.05$, $\lambda_{pv} = 0.05$, $\lambda_{vv} = 0.1$, as highlighted in the tables.

We compare the results obtained with these settings with the results achieved by the two textual approaches (see Table 3). The Latent space Heterogeneous Approval Model (LHAM) outperforms both Support Vector Machine (SVM) and Linear Regression (LR) when predicting the polarity of the posts (around 5 % improvement), and strongly outperforms them when predicting the polarity of users (more than 34 % of improvement in terms of accuracy).

In order to reduce the bias introduced by empirically choosing the values of λ_i, we computed the average performance over all possible combinations in the range $\{0.01, 0.05, 0.1\}$. The results (as reported in the last column of Table 3) show that our method still outperform the baseline algorithms when predicting

Table 1. Best configurations of λ_i for inferring the user polarity. The highlighted line represents the chosen configuration.

λ_{vv}	λ_{pp}	λ_{pv}	P+	R+	F1+	P-	R-	F1-	Acc
0.01	0.01	0.01	0.91	0.841	0.873	0.887	0.93	0.907	0.895
0.01	0.05	0.01	0.91	0.841	0.873	0.887	0.93	0.907	0.895
0.05	0.01	0.01	0.91	0.841	0.873	0.887	0.93	0.907	0.895
0.05	0.01	0.05	0.91	0.841	0.873	0.887	0.93	0.907	0.895
0.05	0.01	0.1	0.91	0.841	0.873	0.887	0.93	0.907	0.895
0.05	0.05	0.01	0.905	0.836	0.868	0.89	0.933	0.91	0.895
0.05	0.05	0.05	0.91	0.841	0.873	0.887	0.93	0.907	0.895
0.05	**0.05**	**0.1**	**0.91**	**0.841**	**0.873**	**0.887**	**0.93**	**0.907**	**0.895**
0.05	0.1	0.05	0.91	0.841	0.873	0.887	0.93	0.907	0.895
0.05	0.1	0.1	0.91	0.841	0.873	0.887	0.93	0.907	0.895
0.1	0.01	0.05	0.91	0.841	0.873	0.887	0.93	0.907	0.895
0.1	0.01	0.1	0.91	0.841	0.873	0.887	0.93	0.907	0.895
0.1	0.05	0.01	0.925	0.839	0.878	0.913	0.953	0.932	0.914
0.1	0.05	0.05	0.91	0.841	0.873	0.887	0.93	0.907	0.895
0.1	0.05	0.1	0.91	0.841	0.873	0.887	0.93	0.907	0.895
0.1	0.1	0.05	0.91	0.841	0.873	0.887	0.93	0.907	0.895
0.1	0.1	0.1	0.91	0.841	0.873	0.887	0.93	0.907	0.895

the polarity of the users, maintaining a 33 % of improvement in terms of accuracy, while maintaining a comparable performance when predicting the polarity of the posts.

In order to fully validate our approach, we tested it with different sizes of training and test sets. Therefore, we randomly split our dataset with different percentages $\{20, 33, 50, 66, 80\}$. Given the small size of the dataset, we perform a cross-validation by repeating the random split 30 times for each percentage, and therefore obtain significant results.

Tables 4 and 5 show the results of posts and users classification, performed by our model and baseline models depending on training set percentage. It is clear from the tables that our model outperforms other approaches in most of the cases, in particular when the size of the training set has a larger number of instances. While the post classification shows a slight improvement by our model over SVM and Linear Regression, for user classification we are able to achieve far better results than text-only based approaches.

While our model improves its performance for larger training set sizes, the other methods do not improve, and their performance can even decrease. The most probable explanation of this behaviour is that short-text posts are very noisy: a text-only approach is therefore more affected by the introduction of more training instances (which are regarded as more noise), while our model is

Table 2. Best configurations of λ_i for inferring the post polarity. The highlighted line represents the chosen configuration.

λ_{vv}	λ_{pp}	λ_{pv}	P+	R+	F1+	P-	R-	F1-	Acc
0.01	0.01	0.01	0.673	0.819	0.738	0.763	0.587	0.661	0.705
0.01	0.05	0.01	0.677	0.819	0.74	0.762	0.594	0.666	0.708
0.05	0.01	0.01	0.629	0.806	0.699	0.643	0.477	0.528	0.644
0.05	0.01	0.05	0.677	0.806	0.734	0.755	0.6	0.666	0.705
0.05	0.01	0.1	0.68	0.819	0.741	0.769	0.6	0.671	0.711
0.05	0.05	0.01	0.639	0.863	0.727	0.813	0.465	0.533	0.667
0.05	0.05	0.05	0.678	0.825	0.743	0.772	0.594	0.668	0.711
0.05	**0.05**	**0.1**	**0.684**	**0.819**	**0.743**	**0.772**	**0.606**	**0.675**	**0.714**
0.05	0.1	0.05	0.671	0.813	0.734	0.756	0.587	0.658	0.702
0.05	0.1	0.1	0.678	0.825	0.743	0.772	0.594	0.668	0.711
0.1	0.01	0.05	0.669	0.794	0.724	0.743	0.594	0.657	0.695
0.1	0.01	0.1	0.676	0.806	0.734	0.755	0.6	0.666	0.705
0.1	0.05	0.01	0.606	0.869	0.707	0.826	0.394	0.481	0.635
0.1	0.05	0.05	0.666	0.806	0.728	0.751	0.581	0.652	0.695
0.1	0.05	0.1	0.669	0.806	0.73	0.751	0.587	0.656	0.698
0.1	0.1	0.05	0.673	0.819	0.738	0.761	0.587	0.661	0.705
0.1	0.1	0.1	0.673	0.806	0.732	0.753	0.594	0.661	0.702

Table 3. Accuracy of users and post classification for different algorithms.

	LR	SVM	LHAM (Best λ_i)	LHAM (Average λ_i)
Users	0.467	0.552	0.895	0.886
Posts	0.66	0.657	0.714	0.680

Table 4. Accuracy of post classification for different sizes of the training set.

% Training set	LR	SVM	LHAM
20	0.613	0.597	0.542
33	0.629	0.620	0.662
50	0.642	0.641	0.718
66	0.679	0.679	0.722
80	0.660	0.669	0.739

Table 5. Accuracy of user classification for different sizes of the training set

% Training set	LR	SVM	LHAM
20	0.466	0.485	0.570
33	0.494	0.521	0.823
50	0.480	0.512	0.986
66	0.467	0.531	0.982
80	0.447	0.507	0.986

able to face this problem with the help of the additional information carried by the edges between different nodes.

The lower performance of LHAM for small percentages of the training set is explained by the behaviour of the Stochastic Gradient Descent Algorithm, which randomly chooses a pair of connected nodes at each iteration. When the number of training instances is small, the chance to pick nodes that are not in the training set will be higher. In this case, the latent representations will mostly depend on the similarity among connected nodes, and less on the correct sentiment polarity.

In order to tackle this problem, we modified Algorithm 1 as follows:

- At the beginning, starting from the training instances we create a list of "allowed" nodes;
- At each iteration, the algorithm must choose a pair of nodes where at least one of the nodes is in the list of "allowed" nodes;
- At the end of each iteration, if one of the chosen nodes was not in the list, it is added; if all the existing nodes have been added, the list is again initialized with the training instances.

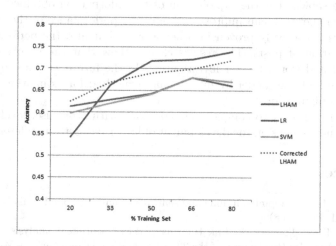

Fig. 2. Accuracy of post classification for different sizes of the training set.

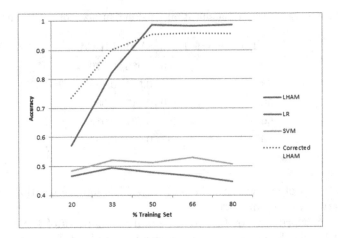

Fig. 3. Accuracy of user classification for different sizes of the training set

The corrected algorithm allows to spread the sentiment polarity information starting from the training nodes, and gradually towards the rest of the network. This permits to outperform the baseline algorithms even when dealing with small training sets both on posts and users classification. At the same time, we maintain a good performance when the training size gets larger (see Figs. 2 and 3).

5   Conclusions

In this work, we proposed a classification approach that is able to infer the polarity of users and posts in a social network, particularly in the case of microblogs (such as Twitter).

We have shown that the exploitation of the information obtained from the heterogeneous network can improve not only the performance of the classification of users (as already proven in other works), but also the performance of the classification of posts. The results clearly show that the proposed model is promising and worth further investigation. In the future we plan to improve the robustness of the model by introducing a method for estimating the best parameter configuration.

Moreover, we want to compare our approach with other user-level polarity classifiers, and to focus on the development of larger datasets on different topics.

References

1. Pang, B., Lee, L.: Opinion mining and sentiment analysis. Found. Trends Inf. Retr. **2**(1–2), 1–135 (2008)
2. Hu, X., Tang, J., Gao, H., Liu, H.: Unsupervised sentiment analysis with emotional signals. In: Proceedings of the 22nd International Conference on World Wide Web, pp. 607–618. International World Wide Web Conferences Steering Committee (2013)

3. Wang, X., Wei, F., Liu, X., Zhou, M., Zhang, M.: Topic sentiment analysis in twitter: a graph-based hashtag sentiment classification approach. In: Proceedings of the 20th ACM International Conference on Information and Knowledge Management, pp. 1031–1040. ACM (2011)
4. Davidov, D., Tsur, O., Rappoport, A.: Enhanced sentiment learning using twitter hashtags and smileys. In: Proceedings of the 23rd International Conference on Computational Linguistics: Posters, pp. 241–249. Association for Computational Linguistics (2010)
5. Go, A., Bhayani, R., Huang, L.: Twitter sentiment classification using distant supervision. Technical report, Stanford (2009)
6. Pozzi, F.A., Fersini, E., Messina, E.: Bayesian model averaging and model selection for polarity classification. In: Métais, E., Meziane, F., Saraee, M., Sugumaran, V., Vadera, S. (eds.) NLDB 2013. LNCS, vol. 7934, pp. 189–200. Springer, Heidelberg (2013)
7. Tan, C., Lee, L., Tang, J., Jiang, L., Zhou, M., Li, P.: User-level sentiment analysis incorporating social networks. In: Proceedings of the 17th ACM SIGKDD International Conference on Knowledge Discovery and Data Mining, KDD 2011, pp. 1397–1405 (2011)
8. Kim, J., Yoo, J., Lim, H., Qiu, H., Kozareva, Z., Galstyan, A.: Sentiment prediction using collaborative filtering. In: Seventh International AAAI Conference on Weblogs and Social Media (2013)
9. Smith, L.M., Zhu, L., Lerman, K., Kozareva, Z.: The role of social media in the discussion of controversial topics. In: 2013 International Conference on Social Computing (SocialCom), pp. 236–243. IEEE (2013)
10. Deng, H., Han, J., Ji, H., Li, H., Lu, Y., Wang, H.: Exploring and inferring user-user pseudo-friendship for sentiment analysis with heterogeneous networks. In: SDM, pp. 378–386 (2013)
11. Lazarsfeld, P.F., Merton, R.K.: Friendship as a social process: a substantive and methodological analysis. In: Berger, M., Abel, T., Page, C.H. (eds.) Freedom and Control in Modern Society, pp. 8–66. Van Nostrand, New York (1954)
12. Pozzi, F.A., Maccagnola, D., Fersini, E., Messina, E.: Enhance user-level sentiment analysis on microblogs with approval relations. In: Baldoni, M., Baroglio, C., Boella, G., Micalizio, R. (eds.) AI*IA 2013. LNCS, vol. 8249, pp. 133–144. Springer, Heidelberg (2013)
13. Jacob, Y., Denoyer, L., Gallinari, P.: Learning latent representations of nodes for classifying in heterogeneous social networks. In: WSDM, pp. 373–382 (2014)
14. Baeza-Yates, R., Ribeiro-Neto, B., et al.: Modern Information Retrieval, vol. 463. ACM Press, New York (1999)
15. Chang, C.-C., Lin, C.-J.: Libsvm: a library for support vector machines. ACM Trans. Intell. Syst. Technol. 2(3), 27:1–27:27 (2011)
16. Fan, R.-E., Chang, K.-W., Hsieh, C.-J., Wang, X.-R., Lin, C.-J.: LIBLINEAR: a library for large linear classification. J. Mach. Learn. Res. 9, 1871–1874 (2008)

Use of Mobile Phone Data to Estimate Visitors Mobility Flows

Lorenzo Gabrielli, Barbara Furletti, Fosca Giannotti,
Mirco Nanni$^{(\boxtimes)}$, and Salvatore Rinzivillo

KDDLAB, ISTI CNR, Via G. Moruzzi 1, 56124 Pisa, Italy
{lorenzo.gabrielli,barbara.furletti,fosca.giannotti,
mirco.nanni,salvatore.rinzivillo}@isti.cnr.it

Abstract. Big Data originating from the digital breadcrumbs of human activities, sensed as by-product of the technologies that we use for our daily activities, allows us to observe the individual and collective behavior of people at an unprecedented detail. Many dimensions of our social life have big data "proxies", such as the mobile calls data for mobility. In this paper we investigate to what extent data coming from mobile operators could be a support in producing reliable and timely estimates of intra-city mobility flows. The idea is to define an estimation method based on calling data to characterize the mobility habits of visitors at the level of a single municipality.

Keywords: Big data · Urban population · Inter-city mobility · Data mining

1 Introduction

Mobile phones today represent an important source of information for studying people behaviors, for environmental monitoring, transportation, social networks and business. The interest in the use of the data generated by mobile phones is growing quite fast, also thanks to the development and the spread of phones with sophisticated capabilities.

The availability of these data stimulated the research for increasingly sophisticated data mining algorithms customized for studying people habits, mobility patterns, for environmental monitoring and to identify or predict events. Some examples include the discovery of social relations studied in [16], where it has been highlighted the existence of correlations between the similarity of individuals movements and their proximity in the social network; the inference of origin-destination tables for feeding transportation models [10]; and, based on roaming GSM data (users arriving from other countries), the study of how visitors of a large touristic area use the territory, with particular emphasis on visits to attractions [11]. For data mining purposes, GSM data proved to be significant in terms of size and representativeness of the sample. In general, having information about the localization or the behavior of human or moving entities permits

© Springer International Publishing Switzerland 2015
C. Canal and A. Idani (Eds.): SEFM 2014 Workshops, LNCS 8938, pp. 214–226, 2015.
DOI: 10.1007/978-3-319-15201-1_14

to build support tools for applications in several domains such as healthcare, coordination of social groups, transportation and tourism.

In this work we propose and experiment an analysis process built on top of the *Sociometer*, a data mining tool for classifying users by means of their calling habits. The calling activities are used to infer the presence of the user and to construct an aggregated and compact call profile. The first prototype of the Sociometer has been developed during the project "Tourism Fluxes Observatory - Pisa", having the aim of producing a presence indicator of different categories of people in the city of Pisa [7]. The project, carried out in cooperation with the Municipality of Pisa, aimed at studying the fluxes of tourists visiting the town in order to evaluate the overall quality of the reception system on the territory, and to install a permanent monitor system. The Sociometer has been tested with positive results on real case studies both in Pisa and Cosenza [8].

In this paper we apply the Sociometer to classify the users moving in the city of Pisa. In particular, we concentrate in the urban area of the city and focus only on the sub-population of visitors – which complements previous analyses performed, mainly focused on residents and commuters, i.e. classes of users visiting the territory on a regular basis. Our objective is to produce statistics that are capable of estimating the probability of observing visitors moving across the urban area rather than arriving and staying in a limited zone. Indeed, such larger-scale visitors represent the group of people that might benefit most from an improved information about city attractions, navigation assistance and public transportation services. Therefore, it is crucial to better understand what kind of mobility (strictly localized vs. over all the city) visitors tend to follow, and in which measure.

The advantage of having defined the call profiles is that the analysis is no more based on the original GSM raw (big and privacy sensitive) data, but on an aggregated privacy-preserving summary of the original data. This allows the Telco operators to disclose only information that satisfy the required level of privacy, respecting the laws and preserving their customers. At the same way the analysts can work with data that are still meaningful. To this aim we also developed a method to measure and handle the privacy risks involved in the distribution of individual habits.

2   Related Works

The use of GSM traces for studying the mobility of users is a growing research area. An increasing number of approaches propose to use GSM data for extracting presence and/or movement patterns and users behavior. We already cited in Sect. 1 the Sociometer [6] as a method for identifying mobility behavior categories starting from call profiles, and the possibility to perform number of analysis about presences and flows of peoples in various cities [7,8]. Among the literature we can recall a famous experiments on analysing GSM data for studying people movement have been run on Rome [3] and Graz [4]. GSM data are used to realize a real-time urban monitoring systems with the aim of realizing a wide range of services for the city such as traffic monitoring and tourists movement analysis. The authors get detailed real time data by installing additional hardware on top of the existing antennas to get an improved location of the users in the networks.

A different approach comes from Schlaich et al. [14] where the authors exploit the GSM handover data - the aggregated number of users flowing between cells - to perform the reconstruction of vehicles trajectories. The objective is to study the route-choice-behavior or car drivers in order to determine the impact of traffic state.

Another use of GSM data is the identification of interesting users places as in [2], where the authors propose a method for the identification of meaningful places relative to mobile telephone users, such as home and work points. They use GSM data (both calls and handovers) collected by the phone operator. The localization precision is the cell which is the same accuracy level of the identified interesting points. They distinguish between personal anchor points like home, work and other person-related places as the locations each user visits regularly, as for example a gym.

In Pereira et al. [12], the authors exploit cellular phone signaling data[1], focusing on the prediction of travel demand for special events. Similar to the previous approach, their analysis identifies the home location: here is defined as starting point of people's trips. However, they observed that mobility data are dependent on mobile phone usage, and this may bias the results. Therefore they propose to integrate the GSM dataset with external data (e.g. ticketing statistics or taxi trips) with the aim of increasing the quantity and the quality of the data, in particular in term of spatial resolution.

Quercia et al. [13] uses GSM data for recommending social events to city dwellers. They combine the locations estimated by mobile phone data of users in the Greater Boston area and the list of social events in the same area. After extracting the trajectories and stops from GSM calls, they crawl the events from the web. Then, they divide the area of Boston in cells and locate each events and each stop in the corresponding cell. Therefore, by crossing the events and the stops, they identify a set of potential users participating to events.

Mobile phone records are analysed also in [1] where the authors propose a visual analytics framework to explore spatio-temporal data by means of SOM (Self-Organizing Map) analysis. They propose a method to cluster the dataset by either of the two dimension and evaluate the resulting aggregation on the other one. Although they show the potentialities of using SOM for analysing mobile phone records, they do not focus on identifying user profiles.

All these approaches, as well others that can be found on the literature, offer different perspectives on how GSM data can be exploited to study the human mobility and the huge potentialities of these kinds of data. Differently from these approaches, the aspect we want to study in this paper are the flows across a city of the a particular category of people: the visitors.

---

[1] These data consist of location estimations which are generated each time when a mobile device is connected to the cellular network for calls, messages and Internet connections.

3 Objectives and Experimental Setting

The purpose of this work is to demonstrate how the massive and constantly updated information carried by mobile phone call data records (CDRs) can be exploited to estimate visitors movements within an urban area and their flows across the observed territory.

In this section, we will first describe what information CDRs contain and we will provide details about the dataset used in the experiments. Then, we will introduce the user categories and the mobility measures we aim at inferring from CDRs.

3.1 Call Detail Records (CDRs)

GSM is a network that enables the communications between mobile devices. The GSM protocol is based on a so called *cellular network architecture*, where a geographical area is covered by a number of antennas emitting a signal to be received by mobile devices. Each antenna covers an area called cell. In this way, the covered area is partitioned into a number of, possibly overlapping, cells, uniquely identified by the antenna. Cell horizontal radius varies depending on antenna height, antenna gain, population density and propagation conditions from a couple of hundred meters to several tens of kilometers.

A Call Detail Record (CDR) is a log data documenting each phone communication that the TelCo operator stores for billing purposes. The format of the CDR used in this work contains a subset of information as follows:

$$< Timestamp, Caller\_id, d, Cell\_1, Cell\_2 >$$

$Caller\_id$ is the anonymous identifier of the user that called, $Timestamp$ is the starting time of the call, d is its duration, $Cell\_1$ and $Cell\_2$ are the identifiers of the cells where the call started and ended (See Fig. 1). Only voice communications are included in the dataset.

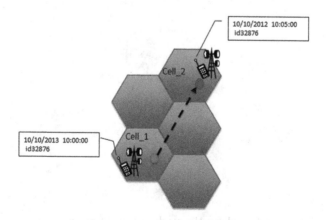

Fig. 1. Exemplification of the cellular network and communication.

The dataset used in this work consists of around 7.8 million CDRs collected from Oct 9th to Nov 9th, 2012. The dataset contains calls corresponding to about 232,200 customers of the Italian TelCo operator *Wind SpA*, with a mobile phone contract (no roaming users are included).

It is important to point out that a major limitation of CDRs is the fact that the localization of individuals occurs only during phone calls, that can lead to an incomplete view of their mobility. We discuss this point in Sect. 4, where we introduce a methodology to partially overcome the incompleteness issue.

3.2   Spatial Granularity

The spatial granularity considered in this work takes into account the spatial resolution of the cells covering the area of study. In the urban area of Pisa, the coverage of each cell is relatively large, therefore it often does not allow a precise relationship between a Point of Interest (POI) and the cell itself. This means

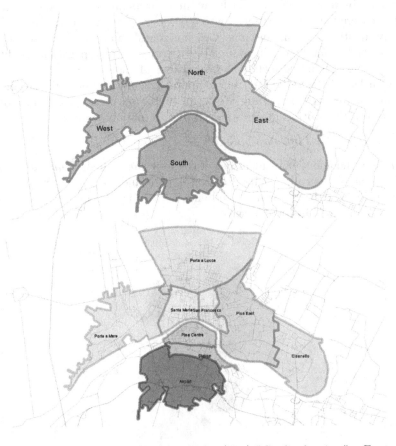

Fig. 2. City partitions adopted for the study: (Top) "Cardinal points" - Four zones (North, South, East, West); (Bottom) "City districts" - Nine areas.

that a cell may contain more than one POI and a POI, if it is large, may belong to more than one cell. Thus, in this study we use a higher level of granularity, and we define two types of partitions of the urban area: "cardinal points" (Fig. 2 top) and "city districts" (Fig. 2 bottom). In the former case the city is divided in four areas according to the cardinal points; while in the latter case the city is divided according to the major districts. Both partitions follow the natural division provided by the Arno River. To better compare the flows measured over the two partitions, each area of the first partition is defined as an aggregation of zones of the second partition.

4 Methodology

The basic idea of the methodology and at the basis of the Sociometer is that the behavior category of an individual within a specific municipality can be inferred by the temporal distribution of his/her presence in the area. For example, people commuting to a municipality for work will usually appear there only during working hours and only during working days – obviously with some exceptions, which however, are expected to be occasional. In this work we are interested in the movements of visitors, a class of users characterized by a sporadic presence on the territory, usually appearing only for a short time period (a few days). As explained in [6], a formal definition of visitors is given by The World Tourism Organization that identifies them as "people traveling to and staying in places outside their usual environment for not more than one consecutive year for leisure, business and other purposes" [15]. In other words, a person is a visitor in an area A if his/her home and work place are outside A and the presence inside the area is limited to a certain period of time T_{to} that can allow him/her to spend some activities in the city. In particular the presence has to be concentrated in a finite temporal interval inside the time window. It should also be occasional therefore, he/she does not appear anymore during the observation period. It is also important to point out the distinction that this definition includes not only the classical *tourism* as visiting cultural and natural attractions, but also the activity related to work, visiting relatives, health reasons, etc.

We already mentioned that CDR may describe the movements of users only partially, since the localization is available only when a user performs a call. For frequent callers, thus, there is a strict correspondence among movements and calls. For users that make low use of their phone, instead, sensing their movements may be underestimated. When analyzing visitors movements, it is crucial to take into account the previous observations. On one hand, the classification of a user u as visitor is based on a narrow period τ where he/she is observed performing a call. Thus, the narrower is the period τ the larger is our confidence that u is a visitor. Obviously, there is still some probability that u may be a local users that uses his/her mobile phone just very seldom, and therefore his/her calling footprint is wrongly classified as that of a visitor.

On the other hand, once we have identified the sub-population of visitors, we want to make inferences about their movements within the city. Since the period of activity of user u within the territory is limited, he/she may be able to perform very few calls, resulting in an underestimation of his/her movements.

In summary, a dependable inference on visitor movements is based on the dualism between these two dimensions: the period of permanence within the area and the number of calls performed during that period. In the next sections we will show how to reason upon these two dimensions to determine the confidence about our predictions.

In the following we summarize the user classification process, at the basis of the quantitative mobility analysis proposed in this paper. The process, introduced in [6], performs a form of active transductive learning, i.e., a process that selects a sample of data to be labeled by the analyst, and exploits that sample to classify the whole dataset. After introducing the individual call profiles (ICFs) (Sect. 4.1), we will describe a semi-automatic methodology for classifying call profiles (Sect. 4.2). In this process, a human expert is asked to manually label a small number of representative call profiles, which are then used to automatically label all other call profiles. After the classification step, we associate each ICP of visitors to the corresponding sequence of CDRs, in order to reconstruct their movements. From the sequence of CDRs we determine an individual indicator stating if a user as crossed one or more city areas.

4.1 Individual Call Profiles (ICPs)

ICPs are the set of aggregated spatio-temporal profiles of an analyst computed by applying spatial and temporal rules on the raw CDRs in order to identify the presences. The resulting structure is a matrix of the type shown in Fig. 3. The temporal aggregation is by week, where each day of a given week is grouped in weekdays and weekend. Given for example a temporal window of 28 days (4 weeks), the resulting matrix has 8 columns (2 columns for each week, one for the weekdays and one for the weekend). A further temporal partitioning is applied to the daily hours. A day is divided in several timeslots, representing interesting times of the day. This partitioning adds to the matrix new rows. In the example we have 3 timeslots (t1, t2, t3) so the matrix has 3 rows. Numbers in the matrix represent the number of events (in this case the presence of the user) performed by the user in a particular period within a particular timeslot. For instance, the number 5 in Fig. 3 means that the individual was present in the area of interest for 5 distinct weekdays during Week1 in timeslot t2 only.

Figure 3 exemplifies the whole process of constructing the ICP from the raw data: starting from the dataset of the calls, the spatio-temporal aggregation rules are applied and the corresponding presences are inferred. The matrix is filled with the number of presences in each time slot. Coloring the slots based on the presence density, we get a simple representation of the profiles that give an immediate idea of the category a user belongs to. In the example the profile is of a resident because the presence is uniform in the whole windows of observation both in the weekdays and in the weekends.

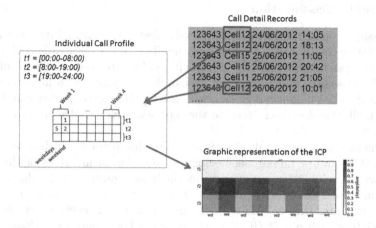

Fig. 3. Example of Individual Call Profile: from the calls, the individual presence is derived

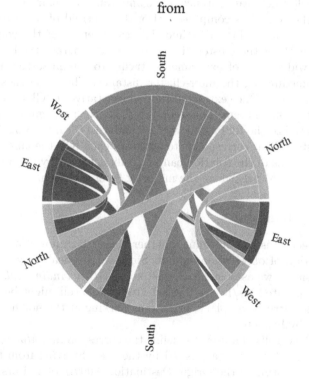

Fig. 4. Visitor flow transitions among cardinal areas according to Fig. 2 (Top).

4.2   Profile Classification

The classification method we propose is composed of two parts. First, we extract representative call profiles, i.e. a relatively small set of synthetic call profiles, each summarizing an homogeneous set of (real) ICPs. This step reduces the set of samples to be classified, which can then be handled manually by a human expert, based on the class definitions given above and his/her own experience and judgment. Finally, the labels assigned to the representative profiles are propagated to the full set of ICPs.

In the first step the standard K-means algorithm is used, which aims to partition n ICPs into k homogeneous clusters, and the mean values of the ICPs belonging to each cluster serves as prototype/representative of the cluster. The algorithm follows an iterative procedure. Initially it creates k random partitions, then, it calculates the centroid of each group, and it constructs a new partition by associating each object (ICP) to the cluster whose centroid is closest to it. Finally the centroids are recalculated for the new cluster, reiterating the procedure until the algorithm reaches a stable configuration (convergence). The similarity between two ICPs, which is the key operation of K-means, is computed through a simple Euclidean distance, i.e. comparing each pair of corresponding time slots in the two ICPs compared. Also, the centroid of a cluster is simply obtained by computing, for each time slot, the average of the corresponding values in the ICPs of the cluster. The choice of the parameter K is made by performing a wide range of experiments, trying to minimize the intra-cluster distance and maximizing the inter-cluster distance. The value chosen as most suitable was K = 100. Once extracted the representatives (RCPs), we asked the domain experts to label them. The second step, i.e. the propagation of the labels manually assigned to the RCPs, followed a standard 1-Nearest-Neighbor (1-NN) classification step. That corresponds to assign to each ICP the label of the closest RCP. Extensions of the solution can be easily achieved by adopting a K-NN classification, with $K > 1$, where the majority label is chosen.

4.3   Mobility Indicator

Our basic objective is to determine whether a user has moved across the city during the period of observation, or not. Since we are dealing with movement patterns of visitors, we associate each visitor to his/her *landing cell*, i.e. the cell where he/she initiated his/her calling activities. This cell might be the airport when the visitor arrives via plane, or the bus parking at the north of the city if he/she arrives by bus, etc.

Given the base cells of a user, we define the corresponding *Mobility Indicator* as the number of distinct areas visited by the user. Starting from the landing cell, we can also estimate the Origin-Destination Matrix of visitors within the city, since the consecutive visit of two areas imply a movement between them – though the incompleteness issue mentioned in previous sections might lead to introduce some errors, since some intermediate visits to other areas might be missed. Figure 4 shows the flows of the visitors among the cardinal areas of our partition obtained with the dataset which spans over a period of one month, as described in Sect. 3.1.

We can appreciate how the incidence of self-loops, i.e. people staying still in a region, is greater in the southern area, which contains the main transportation facilities of the city (airport, train and central bus stations) to arrive to the city. From East and West we cannot appreciate any self loop, suggesting that those routes are mainly used to cross the city.

If we consider the partition in districts (Fig. 5), it is easier to observe a transition among two adjacent districts (e.g., airport (Aeroporto) and train station (Stazione)). It is however difficult to measure large flows across distant districts.

5   Evaluation

In this section we summarize the experimental results obtained by computing some population and flow statistics over the city of Pisa. After the classification step, we identify around 90k users classified as visitors. Since our objective is to

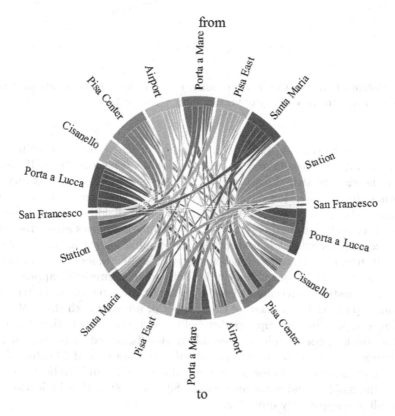

Fig. 5. Visitor flow transitions among districts according to Fig. 2 (Bottom).

determine the percentage of visitors who cross the city to visit different areas, we want to establish the percentage of users with a positive Mobility Indicator. To determine such percentage, however, we have to take into account the limitations about the dualism of precision of the classification and coverage of movement sensing. Not having the support of external evidences to determine a dependable threshold for the two dimensions, we derive a *Mobility Indicator Curve*, connecting the percentage of mobility to a *minimum support threshold* for the observed number of calls for each user.

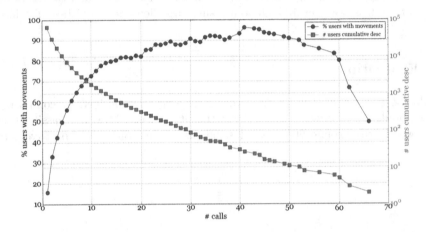

Fig. 6. Mobility Indicator Curve: relationship between the number of calls performed by each user and the probability of visiting more than one zone.

Figure 6 shows the resulting Mobility Indicator Curve for the cardinal area partition (analogous results may be observed for the other partition). If we consider all the visitors with at least one call, the percentage of mobility is very low. This is mainly due to the low duration of each call, thus preventing a user to cross too many cells. Even choosing a very permissive threshold of at least two calls, we can observe that around one third of the population moves across the areas. This percentage increases when selecting a sub-population within an higher minimum call threshold. The curve reaches relatively stable values at around 15 calls – i.e., the sensitivity of the mobility index with smaller thresholds appears to be too high, suggesting to require at least 15 calls. At the same time, the red curve shows an exponential decrement of the number of users for each threshold, thus adopting a large minimum support threshold would result in selecting just a tiny and statistically poor sample. Reasonable trade-offs, aimed at keeping at least some hundreds of users in the sample, should then not exceed 30 calls. Within this range of choices – between 15 and 30 calls as minimum threshold – we can see that the mobility index ranges between 80 % and 90 %, thus indicating that the mobility is apparently quite high.

The publication of the final results cannot put at risk the individual privacy because this information is a simple aggregation that does not contain any sensitive information about the single users. This means that an attacker, by accessing this kind of data, cannot infer any information about a user. The ICP reconstruction instead, may be more problematic for the individual privacy because requires to access the CDR data that contain all information about the user calls. However, since the only information that the analyst needs for performing the analysis is the set of ICPs, we propose an "protocol" where, the computation of the ICPs is delegated to the TelCo operator that sends them to the analyst for the computation of the other steps. As described in [5], we supply to the TelCo operator a tool for evaluating the risk of privacy in disclosing ICPs so that it can decide supply only a subset of data that are compliant to the required level of privacy.

6 Conclusions

In this work we developed an analytical process to determine the probability of observing a population of visitors moving across an urban area. The method is based on a classification step capable of determining the class of mobile phone users by analyzing their call habits. The population of users tagged as visitors is further analyzed by reconstructing their respective movements. To overcome the limitation of partial observation for movements due to individual call habits, we introduce a methodology to relate the observations available for each user and the confidence of the prediction of observing a movement. The experimental results show that visitors have a high tendency of moving across the city, even for coarser spatial granularities.

Acknowledgments. This work has been partially funded by the European Union under the FP7-ICT Program: Project DataSim n. FP7-ICT-270833, and Project Petra n. 609042; and by the MIUR and MISE under the Industria 2015 program: Project MOTUS grating degree n.0000089 - application code MS01_00015.

References

1. Andrienko, G., Andrienko, N., Bak, P., Bremm, S., Keim, D., von Landesberger, T., Poelitz, C., Schreck, T.: A framework for using self-organising maps to analyse spatio-temporal patterns, exemplified by analysis of mobile phone usage. J. Locat. Based Serv. **4**, 3–4 (2010)
2. Ahas, R., Silm, S., Järv, S., Saluveer, E.: Using mobile positioning data to model locations meaningful to users of mobile phones. J. Urban Technol. **17**, 1 (2010)
3. Calabrese, F., Colonna, M., Lovisolo, P., Parata, D., Ratti, C.: Real-time urban monitoring using cell phones: a case study in rome. IEEE Trans. Intell. Transp. Syst. **12**, 141–151 (2011)
4. Ratti, C., Sevtsuk, A., Huang, S., Pailer, R.: Mobile Landscapes: Graz in Real Time. MIT Senseable City Lab, Massachusetts (2005)

5. Furletti, B., Gabrielli, L., Monreale, A., Nanni, M., Pratesi, F., Rinzivillo, S., Giannotti, F., Pedreschi, D.: Assessing the privacy risk in the process of building call habit models that underlie the sociometer. Technical report. http://puma.isti.cnr.it/dfdownload.php?ident=/cnr.isti/2014-TR-011&langver=it&scelta=Metadata

6. Furletti, B., Gabrielli, L., Renso, C., Rinzivillo, S.: Identifying users profiles from mobile calls habits. In: The Proceedings of UrbComp (2012)

7. Furletti, B., Gabrielli, L., Renso, C., Rinzivillo, S.: Turism fluxes observatory: deriving mobility indicators from GSM calls habits. In: The Book of Abstracts of NetMob (2013)

8. Furletti, B., Gabrielli, L., Renso, C., Rinzivillo, S.: Analysis of GSM calls data for understanding user mobility behavior. In: The Proceedings of Big Data (2013)

9. Giannotti, F., Nanni, M., Pedreschi, D., Pinelli, F., Renso, C., Rinzivillo, S., Trasarti, R.: Unveiling the complexity of human mobility by querying and mining massive trajectory data. VLDB J. **20**, 695–719 (2011)

10. Nanni, M., Trasarti, R., Furletti, B., Gabrielli, L., Mede, P.V.D., Bruijn, J.D., Romph, E.D., Bruil, G.: MP4-A project: mobility planning for Africa. In: D4D Challenge @ 3rd Conference on the Analysis of Mobile Phone datasets (NetMob 2013)

11. Oltenau, A.-M., Trasarti, R., Couronne, T., Giannotti, F., Nanni, M., Smoreda, Z., Ziemlicki, C.: GSM data analysis for tourism application. In: Proceedings of 7th International Symposium on Spatial Data Quality (ISSDQ) (2011)

12. Pereira, F.C., Liu, L., Calabrese, F.: Profiling transport demand for planned special events: prediction of public home distributions (2010). www.scienceDirect.com

13. Quercia, D., Lathia, N., Calabrese, F., Di Lorenzo, G., Crowcroft, J.: Recommending social events from mobile phone location data. In: International Conference on Data Mining, ICDM (2010)

14. Schlaich, J., Otterstätter, T., Friedrich, M.: Generating trajectories from mobile phone data. In: The Proceedings of the 89th Annual Meeting Compendium of Papers, Transportation Research Board of the National Academies (2010)

15. Wikipedia. Tourism. http://en.wikipedia.org/wiki/Tourism

16. Wang, D., Pedreschi, D., Song, C., Giannotti, F., Barabasi, A.-L.: Human mobility, social ties, and link prediction. In: Proceedings of the 17th ACM SIGKDD International Conference on Knowledge Discovery and Data Mining, KDD 11. ACM, New York (2011)

An Abstract State Machine (ASM) Representation of Learning Process in FLOSS Communities

Patrick Mukala[✉], Antonio Cerone, and Franco Turini

Department of Computer Science, University of Pisa, Pisa, Italy
{patrick.mukala,cerone,turini}@di.unipi.it

Abstract. Free/Libre Open Source Software (FLOSS) communities as collaborative environments enable the occurrence of learning between participants in these groups. With the increasing interest research on understanding the mechanisms and processes through which learning occurs in FLOSS, there is an imperative to describe these processes. One successful way of doing this is through specification methods. In this paper, we describe the adoption of Abstract States Machines (ASMs) as a specification methodology for the description of learning processes in FLOSS. The goal of this endeavor is to represent the many possible steps and/or activities FLOSS participants go through during interactions that can be categorized as learning processes. Through ASMs, we express learning phases as states while activities that take place before moving from one state to another are expressed as transitions.

Keywords: Process modeling · Abstract State Machines (ASMs) · FLOSS communities · Learning processes

1 Introduction

The idea of process definition entails specifying the activities and flow of occurrences thereof between learning actors within the settings of Free/Libre Open Source Software (FLOSS) communities. The current literature is endowed with extensive exploration, critiques and development of specification languages in software engineering and modeling [1–7]. These languages and associated methods help in simulating and possibly verifying behaviors and functionalities of computer programs before they are developed. Specifically, some works [5, 8] draw attention to an important role of specification methods with regard to producing simulation models. These are models that depict a representation of some functionality as it is expected to occur in a specific domain. Furthermore, there has been an increasing interest in the area of specification languages for process modeling [9–13] and one of them, the Process Specification Language (PSL), provides a set of concepts and terms used for the description of process reengineering, process realization, process simulation etc. [9, 10]. Another specification language that can be used for both software engineering and process modeling is Abstract State machines (ASM) as suggested by Farahbod, Glässer and Vajihollahi [14]. In additional reports on this method [15, 16] Börger gives a detailed annotation of ASM biography since the inception of this area of research.

© Springer International Publishing Switzerland 2015
C. Canal and A. Idani (Eds.): SEFM 2014 Workshops, LNCS 8938, pp. 227–242, 2015.
DOI: 10.1007/978-3-319-15201-1_15

As part of our work, we chose the ASM approach as a way of specifying and defining learning processes because of its implementation success rate under industrial constraints for rigorous process modeling, software and hardware development, as emphasized by Börger, [17] and also because of its practicality and simplicity in documenting the steps from high-level abstraction of specifications to their decomposition until the ground models are produced.

Hence, the goal of this paper is to model learning processes from FLOSS repositories and clearly explain them through ASMs from the initial natural language in which they have been thus far expressed so as to enhance the understanding of learning behaviors and patterns through participatory activities in FLOSS communities. The paper is structured as follows. We briefly discuss Abstract States Machines and their relevance to our work in Sect. 2. Section 3 gives a general description of ASMs constructs and requirements as needed in this context. In Sect. 4 we present the developed ASMs Ground Models and specifications. In Sect. 5 we show how to validate the ASM specification of FLOSS learning processes by process mining FLOSS repositories. Finally, Sect. 6 concludes the paper.

2   Abstract State Machines (ASMs): Motivation

ASMs [14–18] can be understood as extensions of FSM (Finite State Machines) where any desired level of abstraction can be achieved by permitting possibly parameterized locations to hold values of arbitrary complexity, whether atomic or structured: objects, sets, lists, tables, trees, graphs, whatever comes natural at the considered level of abstraction [18]. Contrary to FSM, ASMs represent FSM instructions as control state rules as depicted in Fig. 1 below.

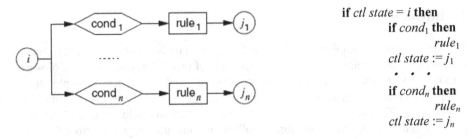

Fig. 1. Viewing FSM instructions as control state ASM rules

Figure 1 depicts an automaton where $i, j_1., j$ are internal (control) states, $cond_v$, for $1 \leq v \leq n$, represent the input condition $i_n = a_v$ (reading input a_v) and $rule_v$, for $1 \leq v \leq n$, represent the output action $out := b_v$ (yielding output b_v), which go together with the ctl $state$ update to j_v. Simply put, these rules represent actions that need to be taken or activities carried out in the event of conditions (if any) being true before moving from one state to another.

The potential of using Abstract States Machines (ASMs) for modeling learning processes in volatile and dynamic FLOSS environments is twofold. First, the ASM approach can help elaborate and express information we gather about activities in FLOSS communities and turn this information into necessary *ground models*. Ground Models are defined as functionally complete but abstract descriptions of sufficient but not more than necessary rigor, which can be read and understood as a representation of the problem to be solved and also contain only what the logic of the problem requires being modeled [17]. Finally, ASMs allow for the implementation and verification of the ground models reliably by refining them as needed step by step and through a hierarchy of intermediate sub-models which represent a major component of the problem [17]. We refer the reader to Börger's work [17] for detailed theory and semantic foundations of this approach.

2.1 Abstract State Machines (ASMs) for Learning Processes in FLOSS Communities

Modeling learning processes through ASMs grew out of a need to express the flow of occurrence for processes. A Ground model provides a simple representation of states, processes and transitions that we believe are fit to explain and give the readers a clear picture of learning processes in FLOSS communities. A number of studies [19–25] provide a lot of grounds for the identification of terms and concepts one can use to identify learning activities, participants and related classes in FLOSS communities.

In the context of our work, we identified two main learning processes in FLOSS communities (Undirected Learning and Directed Learning), with the second learning process (Directed Learning) unfolding from 2 perspectives in 4 different formats, thus totaling the number of processes to 9. These are:

- Undirected Learning: This process can also be referred to as Peer-2-Peer or Reflective Learning. This kind of learning is assumed to take place between any numbers of participants. In this process, any participant can be both a receiver (Novice) and a sender (Expert). At this level, the assumption is that learning occurs between mates with a diversified expertise background who learn from each other.
- Directed Learning: This process refers to involvement of more knowledgeable participants or expert members in helping less expert members to develop their skills with some level of guidance or supervision. The occurrence of the process is twofold:
  - Pulling: This is the process where a participant who is less expert on any topic would initiate a need to learn by reaching out to the more advanced participants that can culminate in a supervised or guided learning process. This can in turn occur according to the four formats as follow:
    - Modeling: In this process, the Expert's activities and actions are systematically monitored and observed by the Novice. This can happen as the receiver aims to emulate the sender given the latter's reputation on their FLOSS contribution. An example could be tracking the sender's commits in SVN, their comments on mailing lists etc.;
    - Coaching: As the term explains, this involves giving direct monitoring and guidance to the requester's and observing his/her performance;
    - Scaffolding: In this process, the sender analyses and determines the receiver's level of capacity and allows him/her the opportunities to acquire

knowledge accordingly. For example, supplying materials (tutorials etc.) on specific problems and a solution approach etc. based on the requester's background.

- Fading: This process depicts involving a requester in practical execution of tasks for skills acquisition. However, as the requester's performance matures, the sender gradually gives them autonomy to apply their skills.

– Pushing: This is the type of directed learning that occurs when the sender takes the initiative to make available opportunities of knowledge acquisition for requesters. Just like the pulling, this process can also be understood in 4 formats: Modeling, Coaching, Scaffolding and Fading.

Therefore, given this classification, one can identify nine learning processes, namely Undirected/Reflective Learning, Directed-Pulling-Modeling, Directed-Pulling-Coaching, Directed-Pulling-Scaffolding, Directed-Pulling-Fading, Directed-Pushing-Modeling, Directed-Pushing-Coaching, Directed-Pushing-Scaffolding and Directed-Pushing-Fading.

3   ASM Requirements and Constructs

In a FLOSS community, the transfer of software engineering skills between participants occurs in an informal fashion but can be tracked through participants' activities. In order to accomplish this, some qualitative works on these activities have helped us identify and formulate the 9 learning processes introduced in Sect. 2.1 through which learning for this purpose occurs in FLOSS communities.

The purpose of building the ASMs is to develop models that can express the occurrence of these learning processes. It is crucial noting that learning in FLOSS for all processes that we have identified happens in three important phases that corresponds to three stages of software engineering skills development. Such phases are: initiation, progression and maturation. For each stage, a number of tasks/activities are carried out by both the Novice (knowledge requester) and the Expert (knowledge provider). Details of these activities in each phase or related thereof are graphically represented in the Ground Models in the next section. While these phases and states apply for all the identified learning processes, the demarcation thereof can be reflected through instances of activities for each learning process. This simply means that for all the identified instances of the learning process, there is a difference in the way the Novice and the Expert would interact. For instance, with regard to an activity such as *CommentOnCode*, an Expert in Reflective Learning process will provide an opinion on improving the commented code or any other observation with an understanding that the code's owner is a peer who can agree or disagree with the suggestions. However, when an explicit relationship has been established like in the context of the Directed-Pulling-Modeling learning process, an Expert reacts mainly to the Novice's comments with the intent to provide guidance with the same *CommentOnCode* activity. The difference in the steps undertaken to fulfill the same activity for these two learning processes lies in the levels of responsibility, role of the Expert and Novice as well as their mutual consideration for both learning processes. In spite of such differences, all the learning processes can be considered through three phases, namely initiation, progression and maturation, which are expanded with related activities respectively in Figs. 2, 3 and 4. The initiation phase sanctions the start of a learning process as can be seen in Fig. 2 while the completion of a learning process can be demonstrated through the Novice ability to undertake activities of the maturation phase as depicted in Fig. 4.

Therefore, the ASM Ground Models depicted below are built based on a number of ASM constructs including states and transitions. Each Ground Model represents a learning phase, with a number of states and activities. These activities are ASM transitions and they determine moving from one state to another. In summary, we have Participants (Novice or Expert) that take part in a learning process (L_P) that occurs through three phases with corresponding states and transitions (activities).

These terms (phases, states and transitions) capture the main constructs that explain the different phases and activities a Novice goes through during a Learning Process. The Expert plays a critical role during these phases as a knowledge provider. The three ASM Ground Models as depicted in Figs. 2, 3 and 4 describe at some extent the interaction Novice-Expert during the Learning Process in terms of activities they perform in each respective phase. For clarity purposes, in order to illustrate the control flow as efficiently as possible, we consider only two participants (one Novice and one Expert) taking part in a learning process at a time.

We can thus express in ASM notation the basic specification that a phase in a learning process L_P can be any of list as enclosed in the brackets, namely initiation, progression and maturation. *∃ Phase: L_P —> {Initiation, Progression, Maturation}*. We can further express that in the initiation phase, a state can take any of the enclosed values (*Observation* or *ContactEstablishment*): *State: Initiation —> {Observation, ContactEstablishment}*. The same applies for the remaining two phases expressed respectively: *State: Progression —> {Revert, Post, Apply}* and *State: Maturation —> {Analyze, Commit, Develop, Revert, Review}*. Finally, for consistency we can also express that two types of participants (Expert and Novice) take part in the learning process as *∃ Participants: Participant ∈ L_P —> {Expert, Novice}*.

4   ASMs Specifications and Ground Models

A Learning Process (L_P) is assumed to take place between any numbers of participants. In this process, any participant can be either a Novice or an Expert depending on the level of expertise and participant's profile. At this level, the assumption is that learning occurs between mates with a diversified expertise background who learn from each other. In Sects. 4.1–4.3 we describe the three phases (initiation, progression and maturation) and, for each phase, activities are identified and described phase-dependently.

4.1   Initiation Phase Ground Model

Two main states explain this phase: *Observation* and *ContactEstablishement*. This simply refers to the steps in which the Novice or Expert will attempt to establish some form of contact between them. As depicted in Fig. 2, in the first state (*Observation*) of the state machine, both the Novice and Expert undertake a number of activities. When a Novice seeks help, he/she can perform activities such as *FormulateQuestion*, and/or

IdentifyExpert and then *PostQuestions or CommentPost,* whereas the Expert can provide help after he/she performs either *ReadMessages* on the mailing lists or *ReadPost* from forums *or ReadSourceCode* as any participant commits code to the project, or *CommentPost.* After completing these activities, we move to the second state (*ContactEstablishement*).

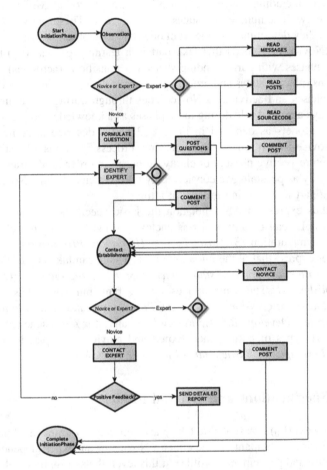

Fig. 2. Initiation ASM Ground Model

In the second state (*ContactEstablishement*) the Novice and/or Expert attempts to make contact in order to establish collaboration or to provide the required help. Hence, the *Novice* at this point, can simply perform *ContactExpert.* If the Expert responds positively, he/she can perform *SendDetailedRequest,* otherwise the cycle is restarted to identifying an expert. The Expert on the other side, just like the Novice seeking to be part of some form of knowledge channel, can perform *ContactNovice* and show interest in helping or simply perform *CommentPost* as shown in Fig. 2.

As said above, this phase of learning occurs for all instances of learning processes, the demarcation lies on two critical factors: the level of the Expert's involvement and the content of messages and deliverables exchanged. In future, we hope to unmask and explain these differences as we empirically explore data from sample FLOSS projects. Nevertheless, at this point one can note that in the context of undirected learning, a Novice can be seen as a participant with considerable knowledge and skills because the exchange is assumed to take place between two colleagues. This could be the default perceptive knowledge exchange in such community environments where participants learn from each other. However, with the remaining of the learning processes, the emphasis is on the formal communication channel that exists between the concerned participants as well as the knowledge gap and disparity between them. This gap makes it possible for some level of mentorship as it allows for modeling, coaching, and fading and scaffolding as previously eluded. Hence, the semantics of activities such as *ContactExpert, ContactNovice, PostQuestions*, and *CommentPost* will vary accordingly although this specification is quite representative of the steps that actually take place in the process of observing occurring activities and possibly establishing these ties.

This description can also be summarized by the following ASM code providing the specification as graphically represented by the Ground Model in Fig. 2.

Let **L$_p$act** = activity occurring in L$_P$ phase;
Let **P** denote Participant in Floss Community in L$_P$ and **P$_{Floss}$** denotes the total number of participants;
Let **P$_e$** and **P$_n$** respectively denote sets of participants that are expert and novice.
The keyword ***Choose*** simply denotes a choice to be made from listed options.

If state = observation **then**
        If participant = n **then**
                FORMULATEQUESTION (n)
                IDENTIFYEXPERT (n)
                Choose L$_p$act **in** (POSTQUESTIONS (e),
                                COMMENTPOST (e)) **do**
                        L$_p$act
        If participant = n **then**
                Choose L$_p$act **in** (READMESSAGES (P$_{Floss}$),
                              READPOST (P$_{Floss}$),
                        READSOURCECODE (P$_{Floss}$),
                                COMMENTPOST (P$_{Floss}$)) **do**
                    L$_p$act
                                      //Move to second state
If state = ContactEstablishment **then**
        If participant = n **then**
                CONTACTEXPERT (n)
                If SENDFEEDBACK (e) **then**
                        SENDDETAILEDREPORT (e)
        Else
    StartInitiationPhase
                IDENTIFYEXPERT (n)
        If participant = Expert **then**
                Choose L$_p$act **in** (CONTACTNOVICE (n),
                                COMMENTPOST (n)) **do**
                    L$_p$act

4.2   Progression Specification and Ground Model

As with the first phase of the Lp, the enactment steps of these activities are quite similar with the only demarcation factors being the level of the Expert's involvement and the content of messages and deliverables exchanged. In this phase, while the Novice involved in the learning process starts gradually performing some apparent activities pertaining either to developing source code, commenting source code and actively engaging in the community discussions, the Expert's role shifts towards assessing and assisting the Novice where needed to ensure that the skills are effectively applied. Like in the next phase, this role is carried out in almost the same way while unleashing the Novice's full autonomous operation.

In this phase, the specifications above and Ground Model provided in Fig. 3 can be summarized as follows. Three main steps take place for both participants after establishing contact. These are *Revert, Post* and *Apply* and they denote important states within this phase.

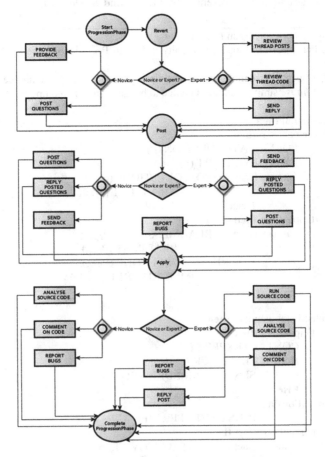

Fig. 3. Progression Phase Ground Model

These activities denote providing some level of feedback after being contacted, then providing the required help for Novice and implementing new knowledge through a set of new activities. In *Revert*, the Expert will then, if she/he accepted the request from the Novice, attempt to perform *ReviewThreadPosts*, where questions or need for clarification have risen, and *ReviewThreadCode*, for the purpose of critiquing and fixing as required if needs be. He/she can also perform *SendReply* in an attempt to answer any direct questions and help requests or just reacting to a discussion in a forum. While the Novice, at this state, can only react to the Expert's help or feedback and provide insights on the extent to which the Expert's input was helpful through *ProvideFeedback* or simply pose more questions through activity *PostQuestions*. In state *Post*, both the Novice and Expert illustrate their activities by performing a number of tasks that can all be grouped under this state. Some of these tasks include: *PostQuestions, ReplyPostedQuestions, ReportBugs* and *SendFeedback*. Hence, the flow of occurrence of these tasks happens as follows: the Novice will, during this state, perform a number of activities in the context of posting. These activities include *PostQuestions, ReplyPostedQuestions* and possibly *SendFeedback*, when needed, while the expert will directly or indirectly perform *SendFeedback, ReplyPostedQuestions (possibly questions and requests from novice), PostQuestions,* in order to enquire more if there is a need for clarity, as well as *ReportBugs,* as a response to Novice's need to understand why some piece of code cannot run properly, for example. In the final state, *Apply,* core development and practical activities are undertaken from both sides. The Novice can start exercising the new acquired skills through activities such as *AnalyseSourceCode,* when he/she looks at new commits, new pieces of code being posted by community members and hence, the novice will also be able to perform *RunSourceCode* on these pieces of code and comment on them through *CommentOnCode* and reporting bugs through *ReportBugs*.

The expert in turn can monitor the Novice through also a set of almost similar activities but for the purpose of evaluating the level of skill acquisition. These activities include *RunSourceCode* and *AnalyseSourceCode*, to identify flaws in the Novice's works, and, if necessary, *ReportBugs, CommentOnCode* and also *ReplyToPost*. Any more activities in this phase could trigger further states, but we set the limit of the scope at this point.

4.3   Maturation Specification and Ground Model

To conclude with the last part of the specifications, as with the two previous phases, most activities here in this phase have gained a certain level of maturation. It means in this phase, the role of the Expert becomes more or less a sporadic assessor that progressively considers the Novice as a colleague and member of the same community. The Novice, on the other hand, can possibly start at some extent new knowledge exchange channels as an Expert, to transfer the newly acquired skills during participation in FLOSS environments. The following specification can be easily understood by looking at the graphical representation in Fig. 4.

In this last phase of the learning process, the activities are presented to assert how the novice has mastered the skills learnt during the learning process. Five main groups of activities make up this phase of the process as referred to as states. These include *Analyze, Commit, Develop, Review* and *Revert.* In the *Analyze* state, the Novice or Expert engage in a set of activities to examine the maturity of the learning process. The Novice is assumed to have acquired enough skills to be able to undertake a set of activities, such as *AnalyzeDiscussions,* in order to actively engage and contribute to comments and posts in the team about topics in the sphere of the skills acquired and possibly becoming an Expert to a new Novice. Activity *AnalyzeSourceCode* consists in analyzing the code (when applied) in order to understand and critique that piece of software and, finally, activity *AnalyzeThreadProgression* is performed in order to be part of a discussion and exchange a channel that engages on a topic related to a new skill learnt. The Expert will perform the exact same activities but tracking the Novice's progress. Thus, these activities include *AnalyzeThreadProgression, AnalyzeSource-Code* and *AnalyzeDiscussions.*

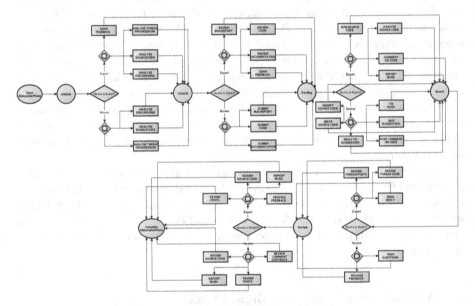

Fig. 4. Maturation ASM Ground Model

In the second state (*Commit*), the assumption is that as the Novice fosters his/her skills on a specific area, he/she can now commit some deliverables at the repositories that can be evaluated and criticized by the community. These activities include *SubmitBugReport,* where the Novice will commit any fix or bug report for the interest of the entire community, *SubmitCode,* where the Novice will commit some code for any piece of software and participate to the project and build reputation for a possible role transition, and also *SubmitDocumentation,* where the Novice is able to submit documentation in terms of requirements elicitation documents, help document, user manuals, tutorials etc. The Expert on the other hand, is assumed to conduct the same activities for monitoring purposes and give feedback as needed.

During the next state (*Develop*), the Novice carries out a number of activities that demonstrate his/her ability to develop. These activities include:

- *FixBugs,* where he/she attempts to fix any reported bugs in the project;
- *GiveSuggestion,* as part of reviewing peers' works, which provide alternatives when needed (for example what the appropriate function might be to perform a particular task etc.);
- *PostCommentOnCode,* in order to make sure that appropriate indicative comments in the source code are posted for enlightenment;
- *ReplyToSuggestion,* to reply and critique suggestion from other experts or novices in an active fashion,
- *WriteSourceCode,* in order to commit pieces of software;
- *ModifySourceCode,* to modify any code and implement suggestion as requested.

In turn, the Expert carries out a number of activities as well during the learning process and can perform *RunSourceCode,* in order to be able to perform *Analyze-SourceCode,* and, if possible, as needed, perform *CommentOnCode* and *ReportBugs* to the benefit of the Novice.

The *Revert* state in this phase is essentially the same state as in the progress phase. This contains all feedback activities between the Novice and the Expert. Three classes or activities occur under this state: *ReviewThreadPosts, ReviewThreadCode* and *SendReply.* The Expert will then, if she/he accepted the request from the Novice, attempt to perform *ReviewThreadPosts,* where questions or need for clarification have risen, *ReviewThreadCode,* for the purpose of critiquing and fixing as required if needs be. The Expert could also perform *SendReply,* in an attempt to answer any direct questions and help requests or just reacting to a discussion in a forum. The Novice, at this state, can only react to the Expert's help or feedback and provide insights on the extent to which the Expert's input was helpful through *ProvideFeedback* or simply pose more questions through *PostQuestions.*

In the last state, called *Review,* the Novice or Expert engage in a set of activities to examine the maturity of the learning process in reviewing a number of posts and artifacts according to the level of competency. The Novice can undertake as part of his/her ability to Review a number of activities that can be assimilated to three main review activities such as *ReviewCommentContents,* in order to contribute to comments and posts in the team about topics in the sphere of the skills acquired and possibly becoming an expert to a new novice, *ReviewPosts,* on mailing lists and forums so as to react as needed to comments and posts related to a particular content that is the subject of learning, *ReviewSourceCode,* which explains the ability to analyze the code (when applied) and identify flaws that can be reported or fixed. The Expert, in this last phase of the learning process, will be performing the same activities as the Novice, but on the Novice's progress work. Hence, he/she will perform *ReviewPosts* on posts from the Novice and react as needed to comments and posts related to a particular content that is the subject of learning. The Expert can also perform *ReviewSourceCode* in order to be able to perform *ReportBugs* and also perform *ProvideFeedback* when necessary.

5   Using Process Mining to Validate the ASM Model

The ASM models as built in this paper form part of the undertaking to identify traces of learning processes from FLOSS repositories. This evidence-based undertaking can be accomplished through process mining. Process mining is a method of reconstructing processes as executed from the event logs [29]. These logs are generated from process-aware information systems such as Enterprise Resource Planning (ERP), Workflow Management (WFM), Customer Relationship Management (CRM), Supply Chain Management (SCM), and Product Data Management (PDM) [28]. The logs contain records of events such as activities being executed or messages being exchanged on which process mining techniques can be applied in order to discover, analyze, diagnose and improve processes, organizational, social and data structures [29]. This can also be understood as the automated discovery of processes from event logs resulting in a generation of a process model (e.g., a Petri net or a workflow net) that describes the causal dependencies between activities [28].

More specifically, the goal of process mining is the extraction of information on the process from event logs using a family of a posteriori analysis techniques. These techniques enable the identification of sequentially recorded events where each event refers to an activity and is related to a particular case (i.e., a process instance) [28]. They also can help identify the performer or originator of the event (i.e., the person/resource executing or initiating the activity), the timestamp of the event, or data elements recorded with the event. Being able to retrieve such information is critical in our endeavor as we attempt to study the generation and originators of learning patterns from data recorded in FLOSS repositories. However, in these repositories, the structure of data files does not correspond to the required format of a log required for process mining. This can be illustrated by the Process Mining Meta Data Model in Fig. 5 below.

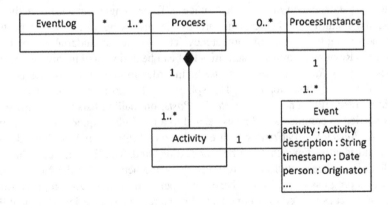

Fig. 5. Process Mining Meta Data Model

The idea as expressed in the model is that a log, an event log that is ready for process mining should abide by a number of structural properties to facilitate its processing and analysis. It should contain data organized and clustered in processes; each of these processes has instances uniquely identifiable with a set of activities. A process instance can also be referred to as a case instance includes a number of events that consist of activities being executed at a given point in time. An example could be a log of an insurance company might contain information about a billing and refund process. A refund process has a number of process instances uniquely identified by the claim number. Activities that should be executed in the refund process may include registering the claim, and checking the insurance policy. An example of an event is "On Thursday September 23, 2010 Alice checks the insurance policy of the persons involved in claim 478-12" [26].

However, in Floss repositories, data can be often found in form of statistical details or email messages exchanged in forums. Therefore, these ASM models will be used to help construct the logs containing all the information we need to represent the learning processes. These models can guide in identifying activities in these data as specified in the model and build an event log on this basis.

Furthermore, the output of process mining plays three important roles. These include discovery, conformance and extension [28]. In discovery, the idea is that a new model is discovered from the event log and it provides insights on processes in the systems. With conformance, there is an a priori model which is used to verify if the events recorded in the log conform to such model; this is used to detect deviations, locate and explain them in order to take appropriate actions. The last role of process mining is extension, where the a priori model is extended or enriched with new aspects, for example the extension of a process model with performance data.

In our context, we intend to use process mining for the second role, which can be referred to as conformance. Rozinat and van der Aalst [26] highlight that the question of conformance arises when there is a need to check for conformity. Given the existence of predefined models that specify how the processes should (or are expected to) be executed as our ASM models, conformance helps determine at what extent these models relate to the actual process models generated as a result of recorded data. For conformance, two techniques are mainly considered to this end, namely Delta Analysis and Conformance Testing.

Delta analysis is defined as a way of comparing the discovered model (process model) with some predefined model while conformance testing attempts to determine the "fit" between these two models [27]. In our case, delta analysis implies comparing the obtained process models as a result of process mining FLOSS repositories with our ASM models. This analysis can help validate the ASM models that describe how learning occurs or provide new insights that can help enrich this area of research and probably lead to their realignment if any discrepancies are detected in order to improve the process as seen in Fig. 6 below.

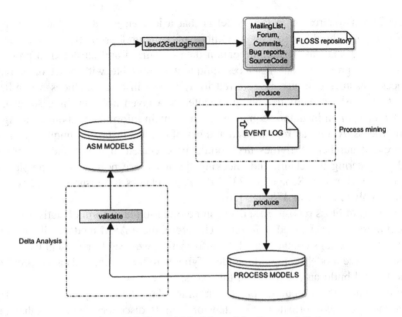

Fig. 6. ASM Ground Model used for Process Mining

6 Conclusion and Future Work

Mining Software Repositories for any purpose has been and still is the heart of numerous endeavors aiming at understanding open source software development. As we set to investigate and understand learning processes in FLOSS communities using process mining, ASM specifications can provide a detailed guideline in acquiring and retrieving relevant data. With the specifications at hands, in order to track learning processes in these environments, one can explore as much as possible data from repositories such as MailingList archives, Bug reports and CVS in order to understand patterns and related learning activities.

Our requirements as specified can be traced on these sets of data at an acceptable level of granularity.

We hope that these ASM specification and Ground Models are enough, at this point at least, to draw a representational idea as to the degree to which our identified learning processes occur in FLOSS communities.

As these activities in different phases unfold and are completed, it is critical to note that the representation of any learning process is enriched with an analysis and description of the impact of newly acquired skills on the Novice's contributions pre and post learning on a given project. In the future, we plan to conduct some empirical experiments based on these specifications in order to explore and analyze these learning processes from FLOSS repositories using Process mining techniques.

References

1. Fensel, D.: Formal specification languages in knowledge and software engineering. Knowl. Eng. Rev. **10**(4), 361–404 (1995)
2. Tse, T.H., Pong, L.: An examination of requirements specification languages. Comput. J. **34** (2), 143–152 (1991)
3. Shaw, A.C.: Software specification languages based on regular expressions. In: Riddle, W.E., Fairley, R.E. (eds.) Software Development Tools, pp. 148–175. Springer, Heidelberg (1980)
4. Harmelen, F.V., Aben, M.: Structure-preserving specification languages for knowledge-based systems. Int. J. Hum Comput Stud. **44**(2), 187–212 (1996)
5. Bjørner, D., Henson, M.C.: Logics of Specification Languages, vol. 18. Springer, Berlin (2008)
6. Cooke, D., Gates, A., Demirörs, E., Demirörs, O., Tanik, M.M., Krämer, B.: Languages for the specification of software. J. Syst. Softw. **32**(3), 269–308 (1996)
7. Tan, Y.M.: Introduction. In: Tan, Y.M. (ed.) Formal Specification Techniques for Engineering Modular C Programs, pp. 1–15. Springer, New York (1996)
8. Overstreet, C.M., Nance, R.E., Balci, O., Barger, L.F.: Specification languages: understanding their role in simulation model development (1987)
9. Gruninger, M., Tissot, F., Valois, J., Lubell, J., Lee, J.: The process specification language (PSL) overview and version 1.0 specification. US Department of Commerce, Technology Administration, National Institute of Standards and Technology (2000)
10. Gruninger, M., Menzel, C.: The process specification language (PSL) theory and applications. AI Mag. **24**(3), 63 (2003)
11. Catron, B.A., Ray, S.R.: ALPS: a language for process specification. Int. J. Comput. Integr. Manuf. **4**(2), 105–113 (1991)
12. Schlenoff, C., Knutilla, A., Ray, S.: Unified process specification language: requirements for modeling process. Interagency Report, 5910 (1996)
13. Schlenoff, C., Ray, S., Polyak, S.T., Tate, A., Cheah, S.C., Anderson, R.C.: Process specification language: an analysis of existing representations. US Department of Commerce, Technology Administration, National Institute of Standards and Technology (1998)
14. Farahbod, R., Glässer, U., Vajihollahi, M.: Specification and validation of the business process execution language for web services. In: Zimmermann, W., Thalheim, B. (eds.) ASM 2004. LNCS, vol. 3052, pp. 78–94. Springer, Heidelberg (2004)
15. Börger, E., Stärk, R.F.: Abstract State Machines: A Method for High-level System Design and Analysis (with 19 Tables). Springer, Heidelberg (2003)
16. Börger, E.: The origins and the development of the ASM method for high level system design and analysis. J. Univ. Comput. Sci. **8**(1), 2–74 (2002)
17. Börger, E.: High level system design and analysis using abstract state machines. In: Hutter, D., Stephan, W., Traverso, P., Ullmann, M. (eds.) FM-Trends 1998. LNCS, vol. 1641, pp. 1–43. Springer, Heidelberg (1999)
18. Börger, E.: The ASM Method for system design and analysis. a tutorial introduction. In: Gramlich, B. (ed.) FroCos 2005. LNCS (LNAI), vol. 3717, pp. 264–283. Springer, Heidelberg (2005)
19. Glott, R., SPI, A.M., Sowe, S.K., Conolly, T., Healy, A., Ghosh, R., West, D.: FLOSSCom - Using the Principles of Informal Learning Environments of FLOSS Communities to Improve ICT Supported Formal Education (2011)

20. Glott, R., Meiszner, A., Sowe, S.K.: FLOSSCom Phase 1 Report: Analysis of the Informal Learning Environment of FLOSS Communities. FLOSSCom Project (2007)
21. Cerone, A.K., Sowe, S.K.: Using Free/Libre Open Source Software Projects as E-learning Tools. Electronic Communications of the EASST, 33 (2010)
22. Fernandes, S., Cerone, A., Barbosa, L.S.: Analysis of FLOSS communities as learning contexts. In: Counsell, S., Núñez, M. (eds.) SEFM 2013. LNCS, vol. 8368, pp. 405–416. Springer, Heidelberg (2014)
23. Rubin, V., Günther, C.W., van der Aalst, W.M., Kindler, E., van Dongen, B.F., Schäfer, W.: Process mining framework for software processes. In: Wang, Q., Pfahl, D., Raffo, D.M. (eds.) ICSP 2007. LNCS, vol. 4470, pp. 169–181. Springer, Heidelberg (2007)
24. Cerone, A.: Learning and Activity Patterns in OSS Communities and their Impact on Software Quality. ECEASST, 48 (2011)
25. Sowe, S.K., Stamelos, I.: Reflection on Knowledge Sharing in F/OSS Projects. In: Russo, B., Damiani, E., Hissam, S., Lundell, B., Succi, G. (eds.) Open Source Development, Communities and Quality. LNCS, vol. 275, pp. 351–358. Springer, New York (2008)
26. Rozinat, A., van der Aalst, W.M.: Conformance checking of processes based on monitoring real behavior. Inf. Syst. 33(1), 64–95 (2008)
27. van der Aalst, W.M.: Business alignment: using process mining as a tool for Delta analysis and conformance testing. Requir. Eng. 10(3), 198–211 (2005)
28. van der Aalst, W.M., Rubin, V., Verbeek, H.M.W., van Dongen, B.F., Kindler, E., Günther, C.W.: Process mining: a two-step approach to balance between underfitting and overfitting. Softw. Syst. Model. 9(1), 87–111 (2010)
29. De Weerdt, J., Schupp, A., Vanderloock, A., Baesens, B.: Process mining for the multi-faceted analysis of business processes—a case study in a financial services organization. Comput. Ind. 64, 57–67 (2012)

A Mathematical Model for Assessing KRAS Mutation Effect on Monoclonal Antibody Treatment of Colorectal Cancer

Sheema Sameen, Roberto Barbuti, Paolo Milazzo$^{(\boxtimes)}$, and Antonio Cerone

Dipartimento di Informatica, Università di Pisa, Pisa, Italy
{sameen,barbuti,milazzo,cerone}@di.unipi.it

Abstract. The most challenging task in colorectal cancer research nowadays is to understand the development of acquired resistance to anti-EGFR drugs. The key reason for this problem is the KRAS mutations produced after the treatment with monoclonal antibodies (mAb). KRAS screening tests done before the start of the treatment are not very sensitive to identify minute quantity of the mutated cells, which can produce resistance to the therapy after the beginning of the treatment. Here we present a mathematical model for the analysis of KRAS mutations behavior in colorectal cancer with respect to mAb treatments. To evaluate the drug performance we have developed equations for two types of tumors cells, i.e. KRAS mutated and KRAS wildtype. Both tumor cell populations were treated with a combination of mAb and chemotherapy drugs. It was observed that even the minimal initial concentration of KRAS mutation before the treatment has the ability to make the tumor refractory to the treatment. Patient's immune responses are specifically taken into considerations and it is found that, in case of KRAS mutations, the immune strength does not affect medication efficacy. Finally, Cetuximab (mAb) and Irinotecan (chemotherapy) drugs are analyzed as first-line treatment of colorectal cancer with few KRAS mutated cells. Results show that this combined treatment is only effective for patients with high immune strengths and it should not be recommended as first-line therapy for patients with moderate immune strengths or weak immune systems because of a potential risk of relapse, with KRAS mutant cells acquired resistance involved with them.

Keywords: Colorectal cancer · Mathematical model · Monoclonal antibody resistance · KRAS mutation

1 Introduction

The World Health Organization (WHO) declared colorectal cancer (CRC) as the second most common cause of cancer mortality in Europe [1]. Monoclonal antibody (mAb) has been introduced as the most promising treatment to fight disease. The development of acquired resistance to the mAb drug, due to KRAS mutations, makes the problem very complex in terms of personalized treatment.

© Springer International Publishing Switzerland 2015
C. Canal and A. Idani (Eds.): SEFM 2014 Workshops, LNCS 8938, pp. 243–258, 2015.
DOI: 10.1007/978-3-319-15201-1_16

We have developed a system of non-linear ordinary differential equations (ODEs) to model the impact of KRAS mutations on the mAb and chemotherapy combination treatment of colorectal cancer. We have studied the behavior of mAb and chemotherapy with respect to patient immune responses and we have explored one mAb drug as a potential candidate for first-line therapy of CRC, in combination with chemotherapeutic drug.

Colorectal Cancer Therapy and KRAS Mutations. Colorectal cancer is, in most cases, caused by the overexpression of epidermal growth factor receptor (EGFR). Monoclonal antibodies are a major breakthrough in CRC therapeutic research because of their anti-EGFR activity [2,3]. The Food and Drug Administration (FDA) approved mAb drugs for colorectal cancer including Cetuximab and Panitumumab [4]. These drugs produce promising results when administered in combination with chemotherapeutic drugs [5,6]. They kill tumor cells in three ways: by directly blocking the EGFR pathway, by enhancing the activity of chemotherapeutic drugs and by enabling antibody-dependent cellular cytotoxicity (ADCC) from natural killer cells.

The emergence of KRAS mutations is the main obstacle to progresses in tumour treatments by monoclonal antibodies. It has been frequently reported that patients having KRAS mutations show no significant response to mAb treatment [7,8]. KRAS mutations are found in approximately 35 %–45 % of CRCs [9–11]. For this reason KRAS mutational status is considered as predictive marker for determining the efficacy of anti-EGFR therapies, and KRAS screening tests are prescribed by physicians before the start of treatments [12]. Only patients having wild type KRAS are eligible for mAb therapy to avoid acquired resistance to drugs in case of mutant KRAS [13]. Interestingly, some patients who have initially only KRAS wild type cells before treatment, still remain irresponsive to the medication because of the emergence of KRAS mutations. There could be two possibilities for this phenomenon: either the mutations are produced by the drug, or there are initially subpopulations of KRAS mutants present in the body which are undetectable by conventional screening tests. Most scientists agree with the second hypothesis because minimal quantities of KRAS mutant cells cannot be detected by simple sequencing techniques, but can only be found by using the sensitive pyrosequencing method [14,15].

Previous Models. Various colorectal cancer mathematical models have been developed for basic tumor cell populations, cell proliferation and for the more complex pharmacodynamic and pharmacokinetics in colorectal cancer treatment [16]. These include models of colon crypts [17–21] and models of chemotherapy for colorectal cancer [22,23]. Recently, DePillis et al. proposed a model which includes both chemo and immunotherapy along with considerations of patient specific immunity parameters. This is a comprehensive model which includes tumor cell and immune cell populations, chemotherapy and monoclonal antibody treatment. Results show the effect of drugs on chemorefractory tumors [26].

The hypothesis of drug resistance of KRAS mutations in colorectal cancer is quite recent. Diaz Jr. et al. recently published a paper in which they proved that pre-existed small number of KRAS mutated cells are responsible for developing resistance to Panitumumab, a monoclonal antibody drug [24]. Another very recent paper by Stites describes a mathematical model which evaluates how different KRAS mutated polymorphisms show different sensitivity to the EGFR inhibitors [25].

The model presented here studies the impact of KRAS mutations on the mAb treatment.

2 Extending DePillis' Model

The purpose of our model is to monitor tumor growth with respect to KRAS mutational status during and after the mAb therapy. Our model is an extension of the model developed by DePillis et al. [26]. We extend DePillis' model by representing tumor cell populations using two equations, Eq. (1) for tumor cells with wild type KRAS and Eq. (2) for mutant KRAS tumor cells. All the other equations for natural killer cells (NK), cytotoxic T lymphocytes (CTL), lymphocytes excluding NK cells and CTLs and medications are as in the original model by DePillis et al. [26]. The model is implemented using the OCTAVE programming environment [27, 28]. For detailed information and parameter values of the model see the DePillis paper [26]. The model includes equations for:

1. wild type tumor cell (Tw) and mutant tumor cell (Tm) populations;
2. patient immune system including, Natural killer cells (N), CD8+ T-Cells (L), Lymphocytes (C) and Interleukins (I);
3. chemotherapy (M) and monoclonal antibody (A) treatment;
4. patient immune strength (D).

We illustrate these four groups of equations in Sects. 2.1–2.4

2.1 Equations for Tumor Cells

Equation for KRAS Wild-Type Tumor Cells. Tumor cells with KRAS wildtype nature go through natural clonal expansion process to form a tumor mass. The only two factors that interrupt the logistic growth of tumor cells are immune system and therapy. This fact is modeled in Eq. (1).

$$\frac{dTw}{dt} = aTw(1 - b(Tw + Tm)) - (c + \xi\frac{A}{h1 + A})NTw$$
$$-DTw - (Kt + KatA)\frac{Tw}{\alpha Tm + Tw}(1 - e^{-\delta TM})Tw - \psi ATw \tag{1}$$

Logistic tumor growth is modeled by term $aTw(1 - b(Tw + Tm))$. The innate immune system of the body fights tumor cells with the help of natural killer cells (term $-cNTw$) and CD8+ T cells (term $-DTw$). Two other ways by which tumor cells experience death are chemotherapy (term $Kt\frac{Tw}{\alpha Tm+Tw}(1-e^{-\delta TM})Tw$) and monoclonal antibody treatment The triple action of monoclonal antibody, which is valid only for KRAS wildtype tumor cells, includes terms for:

- direct killing ($-\psi ATw$);
- killing by enhancement of chemotherapy ($KatA\frac{Tw}{\alpha Tm+Tw}(1-e^{-\delta TM})Tw$);
- killing by assisting natural killer cells ($-\xi\frac{A}{h1+A}NTw$).

Equation for KRAS Mutant Tumor Cells. KRAS mutant cells behave differently from the KRAS wildtypes by disturbing the triple action behavior of monoclonal antibody treatment. The monoclonal antibody is not able to directly kill KRAS mutant tumor cells and also fails to create chemosensitization in KRAS mutants. This fact is modeled in Eq. (2).

$$\frac{dTm}{dt} = aTm(1-b(Tw+Tm)) - (c+\xi\frac{A}{h1+A})NTm$$
$$-DTm - (Kt\frac{Tw}{\alpha Tm+Tw})(1-e^{-\delta TM})Tm \tag{2}$$

Thus Eq. (2) is obtained from Eq. (1) by removing the two terms for mAb induced tumor death in KRAS wildtype tumor cell equation and mAb-induced tumor death by enhancing activity of chemotherapy.

2.2   Equations for Immune Response

Natural killer cells, CD8+ T-Cells, other lymphocytes, and interleukins all play a vital role in creating immediate immune response with the initiation of tumor. Thus, in order to analyze the effect of immune system response and strength on the tumor proliferation we introduce four equations.

Natural Killer Cells. Natural Killer (NK) cells are a fundamental part of host first-line defense system. Their activity is modeled in Eq. (3).

$$\frac{dN}{dt} = eC - fN - (p+pa\frac{A}{h1+A})N(Tw+Tm) + \frac{pnNI}{gn+I}$$
$$-Kn(1-e^{-\delta NM})N \tag{3}$$

They are produced from circulating lymphocytes (term eC) and their activity is stimulated by interleukins (term $\frac{pnNI}{gn+I}$). NK turnover is modeled by term fN. In case of tumor cells NK cells exhibit a special killing mechanism known as "Antibody-dependent cell-mediated cytotoxicity" (ADCC). In this process NK cells recognize tumor cells by special receptors that identify attached antibodies on the surface of tumor cells. After recognition, NK cells release some cytotoxic granules into the tumor cell which consequently cause death. The cytotoxic granules are actually tumor killing resources of NK cell; in case of exhaustion of these resources the NK cells die (term $(p+pa\frac{A}{h1+A})N(Tw+Tm)$). In addition, NK cells may die due to chemotherapy toxicity (term $-Kn(1-e^{-\delta NM})N$).

CD8+ T-Cells. Cytotoxic lymphocytes are part of cell-mediated immunity. They kill target cells by releasing into them specialized granules that program them to undergo apoptosis. They are vital for killing tumor cells. Their activity is modeled in Eq. (4).

$$\frac{dL}{dt} = \frac{\theta mL}{\theta + I} + j\frac{Tw + Tm}{k + T}L - qL(Tw + Tm) + (r1N + r2C)$$

$$(Tw + Tm) - \frac{uL^2CI}{\kappa + I} - Kl(1 - e^{-\delta LM})L + \frac{piLI}{gi + I} \tag{4}$$

CD8+ T cell turnover is modeled by term $\frac{\theta mL}{\theta + I}$ and the breakdown of their surplus in presence of IL-2 is modeled by term $\frac{uL^2CI}{\kappa + I}$. CD8+ T cells activity is stimulated by dead tumor cells, lysed by themselves (term $j\frac{Tw + Tm}{k + T}L$), NK cells (term $r1N(Tw + Tm)$) or the general lymphocyte population (term $r2C(Tw + Tm)$). Interleukins also perform stimulating effect on CD8+ T cells (term $\frac{piLI}{gi + I}$). CD8+ T cell may die because of exhaustion of these tumor killing resources (term $qL(Tw + Tm)$) or due to chemotherapy toxicity (term $Kl(1 - e^{-\delta LM})L$).

Lymphocytes. Lymphocyte count is the most important parameter to be considered while modeling tumors undergoing chemotherapy. Chemotherapy kills normal cells along with the tumor cells; hence, patients are constantly checked for their lymphocyte count during treatment. Reduction in lymphocyte count means weakening of immune system, which makes the body more vulnerable. Lymphocyte activity is modeled in Eq. (5).

$$\frac{dC}{dt} = \alpha - \beta C - Kc(1 - e^{-\delta CM})C \tag{5}$$

Lymphocytes are synthesized in the bone marrow (term α) and their turnover is modeled by term βC. In addition, lymphocytes may be killed by chemotherapeutic drugs (term $Kc(1 - e^{-\delta CM})C$).

Interleukins. Interleukin-2 is a major regulatory factor of immune responses. It belongs to a immune signaling group of cytokines. Interleukin-2 work as an immune response system by increasing the activity of cytotoxic T-cells. Their activity is modeled in Eq. (6).

$$\frac{dI}{dt} = -\mu I + \phi C + \frac{\omega LI}{\varsigma + I} \tag{6}$$

Interleukin-2 is produced in response to activated CD8+ T-cells (term $\frac{\omega LI}{\varsigma + I}$) or by naive CD8+T cells and CD4+T cells in the body (ϕC). Its turnover is modeled by term $-\mu I$.

2.3 Equations for Treatments

In order to monitor treatments, separate equations are defined for chemotherapy (Irinotecan) and monoclonal antibody (Cetuximab). Terms $VM(t) and VA(t)$, in Eqs. (7) and (8), respectively, describe the amount of drug injected with respect to time.

Chemotherapy/Irinotecan. The activity of chemotherapy depends on the concentration of drug present in body at a specific time. This can be understood by the rate of excretion of drug from body, which is modeled by term $-\gamma M$. Chemotherapy using Irinotecan is modeled by Eq. (7)

$$\frac{dM}{dt} = -\gamma M + VM(t) \tag{7}$$

Monoclonal Antibody/Cetuximab. Monoclonal antibodies bind to the epidermal growth factor receptors (EGFRs) present on the surface of tumor cells. As an average cell contains thousands of EGFRs, many molecules of mAb drug are consumed in a single tumor cell. The loss of mAb molecules due to their binding with the tumor (term $\lambda T \frac{A}{h2+A}$) is an important factor to be considered while modeling mAb drug treatment to tumor. The rate of excretion of drug from body is modeled by term $-\eta A$.

$$\frac{dA}{dt} = -\eta A - \lambda T \frac{A}{h2 + A} + VA(t) \tag{8}$$

2.4 Patient Immune Strength Formula

Immune strength, i.e. the effectiveness of CD8+ T-cells, is calculated using Eq. (9). The formula uses the lymphocyte count $'L'$ and tumor mass $'T' = (Tw + Tm)$ along with other parameters to compute immune strength.

$$D = d \frac{(L/T)^l}{s + (L/T)^l} \tag{9}$$

Immune strength D is calculated by considering the following parameters:

d = immune strength coefficient;

l = immune-system strength scaling coefficient;

s = ratio of $(L/T)^l$ (It tells how quickly CD8+ T-cell respond to the presence of tumor)

In our simulation we varied the parameters to generate three types of immune strength values: strong, moderate and weak.

2.5   Initial Conditions and Drug Dosages

The initial conditions for the model are taken from DePillis model except the number of KRAS mutated cells. The initial number of KRAS mutated cells, which can cause resistance to the treatment, is not available in the literature. Thus we assumed a small number for KRAS mutated cells, say 35, because even such a small number of mutated cells is able to cause resistance. The initial conditions for the model are as follows.

$$Tw = 4.65928 \times 10^9$$
$$Tm = 35$$
$$N = 9 \times 10^7$$
$$L = 1.8 \times 10^5$$
$$C = 9 \times 10^8$$
$$M = 0$$
$$I = 1173$$
$$A = 0$$

The parameter values in our model are also taken from DePilis except the rate of chemotherapy induced tumor death, which is reduced to the minimum level because of KRAS mutations. As DePillis, we assume that patients are already gone through first-line chemotherapy and are refractory to the treatment. Therefore, the initial tumor is assumed to have a very large number of cells: 4.65928×10^9. If tumor size becomes less than 2^7 cells during the treatment, it is assumed that the tumor is showing complete response to the therapy. Similarly, tumors which remain larger then 2^7 but do not continue to grow during the treatment are considered to have partial response.

Treatment comprised individual or combination of monoclonal antibody and chemotherapeutic drug, Cetuximab and Irniotecan, respectively. The drugs are administered according to standard FDA approved dosages and timings. For Irinotecan, a $125\,\text{mg/m}^2$ dose is given over 90 min once a week, for 4 weeks. For Cetuximab, a loading dose of $400\,\text{mg/m}^2$ is administered for two hours, followed by a $250\,\text{mg/m}^2$ dose over 60 min given every week for one month.

3   Results

3.1   Monoclonal Antibody Effect on Chemotherapy and Natural Killer Cell Activity

The enhancement of natural killer cells activity induced by mAb therapy is the same for both mutated and wildtype cells. This is represented in both equations by the $-\xi \frac{A}{h1+A} NTw$ term. Chemotherapy has reduced effectiveness against tumor cells during monoclonal antibody treatment because of mutant cells. This is represented in the model by $-Kt\frac{Tw}{\alpha(Tm)+Tw}$. The chemotherapy effectiveness

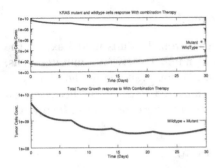

Fig. 1. α value: 10^6 shows rapid decrease in wildtype and increase in mutant KRAS cells (Red: mutant; Blue: wildtype) (Colour figure online)

Fig. 2. α: 10^7 shows gradual decrease in wildtype and increase in mutant KRAS cells (Red: mutant; Blue: wildtype) (Colour figure online)

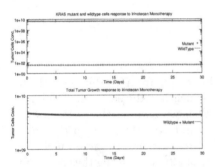

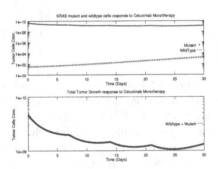

Fig. 3. Irinotecan monotherapy(Red: mutant; Blue: wildtype) (Colour figure online)

Fig. 4. Cetuximab monotherapy(Red: mutant; Blue: wildtype) (Colour figure online)

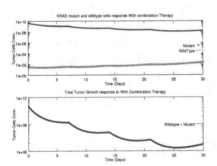

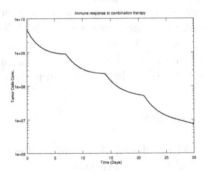

Fig. 5. Cetuximab and Irinotecan as combination therapy with KRAS mutant (Red: Mutant; Blue: Wildtype) (Colour figure online)

Fig. 6. Cetuximab and Irinotecan as combination therapy without KRAS mutant (Red: Mutant; Blue: Wildtype) (Colour figure online)

Table 1. Cetuximab and irinotecan combination therapy

	With KRAS Mutation	Without KRAS mutation
Strong immunity	NR/PR (Fig. 7)	CR (Fig. 8)
Moderate immunity	NR (Fig. 9)	PR (Fig. 10)
Weak immunity	NR (Fig. 11)	NR (Fig. 12)

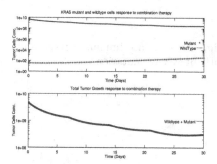

Fig. 7. Moderate Immunity response to KRAS mutation

Fig. 8. Strong Immunity response without KRAS mutation

decreases with the increase of the number of mutated cells. This term is introduced in both the equations of wildtype and mutant tumour cells for controlling the rate of chemotherapy induced tumor death. Kt is the maximum rate of chemotherapy induced tumor death in the absence of KRAS mutant cells. The above term makes the effectiveness of the chemotherapy dependent on the ratio of wildtype and total tumor cells. This ratio is controlled by the parameter α in such a way that, by increasing α, the rate of chemotherapy induced death is decreased with respect to the increase in the mutant population (Figs. 1 and 2). Similarly, by increasing the initial number of KRAS mutated cells or by decreasing the initial number of KRAS wildtype cells, the rate of chemotherapy induced tumor death becomes much lower. Hence, the function clearly models the phenomenon of chemotherapy ineffectiveness, in conjunction with monoclonal antibody treatment, in case of presence of KRAS mutant cells. It is hard to find more realistic values for α as we did not find any clue in the literature about the chemotherapy ineffectiveness rate due to increase in KRAS mutations. In our simulations we used the value $\alpha = 10^7$ because this shows a gradual decrease in the efficiency of the chemotherapy as compared to a too rapid reduction experimented with the smaller value $\alpha = 10^6$.

3.2 Treatment Trial Simulations for KRAS Mutated Colorectal Cancer Tumors

Our model has been evaluated for standard treatments by chemotherapy and monoclonal antibodies for tumors with KRAS mutations. The KRAS mutated

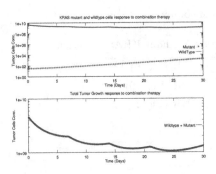

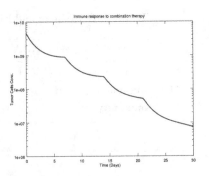

Fig. 9. Moderate Immunity response to KRAS mutation

Fig. 10. Moderate Immunity response without KRAS mutation

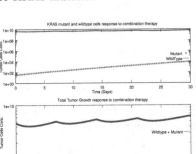

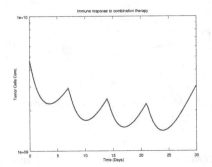

Fig. 11. Weak Immunity response with KRAS mutation

Fig. 12. Weak Immunity response without KRAS mutation

tumors are treated according to standard dosage of drugs and are evaluated for both monotherapy and combination therapy.

Cetuximab and Irinotecan Monotherapy. In accordance with the literature, in our model Cetuximab monotherapy has no impact on colorectal tumors because of the number of elevated KRAS mutated tumor cells (Fig. 4). Similarly, Irinotecan monotherapy has no impact on the tumor because of the chemorefractory status of tumor. Here, no increase in KRAS mutated cells is noticed (Fig. 3). Results show that, although both drugs fail as monotherapies, failure of Cetuximab is specifically caused by an increase in the number of KRAS mutated cells.

Cetuximab and Irinotecan Combination Therapy. For patients presenting metastatic colorectal cancer, Cetuximab and Irinotecan are recommended in combination. We used our model to test the combination of the two drugs. This allowed us to understand the impact of combined therapy on KRAS mutated tumor cells (Fig. 5). KRAS mutated cells grow with the passage of time and KRAS wild type cells start to reduce. However, as the initial number of KRAS mutated cells is very small, their increase is not clearly visible in the figure.

Anyway, even this very low level of KRAS mutated cells is still able to gradually reduce the activity of drugs (Fig. 5). The combination therapy is only effective for KRAS wildtype tumours (Fig. 6).

3.3 Patient Responses to the Therapy

We simulated our model for patients with different immune strengths. Generally, it is believed that a strong immune system both helps the medication and facilitates quick recovery, while patients with weak immunity do not respond well to the medicine. We analyzed the interaction between patient immune strength and treatment in case of mutation development during and after medication. The hypothetical immune strength values are calculated for generating weak, moderate and strong immune responses. These values are generated by the formula for immune strength (Eq. (9)) by changing the values of its parameters.

Our results are summarized in Table 1. Patients without KRAS mutations have complete response (CR), partial response (PR) and no response (NR) for strong, moderate and weak immunity, respectively. With KRAS mutations the immune strength has no significant impact on the treatment. KRAS mutated tumours normally show no response to the treatment but sometimes there is a partial response in presence of a high immune strength. For moderate and weak immunity there is no response at all.

3.4 Cetuximab and Irinotecan as First-Line Therapy

In this section we explore the possibility of using Cetuximab and Irinotecan as first-line therapy. Initial conditions are the same as shown in Sect. 2.5. Patients having weak immunity do not show any significant response to the Cetuximab and Irinotecan as first-line therapy (Fig. 13). Tumor size reduces significantly in patients with moderate immunity, but the number of KRAS mutated cells show a relevant increase (Fig. 14). The response to the therapy is only observed in patients with strong immunity and very low number of initial KRAS mutated cells (Fig. 15).

4 Discussion

Emergence of KRAS mutated status is an alarming situation for colorectal cancer patients being treated with anti-EGFRs. Presence of KRAS mutations in a tumor treated with monoclonal antibodies is a sign of becoming refractory to treatments. In order to understand the phenomenon of developing resistance to the anti-EGFRs we developed a mathematical model with separate equations for KRAS mutant and wildtype cells.

A major problem in colorectal cancer is to identify the behavior of monoclonal antibody therapy in presence of KRAS mutations and the impact of the mutations on other therapies. More specifically, exploring the sensitivity of monoclonal antibody drugs to the chemotherapy and natural killer cells activity

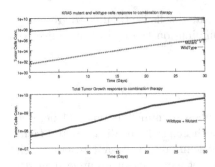
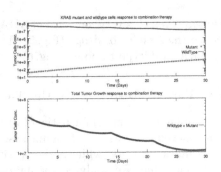

Fig. 13. Cetuximab and Irinotecan as first-line therapy: weak immune response (Red: Mutant; Blue: Wild-type) (Colour figure online)

Fig. 14. Cetuximab and Irinotecan as first-line therapy: moderate immune response (Red: Mutant; blue: Wild-type) (Colour figure online)

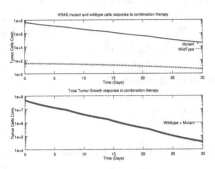

Fig. 15. Cetuximab and Irinotecan as first-line therapy: strong immune response (Red:Mutant; Blue:Wildtype) (Colour figure online)

in the presence of mutations is another key issue in understanding drug efficacy [29]. In case of natural killer cells, Cetuximab has equal enhancing effect on both KRAS mutant and wildtype cells. In other words, KRAS mutational status has no impact on the antibody-dependent cellular cytotoxicity (ADCC) mediated by the drug [32]. Cetuximab has been frequently reported to increase chemotherapeutic activity upon combination with Irinotecan drug in tumor cells [30,31]. Studies show that KRAS mutant cells do not allow Cetuximab to produce such type of chemosensitization [9,13]. In chemo-refractory colorectal cancer with mutated KRAS the chemotherapy failed to induce tumor cell death, not only for mutated cells but also for wildtype cells. The reason for this lies in the heterogeneity of KRAS mutations in colorectal tumors [33–35]. In order to model this phenomenon we have regulated the rate of chemotherapy induced tumor death. We assumed that the effect of chemotherapy decreases with the increase in KRAS mutated cells. Therefore, we cannot take any benefit from the chemosensitization activity of mAb drugs in case of KRAS mutations. The chemotherapy may work effectively only at the beginning of the treatment but then, with the increase of KRAS mutant population, starts to loose its strength.

Patient immune responses play a vital role in oncotherapeutic processes and this role varies from positive to negative with strong to weak immune strength respectively. The immune strength becomes unimportant for KRAS mutated patients because the initially strong immunity turns into a weak one due to the development of secondary KRAS mutations during the treatment [36]. Even with the highest immune strength, the response to the drugs is only partial (sometimes). In our simulations tumor size was set to its maximum and it is considered refractory to the chemotherapy given as first-line to the patients. The reason for adopting these criteria is because Cetuximab is generally given as third- or fourth-line treatment to the patients as final rescue [38, 39]. Hence it is proved that there is no correlation between immune strength and combination treatment for KRAS mutated patients.

The Cetuximab and Irinotecan combination therapy is proved to be very effective as first-line therapy for colorectal cancer but this is true only for KRAS wild-type patients [11, 37]. Although KRAS screening tests are always performed before starting monoclonal antibody treatments, there is a risk of minimal quantities of KRAS mutated cells that are not detected by common sequencing processes of laboratories. In this case critical questions arise about the patient's response to Cetuximab and Irinotecan as first-line therapy. Our results show complete response only in patients with strong immunity. High immune strength means little number of KRAS mutations, so there is a chance that the drug kills wild-type cells quickly and chemotherapy also gets the chance to kill mutant cells. The first-line therapy seems to work also for moderately immune persons but, at the same time, increases the KRAS mutation level, which is a sign of recurrence of disease. Patient responses are also dependent upon the initial KRAS mutant cell concentrations. If the initial mutant level is very low then a complete response can be obtained. However, in case of greater level of initial KRAS mutants, the response is only partial with decrease in tumor size and significant increase in KRAS mutant levels, which doubles the chances of relapse. The relapse after Cetuximab as first-line therapy will be more lethal because of acquired resistance to the drugs due to increased KRAS mutant populations.

5   Conclusion and Future Work

In Cetuximab and Irinotecan combination therapy the rapid increase in levels of KRAS mutations and the partial or no response on the tumor size an indications of the development of resistance to the drugs. Using our model we could measure the level of KRAS mutations that can be tolerated to avoid resistance to anti-EGFRs. This could provide information to stop the anti-EGFR treatment before reaching the threshold value for KRAS mutant cells. The treatment could be switched from anti-EGFR to anti-KRAS drugs. We do not know the clinical perspective about switching treatments, but this could provide a better way to solve the secondary KRAS mutation problem in colorectal cancers.

Patients with stronger immunity can be highly recommended for Cetuximab and Irinotecan as first-line therapy but there is no instrument to accurately judge a person's immunity. Thus there is a potential risk associated with standard dosage cycles of drugs. The failure of the treatment will ultimately lead towards tumor progression with much higher rates. Moreover, the increased number of KRAS mutations makes the problem even more complex by creating resistance against the drugs. The co-occurrence of EGFR and KRAS mutations in a colorectal cancer patient is indeed the worst case scenario. The possibilities of Cetuximab and Irinotecan drugs as first-line therapy for treatment of KRAS mutated colorectal cancer can again be explored by varying dosages and timings of the drugs and also by applying other monoclonal antibodies, e.g. Panitumumab and Bevacizumab.

As future work, we also aim to develop a stochastic computational model for KRAS mutations and combine it with the current mathematical model in order to increase the accuracy of the model.

References

1. WHO/Europe—Colorectal cancer. http://www.euro.who.int/en/health-topics/noncommunicable-diseases/cancer/news/news/2012/2/early-detection-of-common-cancers/colorectal-cancer
2. Deschoolmeester, V., Baay, M., Specenier, P., Lardon, F., Vermorken, J.B.: A review of the most promising biomarkers in colorectal cancer: one step closer to targeted therapy. Oncologist 15, 699–731 (2010)
3. Repetto, L., Gianni, W., Aglianò, A.M., Gazzaniga, P.: Impact of EGFR expression on colorectal cancer patient prognosis and survival: a response. Ann. Oncol. 16, 1557 (2005)
4. Gschwind, A., Fischer, O.M., Ullrich, A.: The discovery of receptor tyrosine kinases: targets for cancer therapy. Nat. Rev. Cancer. 4, 361–370 (2004)
5. Van Cutsem, E., Peeters, M., Siena, S., Humblet, Y., Hendlisz, A., Neyns, B., Canon, J.L., Van Laethem, J.L., Maurel, J., Richardson, G., Wolf, M., Amado, R.G.: Open-label phase III trial of panitumumab plus best supportive care compared with best supportive care alone in patients with chemotherapy-refractory metastatic colorectal cancer. J. Clin. Oncol. 25, 1658–1664 (2007)
6. Martinelli, E., De Palma, R., Orditura, M., De Vita, F., Ciardiello, F.: Anti-epidermal growth factor receptor monoclonal antibodies in cancer therapy. Clin. Exp. Immunol. 158, 1–9 (2009)
7. Parsons, B.L., Meng, F.: K-RAS mutation in the screening, prognosis and treatment of cancer. Biomark Med. 3, 757–769 (2009)
8. Bando, H., Yoshino, T., Tsuchihara, K., Ogasawara, N., Fuse, N., Kojima, T., Tahara, M., Kojima, M., Kaneko, K., Doi, T., Ochiai, A., Esumi, H., Ohtsu, A.: KRAS mutations detected by the amplification refractory mutation system-scorpion assays strongly correlate with therapeutic effect of cetuximab. Br. J. Cancer 105, 403–406 (2011)
9. Karapetis, C.S., Khambata-Ford, S., Jonker, D.J., O'Callaghan, C.J., Tu, D., Tebbutt, N.C., Simes, R.J., Chalchal, H., Shapiro, J.D., Robitaille, S., Price, T.J., Shepherd, L., Au, H.J., Langer, C., Moore, M.J., Zalcberg, J.R.: K-ras mutations and benefit from cetuximab in advanced colorectal cancer. N. Engl. J. Med. 359, 1757–1765 (2008)

10. Amado, R.G., Wolf, M., Peeters, M., Van Cutsem, E., Siena, S., Freeman, D.J., Juan, T., Sikorski, R., Suggs, S., Radinsky, R., Patterson, S.D., Chang, D.D.: Wild-type KRAS is required for panitumumab efficacy in patients with metastatic colorectal cancer. J. Clin. Oncol. **26**, 1626–1634 (2008)
11. Van Cutsem, E., Köhne, C.H., Hitre, E., Zaluski, J., Chang Chien, C.R., Makhson, A., D'Haens, G., Pintér, T., Lim, R., Bodoky, G., Roh, J.K., Folprecht, G., Ruff, P., Stroh, C., Tejpar, S., Schlichting, M., Nippgen, J., Rougier, P.: Cetuximab and chemotherapy as initial treatment for metastatic colorectal cancer. N. Engl. J. Med. **360**, 1408–1417 (2009)
12. Fakih, M.M.: KRAS mutation screening in colorectal cancer: from paper to practice. Clin. Colorectal Cancer **9**, 22–30 (2010)
13. De Roock, W., Piessevaux, H., De Schutter, J., Janssens, M., De Hertogh, G., Personeni, N., Biesmans, B., Van Laethem, J.L., Peeters, M., Humblet, Y., Van Cutsem, E., Tejpar, S.: KRAS wild-type state predicts survival and is associated to early radiological response in metastatic colorectal cancer treated with cetuximab. Ann. Oncol. **19**, 508–515 (2008)
14. Parsons, B.L., Myers, M.B.: KRAS mutant tumor subpopulations can subvert durable responses to personalized cancer treatments. Pers. Med. **10**, 191–199 (2013)
15. Tougeron, D., Lecomte, T., Pagés, J.C., Villalva, C., Collin, C., Ferru, A., Tourani, J.M., Silvain, C., Levillain, P., Karayan-Tapon, L.: Effect of low-frequency KRAS mutations on the response to anti-EGFR therapy in metastatic colorectal cancer. Ann. Oncol. **24**, 1267–1273 (2013)
16. Ballesta, A., Clairambault, J.: Physiologically based mathematical models to optimize therapies against metastatic colorectal cancer: a mini-review. Curr. Pharm. Des. **20**, 37–48 (2014)
17. Johnston, M.D., Edwards, C.M., Bodmer, W.F., Maini, P.K., Chapman, S.J.: Mathematical modeling of cell population dynamics in the colonic crypt and in colorectal cancer. Proc. Natl. Acad. Sci. U.S.A. **104**, 4008–4013 (2007)
18. van Leeuwen, I.M., Byrne, H.M., Jensen, O.E., King, J.R.: Crypt dynamics and colorectal cancer: advances in mathematical modelling. Cell Prolif. **39**, 157–181 (2006)
19. Fletcher, A.G., Breward, C.J.W., Chapman, S.J.: Mathematical modeling of monoclonal conversion in the colonic crypt. J. Theor. Biol. **300**, 118–133 (2012)
20. Murray, P.J., Walter, A., Fletcher, A.G., Edwards, C.M., Tindall, M.J., Maini, P.K.: Comparing a discrete and continuum model of the intestinal crypt. Phys. Biol. **8**, 1478–3975 (2011)
21. Johnston, M.D., Edwards, C.M., Bodmer, W.F., Maini, P.K., Chapman, S.J.: Mathematical modeling of cell population dynamics in the colonic crypt and in colorectal cancer. Proc. Natl. Acad. Sci. U.S.A. **104**(10), 4008–4013 (2007)
22. Monro, H.C., Gaffney, E.A.: Modelling chemotherapy resistance in palliation and failed cure. J. Theor. Biol. **257**, 292–302 (2009)
23. Boston, E.A.J., Gaffney, E.A.: The influence of toxicity constraints in models of chemotherapeutic protocol escalation. Math. Med. Biol. **28**, 357–384 (2011)
24. Diaz, L.A., Williams, R.T., Wu, J., Kinde, I., Hecht, J.R., Berlin, J., Allen, B., Bozic, I., Reiter, J.G., Nowak, M.A., Kinzler, K.W., Oliner, K.S., Vogelstein, B.: The molecular evolution of acquired resistance to targeted EGFR blockade in colorectal cancers. Nature **486**, 537–540 (2012)
25. Stites, E.C.: Differences in sensitivity to EGFR inhibitors could be explained by described biochemical differences between oncogenic Ras mutants. bioRxiv (2014). http://dx.doi.org/10.1101/005397

26. de Pillis, L.G., Savage, H., Radunskaya, A.E.: Mathematical model of colorectal cancer with monoclonal antibody treatments. Brit. J. of Med. and Medical Res. 4(16), 3101–3131 (2014)
27. GNU Octave 3.8.1. http://www.gnu.org/software/octave/
28. Eaton, J.W., Bateman, D., Hauberg, S.: GNU Octave version 3.0.1 manual: a high-level interactive language for numerical computations, CreateSpace Independent Publishing Platform. ISBN: 1441413006 (2009). http://www.gnu.org/software/octave/doc/interpreter
29. Arnold, D., Seufferlein, T.: Targeted treatments in colorectal cancer: state of the art and future perspectives. Gut **59**, 838–858 (2010)
30. Prewett, M.C., Hooper, A.T., Bassi, R., Ellis, L.M., Waksal, H.W., Hicklin, D.J.: Enhanced antitumor activity of anti-epidermal growth factor receptor monoclonal antibody IMC-C225 in combination with irinotecan (CPT-11) against human colorectal tumor xenografts. Clin. Cancer Res. **8**, 994–1003 (2002)
31. Jonker, D.J., O'Callaghan, C.J., Karapetis, C.S., Zalcberg, J.R., Tu, D., Au, H.J., Berry, S.R., Krahn, M., Price, T., Simes, R.J., Tebbutt, N.C., van Hazel, G., Wierzbicki, R., Langer, C., Moore, M.J.: Cetuximab for the treatment of colorectal cancer. N. Engl. J. Med. **357**, 2040–2048 (2007)
32. Wu, L., Adams, M., Carter, T., Chen, R., Muller, G., Stirling, D., Schafer, P., Bartlett, J.B.: lenalidomide enhances natural killer cell and monocyte-mediated antibody-dependent cellular cytotoxicity of rituximab-treated CD20+ tumor cells. Clin. Cancer Res. **14**, 4650–4657 (2008)
33. Vilar, E., Tabernero, J.: Cancer: pinprick diagnostics. Nature **486**, 482–483 (2012)
34. Baldus, S.E., Schaefer, K.L., Engers, R., Hartleb, D., Stoecklein, N.H., Gabbert, H.E.: Prevalence and heterogeneity of KRAS, BRAF, and PIK3CA mutations in primary colorectal adenocarcinomas and their corresponding metastases. Clin. Cancer Res. **16**, 790–799 (2010)
35. Hasovits, C., Pavlakis, N., Howell, V., Gill, A., Clarke, S.: Resistance to EGFR targeted antibodies - expansion of clones present from the start of treatment. The more things change, the more they stay the same (Plus ca change, plus ca ne change pas!. Transl. Gastrointest. Cancer **2**, 44–46 (2013)
36. Smakman, N., Veenendaal, L.M., van Diest, P., Bos, R., Offringa, R., Borel Rinkes, I.H., Kranenburg, O.: Dual effect of Kras(D12) knockdown on tumorigenesis: increased immune-mediated tumor clearance and abrogation of tumor malignancy. Oncogene **24**, 8338–8342 (2005)
37. Folprecht, G., Lutz, M.P., Schöffski, P., Seufferlein, T., Nolting, A., Pollert, P., Köhne, C.H.: Cetuximab and irinotecan/5-fluorouracil/folinic acid is a safe combination for the first-line treatment of patients with epidermal growth factor receptor expressing metastatic colorectal carcinoma. Ann. Oncol. **17**, 450–456 (2006)
38. Pfeiffer, P., Nielsen, D., Bjerregaard, J., Qvortrup, C., Yilmaz, M., Jensen, B.: Biweekly cetuximab and irinotecan as third-line therapy in patients with advanced colorectal cancer after failure to irinotecan, oxaliplatin and 5-fluorouracil. Ann. Oncol. **19**, 1141–1145 (2008)
39. Vincenzi, B., Santini, D., Rabitti, C., Coppola, R., Beomonte Zobel, B., Trodella, L., Tonini, G.: Cetuximab and irinotecan as third-line therapy in advanced colorectal cancer patients: a single centre phase II trial. Br. J. Cancer. **94**, 792–797 (2006)

Sea-Scale Agent-Based Simulator of *Solea solea* in the Adriatic Sea

Cesar Augusto Nieto Coria[1,4], Luca Tesei[1,4(✉)], Giuseppe Scarcella[2],
Tommaso Russo[3], and Emanuela Merelli[1,4]

[1] School of Science and Technology, University of Camerino, Camerino, Italy
{cesar.nietocoria,luca.tesei,emanuela.merelli}@unicam.it
[2] National Research Council - Institute of Marine Sciences Ancona, Ancona, Itlay
giuseppe.scarcella@an.ismar.cnr.it
[3] LESA-TVUR - Laboratory of Experimental Ecology and Aquaculture,
Tor Vergata University of Rome, Rome, Italy
tommaso.russo@uniroma2.it
[4] CINFAI, Consorzio Interuniversitario Nazionale per la Fisica delle Atmosfere e
delle Idrosfere, Sezione di Camerino, Camerino, Italy

Abstract. DISPAS is an agent-based simulator for fish stock assessment developed as a decision making support for the sustainable management of fishery. In this work we enlarge the underlying model of DISPAS allowing it to model and simulate a multi-scale scenario. We retain the currently available spatial scale, able to represent a limited average region of the sea, and we introduce a new spatial macro-scale, able to represent the whole sea. At the macro-scale a single agent represents an area of five square nautical miles and manages groups of fish in different age classes. The interactions among the macro agents permit the exchange of individuals of each class among neighbor areas. A case study regarding the *Solea solea* (Linnaeus, 1758; Soleidae) stock of the northern Adriatic Sea is used to show the intended approach, taking into account the available data, coming from fishery independent scientific surveys.

Keywords: Modeling and simulation · Agent-based modeling · Ecosystem modeling · Common sole · Adriatic Sea · Multi-scale modeling

1 Introduction

Marine ecosystems are undoubtedly an important environmental resource for the life they support and, from a more ordinary point of view, as a source of food through fishing activities, which are a relevant sector of the economy of mostly all of the coastal Countries. Because of its importance, in the last twenty years, a global concern about the sustainable management of marine resources has risen [10]. In particular, as a partial consequence of weak or ineffective fishery management policies, a rising overfishing in the Mediterranean Sea have been put forward by scientists [5]. Within this scenario, national and regional management bodies, with the support of research institutes, are currently cooperating to

© Springer International Publishing Switzerland 2015
C. Canal and A. Idani (Eds.): SEFM 2014 Workshops, LNCS 8938, pp. 259–275, 2015.
DOI: 10.1007/978-3-319-15201-1_17

study, address and try to minimize the impact of fishery both on target species and on their environment.

The northern part of the Adriatic Sea, as part of the Mediterranean Sea, is one area of interest for these studies. Here, flatfish resources are highly vulnerable to certain fishing activities (e.g. rapido trawling [25]) and to anthropogenic impacts, such as the presence of contaminants and the disruption of sea-floor integrity (e.g. dredging for beach nourishment). Within the group of flatfish, the common sole, *Solea solea* (Linnaeus, 1758), is one of the most commercially important species in the Adriatic Sea, which contributes for around 23 % to the overall sole catch of the FAO-GFCM (Food and Agriculture Organization-General Fisheries Council for the Mediterranean) area (Mediterranean and Black Sea; FAO-FISHSTAT source). The majority of this contribution is provided by the northern and central parts of the Adriatic basin, where around 64 % of the common sole catches come from the Italian rapido trawl fleets, 33 % from the Italian, Slovenian and Croatian set netters operating mostly within 3 nautical miles from the coast, and the remaining 3 % from the Italian otter trawlers [9]. In particular, approximately 80 % of sole rapido trawl landings in the area occur during the fall season [7].

In this scenario, marine biologists are required by management bodies to monitor the sole fish stock in order to estimate its current size, determine the impact of the fishing effort and give support for establishing fishing policies to contrast overfishing. Among other initiatives, the SoleMon project [9] was started in order to get fishery independent data, from scientific surveys, about soles in the northern Adriatic Sea. These data are being applied to assess the stock, implementing methodologies typical of the marine ecology sector. As a new promising way of using the available data and supporting the stock assessment, DISPAS (Demersal fIsh Stock Probabilistic Agent-based Simulator) [2,22,23] was introduced. DISPAS is an agent-based simulator that was designed, implemented and validated with the aim of having a tool to simulate how a (demersal) fish stock would react to different scenarios of fishing efforts, considering also seasonal and environmental conditions. The current version of the simulator is able to reproduce an average square kilometer of sea in which each individual fish is represented by an agent. The behavior of each agent is timed and probabilistic. At every time step, simulating one month, any individual grows according to a parametrized growth function. In the same step it is also subject to a natural mortality probability - modeling interaction with other species (not explicitly represented in the simulator) and with the environment - and to a probability of being fished, which can vary at different months and can be set in different ways to express a range of fishing efforts. In [2,22,23] it is shown that DISPAS simulations are able to reproduce with a good degree of accuracy the biomass (total weight of the stock), the abundance (total number of individuals in the stock, divided by age class) and other indices of the considered stock in the target period 2005–2011, as they are established by marine biologists [9].

Studies to evaluate existing *spatial* management regimes and potential new spatial and temporal closures in the northern and central Adriatic Sea have been carried out employing a simple modeling tool [30]. However, a *quantitative analysis* of spatial management options is quite complicated to perform. This is mainly due to the fact that information on the spatial dynamics of fleets and stocks is often unavailable and effective spatial models are difficult to construct [14]. In response to this need, in this work we present the main ideas and machineries that will enable DISPAS to model and simulate a bigger portion of a sea. The main motivation of doing this is to develop a spatial simulator enabling marine biologists to experiment with their hypotheses and data on the spatial distribution of the common sole stock in the northern Adriatic Sea. Our solution is mainly guided by the paradigm of Complex Automata [11–13] that permits the specification of multi-scale simulations in a flexible and general way. In particular, we define a macro model of simulation at the sea scale that is essentially a Cellular Automaton [3,32], with specific features, in which each cell represents an hexagonal area of the sea of approximatively five square nautical miles. The evolution of the individual soles in each area is simulated through a "micro" model that corresponds, ideally, to the current DISPAS implementation. Migration vectors in every possible direction are applied at each time step, which is kept as one month, in order to accomplish the movement of individuals from an area to neighbor areas. To obtain a more efficient multi-scale simulation, in terms of time and space, a strategy for uncoupling of the ideal schema suggested by the Complex Automata paradigm is proposed. This involves a preliminary set of simulations, performed with the currently available version of DISPAS, in order to obtain a "decoupling operator". This operator is used to perform the macro simulation as a standalone process.

The paper is organized as follows. Section 2 introduces some biological and ecological information about the target species (common sole), while Sect. 3 recalls the main features of the current version of DISPAS. In Sect. 4, the paradigm of Complex Automata is introduced to be then adapted, in Sect. 5, to our needs and to the context of our case study. Finally, Sect. 6 concludes.

2 Biological and Ecological Background

The common sole belongs to a family of Soleidae and is a demersal fish. Among other areas, e.g. in the North Sea, it lives in the whole Mediterranean Sea. However, due to particular environmental conditions, the main concentration of soles are in the seabeds of the northern and central part of the Adriatic Sea (FAO GFCM Geographical Sub-Area 17).

Over time, a rising fishing effort has been applied to the sole fish stock; this situation, together with a weak management of the fishery policies, has led to an overfishing situation [29]. An example of the fishery policies that have been applied by the Italian government is the closure of the trawl fishery along the Italian shore (3 nautical miles from the coast) [1]. Another example of fishery management policy is the fishing ban in the summer period (June, July and August), or the legal minimum landing size for sole in the Mediterranean (20 cm; EC reg. n. 1967/2006). Notwithstanding these policies, the fish stock of the common sole in the Adriatic Sea is still overfished and its sustainability is considered at risk [29].

It is well known that the spatial distribution of individuals in a species are in general not random, but depends on biological and environmental factors, e.g. availability of food, climate, temperature and so on. In [9] the data of the SoleMon project were reported. Data in the period 2005–2011 were used to study the distribution patterns of the demersal fish species that inhabit the Adriatic Sea. The results of this work were the determination of the spatial distribution of the common sole in the Adriatic Sea, differentiated by age classes.

In [30], a spatial management of fishing effort patterns was presented, precisely for *rapido trawling* techniques, which is the most important activity targeting the common sole in GSA 17. Two spatial fishing scenarios were proposed: ban the rapido trawling (i) within 6 and (ii) within 9 nautical miles of the Italian coast, from October to December. The aim was to study the impact of this fishing technique on the stock, especially on the sole juveniles, and also the collateral impact on the environment, e.g. habitat degradation by the seabed trawling.

Data from SoleMon (period 2006–2011) and data from Vessel Monitor System (VMS) [26–28], which are about the fishery activity of 100 rapido trawl vessels in the northern and central part of the Adriatic Sea, were used to estimate the spatial pattern of the fleet. It was shown that the bigger fishery effort is applied on the juveniles of the sole (classes from 0 to 2). A significant contribution of the work was the idea of a management policy driven by a spatio-temporal restriction on the fishery zones, especially where the juvenile age classes are concentrated. The works presented above are the main biological references on which we base on, in this paper, for introducing the multi-scale model for DISPAS.

3   DISPAS at Work

In this section we briefly summarize the main features of the current version of DISPAS (Demersal fIsh Stock Probabilistic Agent-based Simulator), underlying some results already obtained [2, 23]. For more details we mainly refer to [22].

DISPAS was developed since the beginning with the aim of studying and supporting fish stock sustainability. The common sole stock of the northern Adriatic Sea was selected as target case study, given the importance of the stock from an ecological point of view and the availability of data (see Sects. 1 and 2). Agent-based modeling [8, 15] was selected as the main paradigm of design, given the vision of introducing in the marine ecology sector a tool using a different approach from the classical ODE- or PDE-based modeling techniques. For modeling the behavior of a single agent, which should emulate an individual fish (a sole), we defined a class of automata called EPDTA (Extended Probabilistic Discrete Timed Automata) [2]. Applying this automaton-based model we can formally specify the behavior of an individual fish, depending on time. We represent the interaction with other species and with the marine environment as probabilities of natural mortality. The fishing effort is also expressed as a probabilities of being fished. All these probabilities depend on time and on the age of the fish.

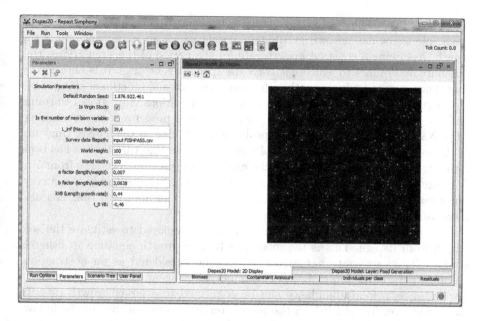

Fig. 1. DISPAS screen shoot.

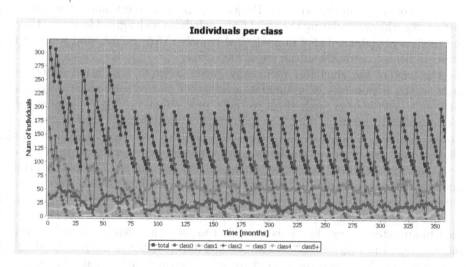

Fig. 2. Number of Individuals chart, divided by age classes, derived from a DISPAS execution.

The simulator has been developed, following the agent-based methodology, on the Repast Simphony suite [19]. DISPAS (see Fig. 1 for a screen shot) is currently able to manage a virtual space of a square kilometer of sea where the sole agents live[1]. The discrete time step of the simulation is equal to one month. Each sole agent has its own attributes, among which an important one is the length. Assuming a constant growth rate for the period of the simulations, this attribute determines to which *age class* the specimens belongs. It is noteworthy that differences in body size within the same age class and functional groups may also occur and could reflect changes in climatic conditions (e.g., global warming and its impacts on phytoplankton [24]) or human pressure (e.g., overfishing; [20]). Natural and fishing mortality probabilities change on the base of time and of the sole age class. The longevity of common sole in the Adriatic Sea has been estimated as 8–10 years [9]. Due to the exploitation pressure, the ages from 5 to 8/10 are not well represented both in the commercial catches and in the survey. For these reasons, a plus group 5+ has been used, an approach that has also been used in [30].

The von Bertalanffy growth equation [31] is employed to estimate the sole length from its age. This is the most widely used growth equation in fisheries studies. Its growth rate parameter, K, can be considered as an abstraction, among others, of the interactions of each individual agent with the environment. For instance, a food abundance can be connected to a larger growth rate. In the current version of DISPAS the parameter K is constant, but in the following versions it will become dependent on time, on space and on environmental conditions, e.g. temperature.

Data coming from the SoleMon Project [9] are used to estimate other parameters, e.g. the ones relating the weight of a sole from its length. Moreover, they are used as abundance index in analytical models (XSA, SCAA, and so on) to estimate fishing mortality in the years 2005–2011.

The user of the simulator can easily create different simulation scenarios or tune the parameters of a simulation in order to first reproduce observed results, as a validation, and, then, to make predictions varying environmental conditions and/or fishing effort. The simulation outcomes are the predicted quantities of agents in a month divided by age classes. They are saved for off-line data analysis and also displayed in charts, with different views on the state of each agent, during the execution of the simulation. As an example, Fig. 2 shows the number of individuals divided per age class in the simulated square kilometer, obtained in one simulation.

The natural mortality probabilities and the fishing probabilities can be specified in an external text file. It is possible to specify a different value for each month along the whole simulation time. It is also possible to instruct DISPAS to create a random value (in a given range) of newborn individuals, which are introduced along the months of the year in which the species is observed to offspring. As an alternative, the simulator can take the information about newborns from an external file. In this case the values are estimated by the user analyzing available data. Finally, a list of other parameters can be set on the GUI of the simulator.

---

[1] The latest version of the simulator can be downloaded from http://giano.cs.unicam. it.

In [22, 23] DISPAS was validated using two different methodologies. The first one was entirely based on SoleMon data. The simulator was instructed to perform 50 different runs and the outputted data about abundance and biomass for each age class were processed offline to determine mean and variance. The resulting curves were compared with real observed data at survey moments, i.e. November of each year from 2005 to 2011. The approximation of real data by the simulated ones was fairly accurate, apart from an overestimation of the stock made by DISPAS in years 2008 and 2009. For a detailed discussion we refer to [22]. The second validation methodology was based on SURBA (SURvey-Based Assessments) [18], a well-established software tool in the context of stock assessment. In particular, SURBA was fed with the simulation outputs of DISPAS and the results were compared with the ones obtained feeding SURBA with the SoleMon data. Also in this case the approximation was fairly good with an overestimation in years 2008 and 2009. The discrepancies are currently under study for further tuning the model by introducing more environmental information (we refer to [22] and to future works for a complete discussion).

4 Cellular and Complex Automata

Different approaches have been introduced in the literature for scaling from a micro-scale simulation to a macro-scale one. Some references can be found in [21], in particular for what concerns agent-based models. In this paper we mainly refer to the strategy suggested by Complex Automata.

Complex Automata (CxA) [11–13] are a computational model in which it is natural to define multi-scale simulations at different time and space scales. CxA are based on Cellular Automata (CA) [3], a well known discrete model that has been applied in several fields: physic, chemistry, theoretical biology, complexity theory and so on [32]. A CA can be informally thought as a *two-dimensional* grid of cells containing variables, which represent the *state* of each cell. The values of such variables change over time in discrete steps using a set of rules that depends on the current state of each cell and on those of its neighbor cells, which can be identified using different topological patterns. For instance, in a two-dimensional grid, a typical neighbor topology is defined as the eight surrounding cells of each cell. In the following we introduce a definition of CAs that is useful for our objectives. We refer to [3] and to the references therein for a full introduction to cellular automata.

Definition 1. *A Cellular Automaton A is a tuple*

$$\langle D(\Delta x, \Delta t, L, T), \mathbb{F}, \Phi, f_{init}, u, O \rangle$$

where:

– *D is the domain, made of spatial cells of size Δx and spanning a region of size L;*

- Δt is the time step and T is the (approximatively) maximal time reached through the evolution of A; i.e. $T/\Delta t$ is the maximal number of iteration steps of execution;
- $\mathbb{F}$ denotes the set of possible states; typically an array of states of dimension $L/\Delta x$, one position of the array representing one cell;
- $f_{init} \in \mathbb{F}$ is the initial state;
- Φ is the update rule according to which every state evolves along time steps;
- u is a function that puts A in communication with external data, i.e. its environment; it is called at each iteration on the domain D;
- O, the observable, is a function that specifies a quantity, calculated from the current state, that is given as an output.

According to the discussion in [4], the update rule Φ is constrained to be in the form of $\Phi = P \circ C \circ B$. This is different from the classical way of describing the updating of a CA at each step and is mainly inspired from Lattice Boltzmann models. As a general description, the *Boundary condition B* is needed for the updating of the cells on the border of the domain D, using some strategy, e.g., in a closed world, the cells on one border are connected to the cells of another border. *Collision C* acts locally on every cell changing the state, according to information gathered in the neighbor cells. *Propagation P* propagates the information calculated during the collision to the neighbor cells. We refer to [4] for a more detailed description. The behavior of a CA A can be described by a generic *main loop* structure, shown in Algorithm 1. Note that *EC*, meaning *Equilibrium Condition*, is a generic predicate on the state indicating that the CA has reached an intended configuration and can stop.

// Initialization of domain, state and time
$D = D_{\text{init}}$; $f = f_{\text{init}}$; $t = 0$;
while *not EC* **do**
    $t = t + \Delta t$; *// time step advances*
    $D = u(D)$; *// domain communicates with external environment*
    // updating: composition of Boundary, Collision and Propagation:
    $f = B(f)$; $f = C(f)$; $f = P(f)$;
    $O_i(f)$; *// outputs the intermediate state observable*
end
$O_f(f)$; *// outputs the final state observable*

Algorithm 1: Main loop of a Cellular Automaton.

The key observation that leads to the definition of CxAs is that it is always possible to connect any two CAs by a flow of data between a pair of the operations of the main loop using well-defined *coupling templates*. Such templates only depend on the spatio-temporal "positions" of the connected CAs in a *Scale Separation Map* (SSM) [13]. An SSM is a two-dimensional map in which temporal and spatial scales can be represented. Consider the SSM shown in the left part of Fig. 3. On the horizontal axis two temporal scales are represented by the pairs $(\Delta t_1, T_1)$ and $(\Delta t_2, T_2)$, corresponding to two CAs, A_1 and A_2. On the vertical axis, two spatial scales are represented by $(\Delta x_1, L_1)$ and $(\Delta x_2, L_2)$. The corresponding regions on the plane are separated. In this case, CAs A_1 and A_2 can be coupled with the so-called "micro-macro" coupling template, that is to say, A_1 operates on a micro spatial-temporal scale, while A_2 operates on a macro spatial-temporal scale. Their executions are coupled connecting the two main loops as shown in the right part of Fig. 3.

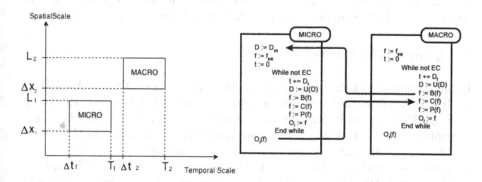

Fig. 3. A Scale Separation Map (left) showing that the two CAs can be coupled by a micro-macro Coupling Template (right) [12].

Definition 2. *A Complex Automaton S is a graph (V, E), where V is the vertex set and E is the edge set, such that:*

- $V = \{A_k \mid A_k \text{ is a CA}\}$,
- $E = \{E_{h,k} \mid E_{h,k} \text{ is a coupling template between } A_h \text{ and } A_k\}$.

Informally, the execution of the particular micro-macro coupling template works in the following way. The macro CA, A_2, starts it execution normally. At each iteration, during the execution of the updating function Φ_2, precisely before the collision step, A_2 calculates *for each* of its $L_2/\Delta x_2$ cells the initial conditions for starting the execution of the corresponding micro CAs of type A_1. Such data are calculated only from the state of the A_2 cells. Each micro CA of type A_1 is executed in parallel with A_2, but it immediately stops due to a blocking receive at the first instruction. This corresponds to the upper arrow of the right part of Fig. 3, which represents the flow of data among the CAs. In these flows the receive is always blocking and the send is always non-blocking. After receiving the initial conditions from A_2, each CA of type A_1 enters its main loop and continues the evolution until the equilibrium condition (at most after time T_1) is reached. After that, it sends the results of its whole evolution back to A_2 (lower arrow in Fig. 3). In the meantime, A_2 was suspended after its collision phase due to the blocking receive. Upon receiving the data from all the micro CAs and adapting the state of each cell accordingly, it restarts performing its current propagation phase. Then, the cycle is restarted.

Note that the whole evolution of all micro cells is performed at every cycle until the end of the macro execution. Thus, the execution time of the described coupling template can be estimated as proportional to the total number of micro steps required for reaching the end of the whole evolution (N_{ex}):

$$N_{ex} \sim \left(\frac{T_1}{\Delta t_1} \left(\frac{L_2}{\Delta x_2} \right) \right) \frac{T_2}{\Delta t_2}$$

This means that the execution of a micro-macro multi-scale simulation can require a very high computational cost, in terms of time, but also of space.

5   Multi-scale DISPAS

In this section we put the basis for the multi-scale version of DISPAS. We mainly get inspiration from the CxA paradigm presented in Sect. 4. However, the multi-scale DISPAS cannot be directly an instance of a CxA model. The first fundamental observation is that the running model of the current DISPAS, which is the natural candidate for the "micro" part of the multi-scale simulation, is a Multi-Agent System (MAS), not a CA. Nevertheless, the Repast Symphony suite, on which DISPAS is developed, gives the possibility of defining a CA in a very simple way. Indeed, the sole agents in DISPAS can be easily placed in a grid of cells, but, as summarized in Sect. 3, their behavior is based on a timed and probabilistic automaton-based model and the fundamental interaction of the agents is with the environment. All in all, the current DISPAS version could be certainly rephrased as a CA, instead of a MAS, but this appears to be an effort with a low pay off and also does not naturally fit the behavioral assumptions that we made on the fish individuals.

As far as the macro part of the simulation - the one at the sea level - is concerned, instead, the paradigm of CA fits particularly well. Indeed, it is possible to divide the area of interest, northern Adriatic Sea, into adjacent cells, each of which contains a certain number of individual per age class. Such individuals evolve using a properly parametrized version of the current DISPAS model and, as a further action, at each step they exchange individuals with neighbor cells using space-dependent migration vectors (see Sect. 5.2 below).

Before proceeding with the specification of the multi-scale schema, it is important to analyze which kind of data are available in the considered scenario, in order to have design directions towards an effective model that can also be validated.

5.1   Available SoleMon Data

The SoleMon project [9] has been surveying, from November 2005 each year in November, sixty seven stations placed in different parts of the Adriatic Sea (see Fig. 4). In each station, fishing samples are performed with the typical catch techniques used for the common sole. The caught soles are then analyzed for determining the total length (which in turn determines the age class), the individual weight, the sex, the maturity stage and several other biological and toxicological indicators.

The important data that are needed in our project are the number of individuals, for each age class (from 0 to 5+), estimated to live in each area. Since some areas of the sea can not be surveyed, in these cases the number of individuals are estimated by interpolation techniques, in particular the Kriging method [16,17] will be used.

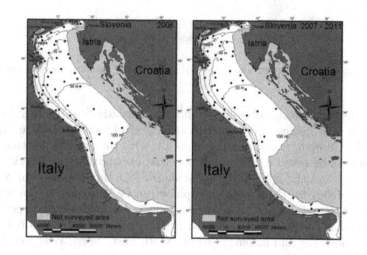

Fig. 4. SoleMon project stations (dots) and not surveyed areas [30].

SoleMon data have also been integrated within a Geographic Information System (GIS). As a result, several shapefiles [6] have been created, each of which maps on the sea the number of individuals (using appropriate ranges), for each age class (see Fig. 5). The spatial distribution of individuals for each age class is studied in [30]. This distribution can be considered an emergent behavior, at the sea level, of the behavior of the common sole in the northern Adriatic Sea, depending also on environmental, geographical, climatical factors as well as on the fishing patterns that are applied at each geographical area. This kind of aggregated data are what we intend to reproduce, as a validation, with the multi-scale version of DISPAS that we are proposing.

5.2   Macro CA Specification

Let us now specify the CA A_s representing the macro model, at the sea level, of the multi-scale DISPAS. Concerning the spatial scale, we consider as Δx_s an hexagonal cell whose area is approximatively 5 square nautical miles (see Fig. 6), that is we take hexagons with side equal to 1.38726 nautical miles. This dimension has been chosen on the basis of the haul length of *rapido trawlers*,

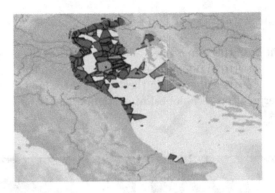

Fig. 5. Adriatic Sea with areas showing the distribution of the common sole age classes.

the main fleet exploiting soles in the northern Adriatic Sea, in order to better standardize their fishing effort in terms of number of hauls and space exploited per day [30]. Moreover, the area is compatible with the average movement that a sole has been observed to perform in the chosen temporal time step Δt_s, which we take as one month (equal to the one-scale DISPAS time step). In this way, the neighbor topology for the Propagation phase can be limited to the surrounding cells of each cell. Finally, the hexagon shape is suitable for representing the migration among adjacent areas. For each cell there are six possible directions of migration (outgoing and ingoing): North, North-East, North-West, South-East, South-West and South.

Fig. 6. Cell representation, with migration directions.

We keep Repast Symphony as the implementation platform, the same on which the current version of DISPAS is implemented. Using the facilities of the platform, the macro CA is represented as a MAS in which each agent is a cell, positioned at certain coordinates, that does not move, and such that all the positioned cells do not overlap. They cover an area corresponding to the northern Adriatic Sea, which is the value of the spatial scale parameter L_s in squared nautical miles. The time scale value of parameter T_s depends on the particular simulation that is performed; typically a number of years between 5 and 10. The state of each macro agent/cell contains the number of sole individuals in each age class currently present in the hexagon area. Notice that, at the sea scale, we loose the resolution of individual fish, keeping only the number of individual per class. These are also the observables O_s output by the CA. The function u_s is the identity function.

Regarding the update function Φ_s, let us analyze the three phases one by one. For the Boundary phase, the cells at the borders, i.e. those in contact with the coast, do not require any particular management. Simply the migration vectors are null towards the land. The Collision phase must consist in a growth, during a month, of the individuals of each age class, which possibly can change class if their new length, through the von Bertalanffy function, make them to get over the threshold of their current class. Furthermore, each individual should be subject to the natural mortality and fish mortality probabilities, correctly parameterized for the considered geographical area. Indeed, there are areas in which the fishing effort is greater than the average and others (called sole sanctuaries in [30]), in which the fishing effort is null.

The Propagation phase acts on the six surrounding cells of each cell. For each cell h_i, it is defined a *migration vector* M_i representing the outgoing probabilistic migration rates, i.e. the probability that a given number of individuals migrates in a certain direction in a considered month. The possible directions are six:

$$M_i(t, \text{ac}) = [\text{N}, \text{Nw}, \text{Sw}, \text{S}, \text{Se}, \text{Ne}]$$

The migration vector depends, in general, on the time t (a month along the simulation), and on the age class ac. In this way, several scenarios can be represented. The estimation of the values of the migration vectors will be crucial for the reproduction of the distribution of the various age classes observed in [30]. This task will be based on the available data and performed in strict collaboration with marine biologists, to exploit biological and environmental information.

At each step, for cell M_i, the number of individuals that are going to migrate, for each age class, in any direction, is probabilistically calculated. Then, one by one the values are propagated to the neighbor cells.

5.3   "Uncoupled" Coupling Template

Ideally, every cell h_i of A_s must be associated with a current DISPAS model, say A_d, adapted to represent five square nautical miles instead of a square kilometer. This would imply only the changing of the initial number of the individuals for each class, then the evolution would follow accordingly. Since the temporal scale of the macro CA A_s and the MAS A_d is the same ($\Delta t = $ one month, $T = N$ years), technically the coupling template is not a micro-macro one. However, it is very similar, the only difference being the fact that the "micro" execution, for each macro cell, consists of only one "micro" step. This mitigates the high computational cost that would be needed to perform the multi-scale simulation. Nevertheless, the computational cost of representing $L_s/\Delta x_s$ MASs of type A_d and let all of them to advance of one month would be still very high in our target scenario.

To further simplify, we perform an abstraction by introducing an operator $\mathcal{C}(t, h, ac)$ that should tell, with an appropriate degree of randomness, for each particular area h, for each month t, how many individuals of age class ac will be present at time $t + 1$ in the same class. The operator should take into account the K growth rate, the natural mortality probability and the fishing probability typical in the particular area h. In this way, the Collision phase of the macro CA A_s corresponds to call, at time step t, the operator $\mathcal{C}(t, h_i, ac)$ for each cell h_i and for each age class ac and to update accordingly the number of individuals for each age class in the cell.

The operator $\mathcal{C}$ can be obtained by using the current version of DISPAS to perform a *preliminary* set of "micro" simulations on each specific 5 square nautical miles area, with specific values for K, for the natural mortality and for the fishing mortality probabilities, as well as for other parameters. The means and variances calculated with these simulations can then be used to define the operator $\mathcal{C}$ in order to perform the macro simulation of A_s. This configures a sort of *"uncoupled semi-micro-macro"* multi-scale simulation, which appears to be suitable for reaching our objective of reproducing the spatial distribution of the common sole age classes in the northern Adriatic Sea area.

5.4   Plausible Scenarios of Simulation

We plan to implement the macro CA simulation on the Repast Symphony suite, developing a new version of DISPAS that retains the current features and adds the possibility to perform the uncoupled multi-scale simulation suggested above. Besides the reproduction of the spatial distribution of the soles, this would also enable the users to set different scenarios of simulation in order to validate the model and/or to perform predictions varying the settable parameters. A non-exhaustive list of such possible scenarios follows.

- An interesting scenario would be, as shown in [30], the reproduction of one or more particular "sanctuary" areas in the Adriatic Sea, i.e. areas in which the fishing effort is null due to technical difficulties of the rapido trawl on irregular sea bottom. In this way the impact of this and other possible sanctuary areas could be evaluated on the stock evolution and on the age class distribution.
- Another possible scenario would be the simulation of fishing bans on particular areas, e.g. those in which a high number of juveniles has been observed, in particular periods of the year. This should have an impact on the abundance of the lower age classes and maybe on the spatial distribution of the higher age classes.
- Finally, it would be interesting to simulate a permanent or periodical fishing ban close to the coast line. This is due to the hypothesis that juveniles mainly stay in this area, at least on the Italian shore below the Po river mouth.

6   Conclusions

We have introduced the basic model for building a new multi-scale version of the DISPAS simulator. The main motivation for the new features comes from the need of studying the spatial distribution of the common sole species in the northern Adriatic Sea. In particular, the new simulator would allow marine biologists to test hypotheses on the movements of the individual fish and would enable the simulation of new sea-scale scenarios to predict the spatial impact of fishing efforts and/or particular temporal measures (e.g. summer fishing bans) on the considered fish stock.

As future work, we plan to implement the defined model on the Repast Symphony agent-based programming suite, retaining the features of DISPAS already implemented. In particular, the current MAS simulation capabilities will be used for the execution of a preliminary phase of the defined multi-scale "uncoupled" coupling template.

Acknowledgments. This work has been supported by the RITMARE Flagship Project funded by the Italian Ministry of University and Research (http://www.ritmare.it).

References

1. AdriaMed Technical Documents: AdriaMed, General outline of marine capture fisheries legislation and regulations in the Adriatic Sea countries. Technical report 14, GCP/RER/010/ITA/ TD14 (rev. 1), (rev. 1), 68 pp., FAO-MiPAF Scientific Cooperation to Support Responsible Fisheries in the Adriatic Sea (2005)
2. Buti, F., Corradini, F., Merelli, E., Paschini, E., Penna, P., Tesei, L.: An individual-based probabilistic model for fish stock simulation. Elect. Proc. Theor. Comput. Sci. **33**, 37–55 (2010)
3. Chopard, B., Droz, M.: Cellular Automata Modelling of Physical Systems. Cambridge University Press, Cambridge (1998)
4. Chopard, B., Falcone, J.-L., Razakanirina, R., Hoekstra, A., Caiazzo, A.: On the collision-propagation and gather-update formulations of a cellular automata rule. In: Umeo, H., Morishita, S., Nishinari, K., Komatsuzaki, T., Bandini, S. (eds.) ACRI 2008. LNCS, vol. 5191, pp. 144–151. Springer, Heidelberg (2008)
5. Colloca, F., Cardinale, M., Maynou, F., Giannoulaki, M., Scarcella, G., Jenko, K., Bellido, J., Fiorentino, F.: Rebuilding mediterranean fisheries: a new paradigm for ecological sustainability. Fish Fish. **14**, 89–109 (2013)
6. ESRI: Shapefile technical description. An ESRI White Paper (1998)
7. Fabi, G., Grati, F., Raicevich, S., Santojanni, A., Scarcella, G., Giovanardi, O.: Valutazione dello stock di Solea vulgaris del medio e alto Adriatico e dell'incidenza di diverse attivita di pesca. Final Report. Technical report, Ministero per le Politiche Agricole e Forestali. Direzione generale della pesca e dell'acquacoltura. VI Piano Triennale della pesca marittima e acquacoltura in acque marine e salmastre 1 (tematica c c6). Programma di ricerca 6-a-74 (133 XVII pp.) (2009)
8. Gilbert, N.: Agent-Based Models. Sage, Thousand Oaks (2008)
9. Grati, F., Scarcella, G., Polidori, P., Domenichetti, F., Bolognini, L., et al.: Multi-annual investigation of the spatial distributions of juvenile and adult sole (solea solea, l.) in the adriatic sea (northern mediterranean). J. Sea Res. **84**, 122–132 (2013)
10. Hilborn, R., Hilborn, U.: Overfishing: What Everyone Needs to Know. Oxford University Press, Oxford (2012)

11. Hoekstra, A.G., Caiazzo, A., Lorenz, E., Falcone, J.-L., Chopard, B.: Complex automata: multi-scale modeling with coupled cellular automata. In: Kroc, J., Sloot, P.M.A., Hoekstra, A.G. (eds.) Simulating Complex Systems by Cellular Automata, pp. 29–57. Springer, Heidelberg (2010)
12. Hoekstra, A.G., Falcone, J.-L., Caiazzo, A., Chopard, B.: Multi-scale modeling with cellular automata: the complex automata approach. In: Umeo, H., Morishita, S., Nishinari, K., Komatsuzaki, T., Bandini, S. (eds.) ACRI 2008. LNCS, vol. 5191, pp. 192–199. Springer, Heidelberg (2008)
13. Hoekstra, A.G., Lorenz, E., Falcone, J.-L., Chopard, B.: Towards a complex automata framework for multi-scale modeling: formalism and the scale separation map. In: Shi, Y., van Albada, G.D., Dongarra, J., Sloot, P.M.A. (eds.) ICCS 2007, Part I. LNCS, vol. 4487, pp. 922–930. Springer, Heidelberg (2007)
14. Holland, D.: Integrating spatial management measures into traditional fishery management systems: the case of the georges bank multispecies groundfish fishery. ICES J. Mar. Sci. **60**, 915–929 (2003)
15. Jennings, N., Wooldridge, M.J.: Agent Technology: Foundations, Applications, and Markets. Springer, Heidelberg (1998)
16. Krige, D.: A statistical approach to some mine valuations and allied problems at the witwatersrand. Master's thesis, University of Witwatersrand, South Africa (1951)
17. Matheron, G.: Principles of geostatistics. Econ. Geol. **58**, 1246–1266 (1963)
18. Needle, C.: Survey-based assessments with SURBA. Working Document to the ICES Working Group on Methods of Fish Stock Assessment, Copenhagen (2003)
19. North, M.J., Collier, N.T., Ozik, J., Tatara, E.R., Macal, C.M., Bragen, M., Sydelko, P.: Complex adaptive systems modeling with repast simphony. Complex Adapt. Syst. Model. **1**(1), 1–26 (2013)
20. Olsen, E.M., Lilly, G.R., Heino, M., Morgan, M.J., Brattey, J., Dieckmann, U.: Assessing changes in age and size at maturation in collapsing populations of atlantic cod (gadus morhua). Can. J. Fish. Aquat. Sci. **62**(4), 811–823 (2005)
21. Parry, H.R., Bithell, M.: Large scale agent-based modelling: a review and guidelines for model scaling. In: Heppenstall, A.J., Crooks, A.T., See, L.M., Batty, M. (eds.) Agent-Based Models of Geographical Systems, pp. 271–308. Springer, Heidelberg (2012)
22. Penna, P.: DISPAS: individual-based modelling and simulation for demersal fish population dynamics. Ph.D. thesis, School of Advanced Studies, Doctoral course in Information science and complex systems (XXVI cycle), University of Camerino (2014)
23. Penna, P., Paoletti, N., Scarcella, G., Tesei, L., Marini, M., Merelli, E.: DISPAS: an agent-based tool for the management of fishing effort. In: Counsell, S., Núñez, M. (eds.) SEFM 2013. LNCS, vol. 8368, pp. 362–367. Springer, Heidelberg (2014). Presented at MoKMaSD 2013
24. Peter, K.H., Sommer, U.: Phytoplankton cell size: intra- and interspecific effects of warming and grazing. PLoS ONE **7**(11), e49632 (2012)
25. Pranovi, F., Raicevich, S., Franceschini, G., Farrace, M., Giovanardi, O.: Rapido trawling in the northern adriatic sea: effects on benthic communities in an experimental area. ICES J. Mar. Sci **57**, 517–524 (2000)
26. Russo, T., Parisi, A., Cataudella, S.: Spatial indicators of fishing pressure: preliminary analyses and possible developments. Ecol. Ind. **26**, 141–153 (2013)
27. Russo, T., D'Andrea, L., Parisi, A., Cataudella, S.: VMSbase: an R-package for VMS and logbook data management and analysis in fisheries ecology. PLoS ONE **9**(6), e100195 (2014)

28. Russo, T., Parisi, A., Garofalo, G., Gristina, M., Cataudella, S., Fiorentino, F.: SMART: a spatially explicit bio-economic model for assessing and managing demersal fisheries, with an application to Italian trawlers in the strait of sicily. PLoS ONE **9**(1), e86222 (2014)

29. Scarcella, G., Fabi, G., Grati, F., Polidori, P., Domenichetti, F., et al.: Stock assessment form of common sole in GSA 17. In: General Fisheries Commission for the Mediterranean, SAC-SCSA Working Group on Stock Assessment on Demersal Species (2012). http://151.1.154.86/GfcmWebSite/SAC/SCSA/WG_Demersal_Species/2012/SAFs/2012_SOL_GSA17_CNR-ISMAR_ISPRA_IZOR_FRIS.pdf

30. Scarcella, G., Grati, F., Raicevich, S., Russo, T., Gramolini, R., Scott, R.D., Polidori, P., Domenichetti, F., Bolognini, L., Giovanardi, O., et al.: Common sole in the northern and central adriatic sea: spatial management scenarios to rebuild the stock. J. Sea Res. **89**, 12–22 (2014)

31. von Bertalanffy, L.: A quantitative theory of organic growth (inquiries on growth laws II). Hum. Biol. **10**(2), 181–213 (1938)

32. Wolfram, S.: A New Kind of Science. Wolfram Media, Champaign (2002)

Research Challenges in Modelling Ecosystems

Antonio Cerone[1]([⊠]) and Marco Scotti[2]

[1] Dipartimento di Informatica, University of Pisa, Pisa, Italy
cerone@di.unipi.it
[2] GEOMAR Helmholtz-Zentrum für Ozeanforschung, Kiel, Germany
marcoscot@gmail.com

Abstract. Ecosystems and their biodiversity have to be protected and preserved as sources of services and goods. The human population controls and modifies ecosystems to improve its health conditions and welfare. The consequences of human activities should be carefully monitored and ecosystems should be managed to protect all of the species and preserve their functioning. The development of strategies for ecosystem management benefits from the use of computational techniques to model the dynamics of species that interact with their abiotic and biotic environment. Life scientists and computer scientists need to work together to define and analyse ecosystem models. However, there is a multifaceted gap between the approaches used in life science and those used in computer science. Such gap is both cultural and technical, and results in a number of challenges. In this paper we identify these challenges and provide technical and cultural proposals for solving them.

1 Introduction

As human activity threatens the functioning of ecological systems by habitat destruction [26], fragmentation [69], climate change [12], and introduction of allochthonous species [27,64], we face the problem of understanding and managing the consequences of these impacts. The goal of environmental policy actions is to preserve biodiversity and ecosystem services. Then identifying the key features responsible for species survival (e.g. absence of a specific pollutant; level of fragmentation of the landscape network; genetic heterogeneity within the population) is the only viable long term solution for managing biodiversity loss.

In population ecology (which deals with the dynamic behaviour of populations, by focusing on the interactions with other species and the abiotic environment), there is a need to combine and coordinate information from different domains. The behaviour of each individual emerges from the complex interplay between social relationships within the population, trophic and non-trophic

We would like to thank Paolo Milazzo for inspiring discussions and for suggesting Dynamic I/O Automata as a possibly appropriate modelling formalism. Discussions with Matteo Pedercini contributed to clarify strengths and weaknesses of System Dynamics (SD). Finally, we also would like to thank the anonymous referees who provided alternative but equally valuable opinions reported in Sect. 5.

C. Canal and A. Idani (Eds.): SEFM 2014 Workshops, LNCS 8938, pp. 276–293, 2015.
DOI: 10.1007/978-3-319-15201-1_18

interactions (e.g. host-parasite and plant-pollinator) with individuals of other species and spatial movements (i.e. dispersal in the landscape network). Linking these organisational levels is still a challenge: an increasing need for hierarchical thinking is present in ecological stoichiometry (community-level patterns concerning the ratios of certain elements [30]), and community genetics (how genetic variance influences ecosystem functioning [38]). Traditional modelling, focusing on macroscopic patterns and adopting a deterministic approach based on average population behaviour (i.e. through the application of ordinary differential equations), is weak in several respects. The inherent stochasticity and variability and the large-scale patterns produced by local rules are important features that should be more thoroughly investigated. Although the importance of these aspects is recognised, novel approaches should be developed to incorporate stochastic dynamics in ecological modelling (e.g. stochastic processes are often modelled by deterministic equations with added random noise).

New tools should be implemented for better understanding how to preserve highly endangered species and plan actions of biodiversity conservation in complex ecological communities. There is a need to improve stochastic modelling for better understanding demographic noise and local interactions, especially in case of small populations. Stochasticity is not a source of unpredictability and randomness; rather, it represents a set of processes that are often neglected in the phase of model design, but that can produce higher-level patterns [23]. Such new tools would help in modelling the link between local and global processes, simulating density dependence [17] and dealing with several other challenges of ecology. Most likely the explicit modelling of hierarchical organisation will be one of the key contributions to ecological research [47,65]. Ecologists emphasised the importance of modelling demographic and environmental stochasticity in metapopulation dynamics [18], investigated fluctuations affecting the densities of populations in communities as a consequence of environmental variability [62], and analysed the effects of random perturbations on cyclic population dynamics [43]. Actions of conservation biology often aim to protect rare species, which are characterised by small population size, with individuals showing a highly heterogeneous behaviour. For these reasons, we argue that stochastic modelling can represent a step ahead in the domain of ecological research. Ecosystem management would benefit from novel computational tools that allow researchers to extend stochastic-based dynamics towards spatial and temporal simulations. Results extracted from these analyses could serve for suggesting best strategies of environmental sustainability and planning actions for biodiversity conservation [52]. In practice, they might aid in planning systems-based conservation strategies [15], defining optimum programmes for managing multispecies fisheries [71], creating sustainable agroecosystems [58], investigating the functioning of bio-geochemical cycles [19], predicting risks of secondary extinction [29], and ranking of conservation priorities [50].

Section 2 reviews the main modelling approaches used in ecosystem science. Section 3 discusses the multifaceted gap between the individual-based modelling used in life science and identifies challenges that emerge from such gap. Section 4 provides technical and cultural proposals for solving the identified challenges and Sect. 5 concludes with some considerations on opinions of other scientists that provide possible alternatives to our proposals.

2   State of the Art and Literature Review

2.1   Mathematical Modelling

Mathematical models [33] are essential in making precise theoretical arguments about the factors affecting observed phenomena. Once validated, mathematical models can be exploited to make predictions about the future evolutions of the system under study.

The use of mathematical models in population biology and ecology is nowadays common practice. Many books describe the basic concepts and the most well-established models [36,46,53,60]. Among the most successful modelling strategies we mention two approaches: age-structured population growth and spatial spread [36]. The first approach allows predictions concerning long-term changes in population numbers based on information about the age at which individuals have offspring and the probabilities of death at different ages. The second approach allows predictions about the future rate of spread of some populations from initial observations. However, the use of mathematical models has also some limitations: for example, such models are often based either on differential equations or on recurrence relations describing how the size of a population changes over time (with continuous or discrete time, respectively). Since differential equations and recurrence relations are deterministic, they are not suitable to model systems whose behaviour could be determined by choices between alternatives associated with probabilities.

Although mathematical models become difficult to be studied analytically when the complexity of the modelled system grows, a large increase in computational power and the development of high-level modelling methods now support the simulation of highly complex models. New methods and tools have been developed to ease the definition of models that are based on differential equations. One of these methods, System Dynamics (SD), developed at the Massachusetts Institute of Technology in the early 1960s, provides a powerful framework to build, simulate and analyse complex models, stressing the relationship between model structure and behaviour [61]. Moreover, the SD method enables a multidisciplinary approach to problems [68], and thus supports the development of comprehensive models for decision-making. Such comprehensive models can be built in a modular way, to allow for some flexibility and adaptability of model structure to different circumstances.

A fundamental characteristic of these models is that system descriptions are very high level, with populations represented as a whole and their dynamics defined top-down in terms of global laws. The internal dynamics is, therefore, a black box. Thus, models can describe neither biological aspects of individuals nor interactions among individuals that are not reflected in global laws controlling the dynamics of the population. A bottom-up definition of the population dynamics, in which population properties emerge through the interaction of individuals, is not possible using SD or methods based on differential equations. Although it is possible to play with the parameters of global laws and identify patterns of changes, such as growth, oscillation and decay, and how these patterns may respond to human intervention, there is actually no way to capture the impact of human intervention at a lower level, e.g. at individual level. For example, imagine that we introduce genetically modified plants that are resistant to chemical treatments in a natural ecosystem, with the purpose of using a given herbicide without leading to the death of the genetically modified individuals, and we know that a side effect (e.g. susceptibility to drought) of this genetic modification is a change in single individual's behaviour. Methods based on differential equations cannot capture the impact of the behavioural changes in single individuals on the population dynamics, unless such a situation has been observed in the past, which is not always the case.

2.2   Individual-Based Models Using Formal Notations

The notion of individual-based model in ecological modelling corresponds to the computer science notion of agent-based model, namely of a model in which there are multiple active entities (the agents), whose behaviour is governed by a set of usually simple rules, that are allowed to interact with each other and move in some virtual environment. A classical example of agent-based modelling notation is that of Cellular Automata [25,45], which consists in a regular grid of cells (usually one- or bi-dimensional), where each cell is associated with a finite number of states and can pass from one state to another depending on the states of adjacent cells in the grid. In the simplest versions of Cellular Automata agents are identified with cells, but there exist extensions in which cells represent positions in the environment, whereas agents are entities that can move from one cell to another, and behave in accordance with the state of the cell and of other agents in the same cell.

A class of modelling notations that are well-known in computer science and can be used to describe populations at the individual level is Petri Nets [59]. Petri Nets, in their most common formulation, are diagrammatic notations consisting of places and transitions, which have been defined with the aim of modelling concurrent systems sharing common resources. Places represent conditions and transitions represent events that may occur when there are agents that satisfy certain conditions. Agents are represented by tokens that can move from one place to another when transitions take place. Petri Nets are one of the simplest and most successful notations of computer science for the description and analysis of concurrent systems. They have also been applied to the modelling of ecological systems [66], also in combination with Cellular Automata [34].

Other recent definitions of individual-based models that exploit formal notations of computer science are based on membrane systems [54]. Membrane systems are distributed parallel computing devices inspired by the structure and the functioning of living cells. A membrane system consists of a hierarchy of membranes, each of them containing a multiset of objects, representing molecules, a set of evolution rules, representing chemical reactions, and possibly other membranes. A model of a population of Bearded Vultures based on membrane systems has been developed using P systems, a formalism belonging to the category of membrane system [20].

The individual-based approach [51] is computationally more expensive than the mathematical modelling approach based on differential equations described in Sect. 2.1, but allows life scientists to explore how the dynamics of a population or of an ecosystem arises from the ways in which individuals interact with each other and with the environment. Due to this computational cost a pure individual-based approach can only be used with populations consisting of a small number of individuals.

2.3   Stochastic Simulation and Individual-Based Models

The limitations of mathematical modelling, the effectiveness of computational models to deal with stochastic aspects, and the level of performances reached by computers in the last few years motivate the increase in the application of computational means in life sciences. In fact, the adjective "computational" is becoming widely used in life sciences to qualify disciplines such as biology, ecology, epidemiology, and so on. However, in these disciplines the adjective "computational" often simply means that stochastic simulation techniques are exploited in order to study properties of mathematical models of systems of interest.

Most stochastic simulation techniques usually consider a relatively small number of classes of individuals, and then use standard probability distributions (binomial, Poisson, etc.) to generate the number of individuals in each class, at each successive time step.

The current trend in the study of population dynamics is to enrich individual-based models with stochasticity, in order to attempt to follow each individual in the population from its birth, through growth, dispersal and reproduction, to death [10]. Such an "individual-based" stochastic approach [51] is computationally more expensive than stochastic traditional approaches, which make use of a small number of aggregate categories, but allows life scientists to explore how the dynamics of a population or of an ecosystem arises from the ways in which individuals interact with each other and with the environment. In this individual-based context, stochastic simulation algorithms such as one of the variants of the Gillespie Algorithm [31,32] generate statistically correct population evolutions.

3   Identification of Research Challenges

Formal analysis techniques of theoretical computer science, such as static analysis and model checking, can be applied to agent-based models in order to verify properties of the described systems. These techniques are well-established in computer science but are practically unknown to life scientists. The rest of this section is organised as follows. In Sect. 3.1 we identify the multifaceted gap between individual-based modelling and formal analysis techniques. Then in Sect. 3.2 we illustrate the research challenges that we encounter in order to fill in this gap.

3.1   A Multifaceted Gap

There is a mutifaceted gap between the individual-based modelling used in life science and the formal analysis techniques used in computer science. This gap can be characterised by the following aspects.

A1 — High-level vs. Low-level Descriptions. *Life scientists* use *high-level* notations that represent models in a visual way annotated with natural language descriptions. Such notations support an almost direct representation of biological and ecological processes. However, the semantics of such models is not formally defined and there is no guarantee that simulations really reflect the intended behaviour of the model. *Formal languages* are based on *low-level* primitives that are close to machine-readable operators, but have to be combined in a complex manner to define high-level biological and ecological processes. Their semantics can be unambiguously defined using mathematical transformations and tools, which, however, obscure the intuition and require deep mathematical skills to be used.

A2 — Extensive Simulations vs. Property Verification. *Life scientists* perform a large number of *simulations* of the same model and then use statistics and/or data mining techniques to extract patterns, oscillations and tendencies in the population dynamics. *Static analysis and model checking techniques* support the characterisation and verification of properties of a model of population dynamics without explicit recourse to simulations.

A3 — Ecological Problem vs. Mathematical Tool. *Life scientists* focus on the *ecological problem* and see mathematical notations and tools as mere instruments to solve their problem. *Computer scientists* normally focus on *mathematical notations and tools* and use simplified and often unrealistic versions of biological and ecological problems to investigate theoretical aspects of such notations and tools.

A4 — Field Data Collection vs. *Ad-hoc* Data. *Life scientists* collect *data in the field* and/or use *historical* data to calibrate their models and run simulations. *Computer scientists* often have to cope with the lack of data to be used for running their models. Thus they are often forced to define *ad-hoc data*, which may not be realistic, with the danger of being biased in choosing data that best illustrate the features and potential of their formal languages and analysis techniques.

A5 — Realistic Models vs. Abstract Models. *Life scientists* tend to include *realistic details* that facilitate the intuitive understanding of the model behaviour and make the model more appealing, but this often increases the computational complexity of the model itself with a negative impact on the efficacy of the analysis techniques. *Computer scientists* define *abstract* models that contain only the details needed for the intended analysis, thus possibly obscuring the understanding of the model behaviour.

A6 — Understand/Control vs. Replication. The final goal of *life scientists* is to be able to *understand* the functioning of the ecosystems and test possible *control* intervention on components of the ecosystem model, aiming to perform adjustments to the system behaviour and evaluate the impact of such intervention on the entire ecosystem. Although the final goal of life scientists has been supported by the mathematical modelling work performed using the SD approach, the use of formal models has been restricted to the *in-silico replication* of the ecosystem evolution without much attention to the evaluation of human intervention impact. To make it worse, as we have seen in Aspect **A4**, since computer scientists typically do not use real data, the ability of replicating reality is mostly just potential and is seldom documented in the literature.

3.2   Research Challenges

A lot of efforts have been devoted during the last decade to the attempt of filling in the gap between individual-based modelling and formal analysis techniques. In spite of such large efforts there are still no conclusive results in this direction and a number of challenges have emerged in the process. In this section we illustrate such challenges and match each of them to the aspects of the gap identified in Sect. 3.1, by using the same top-level sequential number **n** for challenges (**Cn**) as we used for their corresponding aspects (**An**).

C1 — Define an Appropriate Common Language. The definition of a common language that allows life scientists and computer scientists to cooperate in the definition and analysis of models requires the selection of basic biological and ecological processes and their implementation using a formal language. The main challenges in this task are:

>   **C1.1 — Language Expressiveness.** There is a need to define a set of high-level primitives that is sufficiently expressive for life scientists.

>   **C1.2 — Intuitive Semantics.** Each primitive should be associated with a simple semantics that addresses intuition and can be understood without a deep mathematical knowledge.

>   **C1.3 — Correctness of the Implementation.** There is a need to guarantee that the implementation faithfully captures the behaviour resulting from the selected biological and ecological processes.

>   **C1.4 — Modelling Ease.** The use of the primitives in the modelling process should be facilitated through the use of templates, defined operators and modelling frameworks.

C2 — Limitations of Simulation and Verification

C2.1 — Analysis of Simulations. Simulations provide only a sample of possible behaviours rather than a characterisation of all possible behaviours. Moreover, extracting global information from a set of simulations is not an easy task and the outcome of this process may vary depending on the techniques used (i.e. various statistical methods and data mining techniques) and on the assumptions and choices made in applying such techniques (choice of simulation parameters and pieces of information to data mine).

C2.2 — State Space Explosion Problem. The use of verification techniques in a stochastic individual-based approach results in state spaces that grow exponentially with the size of the population; the use of spatiality makes the exponential growth even faster.

C3 — Right Model for a Given Ecosystem.
A cultural challenge is to urge computer scientists to shift the primary focus of their research investigation from the mathematical tool to the ecological problem. The challenge for computer scientists is therefore to be able to define "the right model for a given ecosystem" rather than "the appropriate ecosystem for their own model".

C4 — Data Collection.
There is a need to create multidisciplinary research teams in which life scientists and computer scientists collaborate in all phases of the research: field work planning, data collection, data analysis, model design and implementation, in-silico experiments and their interpretation. In particular, computer scientists cannot use data that have been collected by life scientists for other purposes, but they have to design new field work for collecting appropriate data for their research. The challenge here is for life scientists and computer scientists to define the appropriate form of collaboration, in which the field work is planned by a multidisciplinary research team, is carried out by life scientists and produces data to be analysed by a multidisciplinary research team.

C5 — Right Level of Abstraction.
The model must be defined at an abstraction level sufficiently informative to keep alive the intuition about the system behaviour without including irrelevant details that may have a negative impact on the computational complexity.

C6 — Addressing Policy Support.
The use of formal models to address policy support is a challenging task. SD has been successful in exploring the impact of policy implementation on behaviour of ecosystems [68]. In particular, the use of SD in the T21 modelling framework [1], developed by the Millennium Institute, integrates economic, social and environmental factors to support comprehensive and participatory development planning. However, the T21 approach, and in general any approach based on SD, does not support the modelling of the impact of policy implementation at individual level.

The challenge in using a formal approach for individual-based modelling is the integration of economic, social and environmental factors within the same model.

4   Addressing Challenges

In this section we address the challenges identified in Sect. 3.2 and propose possible strategies and research questions to bridge the gap between individual-based modelling of populations and formal analysis techniques.

The final aim is to develop new theories of population dynamics based on theoretical computer science means. New theories should be based on well-established computer science notations, such as rewrite systems, finite state automata and Petri Nets, adapted and extended to describe population individuals. Moreover, such theories should deal with both deterministic and stochastic behaviours of individuals and take into account spatial movement and landscape dispersal.

4.1   Formal Notation (Addressing Challenge C1)

The events in the life of an individual that are usually of interest for the construction of a population model are birth, death and interactions with other individuals (either conspecific or belonging to different species) and with the environment. Examples of relevant interaction events are those that have some influence on the population size (e.g. mating, predation) or on the life-conditions of the individual itself (e.g. nutrition, migration). All these events are often discrete and may cause new individuals to appear (e.g. to be born, to come from another population in the neighbourhood), and current individuals to disappear (e.g. to die, to leave the local population) or change their states (e.g. from "available to mate" to "pregnant", from "egg" to "larva").

Rewrite Systems. A possible way to model such events is by using rewrite systems [11]. In the rewrite systems approach events may be modelled as rewrite rules, such as $egg \longrightarrow larva$, that is the rule that rewrites a term (egg) into a new one ($larva$). In this way the set of rewrite rules of the model of a population (or a category of individuals in a population) predicts all events that may occur to that population (or to that category of individuals). For example set $\{egg \longrightarrow larva, egg \longrightarrow \epsilon\}$, where $egg \longrightarrow \epsilon$ describes the death of an egg, with ϵ denoting the empty term, predicts all possible events that may occur to an egg.

The occurrence of these kinds of events, however, depends not only on the current state of the individual (e.g. an egg may change to larva, but an adult cannot) but also on the current state of the environment in which the individual lives (e.g. an egg dies if the temperature goes below a specific threshold). In general, in ecological systems we need to deal with a variety of environmental events, whose cause is often unknown or depends on a very complex combination of factors, which are external to the system itself. For example the dynamics of a population of a given species depends not only on the interaction with other species within the same ecosystem, such as predators, prey and competitors, but also on the occurrence of environmental events such as climatic events (i.e. variation of temperature and rainfalls) and events related to habitats (i.e. tree clearing, bushfires, desiccation of a water container, pollution, hunting and human settlement). Therefore, we have to associate a representation of the environment Env with the current term and include in the rule the representation of the environmental condition $cond(Env)$ that enables the rule. Thus the rule that models the death of an egg becomes $cond(Env) : [egg]_{Env} \longrightarrow [\epsilon]_{Env}$. Finally, in order to introduce stochasticity in an individual-based model defined as a rewrite system, rewrite rules are associated with a rate k that describes the frequency with which the rule is used in the computation. Thus the rule that models the death of an egg becomes $cond(Env) : [egg]_{Env} \longrightarrow_k [\epsilon]_{Env}$.

In previous work [11] we assume the existence of a list of external events, with information about the time when these events occur. The occurrence of an external event may modify some environmental information that affects ecosystem evolution, such as temperature, vegetation density, volume of water, level of pollution, size of a population, human density. Moreover, the list of external events may change dynamically. For instance, a bushfire event, which decreases the vegetation density, will be removed from the list of external events after the occurrence of a rainfall event, and will be replaced with a new bushfire event with a later occurrence time. Similarly, a desiccation event, which decreases the volume of a water container will be removed from the list of external events after the occurrence of a rainfall event, and will be replaced with a new desiccation event with a later desiccation time. Lists of external events that contain historical data or data collected through field work are used to calibrate the model. Once calibrated, the model is run together with a new list of external events that describe human intervention and policy implementation.

This approach addresses Challenges **C1.1–C1.3**: the rule construct is sufficiently expressive to describe relevant high-level events such as birth and death (**C1.1**); the semantics of rewriting is quite intuitive even for the stochastic version in which rules are associated with rates (**C1.2**); variants of Gillespie algorithms ensure a correct implementation of the rules (**C1.3**). However, the approach does not address Challenge **C1.4**. This is due to the following two issues: (1) when the number of the details needed for describing the complexity of an organism increases, the set of rules associated with the term that describes a state of that organism also increases and each rule of such set may be affected by a complex combination of environmental conditions and interactions with other individuals; (2) the rate of a rule is not constant but often depends on a complex combination of environmental conditions.

Although the number of different states in which an individual might be is usually quite small, the large number of rules that describes the state transition associated with each state and the complexity of functions describing rule rates make the task of the modeller difficult.

Automata, Process Algebras and Petri Nets. The fact that the number of different states in which an individual might be is usually quite small suggests that some extensions of finite state automata and process algebras with appropriate parallel composition and interaction capabilities could be exploited.

Some interesting work has been carried out in systems biology using modelling languages based on process algebras. Ciocchetta and Hillston developed Bio-PEPA [22], a language for the modelling and analysis of biochemical networks, which is based on PEPA (Performance Evaluation Process Algebra). Although Bio-PEPA can successfully handle some features of biochemical networks, such as stoichiometry and different kinds of kinetic laws, the operators that describe interactions of reactants, products and enzymes do not address intuition and, therefore, do not appeal life scientists. Moreover, Bio-PEPA does not support the modelling of external events, thus lacking an essential feature for modelling ecosystems. Kahramanoğulları et al. [41, 42] developed LIME (Language Interface for Modeling Ecology), a language tool for stochastic dynamic simulation in ecology. LIME supports model definition using a narrative style that facilitates the analysis of parallel, multiple ecological interactions in meta-communities. LIME translates the model description into the BlenX programming language for stochastic dynamical simulation [28]. In BlenX, the propensities of interactions between individual entities can be modelled either as simple rates or in terms of more complex functions (e.g. Holling's type functional responses), and the spatial distribution is described in terms of membership to discrete locations in space (e.g. landscape patches). This discrete description of space might impair the chance of modelling individual dynamics for which exact spatial coordinates need to be known and traced (e.g. fish schooling [48]).

Since births and deaths of individuals must always be described while modelling ecosystems, it would be useful to have a formalism that supports dynamic creation and destruction of components of a parallel composition. A formalism that presents this feature is the Dynamic I/O Automata proposed by Attie and Lynch [4]. An automata-based formalism can be suitably used to build a population model by starting from the description of the events that may happen in the life of each kind of individual. We would need to define an automaton for each kind of individual and compose in parallel as many copies of such automata as individuals of the corresponding kind are present in the initial population. Another important characteristic that makes Dynamic I/O Automata useful in modelling populations of individuals is the ability to dynamically change the signature of an automaton, that is, the set of actions in which the automaton can participate. In this way an automaton describing an individual can change its signature to mimic the evolution of that individual through its maturation stages (e.g. from "egg" to "larva" to "adult"). This is definitely more natural than the destruction of the old term and the creation of a new term that is used to model maturation with a rewrite system.

We might also think of translating a process algebraic model or a constructed parallel composition of automata into a Place/Transition Petri Net. Since the number of kinds of individuals that belong to a population is finite, as well as the number of states of every process/automaton modelling a single individual, a Petri Net could be constructed by considering one place for each state of each process/automaton modelling a kind of individual, and one transition for each transition in any of such process/automaton (by taking into account synchronisations between processes/automata). The translation into Petri Nets would allow some properties of the population dynamics to be verified statically by computing the invariants of the obtained net.

In order to be used for modelling ecosystems, formalisms based on automata, process algebras and Petri nets must be extended aiming to the definition of a complete modelling framework in which also quantitative [9] and spatial aspects [7,8] of population dynamics are taken into account. Quantitative aspects of population dynamics are related with duration, frequency and probability of the events that may happen in the population. Spatial aspects consist of the description of the topology of the population environment, the positions of the individuals in the environment and the movement from one position to another. Several probabilistic, stochastic, timed and spatial extensions of automata and Petri Nets have already been defined and are now well-established in computer science [3,14,44,70]. Similar extensions have also been proposed for other kinds of formalisms such as process algebras [13,37,40,57] and rewrite systems [6,11, 16,21,55,67].

Automata-based and process algebraic formalisms as well as Petri Nets have the advantage that verification techniques, such as model checking, can often be applied easily to them. Moreover, they are usually associated with friendly graphical notations, which make them immediately understandable also to non-specialists. These advantages with respect to rewrite systems clearly address Challenge **C1.4**. However, up to now, we could not identify any approaches based on automata, process algebras or Petri nets that address Challenges **C1.1–C1.2**.

4.2   Analysis Methodologies (Addressing Challenge C2)

Simulation is nowadays one of the most common analysis techniques for models of biological and ecological systems. Simulators can be implemented quite easily by following standard approaches (e.g. Monte Carlo simulation and numerical integration) and can give useful information on the dynamics of the modelled systems with acceptable computational costs. Moreover, simulators for some standard ecological models are available to be used by ecologists and wildlife managers without the need of knowing model details. Furthermore, simulation may characterise the most probable system behaviours and be used for calibration purposes, that is, to validate models against available data.

Concerning formal analysis, model checking and abstract interpretations are well established techniques that can potentially be used to analyse biological and ecological systems. Efficient probabilistic model checkers, such as PRISM [49], are the most promising tools in this sense; modelling notations for ecosystem modelling can be translated into the input language of a model checker. Important work in this direction has been carried out by Romero-Campero *et al.* [63] and by Philippou, Toro and Antonaki [56].

However, in order to deal with quantitative and spatial aspects of population biology and ecology, formalisms must express notions such as position, age, probability and duration, which all together could make the translation into the input language of the model checker not feasible. Consequently, it would be reasonable to translate into the model checker language only fragments of the formalism that are suitable to describe particular classes of biological and ecological systems, whereas new verification techniques should be developed, in which all the quantitative and spatial notions are handled.

Interesting model checking methodologies for stochastic processes have been developed in the last decade. Quantitative properties of stochastic systems are usually specified in logics that explicitly compare the measure of executions satisfying certain temporal properties with thresholds. The model checking problem for stochastic systems with respect to such logics is typically solved by a numerical approach that iteratively computes (or approximates) the exact measure of paths satisfying relevant subformulae; the algorithms themselves depend on the class of systems being analysed as well as the logic used for specifying the properties. Hansson and Jonsson [35] introduced the Probabilistic Computation Tree Logic (PCTL) for specifying properties of Discrete-Time Markov Chain (DTMC) while Baier *et al.* [5] carried out extensive work on model checking of Continuous-Time Markov Chains (CTMC), by defining the Continuous Stochastic Logic (CSL) and developing the proofs of theoretical foundations as well as the model checking algorithms. In general, these model checking approaches, called numerical model checking, have a number of limitations: (1) numerical algorithms work only for special systems that have certain structural properties (e.g. Markov Models); (2) numerical algorithms require a lot of time and space, thus scaling to large systems is a challenge; (3) the logics for which model checking algorithms exist are extensions of classical temporal logics, which are often not the most popular among life scientists.

One way to overcome these weaknesses of numerical model checking could be the search for the right compromise between simulation and model checking. An interesting approach in this direction is *statistical model checking*, which overcomes the disadvantages of numerical model checking at the cost of being less accurate. In this approach the system is simulated for finitely many runs, using hypothesis testing to infer whether the samples provide a statistical evidence for the satisfaction or violation of the specification. Statistical model checking was first introduced by Younes [72] in 2005. The idea underlying statistical model checking is to perform the model checking analysis on a sample of the population rather than the entire population. Although the use of a sample causes a loss in accuracy, statistical model checking provides a mechanism to calculate the size of the sample that ensures the satisfaction of the property with a given probability.

The most basic statistical model checking algorithm considers the probability α of false positive and β of false negative with respect to a given property φ. Then, given a probability p, the algorithm computes two natural numbers, c and n, such that property φ has to be satisfied by c simulations of a Stochastic Discrete Event System $\mathcal{M}$ out of a total of n performed simulations to ensure that φ is satisfied in $\mathcal{M}$ with probability p.

Interest in statistical model checking has been growing during the last five years and a workshop explicitly devoted to statistical model checking has been held for the first time in 2013 [2]. The limited number of applications of statistical model checking to biological systems that have been carried out up to now include the verification of temporal properties of rule-based models of cellular signalling networks [24] and a sophisticated statistical model checking algorithm that uses Bayesian sequential hypothesis testing. This requires fewer system simulations and has the ability to incorporate prior biological knowledge about the model being verified [39].

We believe that statistical model checking has the potential to address Challenge **C2** by realising an optimal compromise between simulation and verification. As a model checking technique it supports the verification of a property, but drastically reduces the number of system simulations, thus overcoming the state explosion problem (Challenge **C2.1**).

4.3   Filling in the Cultural Gap (Addressing Challenges C3–C6)

In Sects. 4.1 and 4.2 we have dealt with the most technical Challenges (**C1–C2**) in filling the gap between the individual-based modelling used in life science and the formal analysis techniques used in computer science. In this section we globally address Challenges **C3–C6** using a *cultural* rather than *technical* perspective.

Challenge **C3** is the most representative aspect of the *cultural gap* between life scientist and computer scientist. Here the need to change culture only involves computer scientists, who should shift their research focus from mathematical tools to ecological problems.

Only after this cultural challenge is solved, the other three challenges (**C4–C6**) can be properly addressed. Moreover, establishing the technical basis of a common language (Challenge **C1**) is the prerequisite that can facilitate the creation of multidisciplinary research teams and their collaboration throughout all research phases from field data collection to interpretation of in-silico experiments (Challenge **C4**). Throughout this continuous collaboration process, multidisciplinary teams should be also facilitated in agreeing on the right level of abstraction for the considered problem (Challenge **C5**) and on the choice of the factors to consider in evaluating and comparing policy implementations and their impact on the ecosystem (Challenge **C6**).

Finally, we must mention that it is opinion of some researchers from both computer science and ecology that cultural differences between the two communities are slowly disappearing. Worldwide there are efforts in proposing multidisciplinary projects, and universities are developing new multidisciplinary educational programmes. We can optimistically expect that future generation of scientists will have the necessary multidisciplinary culture to successfully address Challenges **C1-C6**.

5   Final Considerations

In this paper we have taken an ecology-driven perspective and claimed that it is essential to address all Challenges **C1**–**C6** in order to be able to define an effective framework for modelling ecosystem dynamics.

Some computer scientists, instead, have as their main concern the challenge of designing the appropriate mathematical notations for capturing ecological systems, while dealing with the state-space explosion problem and other technical challenges. In this perspective, the main aim is that of refining frameworks in order to better capture aspects and properties of ecological systems. The use of simplistic or even unrealistic *ad hoc* data, therefore, would be justified by a need to first address Challenges **C1**–**C2**, without taking Aspects **A3**–**A6** into account, with the expectation that, once the theory matures enough, researchers will naturally turn to address Challenges **C3**–**C6**.

In Sect. 4.1 we have surveyed a number of formal notations used in modelling biological and ecological systems and identified which, in our opinion, may be appropriately extended to successfully address Challenges **C1.1**–**C1.4**.

An alternative approach, which has both computer scientists and life scientists among its supporters, favours the adoption of graphical languages similar to the ones typically adopted by ecologists. The main challenges of such approach would be to give a formal semantics to the graphical language and, based on such a semantics, define a translation to a formal language or tool to be used for analysis.

References

1. T21. http://www.millennium-institute.org/integrated_planning/tools/t21/
2. Workshop on statistical model checking. http://rv2013.gforge.inria.fr/workshop.html
3. Alur, R., Dill, D.L.: A theory of timed automata. Theoret. Comput. Sci. **126**, 183–235 (1994)
4. Attie, P.C., Lynch, N.A.: Dynamic input/output automata: a formal model for dynamic systems. In: Larsen, K.G., Nielsen, M. (eds.) CONCUR 2001. LNCS, vol. 2154, pp. 137–151. Springer, Heidelberg (2001)
5. Baier, C., Haverkort, B., Hermanns, H., Kaoten, J.-P.: Model-checking algorithms for continuous-time markov chains. IEEE Trans. Softw. Eng. **29**(7), 524–541 (2003)
6. Barbuti, R., Cerone, A., Maggiolo-Schettini, A., Milazzo, P., Setiawan, S.: Modelling population dynamics using grid systems. In: Cerone, A., Persico, D., Fernandes, S., Garcia-Perez, A., Katsaros, P., Ahmed Shaikh, S., Stamelos, I. (eds.) SEFM 2012 Satellite Events. LNCS, vol. 7991, pp. 172–189. Springer, Heidelberg (2014)
7. Barbuti, R., Maggiolo-Schettini, A., Milazzo, P., Pardini, C.: Spatial calculus of looping sequences. Theor. Comput. Sci. **412**(43), 5976–6001 (2011)
8. Barbuti, R., Maggiolo-Schettini, A., Milazzo, P., Pardini, C., Tesei, L.: Spatial P systems. Nat. Comput. **10**(1), 3–16 (2011)
9. Barbuti, R., Maggiolo-Schettini, A., Milazzo, P., Troina, A.: A methodology for the stochastic modeling and simulation of sympatric speciation by sexual selection. J. Biol. Syst. **17**(3), 349–376 (2009)

10. Barbuti, R., Mautner, S., Carnevale, G., Milazzo, P., Rama, A., Sturmbauer, C.: Population dynamics with a mixed type of sexual and asexual reproduction in a fluctuating environment. BMC Evol. Biol. **12**(1), 49 (2012)

11. Basuki, T.A., Cerone, A., Barbuti, R., Maggiolo-Schettini, A., Milazzo, P., Rossi, R.: Modelling the dynamics of an aedes albopictus population. In: Proceedings of AMCA-POP 2010. Electronic Proceedings in Theoretical Computer Science, vol. 33, pp. 18–36 (2010)

12. Bawa, K.S., Markham, A.: Climate change and tropical forests. Trends Ecol. Evol. **10**, 348–349 (1995)

13. Beaten, J.C.M., Bergstra, J.A.: Real-time process algebra. Formal Aspects Comput. **3**, 142–188 (1991)

14. Beauquier, D.: On probabilistic timed automata. Theoret. Comput. Sci. **292**, 65–84 (2003)

15. Berkes, F.: Rethinking community-based conservation. Conserv. Biol. **96**, 5066–5071 (2004)

16. Bistarelli, S., Cervesato, I., Lenzini, G., Marangoni, R., Martinelli, F.: On representing biological systems through multiset rewriting. In: Moreno-Díaz Jr., R., Pichler, F. (eds.) EUROCAST 2003. LNCS, vol. 2809, pp. 415–426. Springer, Heidelberg (2003)

17. Björnstad, O.N., Fromentin, J.M., Stenseth, N.C., Gjøsæter, J.: Cycles and trends in cod populations. Proc. Nat. Acad. Sci. U.S.A. **96**, 5066–5071 (2009)

18. Bonsall, M.B., Hastings, A.: Demographic and environmental stochasticity in predator-prey metapopulation dynamics. J. Anim. Ecol. **73**, 1043–1055 (2004)

19. Botter, G., Settin, T., Marani, M., Rinaldo, A.: A stochastic model of nitrate transport and cycling at basin scale. Water Resour. Res. **42**, 404–415 (2006)

20. Cardona, M., Colomer, M.A., Pérez-Jiménez, M.J., Sanuy, D., Margalida, A.: Modeling ecosystems using P systems: the bearded vulture, a case study. In: Corne, D.W., Frisco, P., Păun, G., Rozenberg, G., Salomaa, A. (eds.) WMC 2008. LNCS, vol. 5391, pp. 137–156. Springer, Heidelberg (2009)

21. Cavaliere, M., Sburlan, D.: Time–independent P systems. In: Mauri, G., Păun, G., Jesús Pérez-Jímenez, M., Rozenberg, G., Salomaa, A. (eds.) WMC 2004. LNCS, vol. 3365, pp. 239–258. Springer, Heidelberg (2005)

22. Ciocchetta, F., Hillston, J.: Bio-pepa: a framework for the modelling and analysis of biochemical networks. Theoret. Comput. Sci. **410**(33–34), 3065–3084 (2009)

23. Clark, J.S.: Beyond neutral science. Trends Ecol. Evol. **24**, 8–15 (2009)

24. Clarke, E.M., Faeder, J.R., Langmead, C.J., Harris, L.A., Jha, S.K., Legay, A.: Statistical model checking in *BioLab*: applications to the automated analysis of T-cell receptor signaling pathway. In: Heiner, M., Uhrmacher, A.M. (eds.) CMSB 2008. LNCS (LNBI), vol. 5307, pp. 231–250. Springer, Heidelberg (2008)

25. Codd, E.F.: Cellular Automata. Academic Press, New York (1968)

26. Coleman, F.C., Williams, S.L.: Overexploiting marine ecosystem engineers: potential consequences for biodiversity. Trends Ecol. Evol. **17**, 40–44 (2002)

27. Da Silva, J.M.C., Tabarelli, M.: Tree species impoverishment and the future flora of the Atlantic forest of northeast Brazil. Nature **404**(6773), 72–74 (2000)

28. Dematté, L., Priami, C., Romanel, A.: The BlenX language: a tutorial. In: Bernardo, M., Degano, P., Zavattaro, G. (eds.) SFM 2008. LNCS, vol. 5016, pp. 313–365. Springer, Heidelberg (2008)

29. Ebenman, B., Jonsson, T.: Using community viability analysis to identify fragile systems and keystone species. Trends Ecol. Evol. **20**, 568–575 (2005)

30. Elser, J.J., Sterner, R.W., Gorokhova, E., Fagan, W.F., Markow, T.A., Cotner, J.B., Harrison, J.F., Hobbie, S.E., Odell, G.M., Weider, L.W.: Biological stoichiometry from genes to ecosystems. Ecol. Lett. **3**(6), 540–550 (2000)
31. Gillespie, D.T.: A general method for numerically simulating the stochastic time evolution of coupled chemical reactions. J. Comput. Phys. **22**(4), 403–434 (1976)
32. Gillespie, D.T.: Exact stochastic simulation of coupled chemical reactions. J. Phys. Chem. **81**(25), 2340–2361 (1977)
33. Giordano, F.R., Weir, M.D., Fox, W.P.: A First Course in Mathematical Modeling. Brooks/Cole, Cengage Learning, Belmont (2009)
34. Gronewold, A., Sonnenschein, M.: Event-based modelling of ecological systems with asynchronous cellular automata. Ecol. Model. **108**, 37–52 (1998)
35. Hansson, H. Jonsson, B.: A logic for reasoning about time and reliability. Research report SICS/R(0013, SICS) (1994)
36. Hastings, A.: Population Biology: Concepts and Models. Springer, New York (1997)
37. Hennessy, M., Regan, T.: A process algebra for timed systems. Inf. Comput. **117**, 221–239 (1995)
38. Hughes, A.R., Inouye, B.D., Johnson, M.T.J., Underwood, N., Vellend, M.: Ecological consequences of genetic diversity. Ecol. Lett. **11**, 609–623 (2008)
39. Jha, S.K., Clarke, E.M., Langmead, C.J., Legay, A., Platzer, A., Zuliani, P.: A bayesian approach to model checking biological systems. In: Degano, P., Gorrieri, R. (eds.) CMSB 2009. LNCS, vol. 5688, pp. 218–234. Springer, Heidelberg (2009)
40. Jonsson, B., Larsen, K.G., Yi, W.: Probabilistic extensions of process algebras. In: Bergstra, J.A., Ponse, A., Smolka, S.A. (eds.) Handbook of Process Algebra. Elsevier, New York (2001)
41. Kahramanoğulları, O., Jordán, O., Lynch, J.F.: A language interface for stochastic dynamical modelling in ecology. Environ. Model Softw. **26**(5), 685–687 (2011)
42. Kahramanoğulları, O., Lynch, J.F., Priami, C.: Algorithmic systems ecology: experiments on multiple interaction types and patches. In: Cerone, A., Persico, D., Fernandes, S., Garcia-Perez, A., Katsaros, P., Ahmed Shaikh, S., Stamelos, I. (eds.) SEFM 2012 Satellite Events. LNCS, vol. 7991, pp. 154–171. Springer, Heidelberg (2014)
43. Kaitala, V., Ranta, E., Lindstroem, J.: Cyclic population dynamics and random perturbations. J. Anim. Ecol. **65**, 249–251 (1996)
44. Kartson, D., Balbo, G., Donatelli, S., Franceschini, G., Conte, G.: Modelling with Generalized Stochastic Petri Net. Wiley, New York (1994)
45. Kier, L.B., Seybold, P.G., Cheng, C.: Modelling Chemical Systems Using Cellular Automata. Springer, Dordrecht (2005)
46. Kingsland, S.: Modelling Nature: Episodes in the History of Population Ecology. University of Chicago Press, Chicago (1995)
47. Kolasa, J.: Complexity, system integration, and susceptibility to change: biodiversity connection. Ecol. Complex. **2**, 431–442 (2005)
48. Kunz, H., Hemelrijk, C.K.: Artificial fish schools: collective effects of school size, body size, and body form. Artif. Life **9**, 237–253 (2003)
49. Kwiatkowska, M., Norman, G., Parker, D.: PRISM: probabilistic symbolic model checker. In: Field, T., Harrison, P.G., Bradley, J., Harder, U. (eds.) TOOLS 2002. LNCS, vol. 2324, pp. 200–204. Springer, Heidelberg (2002)
50. Lande, R., Engen, S., Swether, B.E.: Stochastic Population Dynamics in Ecology and Conservation. Oxford University Press, Oxford (2003)
51. Lomnicki, A.: Population Ecology of Individuals. Princeton University Press, Princeton (1988)

52. Mace, G.M., Collar, N.J.: Priority setting in species conservation. In: Norris, K., Pain, D.J. (eds.) Conserving Bird Biodiversity. Cambridge University Press, Cambridge (2002)
53. McCallum, H.: Population Parameters: Estimation for Ecological Models. Wiley-Blackwell, New York (2000)
54. Paun, G.: Membrane Computing: An Introduction. Springer, Heidelberg (2002)
55. Pescini, D., Besozzi, B., Mauri, G., Zandron, C.: Dynamical probabilistic P systems. Int. J. Found. Comput. Sci. **17**, 183–204 (2006)
56. Philippou, A., Toro, M., Antonaki, M.: Simulation and verification for a process calculus for spatially-explicit ecological models. Sci. Ann. Comput. Sci. **23**(1), 119–167 (2013)
57. Priami, C.: Stochastic pi-calculus. Comput. J. **38**, 578–589 (1995)
58. Rasmussen, P.E., Goulding, K.W.T., Brown, J.R., Grace, P.R., Janzen, H.H., Körschens, M.: Long term agroecosystem experiments: assessing agricultural sustainability and global change. Science **282**(5390), 893–896 (1998)
59. Reisig, W.: Petri Nets: An Introduction. Springer, Heidelberg (1985)
60. Renshaw, E.: Modelling Biological Population in Space and Time. Cambridge Univerity Press, Cambridge (1991)
61. Richardson, G.P.: Introduction to System Dynamics Modeling with Dynamo. MIT Press, Cambridge (1981)
62. Ripa, J., Ives, A.R.: Food web dynamics in correlated and autocorrelated environments. Theor. Popul. Biol. **64**, 369–384 (2003)
63. Romero-Campero, F.J., Gheorghe, M., Bianco, L., Pescini, D., Jesús Pérez-Jímenez, M., Ceterchi, R.: Towards probabilistic model checking on P systems using PRISM. In: Hoogeboom, H.J., Păun, G., Rozenberg, G., Salomaa, A. (eds.) WMC 2006. LNCS, vol. 4361, pp. 477–495. Springer, Heidelberg (2006)
64. Schea, K., Chesson, P.: Community ecology theory as a framework for biological invasions. Trends Ecol. Evol. **17**, 170–176 (2002)
65. Scotti, M., Ciocchetta, F., Jordán, F.: Social and landscape effects on food webs: a multi-level network simulation model. J. Complex Netw. **1**(2), 160–182 (2013)
66. Seppelt, R., Temme, M.M.: Hybrid low level petri nets in environmental modelling - development platform and case studies. In: Matthies, M., Malchow, H., Kriz, J. (eds.) Integrative Systems Approach to Natural and Social Science. Springer, Heidelberg (2002)
67. Setiawan, S., Cerone, A.: Stochastic modelling of seasonal migration using rewriting systems with spatiality. In: Counsell, S., Núñez, M. (eds.) SEFM 2013. LNCS, vol. 8368, pp. 313–328. Springer, Heidelberg (2014)
68. Sterman, J.D.: Business Dynamics: Systems Thinking and Modeling for a Complex World. McGraw Hill Higher Education, New York (2000)
69. Tigasa, L.A., Vurena, D.H.V., Sauvajot, R.M.: Behavioral responses of bobcats and coyotes to habitat fragmentation and corridors in an urban environment. Biol. Conserv. **108**, 299–306 (2002)
70. Wang, J.: Timed Petri Nets: Theory and Applications. Kluwer Academic Publisher, Boston (1998)
71. Yodzis, P.: Must top predators be culled for the sake of fisheries? Trends Ecol. Evol. **16**, 78–84 (2001)
72. Younes, H.L.S.: Verification and Planning for Stochastic Processes with Asynchronous Events. PhD thesis, Carnegie Mellon University (2005)

Retrieving Points of Interest from Human Systematic Movements

Riccardo Guidotti[1,2]([⊠]), Anna Monreale[1,2], Salvatore Rinzivillo[2],
Dino Pedreschi[1], and Fosca Giannotti[2]

[1] KDDLab, University of Pisa, Largo B. Pontecorvo, 3, Pisa, Italy
{riccardo.guidotti,anna.monreale,dino.pedreschi}@di.unipi.it
[2] KDDLab, ISTI-CNR, Via G. Moruzzi, 1, Pisa, Italy
{salvatore.rinzivillo,fosca.giannotti}@isti.cnr.it

Abstract. Human mobility analysis is emerging as a more and more fundamental task to deeply understand human behavior. In the last decade these kind of studies have become feasible thanks to the massive increase in availability of mobility data. A crucial point, for many mobility applications and analysis, is to extract interesting locations for people. In this paper, we propose a novel methodology to retrieve efficiently significant places of interest from movement data. Using car drivers' systematic movements we mine everyday interesting locations, that is, places around which people life gravitates. The outcomes show the empirical evidence that these places capture nearly the whole mobility even though generated only from systematic movements abstractions.

1 Introduction

The study of human mobility can offer insight into human behavior [5,14]. Traces of human mobility can be collected with a great number of different techniques such as GPS (Global Positioning System) or GSM (Global System for Mobile Communications). The result is a huge quantity of data: about tens of thousand people moving along millions of trajectories. Mobility data can provide a complete description of the places visited and the routes followed by individual users. There are many potential opportunities, and movement data have been recognized by private and public institutions as a valuable source of information to evaluate the habits of people in terms of mobility.

Recent researches in mobility analysis have been extended in order to identify the behaviors that people constantly follow, such as groups of trajectories with common routes [13] or popular destinations [2]. Indeed, a central point in these studies is the concept of *place of interest* [7] in urban mobility environment, i.e. certain places or areas attract individual movements due to their importance. It is worth to point out that people move from one place to another, therefore "places" are not only static geographical objects, but they are also part of people life. The way people move towards these places affects the overall mobility of the environment. Thus, in order to study the relationships between people movements and the places of interest, it is mandatory to have a method that takes into account people's mobility to extract the locations they frequent routinely.

© Springer International Publishing Switzerland 2015
C. Canal and A. Idani (Eds.): SEFM 2014 Workshops, LNCS 8938, pp. 294–308, 2015.
DOI: 10.1007/978-3-319-15201-1_19

Online static datasets of places of interest can be easily exploited to analyze data, and there are plenty of works that enhance their potential. However, capturing real-time human mobility is challenging and often requires expensive frameworks and infrastructures. At any rate, places of interest directly extracted from movement data are more reliable and trustful than those readable from the Web or from public sources. This happens because the last ones are static, rarely updated and, overall, usually related to commercial activities such as bars, hotels, museums and so on.

The method proposed in this paper allows us to extract the places of interest around which our life gravitates. These places are extracted considering how people's everyday systematic mobility is regulated and influenced by them. Using mobility data as a proxy of human mobility and the idea of mobility profiles [13], we introduce a new notion of *Points of Interest* (POIs) explaining how they can be extracted. We test our method on a real case study considering big datasets of *GPS* trajectories. The outcomes show the empirical evidence that these POIs represent nearly the whole mobility even though they are generated only from a systematic movement abstraction. Finally, we propose a wide range of applications for which POIs extracted in such a way can be extremely useful.

The remainder of this paper is organized as follows. Section 2 presents a set of papers extracting places of interest from mobility data. In Sect. 3 are reported some basic concepts to understand the methodology presented in the following. Section 4 illustrates the procedure for the POIs extraction, while in Sect. 5 are reported the experimental results obtained using real datasets. In Sect. 6 are illustrated some possible applications for the proposed methodology. Finally, Sect. 7 concludes the paper.

2 Related Work

In the following are reported some recent works in which the extraction of places (or regions) of interest is a fundamental point. Each one of them explains its own extraction method starting from different types of data. In [2] the authors propose a visual analytic procedure for studying mobility data. Their procedure extracts relevant places from movement data because, for their aim, there is not a predefined set of places (e.g. compartments of a territory division) from which the analyst can select places of interest. In [6,10], the authors generate regions of interest with the purpose of predicting human movements using mobility pattern mining. The regions of interest are obtained by discretizing the working space in a regular grid with cells of small size. Then, the cells not visited are discarded and, by following a density based principle, the cells conceptually belonging to the same points are merged. Similarly, since it is impossible to translate a continuous surface into a graph, different authors in [4] and [12] discretize the territory in cells to apply social network analysis techniques on mobility data. In [8] is proposed an approach based on supervised learning to infer people's motion models from their GPS logs. The authors, first analyze different features to understand the kind of movement performed by the users (car, bus, bike etc.), and then use clustering algorithms to detect stopping points areas. To estimate the physical location of users from traces of mobile devices associated with access points in a wireless network, the authors in [9] characterize popular regions evaluating access points paths with GPS traces. Finally, in [15] it is proposed an approach that is capable of uncovering semantically relevant keywords for describing a location. Also in this case the locations correspond to the access points areas.

3   Preliminaries

Movements are usually performed by people in specific areas and time instants. These people are called *users* or *drivers* and each movement is composed by a sequence of spatio-temporal points (x, y, t) where x and y are the coordinates, while t is the time stamp. We call *trajectory* the movements of a user described by a sequence of spatio-temporal points:

Definition 1 (Trajectory). *A trajectory m is a sequence of spatio-temporal points $m = \{(x_1, y_1, t_1), \ldots, (x_n, y_n, t_n)\}$ where the spatial points (x_i, y_i) are sorted by increasing time t_i, i.e., $\forall 1 \leq i \leq k$ we have $t_i < t_{i+1}$.*

The set of all the trajectories traveled by a user u makes her *individual history*:

Definition 2 (Individual History). *Given a user u, we define the individual history of u as the set of traveled trajectories denoted by $H_u = \{m_1, \ldots, m_k\}$.*

Using the above definitions and following the profiling procedure proposed in [13], we can retrieve the systematic movements of a user u. Thus, we group the trajectories using a density-based clustering (i.e., Optics [3]) equipped with a *distance function* defining the concept of trajectory similarity:

Definition 3 (Trajectory Similarity). *Given two trajectories m and p, a trajectory distance function dist and a distance threshold ε, we say that m is similar to p ($m \sim p$) iff $\text{dist}(m, p) \leq \varepsilon$.*

The obtained result is a partitioning of the original dataset from which we filter out the *clusters* with few trajectories and the one containing noise. Finally we extract a *representative trajectory* from each remained cluster. These representative trajectories are called *routines* and the set of routines is called *mobility profile*. More formally:

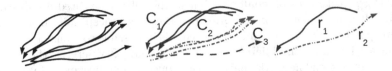

Fig. 1. The user *individual history* (black lines), the clusters identified by the grouping function (C_1, C_2, C_3) and the extracted *individual routines* (r_1, r_2) forming her *individual mobility profile*.

Definition 4 (Routine and Mobility Profile). *Let H_u the individual history of a user u, ms a minimum size threshold,* dist *a distance function and ε a distance threshold. Given a mobility profiling function* profile(H_u, ms, dist, ε) = $\mathcal{M}$, *such that* $\mathcal{M} = \{M_1 \ldots M_k\}$ *where* $M_i \subset H_u$, *we define a routine r_i as the medoid trajectory of a group M_i. The set of routines extracted from $\mathcal{M}$ is called* mobility profile *and is denoted by* $P_u = \{r_1 \ldots r_k\}$.

A *mobility profile* describes an abstraction in space and time of the systematic movements: the user's real movements are represented by a set of trajectories delineating the generic paths followed. Moreover, the exceptional movements are completely ignored due to the fact they will be not part of the profile. Figure 1 depicts an example of mobility profile extraction.

4   Mobility Points of Interest Extraction

In mobility data studies, places or regions can be extracted from raw data through regular territory division. However, relevant places for human mobility do not have regular shapes. Indeed, they may have arbitrary shapes and sizes and irregular spatial distribution. They might even overlap in space; hence, approaches based on dividing the territory into non-overlapping areas (as in [1] and [10]) are not appropriate.

What we are looking for in our study are places of interest that approximate as better as possible human mobility and consequently human behavior. Commonly, *a Point of Interest (POI) is a specific point location that "someone" may find useful or interesting.* Most consumers use the term POIs when referring to hotels, campsites, fuel stations or any other category used in modern navigation systems. In fact, the term is widely used in cartography, especially in electronic variants including GIS, and GPS navigation software. A GPS point of interest specifies, at minimum, the latitude and longitude of the POI. Digital maps for modern GPS devices (e.g. TomTom and Garmin) or GPS navigator applications (e.g. Google Maps and Waze), typically include a basic selection of POIs for the map area. Moreover, there are websites specialized in the collection, verification, management and distribution of POIs which end-users can load onto their devices to replace or supplement the existing POIs. While some of these websites are generic, and collect and categorize POIs for any interest, others are more specialized in a particular category (e.g. as speed cameras).

All the aforementioned type of POIs are strictly related with commercial activities (e.g. bars, restaurants, hotels and shopping centers), public facilitates (e.g. hospitals, schools and universities), leisure sites (e.g. museums and amusement parks). These places are useful to organize a holiday trip or to find a place to spend the evening. At any rate, they do not consider everyday human mobility. Indeed, people constantly follow the same periodic movement during their working day with systematic patterns. Thus, people's visited locations are influenced by the systematic movements of their everyday life. Looking individually at each user, everyone has as most visited POIs her own home, her working place, her

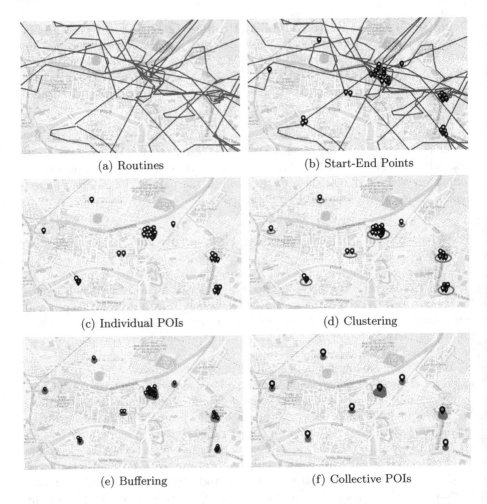

(a) Routines   (b) Start-End Points

(c) Individual POIs   (d) Clustering

(e) Buffering   (f) Collective POIs

Fig. 2. Mobility POIs extraction method.

habitual shopping centers, and maybe her gym and her friends' homes. These POIs are the real interesting locations in individuals routinely life. Thus, from hereafter we will refer to a POI with this latter concept: *a POI is a place that "someone" may find relevant or interesting in her everyday systematic life.*

We propose a new method to extract these POIs in order to understand which are our significant locations and to study how certain places are affected by human systematic mobility. In the following, we illustrate the mobility data-driven procedure to extract POIs from trajectory data. Figure 2 depicts in detail all the steps to retrieve POIs. The systematic behavior of each user can be modeled with the mobility profiles presented in the previous section. Thus, the systematic daily mobility of each user is characterized by her routines (Fig. 2-a). These routines necessarily begin and end somewhere. For profiled users, having a mobility that gravitates around these locations, it results that these places are surely very important for them (Fig. 2-b). We identify these places as *individual POIs* (Fig. 2-c):

Definition 5 (Individual Point of Interest). *Given the mobility profile P_u of a certain user u, then the individual POIs of u is the set I_u such that*

$$I_u = \{p|p = start(r) \vee p = end(r) \; \forall r \in P_u\}$$

where start(.) and end(.) are two functions that given a routine return its start point and its end point, respectively.

We remark that, in this paper, a POI has the meaning of "a place frequently visited by someone" and not the meaning of a public attraction. Therefore, our extraction method allows us to infer not only typical attraction points (because surely there is at least someone working there), but also important places for individual users, such as their home, which are not available in typical public sources. We are able to capture this information thanks to the fact that the GPS signal tells us the position of the nearest parking from the location visited by the user. As we will observe in the following, typically each user frequently visits two places that are with high probability home and work.

From Definition 5 we can notice that, given two different drivers u and v, which systematically park their cars close each other, we have that $I_u \cap I_v = \emptyset$, since each individual POI is represented by GPS coordinates and it is nearly impossible that there is a perfect correspondence. However, these users are following a similar systematic mobility behavior towards the same location, as a consequence the two individual POIs should be geographically considered as a unique *collective* POI. To this aim, given a set of car drivers and considering a certain spatial tolerance, we compute a density-based clustering on the individual POIs and then, we turn each valid cluster and each noise point into a buffered convex shape area representing a collective POI.

Definition 6 (Collective Point of Interest). *Given a set I of individual POIs, then the collective POIs set C_I is defined as*

$$C_I = buffer(convex(clustering(I, \varepsilon)), \varepsilon')$$

In the above definition, ε and ε' are distance values and $clustering(I, \varepsilon)$ is a density-based clustering function that returns clusters composed of individual POIs (Fig. 2-d). Note that two points are considered close enough if their distance is lower than ε. The clusters returned can also be composed of noise points because each noise point represents an individual POI supported by at least a routine and thus, it is relevant for at least one user. $convex(.)$ is a function returning the convex shape of the clusters of the input points. If the cluster contains only one point, then itself is returned. Lastly, $buffer(.)$ is a function that applies a spatial buffer of ε' to the set of input shapes and points (Fig. 2-e). In the following, for the sake of simplicity, we will call a collective POI simply POI. In other words, we can think to a POI as a geographical area with a

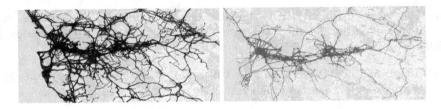

Fig. 3. (Left) A sample of the considered trajectories in Pisa province. (Right) Mobility profiles extracted in Pisa province.

certain extension that is visited frequently by at least one user (Fig. 2-f). Note that two different POIs a and b could be overlapped because of the buffering phase. Anyway, $\varepsilon' < \varepsilon$ ensures that the center of a is not included in b because otherwise the clustering algorithm would have put them in the same cluster because they would have been distant no more than ε.

5   Mobility Case Study

To extract the latent POIs in human systematic mobility we applied the method described above on large provincial trajectory datasets. First of all, we briefly report some consideration about the dataset used and the mobility profile extraction. Then, we describe the study performed to extract reliable POIs and what they represent on the analyzed area. Finally, we show why the extracted POIs represent the overall mobility even though they are built starting from the systematic movements abstractions that are mobility profiles.

5.1   Mobility Dataset

As a proxy of human mobility, we use real GPS traces collected for insurance purposes by *Octo Telematics S.p.A*[1]. This dataset contains 9.8 million car travels performed by about 160,000 vehicles active in a geographical area focused on Tuscany in a period from 1st May to 31st May 2011. Figure 3-left depicts a sample of the considered trajectories. The mobility dataset is geographically and temporally too various to be used for our purposes. Thus, it was split following different principles based on time and geography. In real world, different events may change how people move on the territory. Such events can be unpredictable or not frequent, like natural disaster, but most of them are not. The most regular and predictable event is the transition between working days and non-working days. During Saturday and Sunday, people usually leave their working mobility routines for different paths. Following this concept we filtered out weekend trajectories, maintaining only weekday ones. Another basic issue is that the mobility is not the same in every geographical area. Every area has its own type of mobility with certain characteristics depending on the surface, the topology and the

---

[1] http://www.octotelematics.com/it.

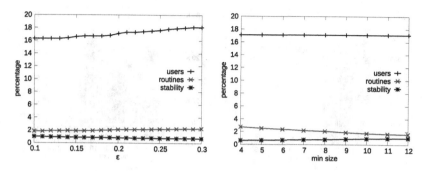

Fig. 4. Profile test ε (left) and min size (right).

number of inhabitants. In order to consider this fact, it was made a geographical filter to split the dataset in provinces by considering for each province all the trajectories that pass through its administrative borders. In this paper we present the results obtained for Pisa, Florence, Siena and Grosseto province.

In order to obtain sound routines we perform some test to set the best parameter to extract reliable mobility profile. Figure 3-right depicts an example of profile extracted in Pisa province modeling the users' systematic movements. The distance function used in the clustering step is *Route Relative Synch* described in [13]. The clustering algorithm used is Optics [3], a density-based algorithm. We study Optics parameters on a subset of 1,000 users in Pisa province. Thus, we vary ε in the range $[0.1, 0.3]$ with step 0.01, Fig. 4-left. The bigger ε is, the more different trajectories are allowed to be clustered together. The threshold *min size*, the minimum number of trajectories that must be in a cluster considered valid, is varied in the range $[4, 12]$, Fig. 4-right. The aspects we consider to tune the values are: *(a)* the dataset coverage, *(b)* the profile distribution per user, and *(c)* the profile stability. From this empirical study we decide to use middle values because the plots obtained do not lead to a clear setting. Anyway, in each plot, after the middle values the curves change more rapidly than before them. We choose ε equal to 0.2, it expresses 80 % of similarity between two trajectories and, a reliable value for *min size* is 8 since a routine is a movement repeated a sufficient number of time during a month.

Figure 5-left shows the number of routines per users in Pisa province where each user has almost one or two routines, which, should correspond to the commute to and from work. Indeed, note that the average number of routines per profile is 2, this is probably due to the home-work-home pattern. In Fig. 5-right the temporal distribution of the trajectories and routines is shown. Here, we can see how the profile set has a working-like trend, highlighting the three peeks during the early morning 5–6, lunchtime 11–12, and late afternoon 17–18. This confirms the previous assumption: mobility profiles are reliable to model systematic movement and thus can be exploited to retrieve systematically visited places.

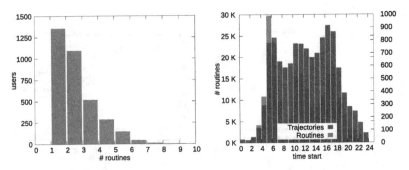

Fig. 5. Routine per user (left), trajectories and routines time start (right) distributions.

5.2 Mobility POIs Extraction Analysis

In the following we analyze the mobility POIs extraction method. Two main issues are considered to build reliable POIs: *(a)* a significant number of POIs must be visited by at least two users otherwise they will be useful only as an individual information in a urban collective scenario, *(b)* POIs shape cannot degenerate, i.e. they cannot be too big, nor too long, nor sausage-shaped. Only two parameters must be considered in POIs extraction process: ε and ε', and, since ε' depends on ε, we study only ε. We tested POIs extraction using the routines of $1,000$ profiled users in Pisa province with $\varepsilon \in [20, 100]$ and step 10. In this case ε in Optics represents the meters of distance between two individual POIs to be considered close. We recall that every POI is important for someone because it is generated by a routine. In order to guarantee both *(a)* and *(b)* we perform an accurate analysis. Thus we study the number of POIs extracted and the average number of users in a POI depicted in Fig. 6-left. We notice that the number of POIs extracted rapidly decreases while the number of POIs with more than one user grows slowly. On the contrary, the average number of user in a POI increases linearly. Moreover, we examined the maximum area and diameter for the POIs extracted, reported in Fig. 6-right. From these lines trend we observe that the maximum values, accordingly to the median and average ones (here not shown), rapidly rise leading to some degenerate POI that collects conceptually different places. Thus, by looking together at these plots, a reasonable value suggested for ε appears to be 50 m. Consequently, we set $\varepsilon' = 45$ to have a remarkable buffer even for individual POIs. In fact, this combination of parameters leads to a good number of POIs neither too big nor too small visited on average by at least two users.

For each province, we obtain a POIs distribution per profiled users telling us that the bigger subset of profiled users stop from 1 to 5 POIs. As it is shown in Table 1, the average number of profiled users per POI in every province ranges from 2 to 4 meaning that, on the whole, a collective points is nearly always visited by at least two users. This happens because, many places (probably home) are visited only by one user, while other social POIs like hospitals and shopping centers are visited by many users. For the home-work-home pattern, the majority of the users visit at least two places. Moreover, still from Table 1,

Table 1. Tuscany mobility POIs statistics. The public source for surface, inhabitants and density is http://en.wikipedia.org/wiki/Tuscany.

Province	Pisa	Florence	Siena	Grosseto
POIs	9,760	12,848	7,299	6,567
Users	20,898	41,724	27,242	14,036
Users profiled	21.05%	11.82%	15.13%	33.24%
Avg users per POI	2.14	3.25	3.73	2.14
Routines	7,383	9,801	6,458	7,281
Surface (km^2)	2,448	3,514	3,821	4,504
Inhabitants	409,251	983,073	268,706	225,142
Density (inh./km^2)	167.2	279.8	81.9	50.0

we note that for every province the number of POIs extracted is not correlated neither with the number of routines, nor with the number of users profiled, nor with the surface. On the contrary, it seems to better correlate with the number of inhabitants.

As final analysis it interesting to observe which are the most visited POIs in every province. Thus we counted how many trajectories present in the initial provincial datasets start and end in every POIs. It emerges that for each provincial dataset there are few POIs visited by many people and many POIs visited by few car drivers, following a long tailed power low distribution. In Fig. 7, depicting semi-log normalized number of visits distributions, we can notice how, despite the difference in number of POIs extracted, all the distributions are quite close. This indicates that the whole mobility is similar with respect to our POIs for the provinces analyzed. This obviously happens because there are some POIs with a role of prevalence, that is more visited, with respect to the others. They are very fascinating places because these POIs are visited both by *systematic drivers* working there and by *occasional drivers*. As an example we can think to the following. Doctors and salesman, working in hospitals and shopping centers

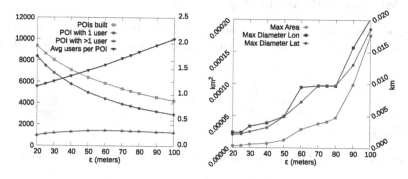

Fig. 6. POI construction test parameter ε (left) POIs numbers, (right) POIs shape.

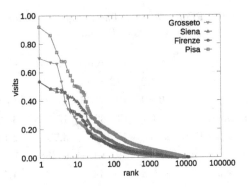

Fig. 7. POIs number of visits distribution for each provincial dataset.

respectively, stop there systematically, while patients and customers just visit these places when they need. The former category, *systematic drivers*, surely belong some routines that start and end there, that is the reason why they have been extracted as POIs. On the other hand, the latter category, *occasional drivers*, belong just several trajectories starting or ending there. However, due to the fact that places like hospitals and shopping centers are attractors for many people, there are many trajectories starting and ending in these places, augmenting in this way the visitors count. Conversely, the great majority of less visited places are POIs for at least a driver by definition, and thus they correspond to homes or to not very frequented working places. Figure 9 shows the ten most visited POIs in Pisa, Florence, Siena and Grosseto. As suggested above, they are mainly big shopping centers, hospitals and car parks close to locations visited very often by many people. We can notice how for every province there are some of these popular POIs out of the main town corresponding to car parks close to big malls. In Fig. 8 is depicted a zoom on the four most visited POIs in Pisa province. As one can see, the POIs areas bound perfectly the car parks close to the real point of interest. This demonstrate the good quality and precision of the mobility POIs extraction method proposed.

5.3 Mobility POIs as Mobility Summary

An important result emerges as a side effect from the POIs extraction process: *the mobility POIs, and thus the mobility profiles, are a good representation of*

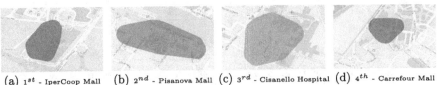

(a) 1st - IperCoop Mall   (b) 2nd - Pisanova Mall   (c) 3rd - Cisanello Hospital   (d) 4th - Carrefour Mall

Fig. 8. The fourth most visited POIs in Pisa.

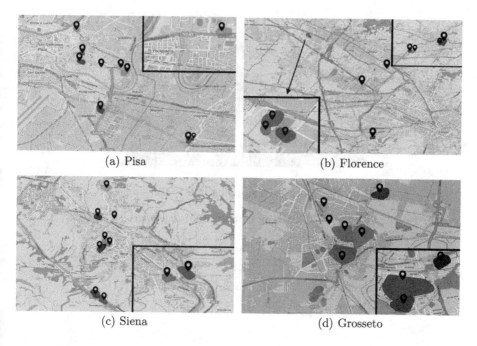

(a) Pisa   (b) Florence

(c) Siena   (d) Grosseto

Fig. 9. Ten most visited POIs in Pisa, Florence, Siena and Grosseto.

the overall mobility. Taking into account that this process starts from the routines and not from all the trajectories, it is interesting to notice that, for every provincial dataset, about 80 % of the trajectories start or end into the POIs extracted. Detailed statistics about coverage are reported in Table 2. Figure 10 shows all the trajectories starting or ending in a little sample of POIs in Pisa. As you can see, the map is almost completely covered by the red lines representing the trajectories. This is a signal that these POIs have an high importance in the overall mobility because they can capture nearly all the route traveled in the considered geographical area. This fact visually reinforces the hypothesis that mobility profiles, that is systematic trajectories, are a good representation of all the mobility. Consequently, mobility POIs are good to capture human mobility. As this assumption appears true, then it is a great simplification to use routines instead of all the trajectories to analyze human mobility. Another confirmation of the strength brought by mobility profiles emerges from the visual inspection of the starting and ending points of the trajectories not starting nor ending in any POIs. It comes out that these places are not really interesting because they do not correspond to important locations but they are almost all private houses which are also occasionally visited by their owners.

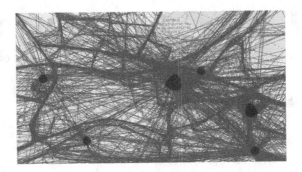

Fig. 10. Trajectories stopping in a POIs sample.

Table 2. Tuscany mobility POIs coverage.

Province	Pisa	Florence	Siena	Grosseto
POIs	9, 760	12, 848	7, 299	6, 567
Trajectories	476, 267	1, 358, 596	478, 424	661, 116
POIs coverage	80.32 %	76.44 %	79.80 %	84.54 %

6 Mobility POIs Applications

There is wide set of mobility applications which need a data driven POIs extraction method to perform different tasks and solve distinct problems. In the following we illustrate a broad range of mobility task where reliable and functional POIs are mandatory in order to obtain good results.

A deep study in mobility data relates to mobility flows and patterns. A mobility pattern represents the regularity of a set of users moving from a place to another, that is, from a POI to another. Thus, in order to deal with worth patterns, interesting POIs must be considered. As in [10], these patterns can be used to solve *mobility prediction* tasks. A mobility prediction is a statement about the place someone will be in the future, often but not always based on experience or knowledge. Prediction tasks use previously extracted movement patterns, which are a concise representation of behaviors of moving users as sequences of places frequently visited with a typical travel time. A decision tree, is built and evaluated with a formal training and test process. Consequently, to produce proper predictions, it is essential to use a sound set of POIs as those extracted by our method.

Another typical application to use our POIs is a *recommendation system*. A recommendation system is a subclass of information filtering system that seeks to predict the "rating" or "preference" that user would give to an item. Recommendation systems have become extremely common in recent years, and are applied in a variety of applications such as mobility. As an example, a recommendation system can exploit the correlation between geographical locations in the space of human behavior, that is, POIs correlation, to suggest new POIs to visit. In [16], for example, by taking into account users travel experience and the subsequent locations visited, the authors learn the location correlation from a large number of user-generated GPS trajectories. Then, by using the POIs correlation, they conduct a personalized location recommendation system, which is evaluated on the basis of a real-world GPS dataset.

Finally, some possible applications are related to *complex network analysis studies* in which the POIs are the nodes of the networks. An example can be found in [11] where the authors analyze the urban mobility and the POIs trying to featuring the places in a city according to how people move among them. Then, they build a POIs network by connecting POIs where trajectories pass. From such a network they extract the communities finding group of places highly connected by people mobility. As another example, a possible mobility data driven analysis could consist in building the bipartite graph of drivers and POIs to investigate the relationship between how the movements of people are affected by the POIs, and how the places themselves are characterized and connected to the mobility of people.

7   Conclusion

One of the most fascinating challenges of our time is to study the global interconnected society, especially, to understand the human mobility. The analysis of movement data and locations of interest has been recently promoted by the wide diffusion of new techniques and systems for monitoring, collecting and storing positional data. In this paper we have shown a novel approach to extract people real POIs from mobility GPS data. We have seen that the procedure is efficient because it does not need all the trajectories present in the data but just a representative abstraction. Moreover, we have observed that the places extracted with the proposed method capture both famous collective POIs and individually important POIs. Finally, as a positive side effect of this study, we have shown that the mobility POIs extracted do not lose in generality even though generated only from systematic movements. A possible future work related to the POIs extraction method consists in adjusting the radius used by the clustering algorithm with respect to the population density of the area in which the POIs are retrieved. Another possible improvements consists in extending the geographical and systematical information given by our POIs with the static and semantic knowledge contained in classical points of interest. That is, we could extend the informative power of our POIs by matching them with common points of interest information saying for example that they are bars, museum, hospital and so on.

Acknowledgements. This work has been partially supported by the European Commission under the FET-Open Project n. FP7-ICT-284715, ICON, and by the European Commission under the SMARTCITIES Project n. FP7-ICT-609042, PETRA.

References

1. Adrienko, N., Adrienko, G.: Spatial generalization and aggregation of massive movement data. IEEE Trans. Vis. Comput. Graph. **17**(2), 205–219 (2011)
2. Andrienko, G., Andrienko, N., Hurter, C., Rinzivillo, S., Wrobel, S.: From movement tracks through events to places: Extracting and characterizing significant places from mobility data. In: 2011 IEEE Conference on VAST. IEEE (2011)
3. Ankerst, M., Breunig, M.M., Kriegel, H.-P., Sander, J.: Optics: Ordering points to identify the clustering structure. In: ACM SIGMOD Record, vol. 28. ACM (1999)
4. Coscia, M., Rinzivillo, S., Giannotti, F., Pedreschi, D.: Optimal spatial resolution for the analysis of human mobility. In: 2012 IEEE/ACM International Conference on Advances in Social Networks Analysis and Mining (ASONAM). IEEE (2012)
5. Giannotti, F., Nanni, M., Pedreschi, D., Pinelli, F., Renso, C., Rinzivillo, S., Trasarti, R.: Unveiling the complexity of human mobility by querying and mining massive trajectory data. VLDB J. Int. J. Very Large Data Bases **20**(5), 695–719 (2011)
6. Giannotti, F., Nanni, M., Pinelli, F., Pedreschi, D.: Trajectory pattern mining. In: Proceedings of the 13th ACM SIGKDD International Conference on Knowledge Discovery and Data Mining. ACM (2007)
7. Hillier, B., Penn, A., Hanson, J., Grajewski, T., Xu, J.: Natural movement-or, configuration and attraction in urban pedestrian movement. Environ. Plann. B **20**(1), 29–66 (1993)
8. Kim, M., Kotz, D., Kim, S.: Extracting a mobility model from real user traces. In: INFOCOM, vol. 6 (2006)
9. Kostakos, V., Juntunen, T., Goncalves, J., Hosio, S., Ojala, T.: Where am i? location archetype keyword extraction from urban mobility patterns. PloS one **8**(5), e6398 (2013)
10. Monreale, A., Pinelli, F., Trasarti, R., Giannotti, F.: Wherenext: a location predictor on trajectory pattern mining. In: Proceedings of the 15th ACM SIGKDD International Conference on Knowledge Discovery and Data Mining. ACM (2009)
11. Ramalho Brilhante, I., Berlingerio, M., Trasarti, R., Renso, C., de Macedo, J.A.F., Casanova, M.A.: Cometogether: discovering communities of places in mobility data. In: 2012 IEEE 13th International Conference on Mobile Data Management (MDM). IEEE (2012)
12. Ratti, C., Sobolevsky, S., Calabrese, F., Andris, C., Reades, J., Martino, M., Claxton, R., Strogatz, S.H.: Redrawing the map of great britain from a network of human interactions. PloS One **5**(12), e14248 (2010)
13. Trasarti, R., Pinelli, F., Nanni, M., Giannotti, F.: Mining mobility user profiles for car pooling. In: Proceedings of the 17th ACM SIGKDD International Conference on Knowledge Discovery and Data Mining. ACM (2011)
14. Wang, D., Pedreschi, D., Song, C., Giannotti, F., Barabasi, A.-L.: Human mobility, social ties, and link prediction. In: Proceedings of the 17th ACM SIGKDD International Conference on Knowledge Discovery and Data Mining. ACM (2011)
15. Zheng, Y., Li, Q., Chen, Y., Xie, X., Ma, W.-Y.: Understanding mobility based on gps data. In: Proceedings of the 10th International Conference on Ubiquitous Computing. ACM (2008)
16. Zheng, Y., Xie, X.: Learning location correlation from gps trajectories. In: 2010 Eleventh International Conference on Mobile Data Management (MDM). IEEE (2010)

WS-FMDS 2014

Path-Sensitive Race Detection with Partial Order Reduced Symbolic Execution

Andreas Ibing[✉]

Chair for IT Security, TU München,
Boltzmannstrasse 3, 85748 Garching, Germany
ibing@sec.in.tum.de

Abstract. This paper presents a combination of symbolic execution and partial order reduction to achieve path-sensitive race detection. The presented approach limits the complexity of symbolic execution of multi-threaded code by applying it with a fixed scheduling algorithm only. Alternative thread interleavings are generated from fixed-scheduling ones with ample set partial order reduction on an abstraction level of thread interactions. Races are detected on the abstraction level. The proposed algorithm is implemented as plug-in extension of Eclipse CDT and evaluated by running it on the race condition test cases from the Juliet suite.

1 Introduction

Data race bugs are introduced in multi-threaded software when the developer forgets to lock a resource which is shared between threads. Races are difficult to find and debug with conventional testing methods only, because they are observed only for certain thread interleavings depending on the scheduler's decisions. Race bugs can only be reproduced in debugging if the scheduling decisions are reproducible, which is why race bugs are sometimes referred to as "Heisenbugs".

Static analysis methods are therefore an attractive approach to race detection. Different static methods offer a trade-off between complexity and accuracy of bug detections. Symbolic execution [1] is a static analysis method which is path-sensitive. It treats program input as symbolic variables and translates operations on them into logic equations. Symbolic execution automatically explores different paths in software and constructs path constraints. It relies on an automatic theorem prover (constraint solver) to decide branch satisfiability and bug conditions. Current symbolic execution engines rely on SAT Modulo Theories (SMT) solvers [2] as logic backend. An overview of symbolic execution tools and applications is given in [3,4].

The manifestation of race bugs depends on the actual thread interleaving, where scheduling points may in principle lie between any neighbouring assembly instructions. On the other hand, most thread actions are independent and commutative, and therefore irrelevant for race conditions. This can be used to analyze only a small number of representative thread interleavings without loss

© Springer International Publishing Switzerland 2015
C. Canal and A. Idani (Eds.): SEFM 2014 Workshops, LNCS 8938, pp. 311–322, 2015.
DOI: 10.1007/978-3-319-15201-1_20

of accuracy [5]. Because the "happens-before" relation is a partial order [6], such approaches are known as partial order reduction techniques [5].

Interesting properties of bug detection algorithms are soundness (no false negative detections) and completeness (no false positives). Because a bug checker cannot be sound and complete and have bounded runtime, in practice bug checkers are evaluated with false positive and false negative detections on a sufficiently large bug test suite. The currently most comprehensive C/C++ bug test suite for static analyzers is the Juliet suite [7]. Among other common software weaknesses [8] it contains race condition test cases. In order to systematically measure false positives and false negatives, it contains both 'good' and 'bad' functions and combines 'baseline' bugs with different data and control flow variants.

This paper combines symbolic execution with partial order reduction to achieve path-sensitive race detection. The proposed algorithm is implemented as plug-in extension of Eclipse CDT. The implementation builds on [9] and extends it to support multi-threading software and to find races. The remainder of this paper is organized as follows. The next section describes symbolic execution of multi-threaded code to find satisfiable program paths with a predefined scheduling algorithm which only depends on the thread identity numbers. Section 3 describes the abstraction of a found path with respect to thread interactions. From abstracted satisfiable paths with fixed scheduling, representatives for alternative thread interleavings are generated with partial order reduction, which is described in Sect. 4. Section 5 then shows how races are detected as overlapping read-write operations in the abstracted interleaving representatives. The algorithm is evaluated in Sect. 6 by running it on the race condition test cases from the Juliet suite. Related work is discussed in Sect. 7, and Sect. 8 discusses the results.

2   Symbolic Execution with Pre-defined Scheduling Algorithm

The symbolic execution engine from [9] is extended to support multi-threading, more specifically Posix threads (pthreads). Symbolic execution is run with a pre-defined scheduling algorithm, and thread interactions are traced as basis for path abstraction. Thread interaction tracing includes thread actions on shared variables.

2.1   Architecture Overview

Starting point is the multi-threaded symbolic execution engine with backtracking described in [9], which can analyze single-threaded C programs. It performs interprocedural analysis and is implemented according to the tree-based interpreter pattern [10]. It relies on an SMT solver as logic backend and translates C code into SMTLib [11] logic equations in the logic of arrays, uninterpreted functions and nonlinear integer and real arithmetic (AUFNIRA).

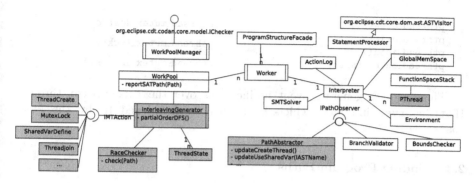

Fig. 1. Architecture Overview. The shaded classes are used to support multi-threading software and to find races.

The architecture is illustrated in Fig. 1. The figure contains the main classes from [9] and the interface IChecker, which makes the plug-in usable from CDT's code analysis framework [12]. Several Workers concurrently explore different parts of a program's execution tree. Each worker has an Interpreter together with a memory system model to store and retrieve symbolic variables (whose values are logic equations). The translation of control flow graph (CFG) nodes into SMTlib syntax is performed by the StatementProcessor (which extends CDT's abstract syntax tree visitor class) according to the visitor pattern [13]. The BranchValidator detects unsatisfiable branches in a program path with the help of the SMTSolver. WorkPool is used as synchronization object between the Workers and the WorkPoolManager.

New classes which have been added to support the analysis of multi-threaded software are shaded. The first addition is the PThread class, so that each thread has its own stack object (the heap is shared). The Interpreter interface IPathObserver is extented to notify about thread interactions. This interface is implemented by PathAbstractor which is described in detail in Sect. 3. If a satisfiable path through the analyzed software is detected, its abstraction is reported to WorkPool for later analysis of alternative thread interleavings (compare Fig. 1). The partial order reduction is implemented in Interleaving Generator. Generated interleavings are passed to RaceChecker for race detection.

2.2 Posix Threads Support

The symbolic execution engine offers the possibility to specify symbolic models of library functions, which is used both for the C/C++ standard library and for the operating system (Posix in this case). Function models are accessed by the Interpreter through the Environment class (compare Fig. 1). Models for Posix threads library (pthreads) function models are currently available for:

- pthread_create()
- pthread_exit()
- pthread_join()
- pthread_mutex_init()

- pthread_mutex_destroy()
- pthread_mutex_lock()
- pthread_mutex_unlock()

These models generate event notifications over the Interpreter through IPathObserver interface, which is in this cased listened to by the Path Abstractor.

2.3   Finding Program Paths

Symbolic execution is run with a fixed deterministic thread scheduling algorithm which depends only on the thread identity numbers. The implementation uses lowest thread-ID first (LTIF) scheduling, i.e. from the active threads the one with lowest thread-ID is scheduled. A thread blocks (becomes inactive) e.g. by trying to acquire a lock already held by another thread or with a join call for a thread which is still alive. The symbolic execution is run with approximate path coverage which is implemented with depth-first search (backtracking the symbolic program state and changing a branch decision, compare [9]). It supports a configurable loop iteration bound and the option to either prune a path when a loop's iteration bound is reached, or to skip out of the loop and bypass the BranchValidator check. In the latter case the loop variables' equations become unknown and are therefore cleared.

2.4   Path-Sensitive Tracing of Shared Variables

In addition to pthread library calls, other relevant thread interactions are read accesses and write accesses to shared variables (usage or definition actions for variables). Whether or not a variable is shared between threads is in principle context-sensitive, i.e. depends on the current program path (including the current function's call context). To trace sharing of variables, the Interpreter and StatementProcessor classes from [9] have been extended. All global variables are marked as shared when they are first accessed. Then the 'shared' property is inferred over data flow constructs like assignments, references, function call parameters and return values etc.. Data structures can be passed to a thread with a pointer at thread creation time (pthread_create()). These thread start arguments are also marked as 'shared'.

3   Abstracting Thread Interactions

Interesting scheduling points lie after each action of a thread which may be relevant to another thread. These thread interaction events are:

- shared variable usage
- shared variable definition
- thread creation
- thread join

- thread exit
- mutex lock
- mutex unlock

These thread events are modelled to implement a joint interface IMTAction, compare Fig. 1. It is possible that multiple events are generated for one source code statement or for one CFG node. Thread events are recorded for each satisfiable path with LTIF scheduling by the PathAbstractor. For each satisfiable path, the sequence of thread events is reported as path abstraction to the Workpool for later analysis.

An example is shown in Listing 1.1, taken from the race tests from [7]. In line 10 the global variable g_good is both used and defined in one statement. The listing is a 'good' function, because the access to the shared variable is guarded with a lock (pthread functions are not directly called in this example, because [7] uses an abstraction layer over Windows threads and Posix threads.). A corresponding 'bad' function uses the global variable g_bad instead of g_good and omits the locking. The abstraction of an interleaving of thread actions with LTIF scheduling for two threads executing the example function is illustrated in Fig. 2 as message sequence chart.

Listing 1.1. Example from [7]. A corresponding observable (abstracted) interaction of three threads, two of them running this functin, is illustrated in Fig. 2.

```
static void helper_good(void *args) {
    int i;
    /* FIX: acquire a lock */
    std_thread_lock_acquire(g_good_lock);
    for (i = 0; i < N_ITERS; i++) {
        g_good = g_good + 1;
    }
    std_thread_lock_release(g_good_lock);
}
```

4 Generating Interleaving Representatives with Partial Order Reduction

From each satisfiable path found by symbolic execution with fixed scheduling, all other thread interleavings corresponding to different scheduling decisions can be generated. They should have the same computation result independent of scheduling decisions. A race condition means that the program result depends on the scheduling decisions. The scheduling points which might be relevant to the program behaviour have been identified by the PathAbstractor. This section describes the generation of the alternative relevant thread interleavings on the path abstraction level. The generated set of interleavings should be of minimal size without degrading the ability to detect races.

The implementation follows partial order reduction with the ample sets approach [14]. The tree of scheduling decisions is traversed on-the-fly, where the tree nodes are maximal sets of independent actions (ample sets). Use or define actions from different threads for shared variables are independent if the variable is not the same. The construction of ample sets reduces the width of the

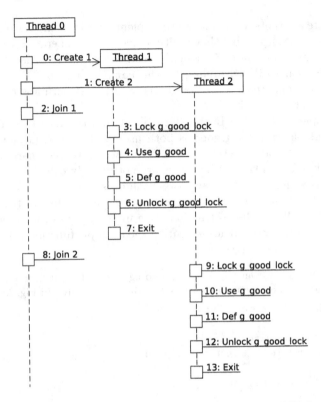

Fig. 2. Example of observable thread interaction with lowest thread-ID first scheduling.

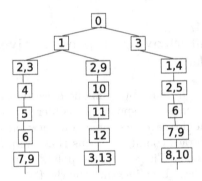

Fig. 3. First levels of ample set scheduling tree for the example in Fig. 2.

scheduling tree and thus the number of generated interleavings. Optimal partial order reduction generates a minimum number of representatives which corresponds to classes of equivalent thread interleavings. The implemented algorithm is listed as pseudo code in Algorithm 1. It is based on depth first search. In each tree node, the enabled actions are divided into ample sets of independent actions. Other actions may be blocked (a thread waiting to acquire a lock held by another thread, or a thread waiting to join another) until they are enabled by other actions. Each ample set is selected for one child node as action set to be executed. An interleaving representative is found if in a tree node there are no more blocked and enabled actions. The representative is generated by backtracking the path from the current node recursively through the parent node (parent ample sets). The first levels of the ample set scheduling tree for the path abstraction in Fig. 2 are shown as example in Fig. 3.

5   Race Detection with Interleaving Representatives

While concurrency bugs in general can involve any number of threads and variables, here we are interested in atomicity violations as overlapping read/write actions to the same variable from different threads. Each interleaving representative is analyzed individually for atomicity violations. An example is shown in Fig. 4. This figure shows an interleaving (not lowest thread-ID first) which corresponds to the 'bad' version of Listing 1.1 where the locking and unlocking operations are omitted. If the analyzed program contains an atomicity violation, then such an interleaving representative is generated by the partial order reduction algorithm from a satisfiable LTIF scheduling path. The algorithm to detect such a race in an interleaving representative is shown as pseudo code in Algorithm 2. It simply goes through the interleaving from start to end and checks for overlapping read/write actions (at least one read and two writes) from different threads to the same variable.

6   Experiments

The presented approach is implemented as plug-in extension to Eclipse CDT (extending [9]) and tested with the available race condition bug test cases (CWE-366) from the Juliet suite [7]:

- CWE366_Race_Condition_Within_Thread__global_int: races on global variables.
- CWE366_Race_Condition_Within_Thread__int_byref: races on variables with access through pointers.

The races are combined with 19 different data and control flow variants for each of both sets [7]. These 38 small test programs consist of 5–7 threads each and contain 'good' as well as 'bad' thread interaction behaviour. The tests were run as JUnit plug-in tests with Eclipse 4.2 on a Core 2 Quad CPU Q9550, on 64-bit Linux kernel 3.2.0.. The symbolic execution engine was configured to run single-threaded, to unroll loops for a maximum of three iterations, and to skip-out further iterations (continue the path skipping the loop while clearing the loop variables' formulas). The races were detected accurately (no false positives or false negatives) except for flow variant 18, in which a goto statement leads to an

```
partialOrderDFS(ThreadStates states_in, ActionSet execute, ActionSet
enabled_in, ActionSet blocked_in) ThreadStates states =
states_in.cloneElements()
ActionSet blocked = blocked_in.cloneElements()
enabled = performActions(execute, blocked)
enabled.addAll(enabled_in)
if enabled.isEmpty() then
    // found representative:
    interleaving = backtrack(execute)
else
    // find ample sets:
    Set<ActionSet> ampleSets;
    ampleSets[0].add(enabled[0])
    enabled.remove[0]
    interator it = ampleSets.iterator()
    forall the actions a in enabled do
        while it.hasNext() do
            ActionSet ample = it.next()
            if fitsAmple(a,ample) then
                ample.add(a)
            else
                ActionSet newSet
                newSet.add(a)
                ampleSets.addLast(newSet)
            end
        end
    end
    // enter next search level
    forall the ActionSet nextExecute : ampleSets do
        // enable backtracking:
        nextExecute.setParent(execute)
        ActionSet nextEnabled
        forall the ActionSet other : ampleSets do
            if nextExecute != other then
                nextEnabled.addAll(other)
            end
        end
        PartialOrderDFS(states, nextExecute, nextEnabled, blocked);
    end
end
```

Algorithm 1. Generating representatives for equivalent interleavings with ample set partial order reduction.

exception in the control flow graph builder of CDT's code analysis framework, and consequently to a false negative detection. The measured runtimes for the accurately decided tests are shown in Fig. 5. A screenshot of error reporting in the GUI is shown in Fig. 6.

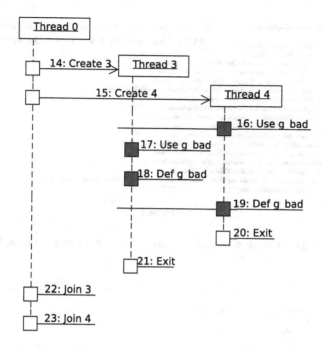

Fig. 4. Race condition, overlapping read/write actions on the same variable g_bad from different threads.

```
forall the actions in interleaving do
    if action instanceof UseSharedVar then
    |   openUses.put(action.getThreadnr(), var)
    else if action instanceof DefSharedVar then
        if openUses.contains(anyOtherThread, var) then
            if futureWrite(otherThread, var) then
            |   atomicity violation found!
            end
        end
    end
end
```

Algorithm 2. Detecting atomicity violations in an interleaving representative as overlapping read/writes.

7 Related Work

Race detection has been a topic for more than 30 years. Dynamic program analysis methods normally rely on an application-level scheduler to make detected bugs reproducible. The dynamic approach inherently leads to false negative detections, since only a subset of program paths and relevant thread interleavings are observed. Prominent examples of dynamic race detection are [15–17].

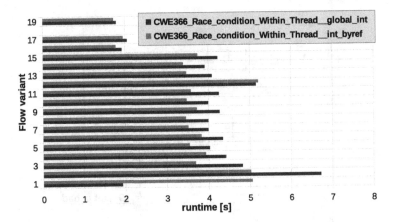

Fig. 5. Benchmark with race condition tests (36 programs) from [7].

```
CWE366_Race_Condition_Within_Thread__int_byref_19.c

static void helper_bad(void *args)
{
    int *p_val = (int*)args;
    int i;
    /* FLAW: incrementing an integer is not guaranteed to occur atomic
     * therefore this operation may not function as intended in multi-
     * programs
     */
    for (i = 0; i < N_ITERS; i++)
    {
        *p_val = *p_val + 1;
    }
}
```

| Problems | Tasks | Console | Properties | Display | Disassemb |

1 error, 0 warnings, 0 others

Description	Resource	Path	Location	Type
▼ ● Errors (1 item)				
⚡ Race condition	CWE366_Race_Condit	/CWE366_Race_(	line 34	Code Anal

Fig. 6. Screenshot error reporting.

Different static analysis approaches offer a trade-off between complexity and accuracy. On the lower complexity side they normally rely on type inference [18–20]. On the more accurate side there are path-sensitive approaches with model checking or symbolic execution [21–24]. Qadeer and Rehof [22] limits the number of generated thread interleavings with a context switch bound. The closest related approach is [24]. It applies symbolic execution with bit-vector logic to an intermediate code representation and uses partial order reduction. It differs from the presented approach in that it does not separate symbolic execution from partial order reduced interleaving generation by fixed scheduling and path abstraction, and it detects races by comparing computation results of different interleavings.

8 Discussion

The presented approach limits the complexity of symbolic execution of multi-threaded code by applying it with a fixed scheduling algorithm only. The handling of loops in the current implementation is problematic. Bounded unrolling misses later bugs after path pruning. The option to skip-out bounded loops and clearing the loop variables' formulas is not sound. It can generate unfeasible paths as feasible and false positive bug detections outside the loop. One improvement might be to add a loop termination check and a live variable analysis to ensure that loop variables are not read later. Another possibility might be to use abstract interpretation with the interval domain to avoid further unrolling. In spite of partial-order reduction the number of generated interleavings currently grows too fast for the presented approach to be useful for practical program sizes. Future work might therefore include application of reduced interleaving coverage criteria (e.g. [25]). This is especially appropriate when only certain concurrency bugs like atomicity violations are targeted.

Acknowledgement. This work was funded by the German Ministry for Education and Research (BMBF) under grant 01IS13020.

References

1. King, J.: Symbolic execution and program testing. Commun. ACM **19**(7), 385–394 (1976)
2. de Moura, L., Bjorner, N.: Satisfiability modulo theories: introduction and applications. Commun. ACM **54**(9), 69–77 (2011)
3. Cadar, C., et al.: Symbolic execution for software testing in practice - preliminary assessment. In: International Conference on Software Engineering (2011)
4. Pasareanu, C., Visser, W.: A survey of new trends in symbolic execution for software testing and analysis. Int. J. Softw. Tools Technol. Transfer **11**, 339–353 (2009)
5. Clarke, E., Grumberg, O., Minea, M., Peled, D.: State space reduction using partial order techniques. Softw. Tools Technol. Transfer **2**(3), 279–287 (1999)
6. Lamport, L.: Time, clocks, and the ordering of events in a distributed system. Commun. ACM **21**(7), 558–565 (1978)
7. United States National Security Agency, Center for Assured Software: Juliet Test Suite v1.1 for C/C++, December 2011
8. Martin, R., Barnum, S., Christey, S.: Being explicit about security weaknesses. In: Blackhat DC (2007)
9. Ibing, A.: Parallel SMT-constrained symbolic execution for eclipse CDT/Codan. In: Yenigün, H., Yilmaz, C., Ulrich, A. (eds.) ICTSS 2013. LNCS, vol. 8254, pp. 196–206. Springer, Heidelberg (2013)
10. Parr, T.: Language Implementation Patterns. Pragmatic Bookshelf, Lewisville (2010)

11. Barrett, C., Stump, A., Tinelli, C.: The SMT-LIB Standard Version 2.0., December 2010
12. Laskavaia, A.: Codan- C/C++ static analysis framework for CDT. In: EclipseCon (2011)
13. Gamma, E., Helm, R., Johnson, R., Vlissides, J.: Design Patterns: Elements of Reusable Object-Oriented Software. Addison-Wesley, New York (1994)
14. Peled, D.: Combining partial order reduction with on-the-fly model-checking. In: Dill, D.L. (ed.) CAV 1994. LNCS, vol. 818, pp. 377–390. Springer, Heidelberg (1994)
15. Savage, S., Burrows, M., Nelson, G., Sobalvarro, P., Anderson, T.: Eraser: a dynamic data race detector for multi-threaded programs. ACM Trans. Comput. Syst. **15**(4), 391–411 (1997)
16. Banerjee, U., Bliss, B., Ma, Z., Petersen, P.: A theory of data race detection. In: PADTAD (2006)
17. Flanagan, C., Freund, S.: FastTrack: efficient and precise dynamic race detection. In: PLDI (2009)
18. Abadi, M., Flanagan, C., Freund, S.: Types for safe locking: static race detection for Java. ACM Trans. Program. Lang. Syst. **28**(2), 207–255 (2006)
19. Voung, J., Jhala, R., Lerner, S.: RELAY: static race detection on millions of lines of code. In: ACM Symposium Foundations of Software Engineering (ESEC-FSE) (2007)
20. Naik, M.: Effective static race detection for Java. Ph.D. thesis, Stanford University (2008)
21. Kahlon, V., Wang, C., Gupta, A.: Monotonic partial order reduction: an optimal symbolic partial order reduction technique. In: Bouajjani, A., Maler, O. (eds.) CAV 2009. LNCS, vol. 5643, pp. 398–413. Springer, Heidelberg (2009)
22. Qadeer, S., Rehof, J.: Context-bounded model checking of concurrent software. In: Halbwachs, N., Zuck, L.D. (eds.) TACAS 2005. LNCS, vol. 3440, pp. 93–107. Springer, Heidelberg (2005)
23. Rabinovitz, I., Grumberg, O.: Bounded model checking of concurrent programs. In: Etessami, K., Rajamani, S.K. (eds.) CAV 2005. LNCS, vol. 3576, pp. 82–97. Springer, Heidelberg (2005)
24. Cordeiro, L.: SMT-based bounded model checking of multi-threaded software in embedded systems. Ph.D. thesis, University of Southampton (2011)
25. Lu, S., Jiang, W., Zhou, Y.: A study of interleaving coverage criteria. In: ECEC/FSE (2007)

Phase-Type Approximations for Non-Markovian Systems: A Case Study

Gabriel Ciobanu[✉] and Armand Rotaru

Institute of Computer Science, Romanian Academy,
Blvd. Carol I no. 8, 700505 Iaşi, Romania
gabriel@info.uaic.ro, armand@iit.tuiasi.ro

Abstract. Non-Markovian systems are usually difficult to represent and analyse using currently available stochastic process calculi. By relying on a combination between the newly introduced process algebra PHASE and the probabilistic model checker PRISM, we examine the dynamics of one such system, which involves a collaborative text review performed by two manuscript editors, and focus on the derivation of quantitative performance measures. We find that approximating non-Markovian transitions through single Markovian transitions is fast, but inaccurate, while employing more complex phase-type approximations is somewhat slow, but considerably more precise.

1 Introduction

In general, stochastic systems are divided into Markovian and non-Markovian systems, based on the temporal properties of their transitions: in the former, the time after which the system leaves any particular state (i.e., performs a transition) does not depend on the time already spent in that state, while in the latter, there is at least one transition between two states which does not satisfy the aforementioned property. A potential shortcoming of current stochastic process calculi refers to the fact that almost all of these formalisms were designed for Markovian systems, which can be expressed in terms of continuous-time Markov chains (CTMCs), and for which a solid mathematical theory exists [15]. This body of theory greatly facilitates performance analysis and allows one to easily derive the exact numerical value of transient, passage time, and steady-state performance measures. However, a sometimes severe downside of this approach lies in having to use only exponential distributions for stochastic variables. This restriction limits the possibility of accurately modelling certain performance variables, such as job service times or process execution times in software/hardware systems, which follow heavy tailed distributions [5], or the durations of pointing gestures in human-computer interaction systems, which follow log-normal distributions [6], to name but a few (for additional examples, see [11]). More specifically, the theory underlying non-Markovian systems is far less developed than that for Markovian systems, which means that performance measures typically cannot be derived analytically (but only approximated). The derivation

C. Canal and A. Idani (Eds.): SEFM 2014 Workshops, LNCS 8938, pp. 323–334, 2015.
DOI: 10.1007/978-3-319-15201-1_21

of these measures is usually performed either by employing non-Markovian formalisms, which rely on discrete event simulation techniques, or by constructing a Markovian system which approximates the behaviour of a non-Markovian system, and then analysing the Markovian system.

With respect to Markovian approximations, modellers typically apply one of two approaches. The first option is that of considering phase-type approximations for transition durations, meaning that non-Markovian transitions are replaced by Markovian processes (consisting of internal states and transitions). Phase-type distributions are adequate for such an enterprise given their strong closure properties (i.e., they are closed under convolution, maximum, minimum and convex mixture, unlike exponential distributions, which are closed only under minimum) and the fact that they can approximate any positive-valued distribution to an arbitrary degree of accuracy [13]. In contrast, the second option is that of ignoring the non-Markovian nature of transition durations: each non-Markovian distribution is replaced with a Markovian (exponential) distribution, such that the means of the two distributions coincide. Preferring one of these options over the other involves making a trade-off between approximation accuracy and size. Phase-type approximations usually produce accurate performance measures, but the resulting models often have a considerable number of states and transitions (e.g., in the order of millions), which makes performance analysis trickier and more time-consuming. Simple exponential approximations tend to generate at least somewhat inaccurate results, but the resulting models are compact and easy to analyze.

In this context, our intention is to examine the accuracy of certain performance measures derived over exponential approximations of non-Markovian systems, with the purpose of showing that the relative errors associated with the performance measures can be quite large, even in situations where simple exponential approximations are traditionally assumed to be quite accurate (e.g., quantitative properties that deal with average case behaviour). The structure of our paper is as follows. In Sect. 2, we describe the syntax and semantics of a new Markovian process calculus, called PHASE, for modelling non-Markovian systems through the use of phase-type distributions. The formalism is parsimonious in terms of syntax and semantics, includes action-based synchronisation, and can be faithfully translated into the stochastic language of the probabilistic model checker PRISM [12]. In Sect. 3 we present a case study involving a hypothetical non-Markovian system (i.e., a collaborative text review scenario) and investigate how well a simple exponential approximation fares against a more elaborate phase-type approximation, expressed as a PHASE model. We are concerned mainly with the cases where the predictions of the two models diverge to a considerable degree, and with the pattern of errors for the simple exponential approximation. We end the paper with conclusions and references.

2   PHASE

In order to allow a better integration of phase-type distributions within stochastic process calculi, we propose a very simple process calculus, inspired by PEPA [10],

PEPA$_{ph}^{\infty}$ [7] and IMC [9], which employs phase-type distributions [14] for transition durations. Our formalism does not put forward any theoretical innovation, given that its syntax is derived from that of PEPA$_{ph}^{\infty}$, while its semantics largely agrees with that of IMC (under the additional assumption that all actions are urgent, and that action non-determinism is solved by uniform schedulers). Instead, the novelty of PHASE lies in the fact that it can be easily implemented in PRISM, which is one of the most advanced stochastic model checkers currently available, supporting the derivation/verification of several types of performance measures (including reward properties). A comprehensive account of how to translate PHASE models into PRISM specifications is given in [4]. For ease of modelling, we restrict our calculus to phase-type representations whose probability of starting in state 1 is equal to 1 (i.e., there is a single initial state), which can therefore be fully specified in terms of their infinitesimal generator matrix. We denote by $PH(A)$ the phase-type distribution whose generator is A. The distribution $PH(A)$ describes the time until absorption for a CTMC of size $ord(A)$ (i.e., the order of A), which we denote by $CTMC(A)$, where state $ord(A)$ is absorbing, and all the other states are transient. The element $A(i,j)$, for $1 \leq i,j \leq ord(A)$ and $i \neq j$, represents the rate of a transition from state i to state j. Furthermore, the element $A(i,i)$, for $1 \leq i \leq ord(A)$, is the negative sum of the rates of all the transitions originating in state i.

Our calculus includes only three operators, namely the *sequential operator*, the *choice operator*, and the *parallel operator*. The full syntax of PHASE can be given as follows, where P_{seq} is a sequential process, P_{par} is a parallel process, α is an action, $(\alpha, PH(A))$ is a phase-type transition, $\{L\}$ is a set of actions, and $n \geq 2$ is a natural number:

$$P_{seq} ::= (\alpha, PH(A)).P_{seq} \mid (\alpha_1, PH(A_1)).P_{seq}^1 + \ldots + (\alpha_n, PH(A_n)).P_{seq}^n$$
$$P_{par} ::= P_{seq} \mid P_{par}^1 \underset{\{L\}}{\bowtie} P_{par}^2$$

The sequential expression $(\alpha, PH(A)).P_{seq}$ indicates that the process performs the action α, after a delay distributed according to $PH(A)$, and then behaves like P_{seq}. The choice expression $(\alpha_1, PH(A_1)).P_{seq}^1 + \ldots + (\alpha_n, PH(A_n)).P_{seq}^n$ indicates a race for execution between the transitions $(\alpha_i, PH(A_i))$, with $1 \leq i \leq n$, such that the first transition to complete (i.e., the transition with the shortest duration) is selected and performed, while all the other transitions are halted and discarded. In other words, the choice operator denotes a competition between processes, via their current transitions, in which the fastest process wins. The parallel expression $P_{par}^1 \underset{\{L\}}{\bowtie} P_{par}^2$ indicates that the processes P_{par}^1 and P_{par}^2 must synchronize whenever performing an action from the *cooperation set* $\{L\}$. This means that, for any action $\alpha \in \{L\}$, if P_{par}^1 finishes a transition $(\alpha, PH(A_1))$, then P_{par}^1 is afterwards blocked and cannot make any further transitions until P_{par}^2 completes a corresponding transition $(\alpha, PH(A_2))$, and vice-versa. The interpretation of this operator is that it forces processes to cooperate on certain transitions (whose actions are included in $\{L\}$), by waiting for each other to complete, therefore generating a shared transition. However, the transitions whose actions are not in $\{L\}$ can proceed unaffected by cooperation.

In addition, no associativity rules are defined for the parallel composition of more than two processes: the order in which the processes are composed must be made explicit through the use of parentheses.

In order to define the formal operational semantics of PHASE, we first separate transition durations from the occurrence of actions, and then we express phase-type distributions in terms of their associated CTMC. More specifically, we make the distinction between *Markovian transitions* and *action transitions*: Markovian transitions, denoted by $\langle r \rangle$ (or $\overset{r}{\Rightarrow}$), indicate a temporal delay drawn from an exponential distribution with a rate of r, while action transitions, denoted by α (or $\overset{\alpha}{\rightarrow}$), indicate the (immediate) occurrence of action α. Next, we translate any sequential expression $(\alpha, PH(A)).P_{seq}^{fin}$ into the following equivalent form, where $o = ord(A)$ and $\oplus$ denotes an internal choice between Markovian transitions (as in classical process calculi, such as PEPA):

$$Int_1 = \langle A(1,1) \rangle.Int_1 \oplus \langle A(1,2) \rangle.Int_2 \oplus \ldots \oplus \langle A(1,o) \rangle.Int_o$$

$$\vdots$$

$$Int_{o-1} = \langle A(o-1,1) \rangle.Int_1 \oplus \langle A(o-1,2) \rangle.Int_2 \oplus \ldots \oplus \langle A(o-1,o) \rangle.Int_o$$
$$Int_o = \alpha.P_{seq}^{fin}$$

As a result, $P_{seq}^{init} = (\alpha, PH(A)).P_{seq}^{fin}$ becomes $P_{seq}^{init} = Int_1$, while $P_{seq} = (\alpha_1, PH(A_1)).P_{seq}^1 + \ldots + (\alpha_n, PH(A_n)).P_{seq}^n$ becomes $P_{seq} = Int_1^1 + \cdots + Int_1^n$. The states $Int_1, \ldots, Int_o$ correspond to the states of $CTMC(A)$, while the values $A(i,j)$, with $1 \le i, j \le o$, correspond to the rates of the transitions from $CTMC(A)$, as described at the beginning of this section. The operational semantics of PHASE, which makes use of both Markovian and action transitions, is given in Table 1, where the transitions above the line form the necessary conditions for the transitions bellow the line to take place. Since the operators $\oplus$, $+$ and $\underset{\{L\}}{\bowtie}$ are commutative, rules $CH1$ through $PAR5$ remain valid when replacing $P1$ with $P2$, and vice-versa.

Rules $SEQ1$ and $SEQ2$ make explicit the (immediate) occurrence of actions, in the case of action transitions, and the passage of time, for Markovian transitions. Rule $CH1$ describes the usual race between the Markovian transitions that produce the phase-type distributions in PHASE. Rule $CH2$ is similar to $CH1$, except that now the race takes place not within a phase-type distribution, but between two (or more) such distributions, as required by the choice operator in PHASE. Next, rule $CH3$ specifies the race policy through which the action associated with the fastest phase-type transition is selected for execution, while the rest of the phase-type transitions (and their corresponding actions) are discarded. The remaining rules refer to the parallel composition of PHASE processes. Firstly, rule $PAR1$ treats the case in which two processes are engaged in Markovian transitions, which means that they do not interact with each other. Secondly, rule $PAR2$ deals with the parallel composition of an action transition and a Markovian transition: given that the action in question does not belong to the cooperation set $\{L\}$, its associated action transition gains precedence over the Markovian transition, due to the immediacy of actions. In contrast, whenever the action is included in $\{L\}$, as in rule $PAR3$, the process that contains

Table 1. PHASE Operational Semantics.

$$(SEQ1) \quad \frac{}{\alpha.P \xrightarrow{\alpha} P} \qquad (SEQ2) \quad \frac{}{\langle r \rangle.P \xRightarrow{r} P} \qquad (CH1) \quad \frac{P_1 \xRightarrow{r_1} Q_1}{P_1 \oplus P_2 \xRightarrow{r_1} Q_1}$$

$$(CH2) \quad \frac{P_1 \xRightarrow{r_1} Q_1 \quad P_2 \xRightarrow{r_2} Q_2}{P_1 + P_2 \xRightarrow{r_1} Q_1 + P_2} \qquad (CH3) \quad \frac{P_1 \xrightarrow{\alpha_1} Q_1 \quad P_2 \xRightarrow{r_2} Q_2}{P_1 + P_2 \xrightarrow{\alpha_1} Q_1}$$

$$(PAR1) \quad \frac{P_1 \xRightarrow{r_1} Q_1 \quad P_2 \xRightarrow{r_2} Q_2}{P_1 \underset{\{L\}}{\bowtie} P_2 \xRightarrow{r_1} Q_1 \underset{\{L\}}{\bowtie} P_2}$$

$$(PAR2) \quad \frac{P_1 \xrightarrow{\alpha_1} Q_1 \quad P_2 \xRightarrow{r_2} Q_2}{P_1 \underset{\{L\}}{\bowtie} P_2 \xrightarrow{\alpha_1} Q_1 \underset{\{L\}}{\bowtie} P_2} \quad (\alpha_1 \notin \{L\})$$

$$(PAR3) \quad \frac{P_1 \xrightarrow{\alpha_1} Q_1 \quad P_2 \xRightarrow{r_2} Q_2}{P_1 \underset{\{L\}}{\bowtie} P_2 \xRightarrow{r_2} P_1 \underset{\{L\}}{\bowtie} Q_2} \quad (\alpha_1 \in \{L\})$$

$$(PAR4) \quad \frac{P_1 \xrightarrow{\alpha_1} Q_1 \quad P_2 \xrightarrow{\alpha_2} Q_2}{P_1 \underset{\{L\}}{\bowtie} P_2 \xrightarrow{\alpha_1} Q_1 \underset{\{L\}}{\bowtie} P_2} \quad (\alpha_1 \notin \{L\})$$

$$(PAR5) \quad \frac{P_1 \xrightarrow{\alpha} Q_1 \quad P_2 \xrightarrow{\alpha} Q_2}{P_1 \underset{\{L\}}{\bowtie} P_2 \xrightarrow{\alpha} Q_1 \underset{\{L\}}{\bowtie} Q_2} \quad (\alpha \in \{L\})$$

the action transition needs to wait for the other process to enable a matching action transition. Finally, rules $PAR4$ and $PAR5$ handle the synchronization between action transitions: those transitions which are not part of the cooperation set proceed independently, while matching transitions with actions in $\{L\}$ are performed simultaneously.

Given that the semantics of PHASE employs both Markovian and action transitions, it is possible to have instances of action non-determinism during the evolution of certain PHASE processes. Somewhat surprisingly, this form of non-determinism is caused by the parallel operator, and not by the choice operator. As an example of action non-determinism, let us consider the following processes:

$$P_1 = (\alpha, PH(A_1)).P_1 \qquad P_2 = (\alpha, PH(A_2)).P_2 \qquad P_3 = (\alpha, PH(A_3)).P_3$$

$$P = (P_1 \underset{\emptyset}{\bowtie} P_2) \underset{\{\alpha\}}{\bowtie} P_3$$

Within P, if the duration of transitions $tr_1 = (\alpha, PH(A_1))$ and $tr_2 = (\alpha, PH(A_2))$ is shorter than that of transition $tr_3 = (\alpha, PH(A_3))$, then tr_3 can synchronize with either tr_1 or tr_2, since both transitions are available for cooperation once the delay associated with tr_3 has elapsed. In order to be able to derive performance measures over PHASE processes such as P, we need to resolve all instances of action non-determinism. Our option in this matter is to assume that the competing alternatives are all equally likely to be chosen (i.e., the winning shared action transition is drawn from a uniform distribution defined over all the competitors)[1]. In the case of P, this results in tr_1 and tr_2 each having a probability of 0.5 to be selected for synchronization.

When reasoning about the behaviour of PHASE processes, it is natural to ignore any intermediate states and transitions, given that their utility is solely technical. Therefore, when we refer to the states and transitions of a sequential PHASE process P, we have in mind only transitions of the form $(\alpha, PH(A))$ and the states that these transitions connect, with respect to P.

3   Case Study

As an illustration of the advantages afforded by using PHASE and PRISM in the modelling of non-Markovian systems, as well as of the errors that can arise when ignoring the non-Markovian nature of transition durations, we focus on a hypothetical instance of collaborative text review. The corresponding system consists of two human manuscript editors, namely Editor 1 (ED1) and Editor 2 (ED2), who must cooperate in processing a set of documents, with the aid of an editing Device (DEV). The structure of the system is shown in Fig. 1.

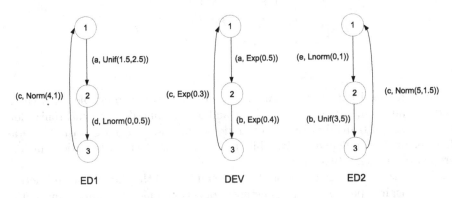

Fig. 1. A collaborative manuscript editing system with non-Markovian dynamics.

Editor 1 first makes adjustments to the graphical elements of the manuscript (i.e., state 1), then works on an unrelated task (i.e., state 2), and, finally, takes part in copyediting the manuscript (i.e., state 3). Meanwhile, Editor 2 begins by dealing with an unrelated assignment (i.e., state 1), then applies certain modifications to the text of the manuscript (i.e., state 2), after which he/she contributes to the copyediting of the manuscript (i.e., state 3). Last, the behaviour of the editing Device can be divided into an initial, an intermediate and a final processing phase (i.e., states 1, 2 and 3, respectively). Moreover, the Editors rely on the Device in order to do their work, meaning that: the first editing

---

[1] If necessary, there are plenty of other solutions for dealing with non-determinism, which employ priority levels and weights, or more advanced schedulers [2].

phase is completed (i.e., action a is performed) only after the Device has finished its initial processing and Editor 1 has made the graphical adjustments; the second editing phase is done (i.e., action b is performed) as soon as the Device has finished its intermediate processing and Editor 2 has made the textual adjustments; finally, the third editing phase is concluded (i.e., action c is performed) once the Device has ended its final processing, and both Editor 1 and 2 have successfully copyedited the resulting manuscript. Also, once an editing session is finished, the Editors immediately start working on a new manuscript (i.e., the system operates in a cyclical manner).

The interactions between the Editors and the Device are implemented through synchronization over shared actions: Editor 1 and the Device have actions a and c in common, while Editor 2 and the Device must perform actions b and c together. The delays for each transition are given by the following distributions: $Unif(LB, UB)$ is a uniform distribution with a lower bound of LB and an upper bound of UB; $Lnorm(M, SD)$ is a log-normal distribution with a mean of M and a standard deviation of SD, on the log scale; $Norm(M, SD)$ is a normal distribution with a mean of M and a standard deviation of SD; $Exp(R)$ is an exponential distribution with a rate of R.

Based on the dynamics of the previously described system, we wish to show the benefits of employing moderately large phase-type approximations for transition durations, in the form of PHASE processes, instead of simply ignoring the non-Markovian nature of the system and modelling each transition as if it were Markovian (i.e., exponentially distributed). To this end, we compare the behaviour of three different formal models for the system depicted in Fig. 1. The first model is expressed in the non-Markovian process calculus MODEST [8]. It is meant to provide an exact representation of the system's evolution, but it relies on discrete event simulation for the derivation of performance measures. In contrast, the second and the third model are expressed in PRISM: the second model implements a PHASE approximation, while the third model is a regular PRISM specification in which non-Markovian transitions are replaced with single Markovian transitions, matched in terms of average duration. Unlike in the case of the first model, performance measures for the last two models can be obtained through the direct application of Markov theory. However, the accuracy of the analysis will differ between the elaborate approximation (involving PHASE and PRISM) and the simple one (involving just PRISM). An extended description of all the models and performance measures is provided in [4].

Since we wish to obtain accurate approximations, in our PHASE model we employ moderately large phase-type representations, having either 1, 10, 15, or 20 phases, corresponding to the exponential, log-normal, normal and uniform distributions, respectively. In order to generate the phase-type distributions, we opt for the tool EMpht [1], since it allows us to impose the requirement that there must be a single initial state for each representation, and also, its pre-specified input distributions already include all the distributions that appear in our example, which means that the input to the fitting algorithm can be provided in an effortless manner. We can now proceed to examine the quality of the

PHASE and simple PRISM approximations. Thus, we compute our performance measures of interest by using stochastic model checking, for the two PRISM models, and discrete event simulation, for the MODEST model. More specifically, we consider four types of quantitative properties supported by PRISM: bounded path properties, unbounded path properties, steady-state properties, and reward properties.

Bounded path properties quantify the probability that a certain behaviour occurs within a particular time interval. In the case of our editing example, we can use such properties in order to estimate the shapes of the temporal distributions associated with a set of events. For instance, we can analyse the duration of the three editing activities of Editor 1, as well as that of a complete editing session. The results of this analysis are displayed in Fig. 2.

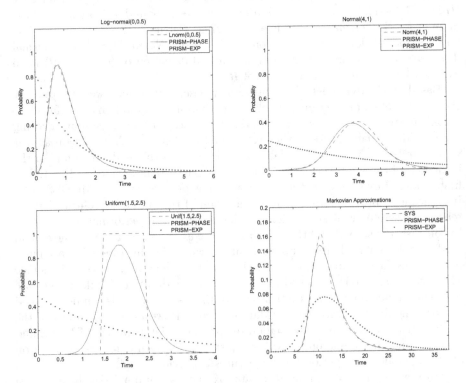

Fig. 2. Transition and editing session durations. PRISM-PHASE = distributions for the PHASE model; PRISM-EXP = distributions for the simple PRISM model.

The figure makes it clear that, although the phase-type representations chosen for the PHASE model are relatively small, they match the initial normal and log-normal distributions quite closely. The only large discrepancy between the PHASE and the MODEST model occurs for the uniform distribution, but this is a direct consequence of the fact that it is difficult for phase-type representations to produce abrupt local variations in probability (e.g., [16]), such as those that take place at the lower and upper bound of uniform distributions. On the other hand, the exponential approximations bear very little resemblance to the any of the non-Markovian distributions, as expected. This is also true with respect to the duration of a full editing session: the PHASE and the MODEST model produce almost identical distributions, whereas the simple PRISM model reproduces only the broad shape of the correct distribution (e.g., its mode), while considerably overestimating the positive skew of the distribution in question.

Next, unbounded path properties are very similar to their bounded counterparts, except for the fact that no temporal constraints are imposed on the behaviour under investigation. For our editing system, we might be curious with respect to the probability that the operation of the editing Device leads to lags in the editing process. These lags appear whenever the Editors have completed they assigned tasks, but the Device has not yet finished incorporating their input within the manuscript. The probabilities for the occurrence of lags, in relation to the action that is delayed by each lag (i.e., actions a, b, and c), are given in the left half of Fig. 3.

Model	$P(a$ lag$)$	$P(b$ lag$)$	$P(c$ lag$)$	$S(a$ lag$)$	$S(b$ lag$)$	$S(c$ lag$)$
MODEST	.376	.386	.234	.060	.087	.062
PHASE	.377	.403	.239	.060	.093	.063
EXP	.500	.520	.315	.068	.133	.071

Fig. 3. Analysis of lag duration and probability of occurrence.

Like in the case of bounded path properties, the PHASE and the MODEST model yield roughly the same results, with the PHASE measures falling within a 10 % range of the MODEST measures. However, the results for the simple PRISM model are markedly inaccurate, missing the actual values by a relative error of 25–35 %. Taken together, the previous two findings suggest that even for very unsophisticated non-Markovian systems such as ours, the use of phase-type distributions, instead of exponential distributions, can significantly increase the accuracy of certain performance measures. In addition, large improvements can be seen even for very basic quantitative properties, such as those measuring the frequency of lags. If we want to have a better look at the extent to which the intricacy of the performance measure influences the size of the error, it is sufficient to calculate the probability that the Editors encounter no lag (of any kind) during a complete editing session: the MODEST and the PHASE models output probabilities of 34.1 % and 32.6 %, while the simple PRISM model predicts a probability of just 16 %. In other words, the relative error is larger than 100 %!

We now move on to steady-state properties, which reflect the percentage of time dedicated to a certain behaviour. For our example, we might wish to learn the relative temporal extent of each type of lag and, more generally, the relative amount of time that the Editors and the Device spend in each of their possible states. The values for the corresponding performance measures are shown in the right half of Fig. 3 and in Fig. 4, respectively.

Model	S(ED1=X)			S(DEV=X)			S(ED2=X)		
	1	2	3	1	2	3	1	2	3
MODEST	.218	.090	.692	.218	.316	.465	.131	.404	.465
PHASE	.219	.090	.691	.219	.312	.469	.120	.411	.469
EXP	.204	.077	.719	.204	.313	.483	.112	.405	.483

Fig. 4. Analysis of state residence times in the long run.

Given that steady-state properties rely heavily on the mean duration of transitions, which are nearly identical for all three of our models, it is not surprising to discover that the models typically agree with respect to the values of said measures. Nevertheless, a few non-negligible relative errors for the exponential approximation can still be detected, namely for the lags, and less pronounced, for state 2 of Editor 1 and state 1 of Editor 2 (i.e., the states where the Editors are not occupied with solving the main task). An interesting point to be made here is that each particular type of lag gives rise to a different pattern of error: a lag - large error for path measure, moderate error for steady-state measure; b lag - large errors for both path and steady-state measures; c lag - small errors for both path and steady-state measures.

Finally, reward properties associate numerical values (rewards) to the states and transitions that make up a certain behaviour, and then compute the expected value of the rewards associated with that behaviour. In our editing example, we can use rewards to determine the average duration of a complete editing session. Once again, the PHASE and the MODEST model are in tight agreement (i.e., 12.597 vs 12.629, respectively), while the exponential approximation produces a value (i.e., 14.712) which is more than 15 % larger than that indicated by the MODEST model.

4   Conclusion

In this paper we employ the novel process calculus PHASE designed specifically for operating with phase-type distributions [3], and the probabilistic model checkers PRISM and MODEST, in order to compare two popular approaches for representing the dynamics of non-Markovian systems: the first approach involves approximating non-exponential (non-Markovian) distributions with moderately elaborate phase-type distributions, in an attempt to capture non-Markovian behaviour as closely as possible; the second approach replaces non-exponential distributions with exponential ones, effectively ignoring the non-Markovian nature of the system. Our intention is to prove that, although the second approach has undeniable merit (e.g., a simple Markovian model is very easy to understand, implement, and analyze), the accuracy of various performance measures is significantly better for the first approach. Thus, we turn our attention to a hypothetical manuscript review system, in which two human manuscript editors interact with an editing device, with the purpose of formatting and copyediting a set of manuscripts. For this system, which features non-exponential transition durations that lead to non-Markovian dynamics, we build and compare three different models: an exact MODEST model, which uses discrete event simulation, a PHASE model, which relies on phase-type distributions, and a simple PRISM model, which relies on exponential distributions. Taking the MODEST model as a reference for the actual behaviour of the system, we examine the accuracy of the PHASE and of the simple PRISM model, in terms of how closely they match the predictions of the MODEST model. More specifically, we compute a set of quantitative measures, in the form of path properties, steady-state properties, and reward properties. These measures are related to both specific and general aspects of the system's evolution, such as the probability of having lags due to the editing devices, or the average duration of an editing session.

Our findings show that the PHASE model approximates the non-Markovian behaviour of the MODEST model in a satisfactory manner, based on a relative error of less than 5–10 % for each of the performance measures being tested. On the other hand, the performance measures generated by the simple PRISM model are often imprecise, which translates into relative error rates as high as 15–30 % (or even greater). The most severe errors occur for path properties, which are known to be quite sensitive to the shapes of the temporal distributions. Nevertheless, in our analysis we also encountered a few sizeable errors for steady-state and reward properties, which should be interpreted as an invitation to caution: even though some properties depend mainly on the means of the temporal distributions, this does not automatically give a modeller the possibility of ignoring other characteristics of the distributions in question (e.g., their skewness), under the assumption that those other characteristics play a negligible role. Furthermore, our results seem to reveal that, given a particular behaviour of interest, the quantitative relation between errors for path properties, on the one hand, and errors for both steady-state and reward properties, on the other hand, is in no way obvious or trivial to predict. Therefore, when employing a simple Markovian approximation, the accuracy of path properties does not immediately guarantee comparable levels of accuracy for steady-state properties, and vice-versa.

All in all, we acknowledge the limited scope of our case study: our PHASE model does not include all the available PHASE operators (e.g., the choice operator), its non-Markovian distributions are of only three types (i.e., uniform, lognormal, and normal), its states and transitions are relatively few in number, and the performance measures being derived are not particularly involved. Therefore, it seems like a natural next step to try to learn how model complexity (expressed in terms of operator diversity, range of temporal distributions, and model size) and property complexity (resulting from the length of the time interval over which the property is computed, as well as from the type and number of operators and variables that are part of the property) interact in determining the accuracy of performance measures, for both phase-type and exponential approximations of non-Markovian systems.

References

1. Asmussen, S., Nerman, O., Olsson, M.: Fitting phase-type distributions via the EM algorithm. Scand. J. Stat. **23**(4), 419–441 (1996)
2. Bernardo, M., Gorrieri, R.: Extended Markovian process algebra. In: Montanari, U., Sassone, V. (eds.) CONCUR 1996. LNCS, vol. 1119, pp. 315–330. Springer, Heidelberg (1996)
3. Ciobanu, G., Rotaru, A.S.: PHASE: a stochastic formalism for phase-type distributions. In: Merz, S., Pang, J. (eds.) ICFEM 2014. LNCS, vol. 8829, pp. 91–106. Springer, Heidelberg (2014)
4. Ciobanu, G., Rotaru, A.: Phase-type approximations for non-Markovian systems. Technical report FML-14-01, Formal Methods Laboratory, Iasi, Romania (2014)
5. Crovella, M.E.: Performance evaluation with heavy tailed distributions. In: Feitelson, D.G., Rudolph, L. (eds.) JSSPP 2001. LNCS, vol. 2221, pp. 1–10. Springer, Heidelberg (2001)
6. Doherty, G., Massink, M., Faconti, G.: Reasoning about interactive systems with stochastic models. In: Johnson, C. (ed.) DSV-IS 2001. LNCS, vol. 2220, pp. 144–163. Springer, Heidelberg (2001)
7. El-Rayes, A., Kwiatkowska, M., Norman, G.: Solving infinite stochastic process algebra models through matrix-geometric methods. In: Hillston, J., Silva, M. (eds.) Proceedings of PAPM 1999, pp. 41–62. Prensas Universitarias de Zaragoza, Zaragoza (1999)
8. Hahn, E.M., Hartmanns, A., Hermanns, H., Katoen, J.-P.: A compositional modelling and analysis framework for stochastic hybrid systems. Form. Methods Syst. Des. **43**, 191–232 (2013)
9. Hermanns, H. (ed.): Interactive Markov Chains. LNCS, vol. 2428. Springer, Heidelberg (2002)
10. Hillston, J.: A Compositional Approach to Performance Modelling. Cambridge University Press, Cambridge (1996)
11. Katoen, J.-P., D'Argenio, P.R.: General distributions in process algebra. In: Brinksma, E., Hermanns, H., Katoen, J.-P. (eds.) FMPA 2000. LNCS, vol. 2090, pp. 375–429. Springer, Heidelberg (2001)
12. Kwiatkowska, M., Norman, G., Parker, D.: PRISM 4.0: verification of probabilistic real-time systems. In: Gopalakrishnan, G., Qadeer, S. (eds.) CAV 2011. LNCS, vol. 6806, pp. 585–591. Springer, Heidelberg (2011)
13. Nelson, R.: Probability, Stochastic Processes, and Queueing Theory. Springer, New York (1995)
14. Neuts, M.F.: Matrix-Geometric Solutions in Stochastic Models: An Algorithmic Approach. Dover Publications, New York (1981)
15. Norris, J.R.: Markov Chains. Cambridge University Press, Cambridge (1998)
16. O'Cinneide, C.A.: Phase-type distributions: open problems and a few properties. Stoch. Models **15**(4), 731–757 (1999)

Quantitative Anonymity Evaluation of Voting Protocols

Fabrizio Biondi$^{(\boxtimes)}$ and Axel Legay

INRIA Rennes, Rennes, France
{fabrizio.biondi,axel.legay}@inria.fr

Abstract. In an election, it is imperative that the vote of the single voters remain anonymous and undisclosed. Alas, modern anonymity approaches acknowledge that there is an unavoidable leak of anonymity just by publishing data related to the secret, like the election's result. Information theory is applied to quantify this leak and ascertain that it remains below an acceptable threshold.

We apply modern quantitative anonymity analysis techniques via the state-of-the-art QUAIL tool to the voting scenario. We consider different voting typologies and establish which are more effective in protecting the voter's privacy. We further demonstrate the effectiveness of the protocols in protecting the privacy of the single voters, deriving an important desirable property of protocols depending on composite secrets.

1 Introduction

Voting is the backbone of the democratic process [15]. To be effective, a voting system must allow the voters to freely express their opinion and elect the public officials that will represent them in the government. An effective voting system guarantees that each vote is counted exactly once, that no malicious agent can tamper with the results of the vote, and that no vote can be traced back to the voter who cast it.

Various traditional and electronic voting systems have been proposed to assure such guarantees. The use of cryptography and certification authorities can guarantee that only eligible voters can vote and that their vote is counted exactly once, and the production of fake credentials can safeguard voters against being coerced to reveal their vote [12]. The anonymity of the vote is harder to guarantee; current proposals include assumptions on the absolute anonymity of the voting channels [12,14] or expect enterprises and universities to provide public proxy servers to hide the IP address of the voter [10]. The problem with these approaches to anonymity is that the anonymity of a vote is considered a qualitative, yes/no property, verifying whether it is possible for an attacker to infer any amount of information about the identity of the voters; this is known as the *possibilistic* approach. The *probabilistic* approach instead considers anonymity as a quantity that can be decreased by the attack of an external agent and by other factor in the voting process including the magnitude of the electoral seat, the electoral formula used, the results of the elections and the number

C. Canal and A. Idani (Eds.): SEFM 2014 Workshops, LNCS 8938, pp. 335–349, 2015.
DOI: 10.1007/978-3-319-15201-1_22

of candidates. Since none of these factors completely compromise anonymity, a qualitative technique has to either ignore them or consider any voting protocol unsafe.

Current approaches to anonymity consider a secret, like the identity of the caster of a vote, as a quantitative amount of information, and use information theory to quantify how much of this secret information is inferred by a malicious attacker [8,9]. This amount is called *information leakage*. The qualitative approach tags as insecure even a negligible amount of loss of information, in practice considering any real system insecure except under very strong assumptions. On the other hand, the quantitative approach allows the analyzer to determine a bound above which a loss of anonymity is considered noteworthy. Quantitative anonymity analysis has been applied among others to study the trade-off between anonymity and utility of operations on databases [2] and to define information-theoretical bounds to differential privacy [4]. To the best of our knowledge, these techniques have not been applied to voting protocols.

Completely automated tools have been created to quantify information leakage for any secret-dependent protocol. Previously we have introduced a theoretical framework to model protocols with Markov chains and efficiently and precisely compute their leakage [5]. We implemented the approach in the QUAIL tool, the first tool able to perform an arbitrary-precision leakage analysis of a non-deterministic secret-dependent protocol [7].

In this work we will use QUAIL to analyze different typologies of electoral formulae. QUAIL considers the combined votes of the voters as a precise amount of secret bits and quantifies precisely how many of these bits are inferred by an attacker able to read the published results of the elections, i.e. the information leakage. Since these results are public, there is no way to avoid this loss of anonymity. Consequently any qualitative method that claims to perfectly guarantee anonymity of the voters is ignoring this non-negative information leakage. By quantifying exactly this amount we establish a lower bound on the amount of anonymity that any implementation or formula can guarantee.

We study two very general typologies of electoral formulae: Single Preference formulae, where each voter expresses a preference for a candidate, and Preference Ranking formulae, where each voter ranks all candidates from the best to the worst. Our results are valid for any electoral formula in the typologies. This classification is traversal to the common division in proportional and majoritarian systems, as it depends only on the way the vote is expressed.

We consider that the secret is not a single entity, but a composite of the secret votes. If we have 10 secrets and each is 2 bits and the leakage of the system is 2 bits, we need to identify whether the leaked information corresponds to the secret of one of the voters or only to general information about the result of the vote. The theoretical bases for the study of leakage of composite secrets are very recent [3], and to the best of our knowledge no large scale study of practical cases has been published.

Our analysis shows the exact impact of the magnitude of the electoral seat and the number of candidates on the anonymity of the vote. The results suggest the data from seats of low magnitude, like hospital seats, should be aggregated before publication to protect the voters' anonymity. Also we show that the leakage on a single voter's secret is strictly less than the leakage on all secrets divided by the number of voters, proving that the voting protocols analyzed are effective in protecting the single voters' secrets. This is a generally desirable property for protocols on composite secrets.

The rest of the paper is organized as follows: Sect. 2 introduces common concepts in probability and information theory and Sect. 3 details the leakage theory and how it is implemented in the QUAIL analyzer. Section 4 presents the two typologies of electoral formulae we analyze and in Sect. 5 we discuss the results obtained. Section 6 explains which problems we are facing in obtaining more results and what steps we are taking to solve them.

2   Background

We define common concepts in probability theory and information theory that are used through the paper. We refer to books on the subject [13] for the basic definitions on probability theory. We call X a *discrete random variable* and $\mathcal{X}$ a *discrete stochastic process*, i.e. an indexed infinite sequence of discrete random variables $(X_0.X_1, X_2, ...)$ ranging over the same sample space S. The index of the random variables in a stochastic process can be understood as modeling a concept of discrete time, so X_k is the random variable representing the system at time unit k.

2.1   Markov Chains

A discrete stochastic process is a *Markov chain* $\mathcal{C} = (C_0, C_1, C_2, ...)$ iff $\forall k \in \mathbb{N}$. $P(C_k|C_{k-1}, ..., C_0) = P(C_k|C_{k-1})$. A Markov chain on a sample space S can also be defined as follows:

Definition 1. *A tuple $\mathcal{C} = (S, s_0, P)$ is a Markov Chain (MC), if S is a finite set of states, $s_0 \in S$ is the initial state and P is an $|S| \times |S|$ probability transition matrix, so $\forall s, t \in S.\ P_{s,t} \geq 0$ and $\forall s \in S.\ \sum_{t \in S} P_{s,t} = 1$.*

We call $\pi^{(k)}$ the probability distribution vector over S at time k and $\pi_s^{(k)}$ the probability $\pi^k(s)$ of visiting the state s at time k. This means that, considering a Markov chain $\mathcal{C}$ as a time-indexed discrete stochastic process $(C_0, C_1, ...)$, we write $\pi^{(k)}$ for the probability distribution over the random variable C_k. Since we assume that the chain starts in state s_0, then $\pi_s^{(0)}$ is 1 if $s = s_0$ and 0 otherwise. Note that $\pi^{(k)} = \pi_0 P^k$, where P^k is matrix P elevated to power k, and P^0 is the identity matrix of size $|S| \times |S|$.

A state $s \in S$ is *absorbing* if $P_{s,s} = 1$. In the figures we will not draw the looping transition of the absorbing states, to reduce clutter. We say that a Markov chain is *one-step* if all states except the starting state s_0 are absorbing. We will usually refer to one-step Markov chains as $\mathbb{C}$.

Let $\xi(s,t)$ denote the *expected residence time* in a state t in an execution starting from state s given by $\xi(s,t) = \sum_{n=0}^{\infty} P_{s,t}^n$. We will write ξ_s for $\xi(s_0, s)$.

We will enrich our Markov chains with a finite set V of natural-valued variables, and for simplicity we assume that there is a very large finite bit-size M such that a variable is at most M bit long. We define an assignment function $A : S \to [0, 2^M - 1]^{|V|}$ assigning to each state the values of the variables in that state. We will use the expression $v(s)$ to denote the value of the variable $v \in V$ in the state $s \in S$.

Given a Markov chain $\mathcal{C} = (S, s_0, P)$ let a *discrimination relation* $\mathcal{R}$ be an equivalence relation over S. We use discrimination relation to quotient one-step Markov chains:

Definition 2. *Given a one-step Markov chain $\mathbb{C} = (S, s_0, P)$ and a discrimination relation $\mathcal{R}$ over S, we define the quotient $\mathbb{C}/\mathcal{R}$ of $\mathbb{C}$ over $\mathcal{R}$ as the one-step Markov chain $\mathbb{C}/\mathcal{R} = (\bar{S}, \bar{s}_0, \bar{P})$ where*

- *$\bar{S}$ is the set of equivalence classes of S induced by $\mathcal{R}$;*
- *$\bar{s}_0$ is the equivalence class of s_0;*
- *for each equivalence class $\bar{s} \in S'$, $\bar{P}_{\bar{s}_0, \bar{s}} = \sum_{s \in \bar{s}} P_{s_0, s}$ and $\bar{P}_{\bar{s}, \bar{s}} = 1$.*

2.2 Information Theory

The *entropy* of a probability distribution is a measure of the unpredictability of the events considered in the distribution [17].

Definition 3. *[13] Let X and Y be two random variables with probability mass functions $p(x)$ and $p(y)$ respectively and joint pmf $p(x,y)$. Then we define the following non-negative real-valued functions:*

- *Entropy $H(X) = -\sum_{x \in X} p(x) \log_2 p(x)$*
- *Joint entropy $H(X,Y) = -\sum_{x \in X} \sum_{y \in Y} p(x,y) \log_2 p(x,y)$*
- *Conditional entropy $H(X|Y) = -\sum_{x \in X} \sum_{y \in Y} p(x,y) \log_2 p(x|y)$*
  $= \sum_{y \in Y} p(y) H(X|Y = y) = \sum_{y \in Y} p(y) \sum_{x \in X} p(x|y) \log_2 p(x|y)$
  $= H(X,Y) - H(Y)$ (chain rule)
- *Mutual information $I(X;Y) = \sum_{x \in X} \sum_{y \in Y} p(x,y) \log_2 \left(\frac{p(x,y)}{p(x)p(y)} \right)$*
  $= H(X) + H(Y) - H(X,Y) \leq \min(H(X), H(Y))$

Since every state s in a MC $\mathcal{C}$ has a discrete probability distribution over the successor states we can calculate the entropy of this distribution. We will call it *local entropy*, $L(s)$, of s: $L(s) = -\sum_{t \in S} P_{s,t} \log_2 P_{s,t}$. Note that $L(s) \leq \log_2(|S|)$.

As a MC $\mathcal{C}$ can be seen as a discrete probability distribution over all of its possible traces, we can assign a single entropy value $H(\mathcal{C})$ to it. The global entropy $H(\mathcal{C})$ of $\mathcal{C}$ can be computed by considering the local entropy $L(s)$ as the expected reward of a state s and then computing the expected total reward of the chain [6]: $H(\mathcal{C}) = \sum_{s \in S} L(s) \xi_s$ If a Markov chain is one-step its entropy corresponds to the local entropy of the initial state s_0.

3 Information Leakage of Markov Chains

3.1 Theoretical Background

We use information theory to compute the amount of bits of a secret variable h that can be inferred by an attacker able to observe the value of an observable variable o after the termination of a protocol. We call this amount *Shannon leakage* or just *leakage*, and it corresponds to the mutual information between the distribution on the secret and the distribution on the observable variable. This analysis assumes the worst possible attacker: the attacker has access to the source code of the protocol and to unlimited computational power.

We will model system-attacker scenarios with Markov chains in which to each state we associate a unique assignment of values to all variables [5]. Then we define leakage as follows:

Definition 4. *Let C be a Markov chain enriched with variable from the set V. Let h represent the secret variables and 0 the variables whose value is observable to the attacker. Then we define the* Shannon leakage *of C as the mutual information $I(0;h)$ between the secret and observable variables.*

Note that to compute leakage we need to have a prior probability distribution over the secret, modeling what the attacker knows before observing the observable output of the protocol. We will assume for simplicity that the attacker knows the possible values of the secret, since he can read the source code and verify which kind of variable holds it, but has no additional information about it.

The modeling of a system-attacker scenario as a Markov chain starts by dividing the system's variables in private and public variables. Private variables, including the secret variable h, are the ones whose value is not defined at compilation time. In each state of the Markov chain a set of allowed values is assigned to each private variable. Public variables, including the observable variable o and the program counter pc, are variable whose value is known to the analyst. On each state a given value is assigned to each public variable.

Given the source code of the system and a prior distribution over the private variables, we have enough information to build the Markov chain semantics C of the protocol, since for each state we can determine its successor states and the corresponding transition probabilities.

We show a simple example, and refer to [5] for the complete semantics. Let secret variable h be a secret bit, observable variable o an observable bit and public variable r a random bit being assigned the value 0 with probability 0.75 and 1 otherwise. We assign to o the result of the exclusive OR between h and r and terminate. We want to quantify the amount of information about h that can be inferred by knowing the value of o. The Markov chain semantics C for the example is shown in Fig. 1a. Each state is enriched with information about the allowed values of private variables and the values of public variables, e.g. in state S_1 secret variable h can be either 0 or 1 and public variable r is 0.

Subsequently we need to model the fact that the attacker has to wait for the protocol to terminate to read the observable output. Equivalently, we can

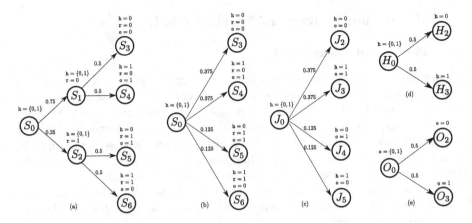

Fig. 1. Bit XOR example: a) Markov chain semantics $\mathcal{C}$. b) Observable reduction $\mathbb{C}$. c) Joint quotient $\mathbb{C}_{|(o,h)}$. d) Secret's quotient $\mathbb{C}_{|h}$. e) Observer's quotient $\mathbb{C}_{|o}$.

say that the attacker is not aware of the internal behavior of the system; this is modeled by hiding in the Markov chain model the internal states, i.e. all states except the initial state and the absorbing states. We call the resulting Markov chain the *observable reduction* $\mathbb{C}$. The observable reduction for the example is shown in Fig. 1b.

Note that the observable reduction is a one-step Markov chain, so we can compute quotients on it following Definition 2. To compute the leakage we need to compute three quotients from the observable reduction:

Joint quotient. The joint quotient process $\mathbb{C}_{|(o,h)}$ models the joint behavior of the secret and observable variables. It is shown in Fig. 1c.

Secret's quotient. The secret's quotient process $\mathbb{C}_{|h}$ models the behavior of the secret variable. It is shown in Fig. 1d.

Observer's quotient. The observer's quotient process $\mathbb{C}_{|o}$ models the behavior of the observable variable. It is shown in Fig. 1e.

Finally we compute leakage as the mutual information $I(0; h)$, as between the secret and observable variable, as explained in Definition 4. To compute it we apply the formula $I(X; Y) = H(X) + H(Y) - H(X, Y)$ from Definition 3, obtaining

$$I(o; h) = I(\mathbb{C}_{|o}; \mathbb{C}_{|h}) = H(\mathbb{C}_{|o}) + H(\mathbb{C}_{|h}) - H(\mathbb{C}_{|(o,h)})$$

meaning that the leakage can be computed as the sum of the entropies of the secret and observable quotient minus the entropy of the joint quotient. In our example we have $(\mathbb{C}_{|o}) = 1$, $H(\mathbb{C}_{|h}) = 1$ and $H(\mathbb{C}_{|(o,h)}) = 1.8112...$, so we conclude that the program leaks $1 + 1 - 1.8112... \approx 0.1887$ bits, or 18.87% of the secret.

3.2   QUAIL Implementation

The QUAIL tool quantifies the Shannon leakage of a probabilistic process in a fully automated way. The user just provides the source code for the process in the QUAIL imperative language, specifying the size of the variables and whether each variable is public, private, secret or observable. QUAIL computes the expected amount of information about the secret variables that an attacker is able to infer by knowing the values of the observable variables after the protocol has terminated and produced output, implementing the theory presented in Sect. 3.1.

The QUAIL language is a WHILE language enriched with for loops, multidimensional arrays and constant declarations. For simplicity all variables are integer variables; the bit length of each variable is defined by the coder at declaration time. Also, assignment to private or secret variables is not allowed, and all variables have to be declared at the beginning of the program. We refer to [1] for the source code and full semantics of QUAIL.

QUAIL is able to handle secret and private variables with a large number of possible values. Alas, the representation of arbitrary probability distributions on such variables on a real machine is untreatable: a probability distribution over a 64-bit variable is composed of $2^{64} \approx 1/8 \cdot 10^{19}$ rational numbers. For this reason QUAIL does not allow the user to define arbitrary prior distributions over the secret, and always assumes that the prior distribution is uniform.

```
1 secret int1 h;
2 observable int1 o;
3 public int1 r;
4 random r := randombit
     (0.75);
5 assign o := h ^ r;
6 return;
```

Fig. 2. Bit XOR example: source code.

The QUAIL source code for the bit XOR example presented in Sect. 3.1 is shown in Fig. 2. In lines 1 to 3 the variables are declared, then in line 4 variable r is assigned value 0 with probability 0.75 and 1 otherwise, and in line 5 variable o is assigned with the exclusive OR of variables h and r.

We save the source code in Fig. 2 in a file bitxor.quail and invoke QUAIL with the command ./quail bitxor.quail -v 0 -p 5 where -v 0 suppresses all output except for the leakage result and -p 5 specifies that we want 5 significant digits in the answer. QUAIL outputs 0.18872 showing that the program leaks ≈ 0.18872 bits of the secret, in accordance to what we computed theoretically in Sect. 3.1.

4   Modeling Voting Protocols

In an election, each voter is called to express his preference for the competing candidates. The *voting system* defines the way the voters express their preference: either on paper in a traditional election, or electronically in e-voting. The voting system also comprehends the additional procedures enforced to guarantee that the voters can vote freely, that they can verify that their vote has been counted and that their vote remains confidential.

After the votes have been cast, the *results* of the vote are published, usually in an aggregated form to protect the anonymity of the voters. Finally, the winning candidate or candidates is chosen according to a given *electoral formula*.

In this section we present two different typologies of voting, representing two different ways in which the voters can express their preference: in the *Single Preference* protocol the voters declare their preference for exactly one of the candidates, while in the *Preference Ranking* protocol each voter ranks the candidate from his most favorite to his least favorite. Since each protocol we model is concerned only about how the votes are expressed and counted and what results are published, each protocol models a number of electoral formulae. For the same reason, the models are valid both for uninominal and multinominal elections.

4.1   Single Preference

The Single Preference protocol typology models all electoral formulae in which each of the N voters expresses one vote for one of the C candidates, including plurality and majority voting systems and single non-transferable vote [15]. The votes for each candidate are summed up and only the results are published, thus hiding information about which voter voted for which candidate. The candidate or candidates to be elected are decided according to the electoral formula used.

Secret and observable encoding. The secrets and observables are modeled by the following lines of QUAIL code:

```
secret array [N] of int32 vote:=[0,C-1];
observable array [C] of int32 result;
```

The secret is an array of integers with a value for each of the N voters. Each value is a number from 0 to $C-1$, representing a vote for one of the C candidates. The observable is an array of integers with the votes obtained by each of the C candidates. The full model for this protocol is shown in the Appendix due to space constraints.

Formal leakage computation. The protocol is simple, and its information leakage can be computed formally, as shown by the following lemma:

Lemma 1. *The information leakage for the Single Preference protocol with n voters and c candidates corresponds to*

$$\log_2 c^n - \frac{1}{c^n} \sum_{k_1+k_2+\dots+k_c=n} \binom{n}{k_1+k_2+\dots+k_c} \left(\log_2 \binom{n}{k_1+k_2+\dots+k_c} \right)$$

The proof for Lemma 1 is in the Appendix. While the lemma characterizes the solution computed by QUAIL for this case, it is very hard to find such a characterization for any process, so in general QUAIL is the best way to obtain a result. We run QUAIL with the command `./quail single_preference.quail -v 0 -p 5` with the same parameters we used in Sect. 3.2 and obtain 1.8112 showing that the leakage of the Single Preference protocol for 3 voters and 2 candidates is ≈ 1.8112 bits.

4.2   Preference Ranking

The Preference Ranking protocol typology models all electoral formulae in which each of the n voters expresses an order of preference of the c candidates, including the alternative vote and single transferable vote systems [15]. In the Preferential Voting protocol the voter does not express a single vote, but rather a ranking of the candidates; thus if the candidates are A, B, C and D the voter could express the fact that he prefers B, then D, then C and finally A. Then each candidate gets c points for each time he appears as first choice, $c-1$ points for each time he appears as second choice, and so on. The points of each candidate are summed up and the results are published.

Secret and observable encoding. The secrets and observables are modeled by the following lines of QUAIL code:

```
secret array [N] of int32 vote:=[0,C!-1];
observable array [C] of int32 result;
```

The secret is an array of integers with a value for each of the N voters. Each value is a number from 0 to C!-1, representing one of the possible C! rankings of the C candidates. The observable is an array of integers with the points obtained by each of the C candidates. The full model for this protocol is shown in the Appendix due to space constraints.

5   Experimental Results

We discuss some of the initial results we have obtained by analyzing the Single Preference and Preference Ranking voting protocols.

Leakage comparison. Table 1 shows the leakage amounts for the Single Preference and Preference Ranking protocols for different numbers of voters and candidates. We note that the results for 2 candidates are identical, since in this case in both protocols the voters can vote in only 2 different ways. The table shows that the leakage for the Preference Ranking protocol is in general lower than the leakage for the Single Preference protocol. Nonetheless we are comparing protocols with a different secret size, so it is more appropriate to compare posterior entropies.

Table 1. Voting protocols: leakage tables for Single Preference (on the left) and Preference Ranking (on the right)

Single	Voters		
Cands	**2**	**3**	**4**
2	1.50	1.81	2.03
3	/	3.12	3.57
4	/	/	4.81

Ranking	Voters		
Cands	**2**	**3**	**4**
2	1.50	1.81	2.03
3	/	2.54	2.96
4	/	/	timeout

Table 2. Voting protocols: posterior entropy tables for Single Preference (on the left) and Preference Ranking (on the right)

Single	Voters			Ranking	Voters		
Cands	**2**	**3**	**4**	**Cands**	**2**	**3**	**4**
2	0.50	1.19	1.97	2	0.5	1.19	1.97
3	/	1.63	2.76	3	/	5.21	7.37
4	/	/	3.19	4	/	/	timeout

Posterior entropy comparison. In Table 2 we show the posterior entropies for the same cases as Table 1. The result confirm that the protocols are identical in case there are 2 candidates, and Preference Ranking is more efficient in protecting the anonymity of the votes than Single Preference.

Table 3. Single Preference voting protocol: entropies and leakage on varying the number of voters, candidates and target voters.

3V-2C	H_O	H_h	$H_{O,h}$	$I_{O,h}$	$I_{O,h}\%$	pH_h
1	1.81	1.00	2.50	0.31	31.1%	0.69
2	1.81	2.00	3.00	0.81	40.5%	1.19
3	1.81	3.00	3.00	1.81	60.3%	1.19

3V-3C	H_O	H_h	$H_{O,h}$	$I_{O,h}$	$I_{O,h}\%$	pH_h
1	3.12	1.58	4.08	0.62	39.1%	0.96
2	3.12	3.16	4.75	1.53	48.5%	1.63
3	3.12	4.75	4.75	3.12	65.6%	1.63

4V-2C	H_O	H_h	$H_{O,h}$	$I_{O,h}$	$I_{O,h}\%$	pH_h
1	2.03	1.00	2.81	0.21	21.0%	0.79
2	2.03	2.00	3.50	0.53	26.5%	1.47
3	2.03	3.00	4.00	1.03	34.0%	1.97
4	2.03	4.00	4.00	2.03	50.0%	1.97

4V-3C	H_O	H_h	$H_{O,h}$	$I_{O,h}$	$I_{O,h}\%$	pH_h
1	3.57	1.58	4.70	0.45	28.7%	1.13
2	3.57	3.16	5.67	1.07	34.0%	2.09
3	3.57	4.75	6.33	1.99	41.9%	2.76
4	3.57	6.33	6.33	3.57	56.3%	2.76

5V-2C	H_O	H_h	$H_{O,h}$	$I_{O,h}$	$I_{O,h}\%$	pH_h
1	2.19	1.00	3.03	0.16	16.7%	0.84
2	2.19	2.00	3.81	0.38	19.3%	1.62
3	2.19	3.00	4.50	0.69	23.2%	2.31
4	2.19	4.00	5.00	1.19	30.0%	2.81
5	2.19	5.00	5.00	2.19	44.0%	2.81

5V-3C	H_O	H_h	$H_{O,h}$	$I_{O,h}$	$I_{O,h}\%$	pH_h
1	3.93	1.58	5.16	0.35	22.3%	1.23
2	3.93	3.16	6.29	0.80	25.5%	2.36
3	3.93	4.75	7.25	1.43	30.1%	3.32
4	3.93	6.33	7.92	2.34	37.0%	3.99
5	3.93	7.92	7.92	3.93	49.6%	3.99

Analysis of Single Preference with variable number of targets. In Table 3 we give detailed results of the analysis of the Single Preference voting protocol, on varying the number of voters, candidates and target voters. The code in bold on the top left corner of a table shows how many voters and candidates are being considered in the experiment, e.g. **4V-2C** means 4 voters and 2 candidates. The column of the left represents the number of target voters for the experiment, i.e. how many votes is the attacker trying to infer. The table reports the following values:

H_O is the entropy of the observer's quotient
H_h is the (prior) entropy of the secret's quotient
$H_{O,h}$ is the entropy of the joint quotient
$I_{O,h} = H_O + H_h - H_{O,h}$ is the information leakage
$I_{O,h}\,\% = I_{O,h}/H_h$ is the percentage of the secret that has been leaked
$pH_h = H_h - I_{O,h}$ is the (expected) posterior entropy of the secret, i.e. the amount
　　of secret that has not been leaked

Discussion. Since the posterior entropy measures how hard it would be for an attacker to learn the secret after observing the results of the voting, we focus on it as the measure of how confidential the votes are after the attack. Note that posterior entropy increases less than linearly with the number of targets, so if we want to learn both the votes of voters Alice and Bob it is more convenient to consider the two votes as a single composite secret than to try to learn the two votes separately. Note also that the posterior entropy when all voters are targets is the same as the posterior entropy when all voters except one are. This is because if all votes except one are known, the last one can be inferred immediately by checking the election's results.

It should also be noted that the percentage of information leaked $I_{O,h}\,\%$ increases with the number of targets, again sublinearly. We argue that this is a desirable property in a protocol designed to protect a secret composed of several subsecrets with the same importance. The property ensures that it is not more convenient for the attacker to try to infer separately every single secret instead of the whole composed secret, so even if it takes less time to infer the secret of 1 target out of 3, the time it would take to infer all 3 secrets one by one is larger than the time required to infer them all at the same time, as we explained in the paragraph above. This guarantees that the posterior entropies for multiple targets are in fact sound. This property also forces the attacker to decide beforehand exactly how many votes he needs to discover to minimize the time needed for the attack.

6   Challenges

6.1   Problem Size

The examples we analyzed consider only a small number of voters and candidates. The algorithm for the precise computation of information leakage is exponential in the size of the secret and the size of the secret grows with the number of voters and candidates, thus QUAIL and any other tool are too slow to analyze large cases. Analyzing the Preference Ranking protocol also requires more time than analyzing the Single Preference protocol, since the former protocol is more complex than the latter and has a larger secret size.

To solve this problem we are implementing a statistical analyzer in QUAIL able to simulate the execution of the protocols a large number of times and to approximate the information leakage value by analyzing the collected data. The statistical analyzer is able to solve larger problems than the standard QUAIL algorithm, since it does not have to analyze the whole space of possible program executions.

6.2   G-Leakage

Information leakage quantifies the loss of information on the whole secret. We have analyzed the behavior of leakage when we consider only some of the votes to be the secret we are interested in, showing how the protocol is efficient in hiding the secret of the single voters.

Recently an extension of information leakage, called *g-leakage* [3], has been proposed exactly to deal with cases in which different subsets of the secret bits have different values for the attacker, as is the case with composite secrets. g-leakage is very general, since it allows for any gain function to be used in top of leakage computation; for this reason it has not yet been implemented in any leakage analysis tool.

We are working to extend QUAIL with g-leakage computation capabilities, allowing us to encode more naturally problems with composite secrets like voting protocols. We expect that the results on the efficiency of the protocols in protecting the single votes will be coherent with the results presented in this paper.

6.3   Implementation Analysis

The protocols we analyze model the abstract behavior of voting systems, giving us theoretical lower bounds on the amount of information leaked by publishing the results of the elections. It would be interesting to compare these theoretical results with actual implementations of voting systems, to evaluate how effective the real systems are in guaranteeing anonymity. Off-the-shelf systems are obviously not written in QUAIL language, so a tool capable of analyzing C or Java code like the ones developed by Phan and Malacaria [16] or by Chothia et al. [11] would have to be used.

A   Appendix

Proof (of Lemma 1). Call h the composite secret about the votes of all voters and O the observable output of the system. Remember that information leakage corresponds to the difference between the prior entropy on the secret $H(h)$ and the posterior entropy on the secret after observing the observable output of the system $H(h|O) = \sum_{o \in O} P(o) H(h|O = o)$.

The secret h has c^n possible values, thus can be encoded in $\log_2 c^n$ bits, thus the prior entropy $H(h)$ corresponds to $\log_2 c^n$.

```
1  // N is the number of voters
2  const N:=3;
3  // C is the number of candidates
4  const C:=2;
5  // the result is the number of votes of
      each candidate
6  observable array [C] of int32 result;
7  // The secret is the preference of each
      voter, from 0 to Cl−1
8  secret array [N] of int32 vote:=[0,C
      l−1];
9  // these bits represent the votes
      received by the voting machine
10 public array [N] of int32 decl;
11 public array [C] of int32 temparray;
12 public int32 pos;
13 // this is just a counter
14 public int32 voter:=0;
15 public int32 candidate:=0;
16 public int32 k:=0;
17 public int32 y:=0;
18 // voting
19 while (voter<N) do
20   while (candidate<C) do
21     if (vote[voter]==candidate) then
22       assign decl[voter]:=candidate;
23     fi
24     assign candidate:=candidate+1;
25   od
26   assign candidate:=0;
27   assign voter:=voter+1;
28 od
29 // transform the secret of each voter
      into the order of the preferences
30 assign voter:=0;
31 while (voter<N) do
32   // build the initial array
33   assign candidate:=0;
34   while (candidate<C) do
35     assign temparray[candidate]:=
        candidate;
36     assign candidate:=candidate+1;
37   od
38   assign k:=C;
39   // find a position
40   while (k>0) do
41     assign pos := decl[voter]%k;
42     assign candidate:=C−k;
43     // update the vote of the candidate
44     assign result[candidate]:=result[
        candidate]+temparray[pos];
45     // remove the element from the
          array
46     assign y:=pos;
47     while (y<C−1) do
48       assign temparray[y]:=temparray[y
          +1];
49       assign y:=y+1;
50     od
51     // update the vote of the voter
52     assign decl[voter]:=decl[voter]/k;
53     // decrease the counter
54     assign k:=k−1;
55   od
56   assign voter:=voter+1;
57 od
58 return;
```

```
1  // N is the number of
      voters
2  const N:=3;
3  // C is the number of
      candidates
4  const C:=2;
5  // the result is the
      number of votes of
      each candidate
6  observable array [C] of
      int32 result;
7  // The secret is the
      preference of each
      voter
8  secret array [N] of int32
      vote:=[0,C−1];
9  // this is just a counter
10 public int32 i:=0;
11 public int32 j:=0;
12 // voting
13 while (i<N) do
14   while (j<C) do
15     if (vote[i]==j) then
16       assign result[j]:=
          result[j]+1;
17     fi
18     assign j:=j+1;
19   od
20   assign j:=0;
21   assign i:=i+1;
22 od
23 return;
```

Fig. 3. Model for the Single Preference protocol (on the left) and for the Preference Ranking protocol (on the right).

For the posterior entropy $H(h|O)$, consider that the possible votes on the candidates form a multinomial distribution, thus the probability $P(o)$ of a given outcome $o \in O$ is $1/c^n$ and the conditional posterior entropy $H(h|O = o)$ where k_i is the amount of votes to candidate $1 \leq i \leq c$ is $\binom{n}{k_1 + k_2 + \ldots + k_c}$. We conclude that

$$I(O, h) = H(h) - \sum_{o \in O} P(o)H(h|O = o)$$

$$= \log_2 c^n - \frac{1}{c^n} \sum_{k_1 + k_2 + \ldots + k_c = n} \binom{n}{k_1 + k_2 + \ldots + k_c} \left(\log_2 \binom{n}{k_1 + k_2 + \ldots + k_c} \right)$$

Voting Protocol Models

Single Preference. The model for the Single Preference protocol is shown on Fig. 3 on the left. Constant N represents the number of voters and constant C the number of candidates. The observable variable `result` is an array with the total votes expressed for each candidate, and the secret variable `vote` is the array with the preference of each voter. The rest of the code just sums up the votes for each candidate.

Preference Ranking. The model for the Preference Ranking model is shown on Fig. 3 on the right. Constant N represents the number of voters and constant C the number of candidates. The observable variable `result` is an array with the total points obtained by each candidate, and the secret variable `vote` is an array with the preference ranking of each voter. For each voter the secret has $c!$ possible different votes, corresponding to the possible complete orderings of the c candidates. The secret vote of each voter is encoded as a number from 0 to $c! - 1$, and then transformed in a preferential order with the algorithm in lines 30–57. The points for each candidate are counted by summing the points given by the preference ranking of each voter.

References

1. QUAIL. https://project.inria.fr/quail/

2. Alvim, M.S., Andrés, M.E., Chatzikokolakis, K., Degano, P., Palamidessi, C.: Differential privacy: on the trade-off between utility and information leakage. In: Barthe, G., Datta, A., Etalle, S. (eds.) FAST 2011. LNCS, vol. 7140, pp. 39–54. Springer, Heidelberg (2012)

3. Alvim, M.S., Chatzikokolakis, K., Palamidessi, C., Smith, G.: Measuring information leakage using generalized gain functions. In: Chong, S. (ed.) CSF, pp. 265–279 (2012)

4. Barthe, G., Köpf, B.: Information-theoretic bounds for differentially private mechanisms. In: CSF, pp. 191–204. IEEE Computer Society (2011)

5. Biondi, F., Legay, A., Malacaria, P., Wąsowski, A.: Quantifying information leakage of randomized protocols. In: Giacobazzi, R., Berdine, J., Mastroeni, I. (eds.) VMCAI 2013. LNCS, vol. 7737, pp. 68–87. Springer, Heidelberg (2013)

6. Biondi, F., Legay, A., Nielsen, B.F., Wąsowski, A.: Maximizing entropy over Markov processes. In: Dediu, A.-H., Martín-Vide, C., Truthe, B. (eds.) LATA 2013. LNCS, vol. 7810, pp. 128–140. Springer, Heidelberg (2013)

7. Biondi, F., Legay, A., Traonouez, L.-M., Wasowski, A.: QUAIL: A quantitative security analyzer for imperative code. In: Sharygina and Veith [18]

8. Chatzikokolakis, K., Palamidessi, C., Panangaden, P.: Anonymity protocols as noisy channels. Inf. Comput. **206**(2–4), 378–401 (2008)

9. Chen, H., Malacaria, P.: Quantifying maximal loss of anonymity in protocols. In: Li, W., Susilo, W., Tupakula, U.K., Safavi-Naini, R., Varadharajan, V. (eds.) ASIACCS, pp. 206–217. ACM (2009)

10. Chen, Y.-Y., ke Jan, J., Chen, C.-L.: The design of a secure anonymous internet voting system. Comput. Secur. **23**(4), 330–337 (2004)

11. Chothia, T., Kawamoto, Y., Novakovic, C.: A tool for estimating information leakage. In: Sharygina and Veith [18], pp. 690–695

12. Clarkson, M.R., Chong, S., Myers, A.C.: Civitas: toward a secure voting system. In: IEEE Symposium on Security and Privacy, pp. 354–368. IEEE Computer Society (2008)

13. Cover, T.M., Thomas, J.A.: Elements of Information Theory, 2nd edn. Wiley, New Jersey (2006)

14. Gritzali, D.: Principles and requirements for a secure e-voting system. Comput. Secur. **21**(6), 539–556 (2002)

15. Norris, P.: Electoral Engineering: Voting Rules and Political Behavior. Cambridge Studies in Comparative Politics. Cambridge University Press, Cambridge (2004)

16. Phan, Q.-S., Malacaria, P.: Abstract model counting: a novel approach for quantification of information leaks. In: Proceedings of the 9th ACM symposium on Information, computer and communications security, pp. 283–292. ACM (2014)

17. Shannon, C.E.: A mathematical theory of communication. Bell Syst. Tech. J. **27**, 379–423 (1948)

18. Sharygina, Natasha, Veith, Helmut (eds.): CAV 2013. LNCS, vol. 8044. Springer, Heidelberg (2013)

Scalable Verification of Markov Decision Processes

Axel Legay, Sean Sedwards[(✉)], and Louis-Marie Traonouez

Inria Rennes – Bretagne Atlantique, Rennes, France
sean.sedwards@inria.fr

Abstract. Markov decision processes (MDP) are useful to model concurrent process optimisation problems, but verifying them with numerical methods is often intractable. Existing approximative approaches do not scale well and are limited to memoryless schedulers. Here we present the basis of scalable verification for MDPSs, using an $\mathcal{O}(1)$ memory representation of history-dependent schedulers. We thus facilitate scalable learning techniques and the use of massively parallel verification.

1 Introduction

Markov decision processes (MDP) describe systems that interleave nondeterministic *actions* and probabilistic transitions, possibly withrewards or costs assigned to the actions [3,19]. This model has proved useful in many real optimisation problems and may also be used to represent concurrent probabilistic programs (see, e.g., [2,4]). Such models comprise probabilistic subsystems whose transitions depend on the states of the other subsystems, while the order in which concurrently enabled transitions execute is nondeterministic. This order may radically affect the expected reward or the probability that a system will satisfy a given property. It is therefore useful to calculate the upper and lower bounds of these quantities.

Figure 1 shows a typical fragment of an MDP. Referring in parentheses to the labels in the figure, the execution semantics are as follows. In a given state (s_0), an action $(a_1, a_2, \dots)$ is chosen nondeterministically to select a distribution of probabilistic transitions $(p_1, p_2, \dots$ or p_3, p_4, etc.). A probabilistic choice is then made to select the next state $(s_1, s_2, s_3, s_4, \dots)$. To each of the actions may be associated a reward $(r_1, r_2, \dots)$, allowing values to be assigned to sequences of actions.

To calculate the expected total reward or the expected probability of a sequence of states, it is necessary to define how the nondeterminism in the MDP will be resolved. In the literature this is often called a *strategy*, a *policy* or an *adversary*. Here we use the term *scheduler* and focus on MDPs in the context of *model checking* concurrent probabilistic systems. Model checking is an automatic technique to verify that a system satisfies a property specified in temporal logic [7]. *Probabilistic* model checking quantifies the probability that a probabilistic system will satisfy a property [9]. Classic analysis of MDPs is concerned with

© Springer International Publishing Switzerland 2015
C. Canal and A. Idani (Eds.): SEFM 2014 Workshops, LNCS 8938, pp. 350–362, 2015.
DOI: 10.1007/978-3-319-15201-1_23

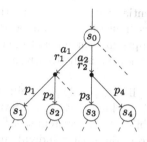

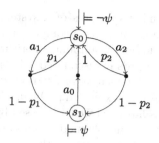

Fig. 1. Fragment of a typical Markov decision process.

Fig. 2. MDP with different optima for general and memoryless schedulers when $p_1 \neq p_2$.

finding schedulers that maximise or minimise rewards [3,19]. The classic verification algorithms for MDPs are concerned with finding schedulers that maximise or minimise the probability of a property, or deciding the existence of a scheduler that ensures the probability of a property is within some bound [4]. Our techniques can be easily extended to include rewards, but in this work we focus on probabilities and leave rewards for future consideration.

1.1 Schedulers and State Explosion

The classic algorithms to solve MDPs are *policy iteration* and *value iteration* [19]. Model checking algorithms for MDPs may use value iteration applied to probabilities [2, Chapter 10] or solve the same problem using linear programming [4]. All consider *history-dependent* schedulers. Given an MDP with set of actions A, having a set of states S that induces a set of sequences of states $\Omega = S^+$, a history-dependent (general) scheduler is a function $\mathfrak{S} : \Omega \to A$. A memoryless scheduler is a function $\mathfrak{M} : S \to A$. Intuitively, at each state in the course of an execution, a history-dependent scheduler ($\mathfrak{S}$) chooses an action based on the sequence of previous states, while a memoryless scheduler ($\mathfrak{M}$) chooses an action based only on the current state. History-dependent schedulers therefore include memoryless schedulers.

Figure 2 illustrates a simple MDP for which memoryless and history-dependent schedulers give different optima for logical property $\mathbf{X}(\psi \wedge \mathbf{X}\mathbf{G}^t \neg\psi)$ when $p_1 \neq p_2$ and $t > 0$. The property makes use of the temporal operators *next* ($\mathbf{X}$) and *globally* ($\mathbf{G}$). Intuitively, the property states that on the next step ψ will be true and, on the step after that, $\neg\psi$ will be remain true for $t + 1$ time steps. The property is satisfied by the sequence of states $s_0 s_1 s_0 s_0 \cdots$. If $p_1 > p_2$, the maximum probability for $s_0 s_1$ is achieved with action a_2, while the maximum probability for $s_0 s_0$ is achieved with action a_1. Given that both transitions start in the same state, a memoryless scheduler will not achieve the maximum probability achievable with a history-dependent scheduler.

The principal challenge of finding optimal schedulers is what has been described as the 'curse of dimensionality' [3] and the 'state explosion problem' [7]:

the number of states of a system increases exponentially with respect to the number of interacting components and state variables. This phenomenon has led to the design of sampling algorithms that find 'near optimal' schedulers to maximise rewards in discounted MDPs. Probably the best known is the Kearns algorithm [13], which we briefly review in Sect. 2.

The state explosion problem of model checking applied to purely probabilistic systems has been well addressed by *statistical* model checking (SMC) [21]. SMC uses an executable model to approximate the probability that a system satisfies a specified property by the proportion of simulation traces that individually satisfy it. SMC algorithms work by constructing an automaton to accept only traces that satisfy the property. This automaton may then be used to estimate the probability of the property or to decide an hypothesis about the probability. Typically, the probability of property φ is estimated by $\frac{1}{N}\sum_{i=1}^{N}\mathbf{1}(\omega_i \models \varphi)$, where $\omega_1, \ldots, \omega_N$ are N independently generated simulation traces and $\mathbf{1}(\cdot)$ is an indicator function that corresponds to the output of the automaton: it returns 1 if the trace is accepted and 0 if it is not. N is chosen a priori to give the required statistical confidence (e.g., using a Chernoff bound [18], see Sect. 4.2). Sequential hypothesis tests (e.g., Wald's sequential probability ratio test [20], see Sect. 4.1) do not define N a priori, but generate simulation traces until an hypothesis can be accepted or rejected with specified confidence. The state space of the system is not constructed explicitly–states are generated on the fly during simulation–hence SMC is efficient for large, possibly infinite state, systems. Moreover, since the simulations are required to be statistically independent, SMC may be easily and efficiently divided on parallel computing architectures.

SMC cannot be applied to MDPs without first resolving the nondeterminism. Since nondeterministic and probabilistic choices are interleaved in an MDP, schedulers are typically of the same order of complexity as the system as a whole and may be infinite. As a result, existing SMC algorithms for MDPs consider only memoryless schedulers and have other limitations (see Sect. 2).

1.2   Our Approach

We have created memory-efficient techniques to facilitate Monte Carlo verification of nondeterministic systems, *without* storing schedulers explicitly. In essence, the possibly infinite behaviour of schedulers is fully specified *implicitly* by the seed of a pseudo-random number generator. Our techniques therefore require almost no additional memory over standard SMC. In doing this, we are the first to provide the basis for a complete lightweight statistical alternative to the standard numerical verification algorithms for MDPs. A further contribution is our derivation of the statistical confidence bounds necessary to test multiple schedulers. These results suggest obvious solutions to problems encountered with existing algorithms that rely on multiple statistical tests (e.g., [11]).

In this work we demonstrate the core ideas of our approach with simple SMC algorithms that repeatedly sample from scheduler space. Practical implementations require more sophisticated algorithms that adopt "smart sampling" (optimal use of simulation budget) and lightweight learning techniques. Some of our results make use of these ideas, but a full exposition is not possible here.

2 Related Work

The Kearns algorithm [13] is the classic 'sparse sampling algorithm' for large, infinite horizon, discounted MDPs. It constructs a 'near optimal' scheduler piecewise, by approximating the best action from a current state using a stochastic depth-first search. Importantly, optimality is with respect to rewards, not probability (as required by standard model checking tasks). The algorithm can work with large, potentially infinite state MDPs because it explores a probabilistically bounded search space. This, however, is exponential in the discount. To find the action with the greatest expected reward in the current state, the algorithm recursively estimates the rewards of successive states, up to some maximum depth defined by the discount and desired error. Actions are enumerated while probabilistic choices are explored by sampling, with the number of samples set as a parameter. The error is specified as a maximum difference between consecutive estimates, allowing the discount to guarantee that the algorithm will eventually terminate.

There have been several recent attempts to apply SMC to nondeterministc models [5,10,11,16]. In [5,10] the authors present on-the-fly algorithms to remove 'spurious' nondeterminism, so that standard SMC may be used. This approach is limited to the class of models whose nondeterminism does not affect the resulting probability of a property–scheduling makes no difference. The algorithms therefore do not attempt to address the standard MDP model checking problems related to finding optimal schedulers.

In [16] the authors first find a memoryless scheduler that is near optimal with respect to a reward scheme and discount, using an adaptation of the Kearns algorithm. This induces a Markov chain whose properties may be verified with standard SMC. By storing and re-using information about visited states, the algorithm improves on the performance of the Kearns algorithm, but is thus limited to memoryless schedulers that fit into memory. The near optimality of the induced Markov chain is with respect to rewards, not probability, hence [16] does not address the standard model checking problems of MDPs.

In [11] the authors present an SMC algorithm to decide whether there exists a memoryless scheduler for a given MDP, such that the probability of a property is above a given threshold. The algorithm has an inner loop that generates candidate schedulers by iteratively improving a probabilistic scheduler according to sample traces that satisfy the property. The algorithm is limited to memoryless schedulers because the improvement process counts state-action pairs. The outer loop tests the candidate scheduler against the hypothesis using SMC and is iterated until an example is found or sufficient attempts have been made. The inner loop does not in general converge to the true optimum, but the outer loop randomly explores local maxima. This makes the number of samples used by the inner loop critical: too many may significantly reduce the scope of the random exploration and thus reduce the probability of finding the global optimum. A further problem is that the repeated hypothesis tests of the outer loop will eventually produce erroneous results. We address this phenomenon in Sect. 4.

We conclude that (i) no previous approach is able to provide a complete set of SMC algorithms for MDPs, (ii) no previous SMC approach considers history-dependent schedulers and (iii) no previous approach facilitates lightweight sampling from scheduler space.

3   Schedulers as Seeds of Random Number Generators

Storing schedulers as explicit mappings does not scale, so we have devised a way to represent schedulers using uniform pseudo-random number generators (PRNG) that are initialised by a *seed* and iterated to generate the next pseudo-random value. In general, such PRNGs aim to ensure that arbitrary subsets of sequences of iterates are uniformly distributed and that consecutive iterates are statistically independent. PRNGs are commonly used to implement the uniform probabilistic scheduler, which chooses actions uniformly at random and thus explores all possible combinations of nondeterministic choices. Executing such an implementation twice with the same seed will produce identical traces. Executing the implementation with a different seed will produce an unrelated set of choices. Individual deterministic schedulers cannot be identified, so it is not possible to estimate the probability of a property under a specific scheduler.

An apparently plausible solution is to use independent PRNGs to resolve nondeterministic and probabilistic choices. It is then possible to generate multiple probabilistic simulation traces per scheduler by keeping the seed of the PRNG for nondetermistic choices fixed while choosing random seeds for a separate PRNG for probabilistic choices. Unfortunately, the schedulers generated by this approach do not span the full range of general or even memoryless schedulers. Since the sequence of iterates from the PRNG used for nondeterministic choices will be the same for all instantiations of the PRNG used for probabilistic choices, the ith iterate of the PRNG for nondeterministic choices will always be the same, regardless of the state arrived at by the previous probabilistic choices. The ith chosen action can be neither state nor trace dependent.

3.1   General Schedulers Using Hash Functions

Our solution is to construct a per-step PRNG seed that is a *hash* of the an integer identifying a specific scheduler concatenated with an integer representing the sequence of states up to the present.

We assume that a state of an MDP is an assignment of values to a vector of system variables $v_i, i \in \{1, \ldots, n\}$. Each v_i is represented by a number of bits b_i, typically corresponding to a primitive data type (*int*, *float*, *double*, etc.). The state can thus be represented by the concatenation of the bits of the system variables, such that a sequence of states may be represented by the concatenation of the bits of all the states. Without loss of generality, we interpret such a sequence of states as an integer of $\sum_{i=1}^{n} b_i$ bits, denoted $\bar{s}$, and refer to this in general as the *trace vector*. A scheduler is denoted by an integer σ, which is concatenated to $\bar{s}$ (denoted $\sigma : \bar{s}$) to uniquely identify a trace and a scheduler. Our approach is to generate a hash code $h = \mathcal{H}(\sigma : \bar{s})$ and to use h as the seed of a PRNG that resolves the next nondeterministic choice.

The hash function $\mathcal{H}$ thus maps $\sigma : \bar{s}$ to a seed that is deterministically dependent on the trace and the scheduler. The PRNG maps the seed to a value that is uniformly distributed but nevertheless deterministically dependent on the trace and the scheduler. In this way we approximate the scheduler functions $\mathfrak{S}$ and $\mathfrak{M}$ described in Sect. 1.1. Importantly, our technique only relies on the standard properties of hash functions and PRNGs. Algorithm 1 is the basic simulation function of our algorithms.

Algorithm 1. Simulate

Input:
  $\mathcal{M}$: an MDP with initial state s_0
  φ: a property
  σ: an integer identifying a scheduler
Output:
  ω: a simulation trace

Let $\mathcal{U}_{\text{prob}}, \mathcal{U}_{\text{nondet}}$ be uniform PRNGs with respective samples $r_{\text{pr}}, r_{\text{nd}}$
Let $\mathcal{H}$ be a hash function
Let s denote a state, initialised $s \leftarrow s_0$
Let ω denote a trace, initialised $\omega \leftarrow s$
Let $\bar{s}$ be the trace vector, initially empty
Set seed of $\mathcal{U}_{\text{prob}}$ randomly
while $\omega \models \varphi$ *is not decided* **do**
  $\qquad \bar{s} \leftarrow \bar{s} : s$
  $\qquad$ Set seed of $\mathcal{U}_{\text{nondet}}$ to $\mathcal{H}(\sigma : \bar{s})$
  $\qquad$ Iterate $\mathcal{U}_{\text{nondet}}$ to generate r_{nd} and use to resolve nondeterministic choice
  $\qquad$ Iterate $\mathcal{U}_{\text{prob}}$ to generate r_{pr} and use to resolve probabilistic choice
  $\qquad$ Set s to the next state
  $\qquad \omega \leftarrow \omega : s$

3.2 An Efficient Iterative Hash Function

To implement our approach, we have devised an efficient hash function that constructs seeds incrementally. The function is based on modular division [14, Chapter 6], such that $h = (\sigma : \bar{s}) \bmod m$, where m is a suitably large prime.

Since $\bar{s}$ is a concatenation of states, it is usually very much larger than the maximum size of integers supported as primitive data types. Hence, to generate h we use Horner's method [12, 14, Chapter 4]: we set $h_0 = \sigma$ and find $h \equiv h_n$ (n as given in Sect. 3.1) by iterating the recurrence relation

$$h_i = (h_{i-1} 2^{b_i} + v_i) \bmod m. \tag{1}$$

The size of m defines the maximum number of different hash codes. The precise value of m controls how the hash codes are distributed. To avoid collisions, a simple heuristic is that m should be a large prime not close to a power of 2 [8, Chapter 11]. Practically, it is an advantage to perform calculations using primitive data types that are native to the computational platform, so the sum in (1) should be less than or equal to the maximum permissible value. To achieve this, given $x, y, m \in \mathbb{N}$, we note the following congruences:

$$(x + y) \bmod m \equiv (x \bmod m + y \bmod m) \bmod m \tag{2}$$

$$(xy) \bmod m \equiv ((x \bmod m)(y \bmod m)) \bmod m \tag{3}$$

The addition in (1) can thus be re-written in the form of (2), such that each term has a maximum value of $m - 1$:

$$h_i = ((h_{i-1}2^{b_i}) \bmod m + (v_i) \bmod m) \bmod m \tag{4}$$

To prevent overflow, m must be no greater than half the maximum possible integer. Re-writing the first term of (4) in the form of (3), we see that before taking the modulus it will have a maximum value of $(m - 1)^2$, which will exceed the maximum possible integer. To avoid this, we take advantage of the fact that h_{i-1} is multiplied by a power of 2 and that m has been chosen to prevent overflow with addition. We thus apply the following recurrence relation:

$$(h_{i-1}2^j) \bmod m = (h_{i-1}2^{j-1}) \bmod m + (h_{i-1}2^{j-1}) \bmod m \tag{5}$$

Equation (5) allows our hash function to be implemented using efficient native arithmetic. Moreover, we infer from (1) that to find the hash code corresponding to the current state in a trace, we need only know the current state and the hash code from the previous step. When considering memoryless schedulers we need only know the current state.

4   Confidence with Multiple Estimates

The Chernoff bound [6,18] and Wald sequential probability ratio test [20] are commonly used to bound errors of SMC algorithms. Their guarantees are probabilistic, such that with specified non-zero probability they produce an incorrect result. If such bounds are used on M schedulers, some of whose true probabilities lie in the interval $(0, 1)$, then as $M \to \infty$ the probability of encountering an error is a.s. 1. In particular, the maximum and minimum estimates will tend to 1 and 0, respectively, regardless of the true values.

To overcome this phenomenon, in Sects. 4.1 and 4.2 we derive new confidence bounds to allow SMC algorithms to test multiple schedulers. We illustrate their use with simple algorithms that sample M schedulers at random, where M is a parameter. These algorithms are the basis of a technique we call "smart sampling", which can exponentially improve convergence. The basic idea is to assign part of the simulation budget to obtain a coarse estimate of the extremal probabilities and to use this information to generate a set of schedulers that contains a "good" scheduler with high probability. The remaining budget is used to refine the set to find the best scheduler. Smart sampling has provided improvements of several orders of magnitude with the illustrated examples and is the subject of ongoing development. Lack of space prevents further discussion.

4.1 Sequential Probability Ratio Test for Multiple Schedulers

The sequential probability ratio test (SPRT) of Wald [20] evaluates hypotheses of the form $P(\omega \models \varphi) \bowtie p$, where $\bowtie \in \{\leq, \geq\}$. The SPRT distinguishes between two hypotheses, $H_0 : P(\omega \models \varphi) \geq p^0$ and $H_1 : P(\omega \models \varphi) \leq p^1$, where $p^0 > p^1$. Hence, to evaluate $P(\omega \models \varphi) \bowtie p$, the SPRT requires a region of indecision (an 'indifference region' [21]) which may be specified by parameter ϑ, such that $p^0 = p + \vartheta$ and $p^1 = p - \vartheta$. The SPRT also requires parameters α and β, which specify the maximum acceptable probabilities of errors of the first and second kind, respectively. An error of the first kind is incorrectly rejecting a true H_0; an error of the second kind is incorrectly accepting a false H_0. To choose between H_0 and H_1, the SPRT defines the probability ratio

$$ratio = \prod_{i=1}^{n} \frac{(p^1)^{\mathbf{1}(\omega_i \models \varphi)}(1 - p^1)^{\mathbf{1}(\omega_i \not\models \varphi)}}{(p^0)^{\mathbf{1}(\omega_i \models \varphi)}(1 - p^0)^{\mathbf{1}(\omega_i \not\models \varphi)}},$$

where n is the number of simulation traces ω_i, $i \in \{1, \ldots, n\}$, generated so far. The test proceeds by performing a simulation and calculating $ratio$ until one of two conditions is satisfied: H_1 is accepted if $ratio \geq (1 - \beta)/\alpha$ and H_0 is accepted if $ratio \leq \beta/(1 - \alpha)$.

To decide whether there exists a scheduler such that $P(\omega \models \varphi) \bowtie p$, we would like to apply the SPRT to multiple (randomly chosen) schedulers. The idea is to test different schedulers, up to some specified number M, until an example is found. Since the probability of error with the SPRT applied to multiple hypotheses is cumulative, we consider the probability of no errors in any of M tests. Hence, in order to ensure overall error probabilities α and β, we adopt $\alpha_M = 1 - \sqrt[M]{1 - \alpha}$ and $\beta_M = 1 - \sqrt[M]{1 - \beta}$ in our stopping conditions. H_1 is accepted if $ratio \geq (1 - \beta_M)/\alpha_M$ and H_0 is accepted if $ratio \leq \beta_M/(1 - \alpha_M)$. Algorithm 2 demonstrates the sequential hypothesis test for multiple schedulers. If the algorithm finds an example, the hypothesis is true with at least the specified confidence.

4.2 Chernoff Bound for Multiple Schedulers

Given that a system has true probability p of satisfying a property, the Chernoff bound ensures $P(|\hat{p} - p| \geq \varepsilon) \leq \delta$, i.e., that the estimate $\hat{p}$ will be outside the interval $[p - \varepsilon, p + \varepsilon]$ with probability less than or equal to δ. Parameter δ is related to the number of simulations N by $\delta = 2e^{-2N\varepsilon^2}$ [18], giving

$$N = \lceil (\ln 2 - \ln \delta)/(2\varepsilon^2) \rceil. \tag{6}$$

Algorithm 2. Hypothesis testing with multiple schedulers

Input:
  $\mathcal{M}, \varphi$: the MDP and property of interest
  $H \in \{H_0, H_1\}$: the hypothesis of interest with threshold $p \pm \vartheta$
  α, β: the desired error probabilities of H
  M: the maximum number of schedulers to test
Output: The result of the hypothesis test

Let $p^0 = p + \vartheta$ and $p^1 = p - \vartheta$ be the bounds of H
Let $\alpha_M = 1 - \sqrt[M]{1-\alpha}$ and $\beta_M = 1 - \sqrt[M]{1-\beta}$
Let $A = (1 - \beta_M)/\alpha_M$ and $B = \beta_M/(1 - \alpha_M)$
Let $\mathcal{U}_{\text{seed}}$ be a uniform PRNG and σ be its sample
for $i \in \{1, \ldots, M\}$ *while* H *is not accepted* **do**
  Iterate $\mathcal{U}_{\text{seed}}$ to generate σ_i
  Let *ratio* = 1
  while *ratio* $< A \wedge$ *ratio* $> B$ **do**
    $\omega \leftarrow$ Simulate$(\mathcal{M}, \varphi, \sigma_i)$
    ratio $\leftarrow \frac{(p^1)^{\mathbf{1}(\omega \models \varphi)}(1-p^1)^{\mathbf{1}(\omega \not\models \varphi)}}{(p^0)^{\mathbf{1}(\omega \models \varphi)}(1-p^0)^{\mathbf{1}(\omega \not\models \varphi)}}$ *ratio*
  if *ratio* $\geq A \wedge H = H_0 \vee$ *ratio* $\leq B \wedge H = H_1$ **then**
    accept H

The user specifies ε and δ and the SMC algorithm calculates N to guarantee the estimate accordingly. Equation (6) is derived from equations

$$P(\hat{p} - p \geq \varepsilon) \leq e^{-2N\varepsilon^2} \quad \text{and} \quad P(p - \hat{p} \geq \varepsilon) \leq e^{-2N\varepsilon^2}, \tag{7}$$

giving $N = \lceil (\ln \delta)/(2\varepsilon^2) \rceil$ to satisfy either inequality.

We consider the strategy of sampling M schedulers to estimate the optimum probability. We thus generate M estimates $\{\hat{p}_1, \ldots, \hat{p}_M\}$ and take either the maximum ($\hat{p}_{\max}$) or minimum ($\hat{p}_{\min}$), as required. To overcome the cumulative probability of error with the standard Chernoff bound, we specify that *all* estimates $\hat{p}_i$ must be within ε of their respective true values p_i, ensuring that any $\hat{p}_{\min}, \hat{p}_{\max} \in \{\hat{p}_1, \ldots, \hat{p}_M\}$ are within ε of their true value. Given (7) and the fact that all estimates $\hat{p}_i$ are statistically independent, the probability that all estimates are less than their upper bound is expressed by $P(\bigwedge_{i=1}^{M} \hat{p}i - p_i \leq \varepsilon) \geq (1 - e^{-2N\varepsilon^2})^M$. Hence, $P(\bigvee_{i=1}^{M} \hat{p}_i - p_i \geq \varepsilon) \leq 1 - (1 - e^{-2N\varepsilon^2})^M$. This leads to the following expression for N, given parameters M, ε and δ:

$$N = \left\lceil -\ln\left(1 - \sqrt[M]{1-\delta}\right)/2\varepsilon^2 \right\rceil \tag{8}$$

Since the case for $p_{\min}$ is symmetrical, (8) also ensures $P(p_{\min} - \hat{p}_{\min} \geq \varepsilon) \leq \delta$. Hence, to ensure the more usual conditions that $P(|\,p_{\max} - \hat{p}_{\max}\,| \geq \varepsilon) \leq \delta$ and $P(|\,p_{\min} - \hat{p}_{\min}\,| \geq \varepsilon) \leq \delta$,

$$N = \left\lceil \left(\ln 2 - \ln\left(1 - \sqrt[M]{1-\delta}\right)\right)/(2\varepsilon^2) \right\rceil. \tag{9}$$

N scales logarithmically with M (e.g., for $\varepsilon = \delta = 0.01$, $N \approx \log_{1.0002}(M) +$ 26472), making it tractable to consider many schedulers. Algorithm 3 is the resulting extremal probability estimation algorithm for multiple schedulers.

Algorithm 3. Extremal probability estimation with multiple schedulers

---

Input:
  $\mathcal{M}, \varphi$: the MDP and property of interest
  ε, δ: the required confidence bound
  M: the number of schedulers to test
Output: Extremal estimates $\hat{p}_{\min}$ and $\hat{p}_{\max}$

Let $N = \lceil \ln(2/(1 - \sqrt[M]{1-\delta}))/(2\varepsilon^2) \rceil$ be the no. of simulations per scheduler
Let $\mathcal{U}_{\text{seed}}$ be a uniform PRNG and σ its sample
Initialise $\hat{p}_{\min} \leftarrow 1$ and $\hat{p}_{\max} \leftarrow 0$
Set seed of $\mathcal{U}_{\text{seed}}$ randomly
for $i \in \{1, \ldots, M\}$ **do**
  Iterate $\mathcal{U}_{\text{seed}}$ to generate σ_i
  Let $truecount = 0$ be the initial number of traces that satisfy φ
  for $j \in \{1, \ldots, N\}$ **do**
    $\omega_j \leftarrow \text{Simulate}(\mathcal{M}, \varphi, \sigma_i)$
    $truecount \leftarrow truecount + \mathbf{1}(\omega_j \models \varphi)$
  Let $\hat{p}_i = truecount/N$
  if $\hat{p}_{\max} < \hat{p}_i$ **then**
    $\hat{p}_{\max} = \hat{p}_i$
  if $\hat{p}_i > 0 \wedge \hat{p}_{\min} > \hat{p}_i$ **then**
    $\hat{p}_{\min} = \hat{p}_i$
if $\hat{p}_{\max} = 0$ **then**
  No schedulers were found to satisfy φ

4.3   Experiments

We implemented Algorithms 2 and 3 in our statistical model checking platform PLASMA [1] and performed a number of experiments.

Figure 3 shows the empirical cumulative distribution of schedulers generated by Algorithm 3 applied to the MDP of Fig. 2, using $p_1 = 0.9$, $p_2 = 0.5$, $\varphi = \mathbf{X}(\psi \wedge \mathbf{XG}^4 \neg \psi)$, $\varepsilon = 0.01$, $\delta = 0.01$ and $M = 300$. The vertical red and blue lines mark the true probabilities of φ under each of the history-dependent and memoryless schedulers, respectively. The grey rectangles show the $\pm \varepsilon$ error bounds, relative to the true probabilities. There are multiple estimates per scheduler, but all estimates are within their respective confidence bounds. Note that the confidence is specified with respect to estimates, not with respect to optimality. Defining confidence with respect to optimality remains an open problem.

In Fig. 4 we consider a reachability property of the Wireless LAN (WLAN) protocol model of [15]. The protocol aims to minimise "collisions" between devices sharing a communication channel. We estimated the probability of the

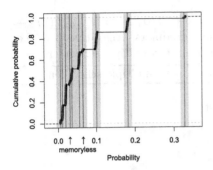
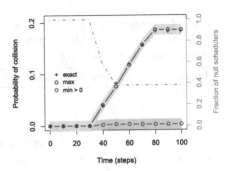

Fig. 3. Empirical cumulative distribution of estimates from Algorithm 3.

Fig. 4. Max. and min. probabilities of second collision in WLAN protocol.

second collision at time steps $\{0, 10, \ldots, 100\}$, using Algorithm 3 with $M = 4000$ schedulers per point. Maximum and minimum estimated probabilities are denoted by blue and red circles, respectively. Maximum probabilities calculated by numerical model checking are denoted by black crosses. The shaded areas indicate the $\pm\varepsilon$ error of the estimates (Chernoff bound $\varepsilon = \delta = 0.01$) and reveal that our estimates are very close to the true values.

To demonstrate the scalability of our approach, we consider the choice coordination model of [17] and estimate the minimum probability that a group of six tourists will meet within T steps. The model has a parameter ($BOUND$) that limits the state space. We set $BOUND = 100$, making the state space of $\approx 5 \times 10^{16}$ intractable to numerical model checking. For $T = 20$ and $T = 25$ the true minimum probabilities are respectively 0.5 and 0.75. Using smart sampling and a Chernoff bound of $\varepsilon = \delta = 0.01$, we correctly estimate the probabilities to be 0.496 and 0.745 in a few tens of minutes on a standard laptop computer.

5   Prospects and Challenges

Our techniques are immediately extensible to continuous time MDPs and other models that use nondeterminism. It is also seems simple to consider MDPs with rewards. Although the presented algorithms are not optimised with respect to simulation budget, in a forthcoming work we introduce the notion of "smart sampling" to maximise the chance of finding good schedulers with a finite budget.

A limitation of our approach is that the algorithms sample from only a subset of possible schedulers. It is easy to construct examples where good schedulers are vanishingly rare and will not be found. Our ongoing focus is therefore to develop memory-efficient learning techniques that construct schedulers piecewise, to improve convergence and consider a much larger set of schedulers.

Acknowledgement. This work was partially supported by the European Union Seventh Framework Programme under grant agreement no. 295261 (MEALS).

References

1. PLASMA project web page. https://project.inria.fr/plasma-lab/
2. Baier, C., Katoen, J.-P.: Principles of Model Checking. MIT Press, Cambridge (2008)
3. Bellman, R.: Dynamic Programming. Princeton University Press, Princeton (1957)
4. Bianco, A., De Alfaro, L.: Model checking of probabilistic and nondeterministic systems. In: Thiagarajan, P.S. (ed.) FSTTCS 1995. LNCS, vol. 1026. Springer, Heidelberg (1995)
5. Bogdoll, J., Ferrer Fioriti, L.M., Hartmanns, A., Hermanns, H.: Partial order methods for statistical model checking and simulation. In: Bruni, R., Dingel, J. (eds.) FORTE 2011 and FMOODS 2011. LNCS, vol. 6722, pp. 59–74. Springer, Heidelberg (2011)
6. Chernoff, H.: A measure of asymptotic efficiency for tests of a hypothesis based on the sum of observations. Ann. Math. Statist. **23**(4), 493–507 (1952)
7. Clarke, E., Emerson, E.A., Sifakis, J.: Model checking: algorithmic verification and debugging. Commun. ACM **52**(11), 74–84 (2009)
8. Cormen, T.H., Leiserson, C.E., Rivest, R.L., Stein, C.: Introduction to Algorithms, 3rd edn. MIT Press, New York (2009)
9. Hansson, H., Jonsson, B.: A logic for reasoning about time and reliability. Formal Aspects Comput. **6**(5), 512–535 (1994)
10. Hartmanns, A., Timmer, M.: On-the-fly confluence detection for statistical model checking. In: Brat, G., Rungta, N., Venet, A. (eds.) NFM 2013. LNCS, vol. 7871, pp. 337–351. Springer, Heidelberg (2013)
11. Henriques, D., Martins, J.G., Zuliani, P., Platzer, A., Clarke, E.M.: Statistical model checking for Markov decision processes. In: 2012 Ninth International Conference on Quantitative Evaluation of Systems, pp. 84–93. IEEE (2012)
12. Horner, W.G.: A new method of solving numerical equations of all orders, by continuous approximation. Philos. Trans. R. Soc. Lond. **109**, 308–335 (1819)
13. Kearns, M., Mansour, Y., Ng, A.Y.: A sparse sampling algorithm for near-optimal planning in large Markov decision processes. Mach. Learn. **49**(2–3), 193–208 (2002)
14. Knuth, D.E.: The Art of Computer Programming, 3rd edn. Addison-Wesley, Reading (1998)
15. Kwiatkowska, M., Norman, G., Sproston, J.: Probabilistic model checking of the IEEE 802.11 wireless local area network protocol. In: Hermanns, H., Segala, R. (eds.) PROBMIV 2002, PAPM-PROBMIV 2002, and PAPM 2002. LNCS, vol. 2399, pp. 169–187. Springer, Heidelberg (2002)
16. Lassaigne, R., Peyronnet, S.: Approximate planning and verification for large Markov decision processes. In: Procecddings of 27th Annual ACM Symposium on Applied Computing, pp. 1314–1319. ACM (2012)
17. Ndukwu, U., McIver, A.: An expectation transformer approach to predicate abstraction and data independence for probabilistic programs. In: Proceedings of 8th Workshop on Quantitative Aspects of Programming Languages (QAPL'10) (2010)
18. Okamoto, M.: Some inequalities relating to the partial sum of binomial probabilities. Ann. Inst. Stat. Math. **10**(1), 29–35 (1958)
19. Puterman, M.L.: Markov Decision Processes: Discrete Stochastic Dynamic Programming. Wiley-Interscience, New York (1994)

20. Wald, A.: Sequential tests of statistical hypotheses. Ann. Math. Stat. **16**(2), 117–186 (1945)
21. Younes, H.L.S., Simmons, R.G.: Probabilistic verification of discrete event systems using acceptance sampling. In: Brinksma, E., Larsen, K.G. (eds.) CAV 2002. LNCS, vol. 2404, pp. 223–235. Springer, Heidelberg (2002)

Towards Synthesis of Attack Trees
for Supporting Computer-Aided Risk Analysis

Sophie Pinchinat, Mathieu Acher$^{(\boxtimes)}$, and Didier Vojtisek

Inria, IRISA, University of Rennes 1, Rennes, France
mathieu.acher@irisa.fr

Abstract. Attack trees are widely used in the fields of defense for the analysis of risks (or threats) against electronics systems, computer control systems or physical systems. Based on the analysis of attack trees, practitioners can define actions to engage in order to reduce or annihilate risks. A major barrier to support computer-aided risk analysis is that attack trees can become largely complex and thus hard to specify. This paper is a first step towards a methodology, formal foundations as well as automated techniques to synthesize attack trees from a high-level description of a system. Attacks are expressed as a succession of elementary actions and high-level actions can be used to abstract and organize attacks into exploitable attack trees. We describe our tooling support and identify open challenges for supporting the analysis of risks.

1 Introduction

Ensuring the security of an information system means guaranteeing data availability, integrity and confidentiality. In this perspective, a preliminary study of the system and its environment, called *risk analysis*, is necessary [4,13]. The discipline of risk analysis aims to identify and evaluate risks that threaten a given system. Current methods follow mostly the same outline: practitioners decompose the system into subsystems and produce a model, then draw up a list of feared events, and finally determine the potential reasons of the realization of these events. The NATO report [11] showed that the current methods are ill-suited to manage the security of complex systems. Formal methods, well-defined formalisms, and analysis tools have the potential to eliminate current barriers. In particular, *attack trees* are widely used in the fields of defense for the analysis of risks (also called threats) against electronics systems, computer control systems or physical systems [1,8,9,12,14,15,18]. Based on the analysis of attack trees, practitioners can define actions to engage in order to reduce or annihilate risks.

Up to now, the construction of attack trees is made by hand, based on knowledge and experiences of analysts and technicians. There are construction and editing tools of attack trees available (e.g., [1,14,15]). This manual effort is time-consuming and error-prone, especially as the size of attack trees can become substantial. Our goal is to create an automated process able to assist practitioners in fulfilling the modeling task. This paper reports on the first steps towards a methodology, the formal foundations as well as automated techniques to *synthesize attack trees* from a high-level description of a system. Though attack

© Springer International Publishing Switzerland 2015
C. Canal and A. Idani (Eds.): SEFM 2014 Workshops, LNCS 8938, pp. 363–375, 2015.
DOI: 10.1007/978-3-319-15201-1_24

trees have deserved a lot of attention [6–10,12,18], we are unaware of existing approaches for (semi-)automatically synthesizing attack trees. Hong *et al.* [3] have addressed synthesis of attack trees, but in a setting lacking the precious hierarchy of actions that enforces the structure of the attack trees. As a result, there is no control over the outcome: deeply flattened and hard to exploit trees can be obtained, precluding a further exploitation by risk analysts and domain experts. For computer system security, Jha *et al.* [5] and Sheyner *et al.* [16,17] proposed an algorithm to automatically generate an attack graph representing the system under consideration. In our case, attack graphs are generated from a description of a system (e.g., a military building). Our methodology allows the user to specify the intended structure through a hierarchy of actions, with flexibility on the adequate level of abstraction to choose. Moreover we do not synthesize scenarios graphs but attack trees.

Our proposed methodology consists in (1) describing the system to protect as an *attack graph (AG)*; (2) extracting the *attacks* (the solution-paths going from an initial state to a final/goal state); (3) gathering all attacks into an *attack tree*. The exploitation of a high-level specification (e.g., a military building) raises the level of abstraction – practitioners (experts of a domain) can more easily express their knowledge and defense objectives. Moreover automating the approach ensures that the presence of all attacks under study are present in the attack tree. We notice, though, that a fully automated synthesis is likely to produce unexploitable (e.g., deeply flatten) trees. Mauw and Oostdijk [9] showed that numerous structurally different attacks trees can capture the same information, out of which a few are readable and meaningful for an expert. An original and crucial feature of our methodology is the support of *high-level actions* to specify how sequences of actions can be abstracted and structured – a high-level action can be seen as a sub-goal. Likewise experts can control the synthesis process and obtain attack trees close to what they have in mind. We formalize *hierarchies of actions* and use standard pattern-matching techniques to compute a so-called *strategies* of the attacks (corresponding to *attack suites* in [9]), that provide abstractions of the attack descriptions. The methodology comes with an environment and a set of languages for generating attacks, specifying high-level actions, and synthesizing attack trees. We illustrate the synthesis process in the context of analyzing risks of a military building. We also identify some open challenges for fully supporting the approach.

Remainder of the Paper. Section 2 introduces a running example in the context of military defense. Section 3 describes background information and notations used throughout the paper. Section 4 defines attack graphs before introducing in Sect. 5 hierarchy of actions, strategies, and attack trees. Section 6 summarizes the paper and describes future works.

2   Motivation and Running Example

To illustrate the motivation of our work, let us consider the example of Fig. 1. Military experts want to protect an armoury, i.e., they do not want that the

Fig. 1. The plan of the armoury to protect

stored weapons fall into the wrong hands. For the sake of risk analysis, we put ourselves in the attacker's shoes and look for the ways to intrude the military building. The armoury consists of six rooms, including a hall monitored by a video equipment and the storage room. The building is guarded by defenders: the attacker (ATK) may meet an agent in one of the rooms, a dog in another. The goal of the analysis is then to find all the *relevant* paths to reach the weapons. Relevant means here that we would like to get the successful attacks that are realistic (no invisibility cloak) and without loops – we would like to avoid the cases where the attacker goes from a room (say A) to the next room (say B), goes back to A, then goes to B, and so on. An example of path, among many others, is that the attacker can cross the hall to go directly into the storage room; to make sure he or she has not been seen, the attacker can cut the video surveillance system. The building of Fig. 1 involves 17 elements (seven doors, five windows, three agents, one camera and the arsenal). The number is substantial since numerous paths and attacks can be envisioned. In practice the complexity can be even higher. The goal of the project we are involved in is to assist military experts in synthesizing attack trees. Specifically we want to generate attacks from the description of a system (e.g., military building) and synthesize, with the help of some directives, a readable attack tree that military experts can exploit afterwards.

Running Example. In the rest of the paper, we will only consider the end of the attack, that is, the intrusion in the storage room. In our running example (Fig. 1), the system consists in a simple room and an attacker who still wants to intrude to steal the weapons located in a locked cabinet of this room. To describe the states of the system, we define the following three two-valued variables: $Pos(ATK) \in \{out., room\}$ (*out.* stands for *outdoor*) which gives the position of the attacker in the system at each moment, $room \in \{opened, closed\}$ which describes the door status, and $cabinet \in \{opened, closed\}$ which tells whether the weapons are easy to reach or not.

3 Preliminary Notations

For a set X, we let X^* be the set of finite sequences over X, and we denote by ϵ the empty sequence. Given two sequences $s_1, s_2 \in X^*$, we let $s_1.s_2 \in X^*$ denote the concatenation of s_1 and s_2. For $x \in X$, we will simply write x for the set $\{x\} \subseteq X^*$. Given a sequence $s \in X^*$ and $Y \subseteq X^*$ a set of sequences over X^*, we let $s.Y$ denote the sequences s, s' where $s' \in Y$ and we $s^{-1}.Y$ be the set of sequences $s' \in X^*$ such that $s.s' \in Y$. For two subsets Y and Z of X^*, we let $Y.Z = \bigcup_{s \in Y} s.Z$; it is the set of sequences obtained by concatenating a sequence in Y with a sequence in Z. We now recall trees, labeled trees and forests.

A *tree* is a finite set $T \subseteq \mathbb{N}^*$ of *nodes* such that: $t.i \in T$ implies $t \in T$ (prefix-closeness), and $t.i \in T$ implies $t.j \in T$, for all $1 \leq j < i$ (left-closeness).

A node $t \in T$ is a *leaf* if $t.1 \notin T$; we write $leaves(T) \subseteq T$ the set of leaves of T. We let $\deg(t)$ be the greatest n such that $t.n \in T$. We write $children(t)$ for the sequence of ordered children of t in T, i.e., the sequence $t.1 \ldots t.\deg(t) \in T^*$. A branch of T is a sequence $i_1 i_2 \ldots i_m$ such that $i_1 i_2 \ldots i_m \in leaves(T)$.

Let Γ be a set. A Γ-*labeled tree* is a structure $\tau = (T, \ell)$ where T is a tree, and $\ell : T \to \Gamma$ is the *labeling function*; Figs. 3(a) and (b) depicts two labeled trees τ_1 and τ_2. We write $w(\tau) \in \Gamma^*$ for the sequence of labels of leaf nodes of τ ordered from left to right. Given a Γ-labeled tree $\tau = (T, \ell)$ and a node $t \in T$, we let $\tau_t = (T_t, \ell_t)$ be the sub-tree of τ rooted at node t defined by $T_t = t^{-1}T$ and $\ell_t(t') = \ell(t.t'), for\ all\ t' \in T_t$.

A Γ-*forest* is a finite ordered set $\{\tau_i\}_{i \in I}$ of Γ-labeled trees.

4 Attack Graphs

We use a standard symbolic representation for dynamic systems, where states are characterized by valuations over a finite set of variables (ranging over a finite domain) and transitions between states correspond to actions.

Figure 2 describes the system of our running example: each state, although numbered, is characterized by a valuation of the relevant variables. Initial states are marked by an ongoing arrow and goal states (those the attacker wants to reach) by double row. We can navigate in this graph following arrows that realize actions; label tc/fl means that either action tc or action fl can be chosen.

Definition 1. *An Attack Graph (AG) over a set of actions* $\mathbb{A}$ *is a structure* $\mathcal{G} = (S, f, I, G)$, *where* S *a finite set of* states, $f : S \times \mathbb{A} \to S$ *a partial transition function,* $I \subseteq S$ *is a set of* initial *states, and* $G \subseteq S$ *is a set of* goal *states.*

The AG $\mathcal{G}_{ex} = (S, f, I, G)$ of Fig. 2 is formally defined by:

- $S = \{1, 2, 3, 4, 5, 6, 7, 8\}$: each state of the system is composed of a combination of the possibles of the variables.
- $I = \{1, 5\}$: the initial sy tates are the states where $Pos(ATK) = out.$ and $room = closed.$

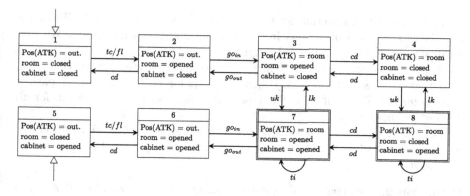

Fig. 2. The AG $\mathcal{G}_{ex}$

- $G = \{7, 8\}$: the final states are the states where attacker is inside and the cabinet opened.
- $\mathbb{A} = \{tc, fl, od, cd, go_{in}, go_{out}, uk, lk, ti\}$ is the set of primitive actions, which respectively means:

Action	Meaning
tc	type the code (door opener)
fl	force the lock
od	open the door
cd	close the door
go_{in}	go inside
go_{out}	go outside
uk	use a key to open the cabinet
lk	lock the cabinet with a key
ti	take item (weapon)

- $f : S \times \mathbb{A} \to S$ the partial *transition function*

f_{tc}	f_{fl}	f_{od}	f_{cd}	$f_{go_{in}}$	$f_{go_{out}}$	f_{uk}	f_{lk}	f_{ti}
$1 \mapsto 2$	$1 \mapsto 2$	$4 \mapsto 3$	$3 \mapsto 4$	$2 \mapsto 3$	$3 \mapsto 2$	$3 \mapsto 7$	$7 \mapsto 3$	$7 \mapsto 7$
$5 \mapsto 6$	$5 \mapsto 6$	$8 \mapsto 7$	$7 \mapsto 8$	$6 \mapsto 7$	$7 \mapsto 6$	$4 \mapsto 8$	$8 \mapsto 4$	$8 \mapsto 8$
			$2 \mapsto 1$					
			$6 \mapsto 5$					

For example, according to f_{tc}, from the state 1, if we apply the action tc, we get into the state 2. Similarly, from the state 5, we get into the state 6 after the application of the same action.

In the rest of this section let $\mathcal{G} = (S, I, G, f)$ be an AG over $\mathbb{A}$. We define *attacks* as sequences of actions from an initial state to a goal state. We first recall standard notion on labeled graphs.

A *path starting from* $s \in S$ in $\mathcal{G}$ is a sequence of states $\pi = s_0 s_1 \ldots s_n$ such that $s_0 = s$ and $\exists a \in \mathbb{A}, f(s_i, a) = s_{i+1}$, for all $0 \leq i < n$. A path π *reaches the set* $S' \subseteq S$ if $s_n \in S'$. A path $\pi = s_0 \ldots s_n$ is *elementary* if, for all $0 \leq i < j \leq n, s_i \neq s_j$.

Let $a_1 . \ldots . a_n \in \mathbb{A}^*$ be a sequence of actions and let $s_0 \in S$. A *path induced by* $a_1 . \ldots . a_n \in \mathbb{A}^*$ is a path $\pi = s_0 s_1 \ldots s_n$ such that $f_{a_{i+1}}(s_i) = s_{i+1}$, for all $0 \leq i < n$.

Definition 2. *An attack in $\mathcal{G}$ is a sequence of actions $a_1 . a_2 . \ldots . a_n \in \mathbb{A}^*$ such that there exists an elementary path from some initial state induced by $a_1 \ldots a_n$ and which reaches the set G. Let $Attack(\mathcal{G})$ be the set of attacks in $\mathcal{G}$; it is finite.*

In $\mathcal{G}_{ex}$, $tc.go_{in}, fl.go_{in}.cd.uk.ti$ is an attack either along path $5, 6, 7$ or path $1, 2, 3, 4, 8, 8$. Also, $tc.go_{in}.cd.ti \in Attack(\mathcal{G}_{ex})$.

5   High-Level Actions and Attack Trees

We first define *hierarchies of actions* used to describe attacks in a more comprehensible way called *strategy*. Then strategies are gathered into an *attack tree*.

5.1   Hierarchy of Actions

The paths extracted from the AG are low-level descriptions of attacks by means of elementary actions. However, sequences of actions may be abstracted as so-called *high-level actions*, explaining some behaviors in a more abstract manner. This abstraction relies on a hierarchy of actions, which may be updated along an analysis process.

Consider our running example. The set $\mathbb{A}$ of elementary actions describe the lowest level actions of level 0, written $\mathcal{H}_0$. "Higher level" actions can be considered for example if one wishes to introduce action *or* for "open room" which may be achieved, or *refined*, by performing either (elementary) actions *tc* ("type the code"), or *fl* ("force the lock"), or *od* ("open the door"). In the same line, one can define the higher-level action *cr* ("close room") uniquely refined as action *cd* ("close the door"). Since higher-level actions *or* and *cr* can be realized by actions of level 0, they would belong to level 1, that is the set $\mathcal{H}_1$. To $\mathcal{H}_1$, we add action *oc* ("open cabinet") refined by performing *uk*, the action *cc* ("close cabinet") refined by performing *lk* ("lock the cabinet with key"), and *tw* ("take weapons") refined either by *ti*, or *cd.ti*, or *od.ti*, or *ti.tw*.

Based on a (somewhat arbitrary) choice of abstraction given by an expert, we get a hierarchy of actions which consists in a set $\mathcal{H}_0 = \mathbb{A}$ of elementary actions, and a set $\mathcal{H}_1$. The latter is formed of actions whose realizations are sequences of actions of level 0. More generally, we should describe a high-level actions of level k by at least a sequence of level $k - 1$, i.e., a sequence containing at least an action of level $k-1$ (no action of level greater than $k-1$). We now formalize the notion of hierarchy of high-level actions.

Definition 3. *A hierarchy over a set of actions $\mathbb{A}$ is a structure $\mathbb{H} = (\{\mathcal{H}_k\}_{0 \leq k \leq K}, \mathcal{R})$ where:*

- *each $\mathcal{H}_k$ ($0 < k \leq K$) is a finite set of high-level actions (HLA), with $\mathcal{H}_K \neq \emptyset$ which forms the top-level actions. $K \in \mathbb{N}$ is the hierarchy level and $\mathcal{H}_0 = \mathbb{A}$ is the set of primitive actions. We let $\mathcal{H} = \bigcup_{0 \leq k \leq K} \mathcal{H}_k$, whose typical elements are $A, B, A', A_1, A_2, \ldots$.*
- *$\mathcal{R} \subseteq \mathcal{H} \times \mathcal{H}^*$ is the set of the refinement rules which satisfies $level(\mathcal{R}(A)) \leq level(A)$, for all action $A \in \mathcal{H}$. In particular, $\mathcal{R}(A) = A$ for all $A \in \mathcal{H}_0$.*

We define $level : \mathcal{H} \to \{0, \ldots, K\}$, the level function, by $level^{-1}(k) = \mathcal{H}_k{}^1$. A hierarchy is strict if for all action $A \in \mathcal{H}$, $level(\mathcal{R}(A)) < level(A)$.

As explained above, we have equipped the AG $\mathcal{G}_{ex}$ with a 2-level hierarchy $\mathbb{H}_{ex}$ over $\mathbb{A}$ defined by $\mathcal{H}_0 = \{tc, fl, od, cd, go_{in}, go_{out}, uk, lk, ti\}$, $\mathcal{H}_1 = \{or, cr, oc, cc, tw\}$ and $\mathcal{H}_2 = \{er, gr, st\}$ and the following refinement rules, where we write $A \rightsquigarrow A_1 \ldots A_n$ instead of $(A, A_1 \ldots A_n) \in \mathcal{R}$, and even use "$|$" on the right-hand side of $\rightsquigarrow$ to mimic standard notations in formal grammar rules; for instance, expression $or \rightsquigarrow tc \,|\, fl \,|\, od$ means that $\mathcal{R}(or) = \{tc, fl, od\}$.

$$
\begin{cases}
er \rightsquigarrow go_{in} \,|\, or.go_{in} \,|\, go_{in}.cr \,|\, or.go_{in}.cr \\
gr \rightsquigarrow go_{out} \,|\, or.go_{out} \,|\, go_{out}.cr \,|\, or.go_{out}.cr \\
st \rightsquigarrow tw \,|\, oc.tw \,|\, tw.lk \,|\, oc.tw.lk
\end{cases}
\qquad
\begin{cases}
or \rightsquigarrow tc \,|\, fl \,|\, od \\
cr \rightsquigarrow cd \\
oc \rightsquigarrow uk \\
cc \rightsquigarrow lk \\
tw \rightsquigarrow ti \,|\, cd.ti \,|\, od.ti \,|\, ti.tw
\end{cases}
$$

with HLAs of level 2 er for "enter room", gr for "get out of room" and st for "steal weapon", and we recall HLAs of level 1: or for "open the room", cr for "close room", oc for "open cabinet", cc "close cabinet", and tw for "take weapons".

5.2 Strategies

Strategies provide high-level descriptions of attacks in the AG. These objects are (forests of) labelled trees whose sequences of leaves describe attacks, while internal nodes of trees are labelled by HLA.

In the rest of this section, we let $\mathcal{G} = (S, I, G, f)$ be an AG over a set of actions $\mathcal{H}_0$, $\mathbb{H} = (\{\mathcal{H}_k\}_{0 \leq k \leq K}, level, \mathcal{R})$ be a hierarchy.

Definition 4. *A strategy over $\mathbb{H}$ is an $\mathcal{H}$-forest $\sigma = \{\tau_i\}_{i=1\ldots n}$ such that for each $\tau_i = (T_i, \ell_i)$, and for every $t \in T_i$, $\ell_i(t) \rightsquigarrow \ell_i(t_1) \ldots \ell_i(t_j)$ is a refinement rule, where $t_1, \ldots, t_j$ are the children of t in T_i. Given a strategy σ, we will write $w(\sigma) = w(\tau_1)w(\tau_2)\ldots w(\tau_n) \in \mathcal{H}_0^*$ for the attack of σ.*

A strategy σ is winning whenever $w(\sigma) \in Attack(\mathcal{G})$.

---

[1] We may sometimes display *level* in the structure.

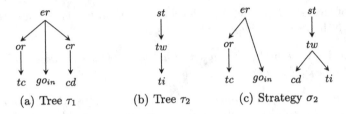

(a) Tree τ_1 (b) Tree τ_2 (c) Strategy σ_2

Fig. 3. Trees τ_1 (a) and τ_2 (b) forming strategy $\sigma_1 = \{\tau_1, \tau_2\}$ such that with $w(\sigma_1) = ti.go_{in}.cd.ti \in Attack(\mathcal{G}_{ex})$. (c) is another strategy σ_2 for $ti.go_{in}.cd.ti$.

The set $\{\tau_1, \tau_2\}$ (see Figs. 3(a) and (b)) represents a winning $\mathbb{H}_{ex}$-strategy σ_1 with two trees, whose attack is $tc.go_{in}.cd.ti$. In essence, branching nodes of a strategy have a conjunctive meaning[2].

It should be noted that there may be several strategies associated to an attack. For instance, strategy σ_1 formed by Figs. 3(a) and (b), and strategy σ_2 of Fig. 3(c) have respectively the same attack $tc.go_{in}.cd.ti$. This phenomenon is typical of a hierarchy of actions that is "ambiguous"[3].

For $w \in Attack(\mathcal{G})$, we let $\Sigma(w) := \{\sigma \,|\, w(\sigma) = w\}$ be the set of strategies associated with w.

Now that we know how to relate attacks in an AG with strategies that exploit the hierarchy of actions, we can gather strategies into a kind of "and-or" trees called an *attack tree*, in the same line as [6].

5.3 Attack Trees

Strategies σ_1 and σ_2 and of Fig. 3, although both abstracting attack $tc.go_{in}.cd.ti$ in $\mathcal{G}_{ex}$, can be distinguished: the former relies on refinement rules $er \rightsquigarrow or.go_{in}.cr$, $cr \rightsquigarrow cd$ and $tw \rightsquigarrow ti$, whereas the latter relies on rules $er \rightsquigarrow or.go_{in}$ and $tw \rightsquigarrow cd.ti$. These alternatives can be expressed using trees including some nodes carrying an "or" semantics.

In the rest of this section, we let $\mathbb{H} = (\{\mathcal{H}_k\}_{0 \leq k \leq K}, level, \mathcal{R})$ be a hierarchy. We consider the signature formed of *and connectors* defined by $\mathcal{C} = \{\bigwedge_j | j \in \mathbb{N}\}$, where $\bigwedge_j$ has *arity* j (see Definition 5).

Attack tree nodes can be labeled by HLAs or by connectors or by the special symbol *win* which actually characterizes the root; label *win* is somehow a "super" high-level action representing the main goal.

Definition 5. *An Attack Tree (AT) over $\mathbb{H}$ is a $(\mathcal{H} \cup \mathcal{C} \cup \{win\})$-labeled tree $\mathcal{T} = (T, \ell)$ such that for all $t \in T$, if $\ell(t) \in \mathcal{C}_k$, then t has k children, and $t \in leaves(T)$ iff $\ell(t) \in \mathcal{H}_0$. Virtual (resp. true) nodes of T are those nodes labeled over $\mathcal{C} \cup \{win\}$ (resp. $\mathcal{H}$).*

---

[2] And even a "sequential" one, i.e. children of the and-node are considered in order from left to right.

[3] As for context-free grammars.

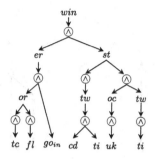

Fig. 4. Attack tree $\mathcal{T}_0$

Definition 6. $\mathcal{T} = (T, \ell)$ *over* $\mathbb{H}$ *is* well-formed *if for any branch* $n_1 n_2 \ldots n_m$ *of* T, *and for any* $1 \le i < j \le m$, *letting* $L = \ell(n_1 n_2 \ldots n_i)$ *and* $L' = \ell(n_1 n_2 \ldots n_j)$, *if* $L, L' \in \mathcal{H}$, *then* $level(L) > level(L')$.

In *well-formed* ATs, the level of actions along a branch strictly decreases; Fig. 4 depicts a well-formed AT over $\mathbb{H}_{ex}$[4].

From strategies to ATs. We can embed strategies into ATs. This embedding consists in (i) explicitly connecting nodes of the trees to the strategy forest, and in (ii) connecting the roots of all the resulting trees via a "*win-then-$\bigwedge$*" mechanism.

We first start explaining (i). Let σ be a strategy over $\mathbb{H}$, and let $\tau = (T, \ell) \in \sigma$. We transform τ into the $(\mathcal{H} \cup \{\bigwedge_j | j \in \mathbb{N}\})$-labeled tree $\hat{\tau} = (\hat{T}, \hat{\ell})$ defined by induction over the height h of τ as follows.

- If $h = 0$, then $\hat{\tau} = \tau$.
- Otherwise, let $\tau_1 = (T_1, \ell_1), \ldots, \tau_n = (T_n, \ell_n)$ be the ordered sub-trees at τ root (hence with lower height). Then
  - $\hat{T}$ is the least set containing all the sets $\{1\}$, $1.1.\widehat{T_1}, \ldots, 1.n.\widehat{T_n}$, and
  - $\hat{\ell}(\epsilon) = \ell(\epsilon)$, $\hat{\ell}(1) = \bigwedge$ and $\hat{\ell}(1.i.t) = \hat{\ell}_i(t)$.

For example, consider the trees τ_1 of Fig. 3(a) and τ_2 of Fig. 3(b); the trees $\hat{\tau_1}$ and $\hat{\tau_2}$ are depicted in Fig. 5(a).

We can now embed strategies into ATs.

Definition 7. *Let* $\sigma = \{(T_i, \ell_i)\}_{i=1,\ldots,n}$ *be a strategy over some hierarchy* $\mathbb{H}$. *The canonical AT associated to* σ *is* $\mathcal{T}_\sigma = (T, \ell)$ *over* $\mathbb{H}$ *defined by:*

- T *is the least set containing all the sets* $\{1\}, 1.1.\widehat{T_1}, \ldots, 1.n.\widehat{T_n}$ *(a node of* T *is then either* ϵ *or* 1 *or of the form* $1.i.y$ *where* $y \in \hat{T_i}$*).*
- $\ell(x) = \begin{cases} win & \text{if } x = \epsilon \\ \bigwedge & \text{if } x = 1 \\ \hat{\ell}_i(y) & \text{if } x = 1.i.y \end{cases}$

---

[4] In figures, we omit the arity of connectors.

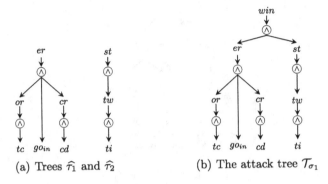

(a) Trees $\widehat{\tau_1}$ and $\widehat{\tau_2}$ (b) The attack tree $\mathcal{T}_{\sigma_1}$

Fig. 5. Trees τ_1 of Fig. 3(a) and τ_2 of Fig. 3(b) transformed before connection and the resulting attack tree $\mathcal{T}_{\sigma_1}$

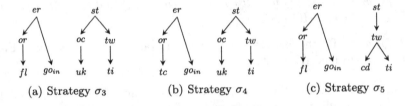

(a) Strategy σ_3 (b) Strategy σ_4 (c) Strategy σ_5

Fig. 6. Strategies included in $\mathcal{T}_0$ of Fig. 4

Clearly, $\mathcal{T}_\sigma$ respects Definition 5, hence it is an AT. Note also that if $\mathbb{H}$ is strict, then $\mathcal{T}_\sigma$ is well-formed. Figure 5(b) depicts $\mathcal{T}_{\sigma_1}$ for strategy σ_1 of Fig. 3.

From ATs to Strategies. A given AT $\mathcal{T}$ naturally denotes a set $\Sigma(\mathcal{T})$ of strategies. Each strategy of $\Sigma(\mathcal{T})$ is obtained by keeping all nodes of $\mathcal{T}$, but by selecting a single child in each $\mathcal{H}$-labeled node of $\mathcal{T}$. Due to lack of space we do not formally define $\Sigma(\mathcal{T})$. Instead, we provide the clarifying following example.

The AT $\mathcal{T}_0$ of Fig. 4 is such that $\Sigma(\mathcal{T}_0) = \{\sigma_2, \sigma_3, \sigma_4, \sigma_5\}$ (where the strategies are given in Fig. 3(c), Fig. 6(a), (b) and (c) respectively), because in $\mathcal{T}_0$ there are two nodes (with HLAs *or* and *st*), with two possible refinements each, hence the four outcomes for $\Sigma(\mathcal{T}_0)$.

Attack Tree Synthesis. We equip ATs with a binary operation $\oplus$ of *merging* with the following guaranteed properties.

– $\oplus$ is associative: $(\mathcal{T}_1 \oplus \mathcal{T}_2) \oplus \mathcal{T}_3 = \mathcal{T}_1 \oplus (\mathcal{T}_2 \oplus \mathcal{T}_3)$, for any ATs $\mathcal{T}_1$, $\mathcal{T}_2$ and $\mathcal{T}_3$.
– $\oplus$ is well-formedness preserving.
– For any two ATs $\mathcal{T}_1$ and $\mathcal{T}_2$,

$$\Sigma(\mathcal{T}_1 \oplus \mathcal{T}_2) \supseteq \Sigma(\mathcal{T}_1) \cup \Sigma(\mathcal{T}_2) \tag{1}$$

It should be noted that Eq. (1) is not an equality. This is illustrated by the AT $\mathcal{T}_{\sigma_2} \oplus \mathcal{T}_{\sigma_3}$ (for strategies σ_2 and σ_3 of Figs. 3(c) and 6(a)), which turns out to correspond to $\mathcal{T}_0$ in Fig. 4, and yet $\Sigma(\mathcal{T}_0) = \{\sigma_2, \sigma_3, \sigma_4, \sigma_5\}$. Actually, the fact that Eq. (1) is an inclusion instead of an equality is harmless since we claim that the extra strategies are in general also winning – indeed, returning to the matter at hand, HLAs would essentially denote sub-goals. Thus, if the main goal decomposes into HLAs e.g., A then B, and if now A can be refined into either A_1 or A_2 and, similarly, if B can be refined into either B_1 or B_2, the main goal cannot be achieved following any of the four combinations $A_1.A_2$, $A_1.B_2$, $B_1.A_2$ and B_1, B_2.

Operation $\oplus$ is central as it provides the last step for synthesizing an AT: from a finite set Σ of strategies, the synthesis is the result of computing

$$\mathcal{T}(\Sigma) = \oplus_{\sigma \in \Sigma} \mathcal{T}_\sigma$$

How this operation can be implemented in a scalable manner is left as future work (see next section).

6   Towards Attack Tree Synthesis

We proposed a mathematical setting to develop procedures that synthesize attack trees. An original and important aspect of our work is that an expert can participate in the synthesis process through the specification of so-called high-level actions (HLAs). We also sketched an end-to-end tool-supported methodology: starting from a high-level description of a system (e.g., a military building), practitioners can generate attacks through model-checking techniques, and eventually exploit HLAs to synthesize readable and well-structured attack trees. We are implementing ATSyRA[5], a tool built on top of Eclipse and upon the mathematical foundations, to support the synthesis methodology with a set of dedicated languages. Our work opens avenues for further research and engineering effort for supporting the analysis of realistic military risks by practitioners.

Interactive Support. The process is likely to be interactive and incremental: experts obtain an attack tree, add some information, re-synthesize, and so on. At different steps of the methodology, there are opportunities to parametrize the synthesis. For instance, experts can typically fine tune the generation of attacks. Currently, the building specification is transformed into GAL [2] (for Guarded Action Language) a simple yet expressive formalism to model concurrent systems. GAL is supported by efficient decision diagrams for model-checking. We use GAL support to generate attacks. Some predicates can be added to *scope* the space in which model checking mechanisms operate over. We can envision the use of specific languages, independent of GAL and at a higher level of abstraction, for easing the generation of attacks considered as relevant. Besides, experts can guide the synthesis of attack trees through HLAs. Re-structuring the hierarchy or abstracting a set of attacks can arise if the resulting attack tree is not satisfactory (e.g., in case the tree is too flat and hard to understand). Some visualisations and suggestions can help an expert for this task.

---

[5] More information about ATSyRA is available online: http://tinyurl.com/ATSyRA.

Scalability. The number of attacks can be huge, especially if the building specification contains numerous elements, leading to numerous possible paths for an attacker. The *scalability* problem impacts two aspects of the methodology. First, the synthesis of attack trees: HLA can help to reduce the complexity, since a hierarchy is pre-defined, guiding a canonical form they should conform. Yet, implementing the merging operator $\oplus$ of attack trees faces the very complex combinatorics induced by pattern-matching-like issues. Heuristics are likely to be needed both for computing the merge of attack trees and for scaling up. Second, we need to only generate relevant attacks. Again, experts can directly tune GAL to scope the generation: some facilities are needed to ease the task.

Attack Defense. Another step in our work consists in the introduction of the defender. We aim to study his or her actions and reactions. We plan to consider game theory and multi-agents systems, keeping close to the clean foundations proposed by [7].

Acknowledgements. This work is funded by the Direction Générale de l'Armement (DGA) - Ministère de la Défense, France. We thank Salomé Coavoux and Maël Guilleme for their insightful comments and development around ATSyRA.

References

1. AttackTree+. http://www.isograph.com/software/attacktree/
2. Colange, M., Baarir, S., Kordon, F., Thierry-Mieg, Y.: Towards distributed software model-checking using decision diagrams. In: Sharygina, N., Veith, H. (eds.) CAV 2013. LNCS, vol. 8044, pp. 830–845. Springer, Heidelberg (2013)
3. Hong, J.B., Kim, D.S., Takaoka, T.: Scalable attack representation model using logic reduction techniques. In: 12th IEEE International Conference on Trust, Security and Privacy in Computing and Communications, pp. 404–411 (2013)
4. ISO, Geneva, Switzerland. Norm ISO/IEC 27002 - Information Technology - Security Techniques - Code of Practice for Information Security Management, ISO/IEC 27002:2005 edition, Section 9 (2005)
5. Jha, S., Sheyner, O., Wing, J.: Two formal analyses of attack graphs. In: Proceedings of the 15th Computer Security Foundation Workshop, pp. 49–63 (2002)
6. Kordy, B., Mauw, S., Radomirović, S., Schweitzer, P.: Foundations of attack–defense trees. In: Degano, P., Etalle, S., Guttman, J. (eds.) FAST 2010. LNCS, vol. 6561, pp. 80–95. Springer, Heidelberg (2011)
7. Kordy, B., Mauw, S., Radomirović, S., Schweitzer, P.: Attack-defense trees. J. Logic Comput. **24**(1), 55–87 (2014)
8. Kordy, B., Piètre-Cambacédès, L., Schweitzer, P.: Dag-based attack and defense modeling: Don't miss the forest for the attack trees (2013). arXiv preprint arXiv:1303.7397
9. Mauw, S., Oostdijk, M.: Foundations of attack trees. In: Won, D.H., Kim, S. (eds.) ICISC 2005. LNCS, vol. 3935, pp. 186–198. Springer, Heidelberg (2006)
10. Mehta, V., Bartzis, C., Zhu, H., Clarke, E.: Ranking attack graphs. In: Zamboni, D., Kruegel, C. (eds.) RAID 2006. LNCS, vol. 4219, pp. 127–144. Springer, Heidelberg (2006)

11. N. Research and T. O. (RTO). Improving Common Security Risk Analysis. Technical report AC/323(ISP-049)TP/193, North Atlantic Treaty Organisation, University of California, Berkeley (2008)
12. Schneier, B.: Attack trees: modeling security threats. Dr. Dobb's J. **24**, 21–29 (1999)
13. Schultz, E.E.: Risks due to the convergence of physical security and information technology environments. Inf. Secur. Tech. Rep. **12**, 80–84 (2007)
14. Seamonster. http://sourceforge.net/apps/mediawiki/seamonster/
15. SecurITree. http://www.amenaza.com/
16. Sheyner, O., Haines, J., Jha, S., Lippman, R., Wing, J.: Automated generation and analysis of attack graphs. In: Proceedings of the 2002 IEEE Symposium on Security and Privacy, p. 273. IEEE Computer Society (2002)
17. Sheyner, O.: Tools for generating and analyzing attack graphs. In: de Boer, F.S., Bonsangue, M.M., Graf, S., de Roever, W.-P. (eds.) FMCO 2003. LNCS, vol. 3188, pp. 344–371. Springer, Heidelberg (2004)
18. Sheyner, O.M.: Scenario Graphs and Attack Graphs. Ph.D. thesis (2004)

On Generation of Context-Abstract Plans

Łukasz Mikulski[1](✉), Artur Niewiadomski[2], Marcin Piątkowski[1],
and Sebastian Smyczyński[3]

[1] Nicolaus Copernicus University, Chopina 12/18, 87-100 Toruń, Poland
lukasz.mikulski@mat.umk.pl
[2] Siedlce University, 3-Maja 54, 08-110 Siedlce, Poland
[3] Simplito Computer Science Lab, Królowej Jadwigi 7/2, 87-100 Toruń, Poland

Abstract. This paper deals with an intermediate phase of resolving
Web Service Composition Problem (WSCP) provided by PlanICS. The
abstract planner discovers a set of abstract plans for a WSCP instance.
The proposed algorithm utilizes the combinatorial structure of this set
and, abstracting from object attributes, browses the space of all potential
solutions taking into account only indistinguishable ones. Finally, the
reported results are validated by checking the attributes valuation and
presumed constraints.

1 Introduction

Following [6], the existing solutions of the Web Service Composition Problem
(WSCP) are mostly based on automata theory [11], situation calculus [2], Petri
nets [7], planning graphs [1], and model checking [16]. In the context of this paper
we consider other approaches to WSCP exploiting partial orders or combinatorial
algorithms.

Peer in [14] extends a Partial Ordering Planning (POP) by adding a set of
causal link patterns that must be avoided by the planner. In the combination
with the replanning algorithm, it is used to solve WSCP. Wang et al. in [18]
construct partial order plans from a pool of atomic services described in OWL-S.

Most of combinatorial approaches in the Web Service domain is related to
compositions based on Quality of Service. For example, Yu et al. in [19] model
WSCP as Multiple-Choice Knapsack Problem and present an algorithm which
maximizes the utility function satisfying the constraints, while Zou et al. in [5]
focus on WSCP in multi-cloud environment. Finally, Höfner et al. in [8] present
an algebraic structure of Web Services, assisting users in WS composition.

In this paper we follow the PlanICS [4] approach. One of its key ideas is to
divide the composition process into several stages. The first phase, called *abstract
planning*, deals with *classes of services*, where each class represents a set of real-
world services, while the second works in the space of *concrete services*. The first
stage produces an *abstract plan*, which becomes a *concrete plan* in the second
phase. It reduces dramatically the number of concrete services to be considered.

This research was supported by the National Science Center under the grants No.
2011/01/B/ST6/01477 and No. 2013/09/D/ST6/03928.

The main goal of the abstract planning phase is to find a number of abstract plans that potentially satisfy a *user query*. Our planners [12,15] deal with this problem by finding plans composed of the same service types that belong to different equivalence classes. From the efficiency point of view, the number of such classes can be exponentially smaller than the number of plans. Each equivalence class is defined by a multiset of service specifications (Fig. 1).

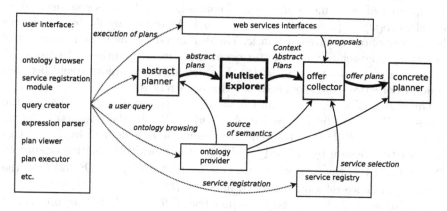

Fig. 1. PlanICS architecture

This paper focuses on the next step of the planning process, which consists in processing the multisets of service types obtained from abstract planners. The module addressing this issue is called Multiset Explorer. Our goal is to generate all significantly different *Context Abstract Plans* (CAPs) composed of the service types from the explored multiset that belong to different partial orders and the difference between utilized objects is more complex than a simple inheritance extension. The motivation behind this consists in the fact that, typically, we would like to have a large selection of plans at our disposal, but we do not want to distinguish between plans, which differ only in the ordering of their context independent services. This observation is strongly related to the original concept of Mazurkiewicz traces [9] – the sets of indistinguishable executions of sequences of partially ordered actions. In this paper we adapt the notion of traces to cut the set of all context-abstract plans.

The rest of the paper is structured as follows. We start with presenting some basic notions which are used in further considerations. In the next section, we build a bridge between assumptions and notations used in PlanICS system and our algorithm. It is followed by the main contribution of the paper – the results of our studies on the combinatorial structure of context-abstract plans. In the subsequent section we utilize this to develop an algorithm solving the problem of searching for the solutions overlooked by the abstract planner. The paper is summarized by short sections containing results of experiments and conclusions.

2   Basic Notions

Throughout the paper we use the standard notions of Set and Formal Languages Theories. In this section we recall the most important definitions.

By an *alphabet* we mean a nonempty finite set Σ, the elements of which are called *letters*. Finite sequences over Σ are called *words*. The set of all words (including the empty word ε) is denoted by Σ^*. Let $w = a_1 \ldots a_n$ be a word. By the alphabet of w we mean $alp(w) \subseteq \Sigma$ consisting of all letters contained in w. Namely, $alp(w) = \{a \in \Sigma \mid \exists_{0 < i \leq n}\ a = a_i\}$. Moreover, by $\#_w(a)$ we denote the number of occurrences of a in w. We also introduce the notion of the *letter occurrence*. The set $occ(w)$ of letter occurrences in w comprises all pairs $\langle a, i \rangle$ with $a \in alp(w)$ and $1 \leq i \leq \#_w(a)$. In what follows we move freely between sequences of letters and sequences of letter occurrences.

Given $R \subseteq X \times X$, $R^0 = \mathbb{I}$ and $R^n = R^{n-1} \circ R$, for all $n \geq 1$. Then (i) the inverse of R is given by $R^{-1} = \{\langle a, b \rangle \mid \langle b, a \rangle \in R\}$; (ii) the symmetric closure by $R^{sym} = R \cup R^{-1}$; (iii) the reflexive closure of R is defined by $R \cup \mathbb{I}$; (iv) the transitive closure by $R^+ = \bigcup_{i \geq 1} R^i$; (v) the reflexive transitive closure by $R^* = \mathbb{I} \cup R^+$; (vi) the transitive reduction by $R^{red} = \bigcap_{Q^* = R^*} Q$; and (vii) the largest equivalence relation contained in R^* by $R^{\circledast} = R^* \cap (R^*)^{-1}$.

A relation $R \subseteq X \times X$ is: (i) symmetric if $R = R^{-1}$; (ii) asymmetric if $R \cap R^{-1} \subseteq \mathbb{I}$; (iii) reflexive if $\mathbb{I} \subseteq R$; (iv) irreflexive if $\mathbb{I} \cap R = \emptyset$; (v) transitive if $R \circ R \subseteq R$; and (vi) total if $R \cup R^{-1} = X \times X$; (vii) equivalence relation if it is symmetric, transitive and reflexive. A set of all equivalence classes of R is denoted by $^X/_R$. An equivalence class containing an element $x \in X$ is denoted by $[x]_R$, or simply by $[x]$ if R is clear from the context.

A relation $R \subseteq X \times X$ is (i) a *(weak) partial order* if it is asymmetric, reflexive and transitive; (ii) a *strict partial order* if it is irreflexive and $R \cup \mathbb{I}$ is a weak partial order. A pair $PS = \langle X, R \rangle$ is a *(strict) partially ordered set* (*poset* in short). A (strict) poset $PS = \langle X, R \rangle$ is called *well-founded* if there is no infinite sequence $\langle x_1, x_2, \ldots \rangle$ of distinct elements from X such that $\langle x_{i+1}, x_i \rangle \in R$.

Let $R \subseteq X \times X$ be a partial order. $F \subseteq X$ is called a *filter* if (i) $F \neq \emptyset$, (ii) $x \in F$ and $\langle x, y \rangle \in R$ implies $y \in F$, and (iii) $x, y \in F$ implies existence of $z \in F$ such that $\langle z, x \rangle \in R$ and $\langle z, y \rangle \in R$. A filter F is *principal* if there exists a minimal element $x \in F$ (called the *principal element*). Note that if poset is well-founded, all its filters are principal.

A *concurrent alphabet* is a pair $\Psi = \langle \Sigma, dep \rangle$, where Σ is an alphabet and $dep \subseteq \Sigma \times \Sigma$ is a reflexive and symmetric dependence relation. The corresponding independence relation is given by $ind = (\Sigma \times \Sigma) \setminus dep$. Ψ defines an equivalence relation $\equiv_\Psi$ identifying words which differ only by the order of independent letters. Equivalence classes of $\equiv_\Psi$ are called *Mazurkiewicz traces*.

With every word $w = a_1 \ldots a_n$ we can associate a strict poset $\langle occ(w), \sqsubset_w \rangle$ induced by the dependence relation over occurrence labels. The relation $\sqsubset_w$ is defined as the transitive closure of the relation consisting of all pairs $\langle a_i, a_j \rangle$ such that $\langle a_i, a_j \rangle \in dep$ and $i < j$. Since an induced poset is a constitutive invariant of a trace, we lift this notion to the level of traces (see [10]).

We emphasize the special case of traces over concurrent alphabets with $dep = \mathbb{I}$. In this case the only important information constituting a trace are the numbers of letters contained in it. This gives a natural correspondence with multisets over Σ and a trace $[w]$ is usually called the *Parikh vector* (of a word w).

Let X be a finite nonempty set. The relational structure over X is a triple $\langle X, ME, SO \rangle$, where (i) $ME \subseteq X \times X$ is a symmetric and irreflexive relation called *mutual exclusion*, and (ii) $SO \subseteq ME$ is an asymmetric and irreflexive relation called *skeleton order*. A relational structure $S = \langle X, ME, SO \rangle$ is *separable* if $SO^{\circledast} = \mathbb{I}$. A strict partial order $PO \subseteq X \times X$ is consistent with a relational structure $RS = \langle X, ME, SO \rangle$ if $SO \subseteq PO$ and $PO^{red} \subseteq ME \subseteq PO^{sym}$. It is easy to prove that for a given relational structure $S = (X, ME, SO)$ there exists a partial order PO consistent with it if and only if S is separable.

Let $RS_1 = \langle X_1, ME_1, SO_1 \rangle$ and $RS_2 = \langle X_2, ME_2, SO_2 \rangle$ be relational structures. We say that RS_1 is equivalent by $rsm : X_1 \to X_2$ to RS_2 (denoted by $RS_1 \equiv_{rsm} RS_2$) if rsm is a bijective function such that $\langle x_1, x_2 \rangle \in ME_1$ iff $\langle rsm(x_1), rsm(x_2) \rangle \in ME_2$, and $\langle x_1, x_2 \rangle \in SO_1$ iff $\langle rsm(x_1), rsm(x_2) \rangle \in SO_2$. We say that RS_1 is equivalent to RS_2 (denoted by $RS_1 \equiv RS_2$) if there exists a function rsm such that $RS_1 \equiv_{rsm} RS_2$.

3 PlanICS Specification

The OWL language [13] is used as the PlanICS ontology format. The concepts are organized in an inheritance tree of *classes*, all derived from the base class, called *Thing*. There are three descendants of *Thing*: *Artifact*, *Stamp* and *Service*.

The branch of classes rooted at *Artifact* is composed of the object types, which the services operate on. The *Stamp* class and its descendants define special-purpose objects, often useful in constructing a user query. Classes derived from *Artifact* and *Stamp* are called the *object types*. Each class derived from *Service*, called the *service type*, stands for a description of a set of real-world services. It contains a formalized information about their activities. A service affects a set of objects (*world before*), and transforms it into a new set of objects (*world after*).

In this section we provide all definitions necessary to formalize the problem of generating CAPs from a multiset. As we operate on types of objects only, in what follows we abstract from the object attributes and stamps. The validation of the found CAP (taking into account object attributes and stamps) is done at the very end. It is realized by calling the external PlanICS library function.

Types and Objects. Let O, P be nonempty sets of objects and object types, respectively. Over the set P we define a binary *inheritance relation* $Ext \subseteq P \times P$ which is transitive and irreflexive (hence also asymmetric and acyclic). Semantically $\langle p_2, p_1 \rangle \in Ext$ means that the type p_2 is extended by the type p_1 (i.e. p_1 is the subtype of p_2). Moreover, we assume that for any triple of types $p_1, p_2, p_3 \in P$ we have that $\langle p_2, p_1 \rangle \in Ext$ and $\langle p_3, p_1 \rangle \in Ext$ implies $p_2 = p_3$ or $\langle p_2, p_3 \rangle \in Ext$ or $\langle p_3, p_2 \rangle \in Ext$ (hence multiple inheritance is excluded). In the complete PlanICS semantics, two types are in the relation Ext if the set of attributes of p_2 is a subset of the set of attributes of p_1.

By an object we mean a labelled instance of a type, namely a pair $\langle id, t \rangle$, where $t \in P$ and id is a unique object identifier. Following [4] we define a function $type : O \rightarrow P$ such that $type(\langle id, t \rangle) = t$. In the context of the system state, the finite set of objects is called a *world*. The set of all worlds is denoted by $\mathbb{W}$.

For a technical reason we define a function $obj : O^{\mathbb{N}} \rightarrow 2^O$ which assigns to every finite sequence of objects the set of objects that are elements of this sequence. We extend this function to the sets of sequences of objects, sequences of sequences of objects, functions with a set of sequences as a codomain and so on. Intuitively, $obj(A)$ means the set of all objects somehow "occurring" in A. We use similar constructions for all maps that transform sets of objects.

Let $X, Y \subseteq O$ and $A \subseteq X$ be sets of objects. We say that $map : X \rightarrow Y$ is *A-invariant* if restricted to A it is an identity function.

Services and Their Specifications. An abstract service specification is a quadruple $spec = \langle name, in, inout, out \rangle$, where in, out and $inout$ are multisets of object types, while $name$ is a service name. Semantically, in is the multiset of types of read-only objects, $inout$ is the multiset of types of objects whose state may be changed, while out is the multiset of types of newly created objects. We also assume that $inout$ and out multisets may not be simultaneously empty. The set of all service specifications is denoted by $\mathbb{S}$.

For a multiset of object types we define a (partial) *context function* $ctx : \mathbb{N}^P \rightarrow (O^{\mathbb{N}})^P$, namely a function that to a given multiset M of types assigns sequences of objects. For $p \in P$ we have $ctx(M)(p)(i) = o_i^p$, for $1 \leq i \leq M(p)$, and undefined otherwise. For every defined value of $ctx(M)(p)(i)$ we require that $\langle p, type(o_i^p) \rangle \in Ext$ (i.e. to p we assign a sequence of objects which types are subtypes of p). Moreover, for $i, j \leq M(p)$ we assume that $i \neq j$ implies $o_i^p \neq o_j^p$. We extend the definition of ctx to the case of service specifications assigning to $spec = \langle name, in, inout, out \rangle$ a quadruple $\langle name, IN, IO, OU \rangle$, where $IN = ctx(in)$, $IO = ctx(inout)$ and $OU = ctx(out)$. We require that the sets $obj(IN)$, $obj(IO)$ and $obj(OU)$ are pairwise disjoint. The specified instance of a service specification is simply called a *service*. The set of all services is denoted by $\bar{\mathbb{S}}$.

We also define an *abstraction function* $abs : \bar{\mathbb{S}} \rightarrow \mathbb{S}$, complementary to the context function ctx. For a given service $\bar{s} = \langle name, IN, IO, OU \rangle$ it returns its specification $spec = \langle name, in, inout, out \rangle$, where for every $p \in P$ $in(p) = |obj(IN(p))|$, $inout(p) = |obj(IO(p))|$, and $out(p) = |obj(OU(p))|$. As the same service (with the same specification) may occur many times in a transformation sequence, we use the notion of a *service occurrence*.

A service $\langle name, IN, IO, OU \rangle$ may be used to transform a world w_1 into the world $w_2 = w_1 \cup obj(OU)$ if $obj(IN) \cup obj(IO) \subseteq w_1$ and $obj(OU) \cap w_1 = \emptyset$, which means that the difference between w_1 and w_2 is precisely the set of newly created objects. This formalizes the assumption that function ctx assigns globally new and unique names to newly created objects. We extend the transforming operation to sequences of services in a natural way.

Let w_1, $w_2 \in \mathbb{W}$ be sets of objects. We say that w_1 is *compatible by map* (or simply *compatible*) with w_2 if $map : w_1 \rightarrow w_2$ is a bijective function such that

$\forall_{o \in w_1} \langle type(o), type(map(o)) \rangle \in Ext$. We say that w_1 is *subcompatible* with w_2 if there exists a set of objects $w_3 \subseteq w_2$ such that w_1 is compatible with w_3.

User Queries. In the approach presented in [4] user query specification has the same structure as a service specification. The core of the user query is a triple of multisets of types $qs = \langle in_q, inout_q, out_q \rangle$. The interpretation of qs is a pair $q = \langle W_{init}, W_{exp} \rangle$, where W_{init} and W_{exp} are sets of worlds called the *initial worlds* and the *expected worlds*, respectively. Since we disregard attributes, W_{init} and W_{exp} became singletons w_{init} and w_{exp}, which have to be consistent with qs, namely $w_{init} = obj(ctx(in_q) \cup ctx(inout_q))$ and $w_{exp} = obj(ctx(in_q) \cup ctx(inout_q) \cup ctx(out_q))$.

Let $q = \langle w_{init}, w_{exp} \rangle$ be a user query. We say that a transformation sequence $\vec{s}$ satisfies q if $\vec{s}$ transforms a world w_{init} into a world w_{fin} and w_{exp} is subcompatible with w_{fin}. The definition of subcompatibility is existential, and matching map used in it may be not unique and each of appropriate substitutions is interesting in terms of the full solution. We have to distinguish between two solutions obtained by two different matchings. Hence, a transformation sequence $\vec{s}$ satisfies the user query $q = \langle w_{init}, w_{exp} \rangle$ by $map : w_{exp} \rightarrow w_{fin}$ if $\vec{s}$ transforms w_{init} into w_{fin} and $\forall_{o \in w_{exp}} \langle type(o), type(map(o)) \rangle \in Ext$.

A solution is presented as a *transformation sequence* $\vec{s}$, namely a sequence of services, which transforms w_{init} into w_{fin}. We denote the set of all transformation sequences which start in w_{init} by $\vec{S}$. Note that all objects used by services contained in $\vec{s}$ must be present in w_{init} or be created before their first use.

4 Partitioning the Solution Domain

In the presented approach, the set of all possible transformation sequences is the solution domain. In this section we discuss the concept of grouping them into sets of indistinguishable solutions. The main idea of this partitioning of the solution domain is depicted on Fig. 2. The components presented there are described in detail in the rest of this section. We fix the user query $q = \langle w_{init}, w_{exp} \rangle$, hence the set $\vec{S}$ of transformation sequences starting from w_{init} is also fixed.

We start from defining two independent notions of indistinguishability of transformation sequences. Their sources are the partial (not total) ordering of concurrent computations leading to the same result and the inheritance relation, which causes the multiplication of a single solution by replacing intermediate objects by their extended substitutes.

Order Indistinguishability. The first identification is based on the theory of Mazurkiewicz traces. It requires the proper definition of a dependence relation on services contained in a given transformation sequence. Let $\bar{s}, \bar{t}$ be services and w_1 is transformed by $\bar{s}\bar{t}$ into w_2. If $\bar{s}$ and $\bar{t}$ operate on disjoint sets of objects the order of their execution does not matter and so w_1 is transformed into w_2 also by $\bar{t}\bar{s}$. We observe the same behaviour when the objects shared by distinct services $\bar{s}$ and $\bar{t}$ are accessed in read-only mode. In both situations mentioned above, it is safe to assume that $\bar{s}\bar{t}$ and $\bar{t}\bar{s}$ leads to the same change of the values of objects

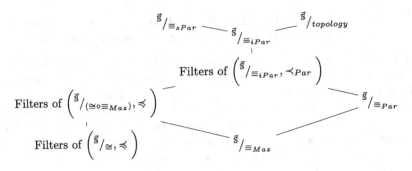

Fig. 2. The partitions of the solution domain.

attributes. This assumption in all other situations is unjustified. Without taking into account the impact of changes made on the values of object attributes it is impossible to determine whether we can harmlessly change the order of $\vec{s}$ and $\vec{t}$.

Formally, let dep be a dependence relation defined as specified above. Then $Maz = \langle \vec{S}, dep \rangle$ is a concurrent alphabet and $\equiv_{Maz} \subseteq \vec{S} \times \vec{S}$ is an equivalence relation. Being a valid transformation sequence is an invariant for equivalence classes of the relation $\equiv_{Maz}$.

Proposition 1. *Let $\vec{s}$, $\vec{t} \in \vec{S}$. If $\vec{s} \equiv_{Maz} \vec{t}$ and $\vec{s}$ satisfies a user query q by map then $\vec{t}$ satisfies q by map.*

Filter Indistinguishability. The source of redundant valid solutions is also the freedom in choosing names of intermediate objects. We say that transformation sequences $\vec{s}$ and $\vec{t}$ are indistinguishable if $\vec{s}$ arises from $\vec{t}$ by one-to-one changing of the object names; we denote it by $\vec{s} \cong \vec{t}$. In such a case we shall report at most one transformation sequence. If $\vec{s}$ differs from $\vec{t}$ not only by objects names but also objects types (with the inheritance preservation) we shall report the more general one only. It leads to the definition of the inheritance relation over transformation sequences.

Let $\vec{s}$ and $\vec{t}$ be transformation sequences. We say that $\vec{s}$ is extended by $\vec{t}$ (or $\vec{t}$ inherits from $\vec{s}$) if $obj(\vec{s})$ is compatible by a inh with $obj(\vec{t})$. Recall that formally it means that $\forall_{o \in obj(\vec{s})} \langle type(o), type(inh(o)) \rangle \in Ext$. We denote it by $\vec{s} \preceq \vec{t}$.

Fact 1. *Let $\vec{s}$, $\vec{t}$, $\vec{u}$ be three transformation sequences. Then (i) if $\vec{s} \preceq \vec{t}$ and $\vec{t} \preceq \vec{u}$ then $\vec{s} \preceq \vec{u}$ (relation $\preceq$ is transitive), (ii) if $\vec{s} \cong \vec{t}$ then $\vec{s} \preceq \vec{t}$, and (iii) if $\vec{s} \preceq \vec{t}$ and $\vec{t} \preceq \vec{s}$ then $\vec{s} \cong \vec{t}$. Hence the relation $\cong \subseteq \vec{S} \times \vec{S}$ is an equivalence relation.*

The above fact justify quotienting the set $\vec{S}$ by the relation $\cong$ and extending $\preceq$ to the case of equivalence classes of $\vec{S}/_{\cong}$ (we keep the notation $\preceq$). The structure of $\vec{S}/_{\cong}$ helps in reporting only essential transformation sequences that satisfy user query. Namely, the following hold:

Proposition 2. *Let $\vec{s}, \vec{t}$ be two transformation sequences. If $\vec{s} \cong \vec{t}$ and $\vec{s}$ satisfies user query q then $\vec{t}$ satisfies user query q.*

Theorem 1. *Let $F \subseteq \vec{\mathbb{S}}/_{\cong}$ be a filter with a principal element $[\vec{s}]$. If $\vec{s}$ satisfies user query q then for all $[t] \in F$, t satisfy user query q.*

The two methods of clustering indistinguishable solutions presented above can be combined. As a result we obtain filters of traces (or traces of filters if we look from the opposite direction). We summarize this facts by the theorem, which is one of the central points of the presented solution.

Theorem 2. *Let $\vec{s}, \vec{t} \in \vec{\mathbb{S}}$ be transformation sequences.*

(i) *Let $\vec{u} \in \vec{\mathbb{S}}$ be such that $\vec{u} \equiv_{Maz} \vec{s}$. If $\vec{s}$ is extended by $\vec{t}$ then there exists $\vec{v} \in \vec{\mathbb{S}}$ such that $\vec{v} \equiv_{Maz} \vec{t}$ and $\vec{u}$ is extended by $\vec{v}$.*

(ii) *Let $\vec{v} \in \vec{\mathbb{S}}$ be such that $\vec{v} \equiv_{Maz} \vec{t}$. If $\vec{s}$ is extended by $\vec{t}$ then there exists $\vec{u} \in \vec{\mathbb{S}}$ such that $\vec{u} \equiv_{Maz} \vec{s}$ and $\vec{u}$ is extended by $\vec{v}$.*

Abstract Partitions of $\vec{\mathbb{S}}$. In the process of browsing all classes of indistinguishable solutions we utilize more abstract partitions of the set of all transformation sequences. We pay attention to maintain compliance with expected form of results. In other words, we do not want to partition any filters of traces.

As a first coarse cut we present an abstract topology which can be seen as a specification for traces. By an abstract topology we mean relations between single service occurrences, which are determined by their common objects. In contrast to traces, we would like to leave as much flexibility as possible (indicating the dependence between two services but leaving their order unspecified).

Formally, we utilize relational structures. We define mutual exclusion relation $ME_{\vec{s}}$ identical as dependence in the case of traces. Two occurrences of services $\langle \bar{x}, i \rangle$ and $\langle \bar{y}, j \rangle$ are in $ME_{\vec{s}}$ if $\bar{x} = \bar{y}$ or $(obj(\bar{x}) \cap obj(\bar{y})) \neq (obj(IN_{\bar{x}}) \cap obj(IN_{\bar{y}}))$. On the other hand, we specify the order on service occurrences only if it is invariant for all transformation sequences containing the same sets of occurrences. Namely, two occurrences of services $(\bar{x}, i)$ and $(\bar{y}, j)$ are in $SO_{\vec{s}}$ if $\bar{x} = \bar{y}$ and $i < j$ or $obj(OUT_{\bar{x}}) \cap obj(\bar{y}) \neq \emptyset$. Note that $SO_{\vec{s}} \subsetneq ME_{\vec{s}}$ and all other conditions (e.g. irreflexivity of $ME_{\vec{s}}$ and $SO_{\vec{s}}$) are satisfied.

Proposition 3. *Let $\vec{s}$ and $\vec{t}$ be transformation sequences. If $\vec{s}$ is extended by $\vec{t}$ or $\vec{s} \equiv_{Maz} \vec{t}$ then $\vec{s}$ and $\vec{t}$ (hence a single reported result) have the same topology.*

The second coarse cut is based on the Parikh vectors of service specifications. It is utilized in [4] where a single valid solution found inside a class causes its exclusion from the further search. Therefore, the cut presented below is very important and embeds Multiset Explorer inside the PlanICS project. The algorithm presented in this paper describes a method of browsing such single class.

Two transformation sequences $\vec{s}$ and $\vec{t}$ are *Parikh specification-equivalent* if the abstractions of their alphabets are equal (denoted as $\vec{s} \equiv_{sPar} \vec{t}$). The relation $\equiv_{sPar}$ is reflexive, symmetric and transitive, hence it is an equivalence relation and we can quotient $\vec{\mathbb{S}}$ by $\equiv_{sPar}$. The obtained equivalence classes are precisely the sets of transformation sequences skipped by the approach from [4] (which may oversight some nontrivially distinct solutions). In what follows we consider only a single equivalence class from $\vec{\mathbb{S}}/_{\equiv_{sPar}}$ and search it for other possible solutions. Hereby, the procedure of browsing all solutions became complete.

Proposition 4. *Let* $\vec{s}, \vec{t} \in \mathbb{S}$. *If* $\vec{s} \equiv_{sPar} \vec{t}$ *then* $|obj(\vec{s})| = |obj(\vec{t})|$.

Parikh Equivalence. To support the last level of partition, we present the context version of Parikh equivalence, based on the inheritance relation (instead of service specification only).

Two transformation sequences $\vec{s}$ and $\vec{t}$ are Parikh equivalent if their topology is not only the same but also implied in the same way by corresponding sets of objects. To formalize that, we first define *Parikh compatibility* of two transformation sequences. We say that $\vec{s}$ is Parikh compatible by *pmap* with $\vec{t}$ if $obj(\vec{s})$ is compatible by w_{init}-invariant *pmap* with $obj(\vec{t})$ and $occ(\vec{t}) = pmap(occ(\vec{s}))$. We denote it by $\vec{s} \prec_{Par}^{pmap} \vec{t}$ (or $\vec{s} \prec_{Par} \vec{t}$ if *pmap* is not important).

Now we introduce *Parikh equivalence* of $\vec{s}, \vec{t} \in \mathbb{S}$ as their simultaneous Parikh compatibility (denote by $\vec{s} \equiv_{Par} \vec{t}$). We also define *Parikh inheritance-equivalence* of $\vec{s}$ and $\vec{t}$ as an existence of $\vec{u}$ Parikh compatible with both $\vec{s}$ and $\vec{t}$ (denoted by $\vec{s} \equiv_{iPar} \vec{t}$). Both $\equiv_{Par}$ and $\equiv_{iPar}$ are equivalence relations. The elements of $\mathbb{S}/_{\equiv_{iPar}}$ and $\mathbb{S}/_{\equiv_{Par}}$ are called *process templates* and *processes* respectively.

The elements of $\mathbb{S}/_{\equiv_{iPar}}$ are fully compatible with all previously presented partitionings. Each process template is completely contained both in classes of $\equiv_{sPar}$ and classes of transformation sequences with the same topology. Every filter, trace and process is completely contained in a process template. The following theorem is crucial from the point of view of our algorithm correctness.

Theorem 3. *Let* $\vec{s}$ *and* $\vec{t}$ *be transformation sequences.*

(i) *If* $\vec{s} \equiv_{iPar} \vec{t}$ *then* $\vec{s} \equiv_{sPar} \vec{t}$, *and* $\vec{s}$ *and* $\vec{t}$ *have the same topology.*
(ii) *If* $\vec{s} \equiv_{Par} \vec{t}$ *or* $\vec{s} \equiv_{Maz} \vec{t}$ *then* $\vec{s} \equiv_{iPar} \vec{t}$.
(iii) *If* $\vec{s}$ *is extended by* $\vec{t}$ *then* $\vec{s} \equiv_{Par} \vec{t}$.

We utilize Parikh compatibility to equip process templates with the algebraic structure. According to Theorem 3, each process template decomposes into processes. The following facts allows to extend the notion of Parikh compatibility to processes and to define a poset on process templates seen as sets of processes.

Proposition 5. *Let* p *and* q *be two processes minimal in the sense of* $\prec_{Par}$. *If* p *and* q *belong to the same process template then* $p = q$.

Finally, we take into account the expected world w_{exp} and matchings between w_{exp} and w_{fin} separating distinguishable solutions. Each solution we are interested in has a form of a filter of traces and is totally contained in a process template (see Theorem 3). It remains to show that relations $\preccurlyeq$ and $\prec_{Par}$ are consistent. We show that each matching identifies a single filter of processes inside a process template which decomposes to the set of expected results.

Proposition 6. *Let* $\vec{s}, \vec{t} \in \mathbb{S}$. *If* $\vec{s} \preccurlyeq \vec{t}$ *then* $[\vec{s}]_{\equiv_{Par}} \prec_{Par} [\vec{t}]_{\equiv_{Par}}$, *while if* $\vec{s}$ *satisfies user query* q *by map and* $\vec{s} \prec_{Par}^{pmap} \vec{t}$ *then* $\vec{t}$ *satisfies* q *by pmap* $\circ$ *map.*

Theorem 4. *Let* $\vec{s}, \vec{t}, \vec{u} \in \mathbb{S}$ *be such that* $\vec{u} \prec_{Par}^{pm_1} \vec{s}$ *and* $\vec{u} \prec_{Par}^{pm_2} \vec{t}$, *and* $\vec{s}$ *satisfies user query* q *by map. If* $\vec{t}$ *satisfies* q *by pmap*$_2 \circ pm_1^{-1} \circ$ *map then there exists* $\vec{v} \in \mathbb{S}$ *such that* $\vec{v} \prec_{Par}^{pm_3} \vec{s}$ *and* $\vec{v} \prec_{Par}^{pm_4} \vec{t}$ *and* $\vec{v}$ *satisfies* q *by pm*$_3^{-1} \circ$ *map.*

5   Algorithm

The main goal of the procedure developed in this paper is to browse all transformation sequences that satisfy a given user query and have the same Parikh vector of service specifications. We present a module Multiset Explorer utilizing the notions presented heretofore. As an input we take the object types from the ontology, the user query $q = (w_{init}, w_{exp})$, and a multiset of service names.

Algorithm 1. Multiset Explorer

Input: A CAP cp (context abstract plan)
Output: List of CAPs equivalent with cp
1 Initialize a class scp of $\equiv_{sPar}$ with cp;
2 **foreach** *each process template tp* **do**
3   Construct bipartite graph G using $obj(tp)$ and w_{exp};
4   **foreach** *process p* **do**
5   Use the topology to construct a dependence relation dep;
6   **foreach** *trace $\tau(p, dep)$* **do**
7   report $minlex(\tau)$;

Having an element of $\vec{\mathbb{S}}/_{\equiv_{sPar}}$ fixed, we start the partitioning by determining a single representative for each subclass. In the first step we divide $\vec{\mathbb{S}}$ into process templates. The chosen representatives are $\prec_{Par}$-maximal. Next we fix the names of the objects produced by the provided services O_{OU} (the objects from OU's) and we determine the most abstract types which they may have. We use those objects, together with w_{init}, to fill all IN's and IO's of provided services respecting the type inheritance (and updating the types of objects from O_{OU}).

Having the single process template T we take one of its maximal element $\vec{s}$ and w_{init}-invariant matching map of w_{exp} with $obj(\vec{s})$ which can be realized for one of the elements of T (as in Theorem 4). For each such matching we compute a filter of processes. Those filters contain transformation sequences which completely cover the set of context-abstract plans satisfying user query. To browse all fitting w_{init} invariant matchings which guaranties subcompatibility with w_{exp} we construct bipartite graph G between objects from $w_{fin} \setminus w_{init}$ produced by the chosen representative and $w_{exp} \setminus w_{init}$. There is an edge E between $o_1 \in w_{fin}$ and $o_2 \in w_{exp}$ if $(type(o_1), type(o_2)) \in Exp$ or $(type(o_2), type(o_1)) \in Exp$. We enumerate all maximal matching in the constructed graph using the algorithm based on [17].

We make some final cuts in the obtained filters of processes FP to report the solution in the assumed form. We start by computing the relational structure RS (topology) which is common (by Theorem 3) for all transformation sequences from FP. Finally, we compute all traces over achieved from RS concurrent alphabet. They induce strict partial orders consistent with RS. We utilize an algorithm from [10] generating all traces with a given Parikh vector and dispose those, which are not consistent with RS. Every obtained transformation sequence (the principal element of a filter of traces) satisfies user query (in a context-abstract sense) and is a final result of Multiset Explorer. The reported results are a subject of further verification made by the external procedure provided in PlanICS which validates them by attributes valuation.

Experimental Results

We implemented Multiset Explorer as a standalone application and made some tests using data randomly generated by Ontology Generator provided by PlanICS.

The experiments have been performed on a computer equipped with 32 GB RAM and 4-core Intel Xeon 2.9 GHz CPU running CentOS 6.5 system. We used SMT solver Z3 [3] as an external procedure called by Abstract Planner. In all experiments we first search for context-abstract plans using Abstract Planner and SMT solver Z3. We fix the maximal number of reported CAPs to 100. Then we make use of all of those CAPs to explore the space of transition sequences Parikh specification-equivalent with solutions found in the first phase.

Table 1. Experiments. In subsequent columns we put a case name, length of solutions we search for, minimal length of existing solution, number of CAPs (at most 100) found by AP and all equivalent with them CAPs founded by Multiset Explorer.

File	dpt	min	AP + Z3 CAPs	AP + Z3 sec.	ME CAPs	ME sec.
nn	5	5	10	22.6	10	1.7
nn	7	5	100	97.7	503	104.2
box	5	4	9	3.7	85760	6.8
box	6	4	25	9.6	2938662	245.2
ont5	5	5	11	18.0	11	1.0
ont5	6	5	100	39.4	200	2.8

file	dpt	min	AP + Z3 CAPs	AP + Z3 sec.	ME CAPs	ME sec.
ont10	11	8	100	293.4	204	23.0
ont10	12	8	100	452.9	275	58.7
ont10	13	8	100	556.7	370	177.0
ont15	11	11	2	285.9	2	6.8
ont15	12	11	100	285.1	134	639.3
ont15	13	11	100	305.1	383	2543.6

The results listed in Table 1 allows to conclude that for solutions of minimal length, Multiset Explorer only confirms their uniqueness. This phenomenon may be caused by the implementation of Ontology Generator. For longer solutions, there are additional distinguishable context abstract plans reported by Multiset Explorer. Their numbers significantly depends on processed ontology. The main reason of noticed blowup is probably the large number of degrees of freedom in choosing additional services and objects which are not used in the creation of expected world. In the case of confirmatory behaviour of Multiset Explorer, the computation times are significantly better than the times of original procedures.

6   Conclusions

The main contribution of the paper is the partitioning of the solution domain for the WSCP. It is used in the presented Multiset Explorer (ME) – a module of PlanICS. ME fills the gap left by abstract planning, i.e., the first stage of resolving WSCP.

To join indistinguishable service sequences into equivalence classes we use the notion of traces. ME utilizes an efficient algorithm for enumeration of all traces with a given Parikh vector (see [10]). This algorithm generates additional traces without any interpretation in WSCP. Improving this part of the module by its full adaptation is one of the straightforward future plans.

Multiset Explorer is intended to be the middle part of PlanICS. The input is taken from abstract planner, while the results are passed to the external validator. Performed tests show that ME has possibilities and limitations comparable to those of Abstract Planner. While at the moment ME is a standalone application, we work on incorporating it into the PlanICS system. As a first step of this integration we have implemented wrappers allowing exchange of data between Abstract Planner and Multiset Explorer.

References

1. Blum, A.L., Furst, M.L.: Fast planning through planning graph analysis. Artif. Intell. **90**(1), 1636–1642 (1995)
2. Chifu, V.R., Salomie, I., St. Chifu, E.: Fluent calculus-based web service composition - from owl-s to fluent calculus. In: ICCP 2008, pp. 161–168 (2008)
3. de Moura, L., Bjørner, N.: Z3: an efficient SMT solver. In: Ramakrishnan, C.R., Rehof, J. (eds.) TACAS 2008. LNCS, vol. 4963, pp. 337–340. Springer, Heidelberg (2008)
4. Doliwa, D., et al.: PlanICS - a web service compositon toolset. Fundam. Inform. **112**(1), 47–71 (2011)
5. Zou, G., et al.: AI planning and combinatorial optimization for web service composition in cloud computing. In: CCV 2010, pp. 1–8 (2010)
6. Li, Z., et al.: Effort-oriented classification matrix of web service composition. In: ICIV 2010, pp. 357–362 (2010)
7. Gehlot, V., Edupuganti, K.: Use of colored petri nets to model, analyze, and evaluate service composition and orchestration. In: HICSS 2009, pp. 1–8 (2009)
8. Höfner, P., Lautenbacher, F.: Algebraic structure of web services. Electron. Notes Theoret. Comput. Sci. **200**(3), 171–187 (2008)
9. Mazurkiewicz, A.: Concurrent program schemes and their interpretations. DAIMI Report PB-78, Aarhus University (1977)
10. Mikulski, Ł., Piątkowski, M., Smyczyński, S.: Algorithmics of posets generated by words over partially commutative alphabets (extended). Sci. Ann. Comp. Sci. **23**(2), 229–249 (2013)
11. Mitra, S., Kumar, R., Basu, S.: Automated choreographer synthesis for web services composition using I/O automata. In: ICWS 2007, pp. 364–371 (2007)
12. Niewiadomski, A., Penczek, W.: Towards SMT-based abstract planning in PlanICS ontology. In: KEOD 2013, pp. 123–131 (2013)
13. OWL 2 web ontology language document overview (2009). http://www.w3.org/TR/owl2-overwiew/
14. Peer, J.: A POP-based replanning agent for automatic web service composition. In: Gómez-Pérez, A., Euzenat, J. (eds.) ESWC 2005. LNCS, vol. 3532, pp. 47–61. Springer, Heidelberg (2005)

15. Skaruz, J., Niewiadomski, A., Penczek, W.: Automated abstract planning with use of genetic algorithms. In: GECCO 2013, pp. 129–130 (2013)
16. Traverso, P., Pistore, M.: Automated composition of semantic web services into executable processes. In: McIlraith, S.A., Plexousakis, D., van Harmelen, F. (eds.) ISWC 2004. LNCS, vol. 3298, pp. 380–394. Springer, Heidelberg (2004)
17. Uno, T.: Algorithms for enumerating all perfect, maximum and maximal matchings in bipartite graphs. In: Leong, H.-V., Jain, S., Imai, H. (eds.) ISAAC 1997. LNCS, vol. 1350, pp. 92–101. Springer, Heidelberg (1997)
18. Wang, B., Haller, A., Rosenberg, F.: Generating workflow models from owl-s service descriptions with a partial-order plan construction. In: ICWS 2011, pp. 714–715 (2011)
19. Yu, T., Lin, K.-J.: Service selection algorithms for web services with end-to-end qos constraints. In: CEC 2004, pp. 129–136. IEEE (2004)

A Coloured Petri Net Approach to Model and Analyse Stateful Workflows Based on WS-BPEL and WSRF

José Antonio Mateo, Valentín Valero, Hermenegilda Macià,
and Gregorio Díaz[✉]

University of Castilla-La Mancha, Campus Universitario s/n, 02071 Albacete, Spain
{JoseAntonio.Mateo,Valentin.Valero,Hermenegilda.Macia,
Gregorio.Diaz}@uclm.es

Abstract. Composite Web services technologies are widely used due to their ability to provide interoperability among services from different companies. Web services are usually *stateless*, which means that no state is stored from the clients viewpoint. However, some new applications and services require to capture the state of some resources after each computation. Thus, new standards to model Web services states have emerged e.g. Web Services Resource Framework (WSRF). In this paper, we present a formal model based on WS-BPEL and WSRF, and we provide a prioritised-timed coloured Petri net semantics for it. This semantics captures the main activities of WS-BPEL, but we also consider other important aspects, both from WS-BPEL and WSRF, such as fault handling, resource management, time-outs and a publish-subscribe system.

1 Introduction

The development of software systems is becoming more complex with the appearance of new computational paradigms such as Service-Oriented Computing (SOC), Grid Computing and Cloud Computing. These systems are characterized by a dynamic environment due to the heterogeneity and volatility of resources and, moreover, the service provider needs to ensure some levels of quality and privacy to the clients in a way that had never been considered. Formal models of concurrency have been widely used for the description and analysis of concurrent and distributed systems. It is then required to develop new techniques to benefit from the advantages of recent approaches such as Web service compositions. In this work, we use the language Web Services Business Process Execution Language (WS-BPEL) [1] to model this composition. In WS-BPEL, the behaviour of each participant (called orchestrator) is defined in terms of invocations to other services.

Although the Web service definition does not consider the notion of state, interfaces frequently provide the user with the ability to access and manipulate states, that is, data values that persist across, and evolve as a result of

Research partially supported by projects TIN2009-14312-C02-02 and TIN2012-36812-C02-02.

C. Canal and A. Idani (Eds.): SEFM 2014 Workshops, LNCS 8938, pp. 389–404, 2015.
DOI: 10.1007/978-3-319-15201-1_26

Web service interactions. The messages that the services send and receive imply (or encourage programmers to infer) the existence of an associated stateful resource. It is then desirable to define Web service conventions to enable the discovery of, introspection on, and interaction with stateful resources in standard and interoperable ways. To this end, a new standard, Web Services Resource Framework (WSRF) [2,5,10], was defined. In addition, it is required to provide notification mechanisms (e.g. publish-subscribe systems) so that each service can be notified about state changes.

The main motivation of this work is to provide a formal semantics for WS-BPEL+WSRF/WSN to manage stateful Web services workflows by using the existing machinery in distributed systems, and specifically a well-known formalism, such as coloured Petri nets extended with time and priorities, which are a graphical model, but they also provide us with the ability to simulate and analyse the modelled system. Notice that our aim is not to provide just another WS-BPEL semantics since WS-BPEL has been widely studied. Nevertheless, we have realised that it is more convenient to introduce a specific semantic model, which covers properly all the relevant aspects of WSRF/WSN (e.g. notifications and resource time-outs) instead of reusing some previous model.

WS-BPEL [1], for short BPEL, is an OASIS orchestration language for specifying actions within Web services business processes. WS-BPEL is therefore an orchestration language in the sense that it is used to define the composition of services from a local viewpoint, describing the individual behaviour of each participant. More specifically, WS-BPEL is a language for describing the behaviour of a business process based on interactions between the process and its partners. At the core of the WS-BPEL process model is the notion of peer-to-peer interaction between services described in Web Services Description Language (WSDL), both the process and its partners are exposed as WSDL services. Thus, a business process defines how to coordinate the interactions between a process instance and its partners through Web Service interfaces, whereas the structure of the relationship at the interface level is encapsulated in what is called a *partnerLink*. These are instances of typed connectors which specify the WSDL port types the process offers to and requires from a partner at the other end of the partner link.

In particular, we will define a web service composition as a set of orchestrators, described by BPEL+WSRF+WSN syntax, which exchange messages through some communication channels, *PartnerLinks*. Moreover, WS-BPEL processes use *variables* to temporarily store data. Variables are therefore declared on a process or on a scope within that process. In our case, there will be a single scope (*root*), so no nesting is considered in our framework. Besides, for simplicity again, we will only consider integer variables.

An orchestrator consists of a main activity, representing the normal behaviour of this participant. There are also fault activities, which are executed upon the occurrence of some unexpected events, or due to some execution failures, respectively. WS-BPEL activities can be *basic* or *structured*. *Basic activities* are those which describe the elemental steps of the process behaviour, such as the assignment of variables (*assign*), empty action (*empty*), time delay (*wait*), invoke a service (*invoke*) and receive a message (*receive*), reply to a client (*reply*), and throw an exception (*throw*). We also have an action to *terminate* the process execution at any moment (*exit*). For technical reasons we have also included an additional activity $\overline{reply}$, which is used when a service invocation expects a reply, in order to implement the synchronization with the *reply* action from the server. On the contrary, *structured activities* encode control-flow logic in a nested way. The considered structured activities are the following: a *sequence* of activities, separated by a semicolon, the parallel composition, represented by two parallel bars (‖), the conditional repetitive behaviour (*while*), and a timed extension of the receive activity, which allows to receive different types of messages with a time-out associated (*pick*).

On the other hand, WSRF [2] is a resource specification language developed by OASIS and some of the most pioneering computer companies, This standard consists of a set of specifications that define the representation of a WS-Resource (web service + associated resource) in the terms that specify the messages exchanged and the related XML documents. These specifications allow the programmer to declare and implement the association between a service and one or more resources. It also includes mechanisms to describe the means to check the status and the service description of a resource, which together form the definition of a WS-Resource.

Here, we can see a WS-Resource as a collection of properties P identified by an address EPR with an associated *timeout*. This timeout represents the WS-Resource lifetime. Without loss of generality, we have reduced the resource properties set to only one allowing us to use the resource identifier EPR as the representative of this property. In addition, in WS-BPEL, we have taken into consideration the root scope only, thus avoiding any class of nesting among scopes, and we have considered fault handling, leaving the other handling types as future work.

Related Work. WS-BPEL has been extensively studied with many formalisms, such as Petri nets, Finite State Machines and process algebras, but there are only a few works considering WS-BPEL enriched with WSRF, and they only show a description of this union, without a formalization of the model. In [16] Slomiski uses BPEL4WS in Grid environments and discusses the benefits and challenges of extensibility in the particular case of OGSI workflows combined with WSRF-based Grids. Other two works centred around Grid environments are [8,12]. The first justifies the use of WS-BPEL extensibility to allow the combination of different GRIDs, whereas Ezenwoye et al. [8] share their experience on WS-BPEL to integrate, create and manage WS-Resources that implement the factory/instance pattern.

Table 1 shows the comparison of the related works where, the columns show the BPEL version considered, the coverage degree of the recovery framework, whether they use WSRF, the formalism they use, the focus area and if the work is supported by a tool.

Table 1. Related works comparison.

Author	BPEL	Rec.	WSRF	Formalism	Focus	Tool
Slomiski [16]	1.0	×	✓	–	Extensibility	×
Ezenwoye [8]	1.0	×	✓	–	Resource management	×
Ouyang [14]	1.0	Part	×	Petri nets	BPEL analysis	✓
Lohmann [7]	2.0	✓	×	Petri nets	BPEL analysis	✓
Dragoni [6]	2.0	✓	×	π-calculus	BPEL recovery framework	×
Qiu [15]	1.0	Part	×	Proc. Algebra	Fault and compensation	×
Farahbod [9]	1.0	Part	×	Finite State Machines	BPEL analysis	×
Busi [3]	1.0	Part	×	Proc. Algebra	Conformance Chor. vs Orch	×
Our work	2.0	Part	✓	Petri nets	Resource management	✓

2 Prioritised-Timed Coloured Petri Nets

Next, we introduce the specific model of prioritised-timed coloured Petri net considered for the translation. We use prioritised-timed coloured Petri nets, which are a prioritised-timed extension of coloured Petri nets, the well-known formalism supported by CPNTools [4]. In Definition 1, we recall the formal definition of coloured Petri nets presented in [11], whereas, in Definition 2, we define the precise model used in this work. We use the classical notation on Petri nets to denote the precondition and postcondition of both places and transitions:

$$\forall x \in P \cup T : {}^{\bullet}x = \{y \mid (y,x) \in A\} \qquad x^{\bullet} = \{y \mid (x,y) \in A\}$$

Definition 1. *A timed non-hierarchical Coloured Petri Net is a nine-tuple $CPN_T = (P, T, A, \Sigma, V, C, G, E, I)$ where:*

- *P is a finite set of places.*
- *T is a finite set of transitions such that $P \cap T = \emptyset$.*
- *$A \subseteq (P \times T) \cup (T \times P)$ is a set of directed arcs.*
- *Σ is a finite set of non-empty colour sets. Each colour set is either untimed or timed.*
- *V is a finite set of typed variables such that $Type[v] \in \Sigma$ for all variables $v \in V$.*
- *$C : P \to \Sigma$ is a colour set function that assigns a colour set to each place. A place p is timed if $C(p)$ is timed, otherwise p is untimed.*
- *$G : T \to EXPR_V$ is a guard function that assigns a guard to each transition t such that $Type[G(t)] = Bool$.*
- *$E : A \to EXPR_V$ is an arc expression function that assigns an arc expression to each arc a such that*

- $Type[E(a)] = C(p)_{MS}$ if p is untimed;
- $Type[E(a)] = C(p)_{TMS}$ if p is timed.

Here, p is the place connected to the arc a. Moreover, MS and TMS are untimed and timed colour sets in Σ, respectively.

$- I : P \rightarrow EXPR_\emptyset$ is an initialisation function that assigns an initialisation expression to each place p such that

- $Type[I(p)] = C(p)_{MS}$ if p is untimed;
- $Type[I(p)] = C(p)_{TMS}$ if p is timed.   □

In this work, we define a subclass of CPN_T, where three functions have been added. First, a *labelling* function is used to label places and transitions. Transitions can be labelled with either strings or nothing. Places are labelled as *entry places, output places, error places, exit places, internal places, variable places* and *resource places*, which, respectively, correspond to the following labels: $\{in, ok, er, ex, i, v, r\}$. Second, a *delay* function to assign a time interval to some transitions. This time interval is uniformly distributed. This is a shorthand for adding this time delay inscription to the time delay inscription of each output arc expression. Finally, the *priority* function assigns priorities to transitions, considering only two levels P_{LOW} and P_{NORMAL} (by default).

Definition 2. *We define a prioritised-timed coloured Petri net (PTCPN) as a tuple (CPN_T, λ, D, π), where:*

- CPN_T *is a CPN according to Definition 1, with the restrictions indicated below.*
- λ *is the labelling function such that*
  - $\lambda(p) = k$, *with* $k \in \{in, ok, er, ex, i, v, r\}$, *if* $p \in P$.
  - $\lambda(t) = q$, *where q is a label with* $t \in T$.
- $D : T \longrightarrow \mathbb{N} \times \mathbb{N}$ *is the delay function.*
- $\pi : T \longrightarrow \{P_{LOW}, P_{NORMAL}\}$ *is the priority function.*   □

In our specific model, a PTCPN will have an only *entry place* p_{in} with colour set *TUNIT* (*UNIT* colour set with time), such that $^\bullet p_{in} = \emptyset$, which will be initially marked with a single token. According to WS-BPEL and WSRF standards, we can distinguish between two kinds of termination: *normal and abnormal*. On the one hand, the *normal* mode corresponds to the execution of a workflow without faults or without executing any *exit* activity. Thus, in our net model, there is an *output place* p_{ok} with colour set *TUNIT*, such that $p_{ok}^\bullet = \emptyset$, which will be marked with one token when the workflow ends normally. On the other hand, a workflow can finish abnormally by means of the execution of an explicit activity (exit or throw) as well as the occurrence of an internal fault in the system. Each PTCPN has also a single *error place* p_{er} with colour set *TUNIT*, which will become marked with one token in the event of a failure, then starting the fault handling activity. In a similar way, the *exit place* (with colour set *TUNIT*) will be marked when the *exit* activity is performed by an orchestrator.

Variable places are denoted by p_v, to mean that they capture the value of variable v. They contain a single token, whose colour is the variable value. We assume that the initial value of all variables is zero so that these tokens have initially value 0. For any resource r in the system we will have two complementary resource places, p_{r_i}, p_{r_a}. The first one will be marked with one token when the resource has not been instantiated or has been released (due to a time-out expiration), whereas the second one becomes marked when the resource is created, its token colour being a tuple representing the resource identifier (EPR), lifetime, and value. All the remaining places will be considered as *internal*. Markings of PTCPNs are defined in the same way as in [11]. The interested reader is referred to [11] for further information.

3   PTCPN Semantics for WSRF/BPEL/WSN

It is worth noting that we have previously presented an operational semantics for this language in a previous work [13].

3.1   Basic Activities

- *Throw, Empty, Assign, Exit* and *Wait* activities:
  These are translated as indicated in Fig. 1, by means of a single transition labelled with the name of the corresponding activity linked with the corresponding terminating place. The time required to execute *assign, empty, throw* and *exit* is negligible, so that the corresponding transitions have a null delay associated. Notice that for the *assign* activity translation we use a self loop between the transition and the place associated with the variable (p_v) in order

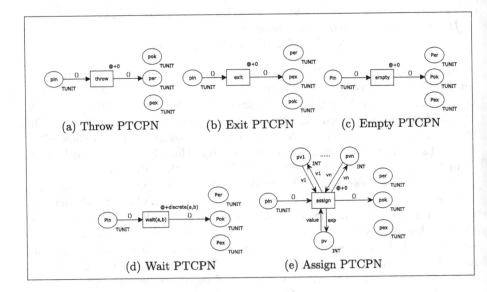

Fig. 1. Basic activities translation

to replace its previous value by the new one, being this new value obtained from an expression (exp) consisting of variables $p_{v1}, \ldots, p_{vn}$ and integers. For the *wait* activity, we have a time interval $[a, b]$ associated, so the delay is randomly selected inside this interval.

Notice the use of a "control" place, to abort all possible remaining activities in the system when either throw or exit are executed. Thus, the idea is that all transitions in the net must be connected with this place, as the different illustrations show.

– *Communication activities:* The model we use is based on the invoke and receive operations, as well as the reply activity that uses a server to reply to a client. We have also added a barred version of reply to synchronise with the response from the client. We have therefore introduced this last activity in our semantics to deal with the request-response operation mode, so the $\overline{reply}$ activity is optional in our syntax.

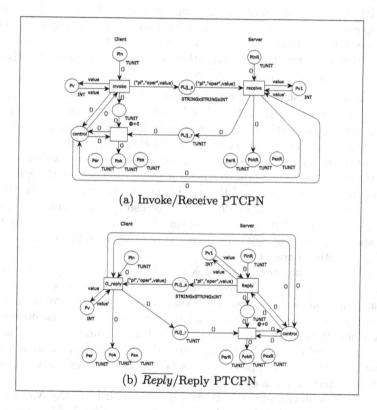

(a) Invoke/Receive PTCPN

(b) $\overline{Reply}$/Reply PTCPN

Fig. 2. Invoke/receive activities translation

Figure 2 shows the translation for both the invoke/receive and the reply/$\overline{reply}$ pairs of activities. Part Fig. 2a of the figure corresponds to the invoke/receive translation, in which the net of the invoke activity is depicted on the left-hand-side part, whereas the receive activity is depicted on the right-hand-side part. There are two shared places, PL_{ij_s} and PL_{ij_r}, which are used to implement the synchronisation between the invocation and reception of services. Both places are associated to the partnerlink used for this communication, denoted here by (i, j), where i and j are the orchestrator identifiers performing those activities. Notice that the value of a single variable is transmitted, which is obtained from the corresponding variable place, p_v. In the same way, the receive activity stores this value in its own variable. The interpretation of Fig. 2b is analogous.

3.2 Ordering Structures

The set of structured activities in WS-BPEL is not intended to be minimal [1], so there are cases where the semantics of one activity can be represented using another activity. Nevertheless, in order to reduce the complexity of our translation, our approach omits many derived activities only dealing with the most important ones from the modelling viewpoint, such as sequence, parallel and choice. For all these cases we provide the translation by only considering two activities. However, the generalization to a greater number of activities is straightforward in all of them.

- *Parallel:* The translation for a parallel activity is depicted in Fig. 3, which includes two new transitions $t1$ and $t2$. The first to fork both parallel activities and the second to join them when correctly terminated. Transition $t1$ thus puts one token on the initial places of both PTCPNs, N_{A_1} and N_{A_2}, in order to activate them, and also puts one token on a new place, p_c, which is used to stop the execution of one branch when the other has failed or the exit activity is explicitly executed in one of them. This place is therefore a precondition of every transition in both PTCPNs, and it is also a postcondition of the non-failing transitions. However, in the event of a failure or an exit activity, the corresponding *throw* or *exit* transition will not put the token back on p_c, thus halting the other parallel activity.
  Notice also that the *error* places of N_{A_1} and N_{A_2} have been joined in a single error place (p_{er}), which becomes marked with one token on the firing of one *throw* transition. In this case, the other activity cannot execute any more actions (p_c is empty), so some dead tokens would remain permanently on some places in the PTCPN. However, these tokens cannot cause any damage, since the control flow has been transferred either to the fault handling activity of the PTCPN, once the place p_{er} has become marked, or the whole system has terminated once the place p_{ex} is marked.
- *Sequence:* A sequence of two activities $A_1; A_2$ (with PTCPNs N_{A_1} and N_{A_2}, respectively) is translated in a simple way by just collapsing in a single place (this will be an internal place of the new PTCPN) the *output* place P_{ok} of N_{A_1}, and the *entry* place of N_{A_2}. The *entry* place of the new PTCPN will be the *entry* place of N_{A_1}. The *output* place of the new PTCPN will be the *output* place of N_{A_2}, and we also collapse the *exit*, *error* and *control* places of both PTCPNs.

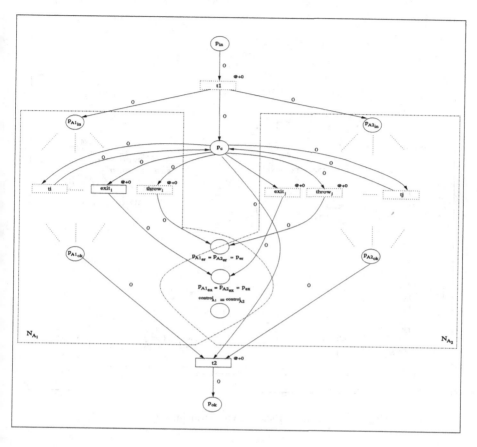

Fig. 3. Parallel activity translation.

- *Pick* $(\{(pl_i, op_i, v_i, A_i)\}_{i=1}^n, A, timeout)$: The <pick> activity waits for the occurrence of exactly one event from a set of events, also establishing a timeout for this selection. The translation is depicted in Fig. 4 where a timer is implemented on the place p_a in order to enforce the firing of transition ta when the timeout has elapsed, thus activating N_A. The colour set INT of the place p_a is timed. To illustrate how this construction works, we define the following example.

Example 1. In this example, there are three actors: two customers and a seller. The customers contact the seller in order to gather information about a specific product identified by id1 and id2, respectively. The seller checks the stock and sends the requested information to the customers. The seller has established a timeout of 24 h to receive requests. Let the orchestrations $O_{c1} = (A_{c1}, empty)$, $O_{c2} = (A_{c2}, empty)$ and $O_s = (A_s, empty)$, the BPEL-RF code for the primary activity of both participants is:

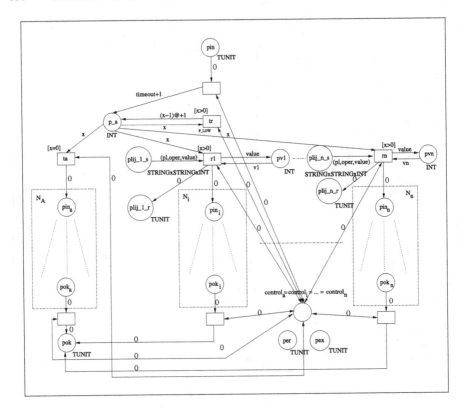

Fig. 4. Pick activity translation.

$$A_{c1} = invoke(pl_1, info, id1); receive(pl_1, inforec1, id_3)$$

$$A_{c2} = invoke(pl_1, info, id1); receive(pl_2, inforec2, id_4)$$

$$A_s = pick(\{(pl_1, info, id_{s1}, reply(pl_1, inforec1, id_3), (pl_2, info, id_{s2},$$
$$reply(pl_2, inforec2, id_4))\}, empty, 24)$$

Looking at Fig. 4, it can be observed that when O_s executes the *pick* activity the input place, p_{in} of the net is marked. Next, transition t_{in} is fired in order to mark the place p_a with the value $timeout + 1$. This timeout is passed as a parameter in the activity and, in this case, its value is equal to 24. Once this place is marked, two possibilities can arise. On the one hand, one of the buyers runs its *invoke* activity before timeout expiration, putting a token in the corresponding input place, $plij_{i_s}$ of the transition r_i, $i \in 1, .., n$, and, then, the behaviour hereafter is the same as in the *receive* activity (Fig. 2). On the other hand, if none of the buyers executes an *invoke* activity, the current time must be increased by means of the transition t_r and the arc inscription @ + 1. Thus, after *timeout* time units without receiving any request, the alarm transition, t_a is fired executing the activity A passed as parameter. It is worthwhile to remark that variable x is used as a countdown timer since CPNTools does

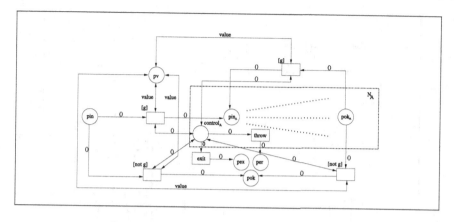

Fig. 5. While activity translation.

not allow to include the *time* function in guards since its inclusion could pose side-effects [4].

- *While* (cond,A): The machinery needed to model this construction is fairly straightforward since we only must check if the repetition condition holds or not in order to execute the contained activity or skip it. Figure 5 shows this translation.

3.3 WSRF-Compliant

Let us now see the WSRF activities, and their corresponding translations.

- *CreateResource (EPR,val,timeout,A)*: EPR is the resource identifier, for which we have two complementary places in Fig. 6, p_{r_i} and p_{r_a}, where the sub-index represents the state of the resource: i when it is inactive and a when it is active. The initial value is *val*, and A is the activity that must be executed when the time-out indicated as third parameter has elapsed.

  We can see in Fig. 6 how the transition *createResource* removes the token from the *inactive* place, and puts a new token on the active place, whose colour contains the following information: resource identifier (EPR), its life-time (max), and its value (val). Transition $t0$ is executed when the lifetime of the resource has expired, thus removing the token from the *active* place, marking again the *inactive* place, and activating N_A. We can also see that the *active* place is linked with a number of transitions, which correspond to the subscribers (we know in advance these possible subscribers from the WS-BPEL/WSRF document). These transitions can only become enabled if the corresponding places $subs_i$ are marked by performing the corresponding activity *subscribe*. The PTCPNs $Ncond_i$ are the nets for the activities passed as parameter in the invocation of a subscribe activity.

- *Subscribe (EPR,cond',A)*: In this case, an orchestrator subscribes to the resource *EPR*, with the associated condition *cond'*, upon which the activity

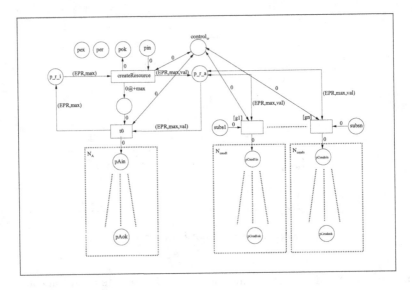

Fig. 6. CreateResource activity translation.

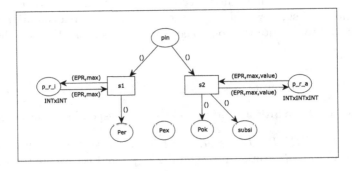

Fig. 7. Subscribe activity translation.

A must be performed. Figure 7 shows this translation, where we can observe that the associated place $subs_i$ is marked in order to allow the execution of the PTCPN for the activity A if the condition g_i holds. On the contrary, if the resource is not active, we will throw the fault handling activity.

– *SetProp (EPR, expr):* In Fig. 8 it can be observed how the new value is assigned to the resource. We omit the translation for the activities *getProp* and *SetLife-Time* since they are similar to this activity.

3.4 Orchestration Translation

Once we have defined the translation for the activities, we can now introduce the definition for the PTCPN at the orchestration level. Notice that all PTCPNs generated for the different orchestrators cooperate to form the entire system (choreography). Let us call N_A and N_f the PTCPNs that are obtained by applying

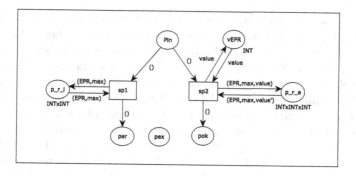

Fig. 8. SetProperty activity translation.

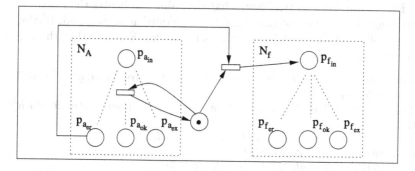

Fig. 9. Orchestration translation

the translation to each one of these activities A and A_f:

$$N_A = (P_a, T_a, A_a, \Sigma_a, V_a, G_a, E_a, \lambda_a, D_a, \pi_a) \qquad \text{(PTCPN for } A)$$
$$N_f = (P_f, T_f, A_f, \Sigma_f, V_f, G_f, E_f, \lambda_f, D_f, \pi_f) \qquad \text{(PTCPN for } A_f)$$

Let $p_{a_{in}}$ and $p_{f_{in}}$ be the initial places of N_A and N_f respectively; $p_{a_{ok}}$ and $p_{f_{ok}}$ their *correct* output places, $p_{a_{er}}$ and $p_{f_{er}}$ their *error* places and, finally, $p_{a_{ex}}$ and $p_{f_{ex}}$ their *exit* places. The PTCPN for the orchestrator is then constructed as indicated in Fig. 9. This PTCPN is then activated by putting one token 0 on $p_{a_{in}}$. However, we can have other marked places, for instance, those associated with integer variables or resources. The other places are initially unmarked.

4 Case Study: Automatic Management System for Stock Market Investments

The case study concerns a typical automatic management system for stock market investments, which consists of $n+1$ participants: the online stock market system and n investors, A_i, $i = 1, \ldots, n$. The complete and detailed version of this case study can be obtained in http://www.dsi.uclm.es/retics/bpelrf/casestudies.htm. Here, the resource will be the stocks of a company that the investors want to buy just in case the price falls below an established limit, which the investors fix previously by means of subscriptions, i.e., an investor subscribes to the resource (the stocks) with a certain guard (the value of the stocks he/she want to pay for it). The lifetime *lft* will be determined by the stock market system and the resource price will be fluctuating to simulate the rises/drops of the stock. Notice that we do not take into account the stock buy process since our aim is to model an investors' information system. Thus, the participants will be notified when their bids hold or the resource lifetime expires. Let us consider the choreography $C = (O_{sys}, O_1, \ldots, O_n)$, where $O_k = (A_k, A_{f_k})$, k=sys, 1,..., n; $Var_{sys} = \{at, vEPR\}, Var_i = \{v_i\}, A_{f_k=exit}$. Variable $vEPR$ serves to temporarily store the value of the resource property before being sent; v_i is the variable used for the interaction among participants, and, finally, at controls the period of time in which the auction is active. Note that the value x indicates the resource value at the beginning, $at0$ is the time that the "auction" is active, and, finally, x_i is the value of the stocks that he/she wants to pay for. Suppose that the variables are initially 0:

$Asys = assign(x + 1, vEPR); assign(at0, at); CreateResource(EPR, lft, x, empty);$
$while(actualTime() <= at, Abid)$
$Abid = getProp(EPR, vEPR); assign(vEPR + bid(), vEPR); setProp(EPR, vEPR);$
$wait(1, 2)$
$A_i = wait(1, 2); subscribe(O_i, EPR, EPR < x_i, Acond_i);$
$pick((pl_i, buy, v_i, empty), empty, at0)$
$Acond_i = getProp(EPR, vEPR); invoke(pl_i, buy, vEPR)$

Here, the function *bid* is used to increase/decrease the stocks value simulating the fluctuation of the stocks price. Next, we present the analysis part.

CPNTools offers us two forms to check the correctness of our system: formal verification and simulation. First, the simulation helps designers to understand how the system exactly works and it is a mean to detect possible errors in early stages of the development process in order to refine the model according the clients' requirements. Besides, formal verification through state space analysis could be done in order to ensure that our system achieves some formal properties such as liveness, deadlock-freeness and so on. In this way, Table 2 shows the results obtained considering 1, 2, 3, 4 or 5 investors. Note that we have considered the following assumptions:

- The "auction" time $at0$ is limited to 10 time units.
- The resource is active during 15 time units ($lft=15$).
- The resource value x is 100 money units.
- The value of subscription of each investor i, x_i, is $x - (9 + i)$, that is, if the system has only one investor its subscription guard will be $x < 90$, whereas with 5 investors, the last investor will have a subscription guard of $x < 86$.
- The function *bid* will fluctuate the stocks price between -2 and 1 in order to simulate that the price only can rise 1 and drop 2 at most each time unit.

We will focus on deadlock-freeness to ensure that the system never gets stuck while the participants have activities to do in their workflow. We have leveraged

Table 2. State space analysis results

Properties	Number of investors				
	1	2	3	4	5
State Space Nodes	3561	7569	16983	50350	89879
State Space Arcs	5203	12843	33271	112101	262215
Time (s)	2	7	23	146	1140
Dead Markings	124	244	454	1108	874

the functions offered by CPNTools to demonstrate that in all dead markings of the system the final place is marked, which leads us to conclude the system has finished correctly. Let us suppose that the final place of this Petri net is called *Pokfinal0* and this final place is marked by a transition when all the participants have finished their execution. For the sake of clarity, we have not drawn this place in each figure. Thus, the next SML code checks when this situation occurs: fun DesiredTerminal n =((Mark.PetriNet'Pokfinal0 1 n) == 1'true), which returns *true* if the place *Pokfinal0* is marked. In addition to this, it is necessary to evaluate the predicate: PredAllNodes DesiredTerminal=ListDeadMarkings(), to check that the list of dead marking contains the marking of the *Pokfinal0* place.

By using CPNTools, we checked that all dead markings hold the predicate *DesiredTerminal*, and, therefore, when the system reaches a dead marking is because system has terminated, which demonstrates the absence of deadlocks in our case study.

5   Conclusions and Future Work

In this paper, we have integrated two complementary approaches in order to improve the definition of business processes models on BPEL by adding the capability of storing their state. We have thus transformed *stateless* business processes into *stateful* business processes. To this end, we have defined a prioritised-timed coloured Petri net model and presented its corresponding semantics to represent the constructions of WS-BPEL and the standard selected for the definition of resources, namely WSRF. Apart from including the notion of state in business processes, our work also includes a publish-subscribe notification system based on WS-BaseNotification, presenting a PTCPN model and its semantics. Thus, an orchestrator can show interest of being notified when a condition holds, e.g., the load of a server exceeds a certain limit. Our approach is based on the one used in CPNTools, allowing us to take advantage of its capability of analysis and verification systems. Moreover, our work in progress is the development of a tool (a beta version can be accessed at: http://www.dsi.uclm.es/retics/bpelrf/) to transform automatically WS-BPEL and WSRF specifications into CPNTools nets. As future work, we plan to study some interesting properties such as safeness, soundness and so on. In addition, it is interesting to define a complete semantics of WS-BPEL and WSRF. Finally, as commented above, we defined an operational semantics in a previous work, so we will demonstrate in a future work the equivalence between both semantics.

References

1. Andrews, T., et al.: BPEL4WS - Business Process Execution Language for Web Services, Version 1.1 (2003). http://www.ibm.com/developerworks/library/specification/ws-bpel/
2. Banks, T.: Web Services Resource Framework (WSRF) - Primer, OASIS (2006)
3. Busi, N., Gorrieri, R., Guidi, C., Lucchi, R., Zavattaro, G.: Choreography and orchestration: a synergic approach for system design. In: Benatallah, B., Casati, F., Traverso, P. (eds.) ICSOC 2005. LNCS, vol. 3826, pp. 228–240. Springer, Heidelberg (2005)
4. CPNTools website. http://cpntools.org/
5. Czajkowski, K., Ferguson, D., Foster, I., Frey, J., Graham, S., Sedukhin, I., Snelling, D., Tuecke, S., Vambenepe, W.: The WS-Resource Framework Version 1.0 (2004). http://www.globus.org/wsrf/specs/ws-wsrf.pdf
6. Dragoni, N., Mazzara, M.: A formal semantics for the WS-BPEL recovery framework. In: Laneve, C., Su, J. (eds.) WS-FM 2009. LNCS, vol. 6194, pp. 92–109. Springer, Heidelberg (2010)
7. Lohmann, N.: A feature-complete petri net semantics for WS-BPEL 2.0. In: Dumas, M., Heckel, R. (eds.) WS-FM 2007. LNCS, vol. 4937, pp. 77–91. Springer, Heidelberg (2008)
8. Ezenwoye, O., Sadjadi, S.M., Cary, A., Robinson, M.: Orchestrating WSRF-based GridServices. Technical report FIU-SCIS-2007-04-01 (2007)
9. Farahbod, R., Glässer, U., Vajihollahi, M.; A formal semantics for the business process execution language for Web services. In: Joint Workshop on Web Services and Model-Driven Enterprise Information Services (WSMDEIS), pp. 122–133 (2005)
10. Foster, I., Frey, J., Graham, S., Tuecke, S., Czajkowski, K., Ferguson, D., Leymann, F., Nally, M., Storey, T., Weerawaranna, S.: Modeling Stateful Resources with Web Services, Globus Alliance (2004)
11. Jensen, K., Kristensen, L.M.: Coloured Petri Nets - Modelling and Validation of Concurrent Systems. Springer, Heidelberg (2009)
12. Leyman, F.: Choreography for the grid: towards fitting BPEL to the resource framework. J. Concurrency Comput. Pract. Exp. 18(10), 1201–1217 (2006)
13. Mateo, J.A., Valero, V., Díaz, G.: An operational semantics of BPEL orchestrations integrating Web services resource framework. In: Carbone, M., Petit, J.-M. (eds.) WS-FM 2011. LNCS, vol. 7176, pp. 79–94. Springer, Heidelberg (2012)
14. Ouyang, C., Verbeek, E., van der Aalst, W.M.P., Breutel, S., Dumas, M., ter Hofstede, A.H.M.: Formal semantics and analysis of control flow in WS-BPEL. Sci. Comput. Program. 67(2–3), 162–198 (2007)
15. Qiu, Z., Wang, S.-L., Pu, G., Zhao, X.: Semantics of BPEL4WS-like fault and compensation handling. In: Fitzgerald, J.S., Hayes, I.J., Tarlecki, A. (eds.) FM 2005. LNCS, vol. 3582, pp. 350–365. Springer, Heidelberg (2005)
16. Slomiski, A.: On using BPEL extensibility to implement OGSI and WSRF grid workflows. J. Concurrency Comput. Pract. Exp. 18, 1229–1241 (2006)

Author Index

Printed in the United States
By Bookmasters